I0882947

IMPERFECT STRANGERS

A volume in the series

The United States in the World

Edited by Mark Philip Bradley, David C. Engerman, Amy S. Greenberg, and Paul A. Kramer

A list of titles in this series is available at www.cornellpress.cornell.edu.

IMPERFECT STRANGERS

Americans, Arabs, and U.S.–Middle East Relations in the 1970s

Salim Yaqub

Cornell University Press
Ithaca and London

Copyright © 2016 by Cornell University

All rights reserved. Except for brief quotations in a review, this book, or parts thereof, must not be reproduced in any form without permission in writing from the publisher. For information, address Cornell University Press, Sage House, 512 East State Street, Ithaca, New York 14850.

First published 2016 by Cornell University Press

Printed in the United States of America

Library of Congress Cataloging-in-Publication Data

Names: Yaqub, Salim, author.
Title: Imperfect strangers : Americans, Arabs, and U.S./Middle East relations in the 1970s / Salim Yaqub.
Description: Ithaca : Cornell University Press, 2016. | Series: The United States in the world | Includes bibliographical references and index.
Identifiers: LCCN 2016006579 | ISBN 9780801448836 (cloth : alk. paper)
Subjects: LCSH: United States—Foreign relations—Middle East. | Middle East—Foreign relations—United States. | United States—Foreign relations—1969–1974. | United States—Foreign relations—1974–1977. | United States—Foreign relations—1977–1981. | Arab-Israeli conflict—1973–1993.
Classification: LCC DS63.2.U5 Y373 2016 | DDC 327.7305609/047—dc23
LC record available at http://lccn.loc.gov/2016006579

Cornell University Press strives to use environmentally responsible suppliers and materials to the fullest extent possible in the publishing of its books. Such materials include vegetable-based, low-VOC inks and acid-free papers that are recycled, totally chlorine-free, or partly composed of nonwood fibers. For further information, visit our website at www.cornellpress.cornell.edu.

Cloth printing 10 9 8 7 6 5 4 3 2 1

To "My Girls"—
Elizabeth Teare and Dorothy Teare Yaqub

Contents

Introduction

> "I can explain," the young man was heard to protest, as bodyguards and onlookers wrestled him onto the steam table and pried the pistol from his hand. It was shortly after midnight on June 4–5, 1968, at the Ambassador Hotel in downtown Los Angeles. The youth had just fired at point-blank range into the back of Senator Robert F. Kennedy's head, moments after Kennedy had thanked his supporters for propelling him to victory in California's Democratic presidential primary. The stricken candidate now lay on the damp floor of the hotel's serving pantry; he would die at a nearby hospital twenty-five hours later. "Let me explain," the young man repeated. ". . . I did it for my country."[1]

Amid the turmoil and grief following the shooting of Senator Kennedy, commentators puzzled over those words. Which country did the gunman mean? He was Sirhan Sirhan, a citizen of Jordan, born twenty-four years earlier in an Arab village on the West Bank, which was now under Israeli occupation. In the 1950s, he had emigrated to America and become a permanent resident. In a June 9 *Los Angeles Times* opinion piece, the journalist A.S. "Doc" Young assumed that Sirhan was claiming the United States as his country. On the surface, Young noted, this was an incongruous assertion.

Senator Kennedy had "soght [*sic*] to turn the country around, to aid the poor, save the cities," and build "a democracy with equal rights and opportunities for all." It was therefore "ironic that a man with the odd name of Sirhan Sirhan should shoot him, claiming: 'I did it for my country.'" Or maybe not so ironic, Young decided after all. Given the violent impulses that had seized the U.S. body politic in recent years, resulting in the assassinations of the senator's older brother, President John F. Kennedy, and of the civil rights leaders Malcolm X and Martin Luther King, Jr.—the latter gunned down just two months earlier—wasn't Sirhan the perfect embodiment of the American spirit?[2]

A June 6 *Boston Globe* editorial saw Sirhan as acting on Jordan's behalf—an assumption with equally nihilistic implications. "So it now develops," the editorial observed, "that Sirhan Bechara Sirhan was a mad man, truly mad. . . . 'I did it for my country. I love my country,' Sirhan is said to have cried out as he watched Sen. Kennedy fall. And thus he proved his madness." The *Globe*'s logic was hard to follow, but it seemed to turn on the fact that, just one year earlier, Israeli forces had occupied Sirhan's native West Bank and physically negated Jordan's claim of sovereignty over the territory. Consequently, "this deluded young Jordanian . . . is in truth a man without a country to love anymore."[3]

The deficiencies in the *Globe*'s analysis—which, in fairness, appeared at a very early stage in the tragedy and was evidently composed even before Kennedy succumbed to his wound—would become clearer in the weeks and months ahead. Sirhan did show signs of mental disturbance, but the political motivations for his crime, while not explaining everything, were intelligible enough. The country he had lost was Palestine, not Jordan, and he believed it was still his to love, and avenge. In 1948, when Sirhan was four years old, the violence attending Israel's creation had forced him and his family to flee their West Jerusalem home for the relative safety of East Jerusalem. Barred by Israel from returning to that home, the Sirhans found refuge in a one-room house in the Old City, sustained by rations from the United Nations Relief and Works Agency. In 1957, they moved to Pasadena, California, where young Sirhan became fluent in English but never felt at home. From childhood he nurtured an abiding hatred of the Zionist movement that had uprooted his family and so many other Palestinians. The Arab-Israeli War of June 1967, erupting exactly one year before the fateful encounter at the Ambassador Hotel, humiliated the Arab world and further devastated Palestinian lives, intensifying Sirhan's rage. As the first anniversary of the June War approached, and in hot pursuit of his party's presidential nomination, Senator Kennedy called for the immediate sale of fifty U.S. Phantom warplanes to Israel, making himself a specific target of Sirhan's wrath.[4]

Most of the facts supporting this political interpretation of Sirhan's crime were publicly available soon after the event, yet such a reading seldom informed mainstream American commentary. Editorials generally treated the murder as a senseless act, though there was some disagreement over whether the madness was limited to Sirhan or extended to a violent American society that had abetted his wild impulses.[5] Even this debate, some felt, granted the tragedy more coherence than it merited. In March 1969, *Newsweek* lamented that Sirhan's murder trial "has notably failed to explain, in any profound way, whatever meaning there may have been behind the Kennedy assassination. Perhaps, as Albert Camus has pointed out, the only way to understand such maniacally absurd events is to see the absurd itself as all the answer there is."[6]

Opinion leaders in the Arab world, by contrast, had no difficulty making sense of Sirhan's act. Although Arab governments and newspapers immediately condemned the murder, some of the latter editorialized that the crime was an understandable, if regrettable, product of Palestinian dispossession. Jordan's *Al-Dastur* called Sirhan "a simple Palestinian who has lost his homeland and has not been able to make his complaint reach the heads of Americans because of the . . . walls erected by Zionist propaganda." Bullets were "his means of expressing his despair."[7] Over the coming months, elements of the newly ascendant Palestinian movement claimed Sirhan as one of their own. A Palestine Liberation Organization (PLO) poster circulated in the spring of 1969 superimposed an image of a gun-toting guerrilla over a portrait of Sirhan, whom it called "a commando . . . not a murderer."[8] Sirhan's status as a Palestinian icon persisted well into the next decade. In 1973, when Palestinian militants seized the Saudi embassy in Khartoum, Sudan, taking two American and several other foreign diplomats hostage, their demands initially included the release of Sirhan, now serving a life sentence for Kennedy's murder.[9]

Of course, there were plenty of Americans who, from the start, grasped the relevance of Middle Eastern politics to Sirhan's crime. Yet many of them had an interest in downplaying the Arab element. Jewish and pro-Israel groups saw little advantage in drawing attention to the Palestinian cause, whose existence posed uncomfortable questions about the circumstances of Israel's birth. Most Americans of Arab descent, mortified by the killing and fearing retaliation, were understandably eager to disavow the perpetrator.

Figure 1. "Sirhan Bishara Sirhan: a commando . . . not a murderer," Palestine Liberation Organization poster, 1969. Art by Ismail Shammout (Palestine Poster Project).

"Sirhan was not thinking about us when he did this thing," an Arab American in Pasadena told a reporter.[10]

In Rapid City, South Dakota, a Lebanese American lawyer had a more personal reason to resent Sirhan. In 1968, James Abourezk had made his first foray into politics, running as a Kennedy delegate in South Dakota's Democratic primary election, held the same day as California's. Kennedy won both races. "Our taste of victory on primary night . . . turned sour as we watched Robert Kennedy's assassination," recalled Abourezk, who in 1970 would be elected to the House of Representatives and two years later win a seat in the U.S. Senate. "I hated Sirhan for doing that to Bobby Kennedy. . . . He assassinated my hero."[11]

Still, some Arab American activists refused to disown the assassin. Like the Arab editorialists, they insisted that Sirhan's offense, while grave, was inseparable from his plight as an uprooted Palestinian. Abdeen Jabara, a young Lebanese American lawyer serving on Sirhan's legal defense team, wanted the defense to foreground the traumas Sirhan had suffered when Israel's creation forced his family into exile. Such a focus, Jabara believed, would serve the defense's agreed-upon strategy of seeking acquittal (or, failing that, a finding of mitigated guilt) on the ground of "diminished responsibility." But the chief defense lawyers rejected Jabara's recommendation. At trial, they touched only glancingly on Sirhan's searing 1948 experience, treating it as just one of several traumas the defendant had suffered during his life—an unconvincing "grab bag for the jury," Jabara later complained. Sirhan was convicted and given a death sentence, which was commuted to life imprisonment after the California Supreme Court voided all pending executions in the state in 1972.[12]

In far more pungent terms, Muhammad ("M.T.") Mehdi, an Iraqi-born activist based in New York, also cited Arab-Israeli inequities. "As we condemn Sirhan's act," he remarked shortly after the shooting, "so we must condemn the Zionist pressures which forced Senator Kennedy to support Israel wrongly against the Arabs." Sirhan's crime "reflects the frustration of many Arabs with American politicians who have sold the Arab people of Palestine to the Zionist Jewish voters." During the trial, Mehdi expressed his own displeasure with the apolitical defense strategy. At one point, he even petitioned the court, unsuccessfully, for permission to replace Sirhan's lawyers with a new legal team.[13]

Over the next dozen years, Abourezk, Jabara, and Mehdi would be ubiquitous figures in Arab-American politics—Abourezk the leading moderate (albeit with a militant temperament), Jabara the unflinching radical, Mehdi the provocative, incessant, and unswattable gadfly.

If Arabs in America could opine about Sirhan, then so, too, could Americans living in the Arab world. Robert Fraga, a young mathematics professor at the American University of Beirut, was a charter member of Americans for Justice in the Middle East (AJME), a Beirut-based organization formed shortly after the 1967 War to acquaint Americans back home with Arab outlooks on the Arab-Israeli dispute. Analyzing the ongoing trial for AJME's newsletter, Fraga cautioned that American handwringing over the senselessness of Sirhan's act served "to obfuscate the political motives for the crime." A guilty verdict was probably appropriate, he wrote, "but I would hope to see mercy" for the defendant, who "acted in accord with his own primitive and not-ignoble sense of right and wrong."[14] Although Fraga himself was to keep a low profile in the years ahead, AJME would, from its Beirut perch, be modestly influential in shaping Arab-friendly discourse in the United States.

Jabara, Mehdi, Fraga, and like-minded critics believed that the United States wielded power in ways that caused dislocation and misery in the Arab world, a damning truth that Sirhan had tried, through his crime, to dramatize to the American public. It stood to reason that the United States should expect further repercussions—"blowback," a later generation would say—for its reckless policies toward the region. It fell to Mehdi, characteristically, to make this warning explicit. "If an American politician supports the [Israeli] invaders against the vanquished," he wrote in a book about the Sirhan case, "he has joined the rank of the invaders, and to the vanquished Palestinian, he is as responsible as the Zionist invaders" and should expect to be treated like them.[15] A more detached observer, surveying a broader Arab canvas, might have paraphrased Mehdi in this way: as the 1960s drew to a close, the United States was playing an increasingly decisive role in the geopolitics of the Middle East; Arab actors were keenly aware of this reality and growing less and less shy about letting Americans know how they felt about it.

In 1968 and 1969, mainstream American commentators had plenty of other urgent issues claiming their attention, and hardly any of them detected this ominous element in Kennedy's assassination.[16] That the tragedy should prompt a rethinking of U.S. Middle East policy simply did not occur to mainstream observers, and the small number exposed to the notion (mainly through Mehdi's writings) dismissed it out of hand.[17] Arab concerns and grievances would intrude on their awareness soon enough.

This book examines U.S. involvement in the Arab world over the dozen years following Sirhan's crime, a period spanning the presidencies of Richard M. Nixon (1969–1974), Gerald R. Ford (1974–1977), and Jimmy Carter (1977–1981) and roughly corresponding to the decade of the 1970s. Exploring the diplomatic, political, cultural, demographic, and psychological dimensions of U.S.-Arab relations, the book argues that the seventies were a pivotal decade in the evolution of that encounter. In the 1970s, Americans and Arabs became an inescapable presence in each other's lives and perceptions, and members of each society came to feel profoundly vulnerable to the political, economic, cultural, and even physical encroachments of the other. It was also in those years that fundamental patterns were entrenched, establishing much of the tone and substance of U.S.-Arab relations as they have unfolded in subsequent decades. In the years since the 1970s, a peculiar irony has marked the U.S.-Arab relationship. In the realm of foreign affairs, we have seen extraordinary and often escalating antagonism between the official policies of the United States and much of Arab society. Domestically, however, Arab Americans and Muslim Americans have been increasingly recognized as a permanent, if highly contested, part of the American community, and important sectors of the U.S. intelligentsia (though by no means all of them) have become more respectful of Arab perspectives on political and cultural issues. It is impossible to understand these more recent patterns without studying the events of the 1970s.

In that decade, Americans and Arabs came to know each other as never before. The decline of European power and influence in the Middle East, the increase in U.S. military and economic assistance to Middle Eastern countries, the growing centrality of the United States to Arab-Israeli diplomacy, and the expansion of U.S. trade with and investment in the region all dramatically raised America's profile in the Arab world (a transformation coinciding, ironically, with a relative decline in U.S. power and influence in most other areas of the globe). Meanwhile, the rise of international terrorism, the Arab oil embargo of 1973–1974, the related increases in the price of Middle Eastern oil, the growing visibility of "petrodollars" in American life, and rising levels of immigration from the Middle East forced ordinary Americans to pay closer attention to the Arab world.

Among both Americans and Arabs, the sense of growing mutual dependence called forth a range of responses. Some sought to rationalize that dependence through accommodation and compromise; others, to break out of it through confrontation and coercion. In the mid-1970s, many Arab actors seemed optimistic that they could parlay their new leverage into a broad accommodation with the United States, entailing a fuller integration of Arab nations into the global economy and a settlement of the Arab-Israeli dispute on terms acceptable to the main currents of Arab public opinion. Important segments of the American political establishment, confronting the perceived limits of U.S. global power, themselves believed that such an accommodation was necessary.

Events in the second half of the 1970s, however, thwarted these hopes. The U.S.-sponsored peace process between Egypt and Israel, while enabling Egypt to recover the Sinai Peninsula, left Israel in possession of Syrian, Palestinian, and Lebanese lands, and so most Arabs angrily rejected it. Lebanon's vicious civil war absorbed the energies and resources of surrounding Arab countries, exacerbated rivalries among them, and thus eroded their strategic leverage on the global stage. At the end of the decade, a series of upheavals involving mostly non-Arab actors—the Iranian revolution, the Soviet invasion of Afghanistan, and the outbreak of the Iran-Iraq war—deepened the Arab world's own polarization and instability, placing the hoped-for accommodation further out of reach. By the early 1980s, U.S.-Arab relations were settling into patterns that would persist over subsequent decades and into the twenty-first century: strategic alignment between the United States and Israel, escalating terrorist attacks by nonstate Arab actors, repeated U.S. military interventions in the Arab world, and rising anti-American sentiment in the region.

Although many of these circumstances were beyond Washington's control, U.S. policies sometimes exacerbated them. A case in point was the American approach to Arab-Israeli peacemaking. Over the half decade following the Arab-Israeli War of 1973, an international consensus emerged over the appropriate resolution of the Arab-Israeli dispute, a consensus that remains substantially unchanged today, despite the absence of a diplomatic process capable of realizing it on the ground. By the late 1970s, most of the world's nations favored a comprehensive settlement entailing Israel's withdrawal from all of the Arab territory occupied in the 1967 War, Arab recognition of Israel, and the establishment of an independent Palestinian state on the West Bank and the Gaza Strip. The forging of this international consensus was a remarkable achievement, made possible by the ascendancy of an independent Palestinian movement that acquired international legitimacy with stunning speed and that, more gradually, moderated its national ambitions to make them compatible with Israel's existence.

As fate would have it, however, the outlines of this comprehensive settlement first emerged during the tenure of secretary of state Henry A. Kissinger, who strongly opposed such a scenario and pushed instead for bilateral agreements between Egypt and Israel. Egypt's removal from the conflict, Kissinger calculated, would ease pressure on Israel to conduct a full withdrawal to the 1967 lines. The Egyptian-Israeli process came to fruition in the Camp David Accords during the presidency of Jimmy Carter. Although Carter himself hoped that Camp David would lead to agreements on other fronts, this did not happen. The Israelis returned the Sinai Peninsula, but Egypt's neutralization allowed them to tighten their hold over the West Bank, the Gaza Strip, the Golan Heights, and parts of South Lebanon (these last areas occupied after 1978). The Egyptian-Israeli peace agreement sharply reduced the likelihood of another full-scale Arab-Israeli War, and indeed none has occurred since 1973. But it also allowed Israel's occupation of other Arab lands to continue indefinitely, intensifying anti-American sentiment among Arabs and further destabilizing the region in ways that later invited U.S. military intervention.

Decisions by Arab actors, too, contributed to the rising mutual antagonism. On the whole, Arab positions on the Arab-Israeli dispute were more conciliatory than American commentators recognized at the time (or since). Yet even moderate Arab leaders were capable of actions that reinforced the worst stereotypes of Arab violence and fanaticism. PLO chairman Yasser Arafat, who after 1974 was increasingly open to an accommodation with Israel, sometimes acquiesced in grisly attacks on Israeli civilians by Palestinian factions. In 1975, the PLO and several Arab states persuaded the United Nations General Assembly to declare Zionism "a form of racism and racial discrimination." While the arguments for the resolution were more cogent than American and Israeli observers acknowledged, the passage of such a measure was hardly conducive to an Arab-Israeli peace settlement, an outcome favored by many of the Arab governments supporting the resolution. Ordinary Americans could be forgiven for concluding that Arabs were not ready for peace.

Less directly, the manner in which some Arab governments wielded the oil weapon helped to destabilize Arab politics and foreign relations. The oil embargo and price hikes goaded industrialized societies to seek out non–Middle Eastern sources of oil, to develop alternative forms of energy, and to implement conservation schemes. By the early 1980s, such measures, though halting and incomplete, had significantly reduced the market share of oil-producing Arab states, causing economic and geopolitical dislocations that would, years later, nourish extremist politics that exacerbated U.S.-Arab antagonism.

Also fueling that antagonism were the dynamics of the Cold War rivalry in the area. In the late 1960s and early 1970s, the Soviet Union's profile in the Arab world, like that of the United States, rapidly ascended. The Soviets offered increased military and economic aid to Egypt, Syria, and Iraq, while stepping in to assist newly proclaimed radical regimes in South Yemen and Libya. But after 1971 Egypt, the most influential Arab state and the centerpiece of Soviet strategy in the region, drifted away from the Soviet camp, and by the late 1970s it had become a U.S. ally. Egypt's defection dealt a crippling blow to Moscow, which over the same period, and partly consequently, lost influence with some of its remaining Arab clients as well. The Soviets' diminished status became clearer in the 1980s, when the United States was able to build up forces in the area, and sometimes intervene militarily, without undue fear of Soviet reaction. But such behavior did encounter fierce indigenous resistance, to which Washington responded with redoubled military measures, provoking further resistance and thus perpetuating the vicious cycle.

Ironically, even as the hopes for U.S.-Arab accommodation dwindled in the second half of the 1970s, Americans of Arab descent were achieving unprecedented visibility, and a measure of acceptance, within the United States. Largely because of the immigration reforms of the mid-1960s, which permitted a marked increase in immigration from "Third World" countries, Arab American communities grew rapidly in the 1970s. This population growth, combined with the political ferment sweeping the Arab world, including the Arab diaspora, after 1967—and combined, too, with the political and social protests animating American society at the time—encouraged a new assertiveness among Arab American activists. Joined by Arab students and residents, and by sympathetic non-Arabs (including U.S. expatriates in Arab countries, such as Americans for Justice in the Middle East), activists like Abdeen Jabara and M.T. Mehdi denounced Zionist ideology, promoted positive images of Arab culture, and sought sympathy for Arab positions in the Arab-Israeli dispute.

In the early 1970s, these efforts had little impact on general American attitudes, but after the 1973 Arab-Israeli War, which focused Americans' attention on the region, Arab American figures and groups began receiving a more respectful hearing in the mainstream media and public institutions. Newspapers and magazines "discovered" Arab Americans and noted their newfound activism and influence. Now ensconced in the U.S. Senate, where he served from 1973 to 1979, James Abourezk provided news outlets with a steady supply of quotable eviscerations of U.S. Middle East policies. In 1975, president Gerald Ford met with a delegation of Arab American leaders to solicit (and then, admittedly, ignore) their views on the Arab-Israeli dispute. The growing recognition of Arab American perspectives was accompanied, in some elite discourses, by more nuanced presentations of Arab society, culture, and politics. In academia, in business, in middle- and high-brow journalism, and within mainstream African American politics (as distinct from Black Muslim and Black Power circles, from which sharp challenges to U.S–Middle East orthodoxies had emanated for years), there was a new receptivity to Arab and Arab American views and aspirations.

By contrast, popular and commercial media (television shows, advertising, adventure literature, and the like), as well as some politically motivated elite discourses (such as the journals, newsletters, and pamphlets of pro-Israel groups), continued to rely on hostile portrayals of the Arab world. Indeed, such portrayals grew more negative in the second half of the 1970s, as international terrorism and the energy crisis took a firmer hold on the public imagination. But this challenge only goaded Arab American activists to become more sophisticated and organized in their media critiques, and they did occasionally persuade popular media outlets to soften their anti-Arab caricatures.

The simultaneous unfolding of these two broad trends—U.S.-Arab hostility and Arab American acceptance—was not merely ironic; the relationship was causal as well. The diplomatic maneuverings that widened the political rift between the United States and the Arab world also had the effect of humanizing Arabs to American audiences. Henry Kissinger's efforts to push Middle East peacemaking onto a bilateral Egyptian-Israeli track, and to persuade other interested parties to give his diplomacy a chance to succeed, required enormous expenditures of time, energy, and political capital. Kissinger spent hundreds of hours in Arab countries. He learned and spoke Arabic phrases, physically embraced Arab leaders, and treated Arab nations as major players on the world stage. These gestures not only flattered Arab leaders (and bought Kissinger the time he needed to launch the Egyptian-Israeli peace process) but also helped to create a somewhat more favorable image of the Arab world within the United States. The pattern was repeated with the culmination of the bilateral process in the late 1970s: Camp David transformed Egypt into an American ally and thus encouraged Americans to view Arabs more positively; by outraging the rest of the Arab world, however, it deepened the geopolitical estrangement.

Focusing more squarely on the domestic American scene, we see a similar dichotomy in the growing importance of petrodollars, which allowed some Americans to gain a deeper understanding of Arab societies while causing others to become more resentful toward them. After 1973, oil-rich Arab states invested extensively in American properties and institutions, laying the basis for economic, cultural, and educational exchanges and for the establishment in American universities of centers and programs devoted to studying the Middle East. At the same time, the rise in Arab investment fueled populist and nativist fears that wealthy Arabs were "buying up America" and gaining a chokehold over the economic, political, and cultural life of the country.

During the 1970s, in sum, global, regional, and domestic circumstances forced Americans and Arabs into unprecedented proximity with one another. This growing intimacy encouraged attitudes of animosity and acceptance that would characterize U.S.-Arab relations in subsequent decades and, indeed, persist into our own era. Drawing on the insights and techniques of diplomatic, political, cultural, and immigration history, *Imperfect Strangers* explores the emergence of this crucial and troubled relationship.

As a glance at its notes will reveal, this book relies heavily on the scholarship of others. Situating it in relation to that scholarship, however, is no simple task. On a very general level, *Imperfect Strangers* resembles studies by Bruce Schulman, Laura Kalman, Daniel Sargent, Thomas Borstelmann, Judith Stein, and others who see the 1970s as a pivotal decade in the evolution of U.S. political, diplomatic, financial, economic, demographic, and cultural history.[18] On another level, also quite general, my work draws inspiration from such historians as John Dower, Naoko Shibusawa, Paul Kramer, Mark Bradley, Frank Costigliola, Petra Goedde, David Engerman, and Mary Ann Heiss. These and other scholars have produced multidimensional studies of modern U.S. relations with particular countries, works that combine informed analysis of official diplomacy with imaginative explorations of the cultural, social, intellectual, and psychological realms that have shaped, challenged, complicated, and illuminated that diplomacy.[19]

In more specific and substantive ways, this book is also clearly indebted to the now voluminous literature addressing aspects of U.S. involvement in the Arab world in the 1970s. Some of these works focus on particular episodes or interactions occurring in that decade;[20] others survey longer time periods that include the seventies.[21] Some analyze U.S. relations with particular countries or groups; others cover U.S. policies regarding much or all of the Middle East.[22] Most of this scholarship centers on official diplomacy; a small but expanding corpus explores the social, cultural, intellectual, and demographic dimensions of America's encounter with the Arab world or the Middle East.[23] My own book draws deeply on works in all of these categories. But because its focus, scope, and arguments are so particular—idiosyncratic, some may say—it is difficult to relate them, as a whole, to any single historiographical position or theme in the literature. My general approach, then, is to engage with individual historiographical issues as they arise in the narrative, rather than make overarching claims at the outset.

Two interpretive issues, however, are sufficiently broad and recurrent to merit mention here. The first concerns Henry Kissinger's post-1973 Arab-Israeli diplomacy, a subject of ongoing debate. Some scholars credit Kissinger with establishing a diplomatic foundation that has underlain most subsequent U.S. efforts at Arab-Israeli peacemaking.[24] Others stress the ephemeral nature of his achievement, noting that a lasting peace, especially between Israel and the Palestinians, remains elusive.[25] Each claim is half-right. Kissinger did leave an enduring diplomatic legacy, but it was a legacy of managing the Arab-Israeli conflict, not of attending to its underlying causes. Egypt's neutralization (the central objective of Kissinger's Arab-Israeli diplomacy) made it extremely unlikely that another full-scale Arab-Israeli war would occur, but it also diminished the prospects for addressing other Arab grievances and thus for achieving ultimate reconciliation. Similarly, the incremental peace process that Kissinger pursued did become the standard pattern of U.S. Middle East diplomacy in later administrations. What few historians have grasped, however, is that Kissinger *deliberately* designed that process to enable Israel's indefinite occupation of Arab land, a function it served in later decades, whatever his successors' intentions.

The second issue concerns the status of Arab Americans within the U.S. body politic. Some scholars of Arab American life have advanced a "de-assimilation" thesis, arguing that, whereas Arab Americans assimilated relatively easily into American society for much of the twentieth century, geopolitical trends taking hold in the 1970s threw that process into reverse. Increasingly, these scholars argue, the dominant society associated Arab Americans with alarming behaviors emanating from the Middle East, such as extortionate oil pricing and international terrorism, and treated the community as an alien and unwelcome presence. Many Arab Americans responded by rejecting assimilation and retaining, or forging anew, bonds of allegiance to their region of origin.[26] *Imperfect Strangers* grants the force of the "de-assimilation" thesis but argues that it tells only half of the story. The international and domestic politics of the 1970s did form a disturbing and sometimes frightening mix that caused many Arab Americans to seek solace, security, and purpose in their Arab identity. Those very circumstances, however, also goaded Arab American activists to engage with the dominant society to seek a redress of grievances, or at least some better public understanding of their concerns. Whatever the outcome of such efforts (and successes were rare and modest), they did afford many activists a greater sense of participation and belonging in the nation's civic life. De-assimilation was just one response to the disorienting experience of being Arab in America; another was redoubled assimilation.

These two interpretive issues are linked in an argument presented above: that Kissinger's diplomatic exertions, while fortifying the Israeli occupation, also modestly enhanced the Arab image within the United States, an outcome of some benefit to Arab American political activism. This claim is indebted to Melani McAlister's broader observation that, since World War II, U.S. Middle East policy "has vacillated between two poles: distance, othering, and containment define the first; affiliation, appropriation, and cooptation constitute the second." McAlister goes on to argue that the affiliating approach predominated in the early postwar decades, only to give way to "distance" and "othering" in the 1970s. While I share McAlister's conclusion regarding the general hardening of U.S. policy in the 1970s, I am struck by the persistence of the softer mode—and by its ironic symbiosis with the harder one.[27]

Readers will note that much of the book is devoted to the Arab-Israeli conflict. This prominence entirely reflects the priorities of historical actors at the time. The struggle against Israel was *the* consuming issue for politically aware Arabs, whether they were government officials, opinion leaders, or ordinary people. That struggle was also central to Arab American activists and to non-Arab Americans who shared their outlook. Even the Lebanese civil war, as we shall see in chapter 7, underscored the priority of anti-Zionism within Arab American activism. To be sure, there were fundamental disagreements within this general anti-Zionist orientation, the chief one pitting those calling for the dismantling of Israel against those open to a diplomatic settlement that left it in existence. But virtually all agreed that Israel's creation had been calamitously unjust to Palestinian Arabs, that Israel's subsequent behavior had been oppressive and belligerent, and that U.S. Middle East policy was scandalously one-sided.

Washington, too, treated the Arab-Israeli dispute as the most important policy challenge it faced in the Middle East—mainly because the Arabs themselves were so preoccupied with the issue and because some of them had turned to Moscow for help. Of all of the region's flash points, this one seemed most likely to spark a potentially catastrophic superpower confrontation. Moreover, following the Arab oil embargo of 1973–1974, U.S. policy makers believed that any resumption of large-scale Arab-Israeli hostilities would be accompanied by another, more crippling embargo. The centrality of this dispute was evident in the terminology prevalent at the time. When government officials or diplomatic reporters spoke of "the Middle East conflict," or used similar words, it was universally assumed that they were referring to the Arab-Israeli dispute. If they meant a different Middle East conflict, they needed to specify it.

I have decided, then, to give that conflict similar prominence in my book. Another historian could make a different choice. An equally valid approach would be to concentrate on topics that received far less official and public attention at the time than they would in later decades—such as international terrorism, political Islam, evangelical Protestantism, gender relations, the politics of the Persian Gulf, and the state of Arab civil society—as a way of unearthing the roots of current concerns. Most of those subjects do appear in the book, but usually only at moments in the narrative when they rose to the top of Washington's Middle East policy agenda or became major public issues in the United States. A central preoccupation of this book, after all, is the interaction of official foreign relations with recurring themes in public discourse.

Of the deferred topics mentioned above, religious affiliation perhaps merits further discussion. Given the centrality of that theme to U.S.-Arab relations since the 1980s, some readers will wonder at its minimal presence in this study. There are countless ways in which religious identity was important to political actors in the 1970s, but it is less relevant to the story *I* am telling. For most of the decade, and with just two significant exceptions—the Lebanese civil war and the general inclination among American Jews to support Israel—religious affiliation was not a broadly defining issue in political relations between Americans and Arabs. Most Arabs were Muslim and most Arab Americans Christian. Arabs and Arab Americans alike, however, offered critiques of U.S. policy that owed much more to pan-Arab solidarity, or to broader political values such as the right of self-determination and the sanctity of human rights, than to religious identity. Similarly, while many American Jews identified with Israel, and many more American gentiles respected this stance, relatively few Americans in the 1970s publicly portrayed the U.S.-Arab encounter as part of an age-old contest between Christendom and Islam.[28] The Iranian revolution of 1978–1979 and the seizure of Mecca's Grand Mosque in 1979 did unleash Islamist forces that would profoundly shape U.S.-Arab relations, but those impacts were still some years in the future. Much the same can be said of American Evangelical activities in and around the Middle East, which were just starting to capture international attention at decade's end. These and similar events appear in my account more as harbingers of a troubled future than as elements of a recurring theme.

Some readers may question my use of the adjectives "pro-Arab" and "Arab-friendly" to describe certain American activists and commentators. Both terms, which I treat more or less synonymously, signify an attitude of sympathy for some core assumptions harbored by nearly all politically aware Arabs at the time: that Israel's creation and subsequent behavior were a terrible injustice to the Arab people; that the Western powers, including the United States, had ridden roughshod over Arab political rights; and that America's political and media establishments were insensitive to Arab concerns. Like Arabs themselves, pro-Arab or Arab-friendly Americans were hardly monolithic in their views—they often disagreed over what to *do* about the various inequities—but they were united in their acceptance of the core assumptions. My terminology aims to capture those commonalities without assuming consensus on every issue.

I should similarly explain my use of the words "moderate" and "radical" in discussing Arab, Arab American, and pro-Arab political outlooks. These terms refer to the character and degree of change that historical actors sought to achieve, and to their level of acceptance of existing power realities. When it came to the Arab-Israeli conflict, a "moderate" typically advocated an Israeli withdrawal from all of the territory occupied in 1967 and an opportunity for Palestinians to exercise sovereignty on a portion of their ancestral homeland; he or she might further argue that such objectives were compatible with U.S. geopolitical interests. A "radical" typically called for the dismantling of the Zionist enterprise, for its replacement by a democratic state representing all of Palestine's inhabitants, and also, perhaps, for the defeat of conservative Arab regimes seen as impediments to political and social progress; such a figure would likely regard the U.S. government as a dangerous adversary. My use of these terms implies no moral or political judgment about the rightness of either course. I am not suggesting that moderates were more reasonable, or radicals more principled, than those taking different approaches. I am simply outlining the two main ways that Arab, Arab American, and Arab-friendly actors challenged the status quo. The categories are archetypes: some figures combined elements of both approaches; some gravitated, over time, from one to the other (usually from radicalism to moderation).[29]

Before we get on with our story, some scene setting may be helpful. Chapter 2 provides brief historical background on Arab American communal and political life; here follows a quick survey of key international antecedents. In the early post–World War II years, Britain and France—especially the former—were the dominant outside powers in the Arab world. Britain had protectorates on the Arabian Peninsula, a large naval presence in the Persian Gulf, and military bases in Egypt, Iraq, Jordan, and Libya. France had protectorates in Tunisia and Morocco and a major colony in Algeria.

In the 1950s and 1960s, mainly as a consequence of indigenous nationalist pressures, the positions of both European powers steadily eroded. Britain relinquished its bases in Egypt and Jordan and was violently ousted from Iraq. In 1968, confronting fierce local resistance in and around the Persian Gulf and empty coffers back home, the British government announced that it would withdraw its military forces from the Gulf region and relinquish control over its Arabian protectorates by the end of 1971. France, meanwhile, had been obliged to grant independence to Tunisia, Morocco, and Algeria, in Algeria's case after a bloody eight-year war.[30]

Even as European power receded, Arabs had to contend with what they almost unanimously regarded as another Western intrusion. The forcible establishment of a Jewish state in Palestine in 1947–1949, with the crucial diplomatic assistance of the United Nations (UN), embittered and traumatized Arabs everywhere, especially as it resulted in the uprooting of a settled Palestinian Arab society. Thwarted in their military efforts to prevent Israel's creation, the Arab states refused to recognize the new state and, with varying degrees of enthusiasm and credibility, proclaimed their determination to liberate Palestine from its Zionist usurpers. Over the next two decades, Egypt and some other Arab countries substantially built up their militaries, but these were no match for Israel's armed forces, which prevailed in nearly every subsequent skirmish. Such circumstances deepened the popular anger in the Arab world, a sentiment increasingly directed at the United States. After all, Washington had prodded the UN to serve as Israel's midwife and was, from that point on, virtually committed to maintaining Israel's existence and security. Although U.S. military aid to Israel was minimal for some years, it became more generous and conspicuous in the early to mid-1960s. In light of this record, even pro-U.S. Arab governments—in Saudi Arabia, Jordan, Lebanon, and elsewhere—had to be circumspect in their public embrace of the United States, especially as they faced withering criticism from self-described "progressive" or "Arab nationalist" regimes in Egypt, Syria, and Iraq.[31]

Meanwhile, as London and Paris disengaged from the Arab world, Washington and Moscow grew increasingly assertive there. Since the 1950s, the United States had proclaimed an interest in preserving the independence and integrity of Middle Eastern countries and had provided modest military and economic assistance to West-leaning governments in Lebanon, Jordan, Saudi Arabia, and Libya, the last of which hosted a U.S. Air Force base. In 1958, U.S. marines landed in Lebanon to support its beleaguered government against combined domestic and external Arab nationalist pressures.

Throughout the 1950s and 1960s, a small U.S. naval force patrolled the Persian Gulf, and a consortium of American oil companies called the Arabian American Oil Company (Aramco) dominated the extraction and marketing of Saudi Arabia's enormous petroleum reserves, as well as furnishing much of the kingdom's physical infrastructure. Over the same period, the Soviet Union provided arms and economic aid to left-leaning regimes in Egypt, Syria, Algeria, and Iraq and, after 1967, to the Marxist government of newly independent South Yemen. In international forums, the Soviets staunchly supported Arab countries' diplomatic claims against Israel.[32] (The United States, too, was formally at odds with Israel on some key issues but seldom buttressed these stances with concrete action.[33])

Heightening the superpowers' interest in the region was the growing importance of Arab oil, located mainly on the eastern side of the Arabian Peninsula and in North Africa. In the early postwar years, the world had experienced an oil glut. In the 1960s, however, rapid industrial development generated a sharp increase in global demand for petroleum, much of it met by stepped-up production in Arab oil fields. The United States itself consumed relatively little Arab petroleum, but Japan and the Western European countries, in whose prosperity and stability Americans had a vital stake, depended overwhelmingly on oil from that quarter. The Soviets, too, were increasingly concerned about oil supplies. Most of Russia's untapped reserves lay in frozen Siberia and thus were difficult and costly to extract. Moscow's moves to improve relations with Baghdad in the late 1960s partly reflected a desire to gain access to Iraqi crude.[34]

The Arab-Israeli War of June 1967 drastically altered the region's geopolitical landscape and created new diplomatic, strategic, and psychological realities that would dominate Middle Eastern politics, and thus U.S. interactions with the Arab world, for years to come. In six days, Israel crushed its Arab enemies, seizing the Sinai Peninsula and Gaza Strip from Egypt, the Golan Heights from Syria, and the West Bank from Jordan. The defeat was especially disastrous for the Palestinian residents of the West Bank and Gaza. Most now found themselves under Israeli military occupation; tens of thousands more were driven from their homes, joining the hundreds of thousands of Palestinians who had become refugees in the late 1940s. The 1967 War and its early aftermath accentuated the Cold War rivalry in the Middle East. Almost immediately, the Soviet Union began rebuilding the shattered militaries of Egypt and Syria, which vowed to win back their lost lands. Without abandoning its own Arab clients (primarily Saudi Arabia, Jordan, and Lebanon), the United States replaced France as Israel's main arms supplier, a move in keeping with president Lyndon B. Johnson's strong attachment to the Jewish state. In retaliation for Washington's pro-Israel stance during the war, Egypt, Syria, Iraq, and some other Arab states severed diplomatic relations with the United States.[35]

Following their victory, the Israelis insisted that any defeated adversary seeking to recover lost territory must first recognize Israel and commence direct, bilateral negotiations with it. They also said they would not return to the pre–June 1967 borders. The standard Arab position was that Israel must withdraw immediately and unconditionally from all of the captured territory, and honor "Palestinian rights" in some (often unspecified) way, before there could be any thought of recognition or negotiation. The implication was that Arab states *would* deal with Israel if it met these demands, and some Arab diplomats said so in private. Hardly any political leaders, however, were willing to endorse this quid pro quo publicly and plainly.[36] Broad segments of Arab opinion adamantly opposed Israel's existence, and rejectionist leaders and commentators were prone to vilify the advocates of compromise, so such reticence was understandable. But it allowed Israelis to claim that Arab society as a whole was unready for peace and that Israel was therefore justified in holding all of the occupied territory as a guarantee of its own security.[37]

These, then, were the experiences and issues that defined the U.S.-Arab relationship as Sirhan made his way to the Ambassador Hotel. His ghastly act failed to draw that relationship to the forefront of the nation's consciousness; such awareness still lay a few years in the future. What the murder did do was deepen the disarray within Robert Kennedy's Democratic Party, heighten a yearning for calm among the American electorate, and thus brighten the prospects of another presidential aspirant, a Republican promising to restore "law and order" at home. Former vice president Richard Nixon eked out a narrow victory in November 1968. He took office the following January expressing concern about the "powder keg . . . in the Middle East," by which he meant, of course, the Arab-Israeli conflict.[38] But the new president's approach to those animosities, at once devious and vacillating, would do little to dampen their explosive potential. Americans would yet hear the echo of Sirhan's fatal shot.

Chapter 1

The Politics of Stalemate

The Nixon Administration and the Arab-Israeli Conflict, 1969–1972

The traveler may not have intended to make headlines, but he did. Arriving in the West Bank town of Jericho on December 9, 1968, former governor of Pennsylvania William Scranton opined to reporters about U.S. Middle East policy. Scranton was paying a fact-finding visit to the Middle East on behalf of president-elect Richard M. Nixon, scheduled to take office six weeks later. "It is important," Scranton told the reporters, "[that] U.S. policy become more even-handed" in the region. Asked to elaborate, he called on "the United States to deal with all countries in the area and not necessarily espouse one." Scranton's statements caused a flurry of apprehension within the Israeli government, as well as among American Jewish groups. Was Nixon planning to abandon the pro-Israel policies of his predecessor, Lyndon B. Johnson? Members of Nixon's inner circle were also concerned, and they hastened to dispel any misunderstanding. At a December 11 press conference, with the terse protectiveness that would become familiar to White House reporters, Nixon's press secretary Ronald Ziegler dissociated his boss from the indiscreet envoy: "His remarks are Scranton remarks, not Nixon remarks."[1]

In fact, Nixon harbored some sympathy for the view that the United States had leaned too far in Israel's direction. During his first year in office, his administration unveiled an ambitious Middle East peace plan that sought to address Arab grievances in ways that alarmed and infuriated Israel. Scranton played no further role in Nixon's foreign policy,[2] but the "evenhanded" spirit was detectable in official U.S. positions on the Arab-Israeli dispute, especially as articulated by Nixon's first secretary of state, William P. Rogers. Nixon, however, realized that alienating Israel and its American supporters carried great political risks. This recognition made him more susceptible to the argument, presented by his national security adviser, Henry A. Kissinger, that evenhandedness was unworkable. But if evenhandedness was unworkable it was partly because Nixon made it so. From the fall of 1969 on, he gave quiet assurances to Israel that undermined the Arab-Israeli policy to which his administration remained formally committed. Occasionally in 1970 and 1971, the president shifted back toward the official positions, but never with enough force or persistence to reverse the pro-Israel drift of his approach to the dispute, a direction underscored by a dramatic increase in U.S. economic and military aid to Israel.[3]

The final collapse of evenhandedness came on the heels of, and partly resulted from, a bold diplomatic initiative emanating from Egypt. In early 1971, having spent many months engaging its adversary in grinding low-level hostilities, Egypt sought a limited agreement with Israel linked to a timetable for a broader Arab-Israeli settlement. The Israelis rejected the overture, and Nixon, loath to antagonize them, acquiesced in this stance. By mid-1972, Cairo was all but convinced that only a resumption of full-scale war could vindicate Egyptian and Arab claims.

In the hierarchy of Nixon's foreign policy priorities in 1969, the Middle East ranked below the Vietnam War, U.S.-Soviet détente, and future relations with communist China. Within the Middle East, the Arab-Israeli conflict outclassed other policy concerns, such as shifting power arrangements in the Persian Gulf area, political upheaval in Libya, and the world's growing dependence on oil, which the Middle East, broadly defined (extending from the Persian Gulf to North Africa), possessed in huge abundance. As important as these latter topics were, it is understandable that Nixon would prioritize the Arab-Israeli conflict, as this was the Middle East issue most likely to spark a superpower confrontation. After all, since 1967 the United States had been Israel's principal source of arms and diplomatic support, and the Soviet Union played a similar role regarding Egypt and Syria, Israel's most formidable military adversaries.

Arabs, too, generally ranked the Arab-Israeli conflict above other regional concerns. For many of them, it was the overriding issue, period, not just within the Middle East. The 1967 defeat was traumatic to Arabs everywhere, even those not subjected to physical violence, military occupation, or forced exile. The catastrophe called into question virtually every element of the Arabs' collective sense of well-being and accomplishment: the security of their borders, the competence of their leaders, the viability of their political systems, the relevance of their ideologies, the efficacy of their educational systems, the pace and extent of their modernization, even the usefulness of their language. The war also created an immediate challenge—Israel's military occupation of large swaths of Arab territory—that virtually all articulate Arabs agreed must be faced without delay. It was possible, of course, to address the long-term and immediate issues simultaneously, and many individuals and groups did just that. Yet the emergency enabled governing elites to treat far-reaching debate over the purpose and performance of Arab institutions as an unaffordable luxury. The tension between these two daunting imperatives, and the sense that preoccupation with one of them precluded due consideration of the other, heightened the feeling of frustration and malaise pervading Arab society after 1967.[4]

Diplomatically, the 1967 War made an eventual settlement of the Arab-Israeli dispute both easier and harder to imagine. On the one hand, the new status quo was so intolerable that Arab governments grew increasingly willing to downplay earlier demands—such as that Israel relinquish the territory it had seized in excess of the 1947 United Nations (UN) partition plan, or that it allow Palestinian refugees to return to their former homes—in order to concentrate on reversing the setback of 1967. As military options were few and daunting (though not, as we shall see, entirely absent), Arab governments were obliged to think pragmatically. After 1967, they grew ever more explicit about their readiness to recognize Israel within its pre-June 1967 borders, provided it vacated the lands occupied in the war and satisfied "Palestinian rights" in some (often unspecified) way.

On the other hand, the 1967 catastrophe permitted the ascendancy of an independent Palestinian movement determined to take matters into its own hands. Since the mid-1960s, two rival organizations had vied for Palestinians' allegiance: the Palestine Liberation Organization (PLO), created by the Arab League in 1964 to provide a harmless outlet for growing Palestinian frustration; and al-Fatah, an independent liberation movement led by a young engineer named Yasser Arafat. Starting in 1965, al-Fatah had conducted guerrilla raids into Israel from Jordan, Syria, and Lebanon, hoping to keep the Palestinian struggle alive and, possibly, to provoke an Arab-Israeli war that liberated the Palestinian homeland. War did come, and it had the contrary effect of extending Israel's control over the remainder of Palestine. Yet the calamity also discredited the Arab regimes that had sought to restrain and co-opt Palestinian militancy. Thus, when al-Fatah's paramilitary operations resumed in early 1968, they captured the imagination of Arab audiences desperate for any signs of effective resistance to Israel. Al-Fatah and Arafat gained enormous prestige, eclipsing the ineffectual PLO leadership. In early 1969, al-Fatah joined the PLO and became its dominant faction; Arafat was named PLO chairman. In the coming years, Arab regimes would meddle in the PLO's affairs and dominate some of its smaller factions, but by and large the organization acted independently.[5]

After 1969, the PLO's stated political objectives were to recover the entire Palestinian homeland and establish a nonsectarian "democratic state" in which Muslims, Christians, and Jews enjoyed equal political rights. The group adamantly rejected any settlement that left Israel in place. In view of the PLO's widespread popularity in the Arab world, and the ability of its various factions to disrupt diplomatic initiatives they opposed, Arab states inclined to compromise with Israel would have to tread carefully. Arafat himself needed to be on his guard. A number of PLO leaders and factions clamored to mount operations that the chairman deemed imprudent, but he could not restrain them too forcefully without jeopardizing his own leadership.[6]

The Persian Gulf, though a lesser concern to both the Nixon administration and pan-Arab opinion, certainly bore watching. In January 1968, Britain had announced that it would complete the withdrawal of its forces from the Gulf region by December 1971, prompting speculation over who would fill the resulting power vacuum. Britain proposed that Iran and Saudi Arabia cooperate with each other, and with the independent Arab states and federations that would succeed Britain's protectorates, to secure the Gulf region. The monarch of Iran, Mohammed Reza Shah Pahlavi, had other ideas. He had long aspired to be the hegemon of the Gulf—the guardian of its pro-Western geopolitical orientation and guarantor of its oil exports. Following Britain's withdrawal announcement, he lobbied Washington for the wherewithal to play this role. Though sympathetic to the shah, the Johnson administration endorsed Britain's more balanced policy, and the Nixon administration initially did so as well.[7]

Already, however, Washington was assuming an international stance that would later dovetail with the shah's regional ambitions. By the late 1960s, a relative decline in U.S. global power, combined with the debacle of Vietnam, had suggested the wisdom of placing stricter limits on America's overseas commitments. In a July 1969 speech, Nixon declared that, while the United States remained committed to its allies, the latter must play a larger role in their own defense. The Nixon Doctrine, as pundits called the statement, was initially designed to explain the progressive withdrawal of U.S. ground forces from South Vietnam. But it soon acquired a broader meaning, justifying the reduction of U.S. forces in other areas where the United States was overextended and signaling a greater reliance on regional proxies: powerful states that could protect Western interests in trouble spots around the globe. Immediately grasping the Nixon Doctrine's implications, the shah redoubled his efforts to persuade the United States to anoint him guardian of the Gulf. But the State Department remained wedded to the balanced policy, and Nixon, at first, did not object.[8] The shah would win him over soon enough.

Two thousand miles to Iran's west, the North African country of Libya was on the cusp of more dramatic change. In early 1969, Libya was sparsely populated, thinly developed, and governed by a pro-Western monarch, King Idris I. It hosted a U.S. airbase, Wheelus Field, which over the last decade had aroused local nationalist resentment. The discovery of oil in the late 1950s had ballooned the country's revenues, yet Libya's industrial, technical, educational, and governmental infrastructures were still rudimentary. Pushing eighty, King Idris was expected to exit the stage shortly (possibly through abdication, as he manifestly disliked his job). His nephew and presumed heir, Crown Prince Hasan, seemed ill equipped to preserve the monarchy, especially against the claims of an officer corps impatient with the government's timidity in exploiting Libya's burgeoning oil wealth. U.S. officials had their eye on a pair of brothers, Abdul Aziz Shalhi and Omar Shalhi, the first an army colonel and the second a close adviser to the king. Perhaps the Shalhis could take power, persuade Idris to step down, and offer the country more dynamic pro-Western leadership. The Nixon administration evidently hoped for such results; it is unclear if it did anything more than hope.[9]

Attracting less U.S. notice was another Libyan army officer, twenty-seven-year-old Lieutenant Mu'ammar Qaddafi. A Bedouin goatherd's son who had started preparing his coup while still a teenager at the military academy, Qaddafi espoused an idiosyncratic blend of socialism, pan-Arab nationalism, and Islamic revivalism. He and a band of loyal comrades planned to seize power on the evening of March 12, 1969. It turned out, however, that the wildly popular Egyptian singer Umm Kulthum was scheduled to perform in Benghazi that night. For the coup plotters to upstage the beloved chanteuse as their first governing act would be the height of political folly, especially as her concert was a benefit for al-Fatah. Moreover, several senior regime officials whom the conspirators planned to arrest would be attending the concert. Apprehending them there would attract general attention and spoil the element of surprise (and only deepen the affront to Umm Kulthum and her huge fan base). Qaddafi and his men decided to await another opportunity.[10]

It was, however, the Arab-Israeli dispute that most concerned the makers of U.S. Middle East policy. And, while the politics of the Persian Gulf and Libya would later become enmeshed in Arab-Israeli affairs, the Nixon administration began by focusing on the dispute's main antagonists. Taking office in January 1969, the administration inherited an ambiguous diplomatic blueprint for addressing the consequences of the 1967 war. In November 1967, the United Nations Security Council had passed Resolution 242, which called for Israel's withdrawal from Arab land in exchange for the Arab states' recognition of Israel's right to live in peace and security. In places, though, the resolution was subject to conflicting interpretation. It did not say explicitly which should come first, the Arab states' recognition of Israel or Israel's withdrawal from Arab territory. Not surprisingly, the Israelis favored the first interpretation and the Arabs the second.[11] Moreover, because the resolution referred to "territories occupied in the recent conflict" rather than "*the* territories," Israel claimed that it was entitled to keep significant portions of that land. At the time of the resolution's passage, however, U.S. officials privately assured the Jordanian government that the omission of the definite article was meant to facilitate only minor alterations in Israel's borders. In a September 1968 speech, President Johnson declared that any such changes "cannot and should not reflect the weight of conquest."[12]

These diplomatic undertakings coincided with escalating violence along the Suez Canal, which separated the Israeli-occupied Sinai Peninsula from the rest of Egypt. Egypt's president, Gamal Abdel Nasser, a formidable and charismatic figure who had led the country since the early 1950s, hankered to reverse the humiliating defeat that the Arabs had suffered in the 1967 War. Since the conclusion of that war, Egypt had conducted sporadic artillery attacks and commando raids against Israeli positions in the Sinai. In the spring of 1969, Nasser ordered that these operations be stepped up. In so doing, he hoped to prevent the military status quo from solidifying and to force the international community to compel Israel's withdrawal from the Sinai and the other occupied Arab territories. Nasser also saw the operations as a way of preparing the Egyptian military for a more ambitious campaign, should outside powers fail to step in. Israel responded to the Egyptian attacks by staging commando raids against Egyptian military bases, power stations, bridges, and dams on the west side of the canal. The conflict became known as the War of Attrition.[13]

To the new Nixon administration, the mounting violence underscored the urgency of pursuing a diplomatic resolution of the Arab-Israeli conflict. The administration was divided, though, over how to proceed. Secretary of State Rogers, to whom Nixon initially assigned primary responsibility for Middle East policy, shared the critique implicit in Governor Scranton's Jericho remarks. Like many other officials in his department, Rogers believed that the Arab-Israeli status quo was deeply damaging to U.S. geopolitical interests. As long as Israel continued to occupy the lands seized in 1967, Arab resentment against the United States would grow, facilitating the spread of Soviet influence, radical Arab nationalism, and Palestinian militancy in the Middle East. Rogers favored a comprehensive settlement whereby the Arab states agreed to make peace with Israel in exchange for Israel's withdrawal from nearly all of the occupied territory. Such a settlement, he wrote Nixon in September 1969, "must be based on a map not very different from the one that existed before the 1967 war."[14]

Opposing Rogers was national security adviser Henry Kissinger, until recently a Harvard political scientist. In 1969, Kissinger had no direct authority over Middle East policy, but he had strong views on the matter and frequently shared them with Nixon. Kissinger noted that two of the Arab states seeking to recover land from Israel, Egypt and Syria, had close ties to the Soviet Union. Helping either country regain territory, he wrote in his memoirs, "would give the Soviets a dazzling opportunity to demonstrate their utility to their Arab friends." Kissinger wanted to delay any settlement until after Arab countries had reduced their ties to the Soviet Union and reoriented themselves toward the United States. This would show "that in the Middle East friendship with the United States was the precondition to diplomatic progress."[15] Cold War strategy aside, Kissinger believed that Israel's American supporters (who were largely, but not entirely, Jewish) had sufficient domestic power to block any U.S. effort to force substantial withdrawals on Israel. After the 1973 Arab-Israeli War, as international pressure mounted for an Israeli retreat to the 1967 lines, Kissinger would further suggest that the Israelis had a point when they claimed that those borders were indefensible. In the earlier years, however, he opposed Rogers's proposals mainly on Cold War and domestic political grounds.

Figure 2. William Rogers, Richard Nixon, and Henry Kissinger confer on Air Force One, 1971. Provided by the Richard Nixon Presidential Library and Museum.

Nixon had sympathy for both Rogers's and Kissinger's positions. While he accepted Rogers's view that resentment over U.S. support for Israel was radicalizing the Arab world and facilitating the spread of Soviet influence, he shared Kissinger's desire to prevent Moscow from reaping the benefits of any Middle East settlement. "In short," writes William B. Quandt, a Middle East scholar who served as a National Security Council (NSC) aide to Kissinger, "Nixon embodied in his own mind the two competing paradigms for how best to tackle the Arab-Israeli conflict."[16]

Domestic politics further complicated Nixon's outlook. Because of American Jews' historical attachment to the Democratic Party, Nixon could never hope to receive the support of most Jews. In fact, Kissinger recalled, "The President was convinced that most leaders of the Jewish community had opposed him throughout his political career"—an attitude Nixon sometimes reciprocated by making anti-Semitic comments in private. At the same time, Nixon took pride in his ability to formulate Middle East policy entirely on the merits, without regard to domestic politics. Whenever he made a move that benefited Israel, he was quick to portray his action as motivated solely by the national interest and to note how little he stood to gain by it politically. During the 1968 presidential campaign, Nixon delivered a prepared speech to a B'nai B'rith convention in which he pledged that the military balance would "be tipped in Israel's favor." Prior to the event Nixon told his speechwriter, William Safire, "You'll see, there won't be a single vote in this for me. They'll cheer and applaud, and then vote for the other guy, they always do. But we're right on the issue, and it wouldn't hurt to say so." "I have always supported the State of Israel," Nixon wrote in a 1971 memorandum to Rogers. "My support, however, has in no way been influenced by the Jewish political lobby in the United States."[17]

Nixon, of course, was protesting too much. He cared deeply about the attitudes of American Jews and believed their opposition should, and could, be blunted. He was right about that last point. By the early 1970s, a host of domestic and international issues—crime, busing, international terrorism, the predicament of Soviet Jews—challenged the traditional liberalism of American Jews, providing the Republican Party with an opportunity to expand its share of the Jewish vote.[18] Throughout his first term, with an eye to his 1972 reelection effort, Nixon never failed to remind Jewish voters that he stood on the "right" side of those issues. Nor could he let them forget his staunch support for Israel. In September 1969, after sending the first installment of fifty F-4 Phantom jets that the U.S. government had agreed to sell to Israel, Nixon wrote to Kissinger demanding an explanation for "the absolute failure of the American Jewish community to express any appreciation by letter, calls or otherwise" for the shipment.[19] More consequentially, Nixon would seek to cultivate Jewish support by distancing himself from, and at times undermining, the initiatives of his own State Department.

Over the course of 1969 the Nixon administration explored prospects for an Arab-Israeli settlement. In Washington, Secretary Rogers and assistant secretary of state for Near East Affairs Joseph Sisco held "two-power" talks with Anatoly Dobrynin, the Soviet ambassador to the United States. In New York, Nixon's UN ambassador Charles Yost conducted "four-power" negotiations with his Soviet, British, and French counterparts. The administration also cooperated with the special UN mediator Gunnar Jarring, whose mission had been authorized by Resolution 242. The purpose of the bilateral and four-power talks was to find some common basis for settling the dispute that Jarring could submit to Israel and the relevant Arab states.[20]

Meanwhile, the War of Attrition escalated. In the summer of 1969, Israel began supplementing its commando raids with air attacks against Egyptian surface-to-air missiles, anti-aircraft gun batteries, and radar stations on the west bank of the canal. By fall, much of Egypt's air defense system lay in ruins. State Department officials fretted about the Israeli onslaught. Few of them had any sympathy for Nasser, who had long publicly disparaged U.S. policy, and some no doubt relished seeing his regime thrown back on its heels. Sharply offsetting this benefit, however, was the political damage the United States incurred through its association with Israel's air attacks. Donald Bergus, chief of the U.S. Interests Section in Cairo (effectively the U.S. ambassador in the absence of formal diplomatic relations), repeatedly warned that Israel's use of U.S.-supplied weapons against Egypt was blackening America's name in the region. To condone such behavior, he cabled home in September, was to allow "the United States to commit hari-kari in the Arab world."[21]

While neither Rogers nor Sisco spoke with Bergus's pungency, both shared his concern about U.S. standing in the area and hoped to salvage it through energetic diplomacy. On October 28, they presented Ambassador Dobrynin with a proposal for an Egyptian-Israeli settlement. In exchange for Israel's withdrawal from all of the Sinai Peninsula, Egypt was to make peace with Israel, allow Israeli vessels safe passage through the Suez Canal and the Strait of Tiran,[22] and agree to the demilitarization of portions of the Sinai. On December 18, Ambassador Yost submitted to the four-power forum a parallel proposal for a Jordanian-Israeli agreement. It called for an Israeli withdrawal from virtually all of the West Bank, a negotiated settlement of Jerusalem's status on the basis of shared Israeli and Jordanian administration of a unified city, and a resolution of the refugee issue involving repatriation of some refugees and resettlement and compensation of the remainder. (Although the State Department did not rule out Syria's eventual inclusion in a settlement, it declined to address Syrian claims because Damascus still rejected Resolution 242.) The above agreements were to be achieved through indirect negotiations among the parties that would, at a later date, give way to direct negotiations.[23]

In a December 9 speech, Rogers publicly outlined the overall approach. While noting that Israel's final borders must be negotiated, he cautioned that "any change in the pre-existing lines . . . should be confined to insubstantial alterations required for mutual security" and—in an exact repetition of Lyndon Johnson's language of fourteen months earlier—"should not reflect the weight of conquest."[24] The new initiative became known as the Rogers Plan.

Kissinger strongly opposed the Rogers Plan, for reasons suggested above: the plan would allow Egypt, a client of the Soviet Union, to recover territory at the expense of Israel, an ally of the United States. He also doubted that Israel would ever accept the plan's provisions. The emerging initiative was indeed generating intense criticism from the Israeli government, American Jews, and other U.S. supporters of Israel. These parties broadly agreed that, in any Middle East settlement, Israel should retain substantial portions of the Arab territories occupied in 1967, including all of East Jerusalem. They were also alarmed at the specter of thousands of Palestinian refugees returning to their former homes. Such an influx, they feared, would undermine Israel's Jewish character. "Any Israeli government which approved this proposal [on refugees]," Israeli prime minister Golda Meir told a visiting U.S. senator in late December, "would be guilty of treason."[25]

Nixon, too, had serious reservations about the Rogers Plan, but he thought there were advantages in allowing Rogers to present it. "I knew that the Rogers Plan could never be implemented," he later wrote, "but I believed that it was important to let the Arab world know that the United States did not automatically dismiss its case regarding the occupied territories or rule out a compromise of the conflicting claims. With the Rogers Plan on the record, I thought it would be easier for the Arab leaders to propose reopening relations with the United States without coming under attack from the hawks and pro-Soviet elements in their own countries."[26]

Cunning in theory, Nixon's approach was unworkable in practice. It was unrealistic to expect the Rogers Plan to sit inertly "on the record." As long as Rogers believed he had presidential backing (and it appears that Nixon encouraged this belief),[27] he was sure to pursue his initiative with vigor. Yet an untrammelled Rogers Plan spelled political danger for Nixon, as the fierce opposition of Israel and its supporters plainly showed. So Nixon, with Kissinger's eager assistance, resorted to covert means to subvert his administration's official Middle East policy.

The undermining of Rogers's efforts began in earnest in the fall of 1969. Kissinger wrote in his memoirs that in late October, after authorizing the State Department to submit its proposal for an Egyptian-Israeli settlement to the Soviets, Nixon "sought to hedge his bets by asking [attorney general] John Mitchell and Leonard Garment—counselor to the President and adviser on Jewish affairs—to let Jewish community leaders know his doubts about State's diplomacy." When the State Department submitted its December 18 paper on an Israeli-Jordanian agreement, Kissinger continued, "Nixon ordered that private assurances be given to Mrs. Meir via Len Garment that we would go no further and that we would not press our proposal."[28] In late December, Israeli ambassador to the United States Yitzhak Rabin privately warned Kissinger that, if the Rogers Plan went forward, he would lead a public campaign in the United States against the initiative. According to Rabin's memoirs, Kissinger replied that Nixon had not yet spoken publicly about the plan. "As long as he himself is not publicly committed, you have a chance of taking action. . . . What you say to Rogers, or against him, is for you to decide. But I advise you. . . . Don't attack the president!" To Rogers, Kissinger craftily suggested that Israeli criticism of the Rogers Plan would enhance the initiative's credibility in the Arab world. "In fact that's what we need. It wouldn't be authentic if the Israelis approved."[29]

Kissinger neglected to tell Rogers that the White House itself was encouraging Jewish and Israeli attacks on the State Department. On October 2, Kissinger had written to Nixon, "As you requested, I told Len Garment to organize some Jewish Community protests against the State Department's attitude on the Middle East situation and Len has promised to take prompt action." Garment later recalled that in January 1970, as Meir began a speaking tour of the United States, Kissinger told Garment, "The president has a little errand for you." Garment was to meet Meir at the airport and "tell her wherever she goes, in all her speeches and press conferences, we want her to slam the hell out of Rogers and his plan." A skeptical Garment called H.R. (Bob) Haldeman, the White House chief of staff, who confirmed that these were Nixon's instructions.[30]

On December 22, 1969, the Israeli cabinet formally rejected the Rogers Plan, calling it "an attempt to appease [Arab states] at the expense of Israel." The next day the Soviet government, too, rejected the plan and informed Washington that the Egyptians (who had authorized the Soviets to speak for them on this matter) had turned it down, too. Egypt never issued a formal rejection of the plan or fully explained its opposition. In scattered statements that fall, Egyptian officials criticized elements of the emerging initiative, such as the provision for eventual direct negotiations and the assumption that demilitarized zones would be established on Arab territory alone. Egyptians also dismissed the Rogers Plan as an attempt to lure Egypt into a separate peace with Israel. The unveiling of the proposed Israeli-Jordanian agreement in December did not silence that complaint; Egyptian officials now criticized the plan for failing to address Syria's claims.[31]

In his memoirs, Mahmoud Riad, Egypt's foreign minister at the time, offered two additional reasons for Cairo's opposition: that Israel had already manifested its rejection of the plan, and that it was clear "that this particular initiative represented only one American trend, that of the State

Department." Similarly, Ashraf Ghorbal, then chief of the Egyptian Interests Section in Washington, wrote in his own memoirs that Nixon's and Kissinger's obvious disdain for the Rogers Plan rendered it "stillborn." Egypt had little incentive to invest political capital in such a scheme.[32]

The Jordanian government was favorably disposed toward the Rogers Plan but could not take the political risk of supporting it alone. It neither accepted nor rejected the plan.[33]

"Rogers and Sisco felt that the Soviets had let the United States down," wrote David Korn, a former State Department official, over two decades later. "The Americans had been ready to take a position at odds with their client, Israel, but the Soviets had been unwilling to do the same with theirs, Egypt."[34] What this assessment missed, of course, was the role of the Nixon White House in abetting Israel's own rejection of the American plan—and, less directly, in encouraging Egypt to keep its distance from it.

In January 1970, the War of Attrition escalated, as the Israeli Air Force (IAF) began conducting "deep penetration" bombing raids into the Egyptian interior, which had been rendered extremely vulnerable by the destruction of Egypt's air defense system. Employing U.S.-supplied F-4 Phantom aircraft, the IAF struck military bases and air force supply depots in the Nile Delta and on the outskirts of Cairo.[35] Alarmed by the raids, in late January Nasser paid a secret visit to Moscow, where he implored his hosts to supply Egypt with new surface-to-air missiles known as SA-3s.[36] According to the Egyptian journalist and Nasser confidant Muhammad Hasanayn Haykal, who went on the trip, the Soviets at first balked at the request but relented when Nasser threatened "to step down and hand over to a pro-American President" should the Russians disappoint him. Over the next several weeks, scores of SA-3s were deployed in Egypt, initially operated by Soviet crews because Egyptians were not yet trained in their use. The Soviets also provided over one hundred MiG-21 aircraft, flown by Soviet pilots.[37]

The arrival of the SA-3s not only forced an end to Israel's deep penetration raids but permitted Egypt to begin laying the basis for further efforts to liberate the Sinai. Fired at an angle, SA-3s had a lateral range of up to thirty-three miles. If stationed on or near the west bank of the Suez Canal, they could make it extremely difficult for Israeli aircraft to fly close enough to attack Egyptian units making a hostile crossing of that waterway. Over the spring of 1970, Egyptian construction crews worked around the clock to build SA-3 sites closer to the canal. The IAF ferociously attacked the construction sites, using napalm to incinerate equipment and people.

As many as two thousand workers eventually died in these raids. But the Egyptian crews persevered, and Israel could not prevent them from inching the missiles toward the canal.[38]

Meanwhile, the Israelis pressed the Nixon administration to sell them an additional twenty-five Phantom and one hundred Skyhawk aircraft. Kissinger favored the sale, arguing that the SA-3 deployments could not go unanswered. From Cairo, however, Donald Bergus warned that selling more planes to Israel would so outrage local opinion as to raise "serious concern re [the] safety of [the] American community in Egypt. I cannot rule out [the] need for evacuation in such a contingency." The State Department extended Bergus's concern to "American material interests and the lives of our citizens in the area" as a whole. Noting that the SA-3s had been deployed in response to Israel's deep penetration raids, the State Department argued that the best way to prevent further Soviet involvement was to urge restraint on Israel and limit its arsenal.[39]

Nixon, characteristically, was swayed by arguments on both sides. Equally characteristically, he fashioned a devious response. On March 23, with the president's blessing, Secretary Rogers announced that the question of additional aircraft to Israel would be held "in abeyance" until further notice. Five days earlier, however, Nixon had met privately with Ambassador Rabin and assured him that the United States would quietly replenish Israeli aircraft lost in the War of Attrition. Rabin should "let Kissinger know if the balance of power was in danger," and Nixon would see to it that Israel got the planes it needed.[40] By this method, the United States could keep Israel armed without generating publicity that further enflamed Arab opinion.

Nixon then made a startling suggestion to Rabin: "I am aware of the introduction of Soviet SA-3s and I hope you knock them out. You can't let them build up." Rabin replied that Israel "would like to knock out the SAMs" but hesitated to attempt this as long as the United States refused to arm Israel publicly. Without such a visible demonstration of U.S. support, Israel would feel too isolated and vulnerable to move directly against Soviet-manned installations. Nixon insisted on the private arms-transfer procedure and dropped the matter of attacking SA-3s.[41] The Israelis would soon skirmish with the Soviets in any case.

Whatever the vicarious appeal of Israeli combat operations, Nixon was willing to let the State Department try its hand at a diplomatic solution. In June, overruling Kissinger, the president authorized Rogers and Sisco to seek a cease-fire over the Suez Canal linked to negotiations for a broader

Arab-Israeli settlement. The initiative, which became known as the second Rogers Plan or Rogers II, called on Egypt and Israel to cease all military hostilities for ninety days and provided for a resumption of Gunnar Jarring's mission, which had been suspended the previous year. On June 19, U.S. diplomats presented the plan to the governments of Israel, Egypt, and Jordan. (Jordan was included because of the key role it was expected to play in any broader settlement.)[42]

For the next several weeks, as Washington tried to sell Rogers II to the parties, the violence over the canal escalated. Although the IAF had ended its deep penetration raids, it continued to strike Egyptian military targets on the canal's western bank. These missions became increasingly hazardous as the SA-3s moved closer to the canal. In several instances the missiles downed Israeli planes, a rare and traumatic occurrence for the IAF. More strikingly, Soviet-piloted MiGs began directly challenging Israeli aircraft flying reconnaissance and bombing missions. On July 30, the IAF shot down five MiGs over the Gulf of Suez. It was a remarkable victory for the IAF, but Israeli leaders had to wonder how Moscow would react to the humiliation.[43]

A simultaneous diplomatic breakthrough prevented (or spared) the Soviets from answering that question. On July 23, Nasser announced his acceptance of the U.S. initiative. According to Muhammad Haykal, who was now Egypt's minister of information, Nasser said that a cease-fire would allow Egypt a "breathing space so that we can finish our missile sites" along the canal. Diplomatically, Nasser did not believe he was committing to anything new, as Cairo had already endorsed Jarring's mission. On July 26, Jordan also accepted Rogers II.[44] The Israelis, however, fiercely resisted the U.S. plan. They suspected, accurately enough, that Egypt would use the cease-fire to continue the buildup of SA-3s along the canal. They also feared that the resumption of Jarring's mission would increase international pressure on them to withdraw from Arab land and repatriate Palestinian refugees. In a July 23 letter to Meir, Nixon promised continued arms deliveries and pledged that the United States "will not press Israel to accept a solution to the [Palestinian] refugee problem that will alter fundamentally the Jewish character of the State of Israel." Nixon also wrote, "No Israeli soldier should be withdrawn from the present lines until a binding contractual peace agreement satisfactory to you has been achieved." These assurances, combined with concern over the escalating confrontation with the Soviet Union—which could grow even more perilous if the Israelis alienated the United States by rejecting its initiative—wore down Israel's resistance. On

July 31, Israel accepted Rogers II. The cease-fire went into effect at midnight on August 7–8.[45]

Almost immediately, evidence surfaced that Egypt was violating the cease-fire. The agreement obligated Egypt and Israel to "refrain from changing the military status quo within zones extending 50 kilometers" on either side of the Suez Canal. In the days preceding the cease-fire's implementation, the Egyptians had scrambled to complete construction on the SA-3 missile sites within their own soon-to-be-restricted zone. Not quite finished by midnight on August 7–8, they continued these deployments, off and on, for some weeks into the cease-fire. The Israelis were the first to notice, providing Washington with photographic evidence of the violations. The State Department—especially Rogers, whose personal prestige was invested in the agreement—initially resisted Israel's claims, but by mid-August U.S. intelligence agencies had confirmed them. Bergus protested to the Egyptian government, which simply denied that any violations had occurred and refused to remove any missiles from the restricted zone. Israel suspended its participation in the Jarring talks, though the cease-fire itself held.[46]

"Stop shooting and start talking" had been Rogers's shorthand for his initiative. Only the first half of the formula had been realized, and even that achievement was tenuous. At the cost of thousands of lives, Egypt had established a network of SA-3s along the west bank of the canal and thus laid the basis for an eventual military crossing. Nasser was determined to resume hostilities once the ninety-day cease-fire expired. His army chief of staff assured him that plans were afoot to get Egyptian units across the canal by early 1971.[47] The timetable was unrealistic, but there was every reason to expect that Egypt would, sooner or later, make an all-out effort to win back the Sinai.

To Nasser's more militant Arab critics, however, Egypt's acceptance of the cease-fire smacked of capitulationism. Iraq, Syria, Algeria, and the PLO accused Nasser of abandoning the Arab cause for a separate deal with Israel. True, Nasser had precedents for accepting Rogers II: Egypt, Jordan, and Syria had agreed to the cease-fire that ended the 1967 War, and Egypt and Jordan had endorsed Jarring's mission. But reaffirming these commitments under the auspices of a U.S. plan was a step too far for Nasser's critics, who denounced the move as "high treason" and a "surrender solution." Nasser cancelled the PLO's radio service, "The Voice of Palestine," which had broadcast from Cairo with his support. In an angry cable to Iraqi president Ahmad Hasan al-Bakr, Nasser asked, "Why do you not send your forces to the front at some time to confront the enemy? . . . The Egyptian people are not fighting this battle from the preacher's pulpit."[48] The message was clear: having fought Israel alone for a year and a half, Egypt was entitled to make its own foreign policy. Nasser's successor would even more jealously guard Egypt's national prerogatives against the claims of pan-Arab solidarity.

On September 6, the day Israel withdrew from the Jarring talks, Middle East politics took a turn for the spectacular. Members of the Popular Front for the Liberation of Palestine (PFLP), a radical faction of the PLO, hijacked four passenger airliners departing from European airports. On one plane, security officers and crew overpowered the militants. Hijackers took a second plane to Cairo airport, released its passengers and crew, and blew it up. The two remaining planes ended up at Dawson's Field, an airstrip in the Jordanian desert, where on September 9 they were joined by a fifth plane hijacked out of Bahrain. Of the hundreds of passengers and crew brought to Dawson's, most were freed within a few days' time, though the hijackers continued to hold about fifty hostages, demanding the release of Palestinians imprisoned in Europe and Israel. Again, the hijackers detonated the empty planes.[49]

The PFLP's plane seizures were the latest, and most audacious, in a string of hijackings that some Palestinian militants had conducted over the previous two years, in their efforts to draw attention to the Palestinian cause and to free jailed comrades. The September hijackings also brought to the fore a basic tension that had developed over that period, concerning the relationship between the Palestinian movement and Arab states bordering Israel.

Since gaining predominant control over the PLO in early 1969, Yasser Arafat and al-Fatah had taken a pragmatic approach to relations with Arab regimes, seeking to maximize the support the PLO received from those governments and to avoid unnecessary conflict with them. The first effort met with considerable success. Egypt continued the practice, begun in 1968, of providing al-Fatah with strong diplomatic backing and modest military aid. In the spring of 1969, Saudi Arabia agreed to furnish the PLO with arms and a $12 million annual subsidy financed by a special tax imposed on Palestinians working in the kingdom. Most other Arab governments offered diplomatic and rhetorical support to the PLO, while a few extended material aid as well.[50]

Because the PLO remained committed to military struggle against Israel, however, Arafat's other pragmatic objective, avoiding friction with Arab governments, proved harder to achieve. Several circumstances made

Jordan and Lebanon attractive staging areas for guerrilla raids into Israel. Both countries had long borders with Israel (and in Jordan's case with the Israeli occupied West Bank). Both, and especially Jordan, had large Palestinian populations that could provide political and logistical support for such attacks. Both, and especially Lebanon, had weak central governments that were ill equipped and reluctant to restrain Palestinian operations. That reluctance, however, exposed Lebanon and Jordan to Israeli reprisal raids. The more lethal the Israeli raids grew, and the more they victimized ordinary Jordanians and Lebanese as well as Palestinians, the less tolerant of Palestinian militancy Amman and Beirut could afford to be. Arafat understood these dynamics and tried to avoid arousing the active hostility of either government. But he could not control all of the PLO's factions, some of which committed acts of air piracy beyond the traditional geographic arena of the Arab-Israeli conflict. Nor could Arafat resist the internal pressure to authorize provocative actions by al-Fatah itself (though al-Fatah's raids were confined to Israel and the occupied territories).[51] Clashes between PLO forces and the host governments were inevitable. And, as both Jordan and Lebanon had close ties to the United States, Washington, too, would be drawn into the fray.

In the late 1960s, Jordan was the main base for Palestinian operations. It was in Lebanon, however, that tensions between the PLO and local authorities first came to a head. In the spring of 1969, Lebanon's Maronite Christian president, Charles Helou, attempted to crack down on PLO groups engaging in cross-border raids into northern Israel. The PLO and pro-Palestinian Lebanese resisted Helou's efforts, and the country was plunged into a months-long crisis. Rashid Karami, Lebanon's Sunni Muslim prime minister, disavowed Helou's policy and called for compromise with the PLO. Iraq and Syria denounced the anti-PLO effort, and Syria sealed its border with Lebanon, damaging its economy. Nasser also criticized Helou's actions, though in more measured tones.[52]

Helou had anticipated such pressures and, in meetings with U.S. ambassador to Lebanon Dwight Porter in May, pleaded for some tangible U.S. support. If the U.S. military could not intervene unilaterally, Helou said, then perhaps it could participate in a UN peacekeeping force that might be stationed in Lebanon. The State Department instructed Porter to commend Helou's courageous stance but urge the president to "avoid looking to external factors as [a] crutch." A UN peacekeeping force "would be exceedingly difficult to arrange"—especially as the Soviets could veto the enabling resolution in the Security Council—"and, even if [it] proved possible, US military participation therein must be ruled out." Porter did not have to explain (because Helou himself had acknowledged this constraint) that the American public's dismay over the Vietnam debacle sharply limited the Nixon administration's freedom of action abroad. Apart from seeking an overall Arab-Israeli settlement, Porter said, about all the administration could do for Lebanon would be to appeal for Israeli restraint and to ask friendly Arab states such as Saudi Arabia and Kuwait to stop financing the PLO. These latter efforts proved only partly successful. Israel pledged to refrain from military action in southern Lebanon for the time being, but no Arab state would agree to defund the PLO, a reflection of the Palestinian movement's enormous popularity throughout the region.[53]

In November 1969, Nasser hosted a meeting between Lebanese and PLO delegations. In the Cairo Agreement, the PLO gained the right to administer Palestinian camps in Lebanon and to conduct cross-border raids into Israel, provided it consulted Lebanese authorities beforehand (a commitment it would honor only loosely). The agreement curbed the Lebanese-Palestinian violence, but at a significant cost to Beirut's authority. Many Lebanese, especially Maronites, felt their government had let them down. They turned increasingly to private militias and redoubled their efforts to acquire arms.[54]

In Jordan, the PLO already possessed a privileged sanctuary. Over the course of 1970, however, a combination of internal divisions and international pressures impelled the organization to seek to improve its position in Jordan, with disastrous results. Arafat and the top al-Fatah leadership did hope for a modus vivendi with Jordan's King Hussein, but they could not easily propagate this view throughout the PLO as a whole. More radical factions insisted that Palestine could not be liberated until "reactionary" Arab regimes—of which Jordan's monarchy was Exhibit A—had first been overthrown. The notion that "the road to Jerusalem goes through Amman," as the PFLP slogan went, had growing appeal among Palestinians, especially the young men who flocked to join the guerrilla organizations after the spring of 1968. Al-Fatah's own recruits were susceptible to this fervor, and the Palestinian movement's explosive growth in 1968–1970 made it difficult for al-Fatah leaders to maintain discipline over the new members. The internal brakes on Palestinian adventurism wore thinner and thinner. By early 1970, PLO militants were in brazen defiance of the Jordanian government, erecting roadblocks on the streets of Amman, engaging the army in sporadic clashes, and openly calling for Hussein's ouster.[55]

Diplomatic developments confirmed the PLO on its collision course with the Jordanian regime. Egypt's acceptance of the second Rogers Plan in July 1970 stirred anger throughout the Arab world, especially among Palestinians. Jordan, too, had accepted the agreement, and Amman was a much softer target than Cairo. On September 1, Palestinian gunmen opened fire on Hussein's motorcade near Amman's airport, almost killing the king. Five days later the PFLP launched its audacious hijacking venture. In addition to seeking the release of Palestinian prisoners held in Europe and Israel, the PFLP clearly hoped to scuttle the Israeli-Egyptian-Jordanian cease-fire. The selection of Cairo airport and Dawson's Field was meant to humiliate both Nasser and Hussein, but the subsequent playing out of the hostage drama on Jordanian soil posed a special challenge to the king.[56]

The PLO Central Committee denounced the hijackings and suspended the PFLP's membership. But the PFLP continued to hold the fifty-odd hostages, and the PLO as a whole remained defiant of Amman's authority. In mid-September, Hussein disbanded his civilian cabinet, formed a military government, and launched an all-out offensive against the PLO. The Jordanian army quickly gained the upper hand, exacting heavy Palestinian casualties. The PLO appealed for support from other Arab countries, especially Iraq, which had stationed troops in Jordan since 1967. The Iraqis stayed out of the battle, but on September 19 a column of Syrian tanks crossed into northern Jordan. Evidently, the Syrian move was aimed not at overthrowing Hussein but, rather, at saving the Palestinians from annihilation and helping them secure an enclave from which to negotiate power-sharing arrangements with the king.[57]

Hussein, however, had reason to fear the worst. In an urgent message to Nixon early on September 21, he warned that the situation was "deteriorating dangerously" and pleaded for "immediate air strikes on invading forces from any quarter." In an appeal to the British government a day earlier, Hussein called, more explicitly, for "Israeli or other air intervention or [the] threat thereof." In a subsequent message to Washington, Hussein specified that any Israeli intervention should be confined to air strikes—from which, presumably, he could more easily disassociate himself than from Israeli ground operations. Hussein also may have feared that, once Israeli troops entered his country, they would never leave. Should ground action become necessary, he insisted, the United States or Britain must conduct it.[58]

Nixon administration officials were in a quandary. If they did nothing, Hussein might fall. Not only would the United States lose a valued ally, but the resulting chaos could trigger a regional war, as Jordan's neighbors rushed to grab parts of its territory or prevent their rivals from doing so. Moreover, Nixon and Kissinger believed that Moscow was behind the Syrian incursion; failing to respond would constitute a major Cold War defeat. (Other U.S. officials questioned this reading.[59]) Yet a direct U.S. intervention on Hussein's behalf, with or without Britain, posed problems of its own. With so many military resources still deployed in Southeast Asia, it was unclear that the United States had the capability to conduct an effective operation in the Eastern Mediterranean. Even if it did, there was the risk of Soviet reaction.[60]

A third course, unilateral Israeli intervention, seemed less objectionable. The Israelis were already on the scene, were better prepared logistically, and had more experience fighting Arab armies and Palestinian groups. While this option, too, carried some potential for escalation, its promised reward made the risks more acceptable. As Rogers remarked on the evening of September 20, "My view is that we should favor it because if the King goes down the drain the GD thing is a total mess. This way it will be a mess, but if they can save the King there is some advantage." In a rare moment of consensus among Middle East policy makers, Nixon, Kissinger, Rogers, and Sisco all supported Israeli intervention. Ideally, air strikes would suffice to turn back the Syrians. If not, Israeli ground forces should move in, despite Hussein's objections.[61]

Over the next couple of days, the Nixon administration sounded out the Israeli government on an intervention in Jordan. The Israelis were noncommittal, seeking to clarify what the administration had in mind. Amid these deliberations, however, Israel visibly mobilized ground forces along the borders with Syria and Jordan.[62] Nixon, meanwhile, placed the 82nd Airborne Division in Fort Bragg, North Carolina, on full alert, increased the alert status of an airborne brigade in West Germany, and ordered ships from the U.S. Sixth Fleet to the Eastern Mediterranean—moves the Soviets were bound to notice. Rogers publicly condemned the Syrian intervention, and the State Department warned Moscow of "the serious consequences which could ensue from a broadening of the conflict."[63]

On September 22 and 23, the tide of battle shifted dramatically in Hussein's favor. The Jordanian military launched air and land offensives against the Syrians, inflicting heavy losses and chasing them back across the border. Several historians have argued that the Jordanians were emboldened, and the Syrians cowed, by the manifestations of U.S. and Israeli support, and surely there is truth to this view.[64] Yet Amman also benefited from the half-heartedness of the Syrian intervention. For reasons that remain unclear—perhaps political divisions within the Damascus regime, perhaps a desire to avoid escalation—the Syrians never threw their full weight behind the intervention and even attempted, unsuccessfully, to disguise their direct involvement. The invading tanks were painted with the markings of the Palestine Liberation Army, a Damascus-backed Palestinian group, and the Syrian air force was withheld from the battle. Whatever its causes, Syria's retreat permitted the Jordanians to concentrate their firepower on the PLO, whose defeat seemed imminent.[65]

By now, however, Hussein faced growing pan-Arab pressure to halt the military campaign and reach an accommodation with the PLO. On September 22, a delegation of Arab leaders headed by Sudanese president Ja'far al-Numayri arrived in Amman to seek a cease-fire. Two days later Numayri smuggled Arafat from Jordan to Cairo, where Nasser had convened an emergency Arab summit meeting. Hussein himself hastened to Cairo. On September 27, in the presence of the assembled heads of state, he and Arafat agreed to end the fighting, which had claimed three thousand to five thousand lives, most of them Palestinian civilians. The cease-fire agreement required both sides to withdraw their forces from Jordan's cities, provided for a prisoner exchange, and established a pan-Arab committee to monitor compliance. It was a measure of Hussein's isolation that Arafat

Figure 3. Emergency Arab summit meeting in Cairo, September 1970; *left to right:* Ja'far al-Numayri (*partly obscured*), Mu'ammar Qaddafi, Yasser Arafat, Gamal Abdel Nasser, and King Hussein. © Bettmann/CORBIS.

could secure such favorable terms, which on several issues treated Jordanian and PLO forces symmetrically.[66]

Brokering the Jordanian-PLO agreement was Nasser's last public act. The next day, after seeing his guests off at the airport, the Egyptian president was felled by a heart attack at the age of fifty-two. Shock and grief swept the Arab world. For nearly two decades, Nasser had embodied the Arabs' struggle for independence and dignity; it was difficult to imagine Middle Eastern politics without him. Although his authority had waned in recent years, especially after the 1967 debacle, he remained an imposing and beloved figure to the end.

Nasser's death had profound implications for Egyptian, inter-Arab, Arab-Israeli, and international affairs; these will be explored later in the current chapter and beyond. The main impact on Jordanian-Palestinian relations was to deprive the PLO of one of its strongest protectors (a role Nasser had continued to play despite the recent disagreement over Rogers II) and thus undermine the September 27 agreement. Over the next several months, while remaining publicly committed to the agreement, Hussein launched what the historian Yezid Sayigh calls a "creeping offensive" against the PLO, seizing control of Jordan's main roads and strategic heights and gradually pushing PLO fighters out of their remaining strongholds. When the PFLP responded with a renewed guerrilla campaign, Hussein moved against the PLO as a whole. By the summer of 1971, the PLO's power in Jordan had been broken, with many of its camps reduced to rubble and its surviving leaders and cadres scrambling for new sanctuaries. Increasingly, the PLO would make its home in Lebanon, a country far less able to withstand full immersion in the politics of Palestinian exile.[67]

As for the events of September 1970 in particular, they, too, had ramifications beyond Jordan. Although Rogers and Kissinger generally agreed on how to address the immediate crisis, the event underscored their deeper differences over Middle East policy, providing some vindication to Kissinger's globalist approach. Perhaps there *were* times when it was preferable to uphold Cold War allies than to push evenhandedly for Arab-Israeli peace. Some scholars go further, arguing that the Jordan crisis convinced Nixon that Israel was a "strategic asset" that could help the United States combat Soviet influence and radical nationalism in the Middle East.[68] This is a dubious claim. While Israel and its American supporters forcefully argued the "strategic asset" case, there is little evidence that Nixon expected to face subsequent crises in which the threat or reality of Israeli intervention in a neighboring country would serve U.S. interests. Rather, the Jordan crisis, by recasting some Middle East conflicts as proxy Cold War struggles, enhanced Israel's *symbolic* status as a loyal ally whose needs and sensitivities merited unusual deference, especially when they clashed with the claims of Moscow's regional clients. This shift in perception would make it harder for successive U.S. administrations to resist Israeli requests for increased military aid or press Israel to be more flexible in Arab-Israeli diplomacy.

At the Arab summit meeting he hosted in his final days of life, Nasser decried King Hussein's assault on the PLO and wearily orchestrated the diplomatic pressures to bring an end to the fighting. Another leader in attendance was far more condemnatory, calling for the immediate dispatching to Jordan of an inter-Arab force. "If we are faced with a madman like Hussein," he said, ". . . we must send someone to seize him, handcuff him, . . . and take him off to an asylum." When King Faisal of Saudi Arabia objected to this characterization of a fellow monarch (Hussein had not yet arrived in Cairo), the critic retorted, "But all his family are mad. It's a matter of record"—a gauche reference to the mental illness that had ended the reign of Hussein's father, King Talal, in 1952. Hussein's assailant was Mu'ammar Qaddafi, who a year earlier had finally seized power in Libya.[69]

Qaddafi's draconian proposal did not prevail at the summit, but his combative presence there proclaimed a new and growing force in Arab politics. After their successful, bloodless coup on September 1, 1969 (beating the Shalhi brothers to the punch by just three days), Qaddafi and his comrades had declared themselves ardent Nasserists who would loyally follow Cairo's revolutionary lead. This was hardly good news, Haykal reported to Nasser following a quick scouting trip to Libya days after the coup. Qaddafi and his men were "shockingly innocent—scandalously pure"; their simplistic approach to international affairs would hinder more than help. In the coming months Haykal, Nasser, and other highly placed Egyptians were by turns bemused and perturbed by Qaddafi's utter lack of worldliness. "What are these? Locusts?" the Libyan asked when served a shrimp platter during a dinner with Nasser. On another occasion, Qaddafi advised that the Arabs "should go straight to an overall war and liquidate Israel." Easier said than done, Nasser replied. To counter Israel's suspected nuclear arsenal, Qaddafi sent his second-in-command, Abdel Salam Jalloud, to Beijing to purchase an atom bomb from the communist Chinese, who politely informed Jalloud that such items were not for sale.[70]

Nixon administration officials were unsure what to make of the new Libyan regime. Its rhetoric was anti-Western, and it immediately demanded that the United States and Britain relinquish their military bases in the country. Still, Tripoli showed no signs of curtailing oil shipments to the West or of cozying up to Moscow, whose Marxist doctrines it disdained on Islamic grounds (Jalloud's Chinese shopping trip notwithstanding). The U.S. airbase, Wheelus Field, had less strategic value than it did a decade earlier, though Washington was hardly eager to be evicted from it.[71] (The United States vacated the base in June 1970.) Over the course of 1970, the Nixon administration evidently considered covert plans for subverting the new regime but abandoned them as infeasible.[72] Meanwhile, the administration sought to influence Libya's behavior by holding up the delivery of eight U.S. F-5 fighter aircraft that King Idris had purchased. The gambit backfired. In the summer of 1970, the Libyans overcame their religious scruples and began buying Soviet arms. Speaking to the U.S. ambassador months later, Qaddafi chided the United States for pushing Libya into the Soviets' embrace. "We both, as Muslims and Christians—people of the book—abhor atheistic communism," he said. "But on political grounds Arabs must be friends to the USSR which befriends them and cannot be with a (Christian) West which befriends Israel."[73] For the moment, Libya's role in the Arab-Israeli dispute was mainly rhetorical. That would change.

On October 15, 1970, an Egyptian popular referendum confirmed Anwar Sadat's appointment as Nasser's successor. Both at home and abroad, Sadat was widely seen as an interim president, someone to occupy the office until a more commanding figure emerged. Not until mid-1971 would he fully establish his authority within Egypt. From the start, however, Sadat showed a willingness to move boldly on the Egyptian-Israeli front, appearing even less patient with the status quo than Nasser had been. Sadat both built on and modified the legacy of his predecessor. In the weeks prior to his death, Nasser had complained about Moscow's slowness in responding to Egyptian arms requests. He had also shown, through his acceptance of Rogers II, a willingness to cooperate with U.S. peace initiatives.[74] Each of those tendencies would be accentuated in Sadat's approach. Sadat would also exhibit far greater substantive flexibility than his predecessor.

In a February 4, 1971, speech, Sadat agreed to renew the Egyptian-Israeli cease-fire again. (The parties had renewed it once already in November 1970.) More significantly, he offered to reopen the Suez Canal, which had been closed since 1967, in exchange for Israel's partial withdrawal from the Sinai "as the first stage of a timetable which will be prepared later to implement the other provisions of the Security Council resolution [242]."

Figure 4. Anwar Sadat, 1971. © Bettmann/Corbis/AP Images.

On February 15, in response to a set of questions posed by Jarring, who had resumed his mission in late 1970, Egypt pledged to conclude a peace agreement with Israel if it fully withdrew from the Sinai and from the other territories occupied in 1967. Never before had an Arab government so publicly contemplated peace with Israel. Equally noteworthy was Egypt's willingness for Israel's withdrawal to be accomplished in stages, a departure from the standard Arab demand for an immediate restoration of the pre-June 1967 borders.[75]

Sadat also made it clear that he wanted the United States, which was uniquely positioned to influence Israel, to spearhead Arab-Israeli diplomacy. On February 8, he dispatched Haykal to tell Bergus "that while discussions through Jarring were acceptable, Sadat felt Jarring would not get anywhere and would take a long time doing so." Actually, Jarring got nowhere pretty fast. On February 26, responding to a similar set of questions from the UN mediator, the Israeli government rejected Sadat's call for a predetermined outcome and said that peace could come only through direct negotiations "without prior conditions." Yet Israel also flatly stated that it would "not withdraw to the pre-June 5, 1967, lines," which sounded for all the world like a prior condition. Unable to bridge the gap between the parties, Jarring again suspended his mission. Sadat renewed his appeal for an American peace initiative, writing Nixon on March 3 that "the United States of America is the sole international party which can bring pressure to bear on Israel" to relinquish the occupied territories.[76]

Rogers was heartened by Sadat's stance. "If, in 1967, we could have gotten from Egypt what they are now willing to give," he said at the February 26 NSC meeting, "Israel would have been delighted with it." Over the next several days, the State Department outlined a detailed strategy for taking advantage of Sadat's overtures: Egypt and Israel would be encouraged to reach a preliminary, or "interim," agreement involving the reopening of the Suez Canal and a substantial Israeli pullback in western Sinai, with the understanding that the United States would then pursue a comprehensive settlement along the lines of the first Rogers Plan.[77]

Kissinger, who thought the Rogers Plan had been killed off in 1970, forcefully opposed State's attempt to revive it. He insisted it was foolish to press for Israeli concessions without getting something from Moscow in return. "With the kind of charter the State Department is now seeking," he wrote in a February 28 memo to Nixon, the United States should have demanded "the removal of Soviet bases from the Middle East," a reference to the Soviet forces stationed in Egypt since early 1970. Kissinger also warned against provoking a politically costly confrontation with Israel. The State Department was proposing "a major approach to the Israelis that they have almost no choice but to reject," he wrote the president on March 9. "You will recall the violent Israeli reaction of January 1970 against the US positions of the previous October and December."[78] Kissinger forbore to mention the part he and Nixon had played in abetting that "violent Israeli reaction."

Nixon, as usual, was of two minds. At the February 26 NSC meeting, he lamented Israel's intransigence, while also saying he "had no confidence at all about the Egyptians" in light of their violations of the Egyptian-Israeli cease-fire the previous summer.[79] Nor, of course, could the political dangers of antagonizing Israel have been far from his thinking. Over the next few weeks, Nixon emitted a flurry of contradictory signals, public and private, designed both to establish his administration's "evenhanded" bona fides and to reassure Israel that it need not make overly painful concessions.[80] Ultimately, though, he blessed the resumption of vigorous diplomacy. In mid-April, he authorized Rogers to travel to the region to pursue an interim Egyptian-Israeli agreement. "This of course has Henry going right up the wall," Bob Haldeman wrote in his diary.[81]

Rogers visited the Middle East in early May.[82] In Cairo, he had a surprisingly encouraging session with Sadat, who welcomed his visitor "with open mind and open heart." Sadat, Rogers reported to Nixon, "is obviously attracted to the idea of being the peacemaker." Sadat made a remarkable pledge. "If we can work out an interim settlement," Rogers quoted him as saying, ". . . I promise you, I give you my personal assurance, that all the Russian ground troops will be out of my country at the end of six months."[83] This was precisely the concession Kissinger had criticized Rogers for failing to extract at the outset, though it was coming from Cairo rather than Moscow. In making the overture, Sadat was not only addressing an obvious U.S. concern but also seeking to placate the fiercely anticommunist Saudi government, which had registered its own dismay over the Soviet presence in Egypt. Though he privately grumbled that "the Saudis have a complex [*'uqda*] about the Russians," Sadat hoped to continue a recent Egyptian-Saudi rapprochement and to receive additional economic assistance from the kingdom.[84]

In Jerusalem, Rogers had a far less productive exchange with Meir and her cabinet. Rogers said that Sadat's peace offer had dramatically altered the situation and merited a positive Israeli response. Meir countered that Sadat's refusal to agree to an indefinite cease-fire gave Israel little incentive to withdraw from its current position along the canal: "If shooting begins [again], this is the best line that Israel can hope for." The Israelis insisted that they could withdraw no more than ten kilometers east of the Suez Canal, that such a withdrawal could not be linked to an overall peace settlement, and that in a final settlement Israel must keep substantial territories in the Sinai and elsewhere.[85]

Egypt's and Israel's contrasting attitudes made a strong impression on Nixon. For some weeks following Rogers's return, the president had little good to say about Israel or its supporters. The Israelis were "sitting tight" on the canal and "not doing a damn thing," Nixon complained to Haldeman on May 10. "The United States just cannot continue to sit in there supporting Israel alone against 100 million Arabs." It was necessary to "keep Henry out of" Middle East policy because he was "taking the Jewish line." Subsequent diary entries by Haldeman continued to record the president's fulminations against Jewish influence, on matters foreign and domestic. Nixon, Haldeman wrote on May 17, was adamant "that . . . we can't play the Jewish game" of permitting Israel to stonewall on a settlement in the hopes that a friendlier Democrat would unseat Nixon in the 1972 election. Discussing drug policy with Haldeman on May 26, Nixon wondered "why all the Jews seem to be the ones that are for liberalizing the regulations on marijuana."[86] As so often happened, Nixon's cogent political observations had awakened cruder habits of mind.

Also on May 26, Nixon sent an "eyes only" memorandum to Rogers strongly encouraging his Middle East diplomacy. Israel's leaders, Nixon wrote, were obviously dragging their feet, knowing it would be all but impossible for the administration to place diplomatic pressure on them once the presidential election season had begun in earnest. But delaying serious diplomacy until after the election was unacceptable; another Arab-Israeli war could break out in the meantime. It was imperative, then, for Rogers to achieve an interim agreement in the summer of 1971. It was also "essential that no more aid programs for Israel be approved until they agree to some kind of interim action on Suez or some other issue. . . . You should put this proposition very hard to them in your conversations."[87]

From Cairo, meanwhile, came indications of Sadat's desire to loosen Egypt's ties to the Soviet camp. In early May, just days before meeting Rogers, Sadat dismissed and arrested 'Ali Sabri, the pro-Soviet secretary general of the Arab Socialist Union (ASU), Egypt's only political party, charging that Sabri had been plotting a coup. Several of Sabri's alleged co-conspirators were jailed as well. In July, Sadat helped Sudan's president, Ja'far al-Numayri, put down an attempted pro-communist coup by arranging for loyalist Sudanese troops stationed in the Suez Canal Zone to be flown back home.[88]

Somewhat complicating the picture was the signing, on May 27, of an Egyptian-Soviet Treaty of Friendship and Cooperation, which reaffirmed the two countries' close political ties and provided for continued Soviet economic and military assistance. Rogers was relaxed about the treaty, seeing it essentially as a sop to the Soviets, who had been disquieted by Sadat's purge of the Sabri faction and hosting of Rogers. "This is just window dressing," Rogers told Nixon on May 28. Kissinger disagreed, warning Nixon in a May 31 memo that "the treaty could give the Soviet Union a veto over the future negotiations."[89] Nixon sided with Rogers. "We must not allow this to be a pretext for escalation of arms to Israel," he wrote on Kissinger's memo. "We should assist only in response to incontrovertible evidence of a Soviet military aid which we evaluate as *significantly* changing the balance of power." Indeed, Nixon still wanted to condition future economic and military aid to the Israelis on their diplomatic flexibility. It was vital, he told Rogers on May 31, that the secretary "be in a position . . . to hold [the prospect of additional aid] over their heads."[90]

Viewing Middle East policy in isolation, one might suppose that Rogers had gained a significant advantage over Kissinger. After all, Nixon was generally heeding Rogers's advice and rejecting Kissinger's, even dismissing the latter as ethnically motivated. But the Arab-Israeli conflict was just one concern among many. Nixon was far more preoccupied with China, Southeast Asia, and nuclear arms control policy, and in those areas Kissinger, not Rogers, was his main partner. Moreover, Kissinger's handling of those other issues would, over the next year, so enhance his stature as to allow him to supplant Rogers in Middle East policy as well.[91] The Israelis didn't know it yet, but they had two reasons for stalling on diplomacy, not just one. A few more months of stubborn immobility would not only extend the issue into the presidential campaign season but bring it under Kissinger's indulgent sway.

As 1972 drew closer, Nixon himself became less eager to press the Israelis. In July, he accepted Rogers's recommendation that Sisco go to Israel to urge greater flexibility on its government. Nixon made it clear, however, that he no longer wished to use military aid as leverage: while in Israel, "Sisco should be . . . firm about the need for some diplomatic progress" but also "conciliatory on the question of Israel's arms needs."[92] Sisco's visit was a flop. Prime Minister Meir was unmoved by his observation that Sadat "would like to use an interim settlement as a way to alter the Soviet presence" in Egypt, focusing instead on the ominous implications of the Soviet-Egyptian friendship treaty. Meir cited reports that Soviet defense minister Andrei Grechko would soon visit Egypt. "What is Grechko going to talk about?" she demanded. "A cultural agreement? Pushkin translated to Arabic?"[93]

The failure of Sisco's trip effectively ended the interim agreement initiative. Nothing short of brutal American pressure could get the Israelis to budge, and the time for applying such pressure had passed. By late summer, Kissinger wrote in his memoirs, "Nixon did not believe he could risk recurrent crises in the Middle East in an election year. He therefore asked me to step in, if only to keep things quiet." Kissinger obliged by establishing a "back-channel" dialogue on the issue with Ambassador Dobrynin. Kissinger's aim "was to explore whether the Soviets were in fact wiling to moderate their proposals; if not, I intended to draw them into protracted and inconclusive negotiations until either they or some Arab country changed their position" of demanding a full Israeli withdrawal from Arab land.[94] Given the unlikelihood of either occurrence, this was essentially a strategy of avoiding serious diplomacy until after Nixon's reelection.

The disabling power of the electoral calendar was a thing to behold. Short of simply ceding territory to Israel, there was virtually nothing the Soviets or the Egyptians could do to advance toward a settlement, at least not before November 1972. During a visit to Washington in September 1971, Soviet foreign minister Andrei Gromyko met alone with Nixon and made a dramatic offer: if Israel relinquished all of the occupied territories, Moscow would withdraw all of its forces stationed in the Middle East and cooperate with the United States to guarantee a peace settlement. Here again was the commitment that Kissinger had faulted Rogers for failing to extract in February, and now it was coming from the Soviets themselves. Still, the idea went nowhere. Meeting the next day with Kissinger (the only other U.S. official to learn of Gromyko's proposal), Nixon described the offer as "a hell of a concession" and urged Kissinger to discuss it with the Soviets. Kissinger did discuss it—in the "protracted and inconclusive" manner later described in his memoirs. Throughout the fall of 1971 he met repeatedly with Dobrynin and dropped vague but tantalizing hints that, following the election, the United States might cooperate with the Soviet Union in implementing a comprehensive Middle East settlement. The details could be worked out in the coming months.[95]

To Egyptians, the collapse of American interest in serious diplomacy was deeply distressing. Back in Cairo for consultations in December, Ashraf Ghorbal lamented to Sadat "that Henry Kissinger and the United States believe that Egypt is a lifeless corpse [*juththa hamida*], and . . . they expect to force Egypt, in the end, to sign an agreement with Israel that amounts to surrender." This brutal policy, Ghorbal said, reflected Kissinger's conviction that the victors of 1967 were entitled to dictate the terms of settlement: "Kissinger, in some of his remarks, did not conceal [his view] that in such situations he who loses the war pays the price."[96]

Also in December, Meir visited Washington and received some remarkable assurances. In response to Meir's insistence that Israel's borders be defensible, Nixon agreed "that you can't go into any of the talks with conditions that you withdraw to . . . any '67 borders." In a departure from the previous pattern of short-term arms transactions, the president pledged to provide military equipment to Israel on a multiyear basis. Nixon also urged Meir not to overreact to State Department pronouncements: "Don't be concerned if our government may speak with two voices here. The voice you need to listen to . . . is mine."[97]

Nixon soon decided to silence that second voice anyway, or at least force it to mimic his own. On January 23, 1972, Haldeman wrote in his diary that Nixon had "a directive . . . about planes to Israel and the Israel-Egypt negotiations" that Haldeman was to convey to Rogers. The president "wants Rogers to know that he expects him to play it politically, that we can't have the American Jews bitching about the plane deliveries. We can't push Israel too hard and have a confrontation. . . . We must not let this issue hurt us politically." Rogers got the message. On February 2, he reported to Nixon that the State Department and the Israeli government had agreed that Israel would receive forty-two F-4 Phantoms and eighty-two A-4 Skyhawks over the next two to three years. (The latter number was raised to ninety a few days later.) The department was determined, Rogers added, to "avoid confrontations with the Israelis on various issues, and [to] avoid putting forward American blueprints to resolve the problem."[98] Foggy Bottom would sin no more.

Kissinger was riding high. Not only had he bested Rogers in Middle East policy making; he was enjoying surprising success in managing the Soviets. Although Dobrynin continued, in back-channel talks, to press for a comprehensive settlement, Kissinger had little difficulty stalling. Plans for Nixon's path-breaking visit to China, which occurred in late February, gave Kissinger a plausible reason to assign the Middle East low priority for some weeks. Moreover, the specter of a Sino-U.S. understanding rattled the Soviets and made them increasingly anxious to ensure the success of their own summit with the Americans, scheduled to take place in Moscow in May. Exploiting his advantage, Kissinger chipped away at the Soviets' expectations regarding the Middle East. Back in the fall, he had suggested that a settlement might be worked out in the spring of 1972 and implemented after November. During a presummit trip to Moscow in April, however, he said that serious bargaining could not begin until after Nixon's second inauguration (assuming his reelection) and that implementation must wait till mid-1973. Leonid Brezhnev, general secretary of the Communist Party's Central Committee, objected that the Arabs would not abide the status quo for that long, but he was clearly unwilling to let disagreements over the Middle East derail a successful summit. Kissinger kept stalling.[99]

From Kissinger's obstructionist standpoint, the Moscow summit succeeded handsomely. When it became clear that neither Nixon nor Kissinger would seriously engage on the Middle East, the Soviets agreed to sideline the issue, acquiescing in a joint communiqué that simply endorsed "a peaceful settlement in the Middle East in accordance with Security Council Resolution 242." Such a settlement, the statement continued, "would open prospects for the normalization of the Middle East situation and . . . a military relaxation in that area." Sadat later wrote that the U.S.-Soviet communiqué "was a violent shock." Considering the Arabs' strategic inferiority, "'military relaxation' . . . could mean nothing but giving in to Israel." To be sure, the relaxation was meant to occur only after the achievement of a (presumably just) settlement. In its sheer blandness, however, the communiqué came across as an endorsement of the status quo.[100]

In July 1972, Sadat jolted the international community by expelling thousands of Soviet military personnel from Egypt, most of them stationed in the country since 1970. What was Sadat up to? In part, the available evidence suggests, he hoped to register his displeasure with the U.S.-Soviet communiqué and prod the Soviets to furnish the arms Egypt needed for a hostile crossing of the Suez Canal. In part, Sadat was responding to a message from Kissinger, conveyed by a Saudi official, that Washington would not press Israel for concessions as long as Soviet troops remained in Egypt. The Soviets, apparently chastened by the expulsion, quickly agreed to provide Egypt with many of the weapons systems they had previously withheld. Kissinger, by contrast, declined to exploit the opening Sadat had created. Certainly, the timing of the move—just a month before the Republican National Convention—argued for inaction. So, too, did Sadat's failure to seek an American quid pro quo prior to acting, an omission that convinced Kissinger he was dealing with a diplomatic lightweight.[101] In 1971, Kissinger had been contemptuous of Rogers for failing to demand the withdrawal of Soviet forces from Egypt, and unmoved when Cairo and Moscow had each offered such a withdrawal as part of a package deal. Now, Kissinger disdained Sadat for bestowing a Soviet withdrawal free of charge.

At about this time, Sadat informed Washington via intermediaries that he was interested in secret, high-level discussions with the U.S. government. Kissinger indicated his willingness to meet with Hafiz Ismail, Sadat's own national security adviser. But Kissinger was in no hurry. As he reminded Nixon in a confidential memorandum months later, "We responded sympathetically [to Sadat's request for a secret dialogue] but did not go immediately into substantive exchanges. This was partly due to our election, partly because of the Vietnam negotiations, but also partly deliberate. We have seen so often that over-eagerness on our part only generates expectations and illusions that far outrun the substantive discussions." Kissinger and Ismail would not meet until February 1973. By then, Egypt's determination to break the cease-fire was nearly unstoppable.[102]

In May 1972, on their way home from the Moscow summit that so distressed Sadat, Nixon and his entourage stopped briefly in Iran. This was the visit during which Nixon famously urged the shah to "protect me" and pledged that Iran could purchase from the United States virtually any conventional weapons it desired. The trip both symbolized and consolidated a new, Iran-centric U.S. policy toward the Persian Gulf region. Over the previous two years, Nixon and Kissinger had dismantled the State Department's more balanced approach and progressively endorsed the shah's bid for regional hegemony; the presidential visit to Iran was an occasion to formalize the emerging understanding.[103] In the coming months and years, America's embrace of the non-Arab shah would color and shape U.S.-Arab relations. It would draw the United States into a grisly battle over domestic power arrangements in neighboring Iraq. Less directly, but more profoundly, it would bind Washington to an Iranian regime whose vulnerabilities it underestimated and whose eventual collapse would scramble the politics of the Arab world.

Nixon's new arrangement with the shah came on the heels of, and subsequently reinforced, a transformation in the pricing system of Middle Eastern and North African oil—itself reflecting the fact that global demand for that commodity now outpaced available supply. In 1970–1971, the major oil producing countries in those regions, sometimes implicitly threatening to nationalize their oil operations, began to insist that Western oil companies accept substantial price hikes. Their leverage dwindling, the companies had little choice but to acquiesce. In what Daniel Yergin describes as a season of "leapfrogging," oil producers sought to outdo each other in imposing ever higher prices on the companies. In September 1970, after lengthy negotiations, Occidental Petroleum accepted a 20 percent increase in the taxes and royalties it paid to the Libyan government, resulting in a thirty-cent-per-barrel increase in Occidental's price, up to the then-impressive rate of

$2.53 per barrel. The other oil companies in Libya were obliged to follow suit. In February 1971, the Persian Gulf countries within the Organization of the Petroleum Exporting Countries (OPEC), led by Iran, compelled the oil companies in their region to accept a thirty-five-cent-per-barrel price increase. Two months later, OPEC's Mediterranean producers won a ninety-cent increase. More important than the numbers was the principle established: producing countries, not companies, were now setting prices.[104]

In addition to raising global energy costs, these early OPEC price hikes had powerful reverberations in Middle Eastern international politics. They enabled the shah to purchase the arms to police the Persian Gulf in the name of the Nixon Doctrine, whetting his appetite for further price increases; they would allow Qaddafi to bankroll increasingly audacious acts of Palestinian adventurism; and they showed Arab leaders that oil was a source of growing power in international affairs. It was only a matter of time, some Western observers warned, before Arab oil producers started using that power to force a change in Washington's pro-Israel policies. "I am concerned," a retired American oil company executive told a House subcommittee in June 1972, "that should these governments feel that they are forced into taking positions where they use oil as a political weapon and threaten or in fact do deprive us of essential energy requirements, there is nothing we can do about that." The oilman insisted he was "not proposing we sell Israel down the river," but his clear implication was that the United States should pay greater heed to Arab positions in the Arab-Israeli dispute.[105]

Such sentiments had little impact on U.S. Arab-Israeli policy, which Kissinger now dominated with Nixon's blessing. Outside of government, however, a scattering of voices protested that Arab perspectives were not receiving a fair hearing in the nation's foreign policies or public discourse. Americans taking this view, many of them possessing ties of kinship to the Arab world, encountered endless frustrations in their efforts to rectify the situation. But they found each other, which was no small thing.

Chapter 2

A Stirring at the Margins

Arab American Political Activism, 1967–1973

In the second week of June 1967, Princeton University's graduating class of 1957 held its tenth-year reunion. The costume theme, announced weeks in advance, was Arabian: attendees were to wear robes, headdresses, sandals, and similar regalia. Days before the event, however, the third major Arab-Israeli war broke out. With violence still raging as the festivities began, reunion organizers wondered if the Arabian motif was appropriate. After hurried deliberation, they decided that members of the Class of '57 would don the robes and headgear for the reunion parade as planned but make it clear that they harbored no sympathy for the Arab armies then going down to ignominious defeat. Some class members would march with their hands raised in surrender. Others would carry signs deriding the Arabs' hapless military performance: "Special Arms Sale—50,000 Rifles, Never Fired"; "See the Pyramids—Visit Israel"; "How D'Ya Expect to Win If Ya Gotta Wear Skirts?" In these ways, the *New York Times* reported, the reunion organizers hoped to demonstrate "that this class, which had nearly 15 per cent Jews and produced a rabbi, was not anti-Semitic"—ignoring the irony that the organizers were seeking such exoneration by denigrating another people. A year and a half later, a Palestinian American member of Princeton's Class of '57 lamented the public's acceptance of the demeaning spectacle.

"Surprisingly, there was no serious complaint made about the really vile taste at work as there might have if any other national or racial group had been similarly insulted," wrote Edward W. Said.[1]

A young professor of English literature at Columbia University, Said wrote those words in an essay titled "The Arab Portrayed," which appeared in a special issue of the *Arab World*, a journal published by the Arab League, in December 1968. The essay surveyed the striking hostility with which American opinion leaders treated Arab subjects, especially when discussing the Arab-Israeli conflict. Indignant and erudite, nimbly traversing the Western canon, "The Arab Portrayed" rehearsed the trenchant critiques that its author would deliver over the next three and a half decades, most famously in his 1978 book *Orientalism*. Yet something about that Princeton vignette stirred the political antennae of Ibrahim Abu-Lughod, the guest editor of the special *Arab World* issue. A Palestinian American political scientist at Northwestern University, Abu-Lughod was starting a one-year term as president of the Association of Arab American University Graduates (AAUG), an advocacy group formed after the 1967 War. He sent a copy of the special issue to Robert Goheen, the president of Princeton University, calling Goheen's attention to "the incident commented upon by Dr. Said."[2]

The reply to Abu-Lughod came not from President Goheen but from his special assistant, David S. Thompson, who despite his modest title was a high-ranking university administrator.[3] Princeton reunions, Thompson wrote, "are conducted by the alumni themselves, who are entirely responsible for the conduct of their classmates. Unfortunately, the behavior of reuning alumni does not always display the maturity and discretion one would expect of adult graduates of this college. . . . The poor taste described by Dr. Said is deeply regretted in Nassau Hall," Princeton's administration building. Thompson promised to convey Abu-Lughod's displeasure "to the alumnus who is chairman of reunions." Thompson added a personal note: "As one who was born and raised in Egypt (my father was on the faculty of Assiut College [an American Protestant missionary school]), I am particularly sensitive to the way in which many Americans, often subtly and unconsciously, conduct themselves so as to give insult to people of other nations and races."[4] It was a small victory, but the AAUG made the most of it. The group published Abu-Lughod's and Thompson's letters on the front page of its June 1969 newsletter, citing the exchange as "a good illustration of how responsible individuals can effectively fight racism against the Arabs in North America."[5]

This two-year sequence of events—from insult to published apology—underscored several themes that marked the emergence of Arab American political activism in the half-dozen years following the Six-Day War. There was, first, the searing experience of June 1967: not just the speed and scale of the Arab military collapse but the gleeful contempt with which many of the dominant voices in American society greeted the humiliation. To possess, in the United States, any conscious ties of kinship to the Arab world at that moment was to court an overpowering sense of alienation and public shame. Second, and consequently, was the awakened determination—manifested individually in Said's essay and more collectively in Abu-Lughod's efforts on behalf of the AAUG—to locate, and protest, the sources of the alienation and thereby begin to expunge the public shame. Third, the episode revealed the limited scope within which Arab American activists could successfully operate. While their Zionist adversaries could command overwhelming majorities in Congress and stymie diplomatic initiatives emanating from the executive branch, Arab Americans had to settle for a statement of regret from a university administrator. But it was a start. Finally, in that administrator's consoling words was a reminder that Arab Americans could find sympathy beyond the confines of their ethnic community, especially among Americans who had lived in the Arab world.

There is a fifth theme, not captured by the Princeton episode but crucial to understanding Arab American political activism from 1967 to 1973: the interplay of accommodationist and defiant tendencies. Openly or implicitly, most Arab American activists confronted the same basic choice: should they pursue a political program that was compatible with the existing state system in the Middle East and with the broad currents of U.S. foreign policy, or should they insist on a bold overturning of those realities? More particularly, should they proclaim that Washington's true interests lay in seeking an "evenhanded" settlement of the Arab-Israeli conflict, one that preserved Israel's existence while ending its occupation of Arab lands seized in 1967 and addressing Palestinian national claims in some way? Or should they demand the liberation of all of Palestine from its Zionist usurpers (and perhaps also, for good measure, the removal of "reactionary" Arab regimes)? The AAUG, the dominant Arab American organization in these years, made moderate-sounding noises in its early months but quickly assumed a radical stance that it maintained for the rest of the period in question. Meanwhile, a latent moderation existed within the Arab American community and probably claimed the quiet allegiance of most of its members. For several years, however, no national Arab American organization existed to articulate this sentiment. It was instead left to non-Arab organizations, often dominated by Americans with personal ties to the Arab world, to bring the cause of "evenhandedness" to national attention. The emergence of the National Association of Arab Americans (NAAA) in 1972–1973 finally introduced a moderate Arab American voice to the national conversation.

The appearance in the late 1960s of sustained and nationally visible Arab American political activism—a novel feature in American life—resulted from profound changes at the community, national, and geopolitical levels. In 1965, about half a million people of Arab background lived in the United States. They had arrived in two main waves. The first wave, from the late 1880s to the start of World War I, consisted overwhelmingly of Christians (Orthodox and Catholic) from what are now Syria and Lebanon. Clustering in cities on the Eastern Seaboard and in the Midwest, these immigrants worked as peddlers, shopkeepers, factory workers, and garment makers. In rural areas, some established small farms or worked as agricultural laborers. The second wave, which started at the end of World War II and continued through the mid-1960s, drew people from a wider set of Arab countries, along with Palestinians displaced by Israel's creation in 1948. Many more of these immigrants were Muslim, and they included a substantial number of university students and professionals.[6]

On the strength of the first wave, as of 1965 about 80 percent of Arab Americans were still Christians of Syrian or Lebanese origin. Collectively, the Syrian/Lebanese expressed pride in their loyalty to the United States, their rapid assimilation into American society, their economic success, and the national prominence that a few of their number—the comedian Danny Thomas, the heart surgeon Michael Debakey, the teen idol Paul Anka—had attained. (The consumer advocate Ralph Nader rocketed to national fame in the spring of 1966.) Most of their associational activity occurred in churches and in an array of loosely federated "Syrian Lebanese American Clubs." The clubs were dedicated to preserving elements of Levantine culture, such as dance and cuisine, and to encouraging young people to marry within the community. For decades, chroniclers of the Arab American experience—primarily activists but sometimes scholars as well—have suggested that, prior to 1967, community members were generally indifferent to Middle Eastern politics and reluctant to identify with the Arab world. Twenty-first-century scholarship has challenged this view, unearthing a range of political organizations active since the 1910s. Initially preoccupied with struggles for Syrian autonomy or independence, such groups grew increasingly pan-Arab in outlook, particularly in their efforts (which came to a futile head in the late 1940s) to dissuade the U.S. government from supporting the establishment of a Jewish state in Palestine. Some Arab American groups and individuals were swept up in the Arab nationalist politics convulsing the region in the 1950s and early 1960s. Others, especially Lebanese Americans concerned for the independence of their ancestral homeland, were discomfited by the phenomenon or downright hostile to it.[7]

The emerging picture, then, is of an Arab American community considerably more attuned to Arab affairs than previously thought, but one still on the cusp of a thoroughgoing transformation. Indeed, in both the United States and the Arab world, the second half of the 1960s brought momentous upheavals that would, in subsequent years, profoundly alter the community's makeup, outlook, and organizing trajectory. The Immigration Act of 1965 abolished the national quota system that had privileged immigration from Northern and Western Europe. After the act went into effect in June 1968, the number of immigrants from the Arab world markedly increased. In 1967, the last year wholly governed by the old quotas, 6,581 immigrants from Arab countries entered the United States. In 1969, the first full year of the new system, 10,742 Arabs arrived. In subsequent years, the annual influx steadily grew. By 1974, about 750,000 people of Arab background lived in the United States, and by 1980 that figure was over a million—more than double the population in 1965. As during the first two postwar decades, the new immigrants came from across the Arab world and included a fresh wave of Palestinians, the latter displaced by the 1967 War.[8]

In theory, the rapid growth of the Arab American community promised to enhance its political clout. Working against this prospect, however, was the fact that many of the fresh arrivals were far too destitute, too lacking in English-language skills, too preoccupied with family needs, and too unaccustomed to American civic life to engage in effective political activism. Still, a sufficient number of them did become politically involved to alter the overall tenor of Arab American associational life, making it more attuned to contemporary Middle Eastern affairs. Moreover, the very vulnerability of the recent immigrants prodded the Arab American organizations to assume an increasingly protective role. *Someone* had to look after the overwhelmed newcomers, and who better than those who had walked in their shoes, or whose parents had done so? Arab American groups had always served this function, of course, but the magnitude of the post-1968 influx was unprecedented. (Also unprecedented, as we shall see in chapter 3, was the extent to which the immigrants' circumstances became enmeshed in Middle Eastern politics.) If the new immigration did not immediately augment the power of Arab American organizations, it did give them a new purpose.

Another set of circumstances, unfolding on a wider national plane, fueled Arab American activism in general while giving an extra boost to the AAUG's brand of militancy. The flourishing in the late 1960s of the antiwar and Black Power movements, and the many subsidiary and parallel social protests they inspired—especially movements for Third World solidarity—created a permissive environment for Arab American activism. By 1970, it was much safer and more acceptable for people with dark complexions, strange names, and in some cases foreign accents to criticize the United States and its allies, and even accuse them of war crimes, than it would have been just a few years earlier. Undoubtedly, this transformation helped to break down the reticence of those who had sought community in the Syrian Lebanese American Clubs, making them more willing to affirm an Arab identity, as many would do within the NAAA. ("Arab Is Beautiful" proclaimed the agenda of a December 1973 meeting of the NAAA board of directors.)[9] The main beneficiaries of the change, however, were Arab Americans already harboring radical temperaments and views.

More broadly, Arab American activists in the late 1960s and early 1970s were catching a wave of racial and ethnic assertiveness, swelled both by activists "of color" stirring the left and by "white ethnics" coalescing in defense of conservative neighborhood values. Boasting their own long heritage of stable and industrious ethnic communities in America, yet occupying a status that some scholars have called "not quite white," Arab American activists drew on each of these emerging demographic and political archetypes.[10] But in one respect their situation departed from both: they were closely associated, by others and themselves, with what U.S. opinion leaders routinely portrayed as the "wrong" side of a bitter international dispute.[11]

The post-1967 Arab-Israeli standoff did more than simply generate hostile stateside attitudes for Arab Americans to combat. It shaped the course of their political activism, reinforcing both its radical and its moderate tendencies. By the summer of 1968, much of pan-Arab political society (as distinct from the deliberations of individual Arab governments) was caught up in the drama of the Palestinian fedayeen—defiant youths who, seeing that the Arab states were in no condition to liberate Palestine, had undertaken to liberate it themselves. The AAUG, founded months earlier on a more anodyne platform, quickly embraced the fedayeen cause. The Palestinian liberationist project, and the accompanying hostility toward Arab regimes that stood in its way, became a driving force behind AAUG activism and remained so into the 1970s. At the same time, Israel's occupation of the lands seized in 1967 planted the seeds of a more pragmatic Arab approach to the crisis. As the occupation dragged on with no end in sight, Arab governments increasingly recognized that only a political settlement could restore the lost territory. Thus by the early 1970s all of the states bordering Israel, including Syria, were inching toward the "evenhanded" scenario that some Americans had advocated since 1967. The emergence of the NAAA in 1972–1973 as a moderate alternative to the AAUG partly reflected this pragmatic turn in Arab diplomacy.

If the new Arab American activism grew out of broad transformations in American and Middle Eastern life, its immediate catalyst was the 1967 War, and in particular U.S. responses to that tragedy. In the Arab American collective memory, the war and its immediate aftermath were a time of rampant anti-Arab hostility, in which much of the American public and news media denigrated the Arab world, often in starkly dehumanizing terms. With important caveats, there is considerable truth to this portrayal. American news coverage of the war was generally factual and straightforward, no doubt reflecting journalists' sincere desire to "get the story right." But the inclusion of some facts instead of others, the use of framing devices that privileged Israeli views, and the occasional reliance on cartoonish stereotypes did portray Arab behavior, both official and societal, as implausibly cruel and fanatical.[12] American commentators, moreover, were often unabashed in their sympathy for Israel, treating its decision to fire the first shot as a justified response to intolerable pressures and threats.

In itself, such partiality did not demonstrate antipathy toward Arabs in general. A persuasive, and surely nonracist, case could be made that Egyptian president Gamal Abdel Nasser and other Arab leaders were deeply culpable for the carnage that suddenly engulfed their region. But some of the pro-Israel commentary suggested a callous indifference to the suffering of ordinary Arabs with no say in state policy. The Egyptian army's collapse in the Sinai Peninsula was, among other things, a vast humanitarian disaster. Thousands of stranded Egyptian soldiers died horribly, some strafed by Israeli aircraft against which they had no defenses, others succumbing to thirst and exhaustion in the blistering desert. Yet the syndicated columnist Frank Getlein saw only humor in the "losses to the Arabs of land, arms, treasure, lives, credibility, shirts, pants and shoes." Even the travails of Arab civilians drew contemptuous responses. "The screams about helping the displaced Arabs have echoed in the [UN] Security Council for endless hours since the war," wrote former New Dealer–turned-columnist Raymond Moley in *Newsweek*, referring to the tens of thousands of Palestinians made refugees by the war. The United States had no responsibility for them, Moley insisted. A *Life* editorial on the broader Palestinian refugee population, titled "1.3 Million Causes of Tension," contained not a word of sympathy for the men, women, and children inhabiting "the hate-filled camps."[13]

A rash of jokes, most of them stressing Arab cowardice and incompetence, swept the country during and after war. How could you tell an Egyptian tank from an Israeli one? The Egyptian tank had backup lights. How fast were the Israelis advancing into Egypt? So fast that the Cairo Hilton was now taking reservations for bar mitzvahs. Another joke had a South Vietnamese general asking Israeli defense minister Moshe Dayan to explain the secret of his success. "Well, to start with," Dayan replies, "it helps if you can arrange to fight against Arabs."[14] Admittedly, the anti-Arab humor was accompanied by a spate of jokes that American Jews—professional comedians and ordinary people alike—told at their own expense, sometimes appropriating anti-Semitic stereotypes. (Why were no Israeli tanks destroyed? Because they didn't have collision insurance. Why did Israeli commanders go only so far into Arab territory? Because they were renting the tanks at eight cents a mile.)[15] But there was a world of difference between spoofing one's own kind and enduring mockery by others, and the existence of the first pattern could scarcely ease the pain that Arabs and Arab Americans felt on account of the second. It's doubtful that many of them were even aware of the self-deprecating Jewish humor, as it seldom appeared in the national print media, circulating instead by word of mouth or via the occasional late-night television variety show. The anti-Arab jokes were published widely, in an atmosphere of sanctioned levity.

In short, Arabs were losers, and no sensible American would wish to emulate them. A cartoon in the December 1967 issue of *Playboy* succinctly captures the sentiment. Behind the scenes of a school Christmas pageant, a little boy in a shepherd's costume, consisting of robe and headdress, looks up at the woman directing the show and asks, "I'm not an Arab, am I?"[16]

The 1967 debacle was traumatic to Arab Americans and Arab residents from all walks of life, but it posed special challenges to academics and professionals, many of whom had arrived in the second, postwar wave of Arab immigration. These people tended to be less rooted in ethnic communities than their working-class counterparts. They lived and worked in white-collar settings where Arabs were few and support for Israel was articulate and often pervasive. Because of their privileged status, they felt a special obligation to challenge what they saw as the distorted, disparaging, callous, and even racist discourse that surrounded them. After all, they had access to facts and insights missing from the national conversation and, in the case of academics, a presence in institutions that shaped public attitudes. More recent immigrants often felt guilty about having left the Arab world for comfortable lives in the West; they simply *had* to speak up for the abandoned homeland. And yet many educated Arabs, like Arabs everywhere, were so stunned by the military defeat that they could scarcely make it intelligible to their own minds, still less interpret it to others. As much as they needed to combat the widespread ignorance and defamation, they also had to explain the Arab predicament to themselves, and each other.[17] Small wonder, then, that the most important Arab American initiative to emerge from this crisis should bear the imprint of "university graduates."

In August 1967, the International Congress of Orientalists held its annual meeting in Ann Arbor, Michigan. During the event, Rashid Bashshur, a sociology professor at the University of Michigan, hosted about fifteen Arab and Arab American attendees, apparently all of them male, at a barbecue in his backyard. After dinner, the group having moved indoors, Bashshur asked his guests to share their thoughts about the Middle East crisis. He later wrote:

> We went around the room, one by one, each of them describing his own feelings. Some recounted their seismic reaction first to the news of Arab victories then the total failure. As I recall most everyone mentioned a feeling of despair, some were simply despondent, some afraid of further retaliation or possible loss of jobs at their institutions as a result of the strong anti-Arab sentiment so rampant at the time. A few mentioned that they did not go to work for several days and avoided talking to colleagues or others when they did. There was also mention of feeling of embarrassment or shame at being Arab.[18]

What to do? Although some of Bashshur's guests proposed individual responses—letters to the editor, approaches to congressional representatives, and the like—the group quickly embraced the idea of launching a collective effort: an organization of "professors and professionals of Arabic extraction" dedicated to addressing, in ways yet to be determined, "the urgent problems facing our communities in the United States, Canada, and in our land of origin." The group authorized Bashshur and Abdeen Jabara, a young Lebanese American attorney based in Detroit, to organize a general conference at which the goals and contours of such an association could be defined.[19]

Bashshur and Jabara were an unlikely pair. Born in Syria in 1933, Bashshur had attended the American University of Beirut before relocating to the United States for graduate study. He did not have an extensive activist background and was politically moderate. Years later, Bashshur lamented the militancy of the organization he had catalyzed, and after 1968 he was only modestly active in it. Jabara, just shy of twenty-seven, was a committed radical. Though born and raised in northern Michigan, he had been steeped from boyhood in the Palestine issue and Arab nationalism, and in the early and mid-1960s he had paid extended visits to the Arab world. Jabara was now active in the anti–Vietnam War, civil rights, and emerging Third World solidarity movements, had close ties to the Socialist Workers Party, and was sharply critical of the U.S. government's behavior around the globe.[20] (In that same month of August 1967, his antiwar activities triggered an FBI investigation that would continue for eight years and eventually enlist the services of the CIA and National Security Agency.)[21] Jabara threw himself wholeheartedly into the new Arab American organization and would serve as its president in 1972. He would also find time to work on Sirhan Sirhan's defense team, edit a newspaper devoted to the Palestinian struggle, defend the civil liberties of Arabs and Arab Americans, and organize Detroit's Arab auto workers. In the decade and a half after 1967, Jabara's was arguably the leading radical voice in Arab American politics.

Despite their differing outlooks, Bashshur and Jabara successfully collaborated on their assigned task. They scheduled the founding conference to take place in Chicago in December 1967, to coincide with the first annual meeting of the Middle East Studies Association. Forty-three Arabs and Arab Americans (now including two women)[22] met at the University of Chicago to approve the bylaws of the Association of Arab American University Graduates, as the organization was to be called. The AAUG would seek "to promote all aspects of knowledge concerning the Arab world, especially in the cultural, scientific and educational fields ... and work to achieve a better understanding in these fields between the United States and Canada and the Arab world." This innocuous mission statement gave little hint of the bracing critiques to come. The attendees named a board of directors and elected Fauzi Najjar, a Lebanese-born social science professor at Michigan

Figure 5. Abdeen Jabara, c. early 1970s. Courtesy of Eastern Michigan University Archives, Ypsilanti, Michigan.

State University, to be the AAUG's first president. Najjar and his successors would each serve a single one-year term, working out of their cities of residence. Across the country, members were encouraged to establish local chapters.[23]

Though calling itself "Arab American," the AAUG was more closely tethered to the Arab half of this identity. Most founding members were Arab-born, and many were more fully invested in Arab affairs than in American ones. "They were Arabs whose heads were in the Middle East," Jabara later said, "but whose feet were here in the United States." While this orientation ensured a high degree of expertise and commitment with respect to the Arab world, it made it harder for the AAUG to appeal to the wider Arab American community or gain a hearing in the U.S. mainstream media. At the same time, simply by functioning politically in the United States, the AAUG could not help bringing its members somewhat more fully into the American fold. As Michael Suleiman, the association's president in 1977, recalled, "Intentionally or not, [the AAUG] worked to make some disgruntled and alienated Arab Americans feel part and parcel of the American political system. Indeed, at times, for some, it gave them a feeling of civic competence."[24]

The AAUG attracted an expanding group of activists and scholars, most of them attached to universities. Quickly assuming a leading role was the aforementioned Ibrahim Abu-Lughod of Northwestern. Although he served as AAUG president in 1969, Abu-Lughod worked mainly behind the scenes, operating for many years as the chief organizer of the group's conferences and publications. Abu-Lughod was adept at bringing new talent into the AAUG. One of his "gets" was Elaine Hagopian, a Syrian American sociologist who had taught with him at Smith College. Principled and exacting, Hagopian labored tirelessly for the AAUG, at lofty and menial tasks alike, and served as its first female president in 1976. Another Abu-Lughod recruit was Edward Said, the AAUG's vice president in 1971. The two had met at Princeton, where Abu-Lughod was a doctoral student while Said earned his bachelor's degree. Said's best-known accomplishment, his 1978 book *Orientalism*, was produced outside of the AAUG's auspices. But Said wrote it largely at the urging of Abu-Lughod, and it was to him and his wife Janet Abu-Lughod, a noted sociologist, that Said dedicated the monograph.[25]

When she first met Said in the late 1960s, Hagopian was unimpressed. "He struck me at that time as a sort of dilettante," she later wrote. "He was elegant in appearance, interested in good food and excellent wine, and he just did not fit the purist image I had of the engaged activist. . . . We were some kind of socialists, leveled by equality. Work—even the most banal—was to be evenly distributed. Somehow, Edward was exempt from this, and I remember being quite annoyed." She revised her assessment after reading Said's work, especially "The Arab Portrayed," the essay Abu-Lughod parlayed into a blow for decency at Princeton. "The original 1968 piece was not only sensitive and brilliant," Hagopian recalled, "but it represented what all of us of Arab origin felt."[26]

In the group's early months, AAUG members differed with one another over political strategy. One division was between those wishing to support

Figure 6. Edward Said addresses the Association of Arab American University Graduates, c. 1970s. Courtesy of Eastern Michigan University Archives, Ypsilanti, Michigan.

Arab causes in militant terms and those preferring to show a more conciliatory face to the U.S. public. Another separated those seeking to forge alliances with other "liberation" movements (at home and abroad) from those determined to keep the focus on the Arab-Israeli issue. In each of these debates, Jabara upheld the first position. In an October 1968 letter, he complained that the AAUG's board of directors was dominated by people "of mild or moderate nationalist feeling who do not verbalize or conceptualize their frustrations into meaningful modes of activity." Years later, Jabara ruefully recalled his inability "to push the AAUG to get out and try to do more coalition building outside of itself" and gain valuable allies.[27] Taking the contrary view on each question was M. Cherif Bassiouni, an Egyptian-born law professor who served as AAUG president in 1970. "[The] Palestinian revolution does not need world revolutions to legitimate it," he stated at a December 1969 AAUG General Assembly meeting, when Jabara and his allies proposed a Third World–oriented resolution. "It can stand on its own merits." ("A good fellow although a right winger," Abu-Lughod privately remarked about Bassiouni a few days later.) Bassiouni also advocated informal dialogue with Israeli officials, at a time when most other AAUG leaders were years away from countenancing such activity.[28]

On one occasion, however, Bassiouni desperately sought to keep Israelis and AAUGers apart. In late 1970, the association held its annual convention at the Orrington Hotel in Evanston, Illinois—just blocks away, it turned out, from an Israeli student convention at which general Yehoshafat Harkabi, the former chief of Israeli intelligence, was the featured speaker. Learning of the AAUG event, Harkabi, who had spent his career studying Arab attitudes, led some ninety Israeli students on a march to the Orrington, requesting a dialogue with the AAUG. Bassiouni, the AAUG's president that year, believed that Harkabi and his group had come in good faith, but most other AAUG leaders saw the approach as an effort to disrupt their convention. Edward Said was especially incensed. He led a group of conventioneers that *he* had been addressing down toward the lobby to intercept the visitors. Thus Bassiouni confronted the strange spectacle of two rival audiences, each led by its speaker, approaching one another on a hotel stairway. He interposed himself between the two groups and, as he later recalled, "extended my arms open, and if I can say so without being taken irreverently, in a Christ-like manner, to try to keep Edward—who was yelling at the top of his lungs 'provocateurs!' leading the crowd behind him—from confronting the Israelis. . . . I literally felt the weight of the bodies from behind and in front as I was asking General Hakarbi [*sic*] to turn back. . . . I was close to being overwhelmed by the situation." Fortunately, the Israelis did turn back before things got truly ugly.[29]

Judging by public declarations, it would appear that single-issue moderates held sway in the AAUG's early months but soon gave ground to militant Third Worlders. In an open letter to president Lyndon Johnson in the spring of 1968, the association commended Johnson's "stand for peace and justice in the world" and urged him to take a similar position in the Middle East, thereby "restoring traditional Arab goodwill for the United States." The assumptions embedded in the letter—that U.S. global power was benevolent and that the Arab-Israeli conflict was separable from other international issues—quickly disappeared from AAUG statements. By December 1969, the AAUG was describing the United States as one of "the imperialist forces" behind "the racist exclusivist State of Israel" and cheering on the Palestinians' "war of national liberation." A year later the association castigated the United States for "pursuing a policy of duplicity and imperialism in the Middle East and the Third World" and for sustaining "colonial," "Fascist," and "racist settler regimes" around the globe. When some Palestinian groups targeted Israeli civilians, the AAUG refused to criticize these acts. The statement released at the group's national convention in November 1972, two months after the attack on the Munich Olympics, pledged "unconditional support [for] the Palestinian Revolution" and "salute[d] the Palestinian Freedom fighters."[30]

The AAUG's membership grew erratically in this period. After a modest first year, during which the association went from 37 members in December 1967 to 79 in September 1968, the group experienced a rapid surge of growth: to 250 members in January 1970, up to 600 by October of that year. Thereafter the rate of expansion slowed; as of October 1973 there were just 925 members.[31] The fastest growth occurred during Bassiouni's presidency and reflected, it appears, a failed attempt on his part to alter the AAUG's political orientation. Instead of confronting the radicals head-on, Bassiouni tried to dilute their strength by rapidly expanding the membership. "The problem," he later recalled, "is the ideologue[s] continued to be vociferous. The new members, who were middle-of-the-roaders, if you will, became disenchanted after the first and second year, and left."[32] Only an exhaustive, person-by-person tracking survey could determine if Bassiouni is correct, but his interpretation is consistent with rates of growth in this period. Chapters of the AAUG proliferated more steadily. They accumulated at the rate of about two per year, reaching a total of thirteen by the summer of 1973.[33]

In its activities, the national AAUG was something of a cross between a political advocacy group and an academic society. It issued public statements on Middle East–related issues and sent messages of protest or praise to U.S. and Arab political leaders. It held annual conventions at which scholars presented papers and from which the AAUG General Assembly issued political resolutions. The conventions' keynote speakers included prominent figures from the nonaligned movement and the international Left, such as the Indian diplomat and politician Krishna Menon, the exiled Greek socialist leader Andreas Papandreou, and the author and activist Shirley Graham Du Bois, widow of W.E.B. Du Bois. The AAUG published anthologies of scholarly articles and, starting in 1979, a scholarly journal, *Arab Studies Quarterly*. Its national newsletter documented all of these activities, touted the achievements of members and chapters, and publicized the efforts of other Arab American and Arab-friendly organizations.

It is difficult to gauge the AAUG's overall impact in the late 1960s and early 1970s. Its influence on executive-branch policy and congressional opinion was surely negligible. Yet its modest visibility in the national news media—through letters to the editor, paid political advertisements, and the occasional op-ed piece—probably shaped public attitudes to some degree. The same can be said of the dinners, lectures, slideshows, and book fairs organized by the chapters. In November 1972, the *New York Times* called the AAUG "the most influential secular group of Arabs in the United States." The statement was accurate, though it mainly reflected the dearth of competition. In academia, the AAUG's national conferences helped to transform the field of Middle East studies in North America, giving new prominence to scholars of Middle Eastern background. The anticolonial perspectives that often informed these scholars' work would render the AAUG's incubation in the International Congress of Orientalists retrospectively ironic.[34]

The AAUG's greatest impact, however, was on its own members. Activists discovered new allies; academics found alternative outlets for their scholarship. On a human level, the AAUG offered solace to a battered and demoralized community. It "brought like-minded people together," Jabara later said, "so that they could not feel as isolated and as marginal as they otherwise felt." Michael Suleiman recalled that participation in the association "gave the members a feeling of camaraderie, a sense that they were not alone." These communal and healing functions were most crucial in the AAUG's early months, when Arabs and Arab Americans were reeling from the 1967 disaster and aghast at the anti-Arab hostility enveloping them. Yet in the spring of 1973 Rashid Bashshur, whose backyard barbecue had launched the whole enterprise, could still argue that seeking a "solution to the problem of our alienation" from U.S. society was one of the AAUG's main reasons for being. "We have to go on because we need each other."[35]

Until the emergence of the NAAA in 1972–1973, the AAUG could claim to be the only national organization speaking politically for Arab Americans. Yet other groups and figures performed portions of this task. The old Syrian Lebanese American Clubs continued to foreground cultural activities but after 1967 were increasingly obliged to address Middle East politics as well. When they did so, they advocated a sort of "soft" Arabism, accepting Israel's existence while criticizing its behavior in the area, highlighting the injustice of the Palestinians' plight, and decrying the loss of Arab goodwill toward the United States on account of misguided American policies.[36] A handful of newspapers—such as the *Heritage* and the *Lebanese American Journal*, both published in New York, and the *American Syrian-Lebanese Leader*, based in Jacksonville Beach, Florida—disseminated the clubs' outlook. Alongside recipes for stuffed grape leaves and profiles of famous Arab Americans like Marlo Thomas and Tiny Tim, these newspapers condemned Israel's military operations in Lebanon and called for U.S. "evenhandedness" in the Middle East.[37]

Covering a very different beat was the Organization of Arab Students in the United States and Canada (OAS). Founded in the early 1950s, the OAS had, by the late 1960s, perhaps a few thousand members in North America, active on scores of campuses.[38] The OAS championed the Palestinian resistance. Although it reportedly received financial assistance from Arab states, it sometimes pressured them to show more spine on the Arab-Israeli issue. In March 1968, 135 OAS members staged a sit-in at the New York headquarters of the Egyptian, Syrian, Jordanian, Iraqi, and Algerian delegations to the United Nations, demanding that Arab governments reject any negotiations with Israel. The OAS formed coalitions with other Third World solidarity movements active on college campuses. The Black Power leader Stokely Carmichael gave the keynote speech at the OAS's 1968 annual convention in Ann Arbor, Michigan. The organization also worked closely with AAUG members, especially Abdeen Jabara, who sometimes offered his legal services. For all its visibility in such circles, however, the OAS had minimal presence in mainstream U.S. discourse and seldom if ever addressed the Arab American experience per se.[39]

Joining in the pro-Arab chorus was an individual who functioned as an institution all by himself. Muhammad ("M.T.") Mehdi, an Iraqi-born activist in New York, headed the Action Committee on American-Arab Relations (ACAAR), which he had founded in 1964. By 1969, Mehdi claimed that ACAAR had twenty thousand members, but the outfit appeared to involve just a handful of people, of whom Mehdi was by far the most visible. Mehdi relished confronting his Zionist antagonists. Whenever Israel's supporters rallied in New York, he and a small band of comrades could be found on the fringes of the event, heckling the throngs and waving placards equating Zionism with Nazism or racism. Mehdi's actions provoked frequent violent attacks by members of the extremist Jewish Defense League (JDL), occasionally leaving the activist bruised and bloodied.[40]

Mehdi had a talent for attracting media attention, and some of his actions were little more than publicity stunts. In October 1970, after a bomb went off in the New York offices of the Palestine Liberation Organization (PLO), Mehdi offered a $5,000 reward for information leading to the arrest and conviction of a JDL member, adding that only $1,000 would be forthcoming if the culprit proved to be an "average sick person." A year later, Mehdi made a public pledge to Democratic senator Henry M. ("Scoop") Jackson of Washington, a staunch backer of Israel who planned to run for president in 1972: if Jackson renounced his pro-Israel stance, ACAAR would give him $1 million and deliver twenty-five to thirty million votes from blacks,

Greeks, Hispanics, and Arab Americans. In January 1973, after Palestinian militants held six diplomats hostage in the Israeli embassy in Bangkok, eventually releasing them in exchange for safe passage out of Thailand, Mehdi ostentatiously paid the Palestinians' $324 hotel bill—as if to suggest that skipping out on the tab was their only offense. For all his antics, however, Mehdi was a boundlessly dedicated advocate who was willing to pay a stiff price for his causes. A May 1974 attack by a group of toughs (including, allegedly, some JDL members) put him in the hospital for three weeks with three fractured vertebrae. The following month ACAAR's offices were destroyed by arson. "They burned everything," Mehdi wrote days after the fire, "books, documents, furniture and office equipment—everything, except, of course, for our determination!"[41]

Outside the Arab and Arab American communities, sympathetic others were swinging into action. In cities across the country, scores of local organizations, and a handful of national ones, sprang up to challenge dominant views and policies on the Middle East. Among the national groups was New York–based Americans for Middle East Understanding (AMEU), founded in 1967 by missionaries, educators, former diplomats, and other professionals to increase Americans' awareness of the history, culture, and politics of the Middle East. Beyond calling for "greater fairness, consistency, and integrity in U.S. foreign policy toward that area," AMEU did not formally espouse any particular policies. But its newsletter, the *Link*, provided a forum for Arab-friendly voices, most of them supporting an "evenhanded" Arab-Israeli settlement.[42] Another national group was American Near East Refugee Aid (ANERA), formed in Washington in 1968 to coordinate existing relief efforts directed toward Palestinian refugees. Although its primary mission was humanitarian, ANERA sometimes made policy pronouncements. In early 1970, for example, it endorsed the Rogers Plan while admonishing the Nixon administration to limit Israel's arsenal and include Palestinians in any future peace negotiations.[43]

A third organization, the American Committee for Justice in the Middle East (ACJME), began locally but quickly acquired a national profile. Formed in 1967 by a group of mostly female activists in Boulder, Colorado, the ACJME compiled materials from anti-Zionist sources and synthesized them into "position papers" that it sent to the national news media, members of Congress, and executive branch agencies.[44] The ACJME had a keen eye for political openings. In the summer of 1968, it secured invitations to testify before the program committees at the Republican and Democratic

National Conventions. (The Democrats gathering in Chicago, it turned out, had other matters vying for their attention.) In October 1969, ACJME organizers gained an audience with undersecretary of state Elliot Richardson, whom they presented with a statement criticizing the Nixon administration for acquiescing in Israeli policies. By then, ACJME chapters had formed in San Francisco, Sacramento, Miami, Boise, and Melbourne Beach, Florida, though some of them appear to have been one-person operations. Like AMEU and ANERA, the ACJME favored an equitable Arab-Israeli settlement, but its criticisms of Israeli and U.S. policies were generally much sharper than those of the other two groups.[45]

Although these non-Arab-identified organizations mainly responded to what they saw as the unfolding needs of the moment, they were also moving into a vacuum created by the decline of an older group. In the 1950s and 1960s, a suspiciously well-heeled organization called American Friends of the Middle East (AFME), headquartered first in New York and later in Washington, had urged Americans to take a more sympathetic view of Arab grievances against Israel and the Western powers. In February 1967, the *New York Times* and the radical journal *Ramparts* published articles describing AFME as a long-standing recipient of clandestine CIA funding. The portrayal was accurate: although AFME was never simply a CIA front, its mission dovetailed with the desire of some CIA officials both to counter Zionist influence at home and to present a friendlier American face to the Arab world. The news stories dealt a devastating blow to AFME's reputation. Critics could now dismiss the group as a creation of official Washington—a cruel irony, considering that by 1967 AFME's Arabist sympathies held little sway in Lyndon Johnson's administration. The revelation was also financially crippling, for the organization was now obliged to forgo the tainted funds. Over the next few years, AFME refashioned itself as a purely philanthropic and educational concern, leaving political advocacy to the likes of AMEU, ANERA, and the ACJME.[46]

One can be reasonably certain that none of these newer organizations received covert U.S. government support,[47] yet AMEU and ANERA, at least, gave off a distinct whiff of the Establishment. Both organizations made places on their boards of directors for oil company executives and retired U.S. diplomats.[48] Both received generous financial support from Aramco, the consortium of American oil companies operating in Saudi Arabia, causing Zionist critics to scoff that the two groups were wholly owned subsidiaries of that sprawling syndicate.[49] As with the CIA-AFME relationship, however, it was more a case of institutions moving in parallel. From the oil companies' standpoint, the Arab-Israeli status quo destabilized the region in ways that threatened their massive holdings and operations. The efforts of AMEU and ANERA to alter the U.S. stance on the conflict, and of ANERA to alleviate the miserable living conditions that helped to fuel Palestinian militancy (which increasingly included attacks on Middle East oil installations)—all this seemed eminently worthy of Aramco's support.

Of course, the Aramco/AMEU/ANERA approach was bound to dissatisfy more radically inclined critics of the U.S.-Israeli relationship. As two such critics, Peter Johnson and Joe Stork, later wrote of this period, "Existing critiques of US support for Israel were inadequate. They came primarily from politically conservative sources, which argued that US support for Israel was not in 'our' interest, as determined by oil company executives and others with ties to the conservative Arab regimes." In late 1970, Johnson and Stork joined with five other young scholar/activists to form the Middle East Research Information Project (MERIP), a loosely run collective based in Washington and Boston. MERIP aired critical perspectives on U.S. policies toward the Middle East and on the region's political economy, approaching the latter with a heavy stress on class analysis. While this mission prompted MERIP to tackle a wide range of issues, Palestine remained its central focus. The group's newsletter, *MERIP Reports*, championed the Palestinian armed struggle, not just against Israel but also against Arab states that attempted to curtail PLO militancy (especially Jordan, whose crackdown against the PLO in September 1970 catalyzed MERIP's founding).[50]

Some American churches, too, were starting to challenge pro-Israel orthodoxies. In May 1969, the National Council of Churches (NCC), which had previously supported Israeli positions, declared that peace in the Middle East rested on two prerequisites: a "home" for Palestinians "that is acceptable to them," and "security for the Jews in the area," whether in Israel or in Arab countries. Innocuous on its face, the statement implicitly rebuked the Israeli and U.S. governments for trying to sideline the Palestinian issue. In June 1970, the NCC urged the Nixon administration not to "escalate the arms race in the Middle East" by sending Israel any more planes.[51] Both statements resulted from vigorous lobbying within the NCC by Frank Maria, a Syrian American representative of the Antiochian Orthodox Christian Archdiocese of North America, and by NCC officers who had worked as educators or Protestant missionaries in the Arab world.[52]

Also in 1970, the American Friends Services Committee (AFSC), the Quakers' social action organization, released a book-length study, *The Search for Peace in the Middle East*. The study envisioned a settlement based on United

Nations Security Council Resolution 242, with two important additions. First, while recognizing that peace required concessions from both sides, the study argued that Israel, as "the militarily dominant power," must act first to break the impasse. Second, it insisted that no settlement would be viable without recognition of the Palestinians' "right of self-determination," though it did not specify how this should be exercised.[53]

Heading the AFSC study group was Landrum R. Bolling, president of Earlham College in Indiana. Bolling tirelessly lobbied the Nixon administration to take heed of the study, but his efforts were deflected.[54] In May 1971, Bolling managed to get a letter on the Middle East to President Nixon, a fellow Quaker. Nixon pronounced the letter "astute" and told his chief of staff, H.R. Haldeman, to provide a copy to secretary of state William Rogers. There is no evidence, however, that Bolling's or the AFSC's views received any further hearing within the Nixon administration.[55] Bolling would have better luck with president Jimmy Carter, serving as a secret U.S. emissary to Yasser Arafat.

A small and embattled group of American Jews also critiqued the Arab-Israeli status quo. Elmer Berger, a Reform rabbi who had fought Zionism since the early 1940s (and helped found AFME a decade later), headed a New York–based outfit called American Jewish Alternatives to Zionism (AJAZ). Although Berger believed that the establishment of Israel had been a tragic error, he did not support its immediate dismantling. Rather, he favored a land-for-peace settlement to be followed by Israel's gradual "de-Zionization"—the elimination of laws and customs that privileged Jews inside Israel (and potentially compromised their status elsewhere), the securing of Palestinian political rights, and the integration of Israel into the Middle East. A handful of other Jewish figures held similar views at the time: the polemicist Alfred Lilienthal, the peace activists Edmund Hanauer and Allan Solomonow, the linguist Noam Chomsky, and the muckraking journalist I.F. Stone. Unlike Berger, these men did not usually foreground their Jewishness, but each had a lifelong familiarity with debates over Zionism, Jewish ethics, and related topics.[56]

There was a final set of contributors to the growing pro-Arab discourse: Americans who had made their homes in the Arab world. Of these, the residents of Lebanon were the most visible and influential. Several factors pushed them to the fore and sharpened their sense of identification with Arab perspectives. The community was large, numbering some five thousand in 1970.[57] Many of its members had spent decades in the Middle East, had Arab spouses, were themselves of Arab background, or had some combination of these experiences. Lebanon hosted the American University of Beirut (AUB), ensuring the presence of a cohort of politically engaged American academics, many of them vocal supporters of Arab causes.[58] The fact that AUB already was a center of Arab nationalist and Palestinian activism encouraged further outspokenness on the part of Americans studying and teaching there. Finally, many U.S. news outlets had stationed their Middle East bureaus in cosmopolitan Beirut, granting expatriate activists a modicum of media exposure back home.

In the weeks following the 1967 War, a group of Americans in Beirut, most of them members of the AUB community, formed Americans for Justice in the Middle East (AJME). The group's mission was to challenge the pro-Israel tilt of U.S. policy and media coverage. Its main activity was the publication of its monthly *Middle East Newsletter*, a compendium of originally produced articles and materials reprinted or translated from the American, European, or Arab press, all tending to promote anti-Zionist perspectives. By the summer of 1968, with the help of some grant money from Aramco,[59] AJME was mailing thousands of copies of the newsletter to American news media, members of Congress, and U.S.-based organizations concerned with the Middle East.[60] The organization also cabled petitions and protests to the U.S. government. AJME soon caught the notice of U.S. media outlets. While the press treatment was generally factual and respectful, *Newsweek*'s description of AJME as a "vociferous . . . pressure group" given to "bombard[ing] the White House, Congress and U.S. publications with cables and letters arguing the Palestinian cause" bordered on disparaging.[61]

Expatriate protests were not confined to words on paper. In April 1970, assistant secretary of state Joseph Sisco visited Beirut and stopped in at the U.S. embassy. Arab demonstrators on the AUB campus, joined by a handful of American students, congregated on a tennis court abutting the embassy and pelted the building with rocks. On Thanksgiving Day 1970, about a hundred Americans, consisting mainly of students from AUB and of teachers and students from the American Community School, marched peacefully to the U.S. embassy to protest military aid to Israel. "Give thanks, not tanks," they chanted.[62]

The activism of AUB students placed university administrators in an awkward position. While they, too, tended to be critical of U.S. military support for Israel (albeit prone to express this view more mildly),[63] they could not ignore the substantial aid—$10 million per year by 1970—that the university received from the Agency for International Development.

Following Sisco's Beirut visit, AUB president Samuel Kirkwood wrote to undersecretary of state Elliot Richardson to express his regret over the violent demonstrations, noting that the disruptive students were few in number, had been swayed by "outside influences," and were being disciplined.[64] An October 1970 *Newsweek* article on AUB, catchily titled "Guerrilla U.," savored the irony that an institution receiving U.S. government support had become a hotbed of pro-Palestinian radicalism. In a letter to *Newsweek*, AUB vice president Robert Crawford protested that it was unfair to hold AUB responsible for the activism of some of its students. While visiting the United States in November, President Kirkwood arranged to be interviewed on ABC TV's *Today* show so that he could dispute the connotations of the "Guerrilla U." label. "It would be most unfortunate," he told officials at the State Department shortly thereafter, "if any movement in the US to denigrate the importance of the University and to cut its sources of USG [U. S. Government] financial support" should gather momentum. AUB kept its funding—and its new nickname.[65]

Elsewhere in the Arab world, American expatriates voiced their own opposition to U.S. policies. In May 1968, Aramco employees in Dhahran, Saudi Arabia, founded a local chapter of AJME. Yet AJME-Dhahran never gained the prominence of the Beirut organization and faded from view after a couple of years. In early 1970, at the height of the Egyptian-Israeli War of Attrition, about two hundred faculty members and students at the American University in Cairo, Americans and Arabs alike, signed a petition to President Nixon protesting U.S. military aid to Israel. "Any additional planes given the Israelis," the petition stated, "can only kill Egyptians, they can never help bring peace."[66]

Despite their wide geographical dispersal, Arab American and Arab-friendly groups achieved impressive coordination. Relying primarily on mail (with the occasional resort to phone calls, telegrams, and personal travel), they kept abreast of each other's activities, publicized those activities among their members, and joined forces on matters of common concern. The ACJME's October 1969 meeting with Elliot Richardson was sponsored by a far-flung set of organizations, including AJME in Beirut, the American Arabic Association of Boston, Elmer Berger's AJAZ in New York, the Middle East Coordinating Committee in Philadelphia, the Committee for Better Arab-American Relations in the Middle East in Birmingham, Alabama, and ACJME chapters in California, Florida, and Idaho. A second list of groups, including the AAUG, AMEU, and ANERA, "wish[ed] to express an interest in this meeting" without sponsoring it. In August 1971, in the wake of Daniel Ellsberg's explosive revelations about Vietnam, the AAUG took out a full-page advertisement in the *New York Times* demanding to know if any "Pentagon Papers on the Middle East" existed. AJME reprinted the ad in the *Middle East Newsletter*—and then sent it back to the United States for further circulation.[67]

While mail was the most frequent medium of communication, personal travel, too, played a crucial role in forging and maintaining pro-Arab networks, especially transnational ones. Arab Americans visited family in the "old country"; U.S.-based professors took sabbatical leaves in the Arab world, and vice versa; students availed themselves of study-abroad opportunities; American missionaries returned home to raise awareness and funds. Such activities were standard fare for émigré and internationally minded professionals and activists, but some overseas encounters entailed more than the usual drama, especially when travelers placed themselves in harm's way for "the cause."

In February 1971, on his way to attend a Palestinian conference in Kuwait, Abdeen Jabara passed through Jordan, where the army was rooting out the remaining pockets of PLO resistance. Approaching Amman at night in a shared taxi, Jabara and his traveling companions (apparently all of them Palestinians) stopped to help a man with car trouble. As they pushed the stalled vehicle, they were suddenly raked with machine gun fire, which killed four of them and wounded Jabara in the shoulder and arm. Jabara was taken to a hospital, where Jordanian police officers soon arrived and pressured him to make a statement blaming the attack on PLO guerrillas. The activist refused, insisting the firing had come from a hillside occupied by the Jordanian army. Jabara was convinced, he later wrote, that the army "had been firing wantonly upon civilians on the street" in a deliberate effort to terrorize the Palestinian population. Released from the hospital, he continued on his journey.[68]

By the time Jabara arrived at the Kuwait conference, U.S. intelligence was on his tail. "Jabara received [a] hero's welcome at [the] symposium," the CIA's Kuwait station reported to headquarters in Langley, Virginia. "Among [the] memorabilia which he had brought with him from Jordan was [a] map of Jordan-Palestine 'soaked with [the] blood of [the] driver' which he brandished about the conference as 'evidence' of Jordanian army guilt."[69] The CIA's reason for monitoring Jabara was never disclosed, but days earlier the FBI's national headquarters instructed the Detroit field office to reopen Jabara's file "to determine if he was affiliated with any Middle East terrorist group."[70] Jabara would soon learn of his government's interest in him, and the discovery would drive his activism into new channels.

Equally remarkable were the efforts of Letitia Greiner, a member of the Boulder group that formed the ACJME. In 1970, Greiner moved to Lebanon to work among Palestinian refugees. "I really wanted, simple as it sounds," she later told a reporter, "to just let these people know that there were human beings in this world who truly loved them and were willing to come and be with them." Greiner founded and directed a school for nurses at a Palestinian-run hospital outside Beirut. In the spring of 1972, outraged by Israeli air raids against Palestinian camps, she proposed that members of the American community "sit in" at Palestinian hospitals and clinics in South Lebanon, in the hope of deterring further attacks. Greiner recruited several Americans for the action and notified the U.S. embassy of the group's intentions. But the PLO, which exercised de facto jurisdiction over the area, denied permission for the action (perhaps for fear that the protesters were U.S. or Israeli spies). In 1973 and 1974, Greiner joined with AJME members and others to organize successive Easter weekend protest marches by Americans in Lebanon, the first from Beirut to the coastal city of Sidon, some twenty-five miles to the south, the second from Sidon to Tyre, twenty-five miles further south. Staged to voice support for Palestinian rights, both marches were amplified by solidarity rallies in several American cities, including a 1974 event in Los Angeles at which Rabbi Berger spoke.[71]

Just as they surmounted geographical barriers, Arab-friendly activists were generally successful in transcending their ideological differences. Figures so marginalized could ill afford to fight among themselves, and they did so only occasionally. Outfits that favored an "evenhanded" settlement between Israel and its Arab neighbors, such as the ACJME, AMEU, and the *Lebanese American Journal*, supported the efforts of groups that stressed the incompatibility of Zionism and justice, like the AAUG, ACAAR, and AJME. The reverse was mostly, but not entirely, true. When the American Friends Services Committee published *The Search for Peace in the Middle East*—which sought to reconcile Palestinian national aspirations with Israel's existence—AJME hailed the study as courageous and distributed copies among its members. The AAUG, by contrast, accused the AFSC of promoting a Palestinian "Bantustan" and darkly hinted that this "group of Quackers" (perhaps an innocent typo) was a "front organization" for the U.S. and Israeli governments.[72] It was an implausible suggestion, made somewhat less so by the revelation, just a few years earlier, of the CIA's covert support for American Friends of the Middle East.

Moderate pro-Arab critics were more receptive to an active U.S. role in the region. A number of them had applauded the diplomacy of Secretary Rogers, while urging him to go further in opposing Israeli policies and recognizing Palestinian claims. By early 1972, however, it was clear that Nixon had abandoned the Rogers Plan and was more interested in placating Israel and its American supporters than in pushing for a Middle East settlement. The president would face the electorate again in November, and, while he had no hope of winning over a majority of American Jews, he *could* realistically seek a substantially larger share of their votes. In February, the syndicated columnists Rowland Evans and Robert Novak wrote that Israel had "broken the State Department's hold over U.S. policy. . . . Given the political realities of a presidential election year, Mr. Nixon is not likely to spoil Israel's triumph for another nine months at least."[73]

Yet the 1972 election season also brought a small ray of optimism for Arab-friendly moderates. In June, James Abourezk, a forty-one-year-old member of the House of Representatives, won the Democratic Party's nomination for the U.S. Senate from South Dakota. Raised on a Sioux Indian reservation, where his Lebanese-born father had run a general store, Abourezk had served in the Navy, tended bar, and practiced law before being elected to the House in 1970. Brash and irreverent, he was a fierce critic of the Vietnam War, the oil and gas industry, and the Bureau of Indian Affairs, which he saw as incompetent and neglectful. He was a protégé of senator George McGovern, another South Dakotan, who that same summer won the Democratic nomination for president.[74]

While in the House, Abourezk had seldom mentioned the Middle East, and he did not much discuss it during his Senate race, either. The statements he did make were cautious and balanced. When a lawyer friend asked about his views in the spring of 1972, Abourezk outlined a scenario similar to that of the Rogers Plan: a land-for-peace settlement, to be pursued through negotiations that could be indirect at first but eventually gave way to face-to-face talks, and a just solution to the Palestinian refugee problem. The congressman then made a pitch for his planned Senate run: "While it would be ridiculous to suggest that a single United States Senator could play any great role in solving this bitter controversy, I do feel that, as an American of Lebanese extraction, but who believes Israel has a right to exist as a state, I would be in a unique and possibly useful position in the Senate to deal with representatives of both sides in this dispute in an effort to promote a just and lasting peace settlement." In September 1972, following the attack at the Munich Olympics, Abourezk addressed the

Middle East on the House floor. As Israeli planes pounded away at Palestinian refugee camps in Lebanon, the congressman deplored the violence of Palestinians and Israelis alike. The United States, he said, should follow "an even-handed policy for all countries in the Middle East."[75] Mostly, though, Abourezk kept quiet about the issue. Perhaps he feared offending the many out-of-state donors his Senate race had attracted.[76] Perhaps he simply assumed that South Dakotans were more concerned about other matters.

Across the country, Lebanese Americans responded enthusiastically to Abourezk's candidacy. Richard Shadyac, a Lebanese American lawyer based in the DC area, formed a nationwide campaign committee and organized fund-raising dinners in Detroit, Miami, Pittsburgh, St. Louis, and other cities. He persuaded Danny Thomas to appear at five events in South Dakota. The surviving campaign materials—the fund-raising letters, the supportive write-ups in the Lebanese American and Arab American press—make no mention of Middle East policy but simply focus on the historic nature of Abourezk's quest to become the first U.S. senator of Lebanese or Arab background. One suspects, though, that the candidate's off-the-record remarks at Lebanese American events gave community leaders some sense of his approach to the issue. In November, Abourezk handily won the election. (His mentor McGovern, however, was crushed by President Nixon, who won 34 percent of the Jewish vote, doubling his share in 1968.)[77]

Although Abourezk had speculated about playing a special role in promoting Arab-Israeli peace, it is unclear how much influence he actually expected to wield on Capitol Hill. He would be one senator out of a hundred, and part of the most junior cohort, at that. The experience of a far more senior colleague was sobering. J. William Fulbright, Democrat of Arkansas, had long championed "evenhandedness" in the Middle East. Yet despite his position as chairman of the Senate Foreign Relations Committee, and despite the stature he had gained as a formidable opponent of the Vietnam War, Fulbright had made no headway in altering the pro-Israel tilt of the Senate. He had been one of only a handful of senators to support Rogers's Middle East diplomacy, or to oppose additional shipments of military aircraft to Israel. When his colleagues moved, in the summer of 1970, to authorize the president to furnish Israel with all of the armaments necessary to maintain "the balance of power in the Middle East," Fulbright tried to block the measure, only to be overruled by an 87–7 vote.[78] If the legendary Fulbright had been so powerless, what could a Lebanese American freshman hope to accomplish?

The answer would be: not much in the Senate, but rather more elsewhere. Like Fulbright, Abourezk would have no discernible impact on his colleagues' pro-Israel attitudes. Nonetheless, his arrival in the Senate in early 1973 coincided with a marked increase in public concern over the deteriorating situation in the Middle East, a concern that turned into deep consternation with the outbreak of war and economic chaos in the year's closing months. These circumstances, combined with an enterprising approach to public relations, would create a substantial audience for Abourezk's views outside the Senate chamber, not just among Arab Americans but in the national media as well. If Jabara could be described as the leading radical in Arab America, then Abourezk was about to emerge as its outstanding moderate—an acerbic moderate, but a moderate nonetheless.

By the time of the 1972 election, a more collective effort to nurture a moderate Arab American alternative was under way. Starting in the fall of 1971, just as Abourezk's Senate campaign was gearing up, Kuwaiti ambassador to the United States Salem Al-Sabah held a series of meetings in Washington, DC, with Dick Shadyac, the chair of Abourezk's Senate campaign committee, and other Arab American business and community leaders. The aim was to consider the formation of an "Arab Community Association" to serve the diverse interests of Arab Americans and to promote Arab political perspectives within the United States. Initially, the meeting participants disagreed over the wisdom of explicitly addressing official U.S. policy toward the Middle East; some worried about provoking an anti-Arab backlash. By early 1972, however, a majority concurred on the need for an Arab American organization that could lobby openly on behalf of policy positions. There was also broad agreement that the new association's prescriptions should be couched "in terms of serving 'the interests of the U.S.A.,'" as Shadyac put it in one of the early meetings.[79]

In April 1972, the new organization, now called the National Association of Arab Americans, was formally incorporated in Washington, DC. Peter S. Tanous, a Lebanese American businessman with close Pentagon ties, became the NAAA's first president. A native of Long Island, New York, Tanous had little background in Arab American or Lebanese American affairs. "Pete . . . had nothing to say, really," Shadyac bluntly recalled, "because he was never involved with our people. We picked him for president . . . because . . . he was a military man. Totally impeccable and clean, a colonel in the army and a typical integrated American. . . . He was perfect for the [NAAA's] image." Whatever the truth of Shadyac's recollection, the available evidence suggests that Tanous was an informed and able steward of the new organization, which he led until mid-1974.[80]

The early documents also show that many of the NAAA's initial officers had come up through the old Syrian Lebanese American Clubs. And, because officers were charged with recruiting members, we can assume that much of the rank and file had similar backgrounds. It was something of a cultural milestone for these Syrian/Lebanese Americans to flock to an "Arab" banner. Shadyac's recollections, while a bit self-serving, illuminate the semantic choice. "Jim [Abourezk] and I came up with that concept of Arab American because the American Jews, the Zionists, were blasting us as Arabs[,] Arabs. Which had a bad connotation." A proud embrace of the label would combat the stigma. Shadyac continued: "Arabs also connoted oil. Now, the vast majority of us were Lebanese . . . probably 80–90% were Lebanese, a few, 5–10% Syrians. . . . Now, there's a lot of love for Lebanon and Syria but there is no political clout in Lebanon or Syria. But if you use the term 'Arab' you got the clout of oil. You are talking about the [Persian] Gulf. So we figured we would . . . use the political clout, 'oil' and money that the Arabs had, and we would package it all together and say we were Arab-Americans." Although the affirmation of Arab identity offended some Lebanese Americans—"We're not camel jockeys . . . we're descendants of the Phoenicians," Shadyac quoted them as protesting—it was, for the community as a whole, an idea whose time had come.[81]

In the ensuing months, the NAAA made modest headway in attracting the attention of official Washington. In February 1973, Tanous and other NAAA leaders met separately with Assistant Secretary Sisco and National Security Council Middle East analyst Harold Saunders, and in April they received an audience with Secretary Rogers himself. In these meetings the NAAA leaders presented themselves as loyal Americans convinced that their government was embarked on a perilous course abroad. Excessive partiality to Israel, they warned, had antagonized Arab opinion to the point of jeopardizing U.S. interests, including access to Middle Eastern oil. The best way to regain Arab goodwill, Tanous told Sisco, was to "approach the [Arab-Israeli] problem with even-handedness, respecting and guaranteeing the rights of all peoples." The U.S. officials were noncommittal but respectful. In May 1973, the *Christian Science Monitor* reported that the NAAA's arrival on the scene represented "a trend privately welcomed by many State Department officials, who feel that the American public, exposed primarily to pro-Israeli propaganda, is not adequately informed about Arab attitudes."[82]

But the NAAA's crowning achievement in 1973 was its first national convention, held in Detroit in June. About a hundred people attended, including several members of the Arab diplomatic corps. The convention addresses, by Senator Abourezk, President Tanous, and other NAAA leaders, were primal and stirring, pitched to a constituency unused to political protest but eager to make its mark. America was the "greatest country in the world," and outstanding "people of our heritage" such as Khalil Gibran, Danny Thomas, and Ralph Nader had helped to make it so. The United States had profited, too, from "the traditional ties of friendship between our great Country and Arab nations." Yet now those ties were strained to the breaking point, and Arab Americans were uniquely situated to salvage the situation. Dancing the *dabke* at club parties was well and good, but it was time to advance to the political arena, where the goal must be "a U.S. Policy in the Middle East that is fair and equitable to all nations in that area." A rousing speech by Minor George, a Cleveland water and sewer contractor representing the Midwest Federation of American Syrian-Lebanese Clubs, surely spoke directly to the experiences of many audience members:

> I am here to say that we have need of a political identity. We have many talks, many hafli's [parties] and I don't think anybody in this room, and I challenge it, outside of myself, has traveled in more cities, and played the deribeke [Middle Eastern drum] and had more fun in dancing. We went thru that stage, [but] the time has come, time has come to flex our muscles. And we finally got a crusade to wake us up out of this hafli binge. . . . I'm not here to break no club up. I want every club to stay where you're at. But I don't want to form another club. I want a National Organization.

Patriotism, contributionism, moderation, awakened duty—these were the touchstones of the NAAA's appeal.[83]

Throughout this formative period, the NAAA's projected relationship with the AAUG was a fraught and delicate question, and both groups positioned themselves cautiously. As early as May 1972, the NAAA made approaches to Abdeen Jabara, the AAUG president that year, assuring him that the NAAA saw its role as complementary to the AAUG's and urging that the two groups work together. Elaine Hagopian, then serving on the AAUG board of directors, warned Jabara against this "attempt to coopt you." But Jabara favored some coordination. At the NAAA's first convention in June 1973, he and twelve other AAUG members were elected to serve on the new group's twenty-seven-person board of directors.[84]

Figure 7. Leaders of the National Association of Arab Americans, 1975; *left to right:* Frank Maria, Minor George, Joseph Baroody, and Joanne McKenna. Each of the three seated figures later served as NAAA president. From the Collection of the Arab American National Museum, Dearborn, Michigan.

Privately, however, Jabara and other AAUG leaders shared Hagopian's wariness, as evidenced by an exchange of memos on the new organization in the spring and summer of 1973. Initiating the discussion, Jabara recommended that AAUGers seek common ground with the NAAA but harbor no illusions about what such an organization could accomplish. "The breach between the United States and the countries of the Arab Middle East," he wrote, "fundamentally emanates out of a systemic defect in the relationship and not out of the non-existence of a pro-Arab political lobby." Ibrahim Abu-Lughod agreed that the AAUG should "welcome others in this thankless task" of correcting misimpressions about the Arab world. But on policy matters there was a "potential conflict" between the two organizations: "NAAA states that it will work for an 'even-handed' American policy in the Middle East. . . . The AAUG has supported the Palestine Revolution and the Arab Liberation Movement. . . . All our statements thus far support efforts to transform the Arab world and to bring about a collapse of American power therein."[85]

Hagopian displayed even less regard for the new organization, though she, too, counseled cooperation. Perhaps it was good thing, she acknowledged, that AAUG members were so heavily represented on the NAAA's board of directors. "I do not think we should leave the field to these characters. They are bad news and opportunists. . . . We should be active in NAAA and attempt to develop our own constituencies within it to get more control and redirect its present 'position.'"[86]

The AAUG did not take over the NAAA. In the coming years, each organization would retain its basic orientation and, as often as not, find occasion to work with the other. Washington seldom came close to pursuing an evenhanded Middle East policy, and so the two groups' disagreement on that point rarely drew to the fore. Both organizations continued to decry U.S. policy in the region, the NAAA lamenting that Uncle Sam was perversely shooting himself in the foot, the AAUG charging that he was predictably pressing his boot to Arab necks.

These, however, were matters for the future. At the moment, life for the AAUG was taking a strange, complicated, scary, but also exhilarating turn. For even as AAUG activists uneasily regarded the emerging NAAA, they knew their government had cast a vastly more suspicious eye on *them*, and on the vulnerable immigrant communities they served. The AAUG's response to this challenge would open new possibilities for Arab American political activism, subtly repositioning it within the nation's civic life.

Chapter 3

From Munich to Boulder

Domestic Antiterrorism and Arab American Communities, 1972–1973

In 1969, the Association of Arab American University Graduates (AAUG) published its first collection of scholarly essays. One of the essays, by the sociologist and AAUG stalwart Elaine C. Hagopian, who also co-edited the volume, took stock of the Arab American experience up to that time. Hagopian observed that Arab Americans had historically enjoyed high levels of economic and social integration into U.S. society. Preoccupied with their advancement in America, they had paid little attention to the politics of the Middle East and had connected with the cultures of their home countries (mostly Syria and Lebanon) only in limited ways. Very recently, however, "the status of Arab-Americans has been affected by the Middle East crisis," and in particular by "the negative image which the strong Zionist groups in this country project of Arab character." The community's only recourse, Hagopian wrote, was to organize in opposition to such defamation "and to speak for justice" in the Middle East. She hoped that Arab Americans would "meet this challenge without being forced to retreat from" their hard-won assimilation. "How peculiar it would be to witness alien pressures forcing an assimilated group to regress to complete ethnicity in order to save its members in an American society to which it had committed itself without reservations."[1]

In a 1975 article in the *Journal of Palestine Studies*, Hagopian revisited the theme of Arab American assimilation and concluded that the "peculiar" scenario had largely come to pass. Three years earlier, ostensibly in response to a horrific act of Palestinian violence at the Munich Olympic Games—but actually, Hagopian maintained, as a result of Zionist political pressure exerted during the 1972 presidential election season—the Nixon administration had begun to monitor and disrupt the domestic activities of Arabs and Arab Americans, violating their constitutional rights and throwing a cloud of suspicion over the entire community, citizens and noncitizens alike. Arab Americans, shocked by the government's challenge to their status, had embarked on what Hagopian called "a process of de-assimilation." Seeing how precarious their position in U.S. society had become, they now sought security and a sense of belonging through closer political and cultural identification with the Arab world. Arab Americans were not only growing increasingly vocal on Middle Eastern political questions but displaying "a resurgence of interest in the Arabic language and culture."[2] Subtly exemplifying the shift was Hagopian's own stance on it. Rather than portraying Arab American activism as the "regress[ion] to complete ethnicity" feared in 1969, the author implied that the community had undertaken a salutary project of political and cultural affirmation.

Decades later, some scholars of the Arab American experience have returned to Hagopian's "de-assimilation" thesis. While occasionally questioning the assumption that Arab Americans assimilated smoothly in earlier decades, they echo Hagopian's claim that the more recent trend has been away from assimilation rather than toward it. This later scholarship coalesced in the aftermath of the attacks of September 11, 2001, when public suspicion of Arab Americans was at or near its peak, and most of the evidence for the revived "de-assimilation" thesis comes from the post-9/11 period.[3] But a number of scholars have located the trend's origins in the 1970s. They argue that the public association of Arab Americans with menacing behaviors emanating from the Arab world in those years—especially terrorism and the use of the oil weapon—transformed the community into a suspect "Other" whose assimilation the dominant society neither expected nor desired. Many Arab Americans responded to their exclusion by forging a stronger sense of identification with their region of origin or, in the case of new immigrants, by holding fast to their Arab identity.[4] Typically, scholars advancing the new "de-assimilation" thesis make only general reference to the events of the 1970s, though some briefly mention the post-Munich situation that Hagopian analyzed. Those who do cite it tend to share her assumption that pro-Zionist politics, not genuine security concerns, drove the Nixon administration's domestic response to the Munich tragedy.[5]

Actually, the administration's motives were not as crudely political as Hagopian and her scholarly successors alleged. The post-Munich investigations of Arabs in America had more to do with addressing a sincerely perceived threat and with preventing other actors from seizing the initiative in antiterrorism policy than they did with appeasing Israel or its American supporters during an election year. That objection aside, the "de-assimilation" thesis has much to recommend it. Since the 1970s, the contentious politics surrounding the Middle East have indeed hindered Arab American assimilation, and the troubled aftermath of the Munich tragedy formed a crucial, early stage in a long-term process of Arab American disaffection from the U.S. mainstream. Joanne McKenna, a Lebanese American from Cleveland, Ohio, told a reporter in 1978 that Washington's domestic response to Munich burdened Arab Americans with "guilt by ethnic association. That's when I became hyphenated."[6] McKenna went on to head the Greater Cleveland Association of Arab Americans and serve as vice president of the AAUG and president of the National Association of Arab Americans (NAAA). Today, the Nixon administration's assault on the civil liberties of Arabs in America—known widely, if imprecisely, as "Operation Boulder"—looms large in the collective memory of Arab Americans, many of whom see it as a "dry run" for the draconian measures directed at domestic Arabs and Muslims in the wake of 9/11.[7]

As powerful as the "de-assimilation" process was, however, it was not the only force at work in the aftermath of Munich (or over the course of the 1970s, as we shall see in later chapters). The very circumstance that alienated Arab Americans from the U.S. mainstream—the perceived anti-Arab character of national policy and public discourse—prodded organized elements of the community, especially within the AAUG, to appeal to that same mainstream for a redress, or at least a recognition, of grievances. This dichotomy marked the decade as a whole but was especially pronounced in the weeks and months after Munich, as Arab Americans both recoiled from the government's attack on Arabs' civil liberties and, with the help of sympathetic non-Arabs, took their case to the executive branch, the courts, and the national media. Arab American activists also addressed their own constituencies, launching information campaigns to advise Arabs and Arab Americans of the rights they enjoyed as inhabitants or citizens of the United States and offering legal services to the targets of official suspicion.

Throughout, the activists presented those targets as sympathetic figures in what was, by the early 1970s, an increasingly recognizable American storyline: the persecution of ethnic minorities or political dissenters by overzealous authorities. The Watergate scandal, which dominated the national conversation after the spring of 1973, reinforced this narrative of official misconduct, and Arab American activists were quick to portray the Nixon administration's antiterrorism measures as abuses of power in the Watergate mold. Meanwhile, the AAUG's Abdeen Jabara, who had himself come under government scrutiny, launched a federal lawsuit against the FBI that further positioned domestic Arabs as victims of Watergate-style excesses. It was "the first time," Jabara recalled, that "we began to link up the whole question of civil rights, Arab-American rights viz-a-viz [*sic*] [the U.S.] constitution."[8] Far from rejecting the American experience, Arab American activists sought to weave their struggle into a national tapestry of repression and dissent.

How successfully they did so is difficult to gauge. The national media were not particularly receptive to the activists' efforts to "Americanize" their campaign against the government's antiterrorism measures. That campaign received little mainstream news coverage and was almost entirely ignored by mainstream commentators. (It is possible, though, that Watergate inhibited the circulation of more explicitly progovernment perspectives on the matter.) Jabara's lawsuit did leave a small but visible mark, forming part of the case law that preceded the creation, in the late 1970s, of a new legal regime for the government's use of domestic surveillance to counter foreign threats. But the activism's most powerful impact was on the activists themselves. In combating the antiterrorism measures, they acquired a fuller sense of participation in, and an enhanced ability to navigate, the nation's political, legal, and journalistic institutions. Perhaps the AAUG's Michael Suleiman had this episode in mind when he later remarked (in a statement quoted in the previous chapter) that working within the AAUG made "some disgruntled and alienated Arab Americans feel part and parcel of the American political system" and "gave them a feeling of civic competence."

The proximate catalyst for these domestic events was an escalation in international violence by elements of the Palestinian movement. Following the final expulsion of the Palestine Liberation Organization (PLO) from Jordan in mid-1971, a shadowy new Palestinian organization emerged with the proclaimed mission of avenging Amman's treachery. Its name was the Black September Organization (BSO), a reference to the month in 1970 in which the Palestinians suffered their initial, and most devastating, defeat by Jordanian forces. The group's leadership was never formally disclosed, but the BSO appears to have been the brainchild of al-Fatah leaders determined to keep the Palestinian movement alive in the aftermath of the Jordanian debacle. The most prominent of these was Salah Khalaf, aka Abu Iyad, a long-standing associate of Yasser Arafat. Although Arafat himself publicly denied involvement in the BSO, he clearly acquiesced in its operations. He was evidently motivated less by approval of those operations than by a desire to preserve his authority within the broader Palestinian movement.[9]

True to its name and avowed purpose, Black September initially focused its wrath on Jordan. In November 1971, BSO militants assassinated Jordanian prime minister Wasfi al-Tal, a leading figure in Jordan's anti-PLO crackdown, in the lobby of a Cairo hotel. Weeks later in London, BSO gunmen opened fire on the car of Jordan's ambassador to Britain, who escaped with a wounded hand. Thereafter, however, the group turned its attention to the primary enemy, ratcheting up both the scale and the visibility of its attacks. In May 1972, four BSO militants took control of a Belgian passenger plane flying from Vienna to Tel Aviv and ordered that it proceed to its scheduled destination, where the hijackers threatened to blow up the plane, along with all of the passengers and crew, unless Israel released over three hundred Palestinian prisoners. After a day-long standoff, Israeli commandos disguised as maintenance workers stormed the plane, killed two of the hijackers, arrested the other two, and freed the hostages, one of whom later died of wounds suffered in the crossfire. The daring rescue operation electrified the Israeli public and fortified the government in its conviction that it should not, and need not, negotiate with hostage takers. The experience also convinced BSO operatives that they must be far more ruthless in the future.[10]

The application of those two lessons ensured a grisly ending to the next BSO operation. Early on the morning of September 5, 1972—ten days into the Olympic Games held in Munich, West Germany—eight BSO operatives broke into the quarters housing the male members of the Israeli Olympic delegation. After killing two Israelis who resisted the intrusion, the attackers took nine other Israelis hostage, barricaded themselves in the residence, and demanded the release of over two hundred Israeli-held prisoners. An eighteen-hour standoff ensued, during which West German officials kept up a dialogue with the hostage takers, persuading them to extend several deadlines and giving them the impression that Israel might release some prisoners. Actually, the Israeli government had told the West

Germans that such a concession was out of the question. The Palestinians, meanwhile, demanded that they be permitted to fly the hostages to Cairo and continue the negotiations there. West German authorities agreed that this could be done. They helicoptered the Palestinians and the hostages to a nearby airbase, where a plane and crew were supposedly being readied for the journey.[11]

The West Germans, however, had no intention of allowing the kidnappers to take the hostages out of the country. In a disastrously ill-prepared ambush at the airbase, Bavarian state police (West Germany's federal authorities were constitutionally barred from using force in the situation) opened fire on some of the Palestinians after they stepped off the helicopters. The Palestinians returned fire, engaging the police in sporadic shooting followed by a tense, hour-long lull, during which the hostages sat bound and helpless in the two helicopters. When armored police vehicles arrived, one of the kidnappers tossed a live hand grenade into one of the helicopters, killing the four hostages on board. Another Palestinian climbed into the second helicopter and machine-gunned the remaining five hostages to death. The shoot-out soon ended with five of the kidnappers dead and three apprehended. A German policeman had also been killed.[12]

Because the world's media had already descended on Munich to cover the Olympics, and because the sustained broadcasting of live images from one side of the globe to the other was still a novel feature of commercial television, the Munich tragedy received unprecedented international attention. The actual violence was shielded from view, but TV cameras trained on the sealed-off Israeli residence transmitted dramatic scenes of West German officials clustering at the entrance to communicate with the kidnappers, of police sharpshooters dressed in tracksuits taking up positions on nearby rooftops, and, most memorably, of a hooded kidnapper stepping out onto the balcony of the residence to survey the scene. "Live terrorist TV," Melani McAlister writes, "was born at the Munich Olympics."[13]

Disseminated so rapidly and so widely, news of the attack shocked the international community, and a broad cross-section of the world's governments immediately condemned the BSO's action.[14] Among Arab states, however, only Jordan denounced the operation outright; King Hussein called it "a crime planned and committed by sick minds." Lebanon expressed "deep regret" over the tragedy while stressing "the state of despair which grips the Palestinian people." Libya's Mu'ammar Qaddafi extolled the attack and provided a martyrs' burial for the five dead BSO kidnappers. The remaining Arab governments either kept silent or blamed the bloody outcome on Israeli intransigence or West German duplicity. These reactions no doubt reflected the assumption that Arab public opinion generally saw the BSO operation as a justified effort to bring the Palestinian cause to the world's attention.[15]

Libya's celebration of the BSO's deed soon became more demonstrative, with ominous implications for Middle Eastern and international politics. In late October, the BSO hijacked a Lufthansa passenger plane, demanding that West Germany release the three hostage-takers apprehended after the Munich standoff. Bonn complied. The freed militants flew to Tripoli, where Qaddafi greeted them as heroes and granted them sanctuary. In the months and years to come, Qaddafi's support for "national liberation" movements was to grow far more concrete and extensive. In addition to forming his own Palestinian paramilitary organization, the National Arab Youth for the Liberation of Palestine, he would bankroll numerous other militant Palestinian groups, some of which perpetrated brutal attacks on Israeli and other civilians. Qaddafi would also support armed insurgencies in neighboring African countries, on the Arabian Peninsula, and in such far-flung locales as the Philippines and Northern Ireland.[16]

Israel's own reaction to the Munich operation was swift and ferocious. Much has been made of the Israeli government's relentless campaign, conducted over the succeeding months and years, to track down and kill all of the known perpetrators of the attack, and that task was indeed a high government priority.[17] But the clandestine assassination program was dwarfed by Israel's overt military response to Munich. On September 8, Israeli warplanes struck ten Palestinian camps in Lebanon and Syria, killing an estimated two hundred people, most of them civilians. A week later Israel conducted a day-and-a-half-long ground invasion of South Lebanon, killing some sixty Palestinian fighters and destroying over a hundred homes they were suspected of using. The number of civilian casualties is unclear, though several civilians were reportedly crushed to death when an Israeli tank ran over their taxi.[18]

As in the past—though now pursued with greater vigor—the Israeli strategy was to compel the Lebanese and Syrian governments to crack down on Palestinian militants operating on their territory. From this perspective civilian casualties, though not officially intended, played a useful role in exerting political pressure on the host governments. Meeting with secretary of state William P. Rogers in Washington on September 25, Israeli foreign minister Abba Eban noted that "if [the] Black September group did not have Arab support its effect would be minor. . . . [Israel's] objectives must be to make Arab states feel [the] seriousness of the matter." Lebanon in particular "should recognize it was in its own interest to act against [the] fedayeen." In a mid-October conversation with Israeli ambassador to the United States Yitzhak Rabin, assistant secretary of state Joseph Sisco brought the Israeli strategy more fully into view. "Over the past weeks and months," Sisco reminded the ambassador, "the US had said little or nothing regarding the number of Israeli raids even in instances where civilian damage had been considerable. . . . We understood . . . that such raids were intended to 'encourage' [the] GOL [Government of Lebanon] to take more effective steps in controlling the guerrillas." Rabin did not dispute Sisco's analysis.[19]

In the United States, mainstream news media were unanimous in their condemnation of the "Munich massacre," as the murder of the eleven Israelis was immediately dubbed.[20] Sounding a ubiquitous theme, the *Chicago Daily News* observed that "the Arab guerrillas who brought death and terror into the Olympic Games declared war on the entire civilized world." The *Detroit Free Press* called the BSO's action "an assault on common decency." A "desecration of basic humanity," pronounced the *Columbia (South Carolina) Record*. Editorials were also universal in expressing understanding for Israel's predicament. "The sympathy of the civilized world," the *New York Times* noted, "goes out to . . . the nation that was the immediate object of this heinous plot." Occasional references to the tragic Jewish history that had preceded Israel's founding—and to the striking fact that this latest outrage had occurred on German soil—accentuated Israel's victim status. A cartoon in the *Cleveland Plain Dealer* depicted a Holocaust memorial, in the form of a tombstone, displaying an updated death toll of 6,000,011.[21]

Journalistic opinion was divided, however, over the extent to which the Israeli reprisal raids were wise or even justified. The *New York Times* ran several editorials cautioning that, while the urge to retaliate was understandable, such action was no substitute for the slow, arduous quest for a diplomatic settlement. Some commentators warned that Israel would lose international standing if it persisted in operations that inevitably harmed innocent bystanders. "Each civilian dead or hurt," the *Los Angeles Times* editorialized, "diminishes Israel's claim to act with the moral approval of the world." *Washington Post* columnist William Raspberry went further, calling the reprisals "illegal air strikes against sovereign states" and urging readers to consider the Palestinians' "legitimate unresolved and largely ignored grievances against Israel." But Raspberry's own newspaper staunchly supported the Israeli raids, and even offered a quasi endorsement of attacks on

Arab civilians. One result of civilian casualties, noted a *Post* editorial, was to place political pressure on Arab governments to curtail Palestinian militancy. "Raids which hit only guerrillas would relieve Beirut and Damascus of political incentive to move against resident guerrillas on their own. . . . If there are strong moral arguments why Israeli raids should be 'surgical,' there is also a harshly practical reason why they should not."[22]

For Arab American and Arab-friendly activists, the sudden upsurge of Arab-Israeli violence was an unsettling experience. Finally, the Palestine issue was receiving sustained coverage in the national media. With Palestinian terrorism serving as the primary frame of reference, however, this was hardly the sort of attention the activists desired. Still, they did what little they could to influence public attitudes on the Munich attack and its aftermath. While most activists deplored the BSO's action, virtually all who did so refused to treat that event in isolation, portraying it as just one episode of a violent saga in which Palestinians were hardly the primary villains. "Munich," wrote John P. Richardson, executive vice president of American Near East Refugee Aid in that group's September/October newsletter, "was only the latest link in a chain of Middle East violence whose roots lie in the upheaval in Palestine in 1948, during which the Palestine Arab people were made a people without a country."[23] In late September, against the backdrop of the Israeli reprisal raids, a coalition of Arab American and Arab-friendly groups in the Greater Boston area issued a statement declaring, "The tragic and deplorable killings in Munich, Lebanon, and Syria are yet another result of the world's failure to halt the vicious cycle of terrorism and counter-terrorism which marks the Arab-Israeli conflict." The "root cause" of that conflict, the statement continued, "is the refusal of Israel to allow three million Palestinian Christians and Moslems to live as first-class citizens in their homeland or even to live in that homeland."[24]

Some Arab-friendly commentators came close to an outright defense of the BSO operation. "We should comprehend the achievements of the Munich action," *MERIP Reports* editorialized. "It has provided a boost in morale among Palestinians in the camps. This . . . is not justification for it, but we understand why those who have been and are once again the targets of Israeli bullets and bombs reject the charge that Munich was 'barbaric.'" In remarks to the *Los Angeles Times*, M.T. Mehdi of the Action Committee on American-Arab Relations stopped just short of declaring the slain Israeli athletes fair game: "Every able-bodied Israeli—man and woman—is required to serve in the army and assumes at least a theoretical responsibility for supporting the Israeli government's policies."[25]

By October, these initial reactions were giving way to alarm over the Nixon administration's own response to Munich: a program of screening, monitoring, interrogation, and deportation that, while officially targeting noncitizens, seemed to cast a stigma on all people of Arab descent in the United States, regardless of nationality. To Arab Americans, this was a galling development, but one that created new and, at times, fruitful possibilities for advocacy on their own behalf and on behalf of those less equipped to fight for themselves.

The Nixon administration's treatment of Arabs in America was part of a larger national response to the Munich tragedy, which posed a number of challenges to the president and his advisers. Most straightforwardly, the sheer brazenness of the BSO operation suggested that Palestinian militants were more desperate and audacious than previously thought and would likely broaden their attacks on international targets, possibly to include the United States. Both internationally and at home, Washington needed more effective means to counter this expanding threat. "We have got to have a plan," president Richard Nixon told national security adviser Henry Kissinger on September 21. "Suppose they kidnap Rabin, Henry, and demand that we release all blacks who are prisoners around the United States, and we didn't and they shoot him? . . . What, the Christ, do we do? . . . We have got to have contingency plans for hijacking, for kidnapping, for all sorts of things that [could] happen around here."[26]

There was also a danger that, should the Nixon administration's response to Munich seem insufficiently vigorous, others might react in ways damaging to U.S. policy interests. Emotions were running high on Capitol Hill, with many Congress members denouncing Arab governments for supporting or failing to curb Palestinian violence. On September 6, both the House and the Senate unanimously passed resolutions calling for the diplomatic isolation of countries that provided aid or sanctuary to terrorists. The resolutions were non-binding, but administration officials feared that more concrete legislation could ensue, with untold diplomatic consequences. Vigorous action was necessary, Joe Sisco observed on September 12, to preempt "unhelpful legislation that may be under consideration."[27]

An even greater danger was that of Israeli overreaction. Within days of Munich, as we have seen, the Israelis launched massive raids into Lebanon and Syria, and they did so with a measure of American indulgence. U.S. officials worried, however, that Israel would exceed this latitude and escalate its attacks to the point of provoking a wider war. On September 6, before any Israeli retaliation had occurred, Kissinger warned Nixon that the Israelis could go so far as to occupy Beirut. "They mustn't do that," the president said. "They can't start a war over this." "I think they might," Kissinger replied; "this is an enormous provocation." With a presidential election approaching, moreover, the Israelis might be counting on Nixon to acquiesce in whatever action they took. "I don't want them to think that they've got you in their hip pocket," Kissinger said. Israel did not capture Beirut, but the attacks it did launch were worrisome enough. Over the coming weeks, Kissinger argued that a strong American response would engender some Israeli restraint. "Kissinger believed," writes the historian Timothy Naftali, "that the United States could slow the Israelis down by showing that it was gearing up institutionally to fight international terrorism."[28]

In short, the Nixon administration needed to take forceful action to meet the terrorist challenge, and to be *seen* to be doing so. The measures it adopted reflected these twin imperatives. It beefed up protection within the United States for foreign diplomats who could be targets of political violence, not just by Palestinians but by other groups as well. It developed contingency plans for managing various terrorist scenarios within the United States. It privately urged Arab governments to dissociate themselves from Palestinian violence and oppose it more forthrightly. And it called on the United Nations General Assembly to take strong action to combat international terrorism. Few expected this last effort to get very far, and the results were indeed disappointing to Washington.[29] Still, Nixon "told Secretary Rogers to consider the UN initiative seriously, since it might just serve to buy time. It serves as a visible reaction to the Israeli outcries." Kissinger agreed: "Of course, nothing will come out [of the UN General Assembly]. Nothing ever comes out. But we could make a lot of statesman-like speeches about curbing terrorism."[30]

All of these steps, genuine and cosmetic, were coordinated by a special Cabinet Committee to Combat Terrorism (CCCT), which Nixon directed Secretary Rogers to create on September 25. Composed of the secretaries of state, defense, justice, and transportation, the directors of the CIA and the FBI, and other top officials, the CCCT was to "consider the most effective means by which to prevent terrorism here and abroad." The CCCT met only once, in early October 1972, though it remained formally in existence until 1977. Its real business was conducted by a working group made up of deputies and staff members, who met regularly over the life of the committee.[31]

With the working group's encouragement and help, government agencies undertook two activities of special relevance to the status of Arabs in

America. The first was the aggressive screening of Arabs seeking to enter the United States, a program known, for obscure reasons, as Operation Boulder. In late September the State Department instituted a five-day waiting period for issuing entry visas to Arab visitors, during which time the names of all visa applicants were to be checked against the records of the CIA, the FBI, the Immigration and Naturalization Service (INS), and the U.S. Secret Service. Applicants found to have associations with terrorist groups would be denied entry. The special screening measures applied not just to Arab nationals but to all "ethnic Arabs" who were not U.S. citizens. An "ethnic Arab" was defined as anyone who had been born in an Arab country or whose parents had come from one. As the left-leaning *National Observer* skeptically noted in November 1972, after Operation Boulder had become public knowledge, "A Brazilian whose parents had emigrated there from Lebanon 30 years before was subject to the U.S. antiterrorist process . . . as much as a grenade-bearing Palestinian youth fresh from a Mideast terrorist camp"—not that the program had netted any grenade bearers, the *Observer* hastened to add. The term "ethnic profiling" was not yet in circulation, but that was what the measures amounted to.[32]

Operation Boulder continued until the spring of 1975, when the State Department concluded that the program was not worth the money and labor it required.[33] Boulder was especially burdensome on U.S. diplomatic posts, which had to devote precious staff hours to processing visa applications and to forwarding names and biographical data to Washington for vetting.[34] At the time of Boulder's termination, 150,000 Arab visa applicants had been screened, but only twenty-three had been denied entry on security grounds. The program's defenders, most prominently represented in the FBI, insisted that even this small number of rejected applicants—who allegedly included ten BSO members who sought to enter the country at the time of Yasser Arafat's November 1974 visit to the UN—represented a significant danger that had been averted. After all, wrote FBI director Clarence M. Kelley, the "carnage resulting from only one Arab terrorist allowed to enter the United States cannot be estimated." Boulder's advocates also argued that the stringent screening procedures had probably dissuaded many other would-be terrorists from applying for visas in the first place. But the State Department believed that Boulder had outlived its usefulness. "It would appear . . . that we are now the lone voice in the wilderness," an FBI official lamented shortly before the program's demise.[35]

The second activity of relevance to Arabs in America, one causing considerable alarm to Arab Americans, was the widespread monitoring of

Arabs already in the country. Technically, the name "Operation Boulder" referred only to the visa screening process, but Arab American activists often applied the term to this part of the antiterrorism policy as well. As of September 1972, some eighty thousand Arab "aliens"—that is, non-U.S. citizens—resided in the United States. The INS undertook to screen all of these individuals "to ensure that their status in the country is legal." Meanwhile, the FBI significantly expanded and systematized an existing practice of investigating the activities and associations of suspect elements within Arab communities. Of particular concern were the estimated nine thousand Arabs studying at American colleges and universities. "Past experience has shown," warned the head of security of the FBI's New York field office, "[that] Arab terrorists utilize those persons of student age to carry out their terrorist plans." Individuals with terrorist ties could be deported.[36]

In the weeks and months after Munich, FBI and INS agents began visiting Arabs in their homes or workplaces and interrogating them about their visa statuses, work habits, associations, and political views. According to testimonies compiled by Abdeen Jabara and the Organization of Arab Students (OAS), some Arabs found to have committed minor violations of their visa terms—such as taking unauthorized employment or failing to report a change of address—were threatened with, and occasionally subjected to, deportation proceedings. A few interviewees were detained for days without trial. Others reported that FBI or INS agents used intimidating or abusive language. An FBI agent told Jamil Azzah, a Palestinian engineer in Kansas City, that the government had evidence of Azzah's membership in a terrorist organization. No charges were filed, and the agent's superior later apologized to Azzah, stating "that such accusations are a tactic sometimes used by agents to obtain information." When Joseph Shikhani, a student at California's San Jose State University, told a visiting immigration officer that he knew his rights, the officer "put his nose at a distance of less than one inch from my nose and said 'you do not know shit.'" From Chicago came reports that FBI agents were taking Arabs on "night rides" and grilling them about their political views and associations.[37]

The scale of this monitoring activity is difficult to determine with precision. In January 1973 the OAS, whose constituents were prime targets of the program, reported that over a thousand students across the country had been questioned, 70 of them arrested, 2 deported, and 27 given "a short notice period to leave the country." In a set of "talking points" prepared a month later, the State Department claimed that, while 282 Arab students had been deemed "deportable," all but 109 of them had been "restored . . .

to legal status." Forty-one of those 109 "had decided to depart from the U.S. voluntarily." The remaining 68 had entered deportation proceedings, but none had yet been deported. There probably was some overlap between the OAS's list of soon-to-be-deported students and the State Department's list of those in the deportation process. The OAS's list also may have included people who had, in the eyes of the State Department, "decided to depart . . . voluntarily." Of course, both the OAS and the State Department were counting only students. In February 1973, *MERIP Reports*, referring to Arabs generally, claimed that 78 individuals had been deported as of early December.[38] Like the OAS, *MERIP Reports* may have been ignoring the "voluntary" category, which indeed was questionable under the circumstances. One suspects that some of the individuals taking that option felt coerced into doing so. No later figures are available, but as the program continued for another few years (albeit less intensively), it is likely that hundreds more were at least questioned.[39]

Although the Cabinet Committee to Combat Terrorism was launched with some fanfare, the Nixon administration did not formally unveil Operation Boulder or the domestic investigations. By early October, however, the national news media were uncovering elements of both initiatives.[40] As the news stories appeared, and as Arabs in the country began hearing personally from the FBI and the INS, Arab American activists swung into action, with AAUG figures taking the lead. Fortuitously, Abdeen Jabara was the AAUG's president at the time. With his legal training, wide "Movement" contacts, and defiant outlook, Jabara would have played a leading role in opposing the antiterrorism measures in any event, but the AAUG presidency added considerable weight to his efforts. Jabara rejected the proposition that the measures were designed to protect the nation from violence. After all, there had been no acts of Arab terrorism on American soil.[41] The only Middle East-related domestic terrorism had been directed at Arab diplomats, apparently the work of the Jewish Defense League (JDL).[42] The government's real intention, Jabara insisted, was to chill pro-Arab and pro-Palestinian activism, especially on university campuses, where Arab students had achieved a high level of political mobilization. Indeed, Jabara and other AAUG members saw the antiterrorism measures as a product of Israeli political pressure, to which the Nixon administration was unusually susceptible in this election year.[43] (As noted, concern about Israeli attitudes did influence U.S. policy, though not in the way that AAUG critics imagined. Nixon and Kissinger hoped to demonstrate that Washington had the terrorism problem well in hand and thereby persuade Israel to exercise restraint in its military reprisals after Munich.)[44]

Under Jabara's leadership, the AAUG launched a multipronged campaign against the government measures. The AAUG took out an advertisement in the *New York Times* accusing the Nixon administration of "playing politics with civil liberties." Attorneys within the association formed the Task Force on Law, which prepared legal guidelines for members. Several task force members offered free legal advice to targeted Arabs in their local communities. Jabara and Cherif Bassiouni, the chair of the task force (and a former AAUG president), wrote letters of protest to high-ranking government officials. Jabara collected testimonies of people caught up in the dragnet and assembled them into an extensive dossier, some of whose contents he shared with allies in the civil liberties community. At his urging, Aryeh Neier, president of the American Civil Liberties Union (ACLU), protested to attorney general Richard Kleindienst, and the left-leaning National Lawyers Guild (NLG) volunteered to defend Arabs in deportation hearings.[45]

U.S. officials were not entirely deaf to the civil libertarians' complaints. After being approached by the NLG's Southern California chapter, George Rosenberg, the district director of the INS, agreed "to go easy" on Arab students in the area who had been forced to supplement their incomes by working under the table. In November 1972, Jabara elicited a small admission of wrongdoing from James F. Greene, the associate commissioner of the INS: "Your charge that some 'students are being asked about their political beliefs and associations . . .' came to me as a surprise since the Service's long standing instructions preclude this line of questioning. When immediate check of field operations established that, at least in several instances, these instructions had not been adhered to they were forcefully reiterated to ensure there will be no further incidents of this nature."[46] The available files document no subsequent instances of politically charged interrogations by the INS. Over the next two years, however, Jabara continued to receive reports that *FBI* agents were quizzing Arabs about their political views and affiliations.[47]

One thing Jabara's files showed from the start was that some interviewees were easily cowed or manipulated by U.S. officials. Out of fear or a naïve desire to be helpful, they made potentially incriminating statements to FBI and INS agents. Ignorance of basic legal rights was most pronounced among working-class Arab immigrants, especially recent arrivals. Almost immediately, then, the AAUG set out to educate Arabs about the rights they enjoyed as inhabitants of the United States. "The *U.S. Constitution*," Jabara wrote to "Members and Friends" in late October, ". . . *applies to all persons within the U.S.* including all aliens, whether permanent residents, visitor, or even illegal entrants. . . . *No one need answer any question or respond to any inquiry from any official source unless the official presents a valid Court Order (Subpoena) to do so*. . . . The validity of the court order itself may be challenged before answering. . . . *All of these rights belong to an individual whether he is arrested or not, but he is not informed of them unless arrested*."[48] The AAUG was assuming an unfamiliar role: interpreter of American legal principles to a foreign-born constituency.

If the government dragnet was an American civics lesson, it was also a crash course in U.S. history. As critics assailed the antiterrorism measures, they found it useful to cite earlier instances of intolerance on the part of U.S. officialdom or American society. In so doing, they situated the targets of the investigations within a national narrative of repression and rehabilitation, associating Arabs with other groups that had been stigmatized, abused, abandoned, but ultimately vindicated by the wider American community. A ready historical comparison was anti-Japanese hysteria during the Second World War. "This policy of singling out an ethnic community as a target for 'special measures,'" Bassiouni wrote President Nixon in mid-October, ". . . is too reminiscent of the early treatment of Japanese Americans during World War II." McCarthyism was another available analogy. In November, Dr. Alan Johnson, associate director of International Student Affairs at California State University, Long Beach, decried the treatment of Arab students at his institution: "We should have learned from the McCarthy days that one of the most effective ways of developing an adverse reaction is to smear a person through assigning guilt by association." In an August 1973 article in the AAUG *Newsletter*, Jabara likened the current anti-Arab climate to "the anti-communist hysteria" of the early Cold War era.[49]

There was another way in which the AAUG Americanized the dragnet's victims: by insisting that U.S. citizens were among them. The association's ad in the *New York Times*, published in late October 1972, stated that the government's draconian measures "have also been applied to Arab-Americans." A few weeks later Jabara publicly claimed that the sweeps were "occurring on a generalized, widespread basis throughout the country, against Arab-Americans, permanent residents, and Arab students."[50] To some extent, the AAUG's references to Arab Americans drew on the fact that the subjects of FBI questioning did include U.S. citizens, a matter discussed below. But they also reflected Jabara's broader theory of the case. As noted, Jabara claimed that the purpose of the investigations was not to thwart terrorism but, rather, to disrupt pro-Arab political activism. To do this, the U.S. government sought "to dampen the informational and associational activities" of the three groups most inclined to engage in such activism: Arab students, Arab permanent residents, and Arab Americans. Noncitizens within this population, and especially students, whose status was more provisional than that of permanent residents, could be silenced through threats to their right to remain in the country. U.S. citizens had to be approached less directly. In part, their "associational activities" could be suppressed by incapacitating the noncitizens with whom they associated. In part, the widespread publicity surrounding antiterrorism measures (accomplished by leaks to newspapers rather than formal announcements) would make "Arabs and Arab-Americans aware that government agents were watching them" and throw "a pall of fear . . . over the entire community."[51]

Jabara's interpretation, which the AAUG as a whole embraced, placed the group's members in a paradoxical position. In the very act of casting their lot with vulnerable foreigners, they made a fresh bid for inclusion in the American polity. The AAUG's *New York Times* ad contained a poignant sentence: "Arab-Americans, long assimilated into the mainstream of American culture, are stunned by their Government's arbitrary *challenge* to their status of equality with other U.S. citizens, which [the investigative] measures necessarily imply." In truth, the claim of long assimilation did not match the experience of most AAUG members. It much better described the situation of the older, Syrian/Lebanese American groups, some of whose organizational representatives were listed as sponsors of the ad.[52] It is possible that the AAUG worded the ad in this way precisely to attract those more assimilationist sponsors. Or it may simply have assumed that stressing the Americanness of the Arab community would most sharply accentuate the injury it was suffering. Either way, the AAUG was planting itself and its constituents firmly within the American tradition.

As mentioned, some U.S. citizens of Arab background were objects of official scrutiny after Munich. Decades later, the FBI disclosed that it had kept Cherif Bassiouni and Edward Said under surveillance during this period, though neither man, apparently, was openly approached by FBI agents.[53] A citizen they did interview was Ihsan Diab, a Palestinian-born pharmacology professor at the University of Chicago.[54] "They [FBI agents] asked me if I sympathized with Al Fatah," he told a reporter in the fall of 1972. "Fatah seeks a democratic state in Palestine . . . where Jews, Moslems, and Christians can all live together. I answered that 90 percent of the 15,000 Arabs in the Chicago area sympathize with Al Fatah!"[55] Another American in whom authorities had an undisguised interest was Jabara himself. The FBI had secretly monitored Jabara since August 1967, focusing first on his opposition to the Vietnam War and then on his Middle East activism. In the aftermath of Munich, the Bureau stepped out of the shadows. Early on the morning of September 15, an FBI agent appeared at Jabara's front door and requested an interview. Jabara refused to talk. The agent left, having no legal right to inquire further.[56]

By now, Jabara had evidence that the FBI's interest in him went well beyond posing a few questions. Back in the spring of 1972, he had received a tip that an unidentified government agency had sent a list of individuals and organizations to a Detroit bank, asking if any of them had accounts there. The list consisted mainly of Palestinian people and groups, but it also included Jabara's name. Jabara sued the bank, which in the ensuing litigation disclosed that the inquiring agency had been the FBI.[57]

After Munich came further signs that Jabara was being watched. There was the FBI visit in mid-September. Then, a month later, just as the dimensions of the antiterrorism policy were looming into view, Jabara spotted a brief report in *Newsweek* that federal agents, in their efforts to combat "Arab terrorism," had "almost double[d] (to about 60) the number of security wiretaps" of domestic subjects. The activist was immediately put on his guard. "I said, 'Surely these must have been people that I talked to,'" he later recalled. "I decided, 'Well, I better do something.'" On October 19, Jabara filed suit in federal district court in Detroit, charging the FBI with spying on him and thus violating his rights under the First, Fourth, Fifth, and Ninth Amendments. "What's happening to me is happening to literally hundreds of people around the United States," he told the *Detroit Free Press*. "The police state tactics the FBI has been employing is [*sic*] the result of my opposition to Zionism."[58]

As it happened, at least one U.S. official shared Jabara's concern about a possible chilling effect on Middle East–related discourse. The day after Jabara filed his lawsuit, Robert Oakley, the political counselor at the U.S. embassy in Beirut, raised what was surely, in the totality of U.S. policy concerns, a miniscule issue: how to respond to visa requests by Arab intellectuals wishing to attend the AAUG's fifth national convention, to be held a month later in Berkeley, California. "The annual AAUG meeting," Oakley wrote to the State Department's Near East Bureau, "is going to provide a very interesting and important (I think) test of what the leading Palestinian and progressive Arab intellectuals think of our [Middle East] policy. If we turn down the key participants because of Boulder, we are playing it

Figure 8. The Palestinian scholar Walid Khalidi addresses the Association of Arab American University Graduates, Berkeley, California, November 1972; AAUG president Abdeen Jabara sits at right. Courtesy of Eastern Michigan University Archives, Ypsilanti, Michigan.

safe from a security point of view, but we will further alienate people who offer at least the faint hope of getting a dialogue going" on the Palestinians' political future.[59]

Whether in response to Oakley's urgings or for reasons of its own, the State Department granted a week-long visa to one Middle East–based Arab participant in the AAUG conference: Walid Khalidi, a Palestinian political science professor at the American University of Beirut with close ties to Yasser Arafat (and a renowned scholar of Palestinian history). As FBI undercover agents mingled with the attendees at Berkeley's Claremont Hotel, hoping to catch wind of violent conspiracies, Khalidi gathered more mundane impressions, which he shared in a cordial meeting with State Department officials in Washington on his way back home. Many Palestinian conferences were "sophomoric," Khalidi said, but "the Arab-American University Conference was helpful, despite certain outbursts of rhetoric. Americans were exposed to various dimensions of the Arab-Israeli and Palestinian problem and there was a constructive dialogue." The professor gently needled his hosts "about his 'forced short stay' and hoped that the next time he came to the United States his visa would allow him more than just seven days." The State Department's recording officer commented that "Khalidi impressed the Department officers as being an effective and moderate spokesman for Palestinians."[60] A flicker of comity in a dark season. In the years to come, and especially during the Carter era, Khalidi would be an important liaison between the United States and the PLO.

In January 1973, Jabara completed his one-year term as AAUG president, but he continued to lead the association's campaign against the antiterrorism measures. He also pressed ahead with his lawsuit, though there was little movement on that front at first. In the Middle East, the events of the ensuing spring did nothing to lessen the animosities that had given rise to the antiterrorism measures. The BSO's killing in March of two U.S. diplomats in Sudan, followed in April by a lethal Israeli operation in Lebanon that many Arabs blamed on the United States (see chapter 4 for both episodes), ratcheted up U.S.-Palestinian tensions. U.S. officials and commentators predicted further Palestinian attacks on American targets.[61] Although the national media featured little commentary overtly supporting the government dragnet, there was every reason to expect that, should Palestinian violence claim additional American victims, and especially should it do so on American soil, domestic support for the draconian measures would be clear and vigorous.

Increasingly, however, the American public's focus was elsewhere. The Watergate scandal, which became the top national story toward the end of April (and which is discussed more fully in the following chapter), created a more favorable atmosphere for Arab American critics of the domestic measures. The late spring brought a flurry of news stories about the Nixon White House's surveillance and harassment of its political enemies: Democrats, antiwar protesters, Black Power activists, even government officials suspected of leaking. These revelations showed that attacks on civil liberties were hardly a thing of the past and that the Nixon administration was eminently capable of the sorts of abuses that Arab American critics alleged. Moreover, some of the Watergate revelations concerned previously undisclosed measures against Arab targets. All of this made it easier for activists to Americanize their campaign against the domestic measures. By presenting themselves as victims of Watergate-style abuses, or as defenders of noncitizens who were so victimized, Arab Americans could now weave their stories into an absorbing national drama unfolding in real time.

On May 24, the *New York Times* revealed the existence of the "Huston Plan," an illegal domestic surveillance program that Nixon had authorized, and quickly rescinded, in the summer of 1970. Among the targets of the program, an anonymous government source told the *Times*, were Arab radicals who had allegedly entered the country on student visas "to conduct sabotage and assassinations."[62] The next day's *Times* quoted an anonymous U.S. intelligence official who disputed this rationale. Certainly, the official acknowledged, "there were Arab students in the United States who were probably financed by [Arab] embassy money who were trying to draw support against Israel." But as far as anyone knew "there were no illegal activities by those students—no recruiting American spies and no bomb throwing." In mid-June, *Newsweek* reported that in the spring of 1972 "FBI agents 'arranged' a burglary" of the offices of the Arab Information Center in Dallas, a branch office of the Arab League, in search of a briefcase containing the names of ninety-four al-Fatah agents operating in the United States and Canada.[63]

The AAUG seized on these revelations and redoubled its rhetorical assaults on the Nixon administration's antiterrorism program. "Watergate Spies Used against Arabs" headlined the June 1973 issue of the AAUG *Newsletter*. The newsletter cited the *New York Times*'s articles on the Huston Plan and highlighted the disagreement between the two anonymous government sources, naturally privileging the one who undermined the case for stepped-up monitoring of Arabs. "It is abundantly clear," the newsletter concluded, "that so-called 'security measures' which do not have an adequate foundation in fact . . . must be condemned as constitutionally impermissible."[64]

Over the summer of 1973, the newsletter continued to run stories on the antiterrorism measures, sometimes using Watergate as a framing device. A column offering legal advice to potential targets of government investigation began with the observation, "The Watergate Hearings have shown to what extent unchecked government activities . . . can get carried away in attempts to silence critics and opponents." Watergate also helped the AAUG make sense of its own institutional travails. When the Internal Revenue Service revoked the AAUG's tax-exempt status in September, the newsletter wondered if the association had somehow found its way onto the infamous White House "enemies list," whose existence, but not all of whose contents, was now public knowledge. After all, "one of the major targets of White House harassment using the Internal Revenue Service were [*sic*] tax-exempt organizations such [as] the AAUG." The AAUG does not, in fact, appear on any of the known versions of Nixon's enemies list.[65]

Watergate also aided Jabara's lawsuit against the FBI. The effort had begun shakily, with Jabara attempting to represent himself. In December 1972, having made little headway in compelling the FBI to furnish information about its investigative methods, Jabara turned again to the ACLU, which in May 1973 agreed to represent him. Perhaps the cascading Watergate revelations persuaded the ACLU that Jabara had a winnable suit. The revelations certainly provided Jabara with a broader sense of the case's potential. In early June, shortly after the *New York Times* broke the Huston Plan story, Jabara wrote to John Shattuck, his new ACLU lawyer, "With regard to the revelations in the Times . . . I am wondering whether we should expand our interrogatories to include break-ins, mail monitoring and phone wire cutting. If you recall, my phone wires were cut in September 1970 in the basement at my home. Neighbors reported seeing men in suits around the house on several occasions. I distinctly recall thinking that it must be the JDL since 'government agents didn't do that kind of thing.'"[66] It may seem odd that a hard-bitten radical like Jabara should have been so trusting of government propriety. Even on the left, however, such sentiments had been easier to harbor in 1970 than they would be just a few years later.[67] In any case, the Watergate revelations now lent national resonance to Jabara's individual complaint. "I was fortunate," the activist later said, "because Watergate was starting to break, and the whole issue about government surveillance and skullduggery was coming to the fore, so I just happened to be segued into that whole trend."[68]

Jabara's and Shattuck's efforts bore fruit. In March 1974, the Detroit district court ordered the government to disclose whether and by what means it had monitored Jabara's activities. Over the ensuing months and years, federal authorities disgorged a remarkably extensive record of their surveillance of Jabara since 1967. In separate filings in May 1974 and February 1975, the FBI admitted it had bugged forty of Jabara's telephone conversations, had exchanged information about him with Jewish, Zionist, and Israeli organizations, and had monitored his appearances at rallies and political meetings. In August 1977, the Bureau disclosed that it had received from the National Security Agency (NSA) the contents of six telephone calls and telegrams that Jabara had made or sent to overseas parties. This was the first time the NSA was forced to identify a person it had subjected to electronic surveillance. The FBI also admitted that it had examined Jabara's bank records, staked out his home, interviewed his neighbors, colleagues, and political associates, and, in the words of the *Washington Post*, "made phony telephone calls to his home to check his whereabouts." Even more ominously, the FBI acknowledged that it had shared information on Jabara's activities with three unidentified foreign governments (two of which were probably Israel's and Jordan's). The Bureau said that its most intensive monitoring had been triggered by a February 1972 CIA report that Jabara "was a cadre member of a Middle East terrorist group" (identified as al-Fatah in an internal FBI document) and that in December 1975 the FBI had closed Jabara's file "in the absence of current subversive activity, or allegation thereof, justifying continuation of current investigation."[69]

In July 1979, the district court judge ruled that the NSA, in furnishing the FBI with summaries of Jabara's intercepted communications, had violated his Fourth Amendment right to be free of "unreasonable searches and seizures." The government appealed, and in October 1982 the Sixth Circuit Court of Appeals overturned the decision. Jabara began preparing an appeal to the Supreme Court. In June 1984 the parties settled: Jabara agreed to drop his lawsuit, and the government formally acknowledged that Jabara had broken no laws and promised to destroy all of the files it had created on him.[70]

Jabara's lawsuit was more consequential in the legislative realm. It was one of a handful of cases that helped persuade Congress to place modest limits on the executive branch's ability to spy on "U.S. persons," that is, American citizens or residents. In the mid-1970s, as part of a broader effort to reassert legislative control over domestic and foreign intelligence procedures (most famously through the hearings chaired by senator Frank Church of Idaho and representative Otis Pike of New York), several Senate and House committees held hearings on the U.S. government's electronic surveillance of U.S. persons. John Shattuck was a frequent witness at these hearings, and *Jabara v. Kelley* joined similar cases, such as *Dellinger v. Mitchell* and *Halperin v. Kissinger*, in supporting Shattuck's brief against unfettered government surveillance.[71] One result of these proceedings was the Foreign Intelligence Surveillance Act (FISA) of 1978, which required the executive branch to obtain a judicial warrant for any extended eavesdropping of communications between U.S. persons and foreign individuals or institutions. FISA was the principal legal regime under which the government engaged in domestic electronic surveillance, until the administration of George W. Bush circumvented it by means of the "warrentless wiretapping" program after 9/11, a practice continued and expanded under the presidency of Barack Obama.[72]

And so, presumably without intending to, in 1972–1973 Jabara and his fellow activists began writing themselves and their communities into an ongoing American saga of resistance, repression, rehabilitation, and renewed struggle. This was primarily a domestic story, touching on the civic status within the United States of individuals possessing kinship ties to the Arab world. Through it all, however, those same activists remained transfixed on their region of origin, which by the summer of 1973 was drifting inexorably toward a violent explosion that would profoundly transform the U.S.-Arab encounter.

Chapter 4

Rumors of War—and War

February–October 1973

On the afternoon of October 6, 1973, Egyptian forces began moving eastward. Under cover of a heavy artillery barrage, thousands of troops crossed the Suez Canal in rubber dinghies and laid down pontoon bridges so that tanks and other heavy equipment could follow behind them. Wielding simple gas-powered water pumps—and using the canal as a virtually inexhaustible water supply—the Egyptians blasted passageways through the high mounds of sand that the Israelis had piled up along the east bank. In these ways, Egypt penetrated an Israeli defensive line that military analysts had considered all but impregnable. A few hundred miles to the northeast, Syrian tanks rolled onto the Israeli-occupied Golan Heights, breaching Israeli defenses along the so-called Purple Line, which had separated Syrian and Israeli forces since 1967.[1] It was the start of a three-week war that not only scrambled the politics of the Middle East but unsettled the international order. Before it ended, oil-producing Arab states had imposed an embargo that imperiled the global economy, and the superpowers had neared the brink of nuclear confrontation.

These events were traumatic but hardly unforeseen. Over the preceding several months, Arab governments had repeatedly insisted that Israel's continuing occupation of Arab lands was intolerable and that, unless the international community intervened to end the occupation diplomatically, Arab countries would seek to end it themselves through military action or economic coercion, or both. World leaders, American oil company executives, and numerous other figures echoed these predictions. Meanwhile, an escalation of Israeli-Palestinian violence further underscored the perils of diplomatic drift. But Richard Nixon's administration—the party best equipped to foster a Middle East settlement—did not act on the warnings, and war came.

This American failure cannot be attributed to misapprehension, at least not on Nixon's part. The president had long recognized the dangers of allowing the Arab-Israeli impasse to continue indefinitely, and he began his second presidential term, in early 1973, determined to press Israel to be more flexible. For such pressure to succeed, however, Nixon needed maximum authority, public support, and room for maneuver, all of which were in short supply once the Watergate scandal became a major national story in the spring of 1973. Control over foreign policy passed increasingly to Henry Kissinger, who lacked Nixon's sense of urgency about the Middle East.

With the October War, however, came an apparent reversal of fortune. In the space of a few weeks, those seeking an end to the Israeli occupation seemed to make a long and gratifying stride toward their goal. Although Egypt and Syria suffered a military defeat, they and the oil-rich states supporting them demonstrated that Arab political grievances, if left unaddressed, could wreak havoc on global order. Kissinger had to abandon his diplomatic complacency and embark on an extended quest for a Middle East settlement. Arabs everywhere could take pride in that accomplishment.

Arab Americans were also encouraged. In cities across the country during the war, thousands of them took to the streets to back Arab claims or criticize their own government's support for Israel. To the casual observer, this unprecedented display of pro-Arab sentiment came out of nowhere. In fact, it drew on experiences and networks that Arab American activists had painstakingly accumulated since 1967. Expected or not, the Arab-friendly outpouring thrilled its participants, creating a mood of optimism and confidence that persisted well after the October War ended.

In the weeks following his landslide reelection victory in November 1972, President Nixon's most pressing foreign policy goal was to conclude a peace agreement with North Vietnam that would enable the United States to withdraw its ground troops from South Vietnam. The agreement was signed on January 27, 1973, a week into Nixon's second term.

Days after that accomplishment, the president began expressing anxiety over the continuing Middle East stalemate, which he blamed primarily on Israeli intransigence. No longer concerned about his own electoral prospects, Nixon believed he could finally launch an initiative that required Israel to make difficult concessions. On February 2 at Camp David, he discussed the impasse with Edward Heath, Britain's prime minister. According to the British transcript of the conversation, Nixon remarked "that every other year the United States Government were inhibited, by one or [an]other of their Elections, from taking any action in relation to the Middle East which would be unacceptable to Israeli opinion. 1973, however, was a year in which they were free from this particular inhibition." The next day Nixon wrote in his diary, "I hit Henry hard on the Mideast thing. . . . We have got to get the Israelis moved off of their intransigent position . . . I am determined to bite this bullet and do it now because we just can't let the thing ride and have a hundred million Arabs hating us and providing a fishing ground not only for radicals but, of course, for the Soviets."[2]

Kissinger was unenthusiastic. He thought little could be accomplished until after Israel's next national elections, then scheduled for late October 1973. Nor did he share Nixon's concern about the consequences of prolonged stalemate. In a February 22 telephone conversation with assistant secretary of state Joseph Sisco, Kissinger argued that the status quo suited U.S. interests and that the Arabs should be left to stew in their own juice. "Give it two years and let enough frustration build up," he said, "and then there is a chance" for a settlement. "The frustration level is at a . . . peak right now," Sisco protested. In a February 23 memorandum to Nixon, Kissinger defended a more modest postponement: "It is difficult to argue that another few months' delay in moving toward a negotiation would be disastrous for US interests." "I totally disagree," Nixon wrote in the margin. "This thing is getting ready to blow." At the bottom of the page, the president added, "The time has come to quit pandering to Israel's intransigent position. Our actions over the past have led them to think we will stand with them *regardless* of how unreasonable they are."[3]

Over the next few days Anwar Sadat's national security adviser, Hafiz Ismail, made his long-awaited visit to the United States. After a brief meeting with Nixon in Washington, Ismail rendezvoused with Kissinger at a private home outside New York City for two days of cordial but fruitless talks. Ismail reiterated Cairo's position that "Egypt could not think in terms of a separate Egyptian settlement unless it is in the context of a general framework of a Middle East settlement," entailing Israel's withdrawal from all the lands occupied in 1967. Such a settlement could be implemented in stages, but "those . . . stages must be interrelated so they can lead to a defined goal." Kissinger cautioned "that US persuasiveness with Israel depends very heavily on the positions that Egypt advances." The United States "must be in a position to answer the question: What is Israel getting out of a proposed agreement?" Arab recognition was the obvious answer, but Kissinger thought further Egyptian concessions were in order. Perhaps, if the Israelis affirmed Egypt's theoretical sovereignty over the Sinai, they might still be permitted to station forces there. Ismail showed little interest in this idea. Sadat had already agreed that an international peacekeeping force could be deployed in the Sinai, and Ismail presumably considered this sufficient to address Israel's security concerns.[4]

Ismail's report of his talks with Kissinger dispirited Sadat. It seemed that Egypt's efforts to meet Israel halfway had made hardly any impression in Washington. "We couldn't pin any hopes on the Americans," Sadat wrote in his memoirs, ". . . as Israel evidently had them completely in her grip." It would be impossible for the United States "to make a move if we ourselves didn't take military action to break the deadlock." The Egyptian newspaper editor Muhammad Hasanayn Haykal, an unofficial adviser to Sadat, wrote that "Kissinger opened neither a door nor a window, nor even the eye of a needle [*thuqb 'ibra*]," for a peaceful settlement.[5]

In mid-March, the Egyptians were further dismayed to learn that, in a meeting with Israeli prime minister Golda Meir two weeks earlier, Nixon had pledged to sell the Israelis scores of sophisticated combat jets and to help them set up their own military aircraft production line. Nixon administration officials had hoped to keep the arrangement quiet, but word of it leaked out. "It was clear from the size of the deal," Haykal recalled, "that the United States was once again underwriting Israel's offensive strike capacity. There was great disillusionment on the Egyptian side."[6]

So much for Nixon's brave talk of cracking down on the Israelis. By now, however, the president was poorly positioned to take charge of Middle East policy. As of mid-March 1973, the Watergate break-in and the inquiries it had spawned remained a relatively minor item in the nation's public conversation. But that was about to change. Weeks earlier, the Watergate burglars had pled guilty or been convicted in a Washington federal district court. Judge John Sirica was threatening lengthy prison terms to compel the defendants to talk, and they were receiving hush money from the White House. Federal prosecutors were investigating attempts by Nixon administration officials to cover up their own involvement in the affair. The Senate had formed a special committee to look into the matter. With so many investigations under way, so many witnesses already or soon to be under oath, the White House's political and legal position was growing ever more precarious. No one understood this better than Nixon himself. By late March, he was spending hours at a time in meandering sessions with his senior aides, waging a desperate but weirdly indecisive campaign to arrange payments to the Watergate burglars, conceal the White House's role in the cover-up, and maneuver surrogates to take the fall should these measures fail.[7]

It would be another month before Watergate became a national obsession. But Nixon was already personally obsessed and had less and less time for the substance of governance. He grew far more sparing in the comments he penned in the margins of policy memoranda, and sometimes he seemed not to read them at all. "On at least one occasion," Kissinger recalled of this period, "Nixon checked every box of an options paper, defeating its purpose."[8] Salvaging his presidency, not averting disaster in the Middle East, had become Nixon's cause.

The Middle East, however, would not wait for Nixon to get his political house in order. Throughout the spring of 1973, Arab-Israeli tensions escalated on several fronts, creating a pervasive mood of crisis and foreboding. Sadat began an ostentatious countdown to war, Palestinians and Israelis sharply raised the stakes of their mutual carnage, and Arab oil emerged, for the first time, as a credible geopolitical weapon. Preoccupied with the domestic scandal, Nixon was hard-pressed to respond intelligently to these unfolding challenges, let alone enact his proclaimed get-tough policy toward Israel. Nor could he make Kissinger do these things for him.

Hafiz Ismail's disappointing mission to the United States confirmed Sadat on a path he had already tentatively chosen. In October 1972, Sadat had instructed the Egyptian military to devise a plan to breach Israel's defenses on the east bank of the Suez Canal and gain a foothold on Sinai territory. Following Ismail's trip, these preparations accelerated, and Sadat supplemented them with a public campaign to alert domestic and international audiences to the growing likelihood of war. On March 26, he announced that "the stage of all-out confrontation" was approaching. Two days later, he appointed himself military governor of Egypt, claiming broad emergency powers. In a March 29 interview with *Newsweek*, Sadat aired his disappointment over Ismail's U.S. visit. "Complete failure and despair sums it up," he said. Egypt was ready for "a final peace agreement with Israel," but Israel had rejected all reasonable terms. "Every door I have opened has been slammed in my face by Israel—with American blessings." Consequently, "the resumption of the battle . . . is now inevitable."[9]

In making these gestures and statements, Sadat apparently had two objectives where the United States was concerned. The first was to dramatize the urgency of the situation and give the Americans a final chance to avert war. The second was to inform them of his wishes and intentions should, as seemed increasingly likely, these warnings fail. If the United States could not launch a peace initiative in time to avert hostilities, then perhaps it could have one ready for their aftermath. In that event, too, Cairo would be prepared to talk—directly to Israel if necessary. "Once our fight resumes," Sadat told *Newsweek*, "I will not be averse to direct negotiations. But not before."[10]

Sadat's public warnings captured the attention of U.S. officials without fundamentally altering their view that Egypt lacked a military option. "Sadat realizes," surmised the U.S. Interests Section in Cairo, "that [the] initiation of hostilities against Israel would trigger [a] major riposte which would threaten Sadat's own position and damage Egypt's military establishment." The "present saber-rattling is designed to raise apprehensions within the US so that we will persuade Israel to become more flexible." Kissinger echoed this analysis, reporting to Nixon that, while Sadat was obviously disappointed in U.S. policy, "he also seems to recognize the disadvantages of military action."[11]

Kissinger and the Interests Section were right about Sadat's awareness of Egypt's military shortcomings. What they missed was the extent to which the Egyptian leader had subordinated military objectives to diplomatic ones. Sadat did not aspire to recapture all, or even much, of the Sinai Peninsula; rather, he hoped to shock the Israelis and the Americans out of their complacency and force them to reconsider Egypt's previous diplomatic overtures. Sadat would, of course, have to avoid a disastrous defeat like the one suffered in 1967, but neither did he require an outright military victory. A credible military performance—especially if it yielded a secure foothold on the east bank of the Suez Canal—would suffice.

The modesty of Sadat's military ambitions becomes clearer when one examines his dealings with Syria, Egypt's ally in the planned military action.[12] In February, the two countries' militaries began detailed operational planning, and in late April Syria's president, Hafiz al-Asad, met secretly with Sadat at the latter's presidential rest house near Alexandria. From these contacts a general plan emerged entailing an Egyptian assault on Israeli forces in the Sinai and a simultaneous Syrian offensive on the Golan.

The military planners identified three time windows in 1973—in May, August–September, and October—during which climatic, lunar, and canal tidal conditions would be optimal. There was not enough time to prepare for May; the attack would occur in the late summer or fall.[13]

Despite the appearance of close coordination, however, Egypt and Syria were pursuing divergent military and political strategies. Egypt's aim, as noted, was not to achieve outright military victory but to revive a stillborn peace process. Sadat knew it would be hazardous for Egyptian forces to advance more than about six miles east of the Suez Canal, as their aircraft and surface-to-air missiles could not provide adequate protection beyond that point. He intended to establish a narrow bridgehead on the opposite bank of the canal and seize whatever diplomatic opportunities emerged. Asad, by contrast, was committed to a far more ambitious Egyptian-Syrian campaign, in which each country attempted to regain all of its lost territory by force. Although Asad doubted that arms would entirely suffice and expected some sort of diplomatic process to follow the war, he placed much greater stress on the military side of the equation.[14]

Remarkably, Asad appears not to have realized how limited Egypt's military objectives were. Sadat evidently feared that Asad would not join the war effort unless assured that Egyptian forces would be fully engaged in the Sinai and able to divert Israeli military resources from the Golan. To secure Asad's participation, Sadat had his military commanders draw up a two-phased plan for the Sinai operation and share it with the Syrians. The first phase called for the Egyptian army to cross the canal and occupy a thin strip on its east bank. The second phase envisioned a subsequent advance to the Giddi and Mitla Passes, some twenty-five miles east of the canal. No one told Asad that, for all practical purposes, only the first part of the plan was to be implemented. General Saad Shazly, the Egyptian chief of staff, wrote in his memoirs that he "was sickened by the duplicity," but he went along with it at the time.[15] Sadat's lack of candor would significantly hamper the Egyptian-Syrian war effort.

As Egyptians and Syrians secretly prepared for battle, Israelis and Palestinians were already locked in deadly combat. For several months, and especially since the Munich attack in September 1972, Israel's intelligence agency, the Mossad, and Palestinian groups had waged a shadowy war across Europe, killing and maiming each other's operatives and officials through gunfire, letter bombs, and planted explosives. The Israeli military also conducted frequent raids into South Lebanon.[16] In early 1973, the struggle acquired a broader geopolitical character, as both sides drew third parties more fully into the conflict. Amid widespread, though erroneous, speculation that Washington was about to launch a Middle East peace initiative, Palestinian groups set out to scuttle the effort (which presumably would ignore Palestinian national claims) by attacking American targets. Israel escalated its operations in Lebanon to foment a crisis that would force Lebanon's government to crush and expel the Palestine Liberation Organization (PLO), as Jordan's had done in 1970–1971.

On the evening of March 1, eight Black September Organization (BSO) gunmen stormed the Saudi embassy in Khartoum, Sudan, where a diplomatic reception was ending. They took several diplomats hostage, including Cleo Noel, the newly appointed U.S. ambassador to Sudan, and George Curtis Moore, the outgoing U.S. chargé d'affaires. The commandos demanded the release of scores of Palestinian prisoners held in Jordan, most prominently Abu Daoud, a recently captured BSO leader; of all Palestinian women prisoners in Israel; of members of the extremist Baader-Meinhof Group imprisoned in West Germany; and of Sirhan Sirhan, now serving a life sentence in California. Within hours, however, the gunmen set aside all of their conditions except for the release of Abu Daoud and the other Jordanian-held prisoners.[17]

In Washington, the State Department assembled a special task force to manage the crisis. The task force members generally agreed that urging Jordan to release the Palestinian prisoners was out of the question. That would show that terrorism worked and imperil future innocents. Yet openly rejecting the terrorists' demands would be dangerously provocative. A more prudent course was to engage the captors in extended discussions unrelated to their demands, get them to break their own deadlines, and wear down their resolve. Eventually, it was hoped, the gunmen would tire of the operation and release the hostages in exchange for safe passage out of the country. A December 1972 standoff at the Israeli embassy in Bangkok, Thailand, in which BSO operatives had taken six diplomats hostage and demanded the release of comrades in Israeli prisons, had ended in this way.[18]

Tragically, there would be no Bangkok solution in Khartoum. At a March 2 press conference, Nixon answered a question about the unfolding crisis, despite the State Department's recommendation that he avoid public comment on it. "We will do everything that we can to get [the hostages] released," the president said, "but we will not pay blackmail." Many State Department officials were aghast to hear Nixon flatly reject the BSO's demands. "It was one thing to decide in one's own inner councils not to make deals or concessions," wrote the former U.S. diplomat David Korn in a book about the incident, "but it was quite another to flaunt one's refusal in the face of armed killers who were holding defenseless hostages."[19] Two and a half hours later, the hostage takers took Noel, Moore, and Belgian chargé d'affaires Guy Eid to the basement of the Saudi embassy and machine-gunned them to death. Early on March 4, the gunmen released the remaining hostages and surrendered to Sudanese police.[20]

The U.S. Foreign Service was rocked by the murders of Noel and Moore, the first American diplomats to fall victim to Palestinian violence. The U.S. ambassador in New Delhi, none other than future ambassador to the United Nations and New York senator Daniel Patrick Moynihan, cabled to ask whether Salah Khalaf (aka Abu Iyad), the suspected mastermind of the operation, had been located. "If we know his whereabouts, I hope by now the son of a bitch is missing a few front teeth."[21] Some Middle East hands, while sharing Moynihan's outrage over the killings, also faulted Washington's partiality toward Israel. "[I] believe most of us, if we must die for our country," cabled U.S. ambassador to Morocco Richard B. Parker, "would rather do so as [a] result of [a] policy moving us towards peace rather than one which appears [to] acquiesce in Israeli territorial expansion. Israeli possession of [the] Sinai and West Bank may be worth [the] lives [of] Israelis, but not those of American diplomats." William R. Crawford, the ambassador to North Yemen, was equally blunt: "Terrorism and [the] loss of American lives are the price we pay for the abandonment of even-handedness."[22]

The State Department was in no position to resuscitate "even-handedness." Four years of William Rogers's losing turf battles with Kissinger had shown the perils of that approach. State instead took a path of much lesser resistance: instructing U.S. embassies in Arab countries to press host governments to get tougher on Palestinian terrorism. Washington's attitude toward Arab governments, the department advised, "will increasingly be strongly affected by [the] degree to which they provide funds and other support to or harbor members [of the] BSO or groups with [a] similar outlook."[23]

The State Department was especially concerned about the situation in Lebanon, where Black September had its operational headquarters and where several BSO leaders—including Salah Khalaf, his front teeth presumably intact—were hiding in plain sight. In mid-March, William Buffum, the U.S. ambassador in Beirut, urged Lebanese president Suleiman Frangieh "to arrest or at the very least expel those who [are] known to be identified directly with terrorist action." Frangieh sympathized with the request but had to be cautious. Confronting the militants too openly would antagonize Palestinians in Lebanon, pro-Palestinian Lebanese, and the Syrian government. Over the next few weeks, Lebanese authorities persuaded PLO chairman Yasser Arafat to pull guerrillas back from the Lebanese-Israeli border but made no move against Khalaf or other Palestinian leaders.[24]

In clearing the border areas of Palestinian fighters, the Lebanese government hoped to deny Israel a pretext for further military action in Lebanon. But the Israelis were not so easily dissuaded. In fact, with Beirut now under pressure from Washington, they saw a golden opportunity to force the issue in Lebanon—to deal a decisive blow that compelled that country's political establishment to crack down on the Palestinians for once and for all. On the night of April 9–10, a seaborne Israeli commando unit landed on Beirut's coastline and met up with undercover Mossad agents, who drove them into the city in rented cars. One group of commandos blew up a headquarters of the Democratic Front for the Liberation of Palestine (DFLP), a leftist PLO organization. Another group broke into the apartments of two Fatah leaders, Yusuf Najjar and Kamal Adwan, and of PLO spokesman Kamal Nasser, killing the three along with Najjar's wife and some guards and bystanders. The raid lasted forty minutes; the commandos were back on the gunboats before the Lebanese army could respond.[25]

The sheer brazenness of this act caused an uproar in Lebanon, among Lebanese and Palestinians alike. How could the Israelis have pulled off such an elaborate operation in the heart of Beirut? The Americans must have helped them, many concluded. Accusations flew that the Israeli infiltrators had entered Lebanon on U.S. passports and that the commandos had escaped in cars bearing U.S. embassy license plates.[26] Other critics focused on the Lebanese army's failure to resist the raid, attributing it to cowardice, incompetence, or outright collusion with Israel. A massive funeral procession for the dead Palestinians turned into a boisterous antigovernment rally. Lebanon's prime minister, Sa'ib Salam, was pelted with oranges and tomatoes when he ventured out to inspect the damage from the raid. Salam in turn blamed the military and called for the army commander's resignation. President Frangieh rejected the demand, and Salam himself resigned.[27]

Over the next few weeks, Lebanon slid into chaos. On April 14, near the port city of Sidon, unknown saboteurs blew up two storage tanks belonging to the U.S.-owned Trans-Arabian Pipeline Company (Tapline). In late April, Lebanese authorities arrested several Palestinian militants for attempting to smuggle explosives into public places. The DFLP retaliated by taking three Lebanese soldiers hostage, prompting the army to surround several Palestinian refugee camps on the outskirts of Beirut. In early May, fighting broke out between the army and PLO groups and quickly spread to other parts of the country. Many Lebanese Muslims and leftists refused to support the anti-PLO effort, while some openly backed the Palestinians.[28]

Syria, too, sided with the PLO, sealing the Syrian-Lebanese border in an attempt to damage Lebanon's economy. Libya's leader, Mu'ammar Qaddafi, urged Palestinians to seize the Beirut airport so that he could supply them with military aircraft. Most other Arab governments opportunistically denounced the Lebanese campaign, even though their own restrictions on Palestinian activities tended to be far more draconian than Lebanon's.[29]

A few days into the violence, Mahmoud Riad, secretary-general of the Arab League (and Egypt's foreign minister from 1964 to 1972), arrived in Beirut to mediate the crisis. Working closely with Hasan Sabri al-Kholi, Sadat's special envoy to Lebanon, Riad met repeatedly with Lebanese, Palestinian, and Syrian leaders in Beirut and Damascus. In the talks, Riad was unexpectedly critical of the PLO, whose actions, he claimed, had exposed Lebanon to Israeli reprisals. He also chided Arab governments for unfairly criticizing the Lebanese government: "We should not make Lebanon alone bear the burden of our fight with Israel." On May 17, Lebanon and the PLO concluded a deal that essentially reaffirmed the Cairo Agreement of 1969, while somewhat tightening government authority over the Palestinian camps. The fighting ended, having claimed over 350 lives.[30]

Throughout the crisis, Cairo strongly supported Riad's mediation efforts, placing itself at odds with Damascus, which continued to denounce Beirut for stifling Palestinian militancy. Robert Houghton, the U.S. chargé d'affaires in Lebanon, cited Egypt's "helpful" and "positive" role, as compared with Syria's "nasty" one.[31] Houghton was pleasantly surprised, but in retrospect we can see how Egypt's and Syria's divergent approaches to Lebanon mirrored their respective attitudes toward the coming war with Israel. Egypt envisioned a limited engagement that cleared the way for a U.S.-brokered peace agreement; a victory for Palestinian militancy could jeopardize that prospect. Syria hoped for a more ambitious campaign, sustained by a wider array of anti-Israeli and anti-Western pressures.

For Lebanon itself, the crisis of April–May 1973 left an ominous legacy. According to the historian Kamal Salibi, "The Palestinian commandos were now convinced that the Lebanese authorities were determined not to rest until they had brought about their final liquidation," a view shared by many pro-Palestinian Lebanese. "As for [many] Christian Lebanese . . . , they were now more convinced than ever that Lebanon could not be truly sovereign until the last traces of the Palestinian military presence in the country had been eradicated." Militias on both sides began preparing in earnest for what they saw as the inevitable showdown, which came two years later.[32]

As the attack on Lebanon's Tapline facilities suggested, access to Middle Eastern oil was a subject of growing sensitivity that spring. Since about 1970, oil specialists had warned that rising global demand for petroleum was allowing oil-producing countries, especially in the Middle East, to gain leverage over Western oil companies and consuming nations alike. By early 1973, with the data showing that U.S. consumption of foreign oil was growing even faster than previously projected—and with the price of such oil steadily rising—the "energy crisis" had become a central theme in the national conversation. In April, James Akins, a State Department oil expert, published an article in *Foreign Affairs* titled "The Oil Crisis: This Time the Wolf Is Here." Akins argued that Western countries, the United States included, had grown dangerously dependent on Middle Eastern oil. The possibility that Arab states might "use oil as a political weapon must be taken seriously," he wrote. Other analysts countered that Arab oil producers were too reliant on Western markets and too divided among themselves to mount an effective embargo. Still, Akins's claims received a respectful hearing in mainstream American news coverage.[33]

One criticism of the Akins thesis was that its author was virtually inviting Arab states to use the oil weapon.[34] No such encouragement was necessary, of course; Arab leaders and commentators were well aware of the transformations in the oil market, and a growing number of them thought the time had come for Arab producers to apply their leverage in the struggle against Israel. On May 15, 1973, the twenty-fifth anniversary of Israel's founding, Libya, Algeria, Iraq, and Kuwait protested the occasion by briefly halting oil shipments to the West. The action was scheduled to last just one hour, but Qaddafi characteristically upstaged his comrades by embargoing Libya's oil for a full twenty-four. Addressing Egypt's parliament that same day, Sadat called on Arab states to use oil to pressure the United States to reduce its support of Israel.[35]

Even Saudi Arabia was entering the fray—a remarkable turnabout for the cautious kingdom. For years, King Faisal had resisted calls to unsheathe the oil weapon, arguing that doing so would damage Arab interests more than Western or Israeli ones. By the spring of 1973, however, the king was reconsidering. The recent changes in the international energy market made the oil weapon seem more potent than ever; perhaps an embargo could succeed after all. Moreover, the risks of *not* politicizing oil were growing. Over the previous two years, Sadat had distanced himself from Nasser's anti-monarchist legacy and drawn closer to Saudi Arabia. Now Sadat was asking for Saudi help; failing to provide it could revive Egypt's hostility. Passivity could also expose Saudi oil facilities in the Middle East, and perhaps within the kingdom itself, to attack by Palestinian militants. The Tapline incident seemed a taste of things to come.[36]

And so, starting in mid-April—much as Sadat had begun to do in March—Faisal issued a series of warnings to the Nixon administration. His message: the Arab-Israeli status quo was intolerable and could not remain insulated from the energy question. Faisal's first gambit was to dispatch his suave minister of petroleum, Zaki Yamani, to Washington for frank talks with top U.S. officials. On April 17, Yamani warned Kissinger that Israel's intransigence "puts friends of the US in a very embarrassing position." Saudi Arabia "is under heavy pressure from the rest of the Arab world. How long it could withstand that pressure he did not know. He hoped the pressure could be removed so that Saudi Arabia could do as much as anyone to solve the oil problem." Kissinger was unimpressed. "There are always 'unemployed intellectuals' who find it fashionable to write dramatically about whatever subject is fashionable at the moment," he told Yamani. "This year the subject is oil."[37]

His minister rebuffed in Washington, Faisal appealed personally to American oil executives. In early May, he warned Aramco president Frank Jungers "that Zionism and along with it the Communists were on [the] verge of having American interests thrown out of the area." Those with a stake in friendly U.S.-Arab ties must "urgently do something to change the posture of the USG [U.S. Government]." Visiting Geneva on May 23, Faisal reiterated his warning to the executives of Aramco's subsidiary companies. "Time is running out," he said; "you will lose everything."[38]

The executives hastened to Washington to carry Faisal's message to Nixon administration officials, including Joe Sisco of the State Department and Harold Saunders of Kissinger's staff. The officials gave little credence to Faisal's warnings. "The general atmosphere encountered," an Aramco vice president reported, "was attentiveness to the message and acknowledgement that a problem did exist but a large degree of disbelief that any drastic action was imminent. . . . The impression was given that some believe H[is] M[ajesty] is calling wolf when no wolf exists except in his imagination."[39]

Kissinger remained dismissive. On May 29, he spoke by phone with deputy secretary of state Kenneth Rush, who had recently met with executives of oil companies operating in North Africa. These men, too, had warned of the dire consequences of neglecting the Arab-Israeli dispute. Rush reported, "All the heads of these companies say we've got to do something to show—to calm this emotional upsurge in the Middle East." "But they are always wrong Ken," Kissinger said. "Every year they have another pet project to calm it, and they are never right."[40]

Meanwhile, Nixon himself faced growing diplomatic pressure to avert a catastrophe in the Middle East. Only the U.S. president, many believed, could persuade Israel to conduct the territorial withdrawals on which a settlement depended. Over the course of that spring, Sadat enlisted the shah of Iran, president Josip Tito of Yugoslavia, and emperor Haile Selassie of Ethiopia to intercede personally with Nixon. Each leader conveyed the message that Sadat was ready for peace but would not shrink from war if his modest terms were rejected. Writing Nixon on their own initiative, president Giovanni Leone of Italy and prime minister Edward Heath of Britain warned that the Arabs were frustrated and embittered by the status quo and liable to lash out desperately against the West. Most of these appeals drew Nixon's bland assurances, oral or written as the occasion demanded, that the president appreciated the gravity of the problem and would spare no effort at a solution.[41]

The sharpest diplomatic prod came from Soviet leader Leonid Brezhnev, who visited the United States for a summit meeting in late June. Brezhnev spent the latter portion of his stay as Nixon's houseguest in San Clemente, California. At ten o'clock on his last evening there, an agitated Brezhnev insisted that Nixon be roused from his bed for an impromptu discussion of the Middle East, which had received only superficial attention in the formal sessions. For an hour and a half, Brezhnev tried to impress on Nixon the severity of the Arab-Israeli impasse. Arab patience had run out, the Soviet leader said, and war could erupt at any moment. The best way to avert disaster would be for the superpowers to agree, immediately, on some principles for resolving the dispute. Those principles should include full Israeli withdrawal from occupied territory, recognition of national boundaries, freedom of navigation through the Strait of Tiran, and international guarantees of the settlement. "If there is no clarity about the principles," Brezhnev warned, "we will have difficulty keeping the military situation from flaring up."[42]

"We can't settle this tonight," Nixon protested. He would consider what Brezhnev had said and get back to him. And anyway, Nixon added, "It would be very easy for me to say that Israel should withdraw from all the occupied territories and call it an agreed principle. But that's what the argument is about." After assuring Brezhnev that "I consider the Arab-Israeli dispute a matter of highest urgency" and that a Middle East settlement "will be our project this year," Nixon brought the meeting to a close.[43]

Brezhnev's premonitory rumblings surely sounded familiar to Nixon, who had made similar noises in February. Yet much had changed in the intervening four months, and especially the previous two, leaving the president with little room for maneuver. Around mid-April, "Watergate" had become a household word for Americans, signifying the likely involvement of high-ranking administration officials in a staggering array of illegal activities, from bugging and burglary to witness tampering and perjury. In late April, Nixon accepted the resignations of his two top aides, White House chief of staff H.R. Haldeman and domestic affairs assistant John Ehrlichman, and of White House counselor John W. Dean, who was already cooperating with federal prosecutors. In mid-May, the Senate's special Watergate committee began holding televised hearings, which transfixed the American public for the next three months. The Watergate hearings brought the question of Nixon's own culpability to the fore, first by providing a forum for Dean's allegations of presidential wrongdoing, then by revealing the existence of the secret White House taping system. Nixon himself had created the evidence that might damn him, if the investigators could only get their hands on it.[44]

Since March, Watergate had monopolized Nixon's time and energy. After April, it had eroded his political authority, an essential resource for effectiveness in Middle East diplomacy. By summer, it was hard to see how the president could demand greater flexibility from Israel and win the bruising domestic battle that would surely ensue. After speaking with Harold Saunders on June 21, a British diplomat reported home that Saunders "alluded to the Administration's especial difficulty in taking steps which might provoke a confrontation with the Jewish lobby and their congressional supporters when they [the administration] have been weakened domestically by the Watergate Affair." In mid-August, Kissinger met in his Washington apartment with Abba Eban and Simcha Dinitz, Israel's foreign minister and ambassador to the United States, respectively. "I must tell you frankly," Kissinger said, "that if it were not for Watergate, there would be great pressures building up now" for Israeli concessions. In view of the scandal, however, "you won't be under pressure from us, probably even [after the Israeli elections] in October."[45]

If Eban and Dinitz quietly celebrated these tidings, their Arab adversaries could only look on in dismay. "The main impact of Watergate," reported the

Washington Post's Jim Hoagland in July, "has . . . been to increase Arab pessimism that a Middle East peace solution can be reached now with American help. The White House is seen as having been so deeply wounded that it cannot undertake a Middle East initiative against a strengthened Congress." Recalling this period in his memoirs, the former Egyptian diplomat Mahmoud Riad wrote that Nixon "was in the turmoil of the Watergate scandal and had rendered himself a hostage to Israeli pressure in the process."[46]

It was all too tempting to find a sinister design in these developments. On a visit to Buenos Aires in late May, Secretary Rogers met with Spanish

Figure 9. A cartoon in the June 9, 1973, issue of *al-Ahram*, Egypt's quasi-official newspaper, shows Israeli prime minister Golda Meir and defense minister Moshe Dayan exploiting Watergate. The upper caption reads, "On the Watergate Question." The bottle on the right is labeled "Aid to Israel." The juice maker on the right is labeled "Nixon's Reelection," and the one on the left is labeled "The Watergate Scandal." The lower caption has Dayan saying, "Excuse me, Mr. Nixon, we had to move you to a new juice maker because the old one isn't working anymore."

foreign minister Gregorio López-Bravo, who reported on his recent conversations with Egyptian diplomats. López-Bravo "stated that Arabs believe that 'Jews are orchestrating and manipulating [the] Watergate affair to divert [the] USG from constructive action in the Middle East.'" "A small number of Arabs," Hoagland continued in his July report, "seem firmly convinced that disclosure of Watergate is yet another Zionist plot aimed at heading off a Middle East peace move that Mr. Nixon was about to make. King Faisal of Saudi Arabia has told foreign visitors that Zionists are behind all current internal problems in the United States, a remark interpreted by one of his aides as applying directly to Watergate." The notion of a Zionist plot was fanciful, but there is no question that the scandal served the Israel/Kissinger strategy of stonewalling on the issue of any land-for-peace agreement.[47]

By now the oil companies, having failed in their private efforts to rouse the Nixon administration, had gone public with their concerns. On June 21, Mobil Oil took out an advertisement in the *New York Times* that described the rapid rise in U.S. dependence on Persian Gulf oil and warned that "political considerations may become the critical element in Saudi Arabia's decisions" regarding its exports. Much as Brezhnev would do two days later in San Clemente, Mobil called for "a settlement in the Middle East, backed by ironclad and credible guarantees from the United States and the Soviet Union . . . that will bring justice and security to all the peoples and all the states of that region. Nobody can afford another war in the Middle East. Nobody. *Nobody*." A month later Otto Miller, chairman of the board of Standard Oil of California (Socal), sent a letter to 262,000 stockholders and 40,000 employees that warned of "a growing feeling in much of the Arab world that the United States has turned its back on the Arab people."[48]

The oil companies' statements ignited a firestorm. Mobil reported that its ad received about seven hundred responses, almost all of them negative. Many of the critics "either returned credit cards or threatened to cease patronizing us." Isaiah L. Kenen, executive director of the American Israel Public Affairs Committee (AIPAC), called Socal's letter "a brazen and outrageous attempt . . . to mobilize a pro-Arab lobby." Zev Yaroslavsky, director of the Southern California Council for Soviet Jewry, accused Otto Miller of seeking to "exchange Jewish blood for Arab oil." Meeting privately with Eban and Dinitz, Kissinger piled on: "The oil men are basically spokesmen for the producing countries. And they are politically stupid."[49]

Most Arab American activists and commentators, by contrast, enthusiastically welcomed the oil company statements. "As loyal Americans, the members of the National Association of Arab Americans congratulates [*sic*] Standard Oil of California . . . on your desire to enhance the United States' posture in the Arab countries," NAAA president Peter Tanous wrote to Miller. Commenting on the Mobil ad, the New York–based *New Lebanese American Journal* displayed an almost mystical faith in oil companies' ability to transform U.S. policy: "Copies of Mobil's ad must have been circulated in Israel's foreign office in Jerusalem; the impact must have been shattering. . . . Historically the most powerful lobbyists in Washington have been in the employ of the great oil companies. . . . Israel will be hard put to counter this lobbying."[50]

To the Association of Arab American University Graduates (AAUG), this was all a bit much. An article in the group's October newsletter, published before the October War, lamented the "confusion . . . generated in recent months among Arab-Americans" by news coverage of international oil politics. The Saudi government, the article maintained, could not possibly be serious about its threats to wage economic warfare against its American patron. Those threats were "hot air balloons" floated to ward off revolution at home. As for the oil companies, they naturally sought to preserve the Saudi regime and saw "a sell out settlement" of the Arab-Israeli dispute—one that left Israel intact and dominant but eased some of the anger in the Arab world—as the best means to that end. Arab oil could be a handy weapon, the article acknowledged, "but only if seen in the context of total mobilization of Arab society and if wielded by Arab forces who are not subject to U.S. government pressure."[51]

Senator James Abourezk, too, was suspicious of the oil companies; his progressive sensibilities demanded no less. On a visit to Lebanon in early August, he told reporters that the energy crisis "was manufactured by public relations firms" working for oil companies eager to jack up gas prices. "The United States should change its policy towards the Middle East," Abourezk proclaimed shortly after returning to Washington, "not because of the energy problem but because it would be right and just to do so."[52]

Abourezk's Lebanon trip, his first to his ancestral homeland, was an unsettling experience. "Visiting the Palestinian refugee camps in Beirut gave me the shock of my life," Abourezk wrote in his memoirs. "Amid the conspicuous affluence of Beirut sat huge rows of squalid tin huts with open sewers running down the middle of the narrow streets that separated them. Palestinian children were . . . climbing up and down on rubble that had been produced by shelling or bombing"—possibly the combined work of Israeli and Lebanese armed forces. In a village in South Lebanon, through which Abourezk and his party drove to reach his parents' home town of

Kfeir, residents "had strung a large canvas sign above the road that read, in Arabic, 'Welcome Senator Sheikh James Abu-rizk,' and in English, 'Fantome Jets made in USA.'" Near the sign was a bomb crater, "which I was told had been made by an Israeli Phantom jet." At the welcoming ceremony in Kfeir, attended by scores of family members, villagers, and local dignitaries, the mayor hailed the famous visitor but also sounded a warning: "We here have always thought of America as the haven for oppressed people. . . . But since America has been giving Israel airplanes and bombs to bomb us here, we now think of America as the oppressor."[53]

"I left Lebanon feeling immensely betrayed," Abourezk recalled. "For most of my adult life I had believed that Israel had been picked on by the Arab countries. . . . To learn in Lebanon that the truth had been stood on its head was an emotional shock to me . . . [and] put me in an angry mood."[54] The conversion story is somewhat overdrawn; Abourezk had been challenging Zionist narratives for several months. Yet the misery and devastation he witnessed in Lebanon sharpened his indignation. This experience, combined with the outbreak of the October War two months later, put the Arab-Israeli dispute at the center of Abourezk's politics, where it would remain for years to come.

Elsewhere in the Middle East, the pace of secret diplomacy was quickening. On August 23, Sadat paid an unpublicized visit to Riyadh, where he told King Faisal that Egypt might soon resume hostilities against Israel. Faisal pledged to use the oil weapon in support of such an operation. He also agreed to double Saudi Arabia's annual subsidy to Egypt to $200 million per year and to provide $500 million in military aid. Sadat proceeded to Kuwait and Qatar, receiving substantial loan pledges from both countries' governments.[55]

On September 10–12, Sadat, Asad, and King Hussein held a summit meeting in Cairo. It was an odd affair. Jordan was not expected to take part in the war, and Sadat and Asad had agreed to keep Hussein in the dark about their plans. They included him in the summit to create a semblance of inter-Arab unity on the eve of war, and perhaps to ensure some Jordanian cooperation once fighting had begun.[56] In the intervals between the three-way talks, which dealt with military preparedness in general terms, Sadat and Asad met secretly to finalize their plans. Hostilities were set to begin on October 6.[57]

Actually, Hussein already knew, or was about to learn, that Egypt and Syria were preparing to break the cease-fire. According to his biographer

Nigel Ashton, in the weeks preceding the October War Hussein received detailed reports on Syrian battle plans from a high-ranking source in the Syrian army. Convinced that war would be disastrous for the Arabs, Hussein told the CIA station chief in Amman that an attack was imminent. The warning appears to have been ignored. It did not fit with the prevailing intelligence assessment that, because the Arabs were sure to lose another war, they would be crazy to start one. Over the summer, U.S. officials had occasionally questioned this conclusion—Kissinger himself felt pangs of unease—but the doubts were too fleeting to dislodge the reassuring consensus.[58]

On September 25, Hussein helicoptered to a Mossad guesthouse outside Tel Aviv for a face-to-face meeting with Prime Minister Meir. This was neither the first nor the last of Hussein's covert meetings with Israeli leaders, but it was surely the most extraordinary. Hussein warned Meir that Egypt and Syria would not tolerate the status quo for much longer and that only vigorous diplomacy could avert an explosion. Syria in particular was in a "pre-jump-off position" for war. After Hussein departed, Meir and her advisers analyzed the king's warning and concluded there was little cause for alarm. Syria would not act without Egypt, and Egypt would not act at all. As a precaution, however, the Israel Defense Forces (IDF) decided to transfer a few more tanks to the Golan to deter or repel any Syrian incursion. "We'll have one hundred tanks against their eight hundred," said IDF chief of staff general David Elazar. "That ought to be enough."[59]

Elazar was not the only one brimming with confidence. In late August, Kissinger scored a final victory in his four-and-a-half-year battle with Rogers when Nixon nominated the former to be secretary of state. A month later Kissinger was overwhelmingly confirmed by a U.S. Senate eager to insulate foreign policy from the ravages of Watergate. (Abourezk, citing Kissinger's involvement in administration wiretapping, was one of seven senators to oppose confirmation.)[60] In a September 5 press conference, Nixon said he had directed his secretary-designate to give "the highest priority" to an Arab-Israeli settlement. Kissinger, however, was lowering expectations. "There won't be a big initiative when I come in," he assured Ambassador Dinitz on September 10. Speaking to a Spanish diplomat on October 4—and taking a small swipe at his predecessor—Kissinger said, "I would emphasize . . . that there would not be a 'Kissinger Plan' for the Middle East."[61]

Two days later, Egypt and Syria launched their offensive, stunning international observers with their rapid successes. By the evening of October 8, the

Egyptians had gotten soldiers and heavy equipment across the Suez Canal, overwhelmed Israel's forward garrisons, advanced about eight miles east of the canal, and beaten back an Israeli counteroffensive. The Syrians, meanwhile, had entered the Golan Heights. Although Israeli forces blunted the attack in the northern and central Golan, two Syrian divisions to the south broke through the Israeli line and quickly advanced toward the eastern shore of Lake Tiberias, part of Israel's western boundary with Syria.[62]

Egypt's and Syria's early achievements produced a wave of euphoria throughout the Arab world, dispelling the defeatism and shame that had lingered since 1967. Arabs at all levels were startled to learn that official reports of battlefield success were not bombastic lies—that Arab armies really had pushed back the Israelis and recovered some lost territory. Ahmad 'Abd al-Karim, then serving as Syria's ambassador in Paris, recalled that "the confirmation of European and even American news agencies that Syrian and Egyptian forces were fighting with incomparable bravery . . . worked wonders in lifting the spirits of the delegation's members." "It seems the Israelis are getting a beating," a villager in South Lebanon said to a reporter. "Let's hope it continues." A Syrian second lieutenant, having seen the enemy "flesh-and-blood and up close," told another reporter that "the myth of the Israeli army . . . has collapsed."[63]

Israel's own reaction seemed to confirm this claim. Having convinced themselves that the Arabs were too weak and ill prepared to go to war, the Israelis were caught unawares by the Egyptian-Syrian offensive. Still, once war was under way Israeli leaders assumed they would quickly defeat their adversaries, as they had done six years earlier. But the failure of the Israeli counteroffensive in the Sinai, coupled with the stunning news that five hundred Israeli tanks had been lost on both fronts in the war's first three days, panicked Meir and her advisers. They appealed to Washington for immediate, massive assistance.[64]

Kissinger later wrote that he and Nixon started "from opposite ends of the emotional spectrum with respect to Israel," an observation borne out by their separate reactions to the outbreak of the October War. "If the Arabs win they will be impossible," Kissinger told White House chief of staff Alexander (Al) Haig on October 7. The next day Nixon predicted to Kissinger, "the Israelis when they finish clobbering the Egyptians and the Syrians, which they will do, will be even more impossible to deal with than before."[65]

Kissinger was the one whose views now mattered. In late September, he had started serving as secretary of state without relinquishing his old position as national security adviser. Thus he controlled both the State

Department machinery and the National Security Council staff, while still retaining his White House office and privileged access to the president. ("We at the White House are very impressed by the leadership that the State Department has received," Kissinger quipped at a news conference during the war.)[66] Nixon, meanwhile, was deeper into Watergate than ever, waging a desperate legal and political battle to retain control of the White House tapes. He was also distracted by the travails of vice president Spiro Agnew, who, embroiled in an unrelated scandal in Maryland, resigned on October 10. These bureaucratic and political circumstances allowed Kissinger extraordinary freedom of action.

Kissinger devised a three-part strategy for managing the war. First, he wanted to ensure that Israel had the means to repel the Egyptian-Syrian attack and even take the offensive. This would teach the Arabs that they would get nowhere by turning Soviet-supplied weapons against an American ally. Second, however, Kissinger hoped to avoid a crushing defeat of Egypt and Syria. The outbreak of the war had convinced him that Arab grievances could not be ignored quite as blithely as before and that a major U.S.-sponsored peace initiative must follow any cease-fire. Such an effort might be futile if the Arabs were too embittered by the war's outcome. Finally, Kissinger sought to prevent the Soviet Union from gaining political influence in the Middle East—indeed, to reduce the influence it already enjoyed.

Kissinger's determination to place limits on Israel's war aims later caused friction between the U.S. and Israeli governments, but for now the two countries' policies were broadly compatible. To help Israel beat back the Arab offensive, and to counter Soviet military assistance to Egypt and Syria, Kissinger arranged for a massive U.S. airlift of arms to Israel. Although it took a few days to get under way, the airlift became one of the largest in U.S. history, with a thousand tons of military equipment pouring into Israel each day during the second half of October.[67]

The airlift was an extraordinary boon to Israel, but the Israelis had a further asset in the poor coordination between Egypt and Syria. Three days into the war, having secured an eight-mile-wide strip of land on the east bank of the canal, the Egyptians dug in and declined to advance further. This "operational pause," as Cairo called it, allowed Israel to divert forces to the Golan Heights. The Israelis not only beat back the Syrian advance in the Golan but struck at military and economic targets elsewhere in Syria. By October 10, they were shelling the Syrian air force headquarters and civilian buildings in Damascus itself. A baffled Asad pleaded with Sadat to resume the Sinai offensive and relieve the pressure on Syria. The Soviet ambassador in Cairo pointedly asked why the Egyptian advance had halted. For a few days, Sadat resisted the pressure, but on October 14 he ordered the army to push on toward the Giddi and Mitla Passes. It was a disastrous decision. As they moved beyond the area protected by their own aircraft and surface-to-air missiles, Egyptian forces came under devastating Israeli attack, losing 250 tanks in a few hours. On the night of October 15–16, Israel broke through the Egyptian line and crossed to the west side of the Suez Canal. Over the next several days the Israelis swung southward, trapping the twenty thousand men of Egypt's Third Army on the east bank.[68]

Even as the Egyptian-Syrian military effort faltered, other Arab pressures were coming to bear. On October 9, amid demands by Arab commentators for a retaliatory oil embargo against nations supporting Israel, the Kuwaiti government called for an urgent meeting of the Organization of Arab Petroleum Exporting Countries (OAPEC) "to debate the role of oil" in the war. The Kuwaiti minister of finance and oil privately assured the U.S. ambassador that Kuwait and Saudi Arabia would try to keep the meeting from imposing overly punitive measures. But Arab hostility toward the United States was deepening, especially after Washington's decision to airlift military supplies to Israel became publicly known on October 13.[69]

Kissinger had long dismissed warnings about the Arab oil weapon. This complacency persisted well after the fighting began and ended only at the moment that events made it untenable. On the morning of October 17, Kissinger and Nixon had a cordial meeting with the foreign ministers of Saudi Arabia, Kuwait, Morocco, and Algeria. The ministers voiced only mild criticism of the airlift and said nothing about curtailing oil shipments. After the meeting, Saudi foreign minister Omar Saqqaf publicly praised Nixon as a peacemaker and statesman.[70] Mistaking politeness for acquiescence, Kissinger remarked at a White House meeting later that afternoon, "We don't expect an oil cut-off now in the light of the discussions with the Arab Foreign Ministers this morning. . . . Did you see the Saudi Foreign Minister come out like a good little boy and say they had had fruitful talks with us?" Reminded that American oil company executives remained anxious about the oil situation, Kissinger scoffed, "They have an unparalleled record of being wrong." As the meeting adjourned, an Associated Press news ticker arrived. The OAPEC members meeting in Kuwait had announced a cutback of total oil production by at least 5 percent immediately and by an additional 5 percent each succeeding month until Israel retreated to the 1967 lines.[71] Kissinger's response to the news is not recorded.

Figure 10. Nixon and Kissinger meet in the Oval Office with Arab foreign ministers, October 17, 1973. *Left to right:* Abdelaziz Bouteflika (Algeria), Sabah al-Ahmad al-Jabir al-Sabah (Kuwait), Omar Saqqaf (Saudi Arabia), Nixon, Kissinger, and Ahmed Taibi Benhima (Morocco). Provided by the Richard Nixon Presidential Library and Museum.

Over the next few days the news got much worse. First, several Arab countries, including Saudi Arabia, opted for an initial production cut of 10 percent, instead of the 5 percent minimum established in Kuwait. Meanwhile, Algeria, Libya, and Abu Dhabi announced total oil embargoes against the United States. Then, on October 20, one day after Nixon announced that he would ask Congress for a $2.2 billion military aid package for Israel, Saudi Arabia imposed its own total ban on oil shipments to the United States. The next day Kuwait, Bahrain, Qatar, and Dubai joined the embargo. The oil cutoff was later extended to the Netherlands and Portugal, both of which were providing logistical support to the U.S. airlift to Israel.[72]

Meanwhile, on October 16, the Persian Gulf members of the Organization of the Petroleum Exporting Countries (OPEC)—Iran and several Arab states—announced a 70 percent increase in the price of crude oil, up to $5.11 per barrel. It was the first of two dramatic price hikes that OPEC imposed in late 1973. Although the embargo and the price increases were formally unconnected, they powerfully reinforced each other. The embargo disrupted the distribution of oil, pushing its price up to previously unimagined heights. Escalating prices allowed Arab states to boost their oil revenues even while reducing production and export.[73] It was a vicious or a virtuous circle, depending on one's outlook.

The Arab oil embargo and OPEC price hikes would soon force millions of ordinary Americans to pay closer attention to the Arab-Israeli conflict. For the moment, however, public interest was largely confined to those with a more immediate stake in the dispute. Most conspicuous were American Jews, who in cities across the country staged massive pro-Israel demonstrations (some of them involving tens of thousands of participants), raised hundreds of millions of dollars, donated thousands of pints of blood, and inundated Congress and the White House with letters, telegrams, and phone calls demanding increased U.S. aid to Israel. The response from the American political establishment was overwhelmingly favorable. Elected officials of both parties spoke at pro-Israel rallies and delivered words of encouragement from the House and Senate floors. In mid-October, following an extensive phone-lobbying campaign by AIPAC, resolutions surfaced in both houses of Congress calling for stepped-up military aid to Israel. These efforts were superseded by Nixon's October 19 request for $2.2 billion for Israel, which Congress approved two months later.[74]

The October War produced another, far less familiar spectacle in American life: a visible and sustained outpouring of pro-Arab support. In what the AAUG *Newsletter* later described as "an unprecedented, historical ethnic Arab awakening in America," thousands of Arabs, Arab Americans, and sympathetic others took to the streets to support the Egyptian-Syrian war effort, oppose U.S. aid to Israel, or call attention to Palestinian claims. For the months of October and November, the newsletter documented "about 60 major rallies in 34 cities in 16 states and the District of Columbia involving 20,600 participants," though the AAUG believed the true figures were much higher.[75] "The pro-Arab wave of protests is also remarkable," the newsletter noted, "for having been completely spontaneous, uncoordinated and without any structure or organization on a national scale." While it is true that national coordination was lacking, many demonstrations were painstakingly organized at the local level, often by chapters of national organizations such as the AAUG and the Organization of Arab Students (OAS).[76] The activism also built on the experience and networks that Arab American groups had developed in recent years. The autumn outpouring had no discernible impact on U.S. policy makers—indeed, it scarcely captured their attention[77]—but it left Arab American activists much more hopeful about their ability to shape American public attitudes in the future.

The first pro-Arab demonstrations were small and relatively inconspicuous. On October 7, M.T. Mehdi of the Action Committee on American-Arab Relations (ACAAR) organized some forty picketers to stand across the street from UN headquarters in New York, where a much larger pro-Israel rally was under way. The following day in Chicago, about fifty demonstrators, organized by the Chicago-based Arab American Congress for Palestine and by local chapters of the AAUG and the OAS, carried signs reading "End Zionist Terror" and "Let My People In" up and down a block of Michigan Avenue.[78]

Pro-Arab events grew rapidly thereafter. On October 9, 350 turned out for a rally at the University of Texas at Austin. Two days later, 250 attended a teach-in at Boston University, and a similar number picketed the White House to protest U.S. military aid to Israel. On Sunday, October 14, still larger crowds turned out in cities across the country: 700 at St. Nicholas Antiochian Orthodox Cathedral in Brooklyn; 650 at St. George Antiochian Orthodox Church in Allentown, Pennsylvania; 1,000–2,000 at the Los Angeles Convention Center; and 2,000–3,000 in Dearborn, Michigan, home to 85,000 Arabs and Arab Americans, the largest such concentration in the country. The Dearborn demonstrators, many of them workers for the Ford Motor Company, gathered outside the United Auto Workers' Local 600 to protest the UAW's purchases of Israeli bonds.[79] "From there," a sympathetic radical journalist wrote, "the protesters marched 70 abreast down Vernor Avenue to the Islamic Mosque in one of the most spirited demonstrations Detroit has seen in years." Demonstrators chanted:

> Nixon, Nixon, don't forget
> Agnew fell and you will yet.
> Keep your bomb, keep your jet,
> No more aid, for your pet![80]

The following week brought a fresh wave of large pro-Arab demonstrations—in New York, Washington, Los Angeles, San Diego, Berkeley, and Columbus, Ohio—though none of them matched the Los Angeles and Dearborn turnouts of October 14. And all of these events were miniscule compared with the competition: a pro-Israel rally at New York's City Hall Plaza on October 14 drew an estimated seventy-five thousand people.[81]

Although pro-Arab and pro-Israeli demonstrators often found themselves in close proximity to one another, there were relatively few acts of violence. Much of the mayhem occurred in New York, where M.T.

Figure 11. Speakers address a pro-Arab rally in Dearborn, Michigan, October 14, 1973 (from AAUG *Newsletter*, December 1973). Courtesy of Eastern Michigan University Archives, Ypsilanti, Michigan.

Mehdi revealed a talent for provoking the ire of the ultranationalist Jewish Defense League (JDL). At the pro-Israel rally on October 7, about twenty JDL members, wearing motorcycle helmets and carrying lengths of pipe, assaulted Mehdi's group of forty picketers, forcing police to break up the scuffle. "These people have no respect for freedom of speech," said Mehdi of his attackers. "Do they think this is Tel Aviv-on-the-Hudson?" At the massive pro-Israel rally on October 14, Mehdi was there with about sixty picketers. Pro-Israeli demonstrators, many wearing JDL symbols, swarmed around police lines and manhandled Mehdi's group. Police hustled the latter into a nearby subway station and onto departing trains. On October 24, as Mehdi addressed a rally at Brooklyn College, JDL members chanting "We want Arab blood" rushed the stage to attack Mehdi and other speakers.[82]

American expatriates in the Middle East also came out in support of Arab positions. On October 16, two hundred demonstrators organized by Americans for Justice in the Middle East gathered in front of the U.S. embassy in Beirut to protest U.S. military support for Israel. The next day a group of Junior Year Abroad students from the University of California published a statement in Beirut's English-language newspaper denouncing U.S. support for the "racist, sectarian state of Israel," which "has displaced countless Palestinians." From Saudi Arabia that same day, 1,419 Aramco employees and family members sent Nixon a cable urging him not to "assist the Israeli government in maintaining its expansionist policies."[83]

Across all of this Arab-friendly activism were some marked differences in outlook and tone. How to position oneself in relation to U.S. global power was a fraught question. One solution was to portray the United States as a benevolent nation and to posit a natural affinity between Americans and Arabs that Zionist machinations had disrupted. At the October 14 rally in Los Angeles, Sabri El Farra of the Islamic Foundation of Southern California extolled the long-standing tradition of "Arab-American friendship." Americans must not be "hoodwinked and dragged into something they have no business in" by "agents of a foreign government." The AAUG's Los Angeles chapter, sounding a patriotic note seldom heard in the national organization's statements, called on "our Government to act in the best interests of the United States, uninfluenced by those whose loyalties apparently lie elsewhere, and to stand by those rights of human decency and integrity which have made this nation great."[84]

Other protesters took a far dimmer view of America's role in the world. Steeped in the militant vocabularies of pan-Arab nationalism, the American New Left, global Marxism, or radical Third Worldism (or combinations thereof), these activists portrayed the U.S. government as malevolently complicit in Israeli misdeeds. During its national convention held in Washington on October 19–21, the AAUG called "for the dismantling of the international Zionist infrastructure, which is aided and abetted by imperialist powers, principally the United States government and the settler-colonialist state of South Africa." Across the country, slogans like "Stop U.S.-Israeli terror against Arab people" and "Defeat US Zionist Aggression" adorned demonstrators' placards. Abdeen Jabara, conversant alike with the Arab intellectuals of the AAUG and the Arab workers and shopkeepers for whom he advocated in Detroit—with both émigrés and immigrants, one might say—understood such disaffection from the American mainstream. For some Arabs, he told a reporter, being in the United States was "like living in the heart of the beast, in a sense, like living in Israel."[85]

Whatever their politics, protesters had to confront the vexed issue of anti-Semitism. The early success of the Egyptian-Syrian war effort caused many American Jews to wonder if Israel itself might be overrun, and this in turn raised the specter of Jewish annihilation. Such fears had little basis in reality but could not be willed away, and so pro-Arab activists took pains to allay any suspicion that they were anti-Jewish. During the October 8 demonstration in Chicago, a young man in a yarmulke confronted the protesters, shouting, "Murderers! Anti-Semites." The demonstrators started chanting, "Jewish people, yes! Zionism, no!" At a rally near the White House on the evening of October 19, the peace activist Edmund Hanauer proclaimed, "As an American Jew, I know you cannot have security for Israeli Jews without justice for Palestinians." The mere mention of Hanauer's Jewishness drew cheers from the crowd. The effect was somewhat spoiled, however, when John M. Sutton, executive director of Americans for Middle East Understanding (AMEU), exhorted the protesters to "write to Tricky Dick, write to Kissinger, write in Hebrew or German, I don't know if he understands English."[86]

Later that same night, the target of Sutton's nativist swipe stole away from a diplomatic dinner and secretly embarked for Moscow. Kissinger's trip was largely a product of the Arabs' declining military fortunes. For the first ten days of the war, Sadat had rejected all calls for a cease-fire, but in an October 16 speech he announced that Egypt would accept a cease-fire if it was linked to an immediate Israeli withdrawal from all occupied territory. This was unrealistic. Soviet premier Alexei Kosygin, then visiting Cairo, showed Sadat aerial photographs revealing that Israeli forces were rapidly expanding their bridgehead on the west bank of the canal and moving to cut off the Egyptian Third Army. Kosygin urged Sadat to accept a cease-fire "in place," whereby the parties stopped fighting and remained indefinitely in the positions they held. On October 19, Leonid Brezhnev invited Kissinger to come to Moscow to work out the terms of such a cease-fire. On October 20, as Kissinger flew to Moscow, Sadat accepted the Soviet cease-fire proposal, provided it be followed by a UN-sponsored conference to achieve a comprehensive settlement of the Arab-Israeli dispute. From Damascus, Asad implored Sadat to reconsider, arguing that the military situation was far from hopeless. But Sadat wanted out and could not be dissuaded.[87]

The Moscow trip brought into focus Nixon's and Kissinger's diverging perspectives on the Arab-Israeli dispute. Although Watergate had prevented Nixon from engaging in vigorous diplomacy for months, he now hoped that Kissinger would conclude a far-reaching agreement with the Soviets on the terms of a general Middle East settlement—much as Brezhnev had urged in June. Kissinger, by contrast, wanted to confine the Moscow talks to a simple cease-fire, with little or no reference to an overall settlement. This would limit the Soviet role in postwar diplomacy and put off the thorny question of Israeli withdrawal.

Late on the evening of October 20, after a few hours of inconclusive discussions with Brezhnev and Soviet foreign minister Andrei Gromyko, Kissinger returned to his guesthouse to find a cable from Nixon. Kissinger, the president instructed, was to engage the Soviets on a comprehensive settlement of the Arab-Israeli conflict: "The current Israeli successes at Suez must not deflect us from going all out to achieve a just settlement now." The United States should use "whatever pressures may be required in order to gain acceptance of a settlement which is reasonable and which we can ask the Soviets to press on the Arabs. . . . I am prepared to pressure the Israelis to the extent required, regardless of the domestic political consequences." Kissinger was appalled. "If I carry out the letter of the President's instructions," he cabled deputy national security adviser Brent Scowcroft, his liaison to Nixon, "it will totally wreck what little bargaining leverage I still have. Our first objective must be a cease-fire. That will be tough enough to get the Israelis to accept; it will be impossible as part of a global deal. . . . We can pursue the course the President has in mind after a cease-fire made with Israeli acquiescence, but not before."[88]

Kissinger could not have chosen a better moment to defy the president. When, later that night, he phoned Al Haig to reiterate his objections, Kissinger found the chief of staff distracted and irritable. "Will you get off my back?" Haig said. "I have troubles of my own." "What troubles can you possibly have in Washington on a Saturday night?" Kissinger asked. Big troubles, it turned out. Earlier that evening, in an event that would become known as the "Saturday Night Massacre," Nixon ordered attorney general

Elliot Richardson to fire the special Watergate prosecutor Archibald Cox, who had demanded that the president surrender potentially incriminating White House tapes. Richardson refused the dismissal order and resigned, as did deputy attorney general William Ruckelshaus. The third-ranking official at the Justice Department, solicitor general Robert Bork, carried out the dismissal. But the public outcry was immediate and deafening—"all hell has broken loose," Haig told Kissinger over the phone—and within days Nixon would be forced to turn over the subpoenaed tapes and appoint a new special prosecutor. Thus the president was ill equipped, to say the least, to control what his secretary of state was saying and doing on the other side of the globe.[89]

The Soviets, too, were in a poor position to challenge Kissinger. With the Israelis closing in on the Egyptian Third Army, Brezhnev and Gromyko were desperate to end the fighting, and they quickly accepted Kissinger's proposal for a narrow cease-fire. The agreed text made no explicit mention of Israeli withdrawal. Instead, it called for "negotiations . . . between the parties concerned under appropriate auspices aimed at establishing a just and durable peace in the Middle East." The negotiations were to follow the principles contained in Resolution 242—"a mandate sufficiently vague," Kissinger gloated in his memoirs, "to have occupied diplomats for years without arriving at agreement."[90]

The text was submitted to the UN Security Council, where shortly after midnight on October 21–22 it passed as Resolution 338. On the morning of October 22, Kissinger headed for home, stopping briefly in Israel to allay Meir's suspicions that he and the Soviets had secretly agreed to force Israel's withdrawal to the 1967 borders. (Seldom had Kissinger's reassurances been more truthful.) That same day Israel and Egypt accepted the cease-fire; on October 23 Syria did so as well.[91]

Despite their formal acceptance of the cease-fire, the Israelis chafed under its requirements. Here was where their interests and Kissinger's finally diverged. Israel, traumatized by a war that had taken it by surprise, wanted to destroy or capture the Egyptian Third Army. Kissinger, though willing to overlook modest Israeli cease-fire violations,[92] sought to prevent Egypt's total humiliation, lest the prospects for postwar diplomacy be ruined. On October 23–24, in defiance of the cease-fire, Israeli forces completed their encirclement of the Third Army, refusing to allow food, water, and medical supplies to reach the stranded soldiers. Sadat sent desperate messages to Moscow and Washington, pleading with both to send troops into Egypt to force Israel to honor the cease-fire.[93] Although Sadat's appeal was intended to inspire U.S.-Soviet cooperation, it inadvertently triggered a superpower showdown.

On the evening of October 24, the Soviet ambassador in Washington, Anatoly Dobrynin, handed Kissinger an urgent message from Brezhnev to Nixon. Brezhnev proposed that the United States and the Soviet Union grant Sadat's request and intervene jointly to enforce the cease-fire. "If you find it impossible to act jointly with us in this matter," Brezhnev added, "we should be faced with the necessity urgently to consider the question of taking appropriate steps unilaterally. We cannot allow arbitrariness on the part of Israel." Kissinger immediately convened a meeting with other top administration officials, including the secretary of defense, the director of Central Intelligence, and the chairman of the Joint Chiefs of Staff, to decide how to respond to Brezhnev's message.[94]

Notably absent from the meeting was the president, who had already turned in for the night. Kissinger had spoken to Nixon by telephone earlier that evening and found him in a morbidly self-pitying mood. The furor over the Saturday Night Massacre was running at full steam, with prominent citizens calling for impeachment. Nixon moaned that domestic critics were motivated by a "desire to kill the President. And they may succeed. I may physically die." From this and other evidence, Kissinger and Haig concluded that Nixon probably was not in the best frame of mind to participate in a superpower showdown. The president slept on.[95]

In their all-night meeting, Kissinger and his colleagues drafted a forceful reply to Brezhnev to be sent in Nixon's name. Insisting that Washington had "no information which would indicate that the ceasefire is now being violated on any significant scale"—a misleading claim, at best[96]—the letter rejected the proposal for joint action in the Middle East. As for unilateral Soviet intervention, "such action would produce incalculable consequences which would be in the interest of neither of our countries." To underscore the message, the meeting participants arranged to have U.S. troops and nuclear forces worldwide placed on heightened alert. Though not publicly announced, the alert was expected to generate extensive signal traffic that the Soviets would detect, leaving them in no doubt about U.S. resolve.[97]

Fortunately, the superpower crisis eased rapidly the next day. Though perturbed by the U.S. alert, the Soviets wisely chose to ignore it. Instead, they seized on a relatively conciliatory passage in the message sent over Nixon's name—pledging to seek Israel's compliance with the cease-fire—and professed satisfaction that the Americans had adopted the Soviet view. Meanwhile, Sadat withdrew his request for U.S.-Soviet intervention and called for the dispatching of an international peacekeeping force that excluded the superpowers. Washington and Moscow endorsed the proposal, and that afternoon the UN Security Council passed Resolution 340, which reaffirmed the cease-fire, demanded that the warring parties return to the October 22 cease-fire lines, and authorized the deployment of a UN peacekeeping force excluding permanent members of the Security Council. Military intervention by either superpower was off the table.[98]

Still, there was the problem of the Egyptian Third Army, which the Israelis continued to besiege in violation of the UN cease-fire. Fearful of alienating Egypt irrevocably, Kissinger demanded that Israel ease the blockade. The Israelis retorted that if the Egyptians wanted relief they could seek it in face-to-face negotiations with Israel. On October 27, Sadat broke the impasse: Egyptian military officers would meet directly with their Israeli counterparts to discuss implementation of the cease-fire, provided that Israel completely ceased its military operations and allowed a single convoy, under UN and Red Cross supervision, to carry nonmilitary supplies to the Third Army. Israel agreed. On October 28, Israeli and Egyptian officers met in a tent in the Sinai desert, at Kilometer 101 on the Cairo-Suez road, for the first direct talks between the two countries' representatives in twenty-five years. The next day the convoy began resupplying the Third Army. The October War was finally over, having taken some 12,000 Egyptian, 3,000 Syrian, and 2,300 Israeli lives.[99]

The cease-fire took hold over a vastly changed geopolitical and psychological landscape. Although Egypt and Syria had suffered a military defeat, their performance had exceeded all expectations. The Israelis had lost their aura of invincibility, and Arabs everywhere felt a surge of confidence and pride. The joint offensive, a Lebanese columnist wrote, showed that the Arabs had "the ability to change the face of history."[100] The nuclear alert and the Arab oil embargo—the latter remained in effect and would soon ravage the global economy—had demonstrated to all the world that the Arab-Israeli status quo was untenable. Even Kissinger had gotten the message. He was now preparing to travel to the Middle East to ensure a smooth implementation of the cease-fire and explore prospects for a broader settlement. Peace on terms acceptable to most Arabs suddenly seemed attainable.

Arab American activists, too, could be satisfied with the role they had played during the war. Drawing on human capital amassed over the previous six years, they had staged an unprecedented demonstration of pro-Arab sentiment. Few of these figures could have had any illusions that their activism directly influenced U.S. policy. If Washington was now showing greater respect for Arab positions, this was almost entirely due to pressures generated from within the Arab world itself. Yet Arab American activists now *could* reasonably aspire to shape public attitudes in the United States, and these in turn might eventually influence national policy. The war and the oil embargo had aroused considerable curiosity about the Middle East among an American citizenry newly accustomed to questioning its political leaders. It was an opportunity the activists could ill afford to miss.

Chapter 5

Scuttle Diplomacy

Henry Kissinger and the Middle East Peace Process, 1973–1976

May 13, 1974—a grueling evening session between Henry Kissinger and Israeli negotiators in prime minister Golda Meir's West Jerusalem office. The secretary of state was two weeks into what would be his longest and most draining round of post-October War negotiations, this one to achieve a disengagement of Israeli and Syrian forces on the Golan Heights. Kissinger had devised a negotiating strategy that, he insisted, was entirely in Israel's diplomatic interests; all it required were some minor Israeli concessions at the outset. Meir and her colleagues were skeptical, offering little for Kissinger to work with. Hours later he would have to fly to Damascus to convey Israel's unpromising stance to Syrian president Hafiz al-Asad. Hours after *that*, no doubt, he would be back in Jerusalem to report on Asad's own adamant position. Not for nothing did they call it "shuttle diplomacy."[1]

His meeting with the Israelis concluded, Kissinger stepped out into the evening air to brave the gauntlet of hawkish Israeli demonstrators who, for days and nights on end, had lined the entrance to Meir's office, furiously demanding that her government make no concessions to Syria. The sentiments fueling such protests went a long way toward explaining Israel's stiff positions in the negotiations. And, whenever Kissinger visited the country, the anger was turned on him. A day earlier, the *New York Times* had reported (erroneously it turned out) that, on one of the White House tapes president Richard Nixon had reluctantly turned over to Watergate investigators, Nixon could be heard referring to "Jew boys" at the U.S. Securities and Exchange Commission. Exploiting this fresh avenue of attack, the Israeli demonstrators chanted, "Jew boy, Jew boy, Kissinger go home."[2]

The next morning Kissinger was in Damascus, riding from the airport to his guesthouse to prepare for his meeting with Asad. As he often did, Syrian foreign minister 'Abd al-Halim Khaddam accompanied Kissinger in the car. The two diplomats enjoyed these rides, easily mixing banter, substantive negotiation, and semiserious rumination on world affairs. On this occasion, Kissinger lamented the "hysterical mood" of the Israeli demonstrators. Khaddam was sympathetic: "Obviously, people like that are not good Jews."[3]

This episode is striking both for what it discloses and for what it obscures. It suggests, first of all, the strange precariousness of the American diplomatic enterprise as Nixon's presidency drew to an early close. With the chief executive almost completely immobilized by domestic scandal, effective control of U.S. foreign policy was now in the hands of a foreign-born diplomat constitutionally barred from holding the nation's highest office. The event also reveals the extraordinary bitterness that Kissinger's diplomacy often elicited from Israelis, a reaction his Jewishness seemed only to intensify. Israelis could not know what Kissinger and Arab leaders were saying behind closed doors (including closed car doors), but there was plenty of public evidence of the post–October War improvement in U.S.-Arab relations, at least when it came to atmospherics. The proposition that Kissinger's diplomacy bolstered Arab nations at Israel's expense—perhaps even to its peril—was widely accepted in Israel, and among its American supporters.

Still, the narrative of Kissinger's antagonistic relations with Israel, while not wholly false, can be misleading. When Kissinger assured Israeli leaders that his diplomatic strategy aimed to fortify Israel's territorial position, he spoke the truth. He really did seek to shield Israel from international pressure to withdraw to the pre–June 1967 borders. The shuttle diplomacy he conducted from late 1973 to late 1975 made extraordinary progress toward that goal. For the price of some modest Israeli concessions on the Sinai Peninsula, and merely a token one on the Golan Heights, Kissinger engineered Egypt's effective removal from the Arab-Israeli conflict, vastly increasing the likelihood that Israel would indefinitely retain major portions of the territory it had seized in 1967. But achieving such a diplomatic coup required convincing Arab leaders, at least for a while, that Washington could and would deliver a full Israeli withdrawal to the 1967 lines. This in turn necessitated an atmosphere of U.S.-Arab comity that perturbed and sometimes alarmed the Israelis.

Back in the United States, the two years following the October War were a time of rapidly growing interest in the Arab world, on the part of policy makers, commentators, journalists, and ordinary citizens. For some Americans, this rising interest translated into greater sympathy for Arab perspectives on international questions, especially the Arab-Israeli dispute. Others, less concerned with the merits of such issues, pragmatically concluded that the Arabs' capacity to disrupt global order had become too formidable for their grievances to be safely ignored. Whatever its motivation, the new attentiveness to Arab outlooks gratified Arab American and Arab-friendly activists, who sensed a historic opportunity to influence their own government's policies toward the Arab-Israeli dispute. In this, the activists would be sorely disappointed. For all the deference Kissinger paid to Arab sensibilities, the relentless thrust of his diplomacy was to sideline the Palestinian issue and maximize Israel's retention of occupied land. Ironically, however, that very deference modestly enhanced the Arab profile in the United States and validated alternative approaches to Arab-Israeli peacemaking. Though the early post-1973 rounds went overwhelmingly to Kissinger, the broader political contest was far from over.

As the October War drew to a close, a new phase in Kissinger's Middle East diplomacy began. Whereas Kissinger had previously avoided extensive personal involvement in the Arab-Israeli dispute, he now threw himself into mediating between Israel and each of its principal Arab rivals, which remained unwilling to deal directly with Israel as long as it occupied their land.[4] Over the next two years, Kissinger made eleven Middle East trips, which together constituted one of the most extraordinary diplomatic performances of the late twentieth century. His challenge was threefold: to end the Arab oil embargo, to achieve a disengagement of forces on the Sinai and Golan fronts, and to establish new diplomatic procedures that sharply reduced the likelihood of another major Arab-Israeli war.

Underlying all of Kissinger's efforts was a basic dilemma. On the one hand, it was clear that Arab grievances could no longer be so easily dismissed. By launching a war that brought the superpowers to the brink of confrontation, and by imposing an oil embargo that seemed destined to wreak havoc on the global economy, the Arab states had shown they could threaten world stability. Consequently, there was growing international pressure for a rapid settlement of the Arab-Israeli conflict involving a full Israeli withdrawal to the 1967 borders in exchange for Arab recognition. Calls for such a resolution emanated not just from the Soviet bloc and Third World nations but from America's own allies, whose dependence on Middle Eastern oil far surpassed that of the United States. In a November 6 declaration, the nine countries of the European Economic Community[5] called on Israel to "end the territorial occupation which it has maintained since the conflict of 1967" and stated that any Middle East settlement must address Palestinians' "legitimate rights." That same day, Japan urged Israel to end its occupation of Arab lands. Although such pronouncements were rarer in the United States, a handful of prominent American figures, such as Arkansas senator J. William Fulbright and former under secretary of state George W. Ball, advocated an Israeli pullback to the 1967 lines coupled with a superpower guarantee of Israel's security.[6] Kissinger could not ignore such views.

On the other hand, Kissinger strongly opposed any effort to push Israel back to the 1967 borders. In his memoirs, he couched his opposition mainly in procedural terms, noting that, under most scenarios, the settlement restoring the 1967 borders was to be reached at an international conference attended by Israel, the principal Arab states, the superpowers, and other interested countries. At such a conference, Kissinger wrote, "all concerned parties would have to agree, and radical elements in the Arab world would have a veto. . . . The Soviet Union would inject itself as the lawyer of the Arab side, putting forth a maximum program that years of experience had taught us was unfulfillable. Our allies, both Europe and Japan, would support the Arab position, leaving us completely isolated."[7] Kissinger did not describe this "maximum program" or explain why it was "unfulfillable." Presumably, though, any proposal enjoying the support of the Soviet Union, Japan, and Western European nations would not have been more drastic than the scenarios described in the previous paragraph. It might even have entailed a superpower guarantee of Israel's security, à la Fulbright and Ball, a measure the Soviet leader Leonid Brezhnev himself had proposed when meeting with Nixon in San Clemente in June 1973.

In truth, Kissinger's objections were less to the forum than to the very idea of a wholesale Israeli withdrawal. Kissinger sympathized with Israel's claim that the 1967 borders were indefensible. "Israel considers that these [borders] would be the end of Israel," he told Gerald Ford in August 1974, shortly after the latter became president. "The country was only 12 kilometers wide in some places. Almost all of Israel would be under SAM coverage"—meaning that surface-to-air missiles stationed on recovered Arab land might deny Israel air superiority over its own territory. That same month Kissinger told Israeli foreign minister Yigal Allon that, while a full Israeli withdrawal from Sinai was conceivable, "I do think it is impossible to accept the 1967 frontiers with Syria, and I think it is impossible with Jordan," a reference to the West Bank.[8]

Even if the 1967 borders could be justified in principle, Kissinger knew Israel would adamantly resist any U.S.-sponsored attempt to impose them. By mobilizing its Americans supporters, Israel might well succeed in blocking such a move, humiliating Washington. Yet the alternative outcome, a successful imposition of the 1967 borders, was even more troubling to Kissinger. Such a result, he told Ford in September 1974, "would be demoralizing [to Israel,] like what was done to Czechoslovakia in '38." The only way to achieve such a withdrawal, Kissinger wrote in his memoirs, would be to force it on Israel "by the threat of economic pressure and diplomatic isolation, thereby threatening its very existence." Kissinger was unwilling to do this to "an ally so closely linked with my family's fate in the Holocaust."[9]

It was a historically freighted line of argument, and a dubious one, too. The 1938 Munich agreement had dismembered Czechoslovakia, whereas a restoration of the 1967 borders would end Israel's occupation of foreign land. Kissinger acted as if there were no middle ground between upholding Israel's conquests and inviting its destruction. Still, it is not altogether surprising that a Jewish refugee from Hitler's Germany should have viewed Israel's challenges through the prism of the Nazi experience.

In any event, Kissinger had to find a way out of his dilemma. He needed some mechanism that created the illusion of progress toward the 1967 borders while ensuring that those borders were never actually restored. It had to appease international demands for Israeli withdrawal even as it neutralized the Arab pressures that generated those demands. The strategy Kissinger devised became known as the "step-by-step" approach. The idea was to launch separate, bilateral, and incremental negotiations between Israel and each of its main Arab antagonists, with the United States serving as mediator. The spectacle of simultaneous, or nearly simultaneous, negotiations on several fronts would appear to heed the worldwide cry for progress toward a comprehensive settlement. It might even convince Arab oil producers to lift their embargo. With any luck, the easing of such pressures would occur well before Israel had been pushed back to the 1967 borders. Kissinger could then establish a new diplomatic framework that all but precluded any further Israeli withdrawals.

Key to this strategy was the attitude of Sadat, who was desperate to end Egypt's conflict with Israel and focus instead on his country's acute economic problems. In his early meetings with Kissinger, Sadat reiterated the standard Arab positions on Israeli withdrawal and Palestinian rights. Kissinger sensed, however, that Sadat might be willing to conclude a separate agreement with Israel, and thereby recover all or much of the Sinai, without absolute assurances that other Arab claims would be satisfied. "My impression is Egypt is eager to talk separately with Israel," he said to Israel's foreign minister, Abba Eban, in late November. "Of all the Arabs I met," he told Golda Meir in mid-December, "he is really an Egyptian nationalist. He mentioned Palestine just enough to be able to say that he mentioned it. . . . The Palestinians I don't think he gives a damn about." If Sadat did make a separate peace that subtracted Egyptian power from the Arab-Israeli equation, the remaining Arab states would find it extremely difficult to resume major hostilities, and again galvanize world opinion, to compel Israel's withdrawal to the 1967 borders. As Kissinger confided to Meir and her top negotiators in February 1974, "Once you have taken Egypt out of confrontation with you altogether, the capability of Syria without Egypt to cause trouble is reduced."[10]

There was another reason to work closely with Egypt. It was becoming increasingly clear that Sadat wanted to take Egypt out of the Soviet orbit and reorient it toward the United States. The Soviets could provide Egypt with arms and diplomatic support, but only the United States could persuade Israel to withdraw from occupied territory. "You hold all the cards here," Sadat remarked during Kissinger's second visit to Cairo, in mid-December.[11] For Kissinger, a tantalizing prospect was coming into view: an Egyptian-Israeli deal that not only eased international pressure for the 1967 borders but dramatically reduced Soviet influence in the Middle East.

Still, Kissinger needed to prevent Sadat's defection from being too rapid or conspicuous, lest Moscow catch wind of it and try to disrupt it. Better yet, Egypt's initial moves toward a separate peace should be draped in the colors of superpower cooperation. The idea, Kissinger told British officials on December 12, was "to push the Soviet Union into the essential cooperation which was required for a settlement, but also to push them to the sidelines." Facilitating this ruse was the language of the cease-fire agreement (subsequently passed as UN Security Council Resolution 338) that Kissinger and Soviet leaders had worked out in Moscow during the October War. The agreement called for "negotiations . . . between the parties concerned under appropriate auspices aimed at establishing a just and durable peace in the Middle East." Although the term "appropriate auspices" was not publicly defined, Kissinger and the Soviets had privately stipulated that it meant loose U.S.-Soviet sponsorship—loose in the sense that U.S. and Soviet diplomats would be present only at the start of the negotiations and intervene only when major issues required superpower involvement. This was a far cry from Moscow's preference for a U.S.-Soviet agreement on the negotiations' outcome, but the Soviets had been desperate for a cease-fire and had quickly accepted Kissinger's terms.[12]

Using the cease-fire agreement as his authority, in November and December Kissinger began organizing an international conference in Geneva, to be sponsored by the superpowers and attended by Israel and the frontline Arab states. The conference, however, would feature no substantive negotiation, at least not in its plenary sessions. The parties would convene in one place, present their official positions, and then break off to pursue separate, bilateral negotiations, with the Egyptian-Israeli negotiation receiving priority. To Kissinger, the real value of the Geneva Conference lay in the international respectability it would confer on Egypt's pursuit of a U.S.-sponsored agreement with Israel. "We strove to assemble a multilateral conference," he later wrote, "but our purpose was to use it as a framework for an essentially bilateral diplomacy. Soviet cooperation was necessary to convene Geneva; afterward, we would seek to reduce its role to a minimum."[13]

The Geneva scheme unfolded more or less according to plan. Sadat, anxious to start a diplomatic process that might relieve Egypt's Third Army, which Israel still encircled, placed no obstacles in Kissinger's way. Sadat also agreed to exchange prisoners of war with Israel and to ease Egypt's blockade against Israeli shipping through the Bab al-Mandeb Strait, the southern entrance to the Red Sea. King Hussein, too, was amenable, seeing the Geneva Conference as an opportunity to reassert Jordan's claim to the West Bank. The Israelis initially balked at attending the conference, fearing it would enable the international community to force an unfavorable settlement on them. They were especially concerned about having to confront Palestinian demands. Kissinger's repeated assurances that Palestinians would be excluded, combined with Nixon's blunt warnings that future U.S. support hinged on Israel's participation in the conference, wore down Israel's resistance, and in mid-December the Meir cabinet agreed to attend. Asad, determined to avoid negotiations until Israel had actually begun withdrawing from Arab land, decided not to go to Geneva. Yet he made no further attempt to undermine the conference and hinted that he might participate later on. Though initially disappointed by Asad's decision to stay away, Kissinger soon realized that Syria's absence would greatly simplify his task of cultivating Sadat.[14]

The Geneva Conference opened on December 21 under the auspices of UN secretary general Kurt Waldheim, whom Washington and Moscow had asked to host the event. The United States and the Soviet Union cochaired the conference, with Israel, Egypt, and Jordan serving as the principal participants. An empty table bearing Syria's nameplate proclaimed the hope that Damascus would eventually take part. (The UN staff even supplied the Syrian table with sharpened pencils and fresh glasses of water.) After opening remarks by Kissinger and Soviet foreign minister Andrei Gromyko, the Middle Eastern foreign ministers delivered tendentious speeches intended mainly for home consumption. The participants then dispersed, pledging to return in January, though in fact the Geneva Conference never reconvened.[15] Kissinger turned to the more meaningful task of pursuing a bilateral Egyptian-Israeli agreement.

Surreptitious by design, Kissinger's Middle East negotiating strategy received almost no notice beyond a tight circle of U.S. and Israeli officials. To most Americans following the news in late 1973, international politics was the story of Western impotence and disarray before a relentless economic assault from the Arab world. In the weeks following the October War, the Arab oil producers continued their embargo, which consisted of two elements: the 5 percent monthly cutback in overall production, and the total ban on exports to the United States and a handful of other nations, such as Holland, Portugal, and South Africa. At the start of the war, the world supply of Arab oil had been 20.8 million barrels per day. By December, it was down to 15.8 million barrels. Also in December, the Organization of the Petroleum Exporting Countries (OPEC) raised the price of oil again, from $5.11 to $11.65 per barrel. Americans were relatively insulated from these wrenching developments: whereas Western Europe and Japan imported 72 percent and 84 percent, respectively, of their oil from the Middle East, the United States got just 11 percent of its oil from the region. But the pivotal role that petroleum played in the American economy, the rapid rate at which American energy consumption had risen in recent years, the integrated nature of the global economy, and profound uncertainty about the future all ensured that the energy crisis would inflict traumatic dislocations on basic patterns of American life.[16]

Just in time for the onset of winter, spiking heating oil costs forced households to turn their thermostats down and businesses and schools to shorten their hours. Utility companies imposed unprecedented price hikes. Department stores scrapped Christmas light displays, harming nearby retailers who relied on the displays to attract customers to their own businesses. Airlines canceled commercial flights, causing major layoffs in the airline industry and the businesses that served it. The national unemployment figure rose from 4.5 percent in October to 5.2 percent in January. Soaring oil prices also caused a spike in the general cost of living—8.8 percent in the last three months of 1973—perplexing economists unaccustomed to addressing recession and inflation simultaneously. By late December, the crisis had acquired its most iconic vignette, replicated at thousands of gas stations across the land: a line of cars, sometimes stretching for blocks, full of anxious and irritable motorists seeking to avail themselves of the day's meager allotment. "They came to the Mobil station on Atlantic Avenue in Brooklyn as nomads to an oasis," reported the *New York Times* in a passage King Faisal might have savored.[17]

Actually, in public recriminations over the oil embargo, Arabs figured less prominently than one might expect. This was, after all, an era in which Americans were increasingly critical of their own leaders, institutions, and cultural practices. A December Gallup poll found that only 6 percent of Americans blamed the energy crisis on the Arab countries, whereas 25 percent blamed the oil companies, which many believed were exaggerating the oil shortage to maximize profits, and 23 percent blamed the U.S. government, which stood accused of failing to plan for the contingency.[18] Elite opinion, too, was relatively easy on the Arabs. True, pro-Israel and conservative commentators spoke darkly of "Arab blackmail." Some wanted the United States to punish Arab countries by refusing to sell them agricultural products.[19] But many other pundits and analysts rejected such talk. Limiting oil shipments, they said, was a rational means of exerting diplomatic pressure, not too different from the economic sanctions Washington had long imposed on Cuba. And a "food embargo" against the Arab world would be counterproductive. The Arabs would buy foodstuffs from the Soviet Union, enabling it to enhance its position in the region. Worse still, they might curtail oil production further or withdraw their assets from Western banks.[20]

In its own public statements, the Nixon administration voiced similar restraint, insisting it had no plans to retaliate against the Arab states and suggesting that the best way to surmount the crisis was to proceed with Arab-Israeli diplomacy. Privately, however, the oil embargo posed a dilemma for Kissinger. He needed to convince Arab governments as a whole that Washington was earnestly addressing their grievances; this would give Sadat political cover for falling in with Kissinger's plans. Yet Kissinger did not want to seem *too* responsive to Arab demands, lest the U.S. government appear weak abroad. "If we permit ourselves to be driven by them," he predicted, "every group of under-developed countries is going to pressure us." In November and December, Kissinger told the Arab oil producers that they had made their point and that it was time for them to end the embargo. If the producers failed to cooperate, he warned, the domestic American backlash might force an end to his Arab-Israeli mediation. In Cairo in early November, Kissinger warned the influential Egyptian newspaper editor Muhammad Hasanayn Haykal (presumably expecting him to spread the word) that "there are many voices demanding that we occupy the oil wells . . . by force"—calls the peace-loving Kissinger could not resist indefinitely. But the embargo continued, provoking neither a U.S. military intervention nor an end to Kissinger's mediation.[21]

"Call it Arab 'blackmail' if you will," wrote a contributor to the *Link*, the newsletter of Americans for Middle East Understanding, "but the oil shortage . . . is forcing Americans to examine the equities of the Arab-Israeli conflict." In the winter of 1973–1974, Arab-friendly figures seized the opportunity created by the oil crisis, calling attention to the unjust status quo that had produced it. Setting the dominant tone of this discourse was a full-page advertisement that the Arab League placed in major American newspapers in December, titled "More in Sorrow than in Anger" (and quietly authored by Elmer Berger, the anti-Zionist rabbi). The ad stated that the Arab oil producers had opted for embargo "to redress an intolerable situation which we have long endured" and only "with the greatest regret and reluctance."[22]

Professing sorrow made good political sense, but in truth pro-Arab commentators were thrilled by the new atmosphere. It really did seem that a historic opportunity to recast U.S.-Arab relations was at hand. In January, the Palestinian-born diplomat and polemicist Fayez Sayegh wrote a friend that "the sudden burst of interest in the Arab situation throughout the United States" had persuaded him to postpone a trip to Kuwait so that he could "respond . . . to requests for lectures from all over the United States and Canada. I'll probably go to Kuwait later in the school year—but this is the time to be *here*." The Association of Arab American University Graduates (AAUG) took heart that so many American citizens and residents were already committed to the struggle. Referring to pro-Arab demonstrations during the October War, the group's December newsletter commented, "Such an outspoken show of unity and identification with the Arab cause is considered to presage a new turn in the history of Arab-American relations, with possible far-reaching consequences in terms of continued U.S. aid to the Israeli government." From his vantage in the U.S. Senate, Jim Abourezk had a clearer view of the obstacles in the way of progress, yet he, too, was optimistic. The United States, he believed, had "a golden opportunity to make peace in the Middle East," provided it was willing to compel Israel to withdraw to the 1967 borders.[23]

If Abourezk's trip to Lebanon the previous August had sharpened his sense of Arab-Israeli inequities, then the October War brought new urgency to the issue. In interviews, on the Senate floor, and on the lecture circuit, Abourezk grew far more outspoken on the issue.[24] The struggle for a more evenhanded U.S. Middle East policy now dominated his politics.

In late December and January, Abourezk took another trip to the Middle East, this time visiting several Arab countries and Israel. He traveled on behalf of the Senate Committee on Interior and Insular Affairs, which had jurisdiction over energy policy, ostensibly to assess how the United States should respond to the oil embargo.[25] As with many congressional "fact-finding" trips, Abourezk discovered what he already knew: in this case, that the best guarantee of a resumption of oil shipments was a less biased U.S. Middle East policy. More newsworthy was an episode spanning his visits to Syria and Israel. Meeting with Asad in Damascus, Abourezk asked about the scores of Israeli prisoners Syria was believed to have taken during the October War. Syria had refused to make the POWs accessible to the Red Cross or release any information about them. Their plight was a charged issue in Israel, and Kissinger, hoping to soften Israeli resistance to a disengagement agreement with Syria, had pressed Asad to furnish a list of prisoners' names. Asad held firm, insisting that Israel must first commit to vacating the Golan. After some prodding of his own, however, Abourezk received Asad's permission to meet briefly with two POWs, captains Yoram Shahar and Ori Shahak, both Israeli Air Force pilots. The prisoners seemed in good health and said they were well treated, though under the circumstances there wasn't much else they could say.[26]

Once in Israel, Abourezk contacted the pilots' families, who on January 13 gathered in the senator's Jerusalem hotel room to hear a tape recording of his meeting with the prisoners. "Mrs. Ida Shahar," wrote an American reporter in attendance, "rocked in her chair, smiling occasionally, laughing, and hiding her face in her arms crossed over her lap as she listened to the voice of her Israeli pilot husband." Hava Shahak asked about reports that her husband had injured his leg parachuting to the ground. Abourezk assured her he had walked without trace of a limp. "That was quite an emotional session for me," Abourezk told his traveling companions after the families left. Captains Shahar and Shahak and the other Israeli POWs would remain imprisoned until summer, as would hundreds of Syrian soldiers held by Israel.[27]

One floor above Abourezk's room in the King David Hotel was a more ample suite, which Kissinger used as his Israeli base of operations. On January 10, he had come for what he thought would be a brief visit to the Middle East, just a few days to establish the framework of an Egyptian-Israeli disengagement agreement for the parties themselves to work out in Geneva. But Sadat persuaded him to remain in the region until an agreement was concluded, and so Kissinger spent the next week traveling back and forth between Egypt and Israel, dispensing with Geneva entirely. The resulting agreement separated the opposing forces and restored a thin sliver of the Sinai to Egypt. In his eagerness for a deal, Sadat made significant concessions, leaving Egypt with far fewer forces in the area than his political and military advisers thought prudent. Sadat's flexibility startled Kissinger. "I'm losing my standing as an expert," he joked to Meir on January 15. "Every time you give me a proposal that I consider outrageous, he [Sadat] accepts it." Three days later, Sadat signed the disengagement document that Kissinger had brought for him and that Meir had signed earlier that morning. Sadat kissed Kissinger on both cheeks and gave him an oral message for Meir: "I am today taking off my military uniform—I never expect to wear it again except for ceremonial occasions." As Kissinger departed the next morning, he got another kiss on each cheek.[28]

"I have kissed my way through the Middle East," Kissinger reported to British officials during a stopover in London on his return home. "If a Foreign Minister doesn't kiss me, I get worried." Kissing was indeed essential to shuttle diplomacy. It was part of a broader effort, launched at the start of Kissinger's diplomatic offensive, to flatter and disarm Arab leaders. In a mid-November phone call to deputy assistant secretary of state Alfred Atherton, who was preparing Kissinger's correspondence with Egyptian foreign minister Ismail Fahmy, Kissinger said, "In every letter to Fahmi, I want first of all some guff that they can use to make them think they have a special relationship to me. . . . And put in some sentence what a great man I think Sadat is." Around this time, State Department Arabists briefed Kissinger on the prevalence of fraternal kissing and embracing in Arab society. Kissinger took the lesson to heart and, throughout his subsequent travels, gamely reciprocated every instance of friendly manhandling.[29]

Kissinger's physical affectionateness with Arab leaders bemused American observers, who in 1973 and 1974 were unaccustomed to seeing men behave in this way. Apart from the inevitable snickering about homosexuality, the standard gloss among American journalists was that such chumminess came at Israel's expense—that Kissinger, as the joke went, was kissing the Arabs and screwing the Israelis. Kissinger playfully encouraged this conceit. "The reason the Israelis don't get better treatment," he told reporters in Tel Aviv, "is that Eban doesn't kiss me." To King Hussein he quipped, "If there are many more pictures of me with my arms around Arabs, . . . I won't be able to go to New York." Israeli leaders went along with the joke, affecting to be miffed by Kissinger's dalliances with Arab men. When Kissinger finally kissed Meir at an Israeli reception in May, the prime minister exclaimed, "I never thought you would kiss a woman!" "I wonder who's kissing 'er now," Eban chimed in.[30]

Kissing the Arabs was serious business, of course, and it hardly redounded to Israel's detriment. It helped to create a diplomatic atmosphere in which it would be easier for Sadat to move toward a separate peace and harder for other Arab leaders to grasp what was happening until it was too late for them to unite in successful opposition to Egypt's diplomacy. "My strategy is to keep the Arab world divided," Kissinger confided to Meir in May. "When I kiss Sadat, understand that objective!"[31]

Yet Kissinger's charm offensive also left a positive legacy for U.S.-Arab relations. The journalist Richard Valeriani later wrote, "Henry Kissinger made the Arabs respectable in America. . . . Kissinger's constant travel to Arab capitals, the pictures of him with Arab leaders, and his positive descriptions of them in his briefings helped change the American concept" and demonstrate "that there were indeed two sides to the story." This was partly deliberate. Kissinger's diplomatic strategy, while heavily tilted toward the Israelis, required them to make *some* territorial concessions, and these would be harder to extract if the domestic American climate was overwhelmingly anti-Arab. "You see," Kissinger told Syrian foreign minister 'Abd al-Halim Khaddam that spring, "every day I'm transforming your leadership from being abstract devils into real leaders with real concerns."[32]

The early rounds of Kissinger's shuttle diplomacy did coincide with a spate of mainstream American news stories detailing how the "new Arabs" defied the old stereotypes: they were pragmatic rather than fanatical, methodical rather than feckless, constructive and broad-minded rather than bitter and vindictive. "Surprisingly," *Newsweek* observed that February, "in light of the grievances both real and imagined that the Arabs hold against the West, the prevailing mood seems to be to let bygones be bygones—if the West will make a genuine effort to help the Arabs achieve an honorable peace."[33] No doubt, these stories mainly reflected journalists' own observations of evolving patterns of Arab self-presentation. Yet it is hard not to conclude that Kissinger's embrace of Arab leaders—literal and figurative—made them more appealing figures in American minds.

The subtleties of Kissinger's diplomatic strategy came more fully into view in February, as the focus shifted from the Sinai to the Golan. Kissinger's goal, as noted, was to achieve a bilateral agreement that permanently withdrew Egypt from confrontation with Israel; the January disengagement agreement was a first step in that direction. Before going any further, however, Sadat needed some camouflage. He could not *appear* to be moving toward a separate peace, which other Arab actors would strongly oppose. To avoid that impression, Kissinger aimed to broker a disengagement agreement on the Golan resembling the one just concluded over the Sinai. With Syria, too, apparently benefiting from Kissinger's peace efforts ("apparently" being the operative word), Egypt would be free to reach a subsequent agreement with Israel.

In the Israeli-Syrian disengagement talks, a key issue was the extent of any Israeli withdrawal from Syrian land. During the October War, Israel had not only pushed Syria back out of the Golan Heights but seized additional Syrian territory. Asad now threatened to break off the disengagement talks if Israel offered nothing more than a restoration of the line that had existed when war started on October 6; Israel must relinquish part of the Golan as well. Meeting with Meir and her negotiating team in Jerusalem on February 27, Kissinger urged that Israel accommodate Asad on this score: "I think for the Syrians any move, even a symbolic move, beyond the October 6th line might make the difference between acceptance and rejection." Specifically, Kissinger thought the Israelis should vacate the Syrian city of Quneitra, which lay just to the west of the October 6 line. This would give Asad something to show for the negotiation and keep him involved in the talks.[34]

If the Israelis made this small concession, Kissinger intimated, it might well be the last one they ever had to make to Syria. He said that as far as *he* was concerned the October 6 line, with a possible modification for Quneitra, "will be the final line. I must also say that whether you can hold that position in the face of certain diplomatic pressures that will arise depends on the degrees to which you can keep Syria isolated, other problems solved, and the energy problem taken out of the way. If you can achieve all these things, I can't believe that the world is going to die on the issue of the Golan Heights."[35]

The key to keeping "diplomatic pressures" at bay, Kissinger insisted, was completing the bilateral peace process with Egypt, and this in turn required a prior deal with Syria:

> Egypt will not be able to talk to you, I believe, until you have disengagement in Syria. . . . However, once you have taken Egypt out of confrontation with you altogether, the capability of Syria without Egypt to cause trouble is reduced, I think. . . . Then you face only Syria. Right now the difficulty is not that Syria has such a great capability, but that Syria can probably under present circumstances still trigger Egypt into renewing hostilities. . . . If, however, one went the route . . . of perhaps not going to the absolute end with Egypt but so close to the end that they'd be in effect politically out of it, then Syria is effectively isolated.

In short, by the time the Syrians realized that there would be no withdrawals on the Golan after Quneitra, it would be too late for them to do anything about it. Meeting separately with Meir earlier that day, Kissinger crisply summed up his strategy: "Some agreement in Syria enables you to settle with Egypt, and then you can ignore the Syrians."[36]

The Israelis were unmoved. In elections held in December, Meir's Labor Party had been returned to office but with fewer seats in parliament. Her government now had to show greater deference to hawkish elements. On March 1, it proposed a disengagement scheme that not only left all of the Golan under Israeli control but also permitted Israeli forces to remain on the newly captured Syrian territory. The offer was so one-sided that Kissinger declined to forward it to Asad, whom he flew to see after his meetings with the Israelis. Instead, Kissinger told Asad that Israel needed more time to formulate a realistic proposal and recommended that the talks be suspended for some weeks. Asad grumbled about Israeli intransigence but accepted the recommendation. He even embraced Kissinger when the latter departed, a gesture Asad had previously, and most un-Arably, withheld.[37]

Accompanying this modest progress on the Syrian front was a far greater achievement on the oil question. In late January, fulfilling a promise he had previously made to Kissinger, Sadat flew to Saudi Arabia to urge an end to the oil embargo. By now King Faisal himself was seeking a face-saving end to the standoff, which had strained relations with Washington, the ultimate guarantor of Saudi security. In February, he and Sadat lobbied fellow Arabs for a suspension of the embargo, arguing that the measure had served its purpose by forcing the United States to reenter the diplomatic fray. Asad insisted that suspension was premature, as Israel had so far withdrawn from just a sliver of the Sinai. But the prospect of a Syrian-Israeli disengagement agreement, coupled with Kissinger's repeated assurances that disengagement would catalyze further Israeli withdrawals, strengthened the Egyptian-Saudi case. Even Algeria, a leading member of the radical Arab camp—and, unlike Syria, a major oil producer—supported suspending the embargo. In mid-March, over Syrian opposition, the Arab oil producers agreed to a suspension, on the understanding that Kissinger would press ahead with Syrian-Israeli disengagement.[38] The term "suspension" implied that the embargo might resume if Kissinger's diplomacy proved unsatisfactory, but in fact the oil weapon had been sheathed for good. Still, the disruptive effects of the five-month embargo, and of the fourfold increase in oil prices, would be felt the world over for years to come.

In late April, Kissinger returned to the Middle East to resume negotiations for a Syrian disengagement agreement. The differences between the parties had narrowed only slightly, but Kissinger thought he detected just enough mutual flexibility to warrant the effort. The Syrian shuttle lasted thirty-four days and involved much harder bargaining than the Sinai disengagement talks had. The Golan is considerably smaller than the Sinai, and the Israelis saw all of the former as vital to their security. They had no intention of giving any of it back and, indeed, hoped to keep much of the additional Syrian territory seized in the October War. For their part, Asad and his top advisers were far more jealous of Syria's prerogatives than Sadat was of Egypt's. Whereas Sadat was prepared to make sweeping material concessions to achieve important but intangible goals, such as a new, trusting relationship with the United States, the Syrians fiercely contested every inch of ground. In this, Kissinger noted, they rather resembled their Israeli antagonists. The shuttle was also physically grueling, requiring Kissinger's party to log 24,230 miles on forty-one flights. Almost everyone on the plane, Kissinger included, came down with diarrhea, and the crew's supply of Lomotil, an antidiarrhetic medication, ran out. Even in this adversity, Kissinger kept his humor. "They're bringing in another shipment of Lomotil for us," he announced to his stricken companions as a huge American C-5-A cargo plane lumbered into Tel Aviv airport during one of his stops.[39]

Substantively, Kissinger had the daunting task of getting both parties to accept the scenario he had outlined in February: Israel's evacuation from all of the Syrian territory captured in the October War and from a symbolic portion of the Golan that included Quneitra. Again, Kissinger told the Israelis that a token concession on the Golan might well obviate any further withdrawals from that territory. "It was almost unanimous in our [negotiating] group," he said to Meir, "that the Israelis should not be asked to give up Golan." The Syrians got a very different message. The Israelis may talk tough, Kissinger told Khaddam, but "Israel is stiffening its back on an issue it can't win, because it's moving back to the 1967 frontiers. So wherever the [disengagement] line is, the direction is an Arab victory." To King Faisal, whom Kissinger saw during a side trip to Riyadh, the assurance was categorical: "The United States supports no claim by Israel to the Golan Heights."[40]

Equal-opportunity duplicity, one might suppose. But Kissinger's dissembling inherently favored the Israelis, who, after all, were in possession of Syrian land and physically capable of holding on to it. The only way to dislodge Israel from the Golan, or any other occupied territory, was through a clear, consistent, concerted, and brutally relentless U.S. campaign directed at that goal. Anything less ensured a continuation of the status quo. It mattered little that Kissinger was promising Arab leaders that the occupation would eventually end if, at the same time, he was telling Israeli leaders it could continue indefinitely. The latter pledges inescapably trumped the former.

There was another, covert dimension to Kissinger's diplomacy over Israeli-Syrian disengagement. Since 1972, under Kissinger's direction, the CIA had joined the Iranian government in providing military and logistical assistance to a Kurdish rebellion inside Iraq. The principal U.S. aim was to weaken Iraq, a client state of Moscow that loudly opposed Arab negotiations with Israel. During his shuttle diplomacy, Kissinger worried that Iraq, which had sent thirty thousand troops to assist Syria during the October War, might somehow disrupt the Israeli-Syrian negotiation, perhaps by triggering hostilities on its own, perhaps by convincing Damascus that there was a viable military alternative to diplomacy. A continuation of Kurdish trouble would keep the Iraqis' attention focused inward. In March 1974, Kissinger told Israeli ambassador to the United States Simcha Dinitz, whose government was also supplying the Kurds, "It is in our interest to keep the Iraqis distracted while we are working on the Syrians."[41]

On May 31, Kissinger finally got the Israelis and Syrians to settle, more or less along the lines of his original scheme.[42] The Golan disengagement agreement was widely hailed as a triumph for American diplomacy and for Kissinger personally. The cover of *Newsweek* featured a soaring, muscle-bound "Super K" in tights and a cape. Kissinger's international stature now exceeded that of Nixon, who, mired in Watergate, was increasingly relegated to a spectator's role. In June, Nixon traveled to the Middle East to enjoy some of the acclaim Kissinger's efforts had generated. The president got his warmest welcome in Egypt, where huge, jubilant crowds lined his motorcade routes. Though no doubt encouraged by Egyptian authorities, the popular enthusiasm was obviously genuine. To millions of Egyptians, Nixon's visit augured not just an honorable exit from war but also a more prosperous future, for the president brought pledges of economic assistance. (Egypt had resumed formal diplomatic relations with the United States in February.) The goodwill was so palpable, Kissinger wrote, that Nixon must have regretted "that Egyptians were not represented on the House Judiciary Committee." Elsewhere in the region the receptions were friendly but more restrained, and, as Kissinger's quip suggests, the visit could scarcely alter the storyline back home. In the weeks following Nixon's return, the accumulated evidence of his role in the Watergate cover-up caused a hemorrhaging of congressional support, including among fellow Republicans. On August 9, Nixon resigned the presidency and was succeeded by Vice President Ford, who had replaced Spiro Agnew in December.[43]

Figure 12. Richard Nixon and Anwar Sadat ride past cheering crowds in Alexandria, Egypt, June 1974. Provided by the Richard Nixon Presidential Library and Museum.

A few hours before Nixon announced his resignation, Kissinger met at the State Department with Sabah Qabbani, the newly appointed ambassador from Syria, which had also recently restored diplomatic relations with the United States. Earlier that day Ford asked Kissinger to stay on as both secretary of state and national security adviser, and Kissinger now assured Qabbani that the United States would remain diplomatically engaged in the Middle East. "I want you to know that there will be continuity of policy," Kissinger said. "You can tell that to your President. There will be no change in this building. That is why everybody you see around here looks so sad."[44] Kissinger could afford to be self-deprecating, for he was then at the apex of his stature and power. Watergate had made him the master of U.S. foreign policy, and Ford's inexperience in world affairs ensured a continuation of that dominance. Kissinger's Middle East diplomacy in particular had won warm applause at home and abroad, and hopes ran high that the triumphs would continue.

The Middle East portfolio was growing more complicated, however, and Kissinger would be hard-pressed to repeat his earlier successes. In the summer of 1974, he began pushing in earnest for an Israeli-Jordanian agreement over the West Bank involving a partial Israeli withdrawal from that territory—or at least conspicuous negotiations in pursuit of that goal. King Hussein was an old friend of the United States who had mostly sat out the 1973 war. It could not appear that Washington was doing less for his country than for Egypt and Syria, which had not only resorted to force but done so with Soviet arms. Moreover, the spectacle of diplomatic progress on a third Arab-Israeli front would give Sadat a pretext for a further bilateral deal with Israel. The Israeli-Syrian disengagement had helped in this regard; a West Bank agreement would help even more.

Kissinger also hoped that a Jordanian-Israeli deal would undercut the Palestine Liberation Organization (PLO), which was making an increasingly credible bid for inclusion in Arab-Israeli diplomacy. Since the end of the October War, Yasser Arafat and other PLO moderates had maneuvered for a Palestinian role in the comprehensive negotiations that seemed likely to ensue, in Geneva or elsewhere. "We . . . knew the Arab states would make peace without us if we did not express our demands in a realistic way," Arafat later told his biographer, Alan Hart. PLO leaders especially feared that Jordan would regain control of the West Bank by diplomatic means. To prevent such a fate, the PLO needed a seat of its own at the bargaining table, and this required a scaling back of Palestinian claims to make them compatible with Israel's existence. The logical course was to embrace a two-state settlement, with the Palestinian state confined to the West Bank and the Gaza Strip or, alternatively, to the area designated as an Arab state in the UN partition plan of 1947.[45] The problem was that a two-state solution violated the PLO's commitment to establish a nonsectarian "democratic state" in all of Mandate Palestine. Openly espousing such a compromise would throw the Palestinian movement into turmoil.

One way around the conundrum was to present a two-state settlement as a way station to a democratic state, not a permanent substitute for it. In early 1974, Arafat's al-Fatah faction joined with two smaller PLO groups, the Syrian-backed al-Sa'iqa and the Marxist Democratic Front for the Liberation of Palestine (DFLP), in drafting a "working paper" on Palestinian aims to be circulated within the PLO. The working paper called on Palestinians to "establish a national authority on any lands that can be wrested from Zionist occupation." The paper insisted, however, that the Palestinians would not recognize or negotiate with Israel, to whose eventual dismantling they remained committed. More militant Palestinian factions excoriated the working paper and vowed to oppose it by all available means. In April, the Popular Front for the Liberation of Palestine–General Command, a South Lebanon–based offshoot of the Popular Front for the Liberation of Palestine, attacked the northern Israeli village of Qiryat Shemona, killing eighteen civilians. In May, three Palestinian men entered a school in Ma'alot, also in northern Israel, and took eighty-five Israeli high school students hostage, an operation leading to the deaths of the hostage-takers and twenty-six Israelis, most of them teenagers. The Ma'alot operation actually was the work of the DFLP, which sought to reestablish its liberationist credentials after being denounced for supporting the February working paper. In response to the attacks, Israel launched air raids against Lebanese villages and Palestinian camps in Lebanon, killing scores of civilians.[46]

Despite the militants' attempts to sabotage it, the al-Fatah/Sa'iqa/DFLP program soon gained wide acceptance within the PLO. In Cairo in June 1974, the Palestine National Council (the PLO parliament in exile) passed a ten-point program declaring that, although the PLO remained committed to recovering all of Palestine, it would meanwhile strive "to establish the people's national, independent and fighting authority on every part of Palestinian land that is liberated." The qualifier "that is liberated" implied that the PLO might eventually settle for something less than all of Mandate Palestine.[47]

The PLO's growing moderation caught the attention of midlevel U.S. policy analysts, several of whom recommended opening a dialogue with the organization. But Kissinger, taking the PLO's most defiant statements at face value, doubted that an organization committed to the "destruction of both Jordan and Israel" could usefully participate in the peace process. Any negotiations over the West Bank, he insisted, must occur between Israel and Jordan. Yitzhak Rabin, who had succeeded Golda Meir as Israel's prime minister in May, was keen on a second agreement over the Sinai that further neutralized Egypt. He showed little eagerness for enduring the domestic backlash that would greet any deal on the West Bank, which is more integral to Zionist ideology than the Sinai. Kissinger cautioned that the PLO was quickly gaining international legitimacy and might soon supplant Jordan as the recognized representative of West Bank Palestinians; Rabin should talk to Hussein while he still could. Rabin kept stalling.[48]

A diplomatic revolution in the fall of 1974 vindicated Kissinger's warning. At their summit meeting in Rabat, Morocco, in October, the Arab states designated the PLO "the sole legitimate representative of the Palestinian people," stripping Hussein of authority to negotiate on behalf of West Bank Palestinians. In November, the UN General Assembly voted overwhelmingly to grant the PLO observer status. Both decisions reflected a growing tendency since the October War—on the part of East bloc states, nonaligned countries, most Arab nations, and a handful of Western European countries—to see the Palestinians as key to a diplomatic settlement of the Arab-Israeli dispute, and the PLO as their obvious representative.[49] That same November, the UN General Assembly invited Arafat to come to New York to address the body in plenary session. It was a memorable scene. As pro-Palestinian and pro-Israeli demonstrators faced off on the streets and plaza outside UN headquarters, the headdress-clad PLO chairman stood at the rostrum and spun a heroic saga of Palestinian resistance to Zionist schemes. Arafat made no mention of his organization's recent flirtation with a two-state settlement, hewing to the more familiar program of a nonsectarian "democratic state" in all of Palestine. But his mere presence at the UN, combined with his symbolic offering of an "olive branch" to his Israeli foes (offsetting the empty holster strapped to his hip), signaled a new realism within the Palestinian movement, whose claims now lay at the forefront of the Arab-Israeli question.[50]

For the PLO and its supporters in the United States, this was a heady moment. Shafiq al-Hout, a close Arafat aide, recalled that his "eyes welled up with tears . . . when I saw some members of the Arab Palestinian community in New York marching towards the United Nations building, carrying Palestinian flags and singing patriotic anthems, in a direct challenge to the groups of Zionist protesters." Describing a reception at the UN following Arafat's speech, the AAUG *Newsletter* reported that "the event, which was directly televised in the Arab world, witnessed numerous stirring moments as Arafat was hugged and kissed by well-wishers who pledged their support for the Palestinian struggle." The AAUG's Elaine Hagopian, invited to meet PLO delegation members staying at the Plaza Hotel, found them "euphoric to be in New York and to have the first glimmers of recognition. There were a number of them running around gleefully on their designated hotel floor. Black Label was flowing freely." Hagopian was put off by such undignified behavior, until she reminded herself that the visitors "were just normal human beings indulging themselves" on the occasion of a stunning success.[51]

Arafat's eclipsing of Hussein was a considerable setback for Kissinger's diplomatic strategy. Still, the secretary of state remained determined to complete Egypt's effective removal from the Arab-Israeli conflict. Ideally, such an operation would unfold in tandem with—and under the political cover of—limited agreements on other Arab-Israeli fronts. But with the West Bank off the table, and with Israel refusing further withdrawals on the Golan, Kissinger decided, in late 1974, to proceed directly to a second Sinai agreement. His challenge was to reconcile the demands of the parties. Egypt wanted Israel to withdraw to the eastern side of the Mitla and Giddi Passes and to relinquish the oil fields at Abu Rudeis and Ras Sudr, in the western Sinai. Israel wanted Egypt formally to renounce its state of belligerency against Israel and to sign an agreement of long duration.[52]

One of the ironies of post-1973 shuttle diplomacy is that the harder Kissinger worked to bolster the Israeli position, the tenser his relations with Israel became. Throughout his efforts, Kissinger argued that a few modest Israeli concessions would go a long way toward neutralizing regional and international pressures for a full restoration of the 1967 borders. Israeli leaders grasped this logic but found it extremely difficult, for domestic political reasons, to deliver even the smallest concessions. So Israel often resisted Kissinger's efforts, and never more ferociously than during the Sinai talks in the spring of 1975.

In March, Kissinger traveled to the region for what he hoped would be a final exertion to arrange a second Sinai agreement. He spent part of his time in Damascus, trying to convince Asad that such an accord would facilitate, not preclude, a further Israeli pullback on the Golan. Asad had seen enough of Kissinger's diplomacy not to be swayed by such happy talk.

Still, he had come to appreciate Kissinger's wit, erudition, and personal attentiveness and thus gave the visitor a warm reception. "Had Asad liked Kissinger less," writes Asad's biographer Patrick Seale, "he would no doubt have been rougher with the man who was threatening to turn his whole environment upside down." Asad also surely recognized that, if by some miracle the Israelis concluded that a further Golan disengagement was in their interest, U.S. mediation would be necessary to bring it off. The two men parted amicably, with few illusions on either side that their diplomatic objectives aligned.[53]

Most of the March trip was devoted to Egyptian-Israeli relations. Here, Kissinger made considerable headway in softening Egypt's position. While balking at formal nonbelligerency, Sadat said he was willing to renounce the use of force against Israel, to cease hostile propaganda in state-controlled media, to ease his country's boycott against Israel, and to allow any new agreement to remain in effect until superseded by another agreement. Sadat also dropped his demand that the agreement be linked to progress on other fronts and pledged not to assist Syria if it resumed hostilities with Israel. To Kissinger, these concessions effectively satisfied Israel's security requirements. Moreover, Egypt was coming under growing pressure from Asad and other Arab leaders not to conclude another bilateral agreement with Israel, so it was crucial that Sadat's stance be vindicated. "Sadat is conceding more

Figure 13. Henry Kissinger and Hafiz al-Asad meet in Damascus, 1975. © Azad/AP/AP/CORBIS.

than I ever thought possible," Kissinger reported to Ford on March 18, "but if he goes beyond a certain point he will be destroyed." Kissinger urged Israel to accept Sadat's terms without further haggling.[54]

The Rabin cabinet had other ideas. Its domestic position was precarious, with hawkish critics accusing it of failing to uphold Israeli security. Although the cabinet agreed to relinquish the oil fields, it refused to vacate the passes and continued to demand formal nonbelligerency. Kissinger was outraged. Egypt's concessions were historic, he lectured the cabinet on March 22. By fixating on nonbelligerency, the Israelis were missing the larger import of Sadat's moves toward a separate peace. Throughout his shuttle diplomacy, Kissinger said, "there was a conviction that this process, while it was in the United States' interest, was also in Israel's interest—splitting all the Arabs, keeping the Soviets out, keeping the Europeans and Japanese quiescent—and that this in itself was a quid pro quo for Israel, and for this reason we thought an agreement would be reached." But Israel's shortsightedness had ruined everything. "All our strategy which we devoted ourselves to for a year and a half is smashed. Let's not kid ourselves; we've failed." Kissinger returned home the next day.[55]

In the wake of the failed shuttle, the Ford administration conducted an ostentatious "reassessment" of its Middle East policy. For several weeks the administration commissioned studies, held high-level meetings, and solicited the views of outside experts. On one level the exercise was a genuine review of policy options in light of the failure of Kissinger's March shuttle. On another level it was a piece of political theater designed to frighten the Israelis into adopting more conciliatory positions. The theatrical component itself operated on two levels. Publicly, Ford, Kissinger, and other administration officials insisted that the reassessment was an innocuous exercise in no way directed against Israel. Privately, the administration considered dramatic changes in U.S. policy—including support for a comprehensive settlement arranged at a reconvened Geneva conference—confident that the Israelis would catch wind of these deliberations and draw the proper conclusions. Kissinger's remarks in successive White House meetings in late March tell the story: "I think we need psychological warfare against Israel. . . . We should keep Geneva dangling. . . . But the press campaign is that this is just a minor misunderstanding and we can go back to business as usual."[56] It was a diplomatic replay of the nuclear alert of October 1973, when an unannounced elevation of the U.S. defense posture generated extensive signal traffic that Moscow was expected to pick up. This time the resulting "chatter" was intended for Israeli ears.[57]

The Israelis got the message. Instead of capitulating, however, they launched a vigorous campaign in the American press and on Capitol Hill to neutralize the administration's pressure. In May, seventy-six U.S. senators sent a public letter to President Ford urging him to support Israel diplomatically and to "be responsive to Israel's urgent military and economic needs." Ford privately scoffed that the letter "could have been written in the Israeli Embassy" and vowed it would have no impact on his decision making, but the episode underscored the political dangers of antagonizing Israel.[58]

In a further challenge to U.S. policy makers, the reassessment unfolded against a backdrop of traumatic and disorienting international events. In April 1975, North Vietnamese forces overran Saigon, sweeping aside the U.S.-backed South Vietnamese regime. That same month the Khmer Rouge took power in Cambodia, and in the coming weeks the Laotian government fell to a communist insurgency. A decade and a half of U.S. involvement in Indochina's wars came to an ignominious end. In the Middle East, on March 25 King Faisal was shot dead by a nephew, for unclear motives. Faisal's brother Khalid assumed the Saudi throne, though another brother, Fahd, the new crown prince, would wield greater de facto authority. In April, simmering animosities in Lebanon erupted in large-scale violence, inaugurating that country's long-dreaded civil war. Initially, the Lebanese crisis made little impression on Ford and Kissinger, but it preoccupied U.S. officials directly assigned to the area.[59]

A regional event that did command Kissinger's attention was the collapse of his secret policy regarding the Iraqi Kurds. Early in March, Iran and Iraq concluded an agreement that clarified, in Iran's favor, the two countries' shared border along the Shatt al-Arab River. In return, the shah withdrew his support for the Iraqi Kurdish rebellion. As Iran had been the rebels' main backer, there was no prospect of continued U.S. or Israeli involvement in the affair. Over the ensuing spring, Kissinger had little choice but to sit impotently by as Iraqi forces crushed the abandoned insurgents and to fend off the desperate pleas of Mustafa Barzani, the Kurdish leader.[60]

Amid all these distractions, the Ford administration pressed ahead with its reassessment, from which three policy options emerged. The first was to resume the search for a Sinai settlement along the lines recently attempted. The second was to encourage Israel to relinquish a larger piece of Sinai in exchange for deeper political concessions from Egypt. The third option was to go to Geneva and unveil a detailed U.S. plan for a comprehensive settlement, involving an Israeli withdrawal from virtually all of the territory occupied in 1967 and some attempt to satisfy Palestinian national claims. No one doubted that Israel would fiercely resist this third course and that Washington would have to apply unrelenting pressure to prevail. Nonetheless, the comprehensive approach was gaining support within the administration and among the U.S. foreign policy establishment generally.[61]

Surprisingly, Kissinger himself advocated a comprehensive settlement. "On balance," he wrote the president on April 21, "the greatest advantage seems to lie with trying for an overall settlement. Trying for another set of interim agreements in the present atmosphere—especially when Syria becomes involved—would generate almost as serious a confrontation with Israel and its supporters as going for an overall agreement." Ford agreed. "I am tilting more and more to a comprehensive settlement," he told Kissinger a week later. "I get the impression there is increased polarization, and to start all over again I don't think it is worth it." On May 8, Ford said to Kissinger, "For us to go back to the step-by-step when Israel is frozen just won't work."[62]

While there is every indication that Ford genuinely favored a comprehensive approach, it appears that Kissinger had grave private misgivings about it. In his memoirs, Kissinger wrote that during the reassessment he made "a private pact with myself: if the step-by-step approach had to be abandoned and the United States was driven to state terms for a settlement, I would resign. The disparity between Israel's perception of its margin of survival and ours would become too difficult to bridge. If we prevailed, we would break Israel's back psychologically; if we failed, we would have doomed our role in the Middle East." Kissinger then made the striking statement quoted earlier in this chapter, about his unwillingness to force withdrawal on "an ally so closely linked with my family's fate in the Holocaust."[63]

Assuming that Kissinger was honestly reporting his private doubts—which were consistent, after all, with his overall record of shielding Israel from outside pressure—how can they be reconciled with his simultaneous support for an imposed comprehensive settlement?[64] A reasonable surmise is that Kissinger was playing a game of diplomatic chicken. In driving U.S. policy toward the brink of a comprehensive settlement (a fate he dreaded nearly as much as the Israelis did), he gambled that Israel would avert this outcome by making the necessary concessions to revive the step-by-step approach.

As it happened, both Egypt and Israel supplied the required concessions, and Kissinger was spared his moment of truth. As early as March 29, Sadat had unexpectedly announced that he would reopen the Suez Canal (closed since 1967) and extend the mandate of the UN peacekeeping force stationed on Egyptian soil. In early June, he proposed that American civilians man observation posts in the Sinai, providing further assurances that Egypt would never resume hostilities there. Sadat's undertakings breathed new life into the step-by-step approach, and Ford and Kissinger pressed the Israelis to respond favorably, subtly wielding the threat of a comprehensive settlement imposed in Geneva. By late June, it appears, Rabin and his advisers had essentially decided to settle, but they spent another two months haggling with the Americans over logistical details. On September 4, 1975, the parties finally signed the Sinai II Agreement. Israel relinquished the Abu Rudeis and Ras Sudr oil fields and withdrew to the east of the Mitla and Giddi Passes; most of the vacated territory became a buffer zone occupied by UN forces and American civilian observers. Without granting formal nonbelligerency, Egypt agreed to refrain from the threat or use of force and to permit nonmilitary cargoes going to and from Israel to pass through the Suez Canal.[65]

Meanwhile, in a series of secret letters to Rabin, crafted by Kissinger and signed by Ford, the United States pledged to provide Israel with additional military and economic aid and to consult closely with it before making any further moves in Arab-Israeli diplomacy. Washington promised to "give great weight to Israel's position that any peace agreement with Syria must be predicated on Israel remaining on the Golan Heights." It also pledged that the United States would refrain from recognizing or negotiating with the PLO as long as it refused to recognize Israel. This self-imposed restriction would prevent the United States from dealing with the Palestinians' chosen leadership until the late 1980s.[66]

The Sinai II Agreement was poorly received in the Arab world. While pro-U.S. governments generally refrained from criticizing the accord in public, some expressed their dissatisfaction privately. "The Saudis very much want Sinai II to succeed," reported the U.S. embassy in Jidda. "They have come to the conclusion, however, that Sadat may have gotten stampeded into a bad bargain." King Hussein agreed. For the Egyptians "to accept almost a state of non-belligerency while most of their territory is still occupied," he told Kissinger, "is too much."[67] Most other Arab actors publicly opposed the agreement, their criticisms ranging from scathing to restrained. The Syrian government "condemn[ed]" this "dangerous setback." Its journalistic mouthpiece, the Damascus newspaper *al-Ba'th*, charged Sadat with "sacrificing the blood of the thousands of martyrs" killed in the October War. The PLO pronounced the agreement "a plot to liquidate the Palestinian cause" that did "not reflect the will of the fighters" in Egypt. More mildly, Algerian foreign minister Abdelaziz Bouteflika called Sinai II an "unequal accord" that favored Israel. Libya's Mu'ammar Qaddafi lamented that "the cause has been sold out" but would not say by whom, leaving Qaddafi watchers to puzzle over such uncharacteristic coyness. (Their best guess was that he was momentarily beholden to Sadat because the latter had tipped him off about a recent coup attempt in Tripoli.)[68]

Arab Americans were also dismayed. The National Association of Arab Americans (NAAA) did not flatly oppose Sinai II but criticized most of its provisions, especially Kissinger's secret pledges (leaked to the press in mid-September) that Israel would receive additional military aid and that Washington would shun the PLO. The AAUG blasted these same elements. But unlike the NAAA, which worried that Sinai II placed an "evenhanded" Arab-Israeli settlement further out of reach, AAUGers presumably would have opposed any agreement with Israel, as they remained committed to "the unconditional liberation of the whole of Palestine" and to the establishment there of "a non-sectarian democratic state"—the PLO's own recent ambiguity notwithstanding. Moreover, while the NAAA refrained from criticizing Egypt, the AAUG (rather like Qaddafi) condemned Cairo's actions in sharp but cryptic terms. Sinai II was partly the handiwork, the AAUG observed, of "certain Arab reactionary forces."[69]

Still, Arab American and Arab-friendly activists could take encouragement from the U.S. public's continuing interest in their concerns. "From all across the country," Americans for Middle East Understanding executive director John M. Sutton had marveled in November 1974, "we are getting the most amazing responses from those who have learned of our efforts." The following February, Rabbi Berger wrote Fayez Sayegh that the American public's "interest in our position is overwhelming, but gratifying."[70] Although the mainstream media had previously taken some notice of Arab American political activism, coverage of the phenomenon grew more extensive in 1975, with several feature stories appearing in national and regional newspapers and magazines.[71] In late June, President Ford invited a delegation of NAAA leaders to meet with him in the White House. The visitors praised the president for "the bold and courageous steps you have taken in reassessing our policies" and urged him to seek a comprehensive settlement without delay.[72] They did not yet know that Ford was already shifting back toward the bilateral track, though this would soon be painfully evident. Policy disappointment coupled with a measure of societal acceptance; such was the emerging, and ironic, pattern of Arab American political life.

In the weeks following Sinai II, Kissinger cautioned Arab leaders not to expect any major U.S. peace initiatives in 1976; a presidential election year was never a good time for difficult decisions on the Arab-Israeli issue. Once Ford was safely elected, however, Washington would launch a serious, comprehensive effort.[73] Kissinger made a special point of reassuring Asad, who had been so critical of the step-by-step approach and the Egyptian-Israeli agreement it produced. In November, Kissinger instructed U.S. ambassador to Syria Richard Murphy to tell Asad "that, when we speak of a major effort in 1977, we are not just talking about procedural ways of continuing the peace process or of further step-by-step arrangements, but of a comprehensive peace settlement that would deal with all aspects of the problem on all fronts—borders, the Palestinians, guarantees, etc." An enticing prospect, but Kissinger, as usual, was not telling the whole truth. Although he did plan to launch an ambitious-seeming initiative in 1977, he expected the effort to bog down when Israel refused to budge from either the West Bank or the Golan; Kissinger could then "settle" for the narrower agreement he preferred. As he summarized the strategy in his memoirs, "We would begin with an attempt to move on all fronts and, failing that, support a major step in a separate Egyptian-Israeli negotiation." Asad placed little stock in Kissinger's promises. By now, however, the spiraling violence in neighboring Lebanon left him little time for Arab-Israeli diplomacy.[74]

Meanwhile, the Ford administration made a small concession to the Palestinians. On November 12, 1975, in prepared testimony before a subcommittee of the House International Relations Committee, deputy assistant secretary of state Harold Saunders stated that the Palestinian question was "in many ways . . . the heart of the conflict." Without proposing any mechanisms for addressing the issue, or relaxing his government's position on contacts with the PLO, Saunders acknowledged that Palestinian claims must be satisfied in some way and pledged that the United States would keep an open mind on the matter. "What is not possible today may become possible," he said. Saunders's statement, which Kissinger and Ford approved in advance, raised expectations that the United States was about to adopt a more accommodating attitude toward the PLO. After the Israelis protested, however, Kissinger publicly dismissed the statement as an "academic exercise" without policy implications. Congressman Lee Hamilton of Indiana, chairman of the subcommittee before which Saunders spoke, suspected that Kissinger had authorized the testimony largely to ease the political predicament of Sadat, whom other Arabs continued to accuse of abandoning the Palestinians. Kissinger confirmed as much in a conversation with

James Callaghan, Britain's foreign secretary. The reason the Palestinian issue had suddenly emerged, Kissinger explained, "was that the Egyptians needed an alibi for their having come to a separate agreement with the Israelis."[75]

Yet Saunders's testimony was not entirely the sterile exercise Kissinger intended. Saunders himself took it more seriously, and he and his colleagues would spend the "down year" of 1976 examining the Palestinian issue. The resulting studies would provide a basis for president Jimmy Carter's much more sincere effort to achieve a comprehensive settlement.[76]

Here, then, was another ironic pattern: in his efforts to fortify Israel's position on the ground, Kissinger helped to carve out some Arab-friendly space in the American political imagination. As we saw, Kissinger's warm and respectful treatment of Arab leaders, though aimed at constructing a diplomatic framework that minimized Israeli withdrawals, had the simultaneous, and partly intended, effect of humanizing Arabs in the United States. Similarly, during the spring 1975 reassessment—conducted to salvage that same diplomatic framework—Kissinger encouraged the circulation of "evenhanded" discourse and engaged in some of it himself. Kissinger's purpose was to spook the Israelis, not to inaugurate a new, comprehensive diplomacy, as sincere advocates of comprehensiveness later learned to their dismay. Writing to George Ball in February 1976, former U.S. high commissioner for Germany and Establishment "wise man" John J. McCloy recalled a private meeting that he, Ball, and other supporters of evenhandedness had held with Kissinger during the reassessment. "I think we all, including Henry, had agreed . . . that an across-the-board approach was then essential rather than the interim solutions," McCloy wrote. "What made Henry change his mind? He never discussed it again with me."[77] Once the bilateral negotiations resumed in the summer of 1975, Kissinger did stop talking about "an across-the-board approach," at least in conversations with other Americans. But his earlier advocacy of comprehensiveness lent impetus to that option in U.S. foreign policy circles.

A case in point was the subsequent release of a challenging yet thoroughly mainstream report on the Middle East. In December 1975, the Brookings Institution, a center-left Washington think tank, unveiled a comprehensive scenario for resolving the Arab-Israeli dispute, entailing Israel's withdrawal from virtually all of the occupied territory, Arab recognition of Israel, and the creation of either an independent Palestinian state or an autonomous Palestinian entity federated with Jordan. The report's authors were sixteen prominent scholars, diplomats, and policy analysts, many with recent experience in government. Two of them, Charles Yost and William Quandt, had served with Kissinger in the Nixon administration, Yost as UN ambassador and Quandt as a National Security Council analyst. During the reassessment, Yost and six other report authors attended a private meeting with Kissinger at which a reinstatement of the 1967 borders emerged as the favored outcome. Kissinger seemed receptive to this view, directing nearly all of his critical questions to the one participant who challenged it.[78] The December Bookings report, while noting that the Sinai II Accord concluded in the interim "still leaves the basic elements of the Arab-Israeli dispute substantially untouched," proceeded on the assumption that Kissinger recognized the "imperative" of pursing a comprehensive settlement in the very near future.[79]

By now, of course, the threat of comprehensiveness had served its purpose, and Kissinger had no use for the Brookings report. In 1977, however, the Carter administration would largely adopt it as the blueprint for its own Middle East peace efforts. In these ways the report resembled Saunders's contemporaneous statement on the Palestinians, another (and more direct) outgrowth of Kissinger's deviousness that would acquire a life of its own.

Shaking the relative calm of these Washington deliberations was a jolting event out of Midtown Manhattan. On November 10, 1975, the UN General Assembly took the extraordinary step of voting to designate Zionism "a form of racism and racial discrimination." Both at the time and subsequently, the UN Zionism debate figured as a stark morality tale, in which the international community either forthrightly called out a new form of colonial oppression or shamefully revictimized the world's surviving Jews.[80] The controversy is better understood as the result of an ongoing and somewhat formulaic anti-Zionist discourse that, against the backdrop of Egypt's moves toward a separate peace with Israel, gained startling and destructive momentum in the second half of 1975.

In fact, the effort to equate Zionism with racism was a substitute for a more drastic measure. Since late 1974, the PLO, Syria, and several other Arab states had advocated Israel's expulsion from the United Nations, on the grounds that Israel had failed to meet the obligations it had accepted upon joining the UN and had then defied numerous Security Council and General Assembly resolutions.[81] Calls for Israel's expulsion emanated from the November 1974 Arab summit in Rabat and from a July 1975 conference of Islamic nations in Jidda. Arab delegations introduced similar measures at the Organization of African Unity conference in Kampala, Uganda, in late July–early August 1975 and at a meeting of nonaligned nations in Lima, Peru, in late August 1975.[82]

Although the expulsion effort reflected a long-standing Arab desire to delegitimate Israel, by the summer of 1975 it had acquired the more specific aim of blocking a second Egyptian-Israeli agreement over the Sinai. Syria, the PLO, and other Arab actors sought to present Cairo with expulsion resolutions it would be obliged to support. This would embarrass Egypt and infuriate Israel, perhaps compelling the latter to pull out of the Sinai negotiations. "The Syrians were obviously delighted, as were the PLO," a British diplomat remarked after the Jidda conference, "to throw a spanner in the Israeli/Egyptian works." Days later Asad's political adviser told Ambassador Murphy that, if Washington showed a genuine willingness to address Syrian and Palestinian claims, "then [the] expulsion campaign could be stopped." But Kissinger had no intention of tackling those issues before the 1976 election (if ever), and the expulsion drive continued.[83]

Passing expulsion resolutions in Rabat and Jidda required little effort; achieving them in Kampala and Lima was a taller order. In mid-July, before the latter two conferences, Kissinger publicly warned that Israel's ouster from the UN could cause a serious reduction in U.S. financial support for the organization. Partly in response to this threat, which if carried out could be devastating to poor countries, both the Kampala and the Lima conferences rejected the expulsion resolutions, opting instead for general condemnations of Israeli policies and Zionist ideology.[84]

Kampala and Lima showed what the traffic would bear: the denunciation of Israel but not its outright banishment from the UN. And so, as the General Assembly convened for its thirtieth session that fall, Egypt's Arab rivals set out to persuade the world body to anathemize Israel's founding creed—and force a reluctant Egypt to join in the campaign. For although Sinai II was signed in early September, opportunities remained for disrupting its implementation and perhaps deterring Sadat from traveling any further down the bilateral road. In October, Syria, Libya, South Yemen, Somalia, and Cuba introduced a resolution in the UN General Assembly's Committee on Social, Humanitarian, and Cultural Affairs (aka the Third Committee) defining Zionism as "a form of racism and racial discrimination."[85]

The anti-Zionist resolution was debated in two UN venues, the Third Committee in October 1975 and the full General Assembly in November. In both forums, the resolution's most effective advocate was Fayez Sayegh, then serving as one of Kuwait's UN representatives. Sayegh noted that the General Assembly's operative definition of racial discrimination, drawn from a 1965 antiracism convention, included ethnic discrimination.[86] Israel's Zionist programs and laws, he argued, amounted to ethnic discrimination against non-Jewish Palestinians. True, Jewishness could be seen as a purely religious identity that a non-Jew might assume through conversion. But Zionists themselves tended to favor an entho-national definition whereby Jewishness, in the overwhelming majority of instances, was an accident of birth. And those born into the Jewish identity enjoyed markedly superior rights under Israel's laws. A case in point, Sayegh observed, was the Law of Return, which permitted a Jew who had never set foot in Palestine to "return" to Israel. By contrast, "the indigenous Palestinian Arab, dislodged in 1948 or 1967, . . . has no such right—because he is not a Jew."[87] Sayegh cited other ways in which Israel's Zionist policies discriminated against non-Jews.[88]

Vehemently opposing the anti-Zionism resolution was the U.S. ambassador to the UN, Daniel Patrick Moynihan, an outspoken supporter of Israel. Moynihan saw the resolution both as a specific attack against the Jewish people and as a broader assault on Western-style democracy. His argument was a curious mixture of towering indignation and legalistic nitpicking. When the ambassador wasn't denouncing the resolution as "infamous" and "obscene," he was objecting that it was imprecisely drafted. The resolution, he noted, called Zionism "a form of racism and racial discrimination," yet the 1965 convention to which it referred provided no definition of racism, only of racial discrimination. "How could we know if Zionism was a form of racism," he later wrote, "if we had never defined racism?" So Moynihan supplied a definition of his own: the belief "that there are significant biological differences among clearly identifiable groups and that those differences establish, in effect, different levels of humanity." Defined this narrowly, the concept seemed to have little bearing on the case. Jews did not constitute a "clearly identifiable group," so discrimination against non-Jews could not be racist.[89]

Having disposed of the racism issue, Moynihan acted as if he had refuted the whole resolution. He ignored the charge of racial discrimination, along with the fact that the definition of this term in the 1965 convention explicitly included ethnic discrimination. He never challenged the evidence of Israel's discrimination against non-Jews. This omission, Sayegh retorted, left the impression that Moynihan "half-agrees with the resolution—that he questions only the statement that 'Zionism is a form of racism,' but does not question the statement that 'Zionism is a form of racial discrimination.'"[90]

On the merits, then, the anti-Zionism resolution was hardly as depraved as Moynihan claimed. The reference to racism was fuzzy, but Sayegh made a credible case that Zionist doctrine and practice did constitute racial discrimination under the accepted definition of the term. Politically, however, the resolution was deeply damaging, and contrary to the diplomatic interests of most Arab governments and the dominant factions of the PLO. Over the last few years these actors had reconciled themselves, or begun to reconcile themselves, to a diplomatic settlement entailing Israel's continued existence within the 1967 borders. This emerging pragmatism had been clear enough to international observers, yet the Israelis had dismissed it as a dangerous mirage. The Arab world was far from ready to make peace, they said, and so Israel must continue to hold, as a guarantee of its security, much of the territory seized in 1967. Under the best of circumstances, overcoming this Israeli resistance would have been a daunting task. Once the anti-Zionism resolution appeared on the UN agenda, it became nearly impossible. How, Israelis would ask, could they even think of returning territory to neighbors so implacably hostile to their national existence? And how could the United Nations, which was hosting the travesty, be permitted any role in future peace efforts? To many of its Arab supporters, the anti-Zionist resolution offered the worst of both worlds: it imperiled the comprehensive settlement to which they were increasingly committed, while still failing to derail Egypt's moves toward a separate peace.

The fate of the resolution was never in doubt. The measure passed in the Third Committee on October 17 and the General Assembly on November 10, on both occasions by comfortable margins. After the final vote, a visibly angered Moynihan strode to the podium and declared: "The General Assembly today grants symbolic amnesty—and more—to the murder of the 6 million European Jews." The United States "will never acquiesce in this infamous act."[91]

Across the United States, public reactions to the anti-Zionism resolution were overwhelmingly negative. Both houses of Congress unanimously passed resolutions condemning the vote.[92] Senator Henry M. "Scoop" Jackson of Washington, a contender for the 1976 Democratic presidential nomination, called the resolution "the worst thing since Hitler." In a Gallup poll taken in late November, only 33% of respondents said the UN was "doing a good job," down from 41% the previous January. Moynihan, by contrast, received stellar reviews. On the day after the General Assembly vote, tens of thousands of Israel's supporters gathered in New York's garment district to hear defiant speeches by senator Jacob Javits of New York, Israeli ambassador to the UN Chaim Herzog, and other prominent figures; applause erupted at every mention of Moynihan's name. Editorialists across the country commended Moynihan's blistering attack on the anti-Zionist resolution.[93]

Figure 14. Daniel Patrick Moynihan addresses the UN General Assembly, c. 1975. UN Photo/Teddy Chen.

The resolution had its American defenders, but they left virtually no mark on the broader landscape of opinion. The principal supporters were anti-Zionist Jews like Rabbi Berger and Edmund Hanauer and more militant elements of the Arab American community, such as the AAUG and M.T. Mehdi.[94] Groups advocating "evenhandedness"—Arab American and otherwise—generally refrained from endorsing the resolution outright, though a number of them circulated, with implicit approval, statements supporting it by Sayegh and others.[95]

A third position, held by Kissinger and many professional U.S. diplomats, was to deplore the resolution *and* Moynihan's reaction to it. According to this view, the ambassador's harsh words had needlessly alienated wavering Third World delegations, converting potential "no" votes into abstentions and potential abstentions into "yeses." Avoiding such defections could not have prevented the anti-Zionist resolution from prevailing in a General Assembly vote, the argument went, but it just might have enabled passage of a procedural motion to keep the measure from coming to a vote in the first place. Moynihan "raised the Zionism question beyond the interest of the United States," Kissinger complained. "We could have won it if [he] had not used the adjectives obscene etc."[96]

Kissinger was especially annoyed by Moynihan's charge, following the General Assembly vote, that the UN was granting "symbolic amnesty" to the perpetrators of the Nazi Holocaust. This was just the sort of extravagant philo-Semitism that so discomfited Kissinger, who usually preferred to avoid drawing attention to his own Jewishness. It also undermined his efforts to avoid unnecessary friction with Arab states while Sinai II was being implemented. After seeing an advance copy of the statement, Kissinger instructed William Buffum, the assistant secretary of state for international organization affairs, to have Moynihan remove the inflammatory passage. "We are conducting foreign policy," Kissinger said. "This is not a synagogue." But either the message failed to get through or Moynihan disregarded it, and the "amnesty" claim remained in the text.[97]

Although most of this anti-Moynihan commentary circulated privately, enough of it leaked out for the ambassador to conclude that his position was untenable. In February 1976, he tendered his resignation to a reluctant Ford, who valued the acclaim Moynihan had drawn to his administration. Later that year Moynihan was elected to the U.S. Senate from New York, a position he would hold for the next quarter-century.[98]

In addition to advancing Moynihan's political career, the Zionism debate gave sharper definition to the emerging phenomenon of neoconservatism—a movement of liberals and former radicals, in many cases Jewish, who over the previous decade had decried what they saw as a harmful leftward turn by the Democratic Party. The first neoconservative cohort, in the late 1960s and early 1970s, had criticized the perceived excesses of the civil rights and anti–Vietnam War movements and the shortcomings of liberal antipoverty policies. A second cohort, emerging in the early 1970s and clustered around Scoop Jackson, had challenged both the dovish positions of McGovernite Democrats and the détente policies of the Nixon and Ford administrations (insisting that neither approach was sufficiently vigorous in upholding American values abroad), while also championing Israel's cause.[99] There was considerable overlap between these two neoconservative groups, best exemplified by Moynihan himself, a leading figure in both.[100]

For virtually all neoconservatives, Moynihan's brief tenure at the UN (from July 1975 to February 1976), and especially his defense of Zionism, provided a thrilling spectacle of unabashed ideological combat. It made neoconservatives surer of their positions and more insistent that their views inform all aspects of U.S. foreign relations, not just public diplomacy. The Zionism debate also drew wide public attention to Moynihan and those who shared his outlook. Several articles and columns on neoconservatism, in some cases introducing the term, appeared in the national press.[101] For the rest of the decade and beyond, neoconservatives would be easily recognizable participants in debates over Middle East policy.

"Moynihan's Moment," as one historian calls it, along with the neoconservatives' arrival on the national scene, further validated the view that Kissinger and the Israelis were fundamentally at odds. In reality, the secretary of state had labored tirelessly and often brilliantly to construct a diplomatic framework that fortified Israel's occupation of Arab land. Unlike the neocons, however, he believed this task was more effectively accomplished without contentious fanfare. Moynihan, as it happened, briefly accommodated this approach in January 1976, when, in one of his last official acts before leaving the UN, he vetoed a Security Council resolution recognizing the right of the Palestinians to establish an independent state in the West Bank and Gaza. Pro-Palestinian resolutions had emanated easily from the General Assembly in recent years; for one to advance this far in the Security Council was a diplomatic milestone. Yet Moynihan kept his cool, calmly explaining that his veto was "not based on antipathy to the aspirations of Palestinians" but rather reflected Washington's view that the proposed measure, by moving beyond Resolution 242, undermined the agreed framework for resolving the dispute. Moynihan even congratulated his Security Council colleagues for holding such a constructive a debate. "The conciliatory tone of this statement," Britain's UN delegation reported home, ". . . helped to defuse criticism of it."[102]

At one point in the January proceedings, however, the familiar feistiness returned. During the lead-up to the Security Council vote on the Palestine resolution, Moynihan was affably mingling in the delegates' lounge when someone asked him if the ongoing debate on the Middle East, in which the U.S. position enjoyed hardly any international support, had isolated the United States. "It's not the United States that is isolated," the ambassador insisted. "It's the world that is isolated."[103]

Moynihan was spoofing his own penchant for provocative hyperbole, but his statement made a weird sort of sense. Over the previous two years, under the aegis of Kissinger (Moynihan's occasional nemesis), the United States had achieved remarkable success in forestalling the coalescence of global forces that, if left unchecked, might well have compelled Israel to retreat to the 1967 lines. Through feints and subterfuges, though exertions at once shamelessly self-promotional and personally draining, Kissinger had eased the Soviets to the sidelines, persuaded Arab oil producers to lift their embargo (thereby blunting the desperation in Western Europe and Japan), and pacified Syria just long enough to pull Egypt out of its confrontation with Israel and into a U.S.-brokered dialogue with that country. The United States now had much greater control over the direction, pace, and scope of Arab-Israeli diplomacy than anyone would have predicted in late 1973. Washington probably could, if it so chose, ensure that Israel indefinitely retained major portions of the occupied territories. The main alternative scenario—a restoration of the 1967 borders and the establishment of an independent Palestinian state—now enjoyed wide international support. Yet Kissinger's maneuverings had largely neutralized the global pressures that might have been mobilized on its behalf.

It was a remarkable diplomatic performance, sufficiently intricate that it yielded consequences not directly related to its object, among them a somewhat more hospitable domestic environment for Arab-friendly activism. Abroad and at home, the struggle to define the contours of an Arab-Israeli settlement would continue.

Chapter 6

Future Shock

The Speculative Mode in American Discourse on the Arab World, 1974–1978

On September 15, 1981, at a posh beach resort hotel in Kuilima, Hawaii, the Organization of the Petroleum Exporting Countries (OPEC) held one of its most consequential meetings. At the start of the session, the oil ministers of Iran and Saudi Arabia announced that their two governments, which had recently assailed each other in a bitter war of words, were about to sign a mutual nonaggression pact. Henceforth, the two nations would work together to propagate Islam throughout the world. To fund this initiative, the Saudi and Iranian ministers proposed that OPEC raise the price of Persian Gulf crude oil from twenty to thirty-eight dollars per barrel. Though taken aback by the announcement, most of the other OPEC ministers warmly welcomed the suggested price hike, which, if generally applied, would substantially boost their own countries' revenues. In a mood of heady exuberance, the ministers approved the price increase by a vote of thirteen to one. The lone dissenter was the Ecuadorian delegate, who cautioned that a near doubling of the price of oil would come as a terrible shock to the industrialized nations. There was no telling how they might react.

The warning was prescient. Over the ensuing weeks, the oil price increase caused massive inflation throughout the world, a condition exacerbated by ill-considered U.S. monetary policy. To maintain Americans' purchasing power, the U.S. Treasury Department drastically stepped up the printing of dollars, causing prices to soar even higher. Soon it cost millions of dollars to buy ordinary household goods, and commercial transactions began to resemble those of Germany in the 1920s. Americans' savings were wiped out overnight; the desperation and rage caused a breakdown of social order. Marauding gangs stalked the land. Reactionary demagogues were not far behind. Conditions were no better in other countries, and in many places, of course, they were much worse. By 1982, global civilization was on the brink of collapse.

On the Brink—that was the title of the dystopian 1977 thriller in which these scenes unfolded. The authors were Benjamin Stein, a young lawyer and former White House speechwriter (who later attained modest fame as an actor, political commentator, and game show host), and his father, Herbert Stein, who had chaired President Nixon's Council of Economic Advisers.[1] In projecting current Middle Eastern realities (or a loose approximation of them) into a near, dire future, the Steins partook of a literary genre that underwent extraordinary growth in the middle years of the 1970s. Over the half decade following the October War of 1973, scores of political thrillers based on events in the Arab world appeared in the United States. Typically, the authors were professional fiction writers mining a rich new vein of popular fascination. But in a number of instances—the Steins were a case in point—journalists, lawyers, bankers, economists, and politicians could not resist dabbling in the genre. With news headlines dominated by challenges emanating from the Arab world, and with humanity's fate seeming to hinge on the international community's responses to those challenges, freewheeling speculation about the region and its relationship to the wider world had become far too important, or at least too enjoyable, to leave to professional novelists.

Just as amateurs swelled the ranks of published fiction writers, so fictional techniques spilled over into nonfiction genres. Even commentators who stuck to the "real world" sometimes inserted speculative elements into their arguments about contemporary Arab affairs. To dramatize the dangers of allowing current trends to continue, or the benefits that would ensue from a bolder U.S. Middle East policy, they crafted alternative scenarios nearly as fanciful as those featured in thriller novels.

Whatever the format, the dominant portrayal was of hostile Arab actors—sometimes a hostile Arab world—seeking to inflict crippling physical, economic, or political damage on the United States or its allies. Implicitly or explicitly, narratives adopting this perspective called for a more robust

U.S. response, taking the form of direct military action, more aggressive police work, or unstinting support for Israel's own efforts to combat Arab threats. Though primarily anti-Arab in tone, these narratives also tended to be highly critical of the United States, depicting American leaders and citizens alike as lacking the character, vision, competence, and grit to meet the Arab challenge. Most fictional works supplied happy (or at least non-catastrophic) endings, but these were often achieved despite, rather than because of, the exertions of American characters. As for the nonfiction pieces, they upheld an ideal of American initiative and success but were pessimistic about the prospects of approaching that ideal.

Meanwhile, a counternarrative found its way into some mid-seventies American thrillers and news commentaries. It resisted the drive to demonize Arab actors and portrayed them in more diverse and human terms. Some versions of the counternarrative sharply criticized America's pro-Israel biases, presenting them as a maddening obstacle to a rational Middle East policy. Yet these alternative portrayals had limited opportunity to influence the national discourse. They were far fewer in number than the anti-Arab narratives, and many of their authors labored under the public suspicion that their sympathy for Arab perspectives was rooted in venality or prejudice. Moreover, some of the Arab-friendly scenarios, especially in news commentaries, engaged in a sort of fear-mongering that lost credibility with the passage of time.

Running through all of these speculative works was the theme of rising and falling fortunes: a sense that Arab wealth, power, and strategic opportunity were on the upswing while the status of the United States—a nation reeling from Vietnam and Watergate, flummoxed by stagflation, paralyzed by a loss of certitude and nerve—was inexorably declining. The coupling of these trajectories was a distinctive feature of American discourse in the 1974–1978 period. For although the perception of American decline persisted into the decade's closing years (and in some ways grew more pronounced), the specter of a united, formidable, and overweening Arab foe became less vivid in the late 1970s. By then, the Camp David peace process had deprived the Arab states of a viable military option against Israel, and the Iranian revolution and its excesses had created a new, non-Arab focus of American alarm in the Middle East. It was in the decade's middle years, then, that the potency of the Arab challenge threw America's failings into sharpest relief, and that American novelists and commentators were most prone to present that challenge as embodying their disappointment in their own country. The purveyors of the dominant narrative lamented

Americans' failure to marshal their still-awesome resources and put the Arab upstarts in their place. The dissenters wondered if their fellow citizens were wise enough to avoid a self-defeating confrontation with the new players on the world stage. All feared that this vexing encounter with Arab power might spell the final chapter of U.S. global ascendancy.

Middle East–themed political thrillers borrowed from a number of existing fictional genres. Some of the novels, in featuring terrorist plots that U.S. authorities sought to foil, were basically police procedurals. At the same time, most of the stories involved a scale of destruction—physical or economic, attempted or actually inflicted—that called to mind the "disaster" themes so prevalent in seventies novels and cinema.[2] Because many of the Middle East–oriented novels were, like *On the Brink*, set a few years after their publication dates, they also bore some affinity with the futuristic, dystopian fiction of the era.[3] This last resemblance was slight, however, as the dystopian works usually took place many decades in the future (or even later) and thus posited a much higher degree of technological or societal transformation. The Middle East–themed novels typically postdated the action just late enough to put a new, imaginary U.S. president in office, to allow radical nationalists to take power in Saudi Arabia, or to introduce some other scene-setting change that could emerge logically from contemporary realities.

Whatever their taxonomy, by the mid-1970s political thrillers touching on Arab themes were all the rage in American publishing. "Every writer," observed the *New York Times*'s crime fiction critic Newgate Callendar in August 1975, "seems to have settled on Arab terrorism for a sure thing." A few months later Callendar quipped, "Books about the Jews, Arabs and the continuing struggle in the Middle East have assumed the status of heavy industry."[4]

In part, this was a continuation of an old pattern. Since the late eighteenth century, American fiction writers had cast dramas of adventure and intrigue in North African and Middle Eastern settings.[5] But there *was* something new in the sheer volume of the output, which underwent a sharp spike after 1967 and an even sharper one after 1973. An extensive list of titles compiled by the historian Reeva S. Simon indicates that forty-six political thrillers involving the Arab world were published in the United States during the half century from 1916 to 1967, as compared with forty-two such titles appearing from 1968 to 1973, and seventy-six from 1974 to 1978.[6] There was also an important qualitative difference. Although the genre had always featured Arab villains who preyed on American protagonists, up through 1973 the harm Arabs did was almost invariably confined to the Middle East, touching only those Americans who ventured to the region. Earlier in the century, American travelers ran afoul of desert bandits, white-slave traffickers, drug smugglers, and sadistic potentates. After 1967, they helped Israelis fight Arabs or got caught in the crossfire of local hostilities. Starting around 1974, however, fictional Arab villains acquired global reach. Through economic warfare, terrorism, and other aggressive means, they began threatening the economic and physical well-being of Americans who never left home. (Such, at least, was the dominant pattern; a small number of American thrillers challenged the genre's preoccupation with Arab bogeymen.)

The starkest form the Arab threat took was, of course, that of outright violence committed on American soil. Long before real-life Arab terrorists plotted the mass murder of American civilians, American novelists were writing the scripts for such outrages. In Richard Graves's *Cobalt 60* (1974), the ruler of an imaginary Persian Gulf emirate attempts to wipe out the entire U.S. Senate by personally stealing into the chamber and spraying senators with radioactive paper clips out of a gun disguised as a camera. In Colin Forbes's *Year of the Golden Ape* (1974), a fanatical Arab nationalist seizes control of the Saudi government and hires a French soldier of fortune to hijack a British oil tanker, smuggle a nuclear bomb on board, and detonate the bomb in San Francisco harbor. In Thomas Harris's 1975 novel *Black Sunday* (released as a movie by Paramount Pictures in 1977), the Black September Organization tries to murder over eighty thousand Americans by sending a Goodyear blimp packed with plastic explosives to blow up the Super Bowl.[7]

In other books, the plots unfold overseas but are aimed at the heart of American governance. In *The Gargoyle Conspiracy*, by Marvin H. Albert (1975), a Moroccan terrorist attempts to assassinate the U.S. secretary of state at a party on the French Riviera. In Alfred Coppel's *Thirty-Four East* (1974), Palestinian commandos kidnap the American vice president when he visits the Sinai Peninsula. In a bizarre coincidence (or is it a coincidence?), the president dies in a stateside plane crash, and the nation is plunged into a bitter constitutional dispute over the proper order of presidential succession.[8]

In still other treatments, Arabs select targets of global significance. In *The Vatican Target*, by Barry Schiff and Hal Fishman (1978), Palestinian hijackers take the Pope hostage. In *The Aleph Solution*, by Sandor Frankel and Webster Mews (1978), Palestinians seize control of the UN General Assembly and threaten to kill the delegates unless they vote to dismantle the state of Israel. To increase the pressure, Palestinians on the outside launch a series of terrorist outrages throughout the world.[9]

In a somewhat more restrained variation on the genre, Arab aggression takes the form of economic sabotage or coercion. In *The Forty-First Thief*, by Edward A. Pollitz, Jr. (1975), the government of Quahrein, an imaginary oil-rich nation in North Africa, learns that General Motors is secretly developing a solar-powered car. Quahrein tries to suppress the new technology by gaining a controlling share of GM stock and, for good measure, assassinating individuals involved in the project.[10] In Ben and Herb Stein's *On the Brink*, as we saw, OPEC's feckless price gouging throws the world into chaos.

Often, these two modes of aggression operate in tandem. The terrorists in *Black Sunday* know that soaring oil prices have already caused many Americans to question the wisdom of supporting Israel; the massacre at the Super Bowl, they hope, will turn that sentiment into a groundswell. In *Year of the Golden Ape*, the logical sequence is reversed. The radical Saudi ruler calculates that the nuclear incineration of San Francisco will so outrage Western leaders that they will call the Arabs "Golden Apes." The slur will inflame Arab opinion, prompting other Arab oil-producing states to cut off oil shipments to Western nations, rendering them powerless to defend Israel.[11] This may read like a parody of the genre, but the novel is devoid of apparent irony.

There is one prominent instance in which Israelis concoct a plot against the West. In Leonard Harris's *The Masada Plan* (1976), Israel comes under devastating attack by the Arab states. Israel's leaders warn the U.S. government that they will detonate nuclear bombs in nine major cities throughout the world, including even Jerusalem (hence the book's title), unless the superpowers impose an immediate cease-fire. Unlike the Arab plots depicted in the other novels, however, the Israeli operation is treated with overwhelming sympathy. With Israelis facing imminent annihilation, the reader is compelled to root for them. And, whereas all of the Arab plots are foiled in the end, the Israeli blackmail succeeds: Washington bows to the threat and, with Moscow's grudging cooperation, forces the Arab states to halt their attack.[12]

Naturally, the Arab aggressors featured in these novels are an unsavory bunch: cruel, ruthless, fanatical, and sexually depraved. Scholars have extensively documented the scope and nature of anti-Arab portrayals in American popular culture of this era, and there is no need to replicate their work.[13] Receiving less attention have been portrayals of Americans' own shortcomings. Repeatedly, Middle East–themed thrillers of the mid-1970s depict the American people and their leaders as too petty, self-absorbed, gun-shy, or legalistic to meet the Arab challenge. In *Year of the Golden Ape*, local authorities, discovering that the hijacked tanker in San Francisco harbor is carrying a nuclear bomb, order an evacuation of the city. One resident hinders the effort by scrambling to salvage her jewelry; the operators of a gas truck sell fuel to stalled motorists at extortionate prices. When Palestinian terrorists take over the UN in *The Aleph Solution*, New York City officials hesitate to make extra demands on the police for fear of provoking a strike. Paralysis has gripped the national government as well. In *Cobalt 60*, American intelligence analysts learn that a gunboat belonging to the hostile Arab nation of Al Hakeer is heading for American shores with threatening missiles on board. When one analyst urges that the gunboat be intercepted, his colleague replies, "We're a long way from the old Cuban missile crisis. We're past the time when we could scratch an overt menace without a Supreme Court decision on the beauty of it all. Besides, it would become public and that would entail a lot of official explanations."[14]

To be sure, all of the Arab plots are thwarted in the end; the conventions of the genre demand no less. Yet these victories are won despite the shortcomings of American society and political culture, sometimes by individual Americans who break away from the herd, sometimes by Israeli agents who launch successful manhunts of their own. The latter pattern is especially noteworthy, for it is often through the prism of Israeli virtue and competence that American failings appear in sharpest focus.

In *Black Sunday* and *The Aleph Solution*, Israeli agents come to the United States to help their American counterparts track unfolding terrorist plots. It soon becomes obvious that the U.S. authorities are out of their depth and that only the Israelis possess the qualities necessary to thwart the enemy's designs. Melani McAlister and Tim Jon Semmerling have written perceptively about the 1977 film version of *Black Sunday*, focusing on David Kabakov, the Israeli Mossad agent who almost single-handedly defeats the Super Bowl plot. Kabakov, they show, is the decisive, resourceful hero who fights for an America too demoralized by the Vietnam experience to fight for itself. This reading also holds true for the original novel, which explicitly links America's inability to handle terrorism to its recent failures in Southeast Asia. The ghost of Vietnam is virtually absent from *The Aleph Solution*, in which U.S. impotence is unexplained. In both stories, though, the Israeli agents are exasperated by the American flaws and tolerate them only to achieve the overriding goal of stopping the terrorists. As Avram Tal, *The Aleph Solution*'s version of Kabakov, reports to an Israeli colleague, "I have been confining myself to Washington. They like to talk here and hold meetings, but they are very difficult to deal with when it comes to action. . . . And they don't know the Arabs. But we have to work with them, at present."[15] The "at present" is key, signaling that in the final showdown Israelis will face their Arab enemies alone, as comes to pass in both *The Aleph Solution* and *Black Sunday*.

Kabakov and Tal know they cannot rely on gentiles for protection. The purple numbers on their arms attest to this truth.[16] But few American characters show any understanding of this tragic history, and many are downright hostile to Jews—a remarkable feature of the genre that has received little, if any, scholarly attention. In the book version of *Black Sunday*, Kabakov attends a meeting with U.S. intelligence analysts and Secret Service agents. "Suddenly Kabakov was acutely aware that he was a foreigner, and a Jew at that. [He knew] that a number of the men in the room were thinking about the fact that he was a Jew. . . . In the minds of these men with their crisp haircuts and law school rings, he was identified with the problem rather than with the solution. The threat was from a bunch of foreigners, of which he was one. The attitude was unspoken, but it was there." In *The Aleph Solution*, an American general privately refers to Tal as "the Jew," suggesting that Tal's ethnicity, not his nationality, is what sets him apart from the U.S. officials with whom he consults.[17]

In other books, the American anti-Semitism is even more pronounced. Americans routinely refer to Israelis as "Jews," and do so with raw distaste. In *The Masada Plan*, a presidential adviser not only calls the Israeli ambassador "the Jewish ambassador" but has "a way of pronouncing the word 'Jew' or 'Jewish' with something close to a built-in sneer." In *Thirty-Four East*, an American general stationed in the Sinai has an affair with an Israeli female liaison officer, enraging his own female aide: "Liz's stomach griped with the nausea of raw jealousy. For an instant she wished with all her heart she could kill the Jew, disfigure her, claw her heavy Jewish breasts, and push nails into her Jewish belly." Another American officer privately disdains the general for "screwing a Jew officer." It is as if there were no Jews serving in the U.S. government or military. In *The Forty-First Thief*, an unscrupulous American oil executive dismisses the argument that Arab oil policies are harmful to U.S. strategic interests: "Bah. Jew chatter."[18]

In light of the unprecedented acceptance and success that American Jews had achieved by the 1970s, the prevalence of the American anti-Semitic archetype is striking. We should recall, however, that the authors of these novels were less than two decades removed from an era in which economic, social, and educational restrictions against Jews were widely accepted in the United States.[19] The attitudes underlying such restrictions would have been apparent to even modestly attentive observers of American society, and unavoidable to those who were themselves Jewish.[20] At the same time, the very fact that Jews had now "arrived" made it easier for writers to call attention to American anti-Semitism and to construct fictional scenarios in which it was pervasive. Hammering away at this theme also sent a geopolitical message: if even the United States was so inhospitable, then surely Jews needed a secure homeland elsewhere.[21]

If a single premise united the thrillers discussed above, it was that the American people and their leaders faced an existential threat from pitiless Arab adversaries but were shamefully ill equipped to meet the challenge. What, in actuality, should be done about this situation was not the explicit concern of the novelists, who after all were in the entertainment business. But many political commentators shared the novelists' bleak outlook and did make real-world recommendations for overcoming the paralysis that seemed to have gripped the American body politic. One of the most common responses, vividly suggested in the thrillers themselves, was to champion Israel's cause; if the United States was unable or unwilling to confront Arab threats, then at least it could provide Israel with the means to confront them itself. The "letter of the 76" of May 1975, in which seventy-six senators demanded that Israel receive unstinting military and economic support, was a conspicuous expression of this view.

Pro-Israel commentary became especially pronounced in the summer of 1976, following one of the most spectacular terrorist incidents of the decade. In late June, militants claiming affiliation with the Popular Front for the Liberation of Palestine hijacked an Air France flight out of Tel Aviv and forced it to land in Entebbe, Uganda. With the help of sympathetic Ugandan authorities, the hijackers moved the 257 passengers and crew into an unused terminal at the Entebbe airport, demanding the release of Palestinian and pro-Palestinian prisoners from jails in Israel and other countries. The hijackers blundered, however, by unilaterally releasing all of the non-Israeli hostages. Israel could now use force without being accused of endangering the citizens of other countries. In a midnight raid in early July, Israeli commandos flew the 2,500 miles to Uganda and slipped into the Entebbe airport. After a skirmish in which all of the hijackers, one Israeli commando, twenty Ugandan soldiers, and three hostages were killed, the rescuers freed the remaining 102 hostages, hustled them onto planes, and returned them to Israel.[22]

By any measure, the Entebbe raid was an extraordinary feat, and Americans across the political spectrum were thrilled and awestruck. It was impossible to avoid contrasting Israel's lightning triumph in Central Africa with America's own drawn-out humiliation in Southeast Asia. "If the United States would have mustered the same spirit the Israelis did in their Uganda mission," wrote the columnist Nick Thimmesch (usually a critic of Israeli militarism), "perhaps the Vietnam ordeal could have ended years before it did." The radio personality Paul Harvey observed, "Israel's . . . example of how to deal with skyjackers should teach us all an important and timely lesson." Accepting the Democratic Party's nomination for vice president in August, senator Walter Mondale of Minnesota seemed to take that lesson to heart. "We reject," he proclaimed to thunderous applause, ". . . the idea that this nation must sit by passively while terrorists maim and murder innocent men, women, and children."[23]

If granting Israel a free hand and seeking to emulate its tough stance on terrorism were popular options, to some commentators they didn't go nearly far enough. A year and a half before the Entebbe raid, a much bolder vision of U.S. power briefly animated the public discourse. In late 1974 and early 1975, a flurry of articles—most of them written by neoconservative intellectuals—agued that the U.S. military should respond to any further use of the oil weapon by seizing the oil fields of Saudi Arabia. Two of these articles were especially prominent: an essay in the January 1975 issue of *Commentary* by Robert W. Tucker, a political scientist at Johns Hopkins University and a leading neoconservative thinker; and a piece in the March 1975 *Harper's* written under the pseudonym "Miles Ignotus," Latin for "Unknown Soldier." The author turned out to be Edward Luttwak, another Johns Hopkins neoconservative who had recently published, under his own name, a shorter version of this argument in the London *Times Literary Supplement*.[24] The *Harper's* article offered the most detailed scenario for breaking the Arabs' oil power. In the event of another embargo, it urged, U.S. Marines should storm the beaches of eastern Saudi Arabia, and the 82nd Airborne Division conduct parachute drops further inland, to secure Saudi oil fields and force them back into production.

Both at home and abroad, the interventionist articles attracted considerable attention, partly because they carried a whiff of official inspiration. In December 1974, the syndicated columnist Jack Anderson reported that unnamed Pentagon officials were discussing "military intervention against the Arabs in case of a new oil embargo." In a January 1975 interview with *Business Week*, Henry Kissinger said that, while he could not foresee U.S.

military action simply to bring down the price of oil, different rules might apply "where there's some actual strangulation of the industrialized world." There is no evidence that the Ford administration seriously considered military intervention. It appears that Kissinger's real purpose, and perhaps that of Anderson's anonymous Pentagon sources, was to make Arab governments think twice about any future resort to the oil weapon. "If we play it boldly," Kissinger told Ford shortly after the interview appeared, "I think we have a fifty percent chance that if there is war there might be no embargo."[25]

Were the interventionist articles part of this government scheme to forewarn Arab oil producers? The *Harper's* piece clearly benefited from some official input, though precisely how much remains uncertain. In 2004, Luttwak discussed his role in the episode with the *Wall Street Journal*. "Mr. Luttwak," the journal reported, "says he wrote the piece after discussion with several like-minded consultants and officials in the Pentagon. . . . Mr. Luttwak says they wanted to demonstrate the merits of 'maneuver warfare,' the use of fast, light forces to penetrate the enemy's vital centers. 'We set out to revolutionize war,' Mr. Luttwak says." Whether Kissinger himself had a hand in the *Harper's* article, or the others like it, is unclear. James Akins, who was then the U.S. ambassador to Saudi Arabia—and who at the time publicly denounced the invasion scenario as the product of "sick minds"—told *Mother Jones* in 2003 that all of the interventionist articles had resulted from "a deep background briefing" by Kissinger.[26] But Akins did not say how he acquired this knowledge, and no other evidence points to Kissinger's role in the articles' production.

Also difficult to gauge is the overall impact of these invasion threats, whether by Kissinger, the neoconservative essayists, or Anderson's anonymous sources. In the short term, the threats caused an uproar in the Arab world and severely strained the Ford administration's relations with the Saudi government, which demanded clarification of U.S. intentions and warned that it was booby-trapping its own oil wells. Without retracting the *Business Week* comments, Kissinger and Ford insisted to the Saudis that the United States had no intention of intervening, and Riyadh warily accepted the assurances.[27] In March 1975, King Faisal was assassinated, and the spat over the invasion threats was shelved and mostly forgotten.

Within the United States, the option of intervening for Persian Gulf oil attracted little public support. Most mainstream commentators agreed that force would be justified only in the direst circumstances. The principal dispute was between those who thought Kissinger had performed a useful service in saying there *was* a point at which Western forbearance would run out and those who saw his warning as needlessly provocative.[28] In a nationwide Gallup poll, only 10 percent of respondents favored military action in the event of another embargo.[29]

Among neoconservatives, however, Tucker's *Commentary* article—which, unlike the *Harper's* piece, had a known author at the time—was hailed as a brilliant analysis of the West's predicament and a devastating critique of the flaccidity of U.S. policy. As Daniel Patrick Moynihan's defense of Zionism would do far more prominently months later, Tucker's article helped to sharpen the neoconservative perspective on foreign affairs, especially relating to the Middle East. Meanwhile, Luttwak's *Harper's* article, and the manner in which it was produced, provided an early instance of cooperation between neoconservative commentators and hawkish officials within the defense establishment, a partnership that would deepen in the coming decades. Some journalists and historians have portrayed the Tucker and Luttwak pieces as the genesis of the "preventive war" doctrine that the administration of George W. Bush championed in the early 2000s.[30] That goes too far, but certainly they were a foreshadowing of things to come.

There were limits, then, to the power of anti-Arab narratives to shape political outcomes. Such narratives could reinforce pro-Israel tendencies, but they could not stimulate a popular appetite for the use of force against Arab adversaries. The picture was further complicated by a set of minor but insistent counternarratives, making the case that Arab actors were being unfairly maligned or that U.S. partiality toward Israel had attained unhealthy proportions. Like the dominant anti-Arab narratives they challenged, the pro-Arab counternarratives grew sharper and more numerous in the middle years of the decade, but they faced special disadvantages as well. These included the sheer force, at least in relative terms, of the dominant narratives; the overreliance of pro-Arab polemicists on pragmatic rather than principled appeals; and the ease with which some of those polemicists could be dismissed as self-interested, unscrupulous, or even bigoted figures.

In political fiction, a handful of works resisted the common portrayal of the Arab world as fanatical and aggressive. Two financial thrillers, *The Crash of '79*, by Paul Erdman (1976), and *The Petrodollar Takeover*, by Peter Tanous and Paul Rubinstein (1975), posited a complex international order in which Arabs were no more blameworthy than most other actors.[31] *The Crash of '79* was by far the more successful of the two, selling four million copies before the calendar rendered it obsolete. (The West German publisher extended the book's shelf life by renaming it *The Crash of '81*.) The fact that the author was an American banker whose international intrigues had briefly landed him in a Swiss jail, from which he launched his second career as a financial fiction writer, no doubt enhanced the novel's credibility and cachet.[32] The book weaves together two main plotlines, a global financial crisis brought about by America's overreliance on petrodollars, and a Middle East war precipitated by the aggressive designs of the shah of Iran (the actual Mohammad Reza Shah Pahlavi, whose ouster in early 1979 Erdman could not have foreseen). Working together, these two events cause a collapse of the world's economy and a reversion of the industrialized nations to subsistence agriculture and barter. Still, the gusto and flair with which the first-person narrator recounts the catastrophe, and the fact that he's doing so from an idyllic Northern California setting where it is difficult to regret the slide into pastoralization, keep the tale from becoming too dispiriting.

While some of *The Crash of '79*'s Arab characters are unsavory, most of them—especially members of the Saudi political and financial elite—are cultivated and restrained players of the international game, men who try, albeit imperfectly, to harmonize their country's interests with the needs of the global economy. The real villain is the power-mad shah, whose bid to dominate the Middle East triggers the final calamity. Also culpable are a handful of renegade Israeli agents who secretly assist the Iranian monarch, though occasional references to the Nazi Holocaust, to the anti-Semitism of American bankers and oil executives, and to Israel's vulnerability place that country's actions in a generally sympathetic light.[33]

The Petrodollar Takeover is even more Arab-friendly. One of its authors, Peter Tanous, was a Lebanese American investment banker and the nephew of Peter S. Tanous, the National Association of Arab Americans' first president. (His partner Paul Rubinstein, a stockbroker and cookbook writer, was the son of the pianist Arthur Rubenstein.)[34] In the book, the Saudi government tries to buy General Motors, enlisting the services of an ambitious young Lebanese American Wall Street trader named John Haddad, who starts surreptitiously purchasing GM stock. The planned takeover becomes public knowledge, provoking an outcry within the United States. Eventually, however, through a shrewd combination of pressure tactics and generous concessions, Haddad and the Saudis persuade the interested parties—the president, Congress, the GM management, and the United Auto Workers—to set aside their nativist misgivings and accept a modified version of the sale. While the book occasionally tweaks the extravagance of wealthy Arabs, it portrays the leaders of oil-producing Arab countries as sophisticated and moderate. Aware that their own success depends on a thriving global economy and good relations with the United States, these leaders take care not to overplay their hand. Instead, the novel expresses disdain for the "Archie Bunker, flag-waving hardhats" in the UAW who oppose the Saudi takeover bid and for the politicians and commentators who exploit workers' xenophobia.[35] Much of the novel's suspense turns on whether Haddad and his Saudi friends can overcome such groundless hostility and show that the "petrodollar takeover" will do no harm.

For all its criticism of prevailing sentiment, *The Petrodollar Takeover* received respectful reviews and generated no visible controversy.[36] This was largely owing, no doubt, to the authors' decision to set the novel in a future era in which the Arab-Israeli dispute had already been settled. Thus the book could criticize anti-Arab attitudes without once mentioning the conflict that had done so much to exacerbate them. Offered up by authors of Arab and Jewish background, *The Petrodollar Takeover* could even be read as a symbolic declaration of truce in the Arab-Israeli conflict. But there was a third dissenting novel that did not in the least shy away from Arab-Israeli controversy. That book, *The Canfield Decision* (1976), by none other than former vice president Spiro Agnew, portrayed the American political and media establishments as outrageously biased in Israel's favor. Agnew wrote the book for the explicit purpose of sparking a debate about the situation. Much to his dismay, however, the controversy he generated tended merely to reinforce the pro-Israel tilt of American public discourse. Worse still for Agnew, he came to exemplify in the public mind the disturbing American archetype—unprincipled, venal, crude, and, worst of all, anti-Semitic—then so prevalent in the thriller genre.

Agnew began his novel almost immediately after resigning the vice presidency in October 1973. The Maryland bribery case that forced his ouster not only saddled him with huge legal fees and tax assessments but also resulted in his disbarment. He needed to make a lot of money quickly but could not fall back on his original profession. Tided over by a $200,000 loan from Frank Sinatra, a close friend, Agnew decided to try his hand at writing. A book of memoirs would have been the traditional choice, but Agnew opted for fiction instead. "I felt it was not appropriate for me to do 'serious' writing now," he wrote in an article published in the *Ladies' Home Journal* in May 1974, when the project was at an early stage. "I am far too bitter. A novel would get me away from the limited perspective of my own troubles. My serious book, the book about my own experiences, will be

Figure 15. The author and his opus, 1977. © Hulton-Deutsch Collection/CORBIS.

written—but not until after the Nixon administration leaves office." (His political memoir, *Go Quietly . . . Or Else*, appeared in 1980.) Creative writing would also be therapeutic. "This book is very important to me," Agnew continued, "—from a financial standpoint, yes, but not solely for that. I want an accomplishment that is all mine that will be respected. . . . When you have been through what I have been through, it is important to reinstill in yourself your confidence and belief in your worth as a human being. And what could be more personal than writing?"[37]

Sinatra was apprehensive. "You're going to write your serious book, aren't you?" Agnew recalled him asking. "I told him yes, but this novel is something I'm going to do first. Francis answered, 'I think you should stick to your serious book. This novel might be misconstrued and affect the serious things you might want to write later.' I assured him that I saw the danger and would be careful to avoid anything connected with reality." Agnew pressed ahead with his literary venture, and by February 1974 he had won a contract from Playboy Press and a reported advance valued at somewhere between $50,000 and $250,000.[38]

Alas, the Chairman of the Board's prescient warning had fallen on deaf ears. Far from avoiding current controversy, Agnew was courting it with a vengeance. He saw his book project as an opportunity to settle scores with the liberal intelligentsia he had battled as vice president. To some extent, Agnew was resurrecting a conservative taunt from the late 1960s and early 1970s: that it was hypocritical for liberals to oppose military assistance to South Vietnam while clamoring to arm Israel to the teeth.[39] But Agnew went a step further. Instead of treating support for Israel as a laudable policy that should be replicated elsewhere—the typical stance of those alleging a liberal double standard—he took the view that such support was a wrongheaded inducement to Israeli intransigence. He had also come to believe that American Zionists (whom he tended to conflate with liberals, ignoring the pro-Israel outlooks of many conservatives and virtually all neoconservatives) were prone to vilify Israel's critics in ways that stifled healthy debate. These were hardly unreasonable positions, but Agnew proved incapable of presenting them with any subtlety or tact.

The novel, which Agnew wrote over the next two years, is set in 1983–1984 and features a fictional American vice president named Porter Newfield Canfield, a liberal Brahman meant to bear no resemblance to everyman Agnew. To ingratiate himself with the liberal media and win his party's presidential nomination, Canfield presents himself as more pro-Israel than the administration he serves, even advocating the transfer to Israel of nuclear-armed intermediate-range ballistic missiles (IRBMs). Unbeknownst to Canfield, a hard-line anticommunist Iranian group called the Persian Protective League (PPL), fearing that the Soviet Union intends to take over Iran under cover of détente, seeks to foment an Arab-Israeli war that will spark a superpower confrontation. The PPL teams up with a militant American Zionist group called Israel Now and Forever, led by a thuggish activist named Yoram Halevi (whose menacing aspect is only slightly softened by a fondness for Earth shoes). The PPL tells Halevi that American media barons have agreed to sell controlling shares of their news operations to Arab investors. Believing the lie, Halevi murders a prominent magazine publisher and makes it appear to be the work of Arab terrorists. In the resulting anti-Arab hysteria, the liberal establishment takes up Canfield's demand that Israel be armed with nuclear missiles, and the president reluctantly complies. Thus emboldened, Israel launches air strikes against its Arab neighbors. A full-scale Arab-Israeli war looms, and with it a terrifying superpower confrontation.

Disaster is averted, but not before the entire liberal commentariat have shown themselves to be the knowing accomplices or feckless stooges of Zionist schemes. In one scene, Vice President Canfield cynically contemplates the pro-Israel opinion leaders he must enlist in his presidential bid: "He was convinced that Israel was the key to his campaign. . . . The American Zionists wanted the American sword to rattle every time a potential attacker made the slightest threat toward their darling. They, who had been the strongest advocates of abandoning Southeast Asia to the communists, were perfectly willing to send war materials, advisors and even armed troops if Israel was attacked." After Halevi kills the magazine publisher and pins the blame on a fictitious organization called Defenders of Arab Militant Nationalism, all hell breaks loose:

> The moderate Arab nations denied any connection with or knowledge of DAMN, but that won them no respite from the fire-spitters in the press and government. There was a mounting swell of sympathy for Israel and much pressure for assuring her of American support. . . . Sensing a receptive audience, the Israelis floated tons of propaganda allegedly documenting plans of an Arab-Soviet attack on them. The plea for IRBM's was intensified, and the American press and public demanded that the Congress and the President of the United States deliver the weapons.[40]

Passages such as these were crude and tendentious but not inherently anti-Semitic, for Agnew had taken pains to target an ideology rather than an ethnicity. Elsewhere in the book, he was less careful. In a Tehran meeting, a PPL activist named Reza tells his comrades,

> American Jews exert an influence on American opinion that is far heavier than their numbers would indicate. They are the strongest single influence

> in the big media—the media with worldwide impact. They control much of the financial community, and through it, large segments of the academic community. Therefore, they heavily affect, through propaganda, the majority of the Congress. Oh, they scream anti-Semitism whenever anyone mentions their power, but it's true. Look at the tortured differentiations that the intellectuals tried to create between aid to Israel and aid to Vietnam. The Viet Cong were oppressed patriots, but the Palestinians were anarchists.

True, these are the words of a foreigner, and a fairly unsympathetic one at that, but Reza's recognition of the Israel/Vietnam hypocrisy—Exhibit A in the Agnevian brief against pro-Israel liberals—establishes the Iranian as an astute observer of the American scene. Another passage, this one in the voice of the omniscient narrator, leaves little doubt as to Agnew's own view. After Canfield gives a pro-Israel speech in Phoenix, the applause is "courteous, but hardly thunderous. After all, less than 15 percent of the crowd was Jewish. Down at the press table, where less than 15 percent was not Jewish, the reaction was ecstatic."[41]

While working on his novel, Agnew launched a business venture that became intertwined with his literary pursuits. In June 1974, he founded Pathlite Inc., an international consulting firm. Soon Agnew was circling the globe, using the contacts he had acquired as vice president to help his corporate clients win contracts overseas. Saudi Arabia was a major target of opportunity. In 1971, Agnew had visited the country and gotten to know King Faisal and other members of the royal family. Pathlite gave him every incentive to maintain those relationships, and in the mid- to late 1970s he travelled frequently to the kingdom and conducted a warm, and occasionally fawning, correspondence with Faisal, his successor King Khalid, and several highly placed Saudi princes.[42]

Critics later charged that Agnew turned against Israel in order to improve his clients' prospects in the Arab world.[43] The accusation missed the mark: Agnew was a true believer. Having staked out an anti-Zionist position, however, he was not above turning it to his business advantage. In the spring of 1976, Agnew proposed to Saudi officials an implicit quid pro quo whereby the kingdom would reward his anti-Zionist activities by giving favorable consideration to his clients' contracting bids.[44] On March 11, he sent two letters to Ali Alireza, the Saudi ambassador to the United States. One letter was addressed to Alireza himself; the other was to be forwarded to Crown Prince Fahd, then serving as Saudi Arabia's first deputy premier. The letter to Fahd described planned publicity for *The Canfield Decision*: "In mid May,

I will be appearing on many national television shows to promote my book, which will be published on May 17th. These TV appearances will provide opportunities to promote our cause, especially because the book deals with the Arab-Israeli question in a way that will infuriate the Zionists. Therefore I will be questioned about my views on Israel." The letter to Alireza described the scheduled television appearances in greater detail and then made a pitch for the Atlantic International Corporation, a U.S. construction firm seeking contracts to build houses and schools in Saudi Arabia.[45]

In an April 5 letter to Fahd, Agnew was more direct. He began with a plaintive recitation of his financial woes, the result of legal and tax penalties "based solely on the testimony of my Zionist accusers"—a reference to some Jewish businessmen in Maryland who had testified against him in the federal bribery case that ended his political career. Agnew then requested Fahd's "personal assistance" in reviewing the bids of several Pathlite clients seeking contracts from the Saudi government, including Atlantic International. "The commission would help me very much," he wrote, with disarming frankness, of one of the bids. In closing, Agnew reiterated his commitment to "crushing the unfair information constantly exercised because of Zionist control of our news media" and pledged to continue the fight even if his clients' bids failed.[46]

Agnew's papers contain no Saudi responses to these letters, and the fate of the other bids is difficult to reconstruct. But later that year Atlantic International concluded an $11 million contract to build schools in Saudi Arabia, and Agnew received an $80,000 commission.[47] Of course, it is possible that the bid succeeded despite, rather than because of, Agnew's bumptious approaches to Alireza and Fahd. In any case, Agnew was lucky that his critics never got their hands on these letters.

Agnew's literary debut was contentious enough as it was. In mid-May, *The Canfield Decision* finally appeared, to a generally hostile reception in the American news media. Many of the objections were aesthetic. Critics ridiculed the book's overly expository dialogue and inept lovemaking scenes (taking special delight in passages that combined those two features). In a review for the *New York Times*, the economist John Kenneth Galbraith cheekily hailed the novel as "a major document on the way English is used in Washington and how the plague can spread." Meg Greenfield of *Newsweek* deadpanned that Agnew's effort "does not represent a clear and present danger to Dostoevsky's reputation." At least now we know the book wasn't ghostwritten, more than one wag observed.[48]

Receiving much sharper criticism were the book's venomous portrayals of Zionists and Jews, and Agnew's further comments on the subject. Just as Agnew had predicted, his novel was released amid a flurry of national television interviews. On NBC's *Today* show, Barbara Walters asked if Agnew really thought a "Jewish cabal" wielded excessive influence in American politics. Agnew replied that "Zionist influences" prevented the United States from adopting "an evenhanded policy in the Middle East." He noted Israel's practice of building Jewish settlements in the occupied territories and said, "I feel that because of the Zionist influences in the United States these matters of aggression are routinely considered to be permissible."[49]

These were defensible claims, but Agnew didn't stop there. Asked by *Newsweek* if he believed that the press was "unduly influenced by Zionist opinion," he said, "I don't think there's any question about that. . . . All you have to do is look around and see who owns the networks, who owns The Washington Post . . . The New York Times. . . . As you look around in . . . the big news business you see a heavy concentration of Jewish people. Now I'm not saying this is wrong. I'm saying it has to color to some extent their comprehension of what takes place." In a *Washington Star* interview, Agnew named names: "For example, CBS, Mr. [William] Paley's Jewish. And this is not said in a defamatory way. Mr. Julian Goodman, who runs NBC, there's a Mr. Leonard Goldenson at ABC. Mrs. [Katharine] Graham of the Washington Post. Mr. Sulzberger of the New York Times . . . how can these people be totally objective where Israel is concerned?"[50]

A storm of outrage descended on Agnew. Editorials across the country denounced his views as bigoted and wrongheaded. (Several news stories and commentaries attributed the phrase "Jewish cabal" to Agnew, even though the words had been Barbara Walters's.) The Anti-Defamation League blasted Agnew's "anti-Semitic canards" and solicited comments from President Ford and former governor of Georgia Jimmy Carter, the presumptive Democratic nominee for president. Both leaders obliged with public statements criticizing Agnew's remarks. Agnew's former speechwriter William Safire and former press secretary Victor Gold wrote opinion pieces disavowing their old boss and insisting he was no longer the man they had served. "Funny, but he didn't *look* anti-Jewish," commented Gold.[51]

Although Agnew was, after a fashion, now championing their cause, Arab American activists generally kept their distance from him, presumably recognizing how radioactive he had become (if not already repelled by his reactionary stances on other issues and by the aura of corruption surrounding him). The exception to this rule was the irrepressible M.T. Mehdi, who, in a late June letter to the former vice president, praised Agnew's efforts to achieve "a better balance in the news" and proposed a meeting to "exchange ideas as to the things we can do in the beloved U.S.A." There is no indication that Agnew responded to the overture; an association with Mehdi could hardly have helped his case.[52]

Addressing the broader public reaction, Agnew indignantly protested that he was no bigot and that, as a son of Greek immigrants, he had long identified with American Jews. He wrote letters to Jewish friends and associates seeking their understanding and advice. Some of the recipients sent compassionate responses, gently suggesting that Agnew might reconsider his inflammatory language. "I know that you are not anti-semetic [*sic*] and I am delighted to learn that you are sensitive to the problems which you have inadvertently created," wrote Cynthia Rosenwald, who had served on Agnew's gubernatorial and vice presidential staffs. Still, "you must . . . try to understand our views based on bitter emperical [*sic*] experience as to the impact of certain phrases." Others seemed to regard Agnew as a lost cause. "I would not presume to tell you what to do or not do," wrote Jerold Hoffberger, part owner of the Baltimore Orioles and president of the Council of Jewish Federations and Welfare Funds. "This is a free country. But . . . when we choose to follow a certain course, we also have to live with the consequences."[53]

For Agnew, the consequences were far from happy. Although *The Canfield Decision* sold well, the controversy it generated thoroughly undermined his effort to challenge pro-Israel biases in American discourse.[54] Agnew was so preoccupied with salvaging his reputation that he could scarcely advance his original thesis, and indeed was obliged to cede some ground. In a July 30 appearance on ABC TV's *Good Morning America*, he acknowledged that his approach was one-sided. But that was no longer the point: "What I'm defending myself against is a charge of anti-Semitism, not the fact that I may be biased—not even the fact that I may be wrong." Poor Agnew even had to give away the book's surprise ending, disclosing to *Newsweek* that "the bad guy turns out to be a South Yemen agent of the Communist Chinese—and not a Jew at all."[55] True enough: Yoram Halevi's real name is Ibrahim Abdullah. Of course, this revelation hardly got Agnew off the hook for his scathing portrayals of American Zionists and their lackeys in the media.

Like their anti-Arab counterparts, the Arab-friendly thrillers had a real-world analogue in political commentary. Indeed, Agnew's literary debut was an unabashed—and spectacularly unsuccessful—effort to bridge the realms of entertainment and advocacy. Other critics of the prevailing view stuck mainly to advocacy, though they, too, sometimes employed a device that had become central to Middle East–themed fiction: the extension of current trends into dark future scenarios. Practitioners of this approach included two of the most influential American proponents of Arab-Israeli "even-handedness" at the time, former Arkansas senator J. William Fulbright and former undersecretary of state George W. Ball.[56] As Democratic Party elder statesmen, Fulbright and Ball had high-level access to U.S. policy makers (though Kissinger privately complained about "idiots like George Ball"), and during the 1976 presidential campaign Ball was on Jimmy Carter's short list for secretary of state, a position awarded to Cyrus Vance.[57] For all their prominence, however, both Fulbright and Ball faced daunting obstacles in their efforts to jolt their fellow citizens into recognizing the dangers of siding too closely with Israel.

Fulbright employed the futuristic approach most conspicuously in a July 1975 opinion piece in the *Washington Star* designed to dramatize the need for a comprehensive settlement entailing Israel's withdrawal to the 1967 borders in exchange for Arab recognition. (Fulbright's long-standing advocacy of such a settlement had infuriated pro-Israel groups and helped to ensure his defeat to Dale Bumpers in Arkansas's Democratic primary a year earlier.) Writing from an imagined vantage point in 1980, Fulbright looked back over a half decade of catastrophes, all resulting from Washington's failure to induce Israel to relinquish the occupied territories. The narrative amounts to the standard Arabist nightmare scenario—another war, another oil embargo—updated to include the neoconservative intervention schemes of late 1974 and early 1975. On day three of the "Ten Days' War" of 1976, which Israel wins, the oil producing Arab states impose an embargo on NATO countries, plunging the West into chaos. Desperate for oil, the United States launches an invasion of Kuwait and eastern Saudi Arabia, only to find that local saboteurs have set the oil fields ablaze. No sooner have the flames been doused than an Arab summit meeting in Khartoum declares jihad against the United States and rescinds previous offers to recognize Israel within the 1967 borders, demanding instead a return to the 1947 UN partition plan, which envisioned a substantially smaller Jewish state. Bombs start going off in American cities.[58]

This is all too much for the American body politic. Politicians who once championed Israel's cause now turn on the Jewish state, echoing the demand that it withdraw to the 1947 partition lines. The narrative ends in the summer of 1980, with Fulbright pondering an invitation to participate in a rally at the Washington Monument supporting the imposition of the 1947 lines. At the rally, the invitation promises, one of that year's presidential candidates, "hitherto regarded as an all-out supporter of Israel, will lead a ceremonial burning of the notorious 'letter of the 76' of May 1975," which called for full military support of Israel. Fulbright declines the invitation, writing to the chief organizer, "I still adhere to my long-standing conviction that Israel is entitled to a secure national existence within its borders of 1967. I am aware that this view is generally considered outmoded, but I adhere to it in the belief that the United States must honor its solemn commitments."[59] Fulbright does not have to add that this whole tragedy could have been avoided had Americans, years earlier, heeded his advice.

Fulbright's real-time message was clear: Israel's true friends were not those who enabled its intransigence but rather were those, like Fulbright himself, who urged Israel to make reasonable concessions for peace. (The Israelis "are so paranoid they don't know their interest," the former senator privately complained to President Ford in July 1975, the same month in which Fulbright's futuristic scenario appeared.)[60] This claim was suggested in the very title of a like-minded piece by George Ball, "How to Save Israel in Spite of Herself," published in the April 1977 issue of *Foreign Affairs*. Like Fulbright, Ball called for a comprehensive settlement to spare Israel, and the world, from catastrophe. Though writing in a more standard argumentative style, he, too, invited readers to imagine the grim scenarios that might unfold in the absence of such a settlement. "Let us suppose," he wrote, "that in the next war Israel's arms prevail and an Israeli column were moving on Damascus." Would the Soviets come to Syria's aid? If so, would Washington sit idly by, or would it counter Moscow's move and thus launch World War III? "Or, as a possible alternative, assume that Arab arms were prevailing and Israel was in imminent danger of invasion. Would the United States use its military might on Israel's behalf? It takes no great prescience to imagine the searing debate that issue would provoke. Nor can one ignore the possibility that, threatened with destruction, Israel might use, or at least threaten to use, nuclear weapons." And whatever happened on the battlefield, Ball noted, the next war would almost certainly trigger another oil embargo, this one far more destructive than the last, given the world's greater reliance on Arab oil.[61]

It is doubtful that these gripping scenarios changed many minds, in part because of the ease with which their authors could be dismissed. For although Fulbright and Ball were respected figures, and although neither carried anything like Agnew's toxic baggage, both faced the suspicion that their views on the Middle East owed more to recently acquired business interest than to political conviction. In fact, each man had come by his opinions honestly and many years earlier. But it didn't help that in 1976 Fulbright registered with the Justice Department as an agent of the United Arab Emirates and soon thereafter became an unofficial adviser to the Saudi government. In the mid- to late 1970s, no feature article on the rising "Arab lobby" was complete if it failed to mention that the enterprise had enlisted the former chairman of the Senate Foreign Relations Committee.[62]

Ball should have been harder to characterize in this manner. His job as a senior partner in the investment firm Lehman Brothers required no particular fealty to Arab interests; the firm's reach was global, and its partners and clients included Israelis and strong supporters of Israel. But nasty rumors circulated anyway. In early 1975, Ball complained to senator Henry M. Jackson of Washington that the latter's aide, Richard Perle, already an influential figure in neoconservative circles, was whispering to reporters that Ball had adopted pro-Arab positions in order to attract Arab clients. Months later a *Washington Post* reporter phoned Ball for his reaction to similar allegations. "I would like to think one could express views with regard to a major aspect of American policy," Ball wrote in reply, "without having those views attributed to some sinister, or selfish, motive." A vain hope. In 1978, when Ball testified before Congress in support of the sale of U.S. military aircraft to Egypt and Saudi Arabia, the syndicated columnist Holmes Alexander wrote that Ball was "speaking for it without a fee (but who does something for nothing?)."[63]

But probably more damaging to Fulbright's and Ball's credibility, at least over the long term, was their reliance on scare tactics. Repeatedly in the mid-1970s, both men predicted that dire consequences would befall the United States if Israel failed to relinquish all of the occupied territories. Pullbacks on the Sinai would not suffice, they warned. If Israel held on to the remaining lands occupied in 1967, the Arab states would launch another major war, bringing the world to economic ruin and, perhaps, the nuclear abyss. Either eventuality would be catastrophic for ordinary Americans, and so all had a vital interest in ensuring that Arab grievances were addressed.[64] But what if these fears were overblown? What if the Israeli occupation continued indefinitely and the Arab reaction did not exceed general resentment against the United States and, at the very most, sporadic or localized acts of violence? In the mid-1970s, there was little in Fulbright's or Ball's rhetoric to suggest that this less dramatic outcome would be intolerable. Although both men occasionally spoke of the issue in moral terms—noting, for example, that the Israeli occupation violated the principle of national self-determination—such critiques were rare and fleeting.[65] Fulbright and Ball evidently assumed that American audiences would be far more responsive to fear-based arguments. This assumption was probably correct, but fearmongering could work only so long as the invoked dangers were believable.

Increasingly, they weren't. The Sinai II Agreement of 1975 provisionally removed Egypt from the Arab-Israeli conflict, an outcome finalized, as we shall see, by the Camp David process of 1978–1979. Without Egypt, Israel's two remaining military antagonists, Syria and the Palestine Liberation Organization, had few prospects for resuming large-scale hostilities, and both parties, in any case, were now enmeshed in the chaos of Lebanon. The Saudis had made it clear that the petroleum weapon would be unsheathed only in the event of another general war, so oil pressures steadily receded as well.[66] There was, to be sure, a lag in Americans' awareness of these realities, at both the elite and the popular levels. Fears of a concerted Arab onslaught persisted well after the geopolitical basis for it had crumbled. By the late 1970s, however, such premonitions were losing their hold on the public imagination, and Fulbright and Ball themselves were obliged to modify their warnings. They continued to sound the alarm against an Arab-Israeli war but did so in vaguer and more perfunctory terms, dispensing with lurid detail. Ball, for his part, increasingly focused on the more diffuse costs—rising Arab antagonism toward the United States, greater localized violence and international terrorism—that a perpetuation of the Israeli occupation would likely entail.[67] There was good reason to worry about these outcomes, too, but they paled in comparison with the apocalyptic visions of the mid-1970s. Nor could they match the actual international challenges Americans faced at decade's end, such as the Iranian revolution and hostage crisis, the Soviet invasion of Afghanistan, and the sharp increase in Cold War tensions.

The foreboding counsels of Fulbright and Ball were best suited to that mid-seventies moment when Arab political actors seemed more united, determined, disciplined, and resourceful than ever before—an impression fostered by such spectacular international events as the October War, the oil embargo, and the Zionism-is-racism vote in the UN. In the second half of the decade, upheavals in Lebanon, in Arab-Israeli diplomacy, in the Persian Gulf region, and elsewhere perturbed and fractured the Arab world, eventually making it appear less coherent and formidable. There would be worries aplenty for U.S. officials entrusted with making and implementing policy toward the region, but the specter of a concerted Arab onslaught was a fading presence in the American mind.

Chapter 7

Fallen Cedar

The Lebanese Civil War and the United States, 1975–1979

On the morning of July 27, 1976, the U.S. government conducted its second and last evacuation of American citizens out of civil war-torn Lebanon. About a hundred Americans, along with some two hundred other foreigners, boarded a landing craft that ferried them from a West Beirut dock to the U.S.S. *Coronado*, a Navy transport ship anchored a few miles out to sea, which was to take them on a two-day voyage to Athens. The evacuation was voluntary, and over twelve hundred other U.S. citizens, most of them of Lebanese ancestry, chose to remain in the country. Among the evacuees were twenty U.S. embassy officials, including Talcott W. Seelye, president Gerald Ford's special representative, sent to Lebanon following the assassination of the U.S. ambassador six weeks earlier. "Don't worry," Seelye said as he boarded the landing craft. "I'll be back." He would not be.[1] Only fifteen U.S. embassy employees stayed behind, twelve of them marines charged with guarding the post. Most of the embassy's files went out with the evacuees. Providing security for the departing foreigners were gunmen from the Palestine Liberation Organization (PLO), the dominant force in that part of the city.[2]

A few miles to the east, on the outskirts of Beirut, other PLO guerrillas fought desperately to relieve the refugee camp of Tal al-Za'tar, which right-wing Christian militias had besieged for weeks, creating hellish conditions for its mostly civilian inhabitants. The rightists bombarded the camp with U.S. weapons and ordinance, supplied by Israel with America's blessing. They also received logistical support from Syria, which months earlier had supported the PLO but now fought in Lebanon alongside the Christian rightists. From Washington, Henry Kissinger celebrated Syria's shift in allegiances, which he had partly facilitated. But he was annoyed with "the damned Christians," whose shelling of Beirut's airport precluded an airborne evacuation of American citizens. Didn't the rightists realize who their ultimate benefactors were?[3]

These events tell little of the agonies Lebanon endured as the civil war touched its nadir in the summer of 1976. But they do hint at the chaotic politics that held Lebanon in its grip and that American diplomats tried, simultaneously, to keep at a safe distance and bend to their own purposes. It was somehow appropriate that, at the very moment of his government's near abandonment of Lebanon, Kissinger was coming to see that he had, through cunning and luck, solved a diplomatic conundrum that had bedeviled him for months. Evidently, the Syrians *could* move into Lebanon to restrain their erstwhile allies without provoking an Israeli response that ignited a wider conflagration. If the United States was powerless to influence Lebanese events directly, or even maintain an effective diplomatic presence in the country, it could still shape the regional environment in which the civil war unfolded and thus keep the crisis contained within Lebanon itself. It was fitting, too, that the effort to remove American citizens from Lebanon entailed another, much smaller, geopolitical inversion. As right-wing Christians inadvertently blocked the aerial departure of American residents—civilian embodiments of the nation on which the rightists pinned their final hopes—smiling PLO guerrillas, with roses nestled in the barrels of their Kalashnikov assault rifles, spirited those residents to a seaborne rescue.

The mostly Lebanese American citizens who stayed behind represented another set of actors in the drama: Americans of Lebanese descent. Those in Lebanon, many living in rural villages, could do little more than seek physical security for themselves and their families. Stateside Lebanese Americans, and Arab Americans generally, were much freer to respond to Lebanon's crisis. Throughout the civil war, many threw themselves into the tasks of appealing for an end to the carnage, raising funds for humanitarian relief, calling for a constructive U.S. role, and outlining the principles for national reconciliation. Overall, though, Lebanese Americans and Arab Americans said less about Lebanon than one might expect. Not until the summer of 1976 did a politically oriented Lebanese American organization with any staying power—the American Lebanese League—form at the national level, and its visibility was low for the next two years. Of the national Arab American groups, the Association of Arab American University Graduates (AAUG) developed a clear, if somewhat facile, analysis of the Lebanese crisis but devoted relatively little energy to purveying it, preferring to focus on the Palestine struggle. The National Association of Arab Americans (NAAA), though overwhelmingly Lebanese American, was even more reluctant to discuss Lebanon, and when it did so it offered platitudes. It, too, much preferred to address the Arab-Israeli conflict. In different ways and to varying degrees, all three organizations seemed daunted by the complexity of Lebanon's crisis. Indeed, their handling of the issue became much more robust in the years after the civil war of 1975–1976 had ended. By then, the crisis had been regionalized in ways that allowed commentators to elide its internal intricacies.

The Lebanese civil war was a struggle for political dominance between two loosely defined coalitions.[4] The first coalition, almost exclusively Christian and commonly referred to as the Lebanese Right, saw Lebanon as a hybrid nation that had as much in common with the Christian West as it did with the Muslim Middle East—more so, in the view of some. Members of this coalition wanted to strengthen Lebanon's geopolitical orientation toward the West and preserve its intricate confessional system, which, based on a 1932 census that had revealed a small Christian majority, distributed political power in ways that favored Maronite Christians. The other coalition, mostly Sunni and Shia Muslims but also including Druze and a substantial number of Christians, was commonly known as the Lebanese Left. It saw Lebanon as primarily Arab in character, wanted to end the country's alignment with the West, and sought either to reform the confessional system so that it accorded more closely with demographic realities (which clearly no longer included a Christian majority) or to abolish confessionalism altogether.[5] The Left also called for the redistribution of Lebanon's economic resources and saw itself as the champion of impoverished Lebanese of all religions, though relatively few poor Christians flocked to its banner.

The emergence of an independent Palestinian movement after 1967, and especially the relocation of the PLO's headquarters from Jordan to Lebanon after 1971, had introduced another axis of conflict. These events transformed South Lebanon into a staging area for PLO attacks against

Israel, provoking, in turn, increasingly lethal Israeli reprisal raids (and preemptive strikes) that victimized Palestinians and Lebanese alike. While most organs of Lebanese opinion portrayed Israel as the primary culprit, a growing number of Lebanese came to resent the PLO for drawing their country into the firing line. A related complaint was that the PLO had established a "state within a state" in Lebanon, challenging the authority of the national government. Mobilizing these sentiments, the Lebanese Right sought to curtail PLO activities within Lebanon or even expel the Palestinians outright. The Lebanese Left, in the name of pan-Arab solidarity, wanted to extend wholehearted support to the Palestinian struggle or at least not stand in its way. Meanwhile, the fact that the Palestinians were overwhelmingly Muslim deepened the controversy over the confessional system. Rightists feared, and Leftists hoped, that the Palestinians' demographic weight would inexorably count against the pro-Maronite status quo, hastening its demise.

To be sure, substantial segments of Lebanon's political elite did not fit easily into either opposing coalition. Within each religious community were political leaders who sympathized with elements of both coalitions' programs. A Sunni politician might favor reform of the confessional system while valuing Lebanon's Western geopolitical orientation. A Maronite might hope to clip the PLO's wings without antagonizing Arab regimes that saw themselves as the Palestinians' protectors.

Even among each coalition's most engaged partisans, one detected a final division: between a willingness to manage the above disputes by accommodation and a drive to attain political objectives by violence. The fault line was by no means permanent or predictable. Political figures willing to compromise at one moment might be impelled at another—by desperation, the prospect of victory, pressure from constituents, or some other incentive—to a resort to arms. Needless to say, the confrontationalism of each side vindicated and intensified that of the other.

Since Lebanon's achievement of independence in 1943, the accommodationist tendency had, for the most part, shakily prevailed. There had been periodic spasms of violence (as, most recently, in the spring of 1973), but leaders of the contending factions had always succeeded in restoring a semblance of calm. In the spring and summer of 1975, however, the impulse toward confrontation became too powerful to subdue. A series of provocations and altercations—bus ambushes, kidnappings, traffic disputes, even, in one case, a scuffle over a pinball game—escalated into pitched battles between rival militias or between unorganized bands of armed youth. The politicians could not agree on how to quell the violence. Rightist leaders wanted to call in the Lebanese army. Leftists and Palestinians objected that the largely Christian officer corps could not be trusted to act impartially. Thus the army was deployed sparingly and to little effect. The leaders did manage to implement a series of cease-fires, but in each case fighting resumed after a few weeks at most.[6]

Although the Lebanese civil war mostly followed a grim internal logic, it also unfolded in response to developments in Arab-Israeli diplomacy. In the summer of 1975, the Ford administration abandoned its brief flirtation with multilateral peacemaking and resumed its sponsorship of bilateral Egyptian-Israeli diplomacy, a decision resulting in the Sinai II Agreement that September. The indefinite postponement of a comprehensive settlement caused dismay throughout the Arab world, but it was especially alarming to two Arab actors with vital stakes in Lebanon: Lebanese Rightists and Palestinians in Lebanon. Rightists had hoped that a general settlement would produce a Palestinian state to which Palestinians in Lebanon would willingly relocate. In March 1976 Dory Chamoun, a Rightist militia leader and the son of former Lebanese president Camille Chamoun, lamented to a Lebanese American businessman that "the USA was making a deal with the Egyptians and therefore left a great dilemma on the doorstep of the other Arab countries of the Middle East—the Palestinian question, which is a cancer on the soul of Lebanon." Following Sinai II, writes the political scientist Fred J. Khouri, some Rightist leaders "concluded that the time had come for a showdown with the Palestinian commando organizations . . . to destroy Palestinian military and political power in Lebanon and to compel the emigration of as many of the Palestinians as possible from their country."[7]

The Palestinians, for their part, were shaken to discover that Egypt was no longer upholding their national claims in Arab-Israeli diplomacy. Deprived of this protection, and facing mounting attacks by the Right, they grew doubly determined to keep their foothold in Lebanon. "U.S. activity in Middle East peace-making," commented the U.S. embassy in Beirut in October 1975, ". . . has some bearing on [the] current Lebanese situation. Palestinians are jittery about their power bases and cannot afford to see [the] Lebanese Left beaten by [the] Christians."[8] It would take several months, however, for the PLO to become fully engaged in the Lebanese civil war.

Arab-Israeli politics drew other actors into the Lebanese fray. Damascus, too, was perturbed by Egyptian-Israeli diplomacy, which threatened to subtract Egyptian military power from the Arab-Israeli equation and thus sharply reduce Syria's strategic leverage against Israel. Seeking to preserve a military option, Syrian president Hafiz al-Asad spent the summer of 1975 trying to forge a joint military command among Syria, Jordan, and the PLO. To be effective, such a command needed access to Lebanon, which served as a natural buffer between Syria and Israel. Lebanon's plunge into anarchy, then, occurred just as Syria's attitude toward Lebanon was growing ever more proprietary, a circumstance that powerfully shaped the subsequent course of the civil war. Syria's early inclination—though this would later change—was to support the Left and the Palestinians, mainly by providing arms and materiel and by infiltrating Syrian-led Palestinian militiamen into the country. Meanwhile, as Damascus's opposition to Egyptian-Israeli diplomacy intensified, Cairo grew increasingly determined to counter Syrian influence in the Arab world. One way it sought to do this was by providing encouragement and small arms to the Lebanese Right, though this approach, too, was subject to change, in response to shifts in Syrian policy. "President Sadat's only rule," writes the veteran Middle East journalist David Hirst, was "to be *for* whoever Asad at any one time was *against*."[9]

The Israelis, who had long sought to cultivate a Christian-dominated Lebanon to counter the hostility of Muslim Arab states, gave covert military assistance to the Right. ("Some of their best friends are Christians," Kissinger quipped.[10]) They extended this aid independently of the U.S. government, which learned about it over the course of the civil war. Washington generally approved of Israel's action, seeing a strong Maronite community as key to Lebanon's pro-Western orientation. At the same time, the United States feared the Maronites were endangering their own position by being politically inflexible. Thus U.S. officials sometimes urged Israel to calibrate its support in such a way as to temper, not abet, the Right's intransigence.[11] It is unclear whether Israel ever followed this advice. The Right did accept some modest political compromises in the spring of 1976, but that probably had more to do with reverses on the battlefield than with any counsels of restraint coming from the south.

Whatever weight one assigns to the Arab-Israeli factor, the civil war escalated sharply in the days and weeks following the signing of Sinai II in early September 1975. During the first half of that month, Leftists and some Palestinians waged nasty skirmishes with Rightists in the north of the country. In mid-September Rightist militias, in protest against the army's inertia, began shelling the central commercial area of Beirut, reducing it to a blasted no-man's land. The fighting soon spread to other parts of the city, and from there to coastal towns south of the capital. In late October, Beirut's luxury hotel district was the scene of savage hand-to-hand combat, as militiamen vied for control of high-rise buildings that could serve as snipers' nests. By now, over three thousand people had lost their lives.[12]

To date, the Ford administration had paid relatively little attention to Lebanon. Over the spring and summer of 1975, Egyptian-Israeli diplomacy consumed most of the energy that top U.S. officials devoted to the Middle East. Lebanon's rapid descent into chaos that autumn, however, caused Washington to take greater notice. The U.S. government's concern centered less on the civil war itself than on other regional actors' likely response to it. The Ford administration was especially worried that Syrian and Israeli forces would enter Lebanon, either independently of each other or in a reactive sequence, and that this in turn would spark a wider Middle East war. At a White House meeting on October 16, Ford asked Kissinger if the United States could send its own forces to pacify Lebanon. "No way," Kissinger replied, citing logistical difficulties and the fact that such a move would find no support in the Arab world. He did not have to mention that the American public and Congress, chastened by the Vietnam experience and dismayed by ongoing revelations of U.S. covert actions abroad, could also be expected to oppose U.S. military action. "Then we have to keep anyone from intervening," Ford commented. "That's right," Kissinger said.[13]

The best way "to keep anyone from intervening" was to work for a political resolution within Lebanon, or at least a reduction of violence there. During October, the U.S. State Department approached a number of foreign governments that seemed well positioned to influence participants in Lebanon's crisis. It asked the Soviet Union to urge restraint on the Lebanese Left, Saudi Arabia and Kuwait to do the same with the Palestinians, and France to call on its traditional clients, the Maronites, to soften their resistance to modest political reform. The department also gently cautioned the Israelis against moving too aggressively in support of Christian militias. In mid-October Malcolm Toon, the U.S. ambassador in Tel Aviv, was instructed to tell Israeli foreign minister Yigal Allon that, while "neither the U.S. nor Israel has any interest in undercutting or weakening the Christians . . . , we have to ask ourselves whether or not there is a point at which the Christian community, by taking too rigid a position against Moslem demands for a greater share of power, may bring to a head the crisis we all hope to avoid and may itself be the principal loser." Allon told Toon "that the Israeli services were not in direct touch with the Lebanese Christian community." Whatever Allon meant by this statement, U.S. intelligence continued to receive reports of Israeli arms shipments to Rightist groups, which showed no sign of moderating their political positions or military tactics. The other U.S. initiatives were likewise ineffectual, and the slaughter in Lebanon continued. "We just cannot seem to influence the situation," assistant secretary of state Joseph Sisco confessed in late October.[14]

Unable to do much else, the U.S. embassy in Beirut concentrated on scaling back its operations and facilitating the departure of American residents. In late October and early November, all embassy dependents and nonessential employees were evacuated, and most other U.S. expatriates left the country voluntarily. From a pre–civil war high of seven thousand, Lebanon's American community dwindled to about two thousand members by the start of November. After brief closures that fall, the American University of Beirut (AUB) and the American Community School (ACS) resumed instruction on a reduced scale. (The shrinkage of ACS was especially pronounced, as its students and faculty consisted primarily of U.S. citizens, who were much more inclined and able to relocate than were the Lebanese, Palestinians, and other Arabs who constituted the bulk of the AUB community.) The American University Hospital, staffed mostly by Arab medical personnel, remained in operation throughout the civil war. Americans for Justice in the Middle East (AJME) likewise stayed afloat, though it had to suspend most of its public programming and could publish its newsletter only sporadically (sometimes sending copies on perilous boat rides to Cyprus for subsequent mailing to the United States); AJME also engaged in small-scale local relief. All of these institutions and many of Lebanon's American residents were clustered in Ras Beirut (meaning "the head of Beirut"), a portion of West Beirut jutting out to the Mediterranean that, with some prominent exceptions, such as the battle over the hotels, escaped the worst ravages of the 1975–1976 civil war. Many other Western foreigners continued to live in Ras Beirut, a pocket of cosmopolitanism in an area generally controlled by Leftist and Palestinian forces.[15]

As fall turned to winter, Lebanon's crisis deepened. On December 6—"Black Saturday," as the date was remembered—Rightist gunmen rampaged through the port area of Beirut, pulling civilians out of their cars, offices, and homes and shooting them if their identification cards showed them to be non-Christian. On that day and the next at least two hundred were killed. The atrocity set off a fresh wave of violence in which civilians were targeted with unprecedented brutality. In January, militias on each side eliminated "foreign" enclaves from the areas they controlled. Rightist gunmen overran Muslim neighborhoods and Palestinian refugee camps astride the main roads connecting Christian East Beirut and the

Maronite-dominated areas northeast of the capital. Scores of civilians were killed and thousands more expelled. The attack on the Palestinians brought the PLO fully into the conflict on the Leftist side. Leftist and PLO militias conquered a handful of Christian towns along the coastal road south of Beirut, slaughtering some of their inhabitants and expelling the rest. Leftist/PLO forces did not, however, harm the many Christians residing in West Beirut. This was partly because the Leftist/PLO coalition, itself religiously diverse, was less committed to sectarianism than was the mostly Maronite Right; partly because the Western powers presumably would not have tolerated an anti-Christian massacre in an area inhabited by so many of their own citizens. As of mid-January, Lebanon's death toll stood at about six thousand.[16]

Back in the United States, the closest watchers of Lebanon's self-destruction, apart from academic and government specialists, were Arab Americans, the majority of whom were of Lebanese descent. Their dominant collective mood, as expressed in declarations by community leaders and treatments in the ethnic press, was one of grief and horror over the scale of the carnage, shame and despair over the senselessness of the conflict. On their face, most of these statements forcefully rejected Lebanon's fratricidal politics; examined more closely, some of them harbored contentious assumptions about the causes of the conflict and thus, implicitly, about which factions were entitled to define Lebanon's future. At the same time, many of these Arab American statements were glancing and formulaic, suggesting that community leaders were still feeling their way through Lebanon's labyrinthine politics. Although distinct, and conflicting, Arab American perspectives on Lebanon emerged in 1975–1976, the intracommunity debate over the country's politics and regional role did not fully coalesce until well after that phase of the civil war had ended.

In November 1975, senator James Abourezk spearheaded the formation of the American Committee for the People of Lebanon (ACPL), one of the first national U.S. organizations to respond to the Lebanese crisis. The ACPL's mission was "to put a national umbrella over the many fund raising efforts being undertaken throughout the United States, to benefit the victims of the disaster in Lebanon." The organization's executive board included Arab American and Lebanese American figures representing a wide array of religious denominations and political perspectives. At the ACPL's founding meeting in Washington, DC, Abourezk insisted that "division and factionalism along religious or political lines cannot become part of this gathering. If anyone here feels that he or she *must* be partisan, or that a non-sectarian effort is not acceptable, now is the time to bail out."[17]

Still, Abourezk could not entirely banish his own political assessments. "Many factors have contributed to the internal warfare in Lebanon," he said in his opening remarks. "The Israeli bombing in the south was calculated to cause dissension over the presence of the Palestinians in Lebanon—and it worked." Here, Abourezk came close to alleging that the Lebanese Right's anti-Palestinian politics were simply the unfolding of an Israeli design. On the whole, though, Abourezk and the other ACPL organizers struck an inclusive note without getting too enmeshed in specifics. A case in point was the group's very name, which referred to "the people of Lebanon" rather than to "the Lebanese people" or simply to "Lebanon." This wording left the door open to efforts on behalf of Palestinians in Lebanon without explicitly mentioning such aid, which some may have considered a diversion from the primary mission.[18]

Indeed, designating worthy objects of humanitarian sympathy was an inescapably political act. Even neutral language could be deployed to make a desired point. In January 1976, Elaine Hagopian, the AAUG's new president, released a statement on Lebanon expressing deep concern "about the survival of the country and <u>all of those who inhabit it</u>"—quite literally underlining her group's commitment to Palestinians. Other community leaders made no pretense of neutrality. In October 1975, the Maronite Center of Youngstown, Ohio, as part of a nationwide campaign by American Maronites, held an "austerity dinner" of rice and lentils to call attention to suffering in Lebanon. In an interview with the local newspaper prior to the dinner, Father Dominic Ashkar of Youngstown's St. Maron church made it clear who the real victims were: "Today in Lebanon we are experiencing a new martyrdom for the Christian faith which we here in America cannot ignore. . . . The assault on Christianity in the East is . . . primarily an attack on the Maronites who represent the last significant vestige of Christianity in that part of the world."[19]

Meanwhile, Arab American groups issued more formal and sustained analyses of Lebanon's deepening crisis, and these brought political differences more clearly to the fore. In late 1975, the AAUG published a pamphlet containing two short essays on Lebanon. The first, by Leila Meo, a political science professor at the University of Massachusetts at Amherst, offered what was quickly becoming a conventional left-of-center analysis of the Lebanese civil war. Internally, she wrote, the conflict was a struggle to achieve "long overdue . . . reform that would bring social justice and political equality to Lebanese citizens"—Muslim and Christian alike—"who remain the poor and underprivileged members of society." Regionally, it was an effort by those same downtrodden elements to bind Lebanon's future to the wider Arab world and promote the Palestinian struggle. "Eliminating the Palestinian resistance will not protect Lebanon from the Zionist blows," Meo wrote. "Only internal Lebanese strength and national solidarity co-extensive with inter-Arab strength and solidarity can prevent Zionist expansion into Southern Lebanon and reclaim Arab lands already conquered by the Zionist state."[20]

The second essay was by Edward Said, professor of comparative literature at Columbia University and still some years away from academic stardom. Said's piece was more elliptical, focusing less on concrete issues than on the seeming inability of any of Lebanon's factions to offer a broadly appealing national vision. Lebanon's predicament, Said wrote, "is a crisis of representation. No single group represents either a decisive majority of people and power or a decisive majority of ideas. The street fighter is not represented by the group or leader in whose name he fights, and vice verssa [*sic*]. . . . Yet people take to the streets fighting, to see what can happen. A vicious way to explore and test, but in Lebanon very few know better."[21]

Said seemed to be declaring a pox on all houses, but upon closer inspection distinct partialities emerged. He coupled blanket expressions of dismay over the senseless violence with targeted criticism of political foes: "There is tremendous waste now in Lebanon; the mood is national suicide. . . . The present fighting is not between two sides, one Christian, one Muslim, one right, one left, one inside patriot, one outside agitator, one good, one bad. Israeli pieties about Lebanon's embattled Christians are fatuous hypocrisy since, aside from using Maronite fantasy to support Zionist exclusivity, Israel has shown comparable piety only for destroying the Arab realities of Palestine." Conversely, imbedded in Said's catalogue of folly were figures pointedly exempt from criticism. After blasting the fecklessness and vacuity of Lebanon's ruling elite, middle class, business community, and intellectuals, Said allowed that "the Palestinians in Lebanon have something to say, but only a handful will listen to them." He then observed that the crisis was partly "about who will, and has a right to, speak for the Arab future. . . . Does metropolitan Cairo have the right to dictate the future with its Sinai deal, or do the villages, slums, camps have it, where the majority lives and suffers? Do traditional politicians speak or should a party? . . . A valueless military-economic alliance or an authentic socio-political movement?"[22] On none of these pairings could the author's own stance be in doubt.

The NAAA, too, tried to make sense of the Lebanese crisis, with less success. In the fall of 1975, Arab American and Lebanese American newspapers published a letter to "Fellow Arab Americans" by former NAAA president Richard Shadyac. Writing on behalf of the NAAA, Shadyac urged Arab Americans to send messages of concern to friends and relatives in Lebanon, to engage in humanitarian relief work, and to pray for Lebanon's salvation. He also ventured some political commentary: "My friends, it is important to keep the problems of Lebanon in perspective. The problems in Lebanon are not problems between Christians and Moslems. Do not let anyone attempt to classify this problem as a religious civil war. The problems of Lebanon are not Palestinian vs. Lebanese. Do not allow anyone to classify the problems in these terms." So what *were* the problems of Lebanon? All Shadyac offered were vague generalities, and assurances that experts were handling the case:

> I am afraid that the problems confronting Lebanon are many and complex. They concern economic issues, political issues, sociological issues and, of course, the problems of external force and pressure being exerted on Lebanon from countries outside the borders of Lebanon. I want to let all of you know that the National Association of Arab Americans has kept in close contact with our State Department and proper officials on the Hill in an attempt to be sure that the United States keeps Lebanon high on its agenda of problem areas.

As unforthcoming as Shadyac's letter was, it appears to have offered the most extended analysis of the Lebanese crisis that the NAAA published in 1975–1976.[23]

Given the dearth of relevant documentation, we can only speculate about the reasons for such reticence. Perhaps NAAA leaders considered it unseemly, or feared that their predominantly Lebanese American constituents would so see it, to offer hard-nosed political analysis in the midst of such overwhelming tragedy. It is also likely that, although most NAAA leaders were themselves Lebanese American, they had little familiarity with Lebanese politics and did not know quite what to make of the civil war. Up till now, their primary frame of reference for understanding the Middle East had been the Arab-Israeli conflict and their own "evenhanded" approach to resolving it. Pre-1975 Lebanon fit comfortably into the evenhanded vision; it could even be seen as its regional embodiment. Lebanon was pro-American *and* pro-Arab, an oasis of liberal entrepreneurialism *and* a haven for Palestinians. The country's rapid disintegration, however, showed that each component of this formula was bitterly opposed by significant segments of Lebanese society. Precisely which components should be rejected and which embraced was, indeed, what the fighting was largely about. For many in the NAAA, this must have been perplexing.

Activists in the AAUG tended to be better informed about Arab politics, including Lebanese politics, partly because many of them had grown up in the region. Even those unfamiliar with Lebanon could draw on ideological paradigms prevalent in AAUG circles—Arab nationalism, Palestinian liberation, Third World solidarity, varieties of socialism—that made the Lebanese civil war intelligible (perhaps a bit *too* intelligible, but that was a different problem[24]). When a conflict pitted the champions of Palestinian militancy, pan-Arabism, and social justice against the guardians of a Maronite-dominated, pro-U.S., bourgeois Lebanon, AAUGers had no doubt about where they stood. For NAAA members, things were less clear.[25]

The Lebanese Right, too, had Arab American defenders, though few of them, perhaps, would have embraced that ethnic label. In May 1976, a group of Lebanese American professionals, most of them Maronites, met in Washington to form the American Lebanese League (ALL). Elias Saadi, a Youngstown, Ohio, cardiologist then serving as president of the National Apostolate of Maronites, was named the ALL's first chairman. The founders later claimed that they formed the new organization only after failing to persuade the NAAA to create a special committee on Lebanon—a plausible assertion, in view of the latter's demonstrated reluctance to tackle the Lebanese crisis. The ALL's declared purposes included "generat[ing] action to protect, promote and sustain the independence, sovereignty, security and stability of Lebanon" and "upholding and maintaining the unique political-social-cultural character of Lebanon."[26] In practice, this meant urging the U.S. government to recognize, and act to address, the danger that non-Lebanese Arab actors, especially Syria and the PLO, posed to Lebanon's independence and cultural distinctiveness. (The ALL's mission would soon be complicated, however, by a brief de facto alliance between Syria and the Lebanese Right.) Initially, the ALL pursued its agenda in muted tones, preoccupied, like other Lebanese American groups, with confronting Lebanon's massive humanitarian and reconstruction needs.[27] After the spring of 1978, however, the league assumed a much higher and more defiant profile.

One of the ALL's more influential founders was Elias El-Hayek, a Lebanese-born Maronite theologian and legal scholar. During the ALL's formative period, El-Hayek drafted a number of position papers that helped to define the new group's outlook and priorities. A case in point was an analysis of the Lebanese crisis, dated April 15, 1976, that he prepared for one of the meetings preceding the ALL's founding in May. To explain that crisis, El-Hayek touched on the many sources of national discord that informed observers of the Lebanese scene had cited in recent months: conflicting visions of Lebanon's internal character and international role, Lebanese Christians' mounting anxiety over the erosion of their demographic strength, the interference of neighboring countries, even the failure of Lebanon's leaders to "pay enough attention to social justice and the concrete needs of the poor."[28]

El-Hayek devoted the bulk of his analysis, however, to the baneful effects of the Palestinian presence in Lebanon. In recent years, el-Hayek wrote, Palestinian refugee camps had become "hotbeds for radical political movements. . . . Communism in all its shapes and forms (Maoism, Leninism, etc) took root and found wide acceptance. . . . As the number of Palestinians increased, their camps became virtual fortresses and their guerrilla organization an army of occupation. . . . The armed presence of these Palestinians in Lebanon destroyed what was left of law and order in the land." Even the non-Palestinian causes of Lebanon's destabilization, El-Hayek noted, were magnified by the Palestinian factor. The country's "economic and social situation was complicated by the problem created by the Palestinian refugees," who swelled the ranks of the disaffected poor. Muslim-Christian tensions "were heightened when the [predominantly Muslim] Palestinians began meddling in the internal affairs of the State of Lebanon, and taking the side of their Moslem co-religionists. In any conflict between the State of Lebanon and the Palestinians . . . [Lebanese] Moslems defended their [Palestinian] co-religionists."[29]

While there was a good deal of truth in these assertions, El-Hayek's preoccupation with the Palestinians left the dubious impression that, but for their presence, Lebanon's other issues could be easily resolved. (On the same day El-Hayek issued this document, bishop Francis M. Zayek, the highest-ranking Maronite cleric in the United States, met with President Ford as part of a religious delegation and stated the claim baldly: "The root problem is the Palestinians. By themselves, the Lebanese would solve their own problems."[30]) Like Dory Chamoun, El-Hayek saw the PLO as a cancer on Lebanon; only by removing the cancer could the nation save itself.

As El-Hayek wrote his analysis, the Lebanese Right's fortunes were falling. The PLO's full entry into the Lebanese civil war in January had bolstered the Left, enabling it to take the offensive. In March, the Lebanese army disintegrated, as Christian and Muslim officers abandoned their commissions to join Rightist and Leftist militias; enlisted men did the same or simply went home. Although the army's dissolution benefited both sides, it was a net gain for the Left because it eliminated a military force that had occasionally supported the Right. In March and April, the tide of battle shifted sharply in favor of the Leftist/PLO coalition, which drove the last Rightist gunmen from Beirut's hotel district and seized a belt of towns in the hills commanding the approaches to the Maronite heartland.[31]

For the Right, this was a moment of profound peril. Salvation, however, would soon arrive from an unlikely quarter. One might suppose that the Leftist/Palestinian successes gratified Syria's president, who had long championed the Palestinian cause and the pan-Arab conception of Lebanon. But Asad was looking a few steps ahead, and he did not like what he saw. It was a virtual certainty that Israel would regard a Leftist/Palestinian victory as intolerable and seek to reverse it militarily. Asad would then face a bleak choice: he could send his own forces into Lebanon to resist the Israeli invasion, with a strong likelihood of defeat, or he could sit on the sidelines and suffer a galling loss of domestic and regional prestige, not to mention the strategic nightmare of having Israeli troops menacing Syria on a new flank.[32]

Unable to countenance a Leftist/Palestinian victory, Asad instead sought to position himself as the sponsor and guarantor of a moderate settlement of the Lebanese dispute. His efforts along these lines had begun in January, when a Rightist defeat first became a serious possibility. With Asad's prodding, Lebanese politicians negotiated a set of principles known as the Constitutional Document. Formally unveiled in February, the document reaffirmed Lebanon's Arab identity, called for a reform of the confessional system to permit non-Christians a somewhat larger share of political power, and provided for a strengthening of the Lebanese government's authority over Palestinian camps. With varying degrees of enthusiasm, most Lebanese politicians endorsed the Constitutional Document. But some Leftist figures, most prominently the Druze leader Kamal Jumblatt, who favored outright abolition of the confessional system, rejected it. The PLO, too, opposed the Syrian-backed plan on the ground that it would unduly restrict Palestinian activity. Tasting victory on the battlefield, these holdouts saw little reason to exercise restraint, and they pressed ahead with their campaign to subdue the Right.[33]

Out of the failure of Asad's political effort arose the scenario for Syrian military intervention; if the hotheads could not contain their ambitions, then outsiders must do it for them. Damascus had already infiltrated hundreds of Syrian-led Palestinian commandos into Lebanon. Over the spring of 1976, they were increasingly deployed to check PLO/Leftist operations. (Egypt, therefore, began shifting its support away from the Right and toward the PLO and the Left.) It soon became clear that Asad's Palestinians were not capable of blunting the PLO/Leftist offensive on their own.[34] Thus in March Syrian officials began a dialogue with their U.S. counterparts about the possible movement of Syrian regular troops into Lebanon.

For decades, journalists and scholars have speculated about the content of this dialogue and its relationship to subsequent events. One of the more persistent theories has been that Asad, in eventually intervening in Lebanon, fell into a Kissingerian trap. According to this view, Kissinger sought to neutralize Syria and the PLO, both of which fiercely opposed his step-by-step approach to Arab-Israeli diplomacy. By luring Syria into Lebanon, he got Syria and the PLO to waste their energies fighting each other, allowing himself a freer hand in the region.[35] While this is surely a tempting thesis, recently declassified U.S. documents (and new scholarship consulting them) show that the idea for intervention originated with Asad and that Kissinger acceded to the venture only after failing to prevent it.

Indeed, when a top Asad aide first suggested, in mid-March, that Syria might send troops into Lebanon, Kissinger strongly opposed the idea. Israel had repeatedly warned Syria to stay out of Lebanon, and Kissinger worried that a Syrian intervention would provoke Israel to respond in kind (even as Asad believed that his *failure* to intervene would ultimately draw Israel into Lebanon).[36] A Syrian-Israeli clash in Lebanon, Kissinger feared, could ignite a wider Arab-Israeli war, provoke an Arab oil embargo, and risk superpower confrontation. In short, it would be a replay of October 1973, with the difference that the Soviets, unable to tolerate yet another defeat of their Arab clients, would adopt a stiffer position than in the past.[37]

Over the next several weeks, Kissinger pursued a multipronged diplomatic initiative designed to keep a Syrian intervention from occurring in the first place or to manage its consequences if prevention failed. In late March, he sent the veteran diplomat L. Dean Brown (who had been the U.S. ambassador in Amman during the Jordanian crisis of 1970) on a mission to Lebanon. Brown's principal assignment was to urge the Lebanese Left, especially Jumblatt, to accept the Constitutional Document and thus facilitate a settlement that made a Syrian military move unnecessary. At the same time, through a variety of channels, Kissinger warned Asad that a Syrian intervention would almost certainly provoke a sharp Israeli response, while seeking clarification on the nature and scope of the contemplated Syrian operation. In a third set of contacts, proceeding on the assumption that intervention could not be avoided, Kissinger shared what he could glean about Asad's intentions with Israeli officials and urged them not to overreact to any Syrian move, while also probing the limits of Israeli tolerance.[38]

In Lebanon, Brown had no success in softening Jumblatt's opposition to the Constitutional Document. The Druze leader continued to demand the abolition of confessionalism, refusing to "rule out a return to arms" if that was the only route to nonsectarian democracy. Reporting back to Kissinger, Brown castigated Jumblatt as an intransigent "nut," even while acknowledging that he championed political norms that "have long been practiced in the West." Despairing of the Lebanese Left, Brown sought authorization to talk directly to Yasser Arafat about ending the fighting—an ironic request, given Brown's role in facilitating King Hussein's suppression of the PLO in 1970–1971. Kissinger, however, refused to relax his ban on negotiating with the PLO, and Brown made no overture to the Palestinians. (In a further irony, after June 1976 the PLO would provide security for the U.S. embassy in Beirut. The Americans were shunning their own soon-to-be protectors.)[39]

The other two prongs of Kissinger's diplomacy—the Syrian and the Israeli—met with modest success. They did not, as some scholars maintain, produce a U.S.-brokered tacit agreement between Syria and Israel over the acceptable scope of a Syrian intervention.[40] But they did permit each country a glimpse of the other's views and intentions and thus an opportunity to calibrate its own actions accordingly. In meetings with U.S. diplomats in late March, the Syrians and the Israelis staked out their positions. The Syrians were thinking of sending troops into Beirut, the Bekaa Valley (in northeastern Lebanon), and some mountain areas; the force would be modest in size and would stay out of South Lebanon. The Israelis listed a number of Syrian actions they would regard as intolerable: "any open and declared Syrian military entrance into Lebanon"; the addition of troops, regular or irregular, that brought existing numbers (currently estimated at one thousand to two thousand irregulars) above "brigade size," or about three thousand men; the introduction of heavy weapons, warplanes, or naval forces; and the movement of Syrian forces more than ten kilometers south of the

Beirut-Damascus highway, a prohibition placing Lebanon's southern third off-limits to Syria. If Syria violated any of these conditions, Israel would occupy South Lebanon. While there were areas of compatibility between the Syrian and Israeli positions, it was hard to get around Israel's opposition to an "open and declared Syrian military entrance into Lebanon."[41]

Still, when Syria sent thousands of additional Palestinian irregulars into Lebanon in the first half of April—bringing the total number of Syrian-controlled troops up to about five thousand, according to a CIA estimate—Israel took no action, even though its "brigade size" limit had been exceeded. "Israel continues to turn a blind eye to Syrian moves," Foreign Minister Allon told Ambassador Toon. Apparently, Damascus had some room for maneuver. Kissinger remained convinced, however, that Israel would not tolerate the introduction of Syrian regulars, and he saw to it that Asad received this assessment.[42]

As Kissinger and his colleagues worked to avert Syrian intervention, they occasionally reflected on the sheer strangeness of the crisis they sought to manage. "We have a really bizarre situation in Lebanon," Kissinger told Ford in late March. "Syria is supporting the conservatives and Christians against the PLO. . . . Egypt is supporting the leftists and the PLO against Syria. The Soviet Union should be supporting Syria, but it also supports the PLO. Israel is, of course, against the PLO." Reporting to the cabinet in mid-April, Kissinger amended this last point: "Israel is opposed to Syrian intervention so objectively is supporting the PLO." Even Joe Sisco, who had overseen the State Department's Middle East diplomacy for nearly a decade, was shaking his head in wonder. "It's weird. It is truly weird."[43]

By summer, Asad had decided he could wait no longer. In the first week of June, twelve thousand Syrian regular troops crossed into Lebanon. As expected, the Syrian forces deployed in the Bekaa Valley and proceeded to Beirut. Yet they also operated in the north of the country and pushed down toward the port city of Sidon, some thirty miles north of the Israeli border, while staying clear of the border area itself. The available evidence suggests that Kissinger had no advance notice of the intervention and that his immediate reaction was one of apprehension over a possible Israeli countermove. In public statements, however, Israeli leaders portrayed Syria's action as an effort to pacify Lebanon that posed no immediate threat to their own country and, indeed, offered distinct benefits. "I will not stand in the way of anyone who wants to subdue Arafat's terrorists," declared Israeli prime minister Yitzhak Rabin. For much of June, Kissinger continued to worry that Israel might change its assessment and enter the fray after all. As the days passed with no Israeli reaction, however, he grew increasingly confident that disaster had been averted.[44]

In fact, Kissinger soon came to see the Syrian move as a near-godsend. Although Asad failed to achieve his maximum objectives of ending the fighting and gaining quick acceptance of the Constitutional Document, he did prevent a military victory by the Leftists and Palestinians, who were obliged to abandon their offensives against the Right and concentrate on resisting the Syrian invasion. Worse still for them, the Syrian presence enabled the Right to mount a counteroffensive of its own. Throughout the country that summer, a fairly consistent pattern emerged. Syrian troops would blockade Leftist and Palestinian strongholds and occasionally shell them from a distance, while Rightists attacked them at closer range. These tactics were most brutally applied to the inhabitants of Tal al-Za'tar, a sprawling refugee camp outside Beirut that was home to thirty thousand Palestinians and Lebanese Shia. Rightists had blockaded Tal al-Za'tar since January. In late June, with Syrian logistical support, they redoubled the siege, and in mid-August they finally overran the camp. At least two thousand residents lost their lives, many of them massacred after the camp had surrendered.[45]

If Kissinger was troubled by the carnage, he gave no sign of it, dwelling instead on the geopolitical windfall. "The PLO is in bad shape," he told Ford in mid-July, at the height of the siege. "We didn't plan it but we have broken the Arab united front." Months later he was still marveling at Washington's good fortune. "I cannot say we planned on the Syrians to grind up on the PLO," he said to former White House counsel Leonard Garment in October, "but it is working out well."[46]

American policy makers did face some tense moments that summer. On June 16, U.S. ambassador to Lebanon Francis E. Meloy, U.S. embassy economic counselor Robert O. Waring, and their Lebanese bodyguard and driver, Zuhair Moghrabi, were abducted and shot to death while crossing from West to East Beirut. The killers appeared to be linked to the Popular Front for the Liberation of Palestine, though the PLO as a whole condemned the act and began providing security for the U.S. embassy, which was located in West Beirut. Immediately, the Ford administration arranged to evacuate as many of the remaining 1,500-odd U.S. residents as would willingly leave the country.[47] On June 20, a U.S. Navy ship transported 116 Americans and 147 other foreigners from Beirut to Athens. PLO forces provided security at the embarkation site. Anxious to avert the least hitch, a top-heavy cluster of U.S. officials, including secretary of defense Donald Rumsfeld and three members of the Joint Chiefs of Staff, monitored the

Figure 16. Deputy national security adviser William Hyland (*standing*) and president Gerald Ford study a satellite photograph of West Beirut during the Ford administration's first evacuation of U.S. citizens from Lebanon, June 20, 1976. Courtesy of the Gerald R. Ford Presidential Library.

evacuation from the Pentagon War Room via a telephone linkup. Ford stayed up till the small hours to keep tabs on the operation.[48]

In mid-July came a new crisis. Through King Hussein, Asad informed Kissinger that Syria had come under heavy Soviet pressure. Moscow was demanding that Damascus end its attacks on the PLO and pull its troops out of Lebanon, or risk a cessation of Soviet economic and military aid. Asad wanted to know what the United States "could do to alleviate pressure . . . if [a] cutoff actually comes." Kissinger assured Asad of U.S. support for Syria's "pursuit of an independent policy" and urged him to specify "how we might be of most help in the face of Soviet pressures." Meanwhile, the Ford administration was preparing a second evacuation, this one an overland convoy heading eastward to the Syrian border. The PLO, which had agreed to provide security along portions of the route, now said it could no longer do so, citing an upswing in violence. Kissinger drew an implausible connection between this development and the Soviet ultimatum to Syria: the PLO, he said, was deliberately obstructing the evacuation as part of a Soviet plot to make life difficult for Asad's new American friends.[49] If the PLO *was* prevaricating about the security situation, it was almost certainly pursuing its own interests, not those of an outside power. As long as hundreds of Americans and other Western foreigners resided in West Beirut, Rightists or Syrians would probably hesitate to launch a full-scale offensive against PLO strongholds there.[50]

Washington resolved the latter issue by opting instead for a second seaborne evacuation, which occurred on July 27, a week after the land convoy would have departed. (Rightist shelling of Beirut's airport, located in an area dominated by the Left, ruled out an aerial evacuation.) Some three hundred foreigners, including about a hundred Americans, boarded another Athens-bound naval vessel, with the PLO again providing security at the loading site. Perhaps to placate U.S. officials, whose complaints about PLO obstructionism had reached Arafat's ears, the Palestinian guards sported red and white roses in the muzzles of their guns. "We thought it would be a nice touch," their local commander explained to a reporter.[51]

The other issue more or less resolved itself as it grew evident, in coming weeks, that Syria would not quit Lebanon and that Moscow would not cut off aid to Damascus. Clearly, the Soviets found the awkwardness of managing two mutually antagonistic clients—Syria and the PLO—preferable to the strategic cost of abandoning the stronger one. (And anyway, Soviet support for the PLO in this period was more verbal than material, much to the dismay of Palestinian leaders.) Arguably, the United States missed an opportunity to draw Syria closer into its orbit, but attempting to engineer such a realignment would have been complicated and risky. Kissinger was content to see Syrian-Soviet relations revert to familiar patterns.[52]

For Americans with a more personal stake in Lebanon, the view was hardly so sanguine. By July 1976, the civil war had killed at least fifteen thousand people, wounded tens of thousands more, and made hundreds of thousands homeless—and no end was in sight. Across the United States, Lebanese Americans witnessed the destruction of their ancestral homeland with a mixture of horror, grief, despair, and gnawing worry. The ordeal was especially painful for those with immediate family in Lebanon. The collapse of Lebanon's mail system often made it impossible to stay in contact with loved ones in the country, or even know their whereabouts. "The last word Habib Akoury of Boston had of his wife and three young children," reported the Associated Press in July, "they had taken refuge in a Beirut cellar with other families. Akoury received that bit of information in a seven-month old letter forwarded from Damascus by a refugee." Maronite pastor Joseph Lahoud labored to console his parishioners at Our Lady of the Cedars of Lebanon Church, also in Boston, while praying for his own parents and siblings, residents of a town in northern Lebanon engulfed by violence. "He knows the town is without water or food," the AP reported. "He doesn't know if his family is still alive." "After all this time, we have lost all feeling," said twenty-three-year old Nagy Baroody of New York City. "Every day we hope that it will end, and every day it goes on."[53]

Compounding the hopelessness was a sense that little could be done to ease Lebanon's misery. Certainly, it was beyond the capacity of ordinary Lebanese Americans or Arab Americans, or of their organizations, to end the fighting. It also appears, although evidence is fragmentary, that relatively little came of the private efforts, urged by Senator Abourezk and others, to generate humanitarian relief for Lebanon.[54] Mainstream news accounts reported local groups' disappointment over fund-raising yields, and the Arab American press occasionally chided readers for failing to do more for the country.[55]

As a senator, Abourezk was uniquely positioned among Arab Americans to seek help from the U.S. government, and he made the most of this privilege. But here, too, success was limited. Over the spring of 1976, Abourezk had consulted with Ford administration officials on the preparation of a request to Congress for humanitarian assistance to Lebanon. In early June, Congress appropriated $20 million in aid, a modest sum in view of Lebanon's staggering needs.[56] Later that summer, Abourezk lobbied Ford about converting a U.S. Navy vessel into a hospital ship that would be docked off of Lebanon's coast but out of artillery range, so that war wounded could safely receive medical treatment. When Ford discouraged the idea as impractical, Abourezk turned to Capitol Hill, where his colleagues also rejected the plan, citing security concerns and the long lead time necessary to ready the ship for service.[57] (So much for the adage "better late than never.")

Meanwhile, Abourezk and Massachusetts senator Edward Kennedy, chair of the Senate Judiciary Committee's subcommittee on refugees, on which Abourezk served, urged the State Department and the Immigration and Naturalization Service (INS) to use discretion they already possessed under the law to make it easier for Lebanese travelers to enter the United States or prolong their stays in the country. Both agencies agreed to relax their visa-granting and enforcement provisions on a case-by-case basis, but they refused to issue any blanket rulings that favored Lebanese haven seekers. At a subcommittee hearing in July, Kennedy denounced the case-by-case approach. He quoted the INS's guidelines, which stated that individual Lebanese visitors could petition to extend their stays if they "find themselves temporarily unable to return to Lebanon because of the civil strife in that country." "Does this not apply to all Lebanese in the United States?" Kennedy demanded. He and Abourezk cited numerous "horror stories" resulting from an overly rigid application of immigration laws: parents separated from underage children; travelers stranded for weeks on end in pricey European cities, sinking into destitution as they awaited permission to join family members in America; students in the United States driven by economic desperation to work under the table, thereby risking deportation. Abourezk attributed these agonies to "calculated bureaucratic obstruction" by the Ford administration, and to the president's personal indifference. Alluding to Ford's frantic efforts to avoid losing the Republican nomination to former California governor Ronald Reagan, the senator drily observed, "There are apparently no uncommitted Lebanese delegates."[58]

Politically, recent events had done little to clarify the Arab American outlook and in some ways had made it murkier. The Syrian intervention received no overt support from national organizations; the main division was between those who opposed the action and those who wished to avoid discussing it. AAUG leaders, outraged by Syria's betrayal of the Palestinians and the Left, were in the first camp. On June 8, President Hagopian sent a telegram to the Arab League expressing the association's "strong opposition to the Syrian invasion of Lebanon which is particularly directed at the popular Lebanese nationalist forces and the Palestinian resistance movement." At its 1976 national convention, held in New York City in October, the AAUG issued a resolution "call[ing] upon Syria to cease and desist immediately from collaborating and conniving with the isolationist [i.e., Rightist] Lebanese forces and their allies, and to withdraw all Syrian forces forthwith." Hagopian granted a brief suspension of the convention so that attendees could protest outside the Syrian mission to the United Nations. These gestures drew complaints from members who still supported the Syrian regime, but Hagopian and the AAUG leadership held firm.[59]

The NAAA and the ALL had much less to say about Syria's intervention. The closest the NAAA came to addressing the topic was in a June 9 statement "urging an immediate ceasefire in Lebanon." As Syrian warplanes pounded away at Palestinian camps outside Beirut, and as PLO fighters fiercely resisted Syrian ground forces attempting to take Sidon, the NAAA expressed "the hope that a united Arab force with Syria and the Palestine Liberation Organization included" would implement the desired cease-fire and "safeguard the peace."[60] If the conflict between the Lebanese Right

Figure 17. James Abourezk and Elaine Hagopian (*both seated*) share a light moment at the AAUG national convention in New York, October 1976; future AAUG president Mujid Kazimi stands at the podium. Courtesy of Eastern Michigan University Archives, Ypsilanti, Michigan.

and the Left/PLO coalition had been difficult to fold into the NAAA's "evenhanded" vision for Middle East peace, then a Syrian-PLO clash was even less assimilable. The NAAA's main foreign policy goal, in 1976, was to persuade Washington that Egyptian-Israeli bilateral agreements were insufficient and that Syrian and Palestinian demands had to be satisfied as well—and indeed *could* be satisfied in a peace settlement that served U.S. geopolitical interests. The NAAA saw no advantage in highlighting disagreements between Syria and the PLO.

The newly formed ALL appears not to have made any political proclamations in the immediate aftermath of the Syrian intervention, focusing instead on Lebanon's humanitarian needs. An ALL recruiting statement authored by Elias El-Hayek, undated but evidently composed in the spring of 1977, did touch on political matters.[61] Yet its language was cryptic, hinting at likely divisions, or feelings of ambivalence, among ALL members. "As Foreign armies occupied Lebanese territory," El-Hayek wrote, explaining Lebanon's predicament, "the alien in Lebanon became the master, and the Lebanese citizen became both alien and refugee in his own country. The invaders imposed a dictatorial rule and the citizens of Lebanon suddenly lost their freedom. The population was exposed to kidnapping, killing, torture and mutilation."[62] El-Hayek's failure to "name names" was probably deliberate. While virtually all of the ALL's emerging constituents would have counted the PLO among the "Foreign armies" ravaging Lebanon, there was, no doubt, some reluctance to attach such a label to the Syrian forces that had recently rescued the Right. Yet who could deny that Syria was now massively interfering in Lebanese affairs? El-Hayek's vague treatment finessed the matter.

By the fall of 1976, the Lebanese civil war was heading for a settlement of sorts. Although Arab governments had generally acquiesced in Syria's intervention in June, the move aroused widespread public criticism in the Arab world. As Syria's offensive against the Left/Palestinian coalition continued that summer, the Arab regimes faced growing pressure to impose some restraint on Damascus. The Saudis in particular had their eye on the U.S. electoral calendar. They realized that once American voters had gone to the polls in November—and regardless of whether President Ford or his Democratic challenger, former governor of Georgia Jimmy Carter, emerged victorious—a fresh opportunity for Arab-Israeli diplomacy would arise. Unless the Arabs got their house in order, the chance would be lost. Asad could not ignore these sentiments. In mid-October, after launching some final, crippling offensives against the PLO and its allies, he accepted a Saudi invitation to attend an Arab summit meeting in Riyadh to address the Lebanese crisis.[63]

The resulting agreement essentially ratified Syria's occupation of Lebanon. It established a thirty-thousand-man Arab Deterrent Force (ADF), consisting almost entirely of Syrian troops, to implement an immediate cease-fire. All factions within Lebanon were to retreat to the positions they had held in April 1975 and surrender their heavy weapons to the ADF. None of the issues in the Lebanese dispute had been resolved, but a combination of exhaustion and the ADF's presence induced the main contending factions to accept the Riyadh agreement. Violence continued at a low level, but large-scale fighting came to an end, creating a lull sufficiently long and noticeable for "the Lebanese Civil War of 1975–1976" to enter history as a discrete event. As many as thirty thousand people lost their lives in the tragedy, and perhaps sixty-five thousand were injured. Hundreds of thousands fled the country or were internally displaced. Property damage was counted in the tens of billions of dollars.[64]

On November 2, the American electorate narrowly rejected President Ford in favor of Governor Carter, ending eight years of Republican rule, and with them the era of Kissinger's dominance in foreign policy. Two days later, Kissinger consoled the president (and himself) that, despite the public's wounding verdict, the Ford administration could be proud of its record in foreign policy. Lebanon was a case in point. "Syria has things under control," Kissinger said, and the Palestinians were "being put in their place." A dangerously destabilizing crisis had been contained, enabling the incoming Carter administration to resume the Arab-Israeli peace process. To be sure, Kissinger had little confidence in the president-elect's abilities. "Carter I think could easily be a one-term President," he told Ford, offering further consolation.[65]

Peace in Lebanon (or what passed for it, anyway) came at a steep cost to the nation's sovereignty and independence. Over the next few years, Syria and Israel imposed unprecedented levels of control over Lebanon's territory and political life, visiting terrible destruction and misery on its inhabitants. One consequence, among many, of Lebanon's geopolitical eclipse was the country's demotion as a U.S. foreign policy issue. Under President Carter, the United States would revert to its pre–civil war practice of treating Lebanon's crises less as a policy area in their own right than as a subset of regional concerns. Not until the early 1980s would Lebanon again rise to the top of the policy agenda—and then it would do so with a vengeance.

Another consequence of Syria's and Israel's domination of Lebanon was a sharpening of political lines among Arab Americans. As Syria and Israel grew ever more enmeshed in the affairs of their common neighbor, Arab American discourse on Lebanon was increasingly regionalized. Discussion of the intra-Lebanese dispute, sparing and tentative to begin with, all but vanished. Replacing it were two competing narratives, one highlighting Israel's offenses against the people of Lebanon, the other focusing on Syria's. While the first perspective was more representative of those calling themselves Arab Americans, the second—precisely because it was anti-Syrian—enjoyed disproportionate influence on Capitol Hill, though it had far less sway over the executive branch.

In the months after the Riyadh summit, Syria tightened its grip over Lebanon, concentrating mainly on neutralizing the Left. In March 1977, Kamal Jumblatt, the most prominent Leftist opponent of the Syrian occupation, was killed by gunmen widely assumed to be under Syrian command. Jumblatt's assassination, along with other Syrian-sponsored anti-Left measures (including a crackdown on news media that fell less heavily on the Right), crippled the Left, which ceased to pose an effective challenge to Lebanon's confessional political system. Asad curtailed the PLO's activities as well, though he had to proceed more cautiously in this area because the PLO enjoyed a degree of diplomatic protection in inter-Arab politics.[66]

Syria's preoccupation with containing Leftist and PLO elements created an opportunity for both the Rightists and their Israeli supporters to strengthen their own positions in Lebanon. Into 1977 the Right continued its efforts, begun during the civil war, to carve out a semiautonomous Maronite enclave northeast of Beirut, a project aided, as before, by clandestine Israeli arms shipments. Meanwhile, in South Lebanon, which Syrian forces generally avoided, Israel began extending its control by means of the South Lebanon Army (SLA), a proxy Christian militia led by a renegade Lebanese Army major named Sa'ad Haddad. The SLA clashed with PLO units operating in the south. In a modest policy adjustment, Asad started to assist those PLO fighters by dispatching Syrian-led Palestinians to join their ranks. The Israelis redoubled their support for the SLA and by the summer of 1977 were sending their own forces on brief forays across the Israeli-Lebanese border.[67]

The skirmishes of 1977 escalated to open warfare in the following year. By early 1978, Israel hankered for an opportunity to impose greater control over South Lebanon. Syria, anxious about Israeli encroachment, drew closer to the PLO and grew less tolerant of Rightist muscle flexing. In

March 1978, a PLO attack on civilians in Israel prompted the Israelis to launch a three-month invasion of South Lebanon. Hundreds of Lebanese and Palestinian civilians were killed, and tens of thousands became refugees. A month earlier, clashes had broken out between Syrian and Rightist forces. Centered mainly in Beirut, the violence continued intermittently over the ensuing year, reaching a crescendo in the summer and fall of 1978 with Syria's massive artillery bombardment of Christian East Beirut. Comparable numbers of civilians, mostly Lebanese Christians, were killed and displaced.[68]

In these ways, both Israel and Syria gave powerful ammunition to their critics, including Arab American ones. Israel's invasion of Lebanon was the focus of most Arab American activism in the spring and summer of 1978. The NAAA, the AAUG, and numerous other Arab-friendly organizations at the national and local levels denounced the invasion in demonstrations, teach-ins, relief drives, newsletters, and letters and telegrams to political leaders and media outlets. In May, the NAAA filed a federal lawsuit charging that Israel's use in Lebanon of American-supplied weapons—including devastating cluster bombs (see chapter 8)—violated the Arms Export Control Act, which required that such weapons be employed only in self-defense. The NAAA withdrew its lawsuit after Israel pulled out of Lebanon later that summer. As usual, Arab American groups differed over how to interpret the U.S. role in the invasion. Whereas the NAAA portrayed Israel as defying the Carter administration's sincere but ineffectual calls for restraint, the AAUG claimed that Israel was "acting in complete collusion with the U.S. government." (In another repetition of old patterns, Jim Abourezk adopted a stance substantively similar to the NAAA's but stylistically in tune with the AAUG's; he exerted little influence over his senatorial colleagues.)[69] On the outrageousness of Israel's behavior, however, there was broad agreement among Arab Americans. For the remainder of the decade, and even more so into the following one, Israeli aggression was the prism through which most Arab American and Arab-friendly groups viewed and presented Lebanon's politics.

Of course, Syria's own military excesses in 1978 permitted an alternative portrayal of Lebanon's plight. Since the Riyadh summit, the ALL had focused mainly on relief and reconstruction efforts, taking occasional rhetorical swipes at Palestinians in Lebanon while saying little, if anything, about Syria.[70] By early 1978, however, the league was increasingly critical of Damascus. "We understand and accept the necessity of foreign intervention in Lebanon in 1976 to put an end to the fighting," the ALL wrote in a February 1978 letter to President Carter. But it now appeared that "the protector has designs on becoming the oppressor."[71]

In May, Robert Basil, a former Pentagon official with close ties to Rightist leaders, was elected president of the ALL. As Syria's military operations in Lebanon escalated, Basil presided over the rapid transformation of the league into an almost single-mindedly anti-Syrian lobbying operation. In newspaper ads, interviews, speeches, and congressional testimony, the ALL accused Syria of seeking to "exterminat[e] the Christian population of Lebanon," "to destroy what remains of their ancient and democratic society," and "to transform Lebanon into a virtual puppet of Syria." In the fall of 1978, the ALL enlisted a Who's Who of Lebanese Rightists to join its stateside campaign. Former foreign minister and Maronite elder statesman Charles Malik, on an extended stay in the United States, spoke at several ALL fund-raisers in the Midwest and on the West Coast. When Dory Chamoun visited Washington, the ALL arranged for him to meet with members of Congress. Bashir Gemayel, a rising star in the Rightist Phalangist militia and a future president-elect of Lebanon—he would be assassinated in 1982 while preparing to take office—appeared on the printed program for an ALL fund-raiser in Los Angeles but seems not to have attended the event.[72]

By the spring of 1979, ALL fund-raising programs were featuring prominent American leaders as well: senators John Glenn and Howard Metzenbaum of Ohio, senator Paul Tsongas of Massachusetts, governor Edward King of Massachusetts, and several House members and mayors. Here, too, there appear to have been some no-shows, but the fact that such figures agreed to speak in the first place testified to the league's rising prominence.[73]

That prominence was almost entirely attributable to the dovetailing of the ALL's positions with those of Israel and its American supporters. Since the summer of 1977, Israeli prime minister Menachem Begin had publicly championed the cause of Lebanese Christians (something his predecessors had done mainly covertly), claiming they faced "annihilation" by Palestinians and Lebanese Muslims. In 1978, Israel's Lebanon policy, like the ALL's, took a sharply anti-Syrian turn. During Syria's bombardment of East Beirut, Israel stepped up its military support for Rightist militias, gathered troops on its border with Lebanon, ostentatiously patrolled Lebanon's coastline with gunboats and helicopters, and shelled PLO positions in West Beirut, all in an apparent effort to boost Rightist morale. The ALL openly welcomed these gestures and made a special effort to cultivate Israel's strongest supporters in Congress, such as senator Daniel Patrick Moynihan of New York, senator Henry ("Scoop") Jackson of Washington, and representative Edward Derwinski of Illinois. In August 1978, with the support of both the ALL and the America Israel Public Affairs Committee (AIPAC), Derwinski persuaded his House colleagues to strip $90 million in economic assistance to Syria from the foreign aid bill. It took an all-out lobbying effort by the Carter administration, which hoped to soften Asad's opposition to the just-concluded Camp David agreement (see chapter 8), to induce the Senate to restore Syria's aid.[74]

Other Arab Americans were contemptuous of the ALL's boisterous championing of Christian Lebanon, and repulsed by its open alliance with Israel. "They don't represent all the Maronites and they certainly don't represent all the Christians," Abourezk scoffed. "What they represent is a small right-wing minority with a lot of money who are determined to use the money and their alliance with Israel to restore themselves to power" in Lebanon. Basil retorted that Abourezk had it backwards: "As far as the American Lebanese community is concerned, Jim Abourezk doesn't represent anyone—and that is a real tragedy." Abourezk had come to Congress with great promise, Basil said, but then "became locked in bitter conflict with the Israelis and the Jewish lobby" and was now subordinating Lebanese interests to Palestinian ones. As for the Israelis, Basil said, they were simply trying to prevent "the demise of another Western-oriented democracy" in the region. Freedom-loving Lebanese should welcome their help.[75]

Whether Basil recognized this or not, it was significant that Abourezk, the NAAA, and other moderate Arab Americans—many of them of Christian Lebanese background—privileged the anti-Israeli narrative over the anti-Syrian one. At any point since 1975 (and especially in 1978, when much of Christian Beirut was genuinely imperiled), the casual observer might have expected such figures to be more susceptible to the appeals of the Lebanese Right. Instead, they generally validated the pan-Arab reading of Lebanon's predicament, assigning to Israel the lion's share of blame. In this respect, the Lebanese civil war was a confirming experience for Arab American moderates. Faced with a series of crises that permitted alternative readings, they doubled down on their pan-Arab commitments.

The Carter administration, too, had little interest in promoting the ALL's cause. Though highly critical of Syria's military conduct in Lebanon, the administration saw no viable alternative, for the moment, to the perpetuation of the ADF's mission in the country, and this meant a continuation of Syria's dominant role. The abrupt removal of Syrian power and influence from Lebanon could well mean a return to the anarchy of 1975–1976.[76]

Over the longer term, Carter and his top foreign policy advisers believed that the best hope for stabilizing Lebanon lay in an Arab-Israeli settlement that addressed Palestinian national claims. On this, the administration agreed with the NAAA and with other moderate Arab American and Arab-friendly commentators—a convergence of views that presented a major opportunity for the advocates of "evenhandedness" in Arab-Israeli diplomacy. Much depended, however, on whether the Carter administration could sustain its own commitment to evenhandedness against the countervailing diplomatic and domestic pressures. An ambitious initiative the administration had launched in early 1977 was already yielding answers to that question.

Chapter 8

Camp David Retreat

Jimmy Carter and Arab-Israeli Diplomacy, 1977–1979

It was, by all accounts, a moving occasion. President Jimmy Carter, on a visit to Jerusalem, stood with Israeli prime minister Menachem Begin at the Wailing Wall and offered a heartfelt prayer. "Oh God," Carter said, "guide the Arabs and Israelis toward a permanent peace." "Amen," murmured his Israeli host. "Oh God," the president continued, "guide the Egyptians and Israelis to real peace and coexistence, with open borders and trade." "Amen," Begin repeated. "Oh God," Carter went on, "guide the Israelis to relinquish to the Arabs all the territory seized since the 1967 Middle East War." Begin cleared his throat: "Mind you, Mr. President, you're only talking to a wall."[1]

This joke, which circulated in Cairo in late 1978, suggested the formidable obstacles facing the advocates of an "evenhanded" Arab-Israeli settlement, a cohort that now included the president of the United States. Upon taking office in January 1977, and with scant appreciation of the resistance he would arouse, Jimmy Carter had launched the most ambitious Middle East peace initiative ever attempted by a U.S. president. Over the next several months, his administration labored to convene an international conference at which the main parties to the Arab-Israeli dispute, including Palestinians, could reach a comprehensive settlement entailing the fullest possible exchange of land for peace and a modest accommodation of

Palestinian national demands. The principal Arab actors, no longer preoccupied with the Lebanese civil war and eager to end the ten-year-old Israeli occupation, generally supported Carter's initiative. The Israelis, by contrast, were deeply suspicious, fearing the U.S. scheme would force them to relinquish more captured territory than they deemed acceptable and to acknowledge the validity of Palestinian claims. Echoing these opposing responses, most Arab American activists were encouraged by Carter's efforts, while American Jewish groups voiced consternation and anger. The Israeli and Jewish positions, needless to say, held vastly greater weight in domestic American politics.

Carter failed to convene the international conference or to achieve a comprehensive peace settlement. In the fall of 1977, taken aback by the intensity of Israeli and Jewish opposition, the president modified his initiative to suit Israeli preferences, angering Arabs instead. Professing dismay over these controversies, president Anwar Sadat of Egypt stunned the world by making a solo visit to Jerusalem to meet Israel's leaders face-to-face. Carter was obliged to put his conference plans on hold and support the new Egyptian-Israeli dialogue. Both Carter and Sadat hoped for an Egyptian-Israeli understanding that paved the way for a broader settlement along the lines envisioned in early 1977. By the summer of 1978, however, Carter had lost his stomach for confronting Israel. His mediation of Egyptian-Israeli talks, though extraordinarily energetic and resourceful, was circumscribed to avoid pressing Israel too hard.

The resulting agreements—the Camp David Accords of September 1978 and the Egyptian-Israeli peace treaty of March 1979—committed Israel to relinquish all of the Sinai Peninsula, and Egypt to make full peace with Israel. Yet they contained no credible provisions for ending Israel's occupation of the remaining Arab territories and thus for resolving the wider conflict. The Arab world recoiled in anger, both at Sadat for leaving his fellow Arabs in the lurch and at Washington for encouraging this abandonment. Ironically, however, even as the bilateral peace process deepened Arab alienation from U.S. policy, it helped to generate a somewhat more fully rounded image of the Arab world, and of Arab Americans, within the United States.

Jimmy Carter came to the presidency harboring what he later called an "unshakable" commitment to Israel's security, a position he attributed, unconvincingly, to his deep Christian faith.[2] Yet he also believed that settling the Arab-Israeli conflict was a vital U.S. interest and that any viable agreement required painful concessions from Arabs and Israelis alike. Carter's thinking bore the imprint of his national security adviser, Zbigniew Brzezinski, a Polish-born academic whom Carter had consulted on foreign policy since 1974. Over that same period, Brzezinski had publicly advocated a comprehensive Middle East settlement entailing a restoration of the 1967 borders (with minor modifications), Arab recognition of Israel, and some form of Palestinian self-determination on the West Bank and the Gaza Strip. He had coauthored the 1975 Brookings Institution report, which proposed a settlement along these lines.[3] Carter prudently kept these ideas out of his campaign speeches, but he recognized their merit and embraced them as president.

Carter's secretary of state, Cyrus Vance, was a former Defense Department official who had said little in public about the Arab-Israeli conflict or any other foreign policy issue. But he was well informed about the region and agreed that a comprehensive settlement was an urgent priority. Vance and Brzezinski would famously clash over other issues (especially U.S.-Soviet relations, on which Brzezinski was more hawkish), but on Arab-Israeli policy they worked relatively harmoniously. It helped that Vance's principal Middle East aides, Alfred Atherton and Harold Saunders, got along

Figure 18. Zbigniew Brzezinski and Cyrus Vance, 1977. Courtesy of the Jimmy Carter Presidential Library.

with William Quandt, their counterpart on Brzezinski's National Security Council (NSC) staff (and another coauthor of the Brookings report). Even more than their superiors, these men were eager to push for a comprehensive settlement.[4]

Indeed, throughout the policymaking bureaucracies of both the State Department and the NSC, there was an unusual degree of consensus regarding Arab-Israeli peacemaking. Most analysts agreed that Henry Kissinger's step-by-step diplomacy had run its course. They could see that the Arab states had no interest in further partial agreements and were insisting on a broad-based settlement that ended the Israeli occupation and addressed Palestinian national claims. Failure to pursue such a settlement could well result in another Middle East war, with all the strategic and economic hazards such an event would entail. The Arabs' firmness, however, was tempered by moderation. With varying levels of explicitness, Egypt, Syria, Jordan, Saudi Arabia, and the dominant factions of the Palestine Liberation Organization (PLO) had signaled a willingness to coexist with Israel if the above requirements were met. On this matter the Arabs themselves showed rare unanimity.[5]

Most U.S. policy analyst believed, therefore, that the time was ripe for an all-out effort to achieve a comprehensive settlement. Their favored approach, which Carter and his top advisers quickly endorsed, was to reconvene the international conference in Geneva that had met briefly in December 1973, only to adjourn indefinitely and lapse into disuse. Opinions varied on details, but the core idea was to bring together Israel, the Arab states, and Palestinian representatives to conclude an overall settlement along the lines outlined above. Carter and his advisers doubted, however, that all of the settlement's terms could be worked out at the Geneva Conference. It would probably be necessary for the parties to reach broad agreement beforehand, through indirect negotiations facilitated by the United States. Geneva would be a forum for ironing out final details and ratifying the settlement.[6]

The U.S. program that emerged in the spring of 1977 was by no means in complete accord with standard Arab positions. It called on the Arab states to commit themselves in advance to the full normalization of relations with Israel, rather than to mere nonbelligerency. It also ruled out an independent Palestinian state, envisioning instead an ill-defined Palestinian "homeland," possibly federated with Jordan. Nor, for reasons discussed below, did the Carter administration support the Arabs' insistence that the PLO be immediately and unconditionally included in any reconvened

Geneva Conference. Unless the PLO substantially altered some of its basic positions, the Americans said, it must step aside and let others represent the Palestinians. On the whole, though, the U.S. approach was more acceptable to the Arabs than it was to the Israelis, who were determined to retain substantial portions of the occupied territories and strongly opposed any sort of Palestinian entity.[7] In the coming months, therefore, Washington's peace efforts encountered much stiffer resistance from Israel and its U.S. supporters than from Arab actors. Carter and his foreign policy team tried to insulate themselves from pro-Israel pressures, but this proved impossible.

Over the spring of 1977, to signal the importance he assigned to his peace initiative, Carter met personally with key Middle Eastern leaders. He hosted successive visits by prime minister Yitzhak Rabin of Israel, president Anwar Sadat of Egypt, King Hussein of Jordan, and Crown Prince Fahd of Saudi Arabia; he met in Geneva with president Hafiz al-Asad of Syria. In the main, Carter had friendly and productive sessions with the Arabs, who encouraged his peace efforts and did not much dwell on their differences with U.S. policy. In a phone call to British prime minister James Callaghan, Carter reported that he was "favourably impressed with the Arab leaders ... They may be wonderful con artists but my impression is that they genuinely want to make some progress." The encounter with Rabin was more difficult. The prime minister was cool and reticent, immune to Carter's attempts at charm. Following a White House dinner, Rabin delivered a senseless snub when he curtly declined an invitation to join Carter as he looked in on his nine-year-old daughter, Amy, asleep in her bedroom. The substantive exchange was no better. Israel, Rabin made clear, did not object to attending the Geneva Conference, only to making meaningful concessions once there. He said that that Israel must retain control of Sharm al-Shaykh, stay on the Golan Heights, and keep substantial portions of the West Bank. Rabin's attitude, Carter later wrote, "caused me to think again about whether we should launch another major effort for peace."[8]

Carter would soon look back on Rabin with nostalgia. In May, Israel held national elections. To the surprise of international observers, the right-wing Likud bloc prevailed, ending a Labor monopoly on political power that had existed since 1948. Menachem Begin, the Likud leader, became prime minister. Carter and his advisers were shaken by this development. In the prestate period, Begin had led a paramilitary group, the Irgun, that committed atrocities against Palestinian civilians. On current issues, his stances were zealous and uncompromising. He believed that all of historical Palestine had been divinely granted to the Jews and that Israel, therefore, must retain all of Gaza and the West Bank, or "Judea and Samaria," as he termed the latter. He insisted that Resolution 242, which obligated Israel to relinquish captured Arab lands, did not apply to the West Bank and Gaza, and he favored a dramatic increase in Jewish settlement of the occupied territories. There was a cruel irony in Begin's elevation at this moment, just months after Carter's own inauguration. As Kathleen Christison writes, "The first U.S. president to recognize the Palestinian stake in the conflict over Palestine confronted the first Israeli prime minister, although not the last, absolutely determined never to cede an inch of territory in what remained of old Palestine."[9]

Begin did establish a new hard-line pattern at the highest level of Israeli politics. At the time of his ascendancy, however, he seemed so far out of the Israeli mainstream as to present what Brzezinski considered a "perverse" opportunity to the Carter administration. "Begin, by his extremism, is likely to split both Israeli public opinion and the American Jewish community," Brzezinski wrote in a May 20 memorandum to Carter. "A position of *moderate* firmness on our part will rally to you in time both the Israeli opposition and significant portions of the American Jewish community," as each of those sectors would favor Carter's peace efforts over Begin's intransigence.[10] Brzezinski's prediction was wide of the mark. The Carter administration never succeeded in driving a wedge between Begin on the one hand and the Israeli opposition and American Jews on the other. Begin's Labor rivals would offer only weak resistance to his security policies and sometimes do so from the right.[11] Many American Jews were indeed discomfited by Begin's election, but they soon got over that reaction and gravitated toward the new prime minister, generally siding with him when he clashed with their own president.[12]

In July, Begin visited Washington to get acquainted with Carter. On a personal level, the meeting was more cordial than the Carter-Rabin encounter in the spring, and Begin showed some flexibility on procedural questions. Israel would attend the Geneva Conference, he said, and it would not object if Palestinians participated, as long as they were part of the Jordanian delegation and not tied to the PLO. Substantively, however, Begin took an even harder line than his predecessor. Like Rabin, he said that Israel should retain part of the Sinai and most of the Golan, but he also rejected any "foreign sovereignty" over the West Bank and Gaza. When the question of a Palestinian homeland arose, Begin had an adviser treat Carter to a brief history lecture, the burden of which was that a Palestinian homeland already existed—in Jordan.[13]

Begin also visited Capitol Hill, where he had a closed-door meeting with the Senate Foreign Relations Committee. Jim Abourezk, a committee member, witnessed what he later called a "nauseating display of senatorial servility." He tried to keep quiet, but when senator Harrison Schmitt of New Mexico, a former astronaut, "asked obsequiously, 'Mr. Prime Minister, do you think the Arabs really want peace?'" Abourezk could take no more. He jumped to his feet and demanded to know why Israel refused to deal with the PLO. "Who does the PLO represent?" Begin rhetorically asked. "They represent the Palestinian Arabs," Abourezk said, "and are at least as legitimate as the Irgun . . . was" before Israel's founding. "Sacrilege!" cried Begin. The PLO rejoiced in the killing of children, he said, whereas the Irgun had always apologized when its operations caused civilian casualties. The heated exchange forced the meeting to an early close. "Abourezk could start a riot in an empty hall," senator John Glenn of Ohio groused to a colleague as everyone filed out. Abourezk wasn't getting along with astronauts that day.[14]

Sacrilege or no, the Carter administration was eager to find a way to include the PLO in negotiations. The Palestinian issue was central to the conflict, and the PLO was the only credible representative of the Palestinian people. The principal obstacle to including the PLO was Henry Kissinger's 1975 pledge to the Israeli government that the United States would not negotiate with the PLO as long as it refused to recognize Israel or accept Resolution 242. In March 1977 in Cairo, the Palestine National Council (PNC), the PLO's legislative body, had reissued its call for the establishment of a Palestinian state on any portion of Palestine that might be liberated. The implication was that a Jewish state could remain on Palestine's unliberated territory, but that was as far as the PNC would go toward recognizing Israel. The PNC also repeated its long-standing rejection of Resolution 242, on the ground that it treated the Palestinian people as nothing more than refugees. Nonetheless, there were indications that PLO chairman Yasser Arafat was encouraged by Carter's support for a Palestinian "homeland" and wished to be included in any peace talks.[15]

Carter and his advisers hoped to find a way around the PLO's objection to Resolution 242. Perhaps, they reasoned, the PLO could be induced to recognize 242 with an accompanying reservation about the resolution's silence on Palestinian rights. As recognition of Israel was embedded in the resolution, such a statement would permit the Carter administration to open a dialogue with the PLO without violating Kissinger's pledge.[16] (Few

U.S. officials noted the irony that, following Begin's ascension in May, Israel itself rejected 242 as it related to Palestinian land.) Throughout the summer of 1977, the administration mounted an extensive, multipronged effort to persuade the PLO to issue a qualified endorsement of 242. Because they could not talk directly to that organization, the Americans relied on third parties, the principal ones being the Egyptian and Saudi governments and two private individuals, Walid Khalidi, a Palestinian political science professor at the American University of Beirut with close ties to Arafat, and Landrum Bolling, an American Quaker educator and foundation head. A friend of First Lady Rosalynn Carter, Bolling was a frequent traveler to the Middle East who also knew Arafat personally.[17]

In his meetings with President Asad and Prince Fahd that spring, Carter asked each leader to see whether the PLO could revisit its position on Resolution 242 and possibly endorse it in qualified form. Fahd, at least, followed through on the request, and in June the PLO responded by telling the Saudis "to ask the Americans to suggest a text of what they [the PLO] might say." Several weeks passed with no American reply, so in mid-July PLO spokesman Mahmoud Abbas (who decades later would serve as PLO chairman and president of the Palestinian Authority) contacted Bolling in Damascus to reiterate the request.[18] Apprised of Abbas's approach, Brzezinski reminded Carter of the PLO-242 initiative. Carter instructed Vance, who was preparing to travel to the Middle East, to pursue the matter.[19]

Arriving in Taif, Saudi Arabia, on August 7, Vance gave a draft statement to his Saudi hosts: "The PLO accepts UN Security Council Resolution 242, with the reservation that it considers that the resolution does not make adequate reference to the question of the Palestinians since it fails to make any reference to a homeland for the Palestinian people. It is recognized that the language of Resolution 242 relates to the right of all states in the Middle East to live in peace." If the PLO delivered this statement, or words to the same effect, the United States would start talking to the organization. The Saudis were optimistic. They told Vance that Arafat, who had himself just visited the Kingdom, was already thinking of issuing of a qualified endorsement of Resolution 242. The PLO's Executive Committee would meet that evening to consider the matter. The next day, however, Vance learned that Arafat had failed to convince hard-liners on the committee to change the organization's stance on 242.[20]

Still, Arafat continued to probe for an understanding with Washington, deploying Professor Khalidi in the effort. In mid-August, Khalidi met with U.S. ambassador to Lebanon Richard B. Parker and asked him what, beyond a mere dialogue with the United States, the PLO could hope to gain by accepting Resolution 242. Would the Americans support a Palestinian state? On August 17, the State Department instructed Parker to tell Khalidi that the question of Palestinian statehood could be resolved only "in the context of the Geneva negotiations. For the U.S. to endorse any particular solution would be to prejudge those negotiations and undermine our ability to play the honest broker role which both sides have asked us to assume." Parker was to remind Khalidi that the United States had already endorsed a Palestinian "homeland" and was committed to the principle of Palestinian "self-determination." These facts, along with the proffered dialogue with Washington, gave the PLO the best available guarantee of success.[21] Parker spoke as instructed to Khalidi, who promised to convey the message to the PLO leadership. The professor warned, however, that the leadership would have difficulty selling the U.S. position to the organization as a whole.[22]

On August 23, Parker cabled home a response. The PLO would issue a statement on 242 that "fits the US requirements," provided the United States agreed to state publicly that it believed:

> A. The PLO represents the Palestinian people;
> B. The Palestinian people should live independently in their homeland; and,
> C. The PLO should participate in negotiations of a settlement which involves their national fate and interests.

Parker commented that these conditions were "considerably more restrained than I had anticipated." While point A might pose difficulties for the United States, "B and C are not much different from what we put to Khalidi. . . . As seen from here we are making progress."[23]

Parker's optimism was short-lived. Two days later, before Washington could formally respond to the proposals, the PLO's forty-member Central Council convened in Damascus. It condemned "United States and Zionist maneuvers" to deny the Palestinian people their right to self-determination and restated the PLO's familiar criticism of Resolution 242. Apparently, this negative response reflected growing doubts among Palestinians that the Americans were acting in good faith. Over the previous weeks, PLO leaders had received conflicting assessments of what to expect if they endorsed Resolution 242. Saudi leaders had initially assured them that the United States would formally recognize the PLO, start negotiating with it, and invite it to participate in the Geneva Conference. The Saudis subsequently provided a more accurate report: Washington would merely open a dialogue with the PLO and recommend its invitation to Geneva, with no guarantee of diplomatic outcomes. The PLO also had gotten wind of an idea Vance had floated on his diplomatic rounds: that, during the months or years in which their final status was being negotiated, the West Bank and Gaza might be placed under a joint Israeli-Jordanian trusteeship. This scheme not only insulted the Palestinians by implying they were not ready for self-government; it threatened to place them at the mercy of two hostile powers. The effect of these impressions was to discredit the argument, presented by Arafat and other PLO moderates, that this was a suitable moment to take a chance on American diplomacy. The Central Council agreed, however, to meet a month later to review the issue.[24]

The Carter administration made a final attempt to bring the PLO into the diplomatic fold. On the evenings of September 9 and 11, Bolling met with Arafat in Beirut and urged him not to squander the opportunity. A dialogue with the United States was no small thing, Bolling said. "By 'dialogue,'" he wrote in his contemporaneous account of the meetings,

> I said I was sure the U.S. Government meant the opening up of a whole range of negotiating issues and processes. . . . I said that the U.S. would *not* make some secret promise that it would guarantee admission of the PLO to the Geneva Conference, nor would it promise the PLO the creation of a Palestinian state. . . . Such promises, if they were given, would be meaningless at this stage. What the U.S. was offering him was the "opening of the gate" to essential PLO participation in the negotiating process and that this could transform the whole situation.[25]

Arafat replied that, as much as he craved a dialogue with the United States, he could not credibly advocate acceptance of U.S. terms. Despite initial indications of much stronger American guarantees, it was now clear that the PLO was being "asked to give everything and get nothing—only a promise of a dialogue and not even acceptance as the sole representatives of the Palestinians, which the Arab states and the United Nations have already accorded us." Moreover, Arafat said, the substantive provisions of the U.S. plan were unacceptable. The plan offered the Palestinians not a full-fledged state but a demilitarized "entity," to be established following a transitional period, lasting perhaps several years, in which Israel and Jordan might be granted trusteeships over the West Bank and Gaza. A trusteeship scenario would be disastrous for Palestinians. "Not only would the Israelis interfere constantly in our affairs," Arafat said, "but King Hussein would have the time to create pressures, threaten people, bribe and corrupt those he could get to follow him so that, in the end, he would destroy our right to have an independent state." No Palestinian could agree to such terms. "Not any of us—hard-liners, moderates, pro-Soviet, pro-Western—none of us."[26]

Still, Arafat was unhappy about his failure to connect with Washington. "We are in a cul de sac," he said. "In the absence of an [American] understanding of the reality of our situation there is a long hard road ahead. But, by secret communication, perhaps we can find a way. We want to find a way." Arafat promised Bolling that he would keep trying to produce a statement on 242 that satisfied the United States.[27]

The chairman did his best. When the PLO's Central Council reconvened on September 20, Arafat argued so strenuously for accepting the U.S. terms that he reportedly broke a glass tabletop with his fist and cut his hand. Again, however, his position was defeated. Several days later Bolling, who had returned to Washington, told Brzezinski that Arafat could not accept 242, even with a reservation, unless the United States guaranteed that a PLO-led Palestinian state resulted from the negotiations. These terms were stiffer than the ones Ambassador Parker had conveyed to Washington a month earlier. The Carter administration suspended its efforts to include the PLO in the Geneva talks.[28]

To some extent, the failure to establish a U.S.-PLO dialogue resulted from misunderstanding. The Americans had never intended to pledge much in exchange for a PLO endorsement of Resolution 242. They would start talking to that organization, but were prepared to do little else. Because PLO leaders had received exaggerated initial reports about what such a concession would yield, however, they were all the more disappointed to learn what was actually on offer. Moreover, Arafat seems not to have realized that this *was* a misunderstanding; he later attributed the discrepancy to "a clear retreat" on Washington's part.[29] Such miscues might have been avoided had the PLO been able to hear directly from U.S. officials, rather than relying on secondhand accounts. It was a self-perpetuating conundrum for PLO moderates: because they had no direct dialogue with the United States, they could not easily remove the misunderstandings that obstructed the establishment of such a dialogue.

Fundamentally, however, PLO leaders understood what the United States was proposing—or at least they did after getting the more accurate Saudi reports—and they rejected it on intelligible grounds. Endorsing Resolution 242 was tantamount to recognizing Israel's legitimacy. To most Palestinian moderates, such recognition was the PLO's final card, to be played only in exchange for the achievement (or at least the imminent prospect) of Palestinian statehood. Carter was asking the PLO to surrender that card for a much lesser reward. Although Arafat himself was willing to do this, few other PLO figures were.

The failure to reach an understanding with the PLO did not dissuade the Carter administration from trying to include Palestinians in the Geneva talks. On September 13, the State Department publicly stated, "The Palestinians must be involved in the peacemaking process. Their representatives will have to be at Geneva for the Palestinian question to be solved." But who, if not PLO leaders, should those representatives be? Since the spring, the administration had considered a formula whereby Palestinian figures not associated with the PLO, or at least not conspicuously so, participated in the conference either as part of a unified Arab delegation or attached to the delegation of one Arab country. Administration officials now pursued this scenario more seriously.[30]

A major obstacle they faced, however, was the wide disagreement among the parties over appropriate procedures for Geneva. Israel and Egypt wanted the Arab countries divided into separate delegations, whereas Syria and Jordan favored a unified Arab delegation. Israel wanted any Palestinian participants to be attached to the Jordanian delegation, a position Jordan rejected. The Carter administration devised a complex scenario for finessing these disagreements. The conference would open with a plenary session at which the Arabs were united in a single delegation that included Palestinians, some of whom could be members of the PLO as long as they "were not well-known." The Arabs would then split up into national delegations, each negotiating with Israel over its separate territorial claims. No Palestinians would be attached to the national delegations, but a special committee formed of Israel, Egypt, Jordan, and the Palestinian representatives would negotiate over the status of the West Bank and Gaza. Meanwhile, a separate committee consisting of Israel, the Palestinians, and a larger group of Arab states would address the issue of Palestinian refugees. In late September, the administration specified these procedures in a "working paper" that it began circulating among the parties.[31]

If the collapse of the PLO initiative failed to shake the Carter administration's determination to tackle the Palestinian question, neither did it improve the administration's relations with Begin, whose intransigence on the issues and zeal for settlement building rankled U.S. officials. On August 28, Carter privately discussed the Middle East with Vance, Brzezinski, and other advisers. The president, Brzezinski noted in a memorandum, "indicated his increasing frustration with the Israeli position and his unwillingness to maintain a policy in which in effect we are financing their conquests and they simply defy us in an intransigent fashion and generally make a mockery of our advice and our preferences." On August 31, Brzezinski attended a dinner party and, according to the diary entry of a journalist in attendance, "said that sooner or later there would have to be a confrontation with Begin over the PLO or the West Bank, even though this would mean a confrontation between Carter and American Jewry."[32]

On September 19, Carter held a contentious meeting in the White House with Moshe Dayan, now serving as Israel's foreign minister. Carter charged "that Israel was taking a very adamant stand and that the Arab side appears to be more flexible." Pressed on the issue of Jewish settlements in the occupied territories, Dayan promised that, while existing settlements would be expanded, Israel would establish no new settlements for one year. (Begin would fail to honor that pledge.)[33] On Geneva procedures, Dayan said that Israel could probably live with a unified Arab delegation that included some Palestinians affiliated with the PLO, provided they were not prominent members of the organization. Dayan urged that the Arabs not be told where this idea originated. "If they know it comes from us," he said, "they will certainly reject it. You should say that we object, and then you can try to force it on us." Carter agreed to this approach.[34] The firm line with Israel seemed to be working.

But maintaining that firmness was no easy task, a reality underscored by an unexpectedly controversial exercise in superpower diplomacy. Since early September, State Department officials had negotiated with their Soviet counterparts over the wording of a joint U.S.-Soviet statement of principles to guide the reconvened Geneva Conference. As the two superpowers were formal cochairs of the conference, the issuing of such a statement was a matter of course, and few Carter administration officials imagined the ritual would raise eyebrows. The statement, moreover, was shaping up to be a bland document. Eager to get the conference under way, the Soviets introduced hardly any contentious issues. They did not insist on PLO participation, and the draft they proposed called for neither a full restoration of the 1967 borders nor the establishment of a Palestinian state. The final version reiterated the main elements of Resolution 242 (without specifically mentioning the resolution) and called for a solution to the Palestinian problem that respected "the legitimate rights of the Palestinian people." Apart from this reference to Palestinian rights, which the Soviets contributed—previous U.S. statements had spoken only of Palestinian "interests"—all the elements of the joint statement were ones the Carter administration would have supplied on its own.[35] The communiqué was issued on October 1.

Despite its moderation, the U.S.-Soviet statement drew a firestorm of protest. The Israeli government, along with a wide swath of American politicians, commentators, and Jewish leaders, blasted the Carter administration for allowing Moscow a prominent role in the negotiations. For years, these critics noted, the United States had steadily pushed the Soviets to the margins of Middle East diplomacy; why was Carter now inviting them back to center stage? Also controversial was the communiqué's reference to "the legitimate rights of the Palestinian people." That phrasing, charged the Conference of Presidents of Major American Jewish Organizations, amounted to "code-words for Israel's destruction."[36]

Stunned by the criticism, Carter scrambled to limit the political damage. He insisted there had been no change in his Middle East policy and noted how conciliatory the Soviets had become on the issue. To a group of pro-Israel Congress members, he said, "I'd rather commit political suicide than hurt Israel"—an odd statement, given where the political dangers actually lay. During an October 4 meeting in New York, Carter assured Dayan that acceptance of the U.S.-Soviet communiqué was not a prerequisite for participating in the Geneva Conference. The next day Vance rewrote the late September "working paper" to exclude any reference to participation by PLO members, even those "not well-known." Carter thought these were minor concessions, but the public impression was of an administration in retreat.[37] That perception helped to trigger a chain of events that brought Carter's Geneva project to an untimely end.

Over the course of the summer, Sadat had grown increasingly apprehensive about evolving plans for Geneva. He had always opposed a unified Arab delegation, fearing it would grant Syria or the Palestinians a veto over Egypt's decisions. Carter's proposal that the Arabs form a single delegation to open the conference was, to Sadat, a step in the wrong direction. There was another way in which the Americans seemed to be backsliding. Initially, the Carter administration had agreed with Sadat that the basic terms of an Arab-Israeli settlement should be worked out in advance of the Geneva Conference, which would serve as a venue for sewing up details and ratifying the final settlement. The parties' numerous disagreements, however, had convinced the administration that this scenario was unworkable. The only feasible approach was to get all the parties to Geneva and force them to start negotiating. Once there, the argument went, they would act more reasonably for fear of being accused of wrecking the conference. Sadat, by contrast, adhered to his original view and was apprehensive about attending a multilateral conference at which basic issues remained unresolved.[38]

Whether through intuition or intelligence gathering, Prime Minister Begin had gained an inkling of Sadat's uneasiness and had, since midsummer, sought to open a secret dialogue with the Egyptian president and thereby interest him in a bilateral agreement. Through the intercession of Romanian president Nicolae Ceauşescu and Morocco's King Hassan, Begin established indirect contact with Sadat, and in mid-September Foreign Minister Dayan—disguised in a wig, a fake mustache, and large sunglasses in place of his distinctive eye patch—secretly flew to Morocco to meet with Hasan Tuhami, Egypt's deputy prime minister. Accounts of the meeting vary, but apparently Dayan intimated to Tuhami that Israel would return all of the Sinai in exchange for full peace with Egypt. Dayan insisted, however, that Sadat must first meet directly with Begin.[39]

The controversy over the U.S.-Soviet communiqué deepened Sadat's doubts about the Geneva scheme. The Carter administration's postcommuniqué assurances to Israel, and especially its revision of the U.S. working paper, caused a general hardening of positions on the Arab side. The PLO declared it would oppose any conference in which it could not openly participate, and Syria said it would not go to Geneva without the PLO. On October 19, Sadat himself wrote to Carter to urge reinstatement of the original U.S. working paper, which envisioned at least a limited PLO role. Carter replied that it would be impossible to get Israel to accept the earlier version; it was time to stop haggling over procedure and go to Geneva. Against this discouraging backdrop, Sadat sounded out Ismail Fahmy, Egypt's foreign minister, on a bold new gambit to break the impasse: a trip to Jerusalem to address the Israeli Knesset and meet Begin face-to-face.[40]

Fahmy was appalled. Visiting Israel would be tantamount to recognizing its legitimacy, he said, something that should occur only at the end of a successful negotiation, not at the outset. Moreover, diplomatic protocol would constrain Sadat from sharply challenging his hosts, who would easily adhere to their hard-line positions. The trip would produce nothing but charges of betrayal from other Arabs. Sadat listened patiently to Fahmy's objections and seemed persuaded by them. But in a November 9 address to the People's Assembly, Egypt's parliament, he declared he would go anywhere for peace, even to Jerusalem to speak to the Israeli Knesset. Accustomed to applauding on cue, the Assembly members reacted warmly to Sadat's statement, which many apparently regarded as nothing more than a rhetorical flourish. As it happened, Yasser Arafat was in the audience as Sadat's guest. Despite his horror at what he was hearing, he felt constrained to join in the applause. Arafat never forgave Sadat for this bit of manipulation.[41]

Egyptian newspapers deleted Sadat's Jerusalem reference from the printed text of the speech, but foreign journalists reported it and the news raced around the world. In Egypt and abroad, there was considerable uncertainty over whether Sadat's words should be taken literally. The Carter administration was also unsure, having received almost no advance notice of the statement.[42] Still, the administration thought it prudent to offer its good offices to follow up on Sadat's proposal. Prompted privately by U.S. officials, and publicly by CBS news anchor Walter Cronkite, in mid-November Begin invited Sadat to come to Jerusalem to address the Knesset, and Sadat quickly accepted the invitation. In Cairo's version of the Saturday Night Massacre, Fahmy resigned in protest and his second-in-command, minister of state for foreign affairs Mohammad Riad, followed suit. The rest of Egypt's foreign policy bureaucracy fell into confused silence. Undeterred by the domestic consternation, or by the cries of dismay emanating from other Arab capitals, Sadat flew to Ben-Gurion Airport on November 19.[43]

What did Sadat seek to accomplish by going to Israel? Doubtless, his ultimate goal was a diplomatic settlement that allowed Egypt to recover the Sinai, end its conflict with Israel, and concentrate on its own increasingly dire economic problems. Less clear is the relationship of this hoped-for bilateral deal to broader Arab-Israeli issues. If Sadat's objective was an agreement whereby Israel relinquished the Sinai and nothing else, then a direct dialogue with the Israelis was the surest route to that destination. It is unlikely, though, that Sadat sought a purely separate agreement in late 1977. In both public and private, he repeatedly rejected such an outcome as unthinkable and insisted that any understanding he reached with Begin would facilitate, not preclude, the reconvening of the Geneva Conference and the achievement of a comprehensive settlement that fully restored Arab territory.[44] Sadat probably did wish to torpedo the Geneva Conference, or at least limit it to a ceremonial function, so that he could negotiate for the Sinai without Arab interference. But he also apparently hoped that the resulting bilateral agreement would be couched in general language committing Israel to an eventual withdrawal to the 1967 lines, the details of which Israel and the other Arabs could work out among themselves. That way, Sadat could claim to have guarded Arab interests even as he focused on recovering Egyptian territory.[45]

But why would Israel agree, even only in principle, to withdraw to the 1967 lines? Because, Sadat maintained, his mission to Jerusalem would transform Israeli public opinion. "The Israeli leadership," he later wrote, "had been able to persuade [the Israeli people that] there was no hope for peace between Israel and the Arabs and had portrayed the Arabs as monsters who wanted only to drive Israel into the sea." Sadat's presence in Israel would discredit this myth and create a constituency for peace among the Israeli public, forcing Begin to deal fairly with all of Israel's Arab adversaries.[46]

The problem with Sadat's reasoning was that it woefully underestimated Begin's determination. The Israeli prime minister was so firm in his conviction that the West Bank and Gaza belonged to the Jewish people, and that Israel was entitled to remain on the Golan, as to be all but immune to domestic pressure on those issues. And anyway, Sadat's visit to Israel did not have the hoped-for effect on Israeli public opinion. The trip did provide palpable evidence, if any was needed, that Egypt was ready for peace, but it could offer no assurances about the attitude of Israel's other neighbors. To the contrary, Sadat's unilateral diplomacy frightened and angered his fellow Arabs, eliciting strident statements from them that left ordinary Israelis even less inclined to respect Arab claims. In the end, having extracted no Israeli concessions beyond the Sinai, Sadat would face the bleak choice of either admitting his gamble had failed or accepting the separate peace he had repeatedly disdained.

Throughout his three-day visit to Israel, and most clearly during his speech to the Knesset on November 20, Sadat did offer a forceful and persuasive presentation of the moderate Arab position. If Israel withdrew to the 1967 lines and allowed the Palestinians to exercise sovereignty on a portion of their former homeland, he pledged, the Arabs would be peaceful, cooperative, and generous neighbors.[47] In the very act of coming to make this case, however, Sadat dismantled the networks of pan-Arab and international support that were crucial to achieving his stated goal. Sadat had accepted Begin's invitation without consulting any other Arab governments. His trip also defied a prohibition, universally accepted among Arabs, against direct diplomatic engagement with Israel as long as it occupied Arab lands. These transgressions aroused alarm and resentment throughout the Arab world and more than offset any credit Sadat may have earned by upholding Arab positions during the visit. In early December, Libya, Syria, Algeria, South Yemen, and the PLO held a conference in Tripoli to condemn Egyptian unilateralism, prompting Cairo to sever relations with those four governments (but not with the PLO, which Sadat could ill afford to disown). Pro-Western Arab governments also criticized Egypt, though in milder terms. Publicly, Sadat acted as if everyone would still be going to Geneva, but the eruption of inter-Arab antagonism cast serious doubt on that prospect. By year's end, it was clear that any resumption of the Geneva Conference must be indefinitely postponed.[48]

This was a major setback for the cause Sadat professed to champion. The conference would have been cochaired by the Soviet Union, which was partial to the Arab side, and conducted according to internationally recognized principles that favored the moderate Arab position, such as the illegitimacy of acquiring territory by war and the right of all people to national self-determination. Having effectively scuttled this advantageous forum, Sadat would find himself facing Begin in bilateral negotiations, brokered by an American president who would try, but seldom manage, to be evenhanded.

The Carter administration was in a quandary over Sadat's initiative and the controversy surrounding it. A direct dialogue between Israel and its most powerful Arab neighbor simply had to receive full U.S. support. Yet Carter and his top advisers much preferred the Geneva option and were dismayed to see it so suddenly imperiled. They wanted to believe Sadat's claim that his visit to Israel had actually helped prepare the way to Geneva, but they soon had to abandon this comforting conceit. The only feasible course, the administration concluded as 1977 drew to a close, was to give full backing to the Sadat-Begin dialogue and hope that it could, at some future date, be broadened to include other Arab parties.[49]

For most Arab American activists, the first three quarters of 1977 had been a period of unusual optimism. In Jimmy Carter, they finally had a president who grasped the urgency of resolving the Arab-Israeli conflict in all of its dimensions, including the Palestinian one. No one doubted the enormous domestic obstacles the president confronted, and Begin's election in May was of course a huge shock. But Carter's persistence in the face of these challenges, and his firmness with Israel on a number of issues, generated considerable goodwill among Arab Americans. These hopeful earlier developments made the events of late 1977, which, in remarkably short order, clouded the prospects for a comprehensive settlement and placed many Arab Americans at odds with U.S. policy, all the more difficult to absorb.

The National Association of Arab Americans had been especially enthusiastic about Carter's approach. Meeting in February 1977 with NSC aide

Gary Sick and the president's assistant for public liaison Margaret Costanza, an NAAA delegation "praised . . . the responsiveness of the Administration to their concerns." In an open letter to Carter in June, NAAA president Joseph Baroody pledged his organization's "whole-hearted support of your efforts to bring about permanent peace in the Middle East," though he urged Carter to do more for the Palestinians. In mid-October, Baroody wrote Minnesota senator Hubert Humphrey, a vocal supporter of Israel, that "the American national interest will be better served by the Administration's current initiatives" than by the reflexive championing of Israeli positions.[50]

The Association of Arab American University Graduates was far less easily impressed, but by fall it, too, was expressing cautious optimism. In an October 3 telegram to Carter, the AAUG applauded the reference to "the legitimate rights of the Palestinian people" in the U.S.-Soviet communiqué issued two days earlier. "At long last," declared AAUG president Michael Suleiman at the group's annual convention later that month, "an American president has had the foresight and the courage to state publicly . . . that the Palestinians have to have a 'homeland.'"[51]

By now, however, the Carter administration was distancing itself from the U.S.-Soviet communiqué and seeking to placate Israel's supporters, a development that not only worried Arab American activists but underscored their dearth of political clout. Amid the uproar over the communiqué, the NAAA prepared an advertisement in support of Carter to run in the *Washington Post*. Before placing the ad, an NAAA officer asked a White House aide if such a move would be helpful. "The White House aide was horrified," the *Post* itself later reported. "The White House would prefer an NAAA statement attacking the President, the aide said—not really in jest." The ad never ran.[52]

The question of Arab American participation in the peace process reemerged a few weeks later, as Middle East diplomacy took a bizarre turn. In early October, Sadat had privately informed Carter that Arafat was eager to get around Washington's unwillingness to include the PLO in the Geneva talks. The chairman wondered if Edward Said of Columbia University, "who is an American professor of Palestinian origin and a very trustworthy man," could represent the Palestinians at Geneva. The Carter administration ignored the idea, but in mid-November Sadat publicly revealed that he had proposed to Carter that the Palestinians' representative be "an American professor of Palestinian origin." Although Sadat supplied no name, speculation immediately focused on Said and another Palestinian

American professor, Ibrahim Abu-Lughod of Northwestern University, a former AAUG president.[53] Approached by reporters on November 15, both men denied that anyone had asked them to represent the Palestinians and, in the words of the *New York Times*, "expressed annoyance . . . over such speculation." Abu-Lughod declined to discuss the matter further. "Keep my name out of the papers," he instructed the *Times* reporter, futilely. Said was more voluble: "My inclination is to say no. . . . It represents a political commitment I may feel in my heart and sentiments, but it doesn't seem practical. I'm principally a scholar and professor and not a full-time political person."[54]

That same day, Egyptian sources identified Said as Sadat's candidate, and public attention on the Columbia professor intensified. The journalist Christopher Hitchens went to dinner at Said's New York apartment and "discovered the sidewalk around his building was alive with cops and 'security' types"—presumably to protect Said in his newfound notoriety. (The physical danger to which Said and Abu-Lughod were now exposed perhaps explains their unhappiness about the publicity.) Said, Hitchens recalled, "was dismayed at Sadat's presumption and embarrassed . . . at the unsolicited attention it had earned him."[55]

Sadat never explained why he chose this moment to unveil the Said scenario. It is noteworthy, however, that Sadat made the revelation just a few days after his speech to the People's Assembly. Perhaps he wished to assure Arab audiences that, even though he was now preparing to visit Israel, he had not forgotten the Palestinians and indeed had devised an ingenious formula to ensure their participation at the Geneva Conference—to which, of course, his trip was but a prelude. That motive may also explain why he presented the idea as his own, not Arafat's. Whatever Sadat's thinking, the Said gambit failed to appease Arab critics and was rejected by Israel in any case.[56] All it did was harass its subject.

In a less crowded hour, Said's and Abu-Lughod's moment in the diplomatic spotlight probably would have attracted considerable attention from other Arab Americans. Amid the turmoil and confusion following Sadat's People's Assembly speech, the episode made little stir. Moreover, the national Arab American organizations were preparing for, and presumably preoccupied with, an imminent meeting with Secretary of State Vance. The meeting took place at the State Department on November 18, the day before Sadat flew to Israel. It was unusual in its size—thirty-five community leaders were invited, twenty-six of whom attended (including Said, who sat in the back and said little)—and unprecedented in its political diversity, with participants ranging from the AAUG on the left, to the NAAA in the center, to the American Lebanese League (ALL) on the right. According to the meeting notes of John P. Richardson, the NAAA's public affairs director, Vance offered the group a generally optimistic assessment. Some procedural hurdles remained along the path to Geneva, he said, but Washington would continue to work on them. Vance "hoped that Mr. Sadat's forthcoming trip to Jerusalem would help break through the psychological barriers that have characterized Arab-Israeli relations." The trip "had the full support of the United States government." Pressed on the Palestinian question, Vance said the United States could not deal directly with the PLO until it accepted Resolution 242. Still, creative means might be devised to permit meaningful Palestinian representation at Geneva.[57]

Reporting on the meeting to the NAAA, Richardson was upbeat: "There was concensus [*sic*] among those who participated . . . that the meeting was successful—both in terms of delegate harmony and of State Department responsiveness." Mary Haddad Macron, a Cleveland activist with ties to both the NAAA and the AAUG, was also encouraged. "Mr. Vance," she wrote to Fayez Sayegh, Kuwait's UN representative, "was very open and . . . receptive to all queries on PLO involvement in the negotiations. . . . It really seemed to be a beginning—at least for them to have some feeling from the Arab American community." But a third participant, former AAUG president Elaine Hagopian, was having none of it. "The whole affair was disgusting," she reported in her own letter to Sayegh. "It was quite clear that the intent was to rally support behind the Sadat affair," a reference to the Egyptian president's imminent visit to Israel. "There is no point in commenting on the Sadat trip," Hagopian wrote. "It is depressing to think of how much energy, talent, resources have been spent [by the Egyptians] on containing their fellow Arabs."[58]

On December 15, a delegation of fifteen Arab Americans, drawn mostly from the previous group and featuring a similar political diversity, met in the White House with Carter himself, along with Brzezinski and other officials. In the interval since the Vance meeting, Sadat had visited Israel and the extent of Arab opposition to that move had become clear. According to Hagopian's meeting notes, Carter and his advisers strongly supported the new Egyptian-Israeli dialogue. The United States would try to bring other Arab parties into the process, they said, but it would build on what Sadat and Begin had started. Carter "said the PLO was given every opportunity to accept 242 and Arafat came close, but did not accept it. . . . Thus, the PLO has eliminated itself from future negotiations." Conspicuously absent was any mention—by Carter, his advisers, or the Arab American visitors—of the Geneva Conference.[59]

Figure 19. Jimmy Carter meets in the White House with representatives of Arab American organizations, December 15, 1977; *left to right:* American Lebanese League chairman Elias Saadi (*with hand partly raised*), William Mansour (unaffiliated), President Carter, NAAA public affairs director John Richardson, AAUG president Michael Suleiman, AAUG president-elect Fouad Moughrabi, and former AAUG president Elaine Hagopian. Across the table, the partly obscured man with long sideburns is NAAA president Joseph Baroody; to his right, also partly obscured, is former NAAA president Richard Shadyac. Courtesy of the Jimmy Carter Presidential Library and the Arab American National Museum.

Several of the Arab American participants criticized what they saw as Washington's demotion of the Palestinian issue. Joe Baroody "indicated NAAA support of the Sadat initiative but cautioned about . . . the need to involve the PLO." AAUG president Michael Suleiman was harsher, insisting "that the Sadat initiative was not historic. It would only be historic if the PLO is recognized. There is nothing with which to be happy about the Sadat effort." In a sharp exchange with Brzezinski, AAUG president-elect Fouad Moughrabi charged that the administration had suffered "a failure of nerve" on the Palestinian question. "The U.S. should deal head on with this," he said, "and put an end to the misery of Palestinians who have suffered so long." Brzezinski countered with icy realpolitik: "Israel is a state. . . . The PLO is not even a Government in exile, and they ask for too much from a position of weakness."[60]

The ALL representatives enthusiastically supported the Sadat-Begin dialogue, on the dubious ground that it would hasten the creation of a

Palestinian state to which Palestinians in Lebanon could relocate. "We need a comprehensive peace settlement that will remove this element from Lebanon," said ALL president Elias Saadi. In a statement that probably caused some eye rolling, the ALL's Paul Corey said "he has great pride in America and asked the President to give 'us' your 'marching orders' so that we may follow."[61]

After the meeting adjourned, many delegation members were dismayed to learn that Carter had publicly aired his criticism of the PLO, and done so more harshly than in the private session. Just before joining the meeting, Carter held a news conference at which he described the PLO's attitude as "completely negative. They have not been cooperative at all. . . . They have completely rejected United Nations Resolution 242. . . . So, I think they have, themselves, removed the PLO from any immediate prospect of participation in a peace discussion." Unlike in the private meeting, Carter made no mention of Arafat's efforts to accommodate the United States. (Nor did he acknowledge Begin's own negative position on Resolution 242.) In an interview with *Paris Match* later that month, Brzezinski summed up the administration's new view: "Bye-bye PLO."[62]

On December 25, Begin arrived at Sadat's winter retreat in Ismailia to start substantive negotiations. Sadat said he was prepared to reach a bilateral agreement with Israel over the Sinai, provided the agreement was couched in a statement of principles that included eventual restoration of the 1967 borders and recognition of the Palestinians' right of self-determination. Begin flatly rejected any withdrawals beyond the Sinai and even there insisted on retaining airfields and Jewish settlements. For the West Bank and Gaza, he proposed an autonomy scheme whereby Palestinians managed their local affairs while Israel remained responsible for the overall security of the territories and retained the right to intervene at will. The Ismailia meeting ended in deadlock. In mid-January 1978, Mohamed Kamel, Sadat's new foreign minister, went to Jerusalem to continue the discussion. When the same impasse emerged, Sadat recalled Kamel, suspended the talks, and appealed to Washington for help.[63]

The Carter administration sympathized with Sadat and in February devised a plan to break the logjam in his favor.[64] The idea was for Sadat to make a proposal that included elements of Begin's Palestinian autonomy scheme but confined them to an interim phase (in contrast with Begin's desire to make the scheme permanent), while also committing Israel to return to the 1967 borders. The Egyptian proposal would include, as well, some unspecified "maximal" demands, perhaps involving a prior guarantee of Palestinian statehood. The United States would respond with its own proposal, consisting of the Egyptian proposal minus the maximal demands, and then "pressure" Egypt to accept the apparent compromise. Once Egypt had done so, the United States would push Israel to accept it as well.

A clever plan, but it went nowhere. Although Sadat endorsed the approach in principle, he was unwilling to delve into the details of interim arrangements for the West Bank, preferring (at least where non-Egyptian territories were concerned) to confine himself to general precepts, such as the need for an across-the-board Israeli withdrawal. He never furnished a proposal that the Carter administration felt it could modify in pursuit of its Machiavellian scheme. Meanwhile, other Middle East–related events complicated U.S. diplomacy. In January, Sadat sought urgent consideration of a pending Egyptian request to purchase about fifty F-5 fighter jets from the United States, a matter he had previously given low priority. In view of the risks Sadat was running for peace, the administration believed it had to grant his request. Yet it also felt obliged, for both diplomatic and domestic political reasons, to take up similar requests by Israel and Saudi Arabia to purchase U.S. military aircraft.[65] All three sales required congressional approval, and the Egyptian and Saudi sales were unpopular on Capitol Hill, on account of Israel's bitter opposition to them. And so, just as it was preparing a complex and risky maneuver to box Israel in on the territorial question, the Carter administration had to wage a draining campaign to persuade Congress to authorize the Egyptian and Saudi arms sales. By May, the administration had prevailed, dealing the pro-Israel lobby a rare defeat. But the effort cost Carter considerable political capital and left him wary of further controversy with Israel.

Also disrupting the administration's efforts was a massive upsurge of violence in the Middle East. On March 11, eight seaborne Palestinian commandos landed on the Israeli coast and hijacked a passenger bus. A shoot-out with Israeli security forces left thirty-seven dead, including six of the commandos. The Palestinians were members of Arafat's al-Fatah organization, a disturbing indication that the PLO chairman, apparently in response to the collapse of the comprehensive peace effort, had abandoned moderation for the time being. On March 14, Israel sent twenty-five thousand troops across its northern border and within days had seized a substantial portion of South Lebanon. Hundreds of Lebanese and Palestinians, mostly civilians, were killed in the invasion, and tens of thousands fled northward. Days later the UN Security Council passed Resolution 425, which demanded an immediate Israeli withdrawal and established a UN peacekeeping force for South Lebanon. The Israelis eventually withdrew, but they retained de facto control of a belt of South Lebanon held by their proxy, the South Lebanon Army. The establishment of such a "security zone" had been a long-standing Israeli goal.[66]

The Carter administration publicly opposed the Israeli invasion and spearheaded passage of Resolution 425. It also got drawn into a controversy over Israel's unauthorized use in Lebanon of a lethal U.S.-supplied weapon. The CBU (cluster bomb unit)-58 functioned by subdividing into multiple explosions that sprayed shrapnel in all directions. The result, wrote the columnist Nick Thimmesch, was "a blizzard of steel fragments over areas as large as 25 acres, causing any humans around to be killed or maimed." Israel had promised that it would use the CBU-58 only in self-defense and only against large-scale military targets. Days into the Lebanon operation, however, the *Washington Post* reported that Israeli forces were dropping CBU-58s in heavily populated areas.[67]

Israel's use of cluster bombs drew sharp condemnation from Senator Abourezk and Arab American groups, especially the NAAA, which was already mobilized on Capitol Hill to support the Egyptian and Saudi arms sales.[68] Less expected, and more effective, was a minirevolt by three moderate House Republicans, Paul Findley of Illinois, Paul N. "Pete" McCloskey of California, and Charles W. Whalen of Ohio. Jointly or individually, they wrote letters of concern to Carter, Vance, Brzezinski, and other officials.[69] Vance publicly acknowledged that Israel "may have" violated the terms under which it had purchased U.S. weapons, though he did not elaborate on this statement and said he was recommending no special action by the president. Privately, however, the State Department protested to the Israeli government, which admitted it had used the CBU-58s improperly and recommitted itself to the original restrictions. Abourezk, who for years had agitated futilely against Israeli military operations in his ancestral homeland, was impressed. "May God love you, Charlie Whalen and Paul Findley," he wrote to McCloskey, "for all you have done in the cause of justice and humanitarianism."[70]

The Carter administration had gotten the Israelis to back down, but it could scarcely savor its victory. As with the Arab arms sales, it feared it was pushing its luck with Begin's government, whose flexibility on the peace process was sorely needed. "The U.S. government," a *Los Angeles Times* editorial noted in April, "seems ready and even eager to drop for now the matter of Israel's improper use of American-supplied cluster bombs in Lebanon last month . . . in view of the current overall political situation in the Middle East." Already, the events of March had caused the Israelis to dig their heels in further. "The terrorist raid and the Israeli military response," Vance wrote in his memoirs, "changed the political atmosphere for our talks with Prime Minister Begin. Before March 14, Begin had been on the defensive on both settlements and withdrawal." After that date, "the possibility of getting Begin to alter his positions on the West Bank and Palestinian questions was virtually eliminated."[71]

By summer, the administration's diplomatic strategy was coming apart. Sadat had not produced a sufficiently detailed set of proposals for the administration to modify. Democratic Party leaders, looking ahead to the midterm elections in November, were growing anxious. According to Carter's memoirs, in late June a group of unnamed Democratic "wise men" urged the president to "stay as aloof as possible from direct involvement in the Middle East negotiations; this is a losing proposition." Vice president Walter Mondale, whose political antennae were especially acute, agreed. In early July, he proposed the appointment of a high-level envoy to whom Middle East negotiations could be delegated; perhaps the good Dr. Kissinger would serve in this role. Vance threatened to resign if the president even considered the idea. In a July 18 memo to Carter, Brzezinski wondered if the administration had "the political strength" for an open confrontation with Israel: "If we go 'public' and then do not prevail, our Middle Eastern policy will be in shambles, and Sadat and others will be either repudiated or will turn in a radical direction. In other words, if we go 'public,' *we must prevail*."[72]

At a July 20 meeting with Brzezinski and other advisers, Carter changed course. According to Brzezinski's paraphrase, the president said "that instead of working against Begin, we should try to work through him." He proposed to facilitate a summit meeting between Begin and Sadat where the two leaders could settle their differences face-to-face. After spending several days mulling over various arrangements, Carter decided he should host the meeting himself. In early August, he invited Begin and Sadat to attend a summit at the presidential retreat at Camp David. Each leader immediately accepted the invitation.[73]

Both the process and the outcome of the Camp David meeting, which took place September 5–17, 1978, bore the imprint of Carter's decision to work "through" Begin rather than "against" him. The president's objective going into the talks, William Quandt later wrote, was to achieve "whatever Begin could be brought to accept without confrontation."[74] As Begin was prepared to concede very little without confrontation—or perhaps with it, either, though that proposition was never tested—he was bound to fare very well in the negotiations.

Throughout the thirteen-day summit, Begin and Sadat seldom met. Their personal chemistry was so poor, and their substantive positions so sharply at odds, that Carter and his team found it best to keep the two leaders apart and work instead on producing an American document that bridged their differences. This procedure suited Sadat, who believed that Carter supported his goal of linking any Egyptian-Israeli agreement over the Sinai to an Israeli commitment to withdraw at some later date to the 1967 lines, with minor modifications. What Sadat failed to realize was that, while Carter did favor this position in the abstract, he was no longer willing to fight for it. Prior to the summit, Carter and his team had ruled out attempting to restore the 1967 borders in favor of a more Israel-friendly objective: coupling a Sinai agreement with an understanding over the West Bank and Gaza that built on Begin's autonomy scheme. Perhaps the Palestinians there could enjoy limited autonomy for a transitional period, during which multilateral negotiations might be held to settle the territories' final status, in accordance with Resolution 242.[75]

Even this looser formula proved overly ambitious, as it ran afoul of Begin's claim that Resolution 242 did not apply to the West Bank and Gaza. So Carter lowered his sights further. While Sadat brooded in his cabin, reluctant as always to be drawn into detailed discussions, the Americans and the Israelis worked out deliberately vague language that abetted Israel's efforts to exempt the Palestinian territories from the provisions of 242.[76] The irony was complete: having bypassed the PLO for the sake of Resolution 242, the Carter administration now bypassed 242 for the sake of Israel.

Meanwhile, Begin drove a stiff bargain on the Sinai, insisting that Israel retain airfields and Jewish settlements on the peninsula. Sadat was outraged. On September 15, he packed his bags and requested a helicopter to fly him to Andrews Air Force Base so he could return home. Carter rushed to Sadat's cabin and, through a combination of dire warnings and desperate pleas, persuaded his guest to stay a bit longer.[77] Over the next two days, the Americans and the Israelis resolved the Sinai issues. In exchange for a U.S. commitment to help build new airfields in southern Israel, the Israelis agreed to relinquish the Sinai airfields. Shortly thereafter, Begin, who had vowed he would never personally order the dismantling of any Jewish settlements, said he would not object if the Knesset, on its own authority, voted to remove the ones in Sinai. He would "finesse it at the Knesset," quipped Carter's chief of staff Hamilton Jordan. By now, Sadat had reluctantly endorsed the murky language on the Palestinian areas. At least he was recovering all of the Sinai, something Begin had shrewdly kept in doubt until the very end.[78]

At a White House ceremony on September 17, Carter, Begin, and Sadat unveiled the Camp David Accords. Several members of the Egyptian negotiating team, whom Sadat had overruled in accepting the agreement, boycotted the ceremony. These included foreign minister Mohamed Kamel, who, as his predecessor Ismail Fahmy had done ten months earlier, resigned in protest. The dissenters saw the Camp David Accords as a thinly disguised blueprint for a separate peace that failed to uphold long-standing Arab claims.[79] They had a good case. The accords consisted of two parts, one dealing with bilateral Egyptian-Israeli relations, and the other with the broader Arab-Israeli territorial dispute. The bilateral section committed Egypt and Israel to sign a peace treaty within three months' time. The treaty would provide for Israel's phased withdrawal from the rest of Sinai over two to three years and for the normalization of Egyptian-Israeli relations while the withdrawal was under way. The treaty would also place limits on the forces each country could deploy along the shared border, authorize the deployment of UN peacekeeping forces on Egyptian (but not Israeli) soil, and assure freedom of passage for Israeli shipping through the Suez Canal and the Strait of Tiran.[80]

The other section of the accords offered a framework for achieving peace between Israel and its other Arab neighbors. Almost all of this section dealt with the West Bank and Gaza. It called on Israel, Egypt, and Jordan to "agree on the modalities for establishing" a self-governing Palestinian authority in the West Bank and Gaza that would exercise limited autonomy for a transitional period not exceeding five years, during which Israel, Egypt, Jordan, and elected Palestinian representatives would negotiate over the territories' final status. Beyond stipulating that the resulting solution "must . . . recognize the legitimate rights of the Palestinian people," the accords did not indicate what sort of Palestinian entity, if any, might emerge from the process. They stated that "a withdrawal of Israeli armed forces will take place" without specifying the extent of that withdrawal. They did not mention arrangements for Jerusalem, or substantively address the claims of Palestinian refugees.[81] Nor was there was any operational linkage between the accords' two sections. The Israeli-Egyptian arrangements would go forward regardless of what happened (or didn't) on the Palestinian front.[82]

Most glaringly of all, the accords were completely silent on Israeli settlements in the West Bank and Gaza. Carter had originally sought a moratorium on the construction of such settlements for the duration of the negotiations over the Palestinian areas—that is, for up to five years—and an earlier draft of the accords contained this provision. Toward the end of the summit, however, Carter deleted the provision from the accords in exchange for Begin's oral promise to address the issue in a side letter to Carter. Yet the letter Begin produced said that Israel would refrain from settlement building for a period of just three months, the time projected for negotiating the Israeli-Egyptian peace treaty. By now, the Camp David Accords had been signed and announced. Carter believed that Begin was misrepresenting their oral agreement and tried to get him to revise the letter, but Begin insisted on his version, and in late September Carter dropped the issue. As if to rub Carter's nose in his defeat, on October 26 Begin announced that Israel would "thicken" some of its West Bank settlements, an activity not covered, he claimed, by the moratorium. The next day Sadat and Begin were jointly awarded the Nobel Peace Prize. "Sadat deserved it," Carter wrote in his diary; "Begin did not."[83]

Some White House aides grumbled that Carter, too, should have received this international honor, but the president got his share of domestic acclaim. Members of Congress, the news media, and ordinary Americans responded extremely favorably to Carter's achievement at Camp David—welcome news to a president who had received low marks for his handling of both domestic and foreign policy. A Gallup poll showed Carter's approval rating jumping from 45 percent at the start of the summit to 56 percent in its immediate aftermath. The president's report on the summit to a joint session of Congress drew rapturous applause. The diplomatic breakthrough also briefly neutralized the view, prevalent among Jewish groups, that the Carter administration was hostile to Israel. A postsummit meeting with Jewish leaders, Carter recalled, "was delightful, full of fun and good cheer, and we welcomed it because it was so rare."[84]

Arab Americans found less to celebrate. In a September 18 statement, the NAAA "welcome[d] the progress toward Middle East peace achieved by the Camp David talks" but noted the accords' weak language on Palestinian issues. "A critical question is whether Israeli intransigence on withdrawal from the West Bank and Gaza Strip in fact changed at Camp David or was merely repackaged." (The NAAA was soon obliged to embrace the pessimistic conclusion.) The AAUG's statement, issued on September 19, was much harsher. It condemned the Camp David agreement as "a total surrender by Mr. Sadat and a victory for Mr. Begin. It is not a framework for peace; it is a blueprint for more conflict and more violence." The ALL, however, "strongly endorsed Camp David."[85]

In the Arab world, reactions to Camp David were overwhelmingly negative. The PLO, Syria, Iraq, Libya, and other self-proclaimed "radical" states condemned the accords as a shameful capitulation to Israeli expansionism. Jordan and Saudi Arabia also criticized the accords but did so in more muted tones, giving the Carter administration some hope of eventually drawing those two countries into a more supportive position. The administration was especially keen on winning over Jordan, as the accords envisioned a key role for it in autonomy negotiations on the West Bank and Gaza. Over the next several weeks, however, both kingdoms grew increasingly critical of the Camp David agreement. The more its provisions were the scrutinized, the worse they looked from an Arab perspective. Meanwhile, Begin's defiant stance on the settlements issue, coupled with his repeated insistence that Israel would never relinquish the West Bank and Gaza, only strengthened the impression that Sadat had bargained away basic Palestinian rights. At an Arab summit meeting in Baghdad in early November, Saudi Arabia and Jordan joined the other states in condemning the Camp David Accords and threatening to suspend Egypt from the Arab League and subject it to economic sanctions if it signed a peace treaty with Israel. Sadat dismissed his Arab critics as "cowards and dwarfs" unwilling to shoulder the responsibilities of international leadership.[86]

Nonetheless, Sadat recognized the potency of the Arab criticism. In the negotiations that now ensued over the Egyptian-Israeli peace treaty—lasting twice the three months projected in the Camp David Accords—he belatedly sought a linkage between the normalization of Egyptian-Israeli relations and progress toward Palestinian autonomy. He proposed that Egypt and Israel delay exchanging ambassadors until the Palestinians had elected and established their self-governing authority. The Carter administration thought this a reasonable suggestion. The Israelis rejected it. They also made it clear that any Palestinian autonomy emerging from the process would be sharply circumscribed. Carter and his advisers were incensed. On November 8, the president wrote in his diary, "It's obvious the Israelis want a separate treaty with Egypt, to keep the West Bank and Gaza, [and] to get as much money as possible from us." "Begin feels he can get away with almost anything," Brzezinski complained a month later. The administration was determined to overcome the prime minister's intransigence. Again there was talk of a showdown with Israel.[87]

Time, however, was working against such a notion. The collapse of the shah of Iran's regime in January 1979 was a severe blow to U.S. prestige. Carter felt growing pressure to achieve a rapid success in the Egyptian-Israeli negotiations to combat the perception, and hence the reality, of diminishing U.S. influence in the region. Moreover, the longer the negotiations dragged on, the more they would become enmeshed in Carter's campaign for reelection in 1980. "I do not believe," Brzezinski wrote Carter on January 23, "that in the approaching election year we will be able to convince the Israelis that we have sufficient leverage over them" to extract meaningful concessions. "We have little time left."[88]

On February 19, Carter convened his Middle East policy team and said it was time to reach a deal. As Quandt, who attended the meeting, recalled, "Carter stated clearly that he did not want a public confrontation with Israel. This was a time for progress on the overall negotiation, with details to be resolved later. Carter acknowledged that he had to take some of the blame for urging Sadat to link the exchange of ambassadors to the establishment of self-government, but Sadat would now have to drop that demand for linkage."[89] Sadat accepted the decision with little complaint. Even more than Carter, he was desperate to avoid a diplomatic failure, which would vindicate his Arab critics. The exchange of ambassadors was decoupled from events on the Palestinian front. Instead, the parties set a "target date" of the end of 1979 (with no consequences if the target was missed) for Egypt and Israel to complete their negotiations for the holding of Palestinian elections.[90]

In a March 26 ceremony on the White House lawn, Sadat and Begin signed the Egyptian-Israeli peace treaty. The treaty gave effect to the bilateral provisions outlined in the Camp David Accords and reiterated the loose scenario for autonomy talks among Israel, Egypt, Jordan, and unspecified Palestinians. Accompanying the treaty, but not formally part of it, was a U.S.-Israeli "memorandum of agreement" essentially committing the United States to side with Israel—through the furnishing of arms and possibly "the strengthening of the United States presence in the area"—in the event Egypt violated the treaty. Mustafa Khalil, Sadat's latest foreign minister, protested the memorandum, but U.S. officials paid him little heed. "Carter had long ago learned," Quandt recalled, "that Sadat would not make an issue out of such matters."[91]

Sadat did attempt a small gesture to placate his Arab critics. His prepared remarks at the signing ceremony, to be delivered in English, called for a U.S.-Palestinian dialogue and "a genuine transfer of authority to the

Figure 20. Anwar Sadat, Jimmy Carter, and Menachem Begin mark the signing of the Egyptian-Israeli peace treaty, Washington, DC, March 26, 1979. Courtesy of the Jimmy Carter Presidential Library.

Palestinians in their land." But Sadat never spoke those words. The pages of his text got stuck together, and he inadvertently flipped past the challenging passage.[92]

The signing of the treaty drew fresh condemnation in the Arab world. Protesters staged rallies and sit-ins, menaced Egypt's embassies, and burned effigies of Carter, Begin, and Sadat. Arafat vowed to "chop off the hands" of those three leaders and suggested that Sadat was courting assassination. Again, Carter administration officials were dismayed to see Saudi Arabia and Jordan joining in the denunciations. Radio Riyadh called the agreement "a black day" in Arab and Islamic history. King Hussein pronounced the situation "unacceptable." The Arab League suspended Egypt's membership, moved its headquarters from Cairo to Tunis, and imposed economic sanctions against Egypt. Meeting with Brzezinski in Cairo just prior to the treaty signing, Sadat had ridiculed his Arab critics as "scarecrows" and "bedouins" whose protests could be ignored. "There will be a hysteric state for one month maximum," he predicted, and then it would blow over. The anger was widespread and vociferous, however, and showed no sign of abating any time soon.[93]

Against this inauspicious backdrop, the Carter administration tried to launch the multilateral autonomy talks envisioned in the Camp David Accords. But no Palestinians of consequence, within the PLO or outside of it, wanted anything to do with the negotiations, which were widely seen as a mechanism for legitimating the Israeli occupation. King Hussein, too, boycotted the talks. In addition to recognizing the political dangers in joining such a process, he was genuinely appalled by the lopsided nature of the Egyptian-Israeli agreements. "Sadat," he told *Newsweek* in late March, "has handed Israel a long-sought opportunity to divide and rule the Arabs." Subsequent Israeli actions seemed to bear out Hussein's claim. In the weeks following the treaty signing, the Begin government authorized new settlement construction on the West Bank and issued guidelines for Palestinian autonomy that further drained the concept of meaning.[94] Carter was furious with the Israelis but showed no sympathy for Hussein's position, either. It was time, he wrote in his diary in July, "to tell King Hussein to get off his ass and help us." But Hussein remained on the sidelines, and no multilateral autonomy talks occurred. Instead, Egypt and Israel held bilateral autonomy talks, which proceeded inconclusively for the rest of Carter's presidency, accompanied all the while by a rapid increase in Israel's settler population.[95]

For Egypt, the treaty with Israel represented the culmination of two long-term processes: Egypt's progressive withdrawal from the Arab-Israeli conflict, and its transfer of allegiances from one superpower to the other. Cairo became a full-fledged client of Washington, its share of U.S. military and economic aid second only to Israel's.[96] Few commentators made much of it at the time, but Camp David was a sharp blow to Moscow's strategic position.

In the days that the Egyptian-Israeli peace treaty was being finalized and unveiled, Carter repeatedly called the treaty "the cornerstone of a comprehensive peace."[97] Much remained to be done, he conceded, but future negotiations, involving Israel's other Arab neighbors, would build on Sadat's and Begin's brave work. A few years out of the presidency, Carter was taking a more sober view of this accomplishment. Begin, he wrote in 1985, had never intended to negotiate seriously over the Palestinian areas, and the treaty with Egypt spared him from having to do so. "With the bilateral treaty, he removed Egypt's considerable strength from the military equation of the Middle East and thus gave the Israelis renewed freedom to pursue their goals of fortifying and settling the occupied territories."[98] Carter stopped short of saying that the Camp David process had thus impeded, rather than aided, the search for a broader settlement, but such a conclusion was hard to escape.

To Arab critics of Camp David, this was a familiar argument; they had made it themselves as the bilateral process unfolded.[99] Behind the intensity of the Arab attacks on Camp David was the crushing realization that the strongest Arab nation was quitting the battle for good and leaving its former allies to fend for themselves. A similar outcry had greeted the Sinai II Agreement of 1975, but that reaction had been tempered by the hope that Egypt would, in the end, draw back from making a full separate peace. The events of 1978–1979 dashed that prospect, and Arabs everywhere were crestfallen and frightened. They were also furious—at the Egyptian leader who had abandoned them and at the American president who had led him astray. For Carter, this was a painful irony. No U.S. president had worked harder to address the core Arab grievances against Israel, especially regarding the plight of the Palestinians. In June 1979, he privately remarked "that his worst mistake would be if he went out of office without addressing the Palestinian question."[100] And yet, despite further attempts to tackle the issue (see chapter 10), Carter would indeed leave it, unresolved, to a successor far less concerned about the fate of the Palestinians.

Camp David yielded another irony: even as the bilateral process aroused widespread and bitter Arab resentment against U.S. policy, it helped to foster a somewhat less negative image of the Arab world within the United States. Since the October War of 1973, Arab perspectives had received a more respectful hearing in the U.S. national media. In public opinion surveys, the tiny percentage of respondents favoring the Arab states over Israel had steadily grown, finally breaking into double digits in October 1977.[101] In November, Sadat made his trip to Jerusalem, an event breathlessly followed by the U.S. media. In the ensuing months the Egyptian president appeared frequently in American news coverage, and his memoir, *In Search of Identity*, was published in English by Harper & Row. In these forums, Sadat offered an appealing persona to American audiences: affable, urbane, moderate, eager for peace. Begin, by contrast, seemed rigid and unimaginative. In some polls in early 1978, Sadat's popularity exceeded Begin's, a remarkable development given the legacy of pro-Israel sentiment in the United States. Ashraf Ghorbal, Egypt's ambassador in Washington at the time, later wrote that Sadat functioned as a one-man lobby for Egypt.[102]

Sadat's ascendancy coincided with a further rise in approval ratings for Arabs in general. In an October 1977 Gallup poll, 46 percent of respondents had said they favored Israel in the Middle East dispute, while 11 percent favored the Arab countries (with the rest stating no preference). By February 1978, those figures were 33 percent and 14 percent, respectively. Later that spring, the pro-Arab figure dipped to 10 percent, but by summer it was back on the rise, reaching 15 percent in January 1979, the high point for the decade.[103]

Contemporary observers frequently attributed the rise in Arab popularity to the diplomatic revolution then unfolding. Shortly after Sadat's Jerusalem trip, *Newsweek* columnist Meg Greenfield wrote that Sadat had "transformed, or at least substantially altered, the American perception of the Arab and his cause. Unlike the set pieces to which we have become accustomed—the oil-rich sheik, the terrorist, the ululating crowd—Sadat was neither alarming nor strange. He was politically plausible and humanly familiar." An April 1978 *New York Times* article agreed that some of the shift in attitudes "reflects the peace initiative begun late last year by President Anwar el-Sadat." Meeting with King Hussein in March 1979, Brzezinski, too, touted the Sadat effect: "Arab stereotypes have often been found offensive in the U.S., but that is changing radically today. . . . Sadat has to be given credit for this change." Even Iraqi vice president Saddam Hussein, though outraged by the substance of Sadat's diplomacy, told a British diplomat that he "saw some psychological value in Sadat's visit to Jerusalem, particularly as it had led to a more favourable Western view of the Arabs."[104] While all of these observations were impressionistic, it seems reasonable to conclude that Sadat had a significant hand in altering U.S. public opinion.

The Egyptian president's role was particularly paradoxical when it came to the Palestinian cause, which Arab opinion leaders universally accused Sadat of betraying. Despite that charge—in large measure because of it—Sadat repeatedly insisted, in public, that no final Arab-Israeli settlement would be viable if it failed to recognize Palestinian claims. Such urgings were especially audible in early 1978, when Sadat's American charm offensive was at its height.[105] Around this time and shortly thereafter, pro-Palestinian activists noted a growing receptivity to Palestinian views among the American public. Sara Gentry, vice president of American Near East Refugee Aid, wrote to members in April 1978, "This year as never before, we've had a flood of mail from people all over the United States." The letter writers, though not necessarily anti-Israel, were "concerned that the Palestinians have been treated unfairly in the past and . . . denied even a part of their historic homeland." A few months later, James Zogby, founder of the Palestine Human Rights Campaign (a recent offshoot of the AAUG), remarked on "the new openness of many in the U.S. to recognize Palestinian rights." This more sympathetic mood had many causes: Begin's intransigence, an increasing awareness of the PLO's willingness to compromise, and the cumulative efforts of Gentry, Zogby, and like-minded activists to call attention to the Palestinians' plight. But the *New York Times* television critic John O'Connor was surely correct when he observed, in January 1979, that "the peace gestures of Egypt's Anwar Sadat have . . . added a new legitimacy to the Palestinian problem."[106]

There was another, more tenuous way that the Egyptian-Israeli peace process enhanced the Arab image within the United States. As noted, in the spring of 1978 the Carter administration rewarded Sadat's peace efforts by asking Congress to authorize the sale of military aircraft to Egypt, a move triggering similar requests for Israel and Saudi Arabia. Overcoming congressional opposition to the Egyptian and Saudi arms sales required an all-out effort by the administration. It not only lobbied strenuously in its own right but also enlisted the support of figures from the foreign policy establishment and corporate sector. In congressional testimony and op-ed pieces, the arms sales' advocates portrayed Egypt and Saudi Arabia as moderate, pro-Western nations whose friendship and well-being were vital to U.S. security. These countries had no interest in attacking Israel, the advocates claimed, only in defending themselves against radical Arab adversaries, regional and domestic. Israel's supporters countered that Egyptian and Saudi moderation was vastly overstated; the arms would indeed pose a threat to Israel. In the end, the Carter administration eked out a narrow victory for the arms package, further validating the benign reading of Egyptian and Saudi intentions.[107]

Among the supporters of the Arab arms sales was the NAAA. (The AAUG denounced the sales as an effort to equip Egypt and Saudi Arabia to police the region on behalf of U.S. imperialism.) Although the NAAA was a minor player in the lobbying campaign, it was repeatedly mentioned in news stories on the subject—a consequence, it seems, of public affairs director John Richardson's tireless cultivation of the media.[108] "We're taken seriously now," Richardson proclaimed in the aftermath of the congressional vote, "particularly since we won on the jet planes issue. We are now an organization which can have some influence on Middle East policy." The *Washington Post* reinforced this view. "The NAAA," it reported in mid-May, ". . . is emerging as the Arab countervoice to the pro-Israel activism of Jewish Americans."[109]

The upshot of these developments was a more fully rounded portrayal of Arabs and Arab Americans in mainstream U.S. discourse. The old stereotypes of fanaticism and backwardness remained, but they were challenged by newer impressions of openness, moderation, sophistication, and success. "There is a new political vocabulary being developed here," Richardson observed, "and it includes the idea that Arabs are people who are important to Americans and not just objects." Jim Abourezk was characteristically sardonic: "It is becoming so trendy to be pro-Arab that I am thinking of switching sides."[110]

Yet the specter of Arab lobbying prowess came with its own problems. By the late 1970s, the notion that Arab interests were using their newfound oil wealth to buy influence on Capitol Hill—and, beyond that, to acquire menacing footholds in the nation's political, economic, and cultural institutions—was increasingly common in American public discourse. Arab oil money was real enough, and its growing visibility introduced new strains of antagonism into the U.S.-Arab encounter, even as it nurtured American constituencies inclined to look favorably on the Arab world.

Chapter 9

Abdul Enterprises

Arab Petrodollars in the United States, 1974–1981

On an autumn afternoon in 1977, a dark-bearded man wearing a traditional Arab robe and headdress, accompanied by two men in Western clothing, paid a courtesy call at Jim Abourezk's U.S. Senate office. The visitor, who spoke no English, presented a card bearing the name Sheik Ongha Biran. He came, one of his companions explained, from Halat al-Bhudi, a small island off the coast of Dubai. The men had not made an appointment, but Abourezk invited them into his office for a chat; the sheik's other companion began snapping pictures. Mentioning his own Arab heritage, the senator greeted the visitor in Arabic. When the sheik made no reply, and then abruptly left with his two associates, Abourezk grew suspicious. The next day Abourezk's staff called the State Department and learned there is no island named Halat al-Bhudi.[1]

Three weeks later, the *National Enquirer* published its exposé. Ace reporter Brian Hogan had donned Arab clothing, jumbled the letters of his name to become Ongha Biran, and found himself the toast of Capitol Hill. Abourezk had been only "the first dignitary to fall over himself trying to befriend the phony sheik." Three other senators, Henry Bellmon of Oklahoma, John Danforth of Missouri, and Gaylord Nelson of Wisconsin, had each cordially received the exotic visitor; the *Enquirer* had the photos to prove it. A perusal of the article suggests that none of the senators displayed anything more than bemused politeness, but the tabloid extracted a damning lesson from the episode. "Anyone wearing an Arab robe and headdress," it observed, "can command VIP treatment in oil-hungry Washington, D.C." The following spring one of Abourezk's home-state papers, the *Pierre Times* (South Dakota), belatedly picked up the "fake sheik" story and made the same point more pungently: "To get to the offices of your elected representative without an appointment, and to have much of oil-hungry Washington crawling on their bellies, all you need to do is wrap a towel around your head and claim you're Sheik Bogus Al-Phoney. In the 202nd year of American independence."[2] Neither newspaper spelled out why congressmen in particular would grovel before a figure like Sheik Onga Biran. Presumably, it was to grab a piece of his fabulous oil wealth—"petrodollars" was the new term of art—for investment in their states and districts, or even for their personal use.

The *Enquirer*'s stunt was unimpressive, and few other news outlets paid it any notice. But it foreshadowed a far more consequential sting operation—quietly launched by the FBI just about the time of Sheik Biran's Senate visit and exposed to public view early in 1980—during which several U.S. congressmen *did* disgrace themselves to get their hands on some tantalizing Arab oil riches, dangled before them by another burnoose-clad imposter. If the Biran visit drew only a trickle of journalistic dismay over official Washington's unseemly interest in Arab petrodollars, then the Abscam affair, as the later episode was called, produced a torrent of such sentiment. Both events reflected a broader concern, prevalent in American society in the mid- and late 1970s, that the circulation of petrodollars was permitting Arab governments and interests a dangerous degree of influence over the nation's economic, cultural, intellectual, and political life.

From Congress, pro-Israeli groups, mass-circulation media, and occasionally the broader public came several distinct, but often overlapping, objections to the influx of Arab petrodollars. Some feared that Arab states would use their growing economic power to disrupt U.S. support for Israel—whether by threatening economic reprisals if Washington persisted in such support, by continuing to boycott American companies that traded with Israel, or by turning American universities into hotbeds of pro-Arab agitation. Some worried that repugnant regimes in Tripoli, Baghdad, Riyadh, and elsewhere would succeed in purchasing a sanitized image in the United States. Some, of a more populist bent, saw Arab petrodollars as an instrument of American corporate aggrandizement. And some (though this sentiment was seldom voiced openly) no doubt recoiled from the specter of swarthy foreigners acquiring assets and enjoying luxuries that few Americans could afford. Underlying all of these concerns was a sense that Arab economic power threatened the independence and dignity of the United States or its people.

Yet if displeasure over the influx of Arab petrodollars was the dominant reaction, many Americans viewed the phenomenon more positively. Members of the foreign policy establishment generally agreed that oil-rich Arab countries would be more cooperative on international issues if they had a larger stake in the U.S. economy. Most of those charged with managing or analyzing that economy—government officials, macroeconomists, financial journalists, and others—understood, as well, the value of Arab investment in an era of stagflation. Many individual businesspeople relied on, or hoped to receive, infusions of capital from Arab sources. When it was politically safe to do so, university administrators welcomed Arab funding of Middle East studies programs, which in turn tended to foster, at least within higher education, more sympathetic attitudes toward the Arab world. Finally, the hostile climate often surrounding petrodollars drew a concerted, and partly successful, effort by Arab Americans to combat anti-Arab stereotypes in public discourse. Abourezk could shrug off the *National Enquirer*'s practical joke; similar antics by the federal government, publicized and sanctioned by the national media, were much harder to ignore.

The most consequential petroleum-related event of late 1973 was not the Arab oil embargo but, rather, the drastic increase in the price that the Organization of the Petroleum Exporting Countries (OPEC) charged for each barrel of oil. In two successive spikes between mid-October and late December, OPEC's per-barrel price rose from $3.01 to $11.65, contributing to an inflationary spiral that ravaged the global economy. Over the next few years, a struggle ensued within OPEC over the appropriate trajectory of oil pricing. While the shah of Iran pushed for additional price increases, eager as always to acquire the revenues to expand his already huge arsenal, the Saudi government tried to bring prices down somewhat. Heedless price gouging, Riyadh warned, would further damage the global economy, harming Middle Easterners along with everyone else. The Saudis also worried about alienating the United States, the ultimate guarantor of the kingdom's security. The U.S. government favored the Saudi position and petitioned the shah of Iran to lower prices—though sometimes in muted tones, on account of Henry Kissinger's partiality for the shah and desire to keep contentious issues from intruding on U.S.-Iranian relations. Whatever the respective weight of these Iranian, Saudi, and U.S. influences, from 1974 to 1978 oil prices were relatively stable, undergoing only a modest nominal increase and even a slight decline when adjusted for inflation. Because the 1973 price hikes had been so dramatic to begin with, however, simply maintaining the new prices ensured that oil-producing countries would continue to reap enormous revenues.[3]

Recognizing this reality, Washington sought to channel the surplus wealth in ways that benefited the United States. Most U.S. officials agreed that, the more oil-rich Middle Eastern countries invested in the United States, the greater would be their stake in the success of the American economy. "OPEC members," predicted a U.S. Treasury Department report in January 1974, ". . . will be significantly less likely to attempt to disrupt the economies where they hold assets. Therefore as their wealth increases, the probability of their pursuing policies designed to hamper other economies[—]like cutting off their oil—is likely to decline." In the coming years, the Treasury and State Departments strongly encouraged Arab countries to invest in American enterprises and deposit funds in American banks. Partly as a consequence of these urgings, but mostly due to the attraction of investing in such a huge and diversified economy, the United States became the largest single destination of Arab capital. By mid-1978, Arab countries had invested some $29 billion in the United States, mostly in the form of bank deposits and purchases of U.S. government securities, with a few billion invested in tangible assets such as real estate, cattle ranching, and food processing companies.[4]

The influx of petrodollars aroused sharp opposition within the United States. Members of Congress, leaders of pro-Israel groups, mass-circulation journalists, and some elite pundits warned that Arab nations might, in a future crisis, punish the United States by abruptly withdrawing their funds from American banks; that Arab investors might gain control of a vital American industry; or that Arab-owned firms might discriminate against Jewish employees or wage economic warfare against Jewish-owned competitors.[5] Executive branch officials, business leaders, macroeconomists, and other elite pundits countered that Arab holdings in the United States made up a small fraction of overall foreign investment, most of which came from Canada and Western Europe; that Arab investment, such as it was, benefited the U.S. economy; and that safeguards already existed to prevent the abuses critics predicted.[6] A failed 1974 effort by Arab investors to acquire a controlling share of the Lockheed Aircraft Corporation, the largest U.S.

defense contractor, seemed to vindicate the Cassandras. Yet defenders of the status quo could clam that the system was working: had Lockheed executives themselves not rejected the takeover bid, existing security-clearance requirements would have blocked its consummation. From 1974 to 1976 Congress considered various bills to tighten restrictions on foreign investment, but the administrations of Richard Nixon and Gerald Ford headed them off.[7]

Congressional critics had somewhat greater success when it came to the Arab economic boycott against Israel, an issue that, while touching mainly on business activity in the Arab world, had the potential to affect the influx of petrodollars into the United States. Since 1948, the Arab states had rejected all economic dealings with Israel. They had subsequently extended the boycott to companies of any nationality doing business with Israel, and then extended it further to companies that did business with those companies. Before the fall of 1973, the Arab boycott was of little international consequence. Thereafter, however, companies throughout the world, including many American ones, proved willing to shun Israel, or other companies that dealt with it, to win contracts in oil-rich Arab countries. Meanwhile, some Arab countries boycotted businesses owned or managed by supporters of Israel, and a number of companies complied with this stipulation as well. Because many of the targeted executives were Jewish, critics claimed that the Arab boycott was anti-Semitic. Spurred on by Jewish and pro-Israel groups, in 1975 and 1976 Congress considered several bills to outlaw compliance with the boycott.[8]

The Ford administration opposed these efforts. A successful antiboycott bill could anger oil-rich Arab states and cause them to retaliate by raising oil prices or curtailing the flow of petrodollars into the United States. To preempt congressional action, President Ford proclaimed his opposition to religious discrimination and vowed that his administration would vigorously prosecute any illegal boycott-related discrimination it discovered. Congress persisted in its antiboycott efforts. Although it failed to pass a bill criminalizing compliance with the boycott, in the summer of 1976 an amendment denying some tax breaks to boycott compliers was successfully attached to a tax revision bill. Unable to get the amendment removed, yet loath to veto a tax bill he deemed vital to economic recovery, Ford signed the legislation.[9]

In response to the antiboycott measure, Saudi leaders privately warned the U.S. government that they might well have to go along with a substantial price increase at the next OPEC meeting, scheduled to convene in

Doha, Qatar, in December 1976. Price restraint was an unpopular position within OPEC, the Saudis said; to uphold it, they must be able to show that the Western powers were acting in good faith. Throughout the fall, Ford and other U.S. officials implored Saudi Arabia not to succumb to the price hawks in the cartel. Assistance in this diplomacy came from an unlikely quarter, and only after Ford had lost the election to Jimmy Carter and was no longer positioned to benefit politically. While visiting the Middle East in mid-November, Senator Abourezk met separately with Saudi Arabia's King Khalid and with Shaykh Zayid bin Sultan Al Nahyan, ruler of the United Arab Emirates (UAE), and urged both leaders to keep pushing for price restraint within OPEC. A major price hike at this moment, Abourezk cautioned, would play into American Zionists' hands and make it harder for the new president to pursue an equitable Arab-Israeli peace settlement.[10]

Abourezk's session with King Khalid was marred by an angry altercation between the senator and the U.S. chargé d'affaires in Saudi Arabia, Hume Horan, who accompanied Abourezk to the entrance to the king's chambers expecting to attend the meeting. Abourezk thought Horan's presence would inhibit frank discussion and insisted on meeting alone with the king. When Horan said that diplomatic protocol required his attendance, Abourezk snarled, "Do you want your nuts cut off?" Horan persisted, relenting only after the Saudi interpreter stated that, because Abourezk had made the appointment, the Saudis "had to defer to his wishes as to who would accompany him."[11]

Despite this inauspicious introduction, Abourezk was able to make his points to King Khalid, as he had done days earlier to Shaykh Zayid. At the December OPEC meeting, Saudi Arabia proposed a six-month moratorium on any price increase; the UAE followed suit. When the other OPEC members voted for a 15 percent increase, the Saudis and the Emiratis decided to raise the price of their oil by just 5 percent. For some months, OPEC followed a two-tiered pricing system. Yet the sheer size of Saudi Arabia's share of the global market—which Riyadh expanded further by boosting its production from 8.5 million to 11.8 million barrels per day—made it impossible for the other OPEC nations to maintain the higher price for long. In July 1977, the organization as a whole settled on a 10 percent increase. Abourezk's influence in this matter is difficult to determine. While Horan was not inclined to give the senator any credit, the U.S. ambassador to the UAE, whom Abourezk did not bar from his session with Zayid, reported that "Senator Abourezk certainly made a very persuasive case."[12]

None of these events did anything to curtail the influx of Arab petrodollars into the United States, where politicians, pundits, journalists, activists, and other opinion leaders remained fixated on the phenomenon, especially its more visible aspects. In news stories on the topic (and regardless of whether the overall tone was alarmist, reassuring, or neutral), a common device was simply to list the various American locales, prominent and obscure, in which oil-rich Arabs had purchased major properties, as if to show how thoroughly the tendrils of Arab economic power had crept into the nooks and crannies of American life. Wealthy Kuwaitis, reported the *New York Times* in November 1974, "recently bought the 3,500-acre Kiawah Island, off the coast of South Carolina. . . . Other [Kuwaiti] interests include half-ownership of the Atlanta Hilton Center, . . . a 27 per cent share in a cattle feeder lot in Idaho, and some undeveloped land in California's San Remo Valley." A June 1975 article in the *Wall Street Journal* noted that the investment portfolio of Adnan Khashoggi, a fabulously wealthy Saudi businessman, "includes two small California banks, part of a heavy-trailer-manufacturing plant in Albuquerque, a minority interest in Arizona-Colorado Land & Cattle Co., and a steak house in Modesto, Calif."[13]

This motif sometimes appeared in fictional accounts as well—and here the tone was more consistently hostile. The protagonist of Harold Robbins's 1974 novel *The Pirate*, a rapacious Arab plutocrat named Baydr Al Fay (reportedly modeled on Khashoggi), is described as having "wound up as the controlling stockholder of a small bank in La Jolla, California, a mail-order insurance company based in Richmond, Virginia, and a home-loan and finance company with forty branches in Florida."[14] In a key plot twist of the 1976 movie *Network*, Howard Beale, the deranged television personality, suddenly turns on his own network, charging during a live broadcast that Saudi investors are about to purchase CCA, the network's parent company. This will be, Beale claims, just the latest in a series of Arab acquisitions. Again, the List: "We all know that the Arabs control 60 billion dollars in this country. They own a chunk of Fifth Avenue, twenty downtown pieces of Boston, a part of the Port of New Orleans, an industrial park in Salt Lake City. They own big hunks of the Atlanta Hilton, the Arizona Land and Cattle Company, the Security National Bank in California, the Bank of the Commonwealth in Detroit. . . . They're all over: New Jersey, Louisville, St. Louis, Missouri. . . . The Arabs are simply buying us!" Although Beale is obviously insane, it quickly emerges that he is right about his network's impending sale to Arab interests. "CCA has two billions in loans with the Saudis," a despondent network executive admits in a closed-door meeting following Beale's broadcast. "And they hold every pledge we've got. We need that Saudi money bad." About the peril of petrodollars, not even a madman can exaggerate.[15]

On real-life network television, especially entertainment programs, portrayals of Arab acquisitiveness could be even more hyperbolic.[16] In a *Charlie's Angels* episode from 1979, the daughter of a wealthy Arab—identified as the owner of "half the oil in Arabia"—signs up for a fifteen-mile footrace. When her father disparages the notion of "running in the streets half dressed," the young woman replies, "Please do not question my motives. After all, I did not question you when you bought Rodeo Drive in Beverly Hills." "Did I buy Rodeo Drive?" the father absently asks an associate. In a 1978 episode of the medical drama *Trapper John, MD*, another oil-rich Arab tries to reward the American surgeon who has performed a lifesaving operation on him. What'll it be? the grateful patient asks. "A harem, perhaps? Your own hospital? The state of Pennsylvania?"[17]

Not only are these fictional Arabs buying up the country; they believe they are exempt from American laws. In the *Charlie's Angels* episode, the "Arabian girl" enters the race despite the objections of her overprotective father, who follows the runners in a chauffeured Cadillac, ordering the driver to proceed over bike trails marked as closed to automobile traffic. In a 1978 episode of *CHiPs*, a "buddy" show about two California highway patrolmen, a pampered and arrogant Arab prince races around in a red Ferrari, grossly exceeding the speed limit. He tries to bribe the patrolmen, causing one of them, Poncherello, to protest that such payoffs are illegal. "I'm above your laws," scoffs the prince. "Someday you're gonna kill somebody, the way you drive," Ponch retorts. "But you cannot buy permission to do it on our beat. Not for all the oil in the Middle East!"[18]

Naturally, such cartoonish depictions of Arab economic power aroused keen resentment in Arab American and Arab-friendly circles. In the second half of the 1970s, a wide array of individuals and organizations castigated the television networks for their insensitivity, though most of these critics addressed the topic only glancingly. An exception was Jack G. Shaheen, a young Lebanese American communications professor at Southern Illinois University at Edwardsville. Without benefit of home recording technology (personal videocassette recorders were only just appearing on the market), Shaheen spent hundreds of hours monitoring the Tube's ceaseless effusions, jotting down scene descriptions and bits of dialogue; his wife helped take notes.[19] He and a student, Joanne Myler, then wrote to network executives (mostly at the middle level), confronting them with the content of their programs and urging them to recognize its harmful character. A frequent rhetorical device, which soon became a staple of Arab-friendly media critiques, was to ask if any other ethnic group could be similarly disparaged. "When you screen ONE DAY AT A TIME," Shaheen wrote a CBS vice president, "substitute Jew or Black for Arab. Does the racism seem more obvious?"[20]

Most network executives, when they replied at all, were polite but unpersuaded. These were fictional portrayals, they said; no one should expect literal accuracy. (Such a response never would have sufficed, of course, in the case of fictional representations containing blatantly anti-Jewish or antiblack stereotypes.) Occasionally, an executive would agree that a particular depiction had gone too far and implement a remedy. "At my direction," CBS vice president for program practices Van Gordon Sauter wrote to Myler in 1977, "CBS recently refused to allow any more airings of an appliance commercial which portrayed an Arab with 75 wives."[21] A tiny victory, but this was about as far as the system would bend. And Shaheen did, over the next few years, cultivate sympathizers in network management who circulated his concerns among their colleagues and thereby may have achieved a slight softening of anti-Arab caricatures.[22] "While we 'never promised you a rose garden,' Jack," Sauter's successor at CBS program practices wrote to Shaheen in 1979, "I think you can see some improvement in terms of Arab portrayals on television." "Never asked for 'a rose garden,'" Shaheen replied. "Just a fair shake. Haven't seen a good camel-jockey—yet!!!"[23]

By now, the professor had gone public with his concerns. In late 1978, after a string of rejections, Shaheen placed an article in the *Christian Century*, a mainline Protestant journal published out of Chicago. In October 1979, the *Wall Street Journal* printed a shorter version of the piece, and meanwhile other versions appeared in several Arab American and Arab-friendly newsletters. The articles documented television's disparagement of Arabs and, in some cases, described the author's mostly quixotic efforts to get the networks to mend their ways. Although television remained his primary focus—the 1984 book version of his critique would be titled *The TV Arab*—Shaheen found defamatory portrayals in many other popular media: films, novels, press accounts, print ads, even syndicated comic strips like "Dennis the Menace" and "Broom Hilda." "I now have to hide the comics from my children," he poignantly observed.[24]

Unfortunately for Shaheen's cause, the rapidly expanding scale of the U.S.-Arab economic encounter, coupled with journalists' fascination with the topic, ensured a regular supply of real-world examples that lent credence to the worst caricatures of gauche and rampant opulence. In 1978, a young Saudi businessman with ties to the royal family purchased a thirty-eight-room mansion in Beverly Hills, California, painted it mint green, installed a shiny copper roof, decorated the perimeter with plastic flowers, and painted the existing nude statuary in natural flesh and hair tones, with the genitalia accentuated in red. The "Sheik's Palace" quickly became a sightseeing attraction. Vendors set up stalls near the site; tour bus companies placed it on their routes. "I'm so embarrassed by it all," complained an unnamed Saudi prince in the area. "This man is behaving like a Texan!"[25] Connections between the Desert Kingdom and the Lone Star State had arisen three years earlier with news reports that a wealthy Saudi had inquired about purchasing the Alamo. He wanted to give it to his son, a pilot trainee in San Antonio who had gushed about the landmark in letters home. Journalistic responses were more amused than indignant. "Arab Can't Buy Mecca of Texans," one headline announced. "Forget the Alamo," counseled another.[26]

In short, the image of the spoiled, filthy rich, bumptiously acquisitive Arab spendthrift, whether drawn from reality or wholly fictional, was far too vivid and ubiquitous for any one critic to banish. Not until 1980, however, would an organized response to the problem materialize. In the meantime, the preoccupation with petrodollars, and with the strange figures who dispensed them, continued to rile American society.

In U.S. academia, a growing number of financial donations from Arab sources, usually earmarked for studying the Middle East, aroused unease, suspicion, or outright hostility. Some of the opposition was crassly xenophobic; some of it reflected genuine concern that particular donor arrangements could compromise the academic integrity of recipient institutions. Whatever its motivation, the criticism strengthened the public impression that Arab actors were intruding on a hallowed sphere. At the same time, Arab petrodollars nurtured academic constituencies that generally viewed the Arab world sympathetically and, in some cases, closely identified with it.

In the half decade following the October War, much of the Arab financial support for American higher education came in the form of tuition. The petrodollar bonanza allowed oil-rich Arab states to send more and more of their young people so seek training abroad. American colleges and universities, desperate to boost enrollments in the post-1973 recession, eagerly welcomed the new students. Between the spring of 1974 and the fall of 1978, the number of Arab students in the United States rose from about 8,800 to about 15,000. The rapid growth in the number of Saudi students—from just over 2,000 in early 1975 to 10,000 in late 1978—accounted for most of this increase. During those same years, moreover, Arab oil producers grew increasingly willing to provide direct financial support to American colleges and universities, especially for the purpose of establishing Middle East studies programs and centers, or enhancing existing ones. By late 1978, at least seventy-five U.S. institutions had accepted program-related gifts from Arab states, a tenfold increase since 1973.[27]

Two of the biggest recipients were Georgetown University and the University of Southern California (USC). Between 1975 and 1980, Georgetown secured a series of donations from Arab countries, totaling some $3.4 million, to launch its Center for Contemporary Arab Studies (CCAS). In 1976, the Saudi government endowed a $1 million chair of Arab and Islamic studies at USC. Two years later, the Saudis encouraged several American companies with interests in the kingdom to pledge as much as $22 million for the establishment at USC of a center for Middle Eastern studies.[28]

Each of these initiatives aroused fierce controversy. The funds Georgetown solicited included $50,000 from Iraq and $750,000 from Libya. Both countries' governments opposed any accommodation with Israel, and Libya's Mu'ammar Qaddafi made little secret of his support for violent Palestinian rejectionist groups. The columnist Art Buchwald castigated the university for taking "blood money," a charge echoed by Jewish and pro-Israel commentators across the county. When Georgetown administrators insisted that neither Libya nor Iraq nor any other Arab donor would impinge on CCAS's academic independence, critics replied that such direct influence was unnecessary, given the political leanings of faculty members involved in the center. The center did feature a number of prominent scholars, such as the political scientists Hisham Sharabi and Michael Hudson, who had sharply criticized the U.S. government's support for Israel and failure to accommodate Palestinian claims; CCAS made no pretense of "balancing" them with pro-Zionist scholars. "The center is not doing a very good job," wrote Nicholas Lemann in the *New Republic*, "of laying to rest people's fears that one of its missions is to propagandize for the Arabs generally and the PLO in particular." As Lemann acknowledged, however, such partiality was hardly unique among university centers. The Center for Strategic and International Studies, also at Georgetown, was consistently hawkish in foreign policy debates, yet few questioned its academic legitimacy.[29] This consideration did nothing to lessen the criticism.

With pressure mounting, in July 1978, Georgetown's president, Father Timothy Healy, returned the $50,000 to Iraq, implausibly explaining that the proffered funds, though much appreciated, were no longer needed. Libya's $750,00 was harder to part with, but a barrage of angry letters from the public, and expressions of pointed concern from influential university trustees (including the prominent U.S. diplomat Max Kampelman), eventually persuaded Healy that the gift was more trouble than it was worth. In February 1981, he returned it as well. This time, Healy made no attempt to console the rebuffed donor, announcing that Tripoli's "growing support of terrorism" made it impossible for Georgetown to retain the gift.[30] The university kept the other Arab donations, however, and a battered CCAS weathered the controversy.

Plans for a Middle East studies center at USC fared less well. In that case, the questionable ground rules for administering the proposed center, as much as its Arabist funding sources, accounted for the public opposition to the scheme. The USC center was largely the brainchild of J. Robert Fluor, chairman of the university's board of trustees and head of a construction firm with far-flung overseas contracts. The vaguely worded agreement that Fluor brokered between USC and the Saudi-friendly corporations, concluded in 1978, appeared to vest administrative control of the Middle East center in a private foundation over which the university had no authority. A revolt by USC faculty, cheered on by pro-Israel groups, produced a spate of negative publicity and compelled the university administration to appoint a special committee to look into the matter. In mid-1979, the committee recommended that the agreement be rescinded, and the USC board of directors, with Fluor's own grudging assent, followed the recommendation. USC's president, tainted by the affair, stepped down.[31]

In the suburbs of Philadelphia, a smaller version of these dramas played out on the campuses of three affiliated Quaker colleges. In the fall of 1977, Swarthmore, Haverford, and Bryn Mawr sought funding for a joint program to strengthen Middle East studies at each school and provide need-based scholarships to Arab students. They obtained a tentative pledge of $590,000 from the Triad Foundation, a philanthropic outfit run by the aforementioned Adnan Khashoggi. A flamboyant jet-setter with dealings in Washington, London, Paris, Beirut, Riyadh, and elsewhere, Khashoggi had made his fortune brokering Western arms sales to his native Saudi Arabia. In 1975, he was enmeshed in a Washington influence-peddling scandal, accused of soliciting bribes from U.S. weapons manufacturers doing business with the kingdom. Two years later, Khashoggi was still dodging a subpoena from the U.S. Securities and Exchange Commission, which sought to question him on the matter.[32]

The association of the colleges' Middle East initiative with such a controversial figure was a real vulnerability, and opponents wasted little time in exploiting it. The moving force behind the opposition was the New York–based American Jewish Committee (AJC), though the organization kept a low profile. "Our participation was not widely known on the campuses and not reported in the public press, as we wished," AJC national program director Ira Silverman later wrote in an internal memorandum. With similar shrewdness, the AJC downplayed the Arab-Israeli issue and focused instead on the incongruity of Quaker colleges taking money from a shady arms dealer. It disseminated derogatory information about Khashoggi among students, faculty, and alumni of the three colleges. Some of this material appeared in the colleges' student newspapers. The *Swarthmore Phoenix* falsely claimed that Khashoggi was under federal indictment. "Say No to Triad," demanded the newspaper published jointly by Haverford and Bryn Mawr. Off campus, the AJC mobilized opposition among Philadelphia's Jewish community and enlisted New York congressman James Sheuer, a Swarthmore alumnus, to exert quiet pressure on his alma mater to pull out of the Triad agreement.[33]

Just days into the protests, Haverford withdrew from the joint project, saying it was inappropriate for a Quaker college to "apply for funds derived so directly from arms traffic." Swarthmore immediately followed suit, citing "the lack of a significant existing base in Middle East studies at Swarthmore"—a deficiency the Triad scheme was presumably designed to rectify. For a time, Bryn Mawr pursued a scaled-down version of the grant. Its president, Harris Wofford, publicly urged the college community "to guard against prejudice, against misinformation, and against the politics of purely personal psychic satisfaction." It was too late. Embarrassed by the publicity, Khashoggi turned down Bryn Mawr's application. "This is a good case history of how we can be effective in working with colleges to limit Arab influence on campus," a triumphant Silverman reported to the AJC.[34]

More often than not, however, the exotic transactions were consummated. In the late 1970s and early 1980s, many other U.S. universities eagerly accepted the Arab world's oil-begotten largesse: $5 million for the study of life sciences at Princeton, $1 million for a chair of Arab studies at Harvard, a reported $100,000 annually for an existing Middle East studies center at the University of Texas, to name just some of the gifts.[35] This was a fortuitous turn for Middle East studies. Since the early 1970s, economic hard times had prompted both the federal government and private American foundations to reduce their support for Middle East and other area studies; the Iranian Revolution of 1978–1979 eliminated another major source of funding for Middle East–related programs.[36] At a key moment, then, financial contributions from the Arab world allowed colleges and universities to meet a rising demand for instruction and research in the languages, history, culture, society, and politics of the Middle East.

The growing importance of Arab funding coincided with, and in some ways furthered, a shift in orientation within Middle East studies. Over the first quarter century after World War II, U.S. Middle East studies had been dominated by European American (and sometimes European) scholars who tended to share official Washington's geopolitical outlook and often aspired to produce scholarship that facilitated U.S. policymaking in the Middle East (even while grumbling that the government never followed their advice). As in other academic areas, the upheavals of the Vietnam era challenged this approach, and by the mid-1970s the field's practitioners were more prone to look askance at American global power. Meanwhile, an influx of students and faculty from Arab countries, combined with the coming-of-age of young Arab Americans who had chosen to study the region, altered the field's demographic character. Increasingly, scholars who personally identified with the Arab world were helping to determine how it was studied in the United States, a phenomenon encouraged by the academic activities of the Association of Arab American University Graduates (AAUG). (Underscoring both themes—the disaffection from U.S. policy and the rising prominence of Arab and Arab American scholars—was the publication of Edward Said's *Orientalism*, which first appeared in 1978 and began to revolutionize Middle East studies in the following decade.)[37] Petrodollars partly enabled this broad transformation, erecting a modest firewall against the animosities they simultaneously stoked.

In the realm of higher education, the tussle over petrodollars was largely a debate about the future: what role could Arab oil money legitimately play in training the citizens and leaders of tomorrow? In national politics, by contrast, the potential impact of petrodollars lay in a more immediate temporal realm. Early in 1979, John B. Connally, a former governor of Texas who had served as Richard Nixon's treasury secretary, announced his candidacy for the Republican presidential nomination. Over the coming months, Connally's ties to Arab business interests, coupled with his unorthodox approach to the Arab-Israeli dispute, raised a flurry of concern about petrodollars' allegedly corrupting influence on the determination of national policy toward the Middle East.

Like any candidate, Connally had his share of weaknesses and strengths, though his tended to be larger and more dramatic than usual. On the negative side, he had been a Democrat until 1973, and a high-ranking one at that, leaving many Republicans to question how sincerely he espoused the tenets of his adopted party. In both politics and business, he had a reputation for cutting corners, and some of the sleaze from the Nixon administration (though little of Watergate itself) had rubbed off on him.[38] In 1974, Connally was tried in federal court for taking an illegal gratuity while serving as Nixon's treasury secretary; his subsequent acquittal did not entirely clear his name. More recently, there were murmurings about his chumminess with Arab investors. In 1977, Connally joined two Saudi businessmen, Ghaith Pharaon and Khalid Bin Mahfouz, in acquiring a controlling interest in the Main Bank of Houston. Soon thereafter Connally's law firm facilitated Pharaon's purchase of stock in the National Bank of Georgia, a transaction involving Bert Lance, Jimmy Carter's scandal-clouded former budget director.[39] In the early months of his campaign, Connally's Arab dealings attracted only modest attention. That would soon change.

On the positive side, Connally was a physically imposing, handsome, articulate, and charismatic figure who radiated confidence and command. His résumé ran the gamut from government to business to military affairs to the law. He seemed to offer just the sort of sure-footed leadership Americans professed to crave as 1980 approached. Moreover, for all his unsavory Nixon ties, Connally had a touch of the JFK mystique. As governor of Texas in November 1963, he had been riding with Jack Kennedy during the latter's ill-fated visit to Dallas and was seriously wounded by the gunfire that killed the president. These circumstances aroused considerable excitement among national news commentators. "Throughout early 1979," writes the political analyst Andrew Busch, "if any candidate had media 'buzz,' it was Connally."[40]

Naturally, Connally and his advisers hoped that the "pluses" would prevail and advance the candidate to the front ranks of the Republican primary field. As of the summer of 1979, however, there was little evidence that the campaign was catching on with Republican voters. Hoping to reinvigorate his candidacy through a bold gesture, Connally asked his top adviser on foreign affairs, Samuel Hoskinson, a former CIA and National Security Council analyst, to draft a major foreign policy speech. The Middle

East was then much in the news: Arabs were still in an uproar over the Egyptian-Israeli peace treaty; the Iranian Revolution had driven up the price of Persian Gulf oil, dramatizing the world's dependence on that commodity. Connally and Hoskinson agreed that a challenging address on the Middle East would be just the thing to distinguish the candidate as a serious thinker in foreign affairs. Moreover, both men sincerely believed that a friendlier posture toward the Arab world would serve America's strategic and economic interests.[41] The resulting speech did set Connally apart from his rivals, though not in a manner that did him any good.

The address, which Connally delivered at the National Press Club in Washington, DC, on October 11, laid out a bold scheme for resolving the Arab-Israeli conflict and securing Western access to Middle Eastern oil. Israel, he said, should withdraw from virtually all of the Arab territories it occupied—not just the Sinai Peninsula—and permit the Palestinians to exercise "their right of self determination" in the West Bank and Gaza. While it was preferable that the Palestinians opt for confederation with Jordan, Connally did not rule out an independent state. In exchange, the Arab states and the Palestinians should recognize and make peace with Israel, agree to the demilitarization of the West Bank, Gaza, and the Golan Heights, and permit Israel "to lease military strong points" in those areas for a time. Further, the Arab oil producers should pledge to export petroleum at stable prices without regard to political disputes. "The Arabs must, in short, forsake the oil weapon in return for Israel's withdrawal from the occupied territories," Connally declared. To guarantee the agreement, the United States should expand its own military presence in the region, perhaps by leasing the airfields in the Sinai that Israel would soon vacate, perhaps by forming a new naval fleet to patrol the Indian Ocean.[42]

In part, Connally was reviving the comprehensive settlement that President Carter had pursued in 1977. The candidate's willingness to countenance a Palestinian state, however, went beyond Carter's vague talk of a Palestinian "homeland." Connally's speech also contained criticisms of Israeli attitudes and policies of a sort that Carter administration officials had expressed only in private.[43] Moreover, while most observers believed that the Arab-Israeli impasse had jeopardized Western access to Middle Eastern oil, and that security on the latter issue probably required progress on the former, no previous U.S. peace plan had explicitly advocated that quid pro quo. Connally's calls for military intervention were an even sharper departure from U.S. policy (though a few months later Carter himself would make similar noises).

The public reaction to the speech was swift and savage, mostly centering on the claim that Connally was proposing to trade Israeli security for Arab oil. "The Connally plan is a travesty," charged the *New Republic*. "It represents the abandonment of an ally, a submission to blackmail." A *New York Times* editorial agreed that the proposal amounted to "cynical offers of ransom." Although Connally had stressed throughout his speech, and continued to stress for weeks thereafter, that Israeli security was an indispensable ingredient of his plan, some critics acted as if he were proposing to liquidate the Jewish state. "Is Mr. Cannally [*sic*] assuring the American people that our energy problem and Arab gouging would go away if Israel would go away?" asked Maxwell Greenberg, national chairman of the Anti-Defamation League. Senator Howard Baker of Tennessee, about to launch his own bid for the Republican nomination, declared, "I am not prepared to accept the sacrifice of Israel as the price of peace in the Mideast or as the hope of moderation in the price of oil."[44] While critics also challenged Connally's ideas about U.S. military intervention, they tended to do so more perfunctorily. Such measures would be unnecessary, many said, as long as Israel itself was well armed.[45]

Accompanying the condemnations were several high-profile resignations and snubs. Rita Hauser, a Jewish member of Connally's foreign policy advisory group (and a prominent figure in Republican Middle East policy circles), angrily left the campaign. "What he did that is inexcusable," she told the *Washington Post*, "is the equation of oil and Israel. It's the straight Saudi line." Another Jewish campaign official, Washington attorney Arthur Mason, also resigned in protest. Across the Northeast, Republican politicians blasted Connally's Middle East proposals. The party chairman in New York withdrew his invitation to the candidate to speak at the state's Lincoln Day Dinner, a major fund-raising event for the party. When Connally appeared as scheduled at other New York fund-raisers, prominent donors stayed away. "Every Rockefeller has turned us down," the New York Republican finance chairman lamented about a Manhattan dinner that brought in a little over $100,000, instead of the projected $750,000. In Philadelphia, Connally was humiliated when the Republican candidate for mayor refused to be photographed with him.[46]

While most critics attacked Connally's positions on the merits, some probed the sinister motives presumed to underlie such perverse stances. Inevitably, ethnic bigotry emerged as a ready explanation. Connally's references to "American interests," the *New York Times* maintained, "are ugly code words that have the effect of blaming Israel and Jews for gas lines."

When Connally appealed in a radio campaign advertisement to "the forgotten American . . . who goes to church on Sunday and believes in prayer in school," the syndicated columnist Richard Reeves saw a disturbing pattern. Connally's pointed exclusion of Jewish voters was of a piece with his criticism of Israel, Reeves wrote, and through both gestures the candidate was "tapping America's real but essentially benign anti-Semitism." In a slyer reference to the prejudice, George Will wrote that "Connally may even become 'the thinking person's Agnew,' which is, of course, a contradiction in terms."[47]

Others focused on Connally's associations with Arab moneyed interests, charging that his Middle East policy positions were venally motivated. "It should not be surprising that Connally was in favor of the Arabs and against Israel," wrote William Loeb, publisher of New Hampshire's conservative newspaper the *Manchester Union Leader*. "He has an Arab partner in the banking business in Houston. He has apparently made many large fees by representing Arab clients." The candidate's Middle East policy, wrote Harvard Law professor Alan Dershowitz and *Moment* editor Leonard Fine in a letter to the *New York Times*, "reflects . . . an unseemly eagerness to please Mr. Connally's Saudi clients at the expense of America's commitment to an honorable peace."[48]

An especially overwrought attack came from the investigative reporter Jack Anderson, who wrote in a December 1979 installment of his syndicated column, "Big John is widely perceived as the darling of Big Business, the mouthpiece of Big Oil and the buddy of the Arabs who are picking American pockets at the gas pumps." Although the column concentrated on Connally's corporate and oil company ties, Anderson closed it by wondering, ominously, "whether [Connally's] profitable links to the Arab oil moguls—which we'll detail in a future column—will prove too bitter a pill to be swallowed by an American public outraged at the financial misery and national humiliation the United States has been suffering at the hands of the Middle Eastern petroleum potentates."[49]

Anderson's promised exposé, appearing in the second week of March 1980, was an anticlimactic rehash of previously published reports on Connally's ties to Arab investors. By now, however, the candidate had abandoned his quest. Connally's strategy had been to downplay the Iowa caucuses and New Hampshire primary (he ran poorly in both states) and seek a strong showing in the South Carolina primary in early March. Success in South Carolina would transform the contest into a two-man race between Connally and the front-runner, former California governor

Ronald Reagan, a matchup Connally believed he could win. But Reagan trounced Connally in South Carolina, and meanwhile another aspirant, former CIA director George H.W. Bush, had emerged as Reagan's main rival. Seeing no path to the nomination, Connally ended his candidacy on March 9.[50]

There were, to be sure, multiple reasons for Connally's failure to connect with Republican primary voters, despite his early promise. On television he came off as too loud and forceful—too "hot" for that "cool" medium, as pundits liked to say. Many voters saw something crass in his wheeler-dealer persona and open fealty to big business. (While this latter concern encompassed suspicions about Connally's ties to "Arab money," it would have existed even if the candidate had completely shunned Arab interests.) The campaign was poorly managed and, for all its fund-raising prowess, succeeded in running out of money.[51]

Still, there can be little doubt that the reaction to Connally's Middle East speech was deeply damaging. Although Jews comprised a tiny share of the Republican voter and donor base, staunch support for Israel was the expected stance within the party. The endlessly repeated accusations that Connally was prepared to sacrifice Israel on the altar of Arab oil, that his campaign rhetoric stigmatized American Jews, that his Middle East policy positions were a function of his dealings with wealthy Arabs—all of this appears to have caused thousands of Republican voters, contributors, activists, and operatives to turn away from Connally or at least slacken in their support. (Specific polling on these questions is sparse, but Connally's biographer called the Middle East speech "political suicide.") The Middle East–related charges were all the more harmful because they tended to accentuate the candidate's other perceived defects, such as his coziness with corporate fat cats and his garish style—a problem captured in a commentator's remark, following the Iowa caucuses, that Connally was "too oily and noisy" for the Hawkeye State.[52]

A few weeks before Connally ended his campaign, Americans were greeted to the stunning news that, in the course of an FBI sting operation, several members of the U.S. Congress had taken what they thought were bribes from wealthy Arabs. If Connally's public positions seemed conditioned, in a general way, by his dealings with Arab businessmen, then here was the corruption in naked form: government services in exchange for suitcases stuffed with Arab cash. True, Connally had transacted with flesh-and-blood Saudis, whereas in this case the Arabs were entirely fanciful. But the congressmen *believed* the Arabs were real, and were all too willing to take their money as the price for services rendered. The American political system, it appeared, was even more vulnerable to foreign political influence than previously assumed. This, at least, was a dominant interpretation within mainstream political society. For many Arab Americans, the episode carried a very different meaning.

The story of Abscam, as the FBI sting operation was called, began in February 1977, when a federal grand jury in Pittsburgh indicted a career swindler named Melvin Weinberg on mail fraud, wire fraud, and conspiracy charges.[53] Several months later Weinberg copped a plea: in exchange for a reduced sentence and the dropping of related charges against his mistress, he would plead guilty and help federal authorities catch other offenders. By late 1977, Weinberg and a team of FBI agents were conducting sting operations in cities along the Eastern Seaboard. At first, their targets were ordinary financial criminals, not politicians. But Weinberg had a knack for fashioning scams out of current events, and the ongoing drama over OPEC and oil prices offered rich possibilities. He began representing himself to sting targets as the agent of an imaginary Arab plutocrat named Kambir Abdul Rahman who headed an equally imaginary company called Abdul Enterprises. Abdul was interested in all manner of business: real estate, construction, entertainment ventures, financial speculation. He was also keen on buying valuable art and would not, Weinberg intimated, look too closely at its provenance. In a New York hotel suite in the spring of 1978, a seller of stolen paintings received an audience with Abdul himself—an FBI agent in a rented headdress who presided benignly, and mostly silently, over Weinberg's handling of the transaction. All of the sting operations involving the fictitious Arab were grouped under the heading "Abscam," an abbreviation of "Abdul scam."

Because so many of Weinberg's phony Arab projects required government licenses, favorable zoning decisions, and other kinds of official authorization, Abscam could not stay out of politics for long. By late 1978, Weinberg and the FBI were in contact with Angelo Errichetti, the exuberantly corrupt mayor of Camden, New Jersey, who also served in the New Jersey state senate. Errichetti was delighted to learn that Abdul Enterprises was thinking of building a casino in Atlantic City (and happy, too, with the bribes that accompanied these tidings); he promised to get the state to issue the necessary permits. It turned out, moreover, that the mayor had acquaintances on Capitol Hill who could render services of their own for a share of Abdul's pile. In the second half of 1979 and into early 1980,

Weinberg and an FBI agent named Anthony Amoroso met with several members of Congress, enlisting them in an array of schemes amounting to government action in exchange for money. Occasionally, a second fake Arab, Abdul's associate Yassir Habib, impersonated by another FBI agent, attended the meetings. Much of the promised government action involved bills in Congress to grant permanent residency to Abdul and Yassir, who, Weinberg and Amoroso claimed, feared being exiled by a revolution in their home country (sometimes identified as the United Arab Emirates, sometimes an unspecified Gulf sheikhdom). In return for pledging these favors, the congressmen came away with suitcases full of cash or with promises of Arab investment in businesses they or their friends owned. Most of these encounters were secretly videotaped.

After the Abscam story broke, journalists expressed surprise that prominent politicians could have fallen for such transparent ruses. Arab American activists, as we shall see, were outraged that these supposed pillars of society had seen nothing amiss in the FBI's crudely stereotypical portrayals of wealthy Arabs. Upon closer examination, however, Abscam's success is easier to understand. For all their later notoriety, the Arab impersonators made few appearances in the actual sting operations, which extended over two years. Abdul was trotted out only once, during Abscam's prepolitical phase, and Yassir used just three times, mostly for bagging a single subject, senator Harrison Williams of New Jersey. (In the mid-1970s, Williams had been a leading advocate of congressional restrictions on the influx of petrodollars; perhaps he understood all too well the destructive temptations they posed.) Although the Abdul impersonation was comically slapdash, the Yassir effort was more credible. The agent playing Yassir, Richard Farhart, was a Lebanese American who spoke some Arabic.[54] The Arabs' cameos were brief and largely ceremonial, in settings in which virtually everyone was stiff and awkward. Spotting a fake in such circumstances couldn't have been very easy.

With the Arabs mainly offstage, the sting targets acquired most of their information about Abdul Enterprises and its schemes from the fast-talking American middlemen, played by Weinberg and Amoroso. And if those middlemen sometimes seemed to exaggerate the Arabs' wealth or stumble over basic facts (as when Weinberg referred to the United Arab Emirates as "One of them . . . what they call emigrant"), that could be chalked up to unsurprising ignorance. Moreover, the manner in which Weinberg and Amoroso kept stalling on Abdul's promises probably enhanced the overall credibility of the scam. Although the FBI could furnish the occasional

Figure 21. Senator Harrison Williams and "Yassir Habib," the imaginary wealthy Arab impersonated by FBI agent Richard Farhart. © AP Photo/FBI.

cash-filled suitcase, it could not produce the tens of millions of dollars that Abdul Enterprises had pledged to invest in American ventures. To explain the endless delays on that front, Weinberg and Amoroso would cite Abdul Enterprises's dysfunctional management or, taking a cue from the headlines, claim that the company's funds were tied up in the banks of revolutionary Iran. (The shah's recent ouster, naturally, made Abdul and Yassir all the more fearful of radical change in their own country.) All of these verbal impressions, working together, conjured up a hustling scenario just quirky enough to be real. Even to a discerning eye, Abscam looked a lot like what it pretended to be: an effort by wealthy Arab businessman to purchase favors from the U.S. government, mounted against a backdrop of chaotic upheaval in the Middle East, entrusted to shady American operatives who knew little about the region.

In early February 1980, in a cascade of leaks, scoops, and hasty official announcements, Abscam suddenly became public knowledge. Senator Williams and seven House members were implicated in the affair; all but one representative would later be tried and convicted of bribery or related charges. The revelations rocked the American body politic. Embarrassed congressional leaders demanded that the Department of Justice turn over its evidence so that Congress could investigate its own. The Justice Department refused, arguing that legislative probes would compromise federal trials.[55] Editorial opinion was divided between those decrying the targeted congressmen's greed and dishonesty and those accusing the FBI of entrapping its victims with manufactured crimes.[56] Some commentators chided fellow journalists for airing lurid charges against individuals who had not yet had their day in court.[57] In letters to newspapers and the FBI, ordinary Americans expressed all of these views, but disgust with Congress appears to have been the dominant sentiment. "A wonderful job," wrote an admirer to FBI director William Webster. "Hang them all."[58]

For Arabs and Arab Americans, Abscam presented a different sort of outrage. A series of events in which no actual Arabs had participated was now raising, with unprecedented vividness, the specter of Arab subversion of American democracy. The Arab League denounced Abscam as a "campaign . . . to distort the Arab image through a dirty operation of investigation by F.B.I. agents into a purely internal matter"; the league demanded that Washington apologize to "the Arab people." The *Christian Science Monitor* reported that U.S. ambassador to Saudi Arabia John C. West "has told personal friends recently that reaction to Abscam in the kingdom has made contact difficult with close Saudi acquaintances." Traveling in Saudi Arabia shortly after the Abscam revelations, executive director of the U.S.-Arab Chamber of Commerce Mohamed Baghal found the FBI sting an unavoidable topic of conversation. "Wherever I went," he recalled, "I was asked, 'Why should we do business with a people who are insulting us?'" To contain the diplomatic damage, attorney general Benjamin Civiletti and White House spokesman Hodding Carter each issued qualified apologies to the Arab nations, expressing "regret" that the FBI's investigative procedures had caused any offense.[59]

A more sustained reaction came from organized Arab Americans. Within days of Abscam's unveiling, the National Association of Arab Americans and the AAUG condemned the FBI sting operation. Referring to initial (and erroneous) news reports that Abscam was an abbreviation of "Arab scam," the NAAA asked Americans to "reflect on the impact of an FBI operation that, instead of being called 'ABSCAM,' was . . . called 'JEWSCAM.'" The AAUG similarly wondered, "Could the F.B.I. have used a different ethnic group without due consideration to the consequences?" M.T. Mehdi, characteristically, put the question more sharply. "Couldn't the F.B.I. have used a waspish character, nondescript, or an oil-rich Venezuelan, Nigerian or an Israeli businessman to pose as the corrupting agent?" he cabled Civiletti.[60]

Jim Abourezk, who had left the Senate a year earlier (having decided not to seek reelection in 1978), was also getting into the act. Although his first recorded comment on Abscam was a quip—he said he was launching a consulting service to help members of Congress distinguish "the real Arabs from the FBI agents"—Abourezk recognized the scandal's serious cultural implications. Calling Arab Americans "the last ethnics in America who can be demeaned and stereotyped without a public outcry," he announced that he was forming a new national organization, the American-Arab Anti-Discrimination Committee (ADC), with the mission of combating such abuses in the future.[61]

Pushing back against defamation and discrimination had long been a feature of Arab American activism. The NAAA and the AAUG had frequently critiqued anti-Arab portrayals in news reporting, cinema, television, advertising, and textbooks. (And Jack Shaheen had embarked on a one-man crusade against such disparagement on television.) Both groups, especially the AAUG, had also fought to uphold the civil rights of Arab Americans and Arabs residing in the country. Yet neither organization had placed these tasks at the top of its agenda. "We are very much in need of a single issued, funded, staffed organization in this area," Abdeen Jabara wrote to Abourezk in March 1980, accepting the latter's invitation to join the new committee. Over the previous year, Abourezk had lobbied the NAAA to establish an antidiscrimination subcommittee. It could be run by James Zogby, the energetic director of the Palestine Human Rights Campaign (PHRC). "I'll raise the money and you do the work," Zogby recalls Abourezk telling him. But the NAAA was unenthusiastic, and the proposal languished. Immediately following the Abscam revelations, Abourezk renewed the suggestion that he and Zogby collaborate, this time in a stand-alone organization. Zogby left the PHRC and became, with Abourezk, ADC codirector.[62]

Following a planning meeting in Washington in May 1980, attended by Abourezk, Zobgy, Jabara, and other prominent Arab Americans, and the opening of a national office in the city four months later, the ADC expanded rapidly. Activists across the country, many of them AAUG or NAAA veterans, began forming local chapters, spurred on by Abourezk's offer to speak at inaugural banquets. In December 1980, Zogby could report that seventeen chapters had been established or would open their doors within the next few months. By the fall of 1981, the organization had five thousand members. Over the same period, the national office issued a number of short, polished studies on media portrayals of Arabs. The first two studies, on Abscam and children's entertainment, were authored by Jack Shaheen. A newsletter, *ADC Report*, updated members on national and local activities.[63]

Figure 22. Print advertisement for the Preston Company of Lowell, Massachusetts (from *ADC Report* #5 & #6, March/April 1981). From the Collection of the Arab American National Museum.

Working together, the chapters and the national office developed a formula for racking up small but heartening victories against anti-Arab defamation. Local activists would identify a conspicuous but correctable abuse in their area, such as a demeaning advertising billboard or storefront display, and complain to the offending party with letters and phone calls. The national office would follow up with objections of its own, sometimes supplementing them with complaints to the Better Business Bureau or, if radio or television was involved, the Federal Communications Commission. On several occasions in 1980–1981—in Colorado, Florida, Massachusetts, New York State, and elsewhere—the sponsors of the offensive portrayals agreed to discontinue them, sometimes with forthright contrition. They had thought the depictions were harmless fun and had no idea anyone could be hurt by them.[64]

Not all of the exposed offenders were so gracious. The Preston Company of Lowell, Massachusetts, marketing charcoal briquettes known as "Sheeks," produced a print ad urging customers, "Save oil & other high cost fuels—burn Sheeks." An accompanying drawing showed a figure in a robe and headdress hovering over a flaming barbecue. From across the country, ADC members protested to the Preston Company, whose lawyer responded with what the ADC called "a highly insulting letter in which he made crude reference to sexual practices of Arabs." Soon thereafter Preston announced it was pulling Sheeks from the market. The ADC declared victory, but the company's owner, John Preston, told the *Los Angeles Times* that the product was being withdrawn only temporarily, on account of labor problems at the manufacturing plant. He hoped to sell more Sheeks in the future. Addressing the controversy in the *Chicago Sun-Times*, the columnist Roger Simon told his readers, "Some of you may find that ad mildly amusing, but there are a couple million Arab Americans in this country who don't quite see the joke."[65] It is hard to say which revealed more about the Arab American predicament: the Preston Company's vicious incitement, or Simon's bland validation of the impulse to laugh the matter off.

By now, Arab American activists were facing new challenges. The extended captivity of U.S. embassy personnel in non-Arab Iran had aroused hostility in the United States toward Middle Easterners in general, some of it directed at Arabs and Arab Americans. And the increasingly bizarre and violent behavior of Libya's Mu'ammar Qaddafi certainly wasn't helping matters. Both phenomena were part of a wider array of Middle Eastern crises that grew increasingly enmeshed with one another as the new decade began. It was a disorienting situation for Arab American activists, and a vexing one for U.S. officials charged with making policy for the area.

Chapter 10

The Center Cannot Hold

Americans, Arabs, and the Wider Middle East, 1979–1980

On November 8, 1979, Walter Fauntroy, delegate to the U.S. Congress from Washington, DC, wrote to president Jimmy Carter. Though a nonvoting member of the House of Representatives, Fauntroy was an influential figure in the Congressional Black Caucus, admired for his vigorous advocacy on behalf of the nation's disadvantaged and his prior leadership in the civil rights movement. On this occasion, however, the delegate's concern was the troubled Middle East. Days earlier, over sixty Americans had been taken hostage in Iran, and Fauntroy hoped the president would "leave no non-violent stone unturned in an effort to ensure their safe release." One such stone could be "an appeal to the P.L.O. and its Chairman, Yasser Arafat, to use his good offices, as he did during the Lebanese Civil War, to save the lives of American citizens." Citing "outward indications" that the Palestine Liberation Organization was already willing to intercede with Iran on the hostages' behalf, Fauntroy urged Carter to endorse a Palestinian mission of mercy. That Fauntroy could imagine the PLO playing such a helpful role is not surprising. Weeks earlier, he had traveled to the Middle East as part of a Southern Christian Leadership Conference delegation and participated in a cordial meeting with Arafat. The experience had deepened Fauntroy's conviction that the PLO must be included in Middle East peace negotiations.[1]

If the organization was prepared to assist Washington in the current crisis, then this, too, should be encouraged.

In fact, Arafat had already decided to send a delegation on the hostages' behalf; it departed from Beirut to Tehran on the day Fauntroy wrote his letter. Despite a chilly reception, the PLO delegates pressed their Iranian hosts to show some lenience toward the hostages. On November 17, Ayatollah Ruhollah Khomeini, Iran's spiritual leader, announced the release of thirteen black and female captives; they were home by Thanksgiving. The PLO, it was reported, had urged the freeing of the African Americans in recognition of the vocal support it had recently received from black American leaders.[2] Over the next few weeks, the PLO tried, unsuccessfully, to get the remaining hostages released. They would be held until January 1981.

Fauntroy's call for PLO mediation, and the partly successful diplomacy that ensued, suggested the remarkable fluidity that U.S.-Arab relations had acquired by the end of the 1970s. Dismayed by Washington's failure to address the core issues of the Arab-Israeli dispute, a growing number of nonofficial American actors—of whom Fauntroy and his colleagues were just the most conspicuous—injected themselves into Middle East diplomacy. The PLO welcomed the participation of these disaffected elements of the American elite, but there was little change in the official U.S. approach to the peace process, which remained stalled in the aftermath of the Egyptian-Israeli treaty. More idiosyncratically, the Libyan government conducted its own effort to engage nonofficial Americans, an initiative that only intensified as the two countries' governmental relations plummeted. American policy makers were often discomfited by the appearance of these new actors on the diplomatic stage. Yet in a handful of endeavors, such as the effort (ultimately unsuccessful) to draw Palestinians into the peace process or the campaign to free the American hostages in Tehran, amateurs showed they could play useful roles.

That events in non-Arab Iran had become part of the U.S.-Arab encounter suggested another kind of fluidity. In 1979 and 1980, traumatic upheavals occurring largely or entirely outside of the Arab world—the Iranian Revolution, the Soviet invasion of Afghanistan, the outbreak of the Iran-Iraq War—reverberated through Arab societies, shaping their internal politics and relations with one another. Increasingly, U.S. relations with Egypt, Saudi Arabia, Libya, the PLO, and other Arab actors were conducted in a broader regional perspective and often with an eye to non-Arab developments. Everything, it seemed, was connected to everything else.

Of all the upheavals on the Arab periphery, none aroused greater American anxiety than those shaking the oil-rich Persian Gulf. The Iranian

Revolution extinguished a key U.S. ally on the Gulf; Moscow's move into Afghanistan placed Soviet forces alarmingly close to that waterway; the Iran-Iraq War threw the area into physical turmoil. If the Gulf region was to remain economically integrated with the West, American officials concluded, then the United States must take greater responsibility for its defense. And so, as the decade drew to a close (taking, it turned out, Carter's presidency with it), the United States declared its willingness to use armed force to keep the Soviets out of the Gulf region, cultivated allies in and around the area, and began building up its own military capabilities there. In these ways Americans claimed a proprietary interest in the Gulf that would, in years to come, repeatedly propel them into armed conflict.

At the start of 1979, the Iranian Revolution seized the lion's share of attention that U.S. policy makers devoted to the Middle East. In mid-January, the shah fled the country, and over the next few weeks his government collapsed. In early February Khomeini, exiled for a decade, returned to preside over an interim government. Although the fall of the shah was a huge setback for the United States, the Carter administration initially hoped for productive relations with the new government, which disdained communism and included moderate figures. Meanwhile, Iranian events posed other serious challenges. The disruptions of the revolution forced a complete cessation of Iranian oil exports from December 1978 to March 1979. Other oil-rich countries, most crucially Saudi Arabia, promptly increased their production, limiting the total shortfall to just 4 or 5 percent when measured against world demand. But panicked expectations of a much larger drop-off, and opportunistic price hikes by exporting countries, caused a 150 percent increase in the price of oil. It got worse. After Iranian oil returned to the market in March, the Saudis lowered their production from 10.1 million to 8.5 million barrels per day, unleashing more panic buying and price gouging. Meanwhile, the temporary Iranian cutoff had a delayed impact on the supply of gasoline. Refineries accustomed to Iranian light oil had difficulty handling the heavier crudes they had been required to purchase as a substitute. By June, American drivers were languishing in gas lines, as they had done in the bad old days of 1973–1974.[3]

The Iranian Revolution rattled the leaders of Saudi Arabia and other conservative Arab states in the Gulf. If close ties to the United States could not save the shah, then how confident could those leaders be about their own futures? The conservative regimes had long worried about potential domestic dissent, especially along radical nationalist and pro-Palestinian lines, and they smelled trouble in the air. The U.S.-brokered Camp David agreement, formalized by the Egyptian-Israeli peace treaty in March, was deeply unpopular in the Arab world and had thrown pro-U.S. Arab governments on the defensive. A simultaneous buildup of Soviet arms in nearby Ethiopia, coupled with a brief war in February and March that pitted Soviet-supplied South Yemen against the other Yemen to the north, heightened the Gulf conservatives' sense of beleaguerment.[4]

The Saudis appealed to Washington for protection from what they portrayed as a gathering Marxist/nationalist onslaught. The message was twofold: do something *about* the Soviets, and something *for* the Palestinians. Actually, there was scant evidence of Soviet involvement in the Yemeni conflict beyond the arming of South Yemen, nor was the latter clearly the aggressor. Nonetheless, the United States airlifted weapons to North Yemen and sent its own planes and ships to patrol the area. While these moves were of questionable military utility, they pleased the Saudi government and restored some of its confidence in the United States. Still, when the Carter administration proposed expanding the U.S. military presence in Saudi Arabia, the Saudis balked at the idea. They wanted American protection, but not in such a conspicuous manner.[5]

On the Palestine issue, the administration could offer little more than the Palestinian autonomy negotiations mandated by the Egyptian-Israeli peace treaty. Egypt and Israel were scheduled to begin those talks in May (Jordan refused to participate), and President Carter had appointed a special envoy, former U.S. trade representative Robert Strauss, to oversee the process. Although the treaty authorized no separate Palestinian delegation, Palestinians who resided in the West Bank or Gaza and were unaffiliated with the PLO could join the Egyptian delegation. These stipulations, however, were largely academic. As long as both the PLO and Jordan adamantly opposed the autonomy talks, no local Palestinians with any following would consent to take part in them.[6] There seemed little prospect, then, of rendering the current peace process palatable to any Arab actors outside of Egypt's government.

In the House of Representatives, a moderate Republican from Illinois had his own problems with the post–Camp David peace process. Since the early 1970s, Paul Findley had challenged U.S. policies toward the Arab-Israeli conflict. Through its excessive attachment to Israel, he believed, the United States was alienating the strategically vital Arab world and negating its own professed commitment to the right of self-determination. More recently,

Findley had focused on Washington's unwillingness to negotiate with the PLO as long as it refused to recognize Israel. Though disdainful of this U.S. policy, the congressman chose not to confront it head-on. Instead, he set out to elicit conciliatory statements from the PLO that could, at least under a loose interpretation of the ban, be regarded as satisfying U.S. conditions for a dialogue. Starting in January 1978 and continuing well into the following decade, Findley traveled frequently to the Middle East and held several meetings with Yasser Arafat, seeking to commit the chairman to a form of words that Washington might accept.[7]

The most important of these meetings occurred on November 25, 1978. Receiving Findley in a Damascus apartment, Arafat assailed the recently signed agreement between Egypt and Israel. "Camp David is a disaster for us," he said. "You have put a U.S. legal umbrella over Israeli control of the West Bank. Why legalize this new slavery for Palestinians?" The agreement also meant that "Egypt had withdrawn from the field"; Sadat would soon be overthrown for his treachery. Findley, expressing the hope "that you won't give up on the United States," urged Arafat to make a generous statement that would enable the Carter administration to start a dialogue. The chairman agreed to try. Working with Findley late into the night, and carefully weighing every word, Arafat dictated the following pledge: "The PLO will accept an independent Palestinian state consisting of the West Bank and Gaza, with connecting corridor, and in that circumstance will renounce any and all violent means to enlarge the territory of that state. I would reserve the right, of course, to use non-violent means, that is to say diplomatic and democratic means to bring about the eventual unification of all of Palestine. We will give de facto recognition to the State of Israel. We would live at peace with all of our neighbors."[8] This was a logical extension of earlier statements by Arafat, but more comprehensive and explicit than anything he had previously said.

"I was elated," Findley later recalled, "perhaps too much so." He immediately publicized Arafat's statement, calling it "a major concession" that "meets the essential conditions" for a U.S.-PLO dialogue. He returned to Washington and repeated this argument in a private meeting with Carter's national security adviser, Zbigniew Brzezinski, to whom he gave a typescript of Arafat's statement.[9]

The results were disappointing. As with previous PLO trial balloons, Arafat declined to repeat his pledge in public. A PLO spokesman in Beirut said that Findley's rendering of Arafat's remarks was "not quite accurate," though the spokesman's own version did not substantively contradict it.[10]

The PLO's representative in France explicitly reaffirmed Arafat's pledge as given to Findley, but added that the undertaking was not official policy until the Palestine National Council approved it. These facts, combined with criticism of the pledge by more militant Palestinians, persuaded the State Department that Arafat's statement was not sufficiently "unambiguous" to justify talks with the PLO.[11]

Findley tried again. In an April 1979 memorandum to Carter, he noted that Arafat had climbed out on a limb and could not remain there for long. A retreat by him would strengthen Palestinian extremism and further destabilize a region already in turmoil over the Iranian Revolution. Responding on Carter's behalf, assistant secretary of state for congressional relations Douglas Bennet reiterated that the PLO had not satisfied the U.S. conditions. If other Palestinians sought a role in the peace process, they could join the upcoming autonomy talks as part of the Egyptian delegation.[12]

Actually, the Carter administration was more sympathetic to Findley's suggestion than it let on, and this sympathy had everything to do with the autonomy talks Bennet touted. As mentioned, no Palestinians of any significance would participate in the talks. Thus only Egyptian, Israeli, and U.S. officials showed up for the negotiations that commenced in Beersheba, southern Israel, on May 25. Because it could not credibly represent the Palestinians, and was already dangerously isolated in the Arab world, Egypt had minimal flexibility in the talks, which soon bogged down. By summer, fearing the exercise would be fruitless as long as it remained bilateral, the Carter administration was pushing anew for Palestinian participation. Perhaps the PLO's hostility to the autonomy talks could be softened somehow, providing local Palestinians the political cover to take part.[13] It seemed unrealistic, though, to expect the PLO to moderate its position if the United Sates would not even talk to it. And so, much as it had done two years earlier, the U.S. government set out to overcome its self-imposed ban on dealing with the PLO.

An initiative in the UN Security Council provided the occasion. In May, the PLO's UN representative, Zehdi Terzi, began calling for a new Security Council resolution similar to the one the United States had vetoed in January 1976; it would demand Israeli withdrawal from the occupied territories and support Palestinian statehood. Although the United States would surely veto the new resolution as well, that would suit the PLO and its supporters. Having again demonstrated the Security Council's impotence on the Palestine question, they would seek passage in the UN General Assembly of a resolution condemning the Egyptian-Israeli peace treaty and imposing sanctions against Israel. The General Assembly resolution would be nonbinding, Terzi privately acknowledged, but it would "embarrass Israel and her friends."[14] The Arab delegations, with the Kuwaitis in the lead, began circulating drafts of the PLO-inspired Security Council resolution.

At the State Department, assistant secretary of state for Near Eastern affairs Harold Saunders had a different scenario in mind. Instead of vetoing the proposed resolution and playing into the PLO's hands, perhaps the United States could work for an acceptable resolution, by either amending the Arab draft or offering one of its own. If the resulting language explicitly reaffirmed Resolution 242 and spoke of something vaguer than Palestinian statehood—such as, say, a Palestinian right to "self-determination"—then the United States could conceivably support it. And, if the PLO publicly embraced that resolution, such a gesture might satisfy U.S. conditions for opening a dialogue with the organization. This would be a significant impetus to Middle East diplomacy, Saunders told a British diplomat, "comparable to Sadat's trip to Jerusalem." Carter approved the UN initiative, which his administration pursued in July and August.[15]

As in 1977, however, in order to create the conditions for direct talks with the PLO, U.S. officials would first have to conduct indirect talks with it. Most immediately, they needed to persuade the PLO not to push for its maximal draft until the United States had a chance to propose its own, softer draft. But this could take some time, for the Carter administration was then juggling several domestic and international crises: soaring energy costs, a deteriorating economy, a cabinet shake-up, and another contretemps with Israel over its unauthorized use of U.S.-supplied weapons in Lebanon. Through intermediaries—Findley, Walid Khalidi, and probably Landrum Bolling—in late July the administration asked if the PLO would consent to a postponement of the Security Council's consideration of the resolution.[16] The PLO agreed, and on July 31 the Security Council deferred the item until late August.[17]

All the while, American anxieties over the oil situation continued to mount, and few could separate those concerns from U.S. policy on Palestine. In early July, following weeks of uncertainty, Saudi Arabia announced a production increase from 8.5 to 9.5 million barrels per day, a move that promised to blunt the upward spike in oil prices. Pundits welcomed the news but feared the Saudis would soon demand something in return. Riyadh had already complained about Washington's failure to address Palestinian claims. How long before this sentiment started to impinge on Saudi oil policies?[18] U.S. officials, too, were worried. "There is a significant body of opinion in the administration here," reported the British embassy in Washington on August 9, "which has concluded that the Americans are going to have to find means of recognising and dealing with the PLO if they are going to . . . heal their breach with Saudi Arabia and avoid the risk of a return to domestic 'gas lines.'" The following evening a National Security Council staffer sent an ominous report to Brzezinski: according to John West, the U.S. ambassador to Saudi Arabia, "a U.S. veto on Palestinian rights would severely damage bilateral relations and would foreclose further Saudi assistance and cooperation on oil pricing and production issues."[19]

The countervailing diplomatic pressures were no less intense. Israel was in an uproar over the Carter administration's UN maneuverings, whose underlying purpose—finding a way to talk to the PLO—was plain to see. Even if the PLO recognized the Jewish state, Israeli officials insisted, they would never consent to that organization's inclusion in peace talks. "Nobody," vowed foreign minister Moshe Dayan, "will be able to bend us and impose on us something unfavorable."[20] Israel's stridency raised doubts in Egypt about the wisdom of the UN initiative. If the controversy continued, Israel might pull out of the autonomy talks, leaving Sadat with nothing to show for his diplomacy but a separate peace with Israel. When Robert Strauss, Carter's special Middle East envoy, visited Cairo in mid-August, an agitated Sadat urged a halt to America's quest for a new UN resolution. Even a U.S. veto of the Arab draft, he implied, would be less politically damaging. Sadat's vehemence caught U.S. officials off guard.[21]

The Carter administration was in a bind. Pursuing a UN initiative strongly opposed by Israel and Egypt alike would be an extremely hard sell, both diplomatically and domestically. Yet failing to engage the Palestinians could doom the autonomy talks, radicalize the PLO, and further antagonize Saudi Arabia, with potentially dire economic consequences. Daunted by the dilemma, and overwhelmed by other crises, the administration requested a further, indefinite postponement of the Security Council's consideration of the Palestine item. The delay was granted on August 24.[22]

By now, the UN initiative had become enmeshed in American ethnic politics, in a controversy that activated latent tensions in Carter's governing coalition. The event would also, in short order, mobilize new American sympathies for the moderate Palestinian cause, even while torpedoing a diplomatic effort that might have advanced it. The U.S. ambassador to the UN was Andrew Young, the first African American to hold that position. A former congressman and civil rights leader, Young was a freewheeling and outspoken figure who often chafed against the restrictions of his diplomatic post. On July 26, as part of the general U.S. effort to slow down the PLO's diplomacy—but acting on his own—Young met briefly in New York with Zehdi Terzi, the PLO's UN representative, and asked if the PLO would accept a delay in the consideration of its own resolution. Terzi promised to convey the request to Arafat, who, having received similar appeals through other American channels, agreed to a postponement days later.[23]

Over the next couple of weeks, the Israeli government got wind of the Young-Terzi meeting and tipped off a *Newsweek* reporter, who asked the State Department about it. When the department sought an explanation from Young, he falsely claimed that the meeting had been purely social. He then gave Israel's UN ambassador a truthful account of the meeting, hoping that a full disclosure would persuade the Israelis to let the matter rest. Instead, Israel protested to the State Department that Young had violated the U.S. ban on negotiations with the PLO. Young now admitted to his American colleagues that the encounter with Terzi had been substantive. Young probably would have been forgiven for the meeting itself, but his initial lack of candor infuriated secretary of state Cyrus Vance, who compelled him to submit his resignation. Carter agonized over the situation. Young was a close friend and ally, an embodiment of his administration's commitment to black Americans. Yet Young had angered American Jews, whose support for the president had dwindled after so many American controversies with Israel. Vance, moreover, was insisting that Young had to go. Carter accepted the resignation on August 15. "It is absolutely ridiculous," he lamented in his diary, "that we pledged under Kissinger . . . that we would not negotiate with the PLO." Young was willing to use the same adjective in public. The ban on dealing with the PLO, he said in a television interview days later, "is kind of ridiculous."[24]

News of Young's resignation produced a surge of anger throughout the black community. To all appearances, the highest-ranking African American in the Carter administration had been humiliated and expelled to assuage Israeli and Jewish sensibilities. Long-smoldering grievances against organized American Jewry—over busing, affirmative action, support for Israel, and other issues—burst into flame. Several of the more established civil rights leaders rushed to contain the reaction. While they, too, were dismayed to see Young forced out, they insisted that their quarrel was with the State Department, which in their view had applied the anti-PLO policy inconsistently, not with Israel or American Jews.[25] But many other black leaders and commentators kept the controversy alive by scrutinizing the U.S. policy

Figure 23. Andrew Young and Jimmy Carter, 1977. Courtesy of the Jimmy Carter Presidential Library.

that Young had violated. Why *wouldn't* the United States talk to the PLO? Weren't the Palestinians key to a viable Arab-Israeli settlement? Wasn't it obvious that the PLO was their representative? Over the next several weeks, these and similar questions preoccupied the black community. Exasperation with perceived Israeli intransigence, and with American Jews who abetted it, was the dominant theme.

To many casual white observers, this forceful response probably seemed to come out of nowhere. In fact, over the previous half decade critical perspectives on Israeli behavior had quietly taken hold within the African American mainstream (as distinct from Black Muslim and Black Power circles, where anti-Zionist sentiments had been prevalent for many years). Like Americans generally, African Americans had, after 1973, become more familiar with Arab and Palestinian narratives and less inclined to view Israel in a heroic light. Over the same period, Israel's increasingly cooperative relationship with apartheid South Africa had aroused the ire of some black activists and commentators, especially members of the policy advocacy group TransAfrica, founded in 1977. Another group formed in 1977, the Palestine Human Rights Campaign (PHRC), reinforced the critical trend of mainstream African American discourse. As its name suggested, the PHRC advocated on behalf of Palestinians' human and political rights. A principal strategy of the campaign was to enlist the support of non–Arab American activists in churches, the peace movement, and civil rights groups. The outreach succeeded; over the next two years, several prominent black political figures, including the civil rights leader Ralph Abernathy and Michigan congressman John Conyers, served on the PHRC's board of directors or participated in its activities.[26]

In June 1979, the Association of Arab American University Graduates arranged for a delegation of black journalists and activists to tour Palestinian refugee camps in Lebanon recently subjected to Israeli air raids. The delegation included members of Operation PUSH (People United to Save Humanity), the Reverend Jesse Jackson's Chicago-based social justice organization. Jackson's wife, Jacqueline Jackson, a senior officer in PUSH, went on the trip. The AAUG *Newsletter* reported that Ms. Jackson, after attending some children's events, "spoke of her pain and embarrassment in realizing how much of the children's suffering had been inflicted through weapons and policies originating in the United States."[27]

In view of this recent background, it is not surprising that the most coherent and sustained black response to Young's ouster was a frontal challenge to pro-Israel orthodoxies and taboos. A week after the resignation, Joseph Lowery, president of the Southern Christian Leadership Conference, held his own meeting with Zehdi Terzi and announced the SCLC's support for a Palestinian "homeland" coexisting with Israel. Operation PUSH and the National Association for the Advancement of Colored People issued similar statements. "To be pro-Palestinian does not mean I am anti-Israel," declared Wyatt Tee Walker, an SCLC member and pastor of Harlem's Canaan Baptist Church, but "all you have to do is go to a Palestinian refugee camp one time and you will know that the Palestinians are the niggers of the Mideast." In an open letter to President Carter, TransAfrica detailed Israel's military ties to South Africa and noted the increasingly widespread view "that Israel and South Africa represent examples of a similar phenomenon, 'settler colonialism' or arrogant, aggressive racialism. Americans should have enough influence with Israel to change and negate the growing reality of this charge."[28]

To the complaint that they were overstepping their bounds, the black dissenters replied that Middle East policy was of direct concern to their constituencies. America's pro-Israel policies, Lowery warned, could provoke an Arab oil embargo that would be disproportionately harmful to African Americans: "It would be like America catching a cold and black folks developing pneumonia." Walter Fauntroy, the DC delegate to Congress, argued that the festering Middle East dispute could erupt into full-scale violence and exact a still heavier toll. "Should the United States become drawn into a war in the Middle East," he said, "black Americans will . . . be called upon to sacrifice their lives." (Months later, Jesse Jackson would vividly combine these two scenarios: "Blacks have a vital interest in peace in the Middle East because in a hot war we will die first and in a cold war over oil, we will be unemployed and freeze first.")[29]

In late September and early October, Lowery and Jackson led separate delegations to visit the Middle East. Jackson's trip, which was more extensive than Lowery's, and headed by a younger, more charismatic, and more media-savvy figure, attracted greater attention. Trailed by American television crews, Jackson addressed a prayer breakfast in East Jerusalem, led West Bank Palestinians in his trademark "I am . . . somebody" chant, visited a war-damaged refugee camp in South Lebanon, and, in a move that left many pro-Israel Americans embittered for years, had three friendly meetings with Arafat in Beirut. Jackson did challenge the PLO chairman to commit himself unequivocally to peaceful coexistence with Israel. Arafat reaffirmed his readiness for diplomacy, though in terms that fell short of his pledge to Congressman Findley the previous November.[30] Findley, who had facilitated Jackson's appointment with Arafat, was nonetheless impressed with what Jackson and other black leaders had accomplished. In an interview with the *Chicago Tribune*, the congressman "said the current wave of black support for the Palestinians has created the best opportunity to date for the Palestinians to make their case in this country."[31]

Arab American activists seemed to agree, and they did what they could to exploit the opening. Fortuitously, the weekend on which the PHRC held a national conference in Washington fell right between Lowery's return from and Jackson's departure for the Middle East. Both leaders were invited to address the conference, and they did so in rousing speeches that further identified the struggle for racial justice at home with the quest for an equitable Arab-Israeli settlement. The AAUG offered to help cover the travel costs of the black delegations, but the offer was declined. Instead, a number of AAUG members in Chicago joined with other Arabs and Arab Americans to raise several thousand dollars for Jackson's Operation PUSH. In Washington, when Fauntroy's call for dialogue with the PLO provoked attacks from Jewish groups, the National Association of Arab Americans (NAAA) rushed to his defense. Jackson, Lowery, and Fauntroy were featured speakers at the AAUG's annual convention in Washington that November.[32]

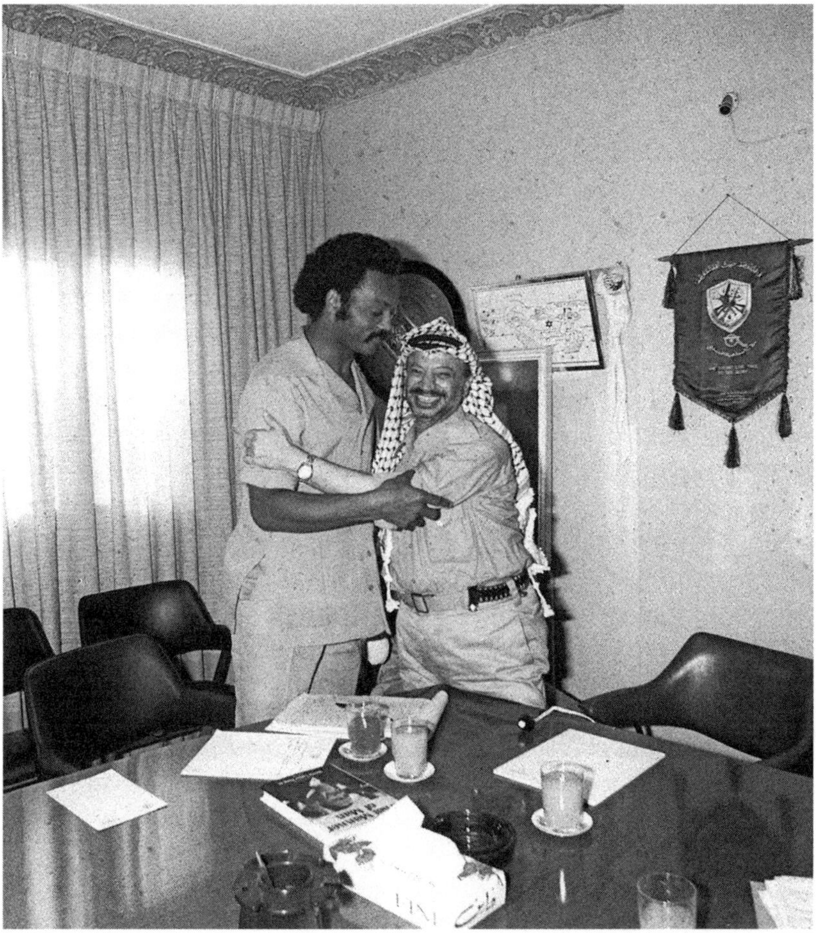

Figure 24. Jesse Jackson meets Yasser Arafat in Beirut, September 1979. © AP/AP/CORBIS.

Although the Young controversy shortly died down, it left an enduring mark on black politics. From now on, African Americans would participate far more vocally in the national discourse on the Middle East, taking positions generally more sympathetic to Arabs and Palestinians than those found in the U.S. mainstream. It became customary for black leaders to speak at Arab American conventions. When Jim Abourezk launched the American Arab Anti-Discrimination Committee (ADC) early in 1980, Congressman Conyers and Delegate Fauntroy attended the first organizational meeting. Over the coming years, a small but outspoken contingent of black congresspeople—Conyers, Fauntroy, Mervyn Dymally, Gus Savage, Cynthia McKinney, and others—would push for more Arab-friendly U.S. policies, often in coordination with Arab American organizations. In his campaigns for the Democratic presidential nomination in 1984 and 1988, Jesse Jackson not only challenged received wisdom on Middle East policy but also granted Arab Americans a prominent place in his Rainbow Coalition. The distinguished psychologist Kenneth Clark was on to something when he said, in the hectic days following Young's resignation, that black Americans were issuing a "declaration of independence."[33]

As for the UN initiative that provoked the controversy, it became, in turn, a casualty of the uproar. With the Security Council's second postponement of the Palestine item in late August, U.S. officials had more time to seek language that they and the PLO could agree on. But the Carter administration was now on the defensive, assailed by blacks from one direction and Israelis and Jews from the other. Robert Hunter, Brzezinski's top Middle East aide, told British diplomats in late September "that in the aftermath of the Andy Young affair there was no political will in Washington to go down this road again." The PLO and the other Arabs could do as they wished in the Security Council; the United States, reverting to form, would probably veto the result. If such a stance augured ill for both the autonomy talks and U.S.-Saudi relations, then so be it.[34] Indeed, the autonomy negotiations would continue to go nowhere, before sputtering out altogether in the early 1980s. But the other feared consequence, punitive Saudi action on oil production, did not materialize. Subsequent events, in the Persian Gulf region and in lands further east, would cause the Saudis to value more highly their strategic relationship with the United States, despite their growing dismay over Palestine. The absence of Saudi economic retaliation would transform what U.S. officials had previously considered an untenable Arab-Israeli status quo into something they could tolerate for the time being.

On September 1, 1979, at the height of the American furor over Young's resignation, the Libyan Arab Republic celebrated its tenth anniversary. Addressing a massive rally in Benghazi, Mu'ammar Qaddafi extolled the revolution he had led, while lashing out at his regional foes. "Sadat's treachery has brought shame on the Arab nation," he said, "but the Arabs are determined to confront and crush the [Zionist] enemy." Possessing vast material and human resources, the Arabs were "capable of wiping out the enemy, despite its support from the United States." In a set of bleachers behind the gesticulating leader sat a round-faced man with sandy hair, horn-rimmed glasses, and a toothy smile that was vaguely familiar. Billy Carter, First Brother of the United States, was back to visit his Libyan friends.[35]

The scene captured the Libyan regime in wild flux, waging an increasingly bizarre campaign to cultivate support among American private citizens, while veering with gathering speed onto a collision course with Washington. Things had not always been so volatile. From mid-1977 to mid-1979, Libya and the United States had made cautious, halting moves toward improving their relations, which had become seriously strained in the Nixon-Ford years—a consequence of Washington's central role in the Egyptian-Israeli peace process, which Qaddafi vociferously opposed, and of Libya's growing complicity in terrorist and subversive activities in the Middle East and beyond. While these differences remained sharp into the early Carter years, neither country had an interest in a complete rupture. Ten percent of U.S. oil imports came in the form of Libyan crude; those shipments amounted to 40 percent of Libya's total oil production. Moreover, the Libyans still hoped to gain possession of eight C-130 military transport planes they had purchased years earlier from the Lockheed Corporation. Since 1973, the U.S. government had refused to license the planes' export, citing Libya's disruptive international behavior. Washington was also holding up the delivery of some commercial airliners that Libya had ordered from Boeing, lest they be converted to military use.[36] Tripoli clearly wanted the planes, but what political price, if any, would it pay to get them?

In June 1977, Qaddafi publicly proposed that Libya and the United States return ambassadors to each other's capitals; since 1973 their embassies had been headed by lower-ranking officials. The State Department responded that Libya would first have to stop supporting international terrorism and reduce its opposition to Arab-Israeli peace efforts. The Libyans initially seemed to regard these conditions as nonstarters, but they kept trying to improve relations. In September, the Libyan government agreed to compensate Texaco and Standard Oil for losses incurred when their Libyan subsidiaries were nationalized in 1973–1974. In the fall of 1978, Libya adhered to the Hague Hijacking Convention and provided written assurances that the American civilian planes would not be used for military purposes.[37] By this time, U.S. intelligence reports revealed no direct Libyan involvement in terrorist acts for over a year. In November, the Carter administration licensed the shipment of two Boeing 727 aircraft. Early in 1979, it allowed the shipment of three 747s.[38] Though pleased with these decisions, the Libyans still hankered for the C-130s.

Meanwhile, Libya pursued a separate, more public diplomatic initiative. Known as the "People to People" program, it entailed forging relationships with influential segments of American society—in universities, businesses, labor unions, civil rights groups, religious organizations, state governments, and elsewhere—in the hope of altering, over time, the U.S. government's policies toward Libya. The most extensive undertaking in this vein was the "Arab-American Dialogue," a conference in Tripoli in October 1978 at which about a hundred Americans and an equal number of Arabs (mostly Libyans) gathered to exchange views on international issues. The American attendees, whose expenses were paid in full, included several prominent and generally Arab-friendly figures, such as former senator J. William Fulbright, Pan American Airlines chairman (and father-in-law of Jordan's King Hussein) Najeeb Halaby, and Georgetown professor and current NAAA president Hisham Shirabi. A former NAAA president, Richard Shadyac, organized the American delegation.[39] He would soon figure more conspicuously in the U.S.-Libyan encounter.

Months earlier, the Libyans had made contact with another prominent American, who seemed to offer a surer entrée into the Carter administration's deliberations. In 1978, Billy Carter was widely seen as a fun-loving "good old boy" with modest accomplishments, an earthy vocabulary, and a disarming ability to laugh at himself—an appealing complement to his earnest, moralistic, and high-achieving older brother. Billy, in fact, was a deeply troubled man, mired in debt and sinking toward the nadir of a lifelong struggle with alcoholism.[40] Perhaps Libyan officials were unaware of these circumstances and gravitated toward Billy simply because of his family connection. Perhaps they knowingly tried to exploit his personal vulnerabilities. In any event, they would accomplish little for their efforts beyond enabling Billy to inflict serious damage on himself and his brother.

In the spring of 1978, an Italian American businessman with dealings in Libya, working in league with Libya's ambassador to Italy, persuaded Billy and several of his Georgia cronies that good money could be made in oil-rich Libya. In September 1978, Billy flew to Libya at its government's expense, receiving VIP treatment. In January, a Libyan delegation, led by Ahmed Shahati, head of Libya's Foreign Liaison Office, arrived in Atlanta to be feted by Billy and his associates. The delegation proceeded to other American destinations, with Billy accompanying it for a time. Over the course of these contacts, the Libyans complained to Billy about the blocked C-130s, and Billy asked U.S. officials about their status. There is no evidence, however, that he advocated for the planes' release.[41]

Figure 25. Billy Carter receives a memento from the mayor of Tripoli, Libya, September 1978. © AP Photo/San Diego Union.

Meanwhile, Billy mulled over his business options, eventually deciding that he wanted to import Libyan oil. Shahati promised to seek an oil allocation from his government. The allocation did not materialize, though Billy later received $220,000 in loans from Libya. P. Edward Haley plausibly speculates that the Libyans never intended to set Billy up as an oil importer but instead calculated that, if he received the loans and nothing else, he would be more susceptible to their influence. Without the ability to establish his lucrative import business, he would be hard-pressed to repay his Libyan creditors, and beholden to them for any debt forgiveness. In exchange for this financial support, the Libyans no doubt hoped Billy would lobby for the release of the C-130s. They also may have imagined, naïvely enough, that he would bring a pro-Libyan perspective into Jimmy Carter's inner circle. Whatever the motivation, several U.S. officials, including the president, surmised early on that Tripoli's interest in Billy was more political than commercial. They tried to dissuade him from his Libyan venture, but the warnings were half-hearted and Billy brushed them aside.[42]

On the diplomatic front, U.S.-Libyan relations were deteriorating. In February 1979, Libyan troops intervened in Uganda in a failed attempt to prevent its president, the murderous Idi Amin, from being overthrown by Tanzanian and dissident Ugandan forces. Libya used its existing fleet of C-130s, as well as some 727s, to ferry military supplies into Uganda. While there was no evidence that these were the same 727s released in November, the Carter administration felt compelled to reverse its more recent decision regarding the 747s, which were still under manufacture. The renewed ban was implemented in May.[43]

Over the next few months, U.S.-Libyan relations grew increasingly contentious. U.S. officials expected some sort of retaliation for the 747 reversal, but they could not predict what form the riposte might take. Both publicly and privately, Qaddafi and other Libyan officials hinted at an oil embargo against the United States. In August, Qaddafi wrote to Carter on the Palestine issue, closing with the ominous observation that "once we have lost everything and have nothing else to lose, then we can only make others lose as well." The Libyans had their own fears. They charged that Egypt, which had recently gathered troops along its western border, was preparing to attack Libya with U.S. encouragement. The State Department privately informed the Libyan government that an Egyptian attack on Libya would "not be in the interests of the United States." The statement accurately reflected U.S. policy, yet its very blandness seemed calculated to stir unease. In October, Secretary Vance had a cordial but unproductive meeting in New York with Libyan foreign minister Ali al-Turayki. Vance noted that Libya's mischief making hindered an improvement in relations. Turayki wondered why the Americans were being difficult about the 747s. "In other words," wrote a British diplomat after receiving a report of the meeting, "the dialogue of the deaf had continued, but with a smile."[44]

By now, genteel encounters of the Vance-Turayki sort, whatever their substance, were rapidly falling out of fashion in Tripoli. In his September 1 anniversary speech, Qaddafi had called for an overhaul of Libya's diplomatic institutions. The existing diplomatic establishment, he said, employed too many holdovers from the monarchical era and was riven with "nepotism and extravagance." Ordinary Libyans abroad should therefore march on Libya's embassies, replace the existing diplomats, and transform the facilities into "Libyan people's bureaus." The next day, small groups of Libyans, many of them students, peacefully occupied Libya's embassies in Washington, London, Paris, Madrid, Athens, and other capitals. The new "people's bureaus" answered not to Turayki's Foreign Ministry but to Shahati's Foreign Liaison Office, which was quickly emerging as Qaddafi's favored instrument of diplomacy. By year's end, the Foreign Liaison Office would enjoy sole jurisdiction over relations with countries hosting people's bureaus. As Qaddafi explained it, the Libyan revolution was approaching the ideal state in which government structures were abolished and the people ruled directly; the changes in the diplomatic apparatus reflected this happy circumstance.[45] A more plausible surmise is that Qaddafi sought to maximize his personal control over Libya's foreign relations by empowering zealous loyalists who would be less encumbered by traditional diplomatic restraints. Not only would such figures be more responsive to Qaddafi's whims; they could be disavowed as misguided enthusiasts when they acted too brazenly.

The implications for U.S.-Libyan relations of Qaddafi's turn to "people's diplomacy" would become glaringly evident the following spring. A hint of them was detectable in the closing weeks of 1979, against the backdrop of a consuming crisis occurring two thousand miles to Libya's east. On November 4, militant Iranian students broke through the gates of the U.S. embassy in Tehran, overpowered marine guards, and took scores of embassy employees captive. The students claimed that the embassy was part of a conspiracy to restore the old regime. By physically seizing the premises, they would stop the plan in its tracks. It was at first widely assumed, including by the students themselves, that Iranian authorities would intervene to free the Americans, as had happened during a similar standoff several months earlier. Instead, Ayatollah Khomeini publicly blessed the students' action, making an early release politically impossible inside Iran (and causing the ouster of moderates from Iran's government).[46] The detainees became hostages, and their release President Carter's top foreign-policy objective for the rest of his term.

Though unfolding in a non-Arab country, the Iranian hostage crisis would affect the content and tenor of U.S. diplomacy across the Arab world. Its chief impact on U.S.-Libyan relations was to cause Carter administration officials to regard Libya as a potential source of assistance in this distressing situation. Libya had loudly championed the Iranian Revolution and continued to do so in the immediate aftermath of the embassy takeover, without specifically endorsing that action. Perhaps Qaddafi had sufficient credibility with the Iranians to make an effective appeal for the hostages' release. Administration officials also looked anew at Billy Carter's Libyan ties; maybe some good *could* come of them. In late November, Brzezinski requested that Billy contact his Libyan friends. Billy arranged for Ali Houderi, head of Libya's new People's Bureau in Washington, to come to the White House to meet with Brzezinski, who asked if Libya could intercede with Iran. Days later Qaddafi passed word to the administration that he had sent a delegation to Khomeini, presumably to appeal for the hostages' release. Nothing more was heard of the effort.[47]

In fact, there had been no reason to expect that Tripoli could sway Tehran on the hostage issue, for the simple reason that the Iranians, and Khomeini especially, were furious at Qaddafi. In August 1978, a prominent Iranian-Lebanese Shia cleric named Musa al-Sadr had disappeared while visiting Libya. The Libyan government could not explain this development, and many suspected foul play on Qaddafi's part. Al-Sadr was a revered figure among Iranian Shia and was related to Khomeini by marriage. Since coming to power in early 1979, the new Iranian government had demanded from Libya an accounting of al-Sadr's fate; none was forthcoming. If Qaddafi did have something to do with the cleric's demise, he was now surely kicking himself for having selected a victim who would posthumously acquire such powerful advocates. At any rate, and despite his protestations of pan-Islamic solidarity, Qaddafi was in no position to lobby the Iranians on behalf of the American hostages.[48]

For Billy Carter, the seizure of the U.S. embassy in Tehran had presented an opportunity for him to demonstrate his usefulness to Libya. After all, he had just gotten a Libyan diplomat admitted to the White House, the first time this happened during Jimmy's presidency. On the heels of the Brzezinski-Houderi meeting, Billy scrambled to obtain the elusive Libyan oil allocation and line up agreements with third parties who had been promised a share of the bonanza.[49] But the allocation never materialized, and his heady schemes came to naught. All that resulted was a damning paper trail that would, in the following year, make life miserable for Billy and his brother.

Meanwhile, the U.S. and Libyan governments had been plunged into a fresh crisis. On December 2, about two thousand Libyan demonstrators, many chanting pro-Iranian slogans, converged on the U.S. embassy in Tripoli. Some of the protesters broke into the building and set fire to it, damaging the lower floor and forcing the staff to flee. Libyan security forces did not intervene. Given the nature of Libyan civic life at this time, it is virtually certain that the demonstrators acted with official blessing, though their violence may have exceeded the government's expectations. Qaddafi insisted that the entire event was spontaneous. "We were surprised by the attack," he told a *New York Times* reporter. "We couldn't save the embassy from this tide of anger by the masses here. The masses impose their will." The Carter administration demanded that Libya apologize for the security breach, pay compensation for the damage, and pledge fuller protection of American residents in the future. After several days of prickly resistance, Tripoli more or less accepted Washington's terms.[50] Prudence prevailed on this occasion. Months later, "the masses" would play a more sustained and alarming role in Libyan policy.

If the Libyans were unable to influence Iranian behavior, then another set of Arab actors proved more effective—though these intermediaries had to be, themselves, approached through intermediaries. The notion that the PLO might intercede on the hostages' behalf sprang immediately to many minds. Arafat had excellent relations with the Islamic republic and clearly longed for a dialogue with the United States. He had both opportunity and motive to do Washington this big favor. As we saw, on November 8 Walter Fauntroy wrote to Carter encouraging him to seek the PLO's help. Two days earlier, Congressman Findley had phoned PLO headquarters in Beirut and urged that the PLO send a mission to Tehran. That evening, former attorney general Ramsey Clark called Beirut with the same message. The Carter administration had just asked Clark to accompany William Miller, an ex–Foreign Service officer, on a trip to Iran to seek the hostages' freedom. It is unclear if Clark's request for PLO assistance came at his own initiative or was officially inspired.[51] On November 7, Findley announced that the PLO had adopted his suggestion and was sending a delegation to Iran. Other testimony places the idea for an Iran mission within Arafat's inner circle. Walid Khalidi, who was then in Beirut, remembers approaching Arafat upon learning of the hostage situation and saying, "We're not going to get somebody as well disposed towards us as Carter for a long, long time. Therefore, we must do everything to help him." Arafat, Khalidi recalls, "understood immediately."[52] One suspects that Arafat was already thinking along such lines and needed no prodding from Khalidi, Clark, or Findley.

Both publicly and privately, the Carter administration encouraged the PLO's mission, which flew to Iran on November 8. That same day, Clark and Miller arrived in Istanbul, en route to Tehran. Before the American envoys could continue their journey, the Iranian government announced it would refuse to receive them, so the two remained in Istanbul and tried to negotiate with Iran via unnamed PLO officials there. The effort failed, and in mid-November Clark and Miller returned home. The PLO delegation, a three-man team led by chief of military operations Abu Walid (aka Saad Sayel), had difficulties of its own. Khomeini insisted that Iran would not negotiate with the United States, via the PLO or in any other way, and the militant students holding the hostages echoed this position. Backpedaling, the PLO announced that its delegation was in Iran not to mediate over the hostages but simply to demonstrate solidarity with the Islamic republic.

Yet the delegation stayed on in Tehran and quietly urged Iranian leaders to make a conciliatory gesture, advice Arafat underscored in phone calls from Beirut. At the UN on November 14, Secretary Vance told a British diplomat that "the PLO had the 'inside track' at present and it was important that any other initiatives should not cut across what they were doing."[53]

Vance's confidence was modestly vindicated. Three days later, Khomeini authorized the release of the thirteen black and female hostages. The PLO, the *Washington Post* reported, had proposed freeing the African Americans "in recognition of its own rapprochement with American blacks" following the Andy Young affair. Khomeini publicly justified their release by noting that "blacks for a long time have lived under oppression and pressure in America." As for the female hostages, "Islam reserves special rights for women." Whatever Khomeini's true motives, U.S. officials were obliged—if only behind closed doors—to acknowledge the PLO's hand in producing the encouraging result. In an oral message to Arafat, which had to pass through two other mouths before reaching the chairman's ears, Vance said he "appreciate[d] the role the PLO played to bring about the release of the thirteen hostages."[54] Brzezinski privately noted that the PLO "had been decisive" on the matter.[55] Administration officials did not make such statements in public.

The release of the thirteen hostages raised hopes that the remaining fifty-two Americans might soon be freed as well. For the next few weeks, the PLO pursued this prospect, conducting separate dialogues with Tehran and Washington and occasionally conveying messages from one capital to the other. The PLO could talk to the Iranians directly. To communicate with the Americans, it dispatched Khalidi to hold a series of clandestine meetings with U.S. ambassador to Lebanon John Gunther Dean in various Beirut apartments. "We met like . . . secret lovers," Khalidi recalls. With Khalidi's input, the State Department floated a scenario for resolving the crisis: once all the hostages were released, the Iranians would be afforded a suitable venue, such as the UN Security Council or the International Court of Justice, where they could air their long-held grievances against the shah and his American backers. The Iranians, however, insisted they would release no additional hostages until the shah, who was receiving medical treatment in the United States, returned to Iran to face trial there. To the Americans this was out of the question.[56]

By December, the PLO was pulling back from the hostage issue. The gap between Washington and Tehran was unbridgeable for the moment, and the Americans clearly had no intention of relaxing their conditions for an open dialogue with the PLO. All Arafat had accomplished for his pains was to alienate his Iranian friends and exacerbate divisions within the PLO, whose militant factions, and even some al-Fatah elements, were dismayed to see yet another unrequited concession to the United States.[57] When it came to the hostages, Washington must seek help from some other quarter.

Khalidi, by now, had a new concern. On December 6, he told Ambassador Dean of reports that a young cleric in Khomeini's circle planned to send thousands of "volunteers" to South Lebanon to help the Palestinians fight Israel. Such a move, Khalidi said, would give the Israelis "a pretext to sweep all the way up to the Litani," a river lying some twenty miles north of the Israeli-Lebanese border. He urged that the U.S. government discuss the matter with Saudi Arabia's Crown Prince Fahd, "who should use his influence with Arafat to oppose such an Iranian venture."[58] It was a strange and portentous request: strange because Khalidi was seeking to activate a cumbersome diplomatic relay—from Beirut to Washington to Riyadh back to Beirut—to influence the behavior of a man he regularly met face-to-face; portentous because Khalidi was calling attention to a phenomenon—Iranian-backed militancy in Lebanon—that would profoundly shape Middle Eastern politics for decades to come.

The Iranians were not the only religious enthusiasts taking an interest in South Lebanon. In September 1979, a radio station called The Voice of Hope, the brainchild of George Otis, a California evangelist, had begun broadcasting from the area controlled by major Sa'ad Haddad's South Lebanon Army, which itself operated under Israeli auspices. In addition to its mix of gospel music, country-and-western tunes, and inspirational Christian messages, The Voice of Hope aired reports from Israel's official news service. It would also, in the coming months, grant regular opportunities for Major Haddad to come on the air to rally his forces or threaten violence against Lebanese villages that harbored Palestinian fighters. Otis disclaimed responsibility for this more menacing content, portraying it essentially as rent owed to the generous commander who, with Israel's blessing, had allowed The Voice of Hope to operate in the area. "If Major Haddad wants to make an announcement over the air or comfort his people, he's earned it," Otis said. "I don't understand Arabic so we don't know what he's said and it's none of our business." In fact, the American evangelist was zealously committed to Christian Zionism—the belief, increasingly prevalent among American Protestants, that Israel's modern creation and recent conquests were the unfolding of God's plan. The Voice of Hope would later join the broadcasting empire of the televangelist Pat Robertson.[59] Here, too, a new era was dawning.

The attacks on the U.S. embassies in Tehran and Tripoli were among several traumatic and globally prominent events roiling the Muslim world in the closing weeks of 1979. On November 20, during the annual pilgrimage to Mecca, a group of extreme Wahhabi purists seized control of Mecca's Grand Mosque, taking hundreds of pilgrims hostage. The insurgents sought an apocalyptic showdown with the Saudi government, which they believed had betrayed the tenets of Islam, in part by allying with the United States. Over the next two weeks, Saudi security forces launched a series of unsuccessful assaults on the insurgents before finally retaking the mosque, leaving hundreds of casualties among security forces, insurgents, and hostages alike. The surviving ringleaders were executed. On November 21, Pakistani demonstrators, incited by false reports that the United States was behind the seizure of the Grand Mosque, overran and set fire to the U.S. embassy in Islamabad. Two American servicemen, two Pakistani embassy staff members, and two protesters were killed. In late December, eighty thousand Soviet troops invaded Afghanistan to prop up its Marxist regime against a formidable Islamist rebellion. The Mujahidin, as the rebels were known, took up arms against the Soviet occupiers.[60]

To Western observers at the time, the common element in these events was a new, general tendency toward Islamist insurgency, directed in most instances against the United States and its local allies and, in the final case, against the Soviet Union and *its* proxy. Years later, it became clear that a more particular strain of Islamist militancy—the Sunni fundamentalism later championed by the al-Qa'ida network—had gained self-awareness, confidence, vision, and impetus from the upheavals in Saudi Arabia, Pakistan, and Afghanistan. This was a vast transnational story, extending well into subsequent decades and well beyond the Arab world. But it did have, in President Carter's final year, a crucial Arab dimension, involving mainly Saudi Arabia and Egypt. In its relations with both countries, the Carter administration unwittingly helped to incubate virulent forces that would, a generation later, menace the United States and its allies.

Carter was alarmed by Moscow's move into Afghanistan, fearing the start of a Soviet campaign to dominate the oil fields and sea-lanes of the Persian Gulf. Much of his administration's reaction, therefore, centered on bolstering the Western position in the Gulf region, a subject discussed below. Washington also set out to challenge the Soviets in Afghanistan itself, mainly by working with regional allies to provide arms, training, and logistical support to the Mujahidin. The most important of these allies was Afghanistan's neighbor Pakistan. But a close second was Saudi Arabia, which leapt at the opportunity to play a conspicuous role in the new campaign. Saudi leaders were shaken in the aftermath of the Grand Mosque rebellion, which had posed a frontal challenge to the government's religious legitimacy, both domestically and in the Muslim world. By supporting the Afghan jihad, Riyadh could reassert its claim to Islamic leadership at home and abroad. And so, in the months following the Soviet invasion, the Saudi government opened its vast coffers to the Mujahidin, encouraging private fund-raising for the same cause by Saudi Islamic institutions. The Saudi intelligence agency coordinated with its American and Pakistani counterparts (and occasionally competed with them) to cultivate promising Afghan commanders. Wahhabi clerics blessed the whole enterprise, while sometimes promoting their own Afghan favorites. Also flocking to the cause were hundreds of Saudi individuals: intelligence agents, paramilitary recruits, religious volunteers, and private contractors. One of the contractors, the scion of a wealthy and influential Saudi family, was a soft-spoken youth named Osama bin Laden.[61]

Sadat, too, saw the Afghan war as an opportunity to burnish his Islamic credentials. However harshly the world's Muslims might assail him—for the condemnation of Camp David was pan-Islamic as well as pan-Arab—*he* would never abandon *them*. In the early weeks of 1980, Sadat publicly embraced the Mujahidin, announcing that Egypt was providing them arms and training. Behind the scenes, he conferred with Brzezinski and arranged for the transfer to the Mujahidin of weapons and ammunition that Egypt had previously acquired from the Soviet Union (and that the United States was replenishing with more up-to-date munitions). Sadat also opened Egyptian airbases to the U.S military, enabling it to project air power into the Persian Gulf region. As from Saudi Arabia, a stream of Egyptian volunteers began flowing into Pakistan for subsequent deployment in Afghanistan. None of these developments, however, appeased the Muslim Brotherhood or other ultraconservative Egyptian Islamists. Taking Sadat's pro-Mujahidin policies for granted, they continued to vilify his peacemaking with Israel and pro-U.S. stances. Egyptian soldiers harboring such views would assassinate the president in October 1981.[62]

Back in the United States, Arab American activists persisted in their efforts to challenge pro-Israel narratives, a project aided, in some measure, by Israeli prime minister Menachem Begin's provocative policies.[63] Increasingly, however, crises emanating from other parts of the Middle East intruded on the activists' work. The Iranian hostage issue stirred a groundswell of hostility among Americans, sometimes taking the form of indiscriminate rage against all things perceived to be Middle Eastern or Islamic. Iranians in America were harassed and assaulted, fates sometimes visited on others with dark complexions, such as South Asians, Latin Americans, and people of Arab descent. (With their beards, turbans, and long tunics, Coptic clergymen and Sikhs were especially vulnerable.)[64] "The taking of the hostages in Iran, and the resulting confusion between Arab and Iranian," lamented the NAAA *Voice*, "have severely affected public efforts to mobilize support for our concerns." Still, the NAAA and other Arab American groups did what they could to combat defamatory portrayals of Islam, to distinguish Iranians from Arabs and Arabs from Muslims, and to decry Americans' failure to condemn Israel's misdeeds as readily as Iran's.[65]

Libyan affairs, too, were becoming a source of uncomfortable publicity for Arab Americans. In July 1980, Carter's reelection campaign announced it was severing its ties to Richard Shadyac, whom it had recently appointed to head an Arab American committee to work on the president's behalf. The problem was Shadyac's relationship with Libya, which had not ended with the "Arab-American Dialogue" in Tripoli in 1978. A second dialogue was scheduled for Washington that fall (it would later be cancelled), and Shadyac was again organizing the American participants, a service for which the Libyans paid him $4,000 a month. Shadyac also provided legal representation to Libya's People's Bureau in Washington. On account of these activities, he had been obliged to register with the U.S. Justice Department as a foreign agent. This was hardly an optimal profile for the representative of an American presidential campaign, especially as the term "foreign agent" left the erroneous impression that Carter's reelection effort had been infiltrated by Libyan spies. Amid howls from pro-Israel groups, embarrassed campaign officials said they had known nothing about Shadyac's Libyan ties and had terminated his involvement as soon as they learned of them.[66] The NAAA's protest that the reelection campaign had "cast aspersions on Arab-American political activism" carried little weight in an administration eager to shore up its eroding pro-Israel support.[67]

The Shadyac affair was all the more conspicuous because it occurred just as Billy Carter's own dealings with Libya became a major national story. Although some of these activities had previously come to light, July 1980 was the month for the most dramatic revelations: that Billy had received $220,000 from Libya, that the Carter administration had sought his help in reaching out to Tripoli on behalf of the American hostages, and that Billy, too, had had to register as a foreign agent. That same month, a special subcommittee of the Senate Judiciary Committee opened hearings on the matter, assuring a steady stream of additional revelations and lurid detail. The subcommittee found no serious legal violations, though it harshly criticized Billy's opportunism and fecklessness (qualities that largely canceled each other out) and chided the president's passivity in the face of his brother's poor judgment. The publicity was acutely embarrassing to both Carters, and it deepened the public impression of presidential ineptitude.[68]

Both "Billygate" and the Shadyac flap occurred against the backdrop of rapidly deteriorating relations between the United States and Libya. If the long-term cause of this downturn was a shared failure to resolve festering disagreements over Palestine, terrorism, subversion, and aircraft purchases, then the proximate cause was Libya's increasingly blatant rejection of diplomatic norms. The conversion of Libya's embassies to people's bureaus grew out of a domestic campaign to "democratize" Libya by placing more and more sectors of its economy and government under the jurisdiction of "people's committees." As in the diplomatic realm, Qaddafi apparently hoped to eliminate institutional impediments to his rule and cultivate cadres who would answer more directly to him. Within Libya, these changes were economically and politically disruptive, arousing opposition among members of the merchant and educated classes. In the spring of 1980, the government cracked down on the dissenters, arresting thousands, trying hundreds for corruption, and conducting several extrajudicial killings.[69]

The regime also turned its attention to the Libyan diaspora. On April 27, Qaddafi demanded that all Libyan dissenters living abroad return home immediately. Those defying the order "will be liquidated wherever they are." Already, Libyan assassins and goons were killing, maiming, and harassing Libyan exiles in Europe. Libyan officials made no effort to conceal their hand and sometimes openly gloated that the regime's critics had received their comeuppance. But Qaddafi himself occasionally posed as a dismayed bystander, a remarkable stance considering his own menacing words on the topic. The reason he had called Libyan dissenters home, he told ABC television in mid-May, was to *protect* them from the long arm of the people's committees.[70]

As of the spring of 1980, no Libyan exiles had been killed in the United States, but the State Department had received numerous reports that Libyan operatives—some with clear ties to the People's Bureau in Washington—were harassing and intimidating Libyan dissenters in the United States, especially students. In early May, the State Department sought to expel four People's Bureau officials it believed had been involved in such activities. The officials refused to leave, insisting they were students, not diplomats.[71] They then barricaded themselves inside the People's Bureau. The standoff presented an unusual legal conundrum. If, as they claimed, the officials were not diplomats, then the U.S. government could not deport them without judicial process. If they *were* diplomats, then the People's Bureau was an inviolable sanctuary. In the first instance, they could be apprehended but not expelled; in the second, expelled but not apprehended. Still, U.S. authorities had logistics on their side. With the building surrounded by a police and FBI cordon, they informed the chief of mission, Ali Houderi, along with Dick Shadyac (whose legal gig was surely growing more interesting by the day), that the Libyan officials would receive no food, water, or electricity as long as they remained holed up. A week later, the officials relented and agreed to return home.[72]

Arab American organizations mostly ignored Tripoli's provocative behavior, which was at best a distraction from the issues they favored and at worst an outrageous spectacle involving a regime they had treated with deference. The fact that Shadyac was a former NAAA president must have been awkward for that organization. The same could be said of the glowing coverage that the NAAA *Voice* had bestowed on Qaddafi's leadership in 1976 and 1977.[73] Within the AAUG, Libya's strong support for the Palestinian struggle had won some admiration. Still, an international campaign to liquidate political dissenters was a bit much. In an April 30 telegram to Qaddafi, the AAUG cited press reports that "allege the assassination of several Libyans in Europe. . . . We respectfully request that you respond to these allegations since we wish to respond to any unfounded attacks on the Libyan revolution." The reply came from Houderi, who, far from denying the charge, wrote that punishment of "treasonous anti-revolutionary Libyan elements" was essential "to safeguard our revolution and its great achievements." The AAUG excerpted the chilling exchange, without comment, in its July–August newsletter. Apart from a cryptic reference in the next newsletter, the AAUG appears to have said nothing further on the matter.[74] Presumably, the group's leadership hoped to avoid antagonizing or embarrassing pro-Tripoli members. Within both the AAUG and the NAAA, moreover, there was a reluctance to criticize, and indeed some impulse to defend, an Arab regime on the receiving end of such harsh and widespread American censure.[75]

In June, perhaps concluding that he had pushed his luck far enough—or that the troublesome exiles were sufficiently pruned back—Qaddafi called a halt to the overseas assassination program, and thereafter the violence abated. But it didn't end entirely: on October 14, Faisal Zagallai, a Libyan graduate student in Fort Collins, Colorado, was shot and seriously wounded by an unidentified white man. Months earlier, Zagallai's name had appeared on a list of regime critics Tripoli had slated for assassination. In April 1981, authorities would arrest Eugene Tafoya, a former Green Beret, and charge him with attempted murder. Documents and other items in Tafoya's possession linked the suspect to Libya, as well as to a secret arms-dealing network run by a renegade U.S. intelligence officer named Edwin P. Wilson—a subject for a book of its own.[76]

In the final weeks of Carter's presidency, U.S. officials still lacked firm evidence of Libyan involvement in the Zagallai attack, yet relations between the two countries continued their rapid slide. Two new issues greased the descent. In December 1980, thousands of Libyan troops intervened in neighboring Chad to confront a Chadian faction supported by America's ally France, which later sent its own forces into the country. Meanwhile, the U.S. and Libyan air forces waged what the *New York Times* called "a war of nerves" above the southern Mediterranean, as the United States asserted its right to fly over international waters Libya claimed as its own. Libyan fighters shadowed the U.S. planes and, on one occasion in September 1980, unsuccessfully tried to shoot one of them down.[77] Repeatedly in the coming decade, off the Libyan coast and elsewhere, Americans and Libyans would clash with more lethal effect.

That same September brought another, vastly more consequential military event. On the 22nd, following a series of escalating border clashes, Iraq launched extensive air attacks against Iran and followed them the next day with a full-scale land invasion. Iraq sought to punish Iran for its political incitement of Iraqi Shia and to force a revision of the 1975 Shatt al-Arab agreement (see chapter 5), under whose terms Baghdad chafed. Saddam Hussein, who had become Iraq's president in July 1979, evidently gambled that Iran was so weakened by revolutionary upheaval that it would collapse under the Iraqi onslaught and quickly accede to its neighbor's demands. But the Iraqi operations were poorly executed, and Iran retaliated with costly air attacks on Iraqi cities, military installations, and oil facilities. Far from surrendering, Tehran declared it would keep fighting until Hussein's government was overthrown. It was the start of a vicious, grinding conflict that would last eight years and cost over a million lives on both sides.[78]

The outbreak of the Iran-Iraq War was the fourth in a series of traumatic events in 1979–1980 that, by altering either the geopolitics of the Persian Gulf region or American perceptions of those geopolitics, made the U.S. posture toward the Gulf increasingly anxious and militarized. The first jolt, the collapse of the shah's regime in early 1979, had prompted a significant expansion of U.S. military capabilities in the area. The Carter administration began planning for a "rapid deployment force" that could be sent into theaters where the United States lacked forward bases. Meanwhile, to enhance its ability to project power into the Gulf, and unable to establish a base in Saudi Arabia, the administration concluded limited basing rights agreements with Oman, Somalia, and Kenya. The second shock, Iran's seizure of the U.S. embassy in November, got Americans thinking about specific military actions, such as a mission to rescue the hostages or a punitive attack on Iran if the hostages were killed or harmed. (A rescue attempt would fail disastrously in April 1980.) December 1979 brought the third shock, the Soviet invasion of Afghanistan, which hardened the administration's diplomatic and military stances across the globe and aroused particular concern about the Gulf. "An attempt by any outside force to gain control of the Persian Gulf," Carter proclaimed in January, ". . . will be repelled by any means necessary, including military force." The Carter Doctrine, as this statement was called, lent greater purpose and urgency to the military buildup the president had launched several months earlier.[79]

Iraq's attack on Iran the following September was yet another dramatic disruption.[80] If the invasion of Afghanistan was significant primarily for the manner in which it altered the U.S. international outlook, as well as for its subsequent, indirect role in nurturing extremist forces that would gain prominence years later, then the Iran-Iraq War transformed regional and inter-Arab politics in more immediate and direct ways. These transformations created new challenges and opportunities for U.S. diplomacy that were sketchily visible to Carter and his advisers during their final months in office, though in most cases it remained for their successors to act on them.

The war split the Arab world. King Hussein of Jordan immediately and wholeheartedly endorsed the Iraqi war effort. After some hesitation, and less enthusiastically, Saudi Arabia, Kuwait, and most of the other Gulf Arab sheikhdoms also supported Iraq. Syria and Libya sided with Iran. Egypt, still shunned by the other Arab states on account of Camp David, remained officially neutral for the time being. Secretly, however, Sadat passed intelligence information and Soviet-supplied weapons to Iraq (apparently hoping this would ease his inter-Arab isolation), while also urging that the United States clandestinely arm Tehran "to prevent Iran from turning in desperation to the Soviets"—a broad foreshadowing of Washington's own convoluted approach to Gulf politics in the ensuing decade.[81]

The Carter administration immediately proclaimed its neutrality in the Iran-Iraq War and its desire for a peaceful resolution. The administration saw little advantage, however, in making heroic diplomatic efforts to end the hostilities. The parties' positions were so far apart that any serious peace initiative would likely enrage one side or the other, with untold consequences. Moreover, U.S. officials speculated, a continuation of the conflict might create an incentive for Iran to bargain more seriously on the hostage front. The longer it fought, the more spare parts the Iranian military would need for the American weapons it had acquired during the days of the shah; perhaps Washington's furnishing of those items could be part of a package deal that included the hostages' release. The discovery that Iran was already acquiring spare parts from Israel and private European arms dealers, however, diminished this hope.[82]

In late September, the Saudi government, fearing Iranian attacks on the Kingdom's oil fields, urgently requested that the United States station Airborne Warning and Control Systems (AWACS) planes and air defense equipment on Saudi territory. Secretary of state Edmund Muskie, who had replaced Cyrus Vance in May, argued that granting the Saudi request would violate America's declared neutrality and be unduly provocative to the Soviet Union. Brzezinski and secretary of defense Harold Brown countered that defending Saudi oil fields was a vital Western interest that the Soviets surely recognized. Moreover, Brzezinski noted, the Saudis' eagerness for U.S. help presented "a unique opportunity to consolidate our security position in a manner which even a few weeks ago would have been not possible. . . . We would miss a major strategic opportunity if we fail to exploit this." Carter agreed and sent the equipment. The move *was* provocative, but not to the adversary Muskie imagined. Voicing a critique that Osama bin Laden would issue far more audibly years later, Qaddafi castigated the Saudi government for permitting the stationing of U.S.-piloted AWACS planes on Saudi soil. The holy places of Islam, he charged, had fallen "under U.S. occupation."[83]

Meanwhile, U.S. officials wondered what impact the war might have on the stalled Arab-Israeli peace process. There was some possibility, noted a

State Department memorandum in mid-October, that dismay over the Gulf carnage would "strengthen the resolve of Arab moderates"—presumably Jordan, Saudi Arabia, and the mainstream of the PLO—"to explore practical ways of resolving their dispute with Israel." Of course, the war could have the opposite effect of hardening attitudes among some or all parties to the Arab-Israeli dispute. In that event, the memo continued, the ongoing hostilities in the Gulf might make the resulting stalemate more manageable: "If we have to hunker down with Egypt and Israel and face a hostile Middle East, a sustained, smoldering conflict in the east that keeps Iraq bogged down and the Arabs bickering among themselves may at least provide the easiest circumstance in which to face this prospect."[84] Here was a remarkably prescient forecast of Middle Eastern geopolitics in the ensuing decade.

The Carter administration also worried about dislocations in global oil markets—for good reason, as the fighting in the Gulf quickly removed almost four million barrels per day in combined Iranian and Iraqi exports. But two factors mitigated the shortfall and prevented, for the moment, a sharp spike in oil prices. The first was a recent drop in global demand, resulting from conservation measures pursued by industrialized nations over the last few years and from a buildup in the inventories of oil companies determined to avoid repeating the shortages of early 1979. The second factor was Saudi Arabia's decision in mid-October to increase its production from 9.5 to 10.4 million barrels per day. Economists cautioned, however, that an extended shortfall would eventually drive prices upward.[85]

From Saudi Arabia, Ambassador West sounded a more pointed warning. "By producing above 10 MBD," he reported in late October, "the Saudis place a great strain on their equipment"; thus the high rate of production could not continue much longer. Even if that rate were physically sustainable, the Saudis' political incentive to keep up production would surely diminish. Once Saudi gratitude for the AWACS deployment faded, West predicted, frustration over Washington's failure to address the Palestine issue would reassert itself. "I would expect that the oil weapon would be used by the Saudis softly and even diplomatically. Such an approach would probably first involve a reversion to the 8.5 MBD ceiling and then the experiencing of 'technical difficulties' which gradually reduced the production to approximately 5 MBD." If the administration wished to avoid this fate, West advised, it would have to be far less tolerant of the Israelis' settlement activity, their inflexibility over the occupied territories, and their provocative use of American-supplied weapons in Lebanon.[86] West was correct to predict a significant reduction in Saudi output in the near future, but wrong to suppose that that decision would have anything to do with the Palestine issue.

Whatever the accuracy of West's forecasting, the Carter administration was in no position to act on his recommendation. On November 4, the American electorate would decide whether Carter should receive a second presidential term, and things were not looking good for the incumbent. The country was enduring what was then the worst economic downturn since the Great Depression, and there was widespread unhappiness over Carter's handling of the crisis. An unsuccessful though potent primary challenge by senator Edward Kennedy of Massachusetts had revealed significant dissatisfaction among liberals in Carter's own Democratic Party. And the Iranians continued to hold the hostages. By October, there were indications that Iran might release the hostages under certain conditions, such as a U.S. pledge of noninterference in Iranian affairs and the unfreezing of Iranian assets in American banks. (The shah's death in July had eliminated the possibility of his repatriation to face trial.) On account of internal divisions, however, Iran's parliament did not announce a formal negotiating position until November 2, leaving too little time to reach a deal before Americans went to the polls.[87]

The Arab-Israeli conflict was not a top issue in the 1980 election, but the frequent accusation that Carter lacked sympathy for Israel was a burden he could ill afford. Kennedy had made that charge during the Democratic primaries, and Carter's Republican challenger, Ronald Reagan, hammered away at it in the general election. Reagan offered the traditional moral arguments for unstinting U.S. support for Israel, while folding them into a broader vision of global anticommunism. "The U.S. must do everything it can to keep the Soviet Union out of the Middle East," he declared. "The fall of Iran increased Israel's value as perhaps the only remaining strategic asset in the region on which the United States can rely." Carter's attempts to extract diplomatic concessions from Israel, Reagan suggested, showed an alarming disregard for the security of a vulnerable ally. In his own defense, Carter stressed the elements of his Middle East record that tended to please Israel's supporters, such as the Egyptian-Israeli peace treaty, yet he could scarcely disown his recent efforts to include Palestinians in the peace process, moves Reagan disparaged as feckless and disloyal.[88]

Election Day brought disaster for the president and his party. Reagan handily defeated Carter, and the Republicans took back the Senate, which they had not held since the mid-1950s. Only the House remained in Democratic hands. A dejected but determined Carter threw himself into the task of securing the hostages' release while still in office. With the help of Algerian mediation, he achieved an agreement, though the hostages were not freed until minutes after Reagan's inauguration on January 20, 1981.[89]

What would a Reagan presidency mean for U.S. relations with the Arab world? During the final weeks of the campaign, and even more so in its aftermath, Middle East watchers scoured the public record for clues. The AAUG *Newsletter* called Reagan's Middle East advisers a "rollcall of extremists," figures with interventionist leanings and shadowy ties to the Israeli right.[90] Officials at the British Foreign Office, though themselves now serving the staunchly rightist government of prime minister Margaret Thatcher, expressed bemusement at "some of the wild ideas being bruited about" by Reagan's people, among them that the United States should embrace Israel as its primary strategic ally in the Middle East, that the Saudis would acquiesce in this arrangement as long as they were protected from the Soviet menace, and "that the answer to the Middle East is a new alliance between like-minded anti-communists such as Israel, Egypt, Jordan and Saudi Arabia." The very unrealism of these proposals furnished some comfort to their critics. As a British official remarked in mid-October, after hearing of a Reaganite scheme to place Israel at the center of anti-Soviet strategy in the region, "This view was so clearly nonsensical that it could not survive for long if Mr Reagan did come to power."[91]

Others believed that Reagan and his advisers would, of their own accord, take a more balanced approach to the area, in recognition of America's extensive economic and strategic interests in the Arab world. Immediately after the election, Andrew Young, busy with consulting and public speaking since leaving his UN post, privately predicted "that Reagan may be better able to deal with the M.E. problem than Carter (because of ties with big oil!)." In mid-December, John Richardson of the NAAA told a British diplomat that, while "committed Zionists" had influenced the president-elect, "Mr Reagan's closest associates were people of a nationalist turn of mind with close connections with big business who were not likely to be especially sympathetic to the pretensions of Israel." Even Qaddafi was placing his faith in sensible American conservatism. "We feel the Republicans have always been closer to the Arab cause than the Democrats," he said at a Tripoli press conference in late November. Prematurely promoting the man who would call him the "mad dog of the Middle East," Qaddafi "firmly welcome[d] the election of President Reagan."[92]

In light of the events of the last seven-odd years, and even accounting for the decline of Arab leverage over the previous two or three, it was not unreasonable to suppose that the Arab world's economic and strategic significance still sufficed to command some deference from Washington, the swagger of the incoming president notwithstanding. But the regional and international forces that had recently eroded the overall Arab position were about to acquire unstoppable momentum, with profound and wrenching consequences for the U.S.-Arab encounter in decades to come.

Epilogue

World opinion was still reeling from the atrocity when the Arab diplomats hastily convened. Days earlier, on September 16–17, 1982, right-wing Lebanese gunmen allied with Israel had rampaged through Sabra and Shatila, two Palestinian refugee camps on the outskirts of Beirut, slaughtering hundreds of civilians. The massacre occurred against the backdrop of Israel's massive invasion of Lebanon, conducted with U.S.-supplied arms and a measure of American acquiescence ill concealed by mild reproaches. Moscow had loudly denounced the invasion but seemed powerless to influence events in Lebanon; it could do little more than fume on the sidelines as Washington dominated diplomatic efforts to resolve the crisis. Now, following the butchery in the camps, a tide of revulsion swept over the globe, and Arab society was in an uproar. At Yasser Arafat's request, the Arab League called an emergency meeting of Arab foreign ministers in Tunis. Once there, the ministers condemned the massacre and charged that the United States bore "moral responsibility" for it. But they rejected the PLO's demand for an Arab oil embargo and for other economic sanctions against the United States.[1]

In the pages of the *Wall Street Journal*, an Egyptian American reporter named Youssef Ibrahim pondered "this seeming contradiction in words and deeds" on the part of Arab governments. The best explanation for it, he found, came in "background" conversations with U.S. government officials, American oil company executives, and "Arab oil industry decision makers." These figures all agreed that Arab states' reluctance to confront the United States, despite their outrage over events in Lebanon, was "a manifestation of the new relationship between major Arab oil producers and the U.S. that has been fashioned since the Arab oil embargo of 1973." In the intervening years, Arab investment in the U.S. economy had become so extensive that any effort to damage that economy was bound to harm the Arab countries as well. The industrialized nations, moreover, had built up significant oil reserves, leaving Arab petroleum exporters with far less international leverage than they had wielded a few years earlier. Finally, many Gulf Arab states had become "so dependent for their security upon the U.S. military and strategic forces that they can ill afford to alienate Western friends." "Let's face it," an unnamed U.S. official told Ibrahim. "They need us a lot more than we need them." The reporter's Arab sources did not disagree. "There is no point of talking about the 'oil weapon' or the 'money weapon,'" a senior government minister acknowledged, "until the Arab world gets its act together."[2]

The international events surrounding Israel's invasion of Lebanon, and Ibrahim's sobering discussion of their import, underscored the destabilizing transformations taking hold in the U.S.-Arab encounter as the 1980s unfolded—inaugurating a new era in the relationship that, in broad outlines, persists to this day. The most basic change was a collapse of strategic leverage enjoyed by Arab actors. Several years earlier, and especially in the early aftermath of the 1973 War, Arab states could credibly threaten to reignite large-scale hostilities against Israel, to enlist Soviet power on their behalf, and to turn the oil weapon on any industrialized nations that stood in their way. By the early 1980s, all three of these scenarios had lost credibility, and they would grow even less plausible with the passage of time. The United States, by contrast (and in large measure consequently), had become more dominant and confident, displaying less reluctance to endorse Israeli military actions or to flex its own muscles in the Arab world. These circumstances infuriated and humiliated Arabs everywhere, and opposition to U.S. policies was growing more bitter and widespread. Starting just months later, some of that opposition would take the form of violent attacks against American targets, provoking, in turn, more naked exertions of U.S. military power. Washington could launch these ventures with little fear of Soviet interference, though the local resistance would be trouble enough. The post–Cold War era began a decade early in the Middle East.

With all that, the Arabic byline adorning the piece in the *Wall Street Journal*, where Youssef Ibrahim served as a staff reporter and, later, as a senior Middle East correspondent and energy editor, was a reminder that Arab Americans had become a more visible and accepted presence in some areas of American life.[3] This phenomenon, too, would persist in the years ahead—though it also would be accompanied, and sometimes obscured, by forces tending to marginalize Arab Americans and their political outlooks.

Anwar Sadat's assassination in October 1981, at the hands of Egyptian Islamists outraged by his peace treaty with Israel and recent crackdown on their political activities, failed to alter Egypt's geopolitical stance. Sadat's successor, Husni Mubarak, reaffirmed his government's commitment to formal peace with Israel, and in April 1982 Israel completed its withdrawal from the Sinai Peninsula. These events consummated the subtraction of Egyptian power from the Arab-Israeli equation, solidified Egypt's status as a U.S. client state, and provided final confirmation of Moscow's strategic and diplomatic defeat in the Arab-Israeli arena. Into the 1980s, the Soviet Union continued to cultivate Arab clients, and its diplomatic positions on the Arab-Israeli dispute were generally in keeping with mainstream Arab views. But it grew less and less relevant to regional diplomacy, whereas the United States, despite its declining popularity within Arab societies, remained central to any future Arab-Israeli peacemaking. The Soviets could provide Arab actors with arms and diplomatic support, but only the Americans had the ability (in theory, at least) to induce Israel to withdraw from the Arab territories it still occupied.

This situation was frustrating to the Soviets, but truly maddening to Arabs committed to a resolution based on mutual compromise. By the early 1980s, the vast majority of the world's nations—the Soviet Union and East bloc, much of the Third World, some Western European countries, most Arab states and the PLO—favored a settlement involving Israel's withdrawal to the 1967 borders and the establishment of a Palestinian state in the West Bank and Gaza.[4] The only significant holdouts regarding this scenario were the United Sates and Israel, yet their opposition sufficed to block its realization. Israel had the raw ability to retain the occupied territories, as long as it received adequate military and diplomatic support. The United States had both the ability and the inclination to provide that support.

Why Washington was so inclined had everything to do with the diplomatic legacy Henry Kissinger bequeathed. When Kissinger began his shuttle diplomacy in late 1973, the U.S. government faced formidable international pressure to push for Israel's retreat to the 1967 lines, and equally formidable domestic pressure to spare Israel the necessity of large-scale withdrawal. The sine qua non of the international pressure, Kissinger quickly grasped, was the possibility of another general Arab-Israeli war. Each of the related coercive elements—the threatened resumption of oil pressures, a potential superpower confrontation—needed the outbreak of hostilities to trigger it. So Kissinger methodically dismantled the triggering mechanism. His Egypt-centered diplomacy, which came to fruition under Jimmy Carter, drastically reduced the likelihood of another full-scale war, sharply diminishing, in turn, the international pressure for Israeli withdrawal. Yet the countervailing domestic pressure remained as robust as ever, and it would have far more impact on the policies of later U.S. administrations than would what remained of the international pressure. The consequence over the succeeding decades, with precious few exceptions, was a series of convoluted U.S. peace initiatives that focused obsessively on the modalities of Israel's negotiations with various Arab partners while evading discussion of substantive outcomes, especially regarding final borders.[5] The time expended on these efforts allowed Israel to solidify its hold on the occupied territories, placing a viable two-state settlement further out of reach.

The 1980s also marked the resumption of direct U.S. military intervention in the Arab world, a practice generally avoided since president Dwight D. Eisenhower sent marines to Lebanon in 1958.[6] While these latter-day adventures entailed considerable risks, military interference by the Soviet Union was almost never one of them. The United States did, however, encounter vigorous and sometimes brutally effective resistance from indigenous Arab actors.

Events in Lebanon in the early 1980s bear out the claim. In June 1982, Israel invaded Lebanon to crush PLO forces based in that country. With Egyptian military power now completely removed from the strategic picture, Israel could launch the operation without fear of disturbance on its southwestern flank. The invasion did bring Israel into confrontation with Syrian forces already occupying Lebanon, but these did not pose an especially formidable threat. The Israeli air force destroyed eighty-five Syrian planes without losing a single plane of its own. Moscow partially replenished these losses but otherwise took little action, allowing Washington to monopolize the diplomacy surrounding the crisis and to contribute marines to a multilateral peacekeeping force in Lebanon that excluded the Soviets. The U.S. intervention soon soured. The marines became a target of some of the country's warring factions, especially Lebanese Shia who had borne the brunt of Israel's invasion. In October 1983, a suicide bomber—apparently a Syrian-backed Lebanese Shia—drove a truck filled with explosives into the marines' headquarters, killing 241 servicemen. Months later, president Ronald Reagan withdrew the marines.[7] These events were a humiliating setback for the United States, but they also indicated a new pattern in the international politics of the Middle East. From now on, the only physical resistance to American power in the region would be mounted by indigenous rather than outside actors.

One of those indigenous actors was Libya's Mu'ammar Qaddafi, whose flouting of diplomatic norms had intensified in the closing months of Carter's presidency. Over the next several years, goaded in part by President Reagan's efforts to weaken and isolate Libya, Qaddafi stepped up his challenges against the United States and the West. Libya's army waged a proxy war against French forces in neighboring Chad; its air and naval forces tangled with their American counterparts when the latter ventured into international waters Libya claimed for itself; the terrorist activities that Tripoli sponsored abroad were increasingly directed at American and Western targets. In April 1986, U.S. warplanes struck several government and military installations in and around Tripoli, killing nearly a hundred. Although Libya was a major recipient of Soviet arms, Moscow confined itself to verbal protests and offers to replenish its client's arsenal. The December 1988 bombing of a Pan Am passenger plane over Lockerbie, Scotland, killing 270 people, including 180 Americans, appears to have been Qaddafi's retaliation for the 1986 raid. In the early 1990s, domestic concerns drew Qaddafi's energies inward, and over the next two decades U.S.-Libyan tensions were muted, though they resumed with a vengeance in the months preceding the regime's overthrow (and Qaddafi's personal demise) in 2011.[8]

Taking on a different coloration, but manifesting the same underlying reality of rising U.S. dominance in the 1980s, were America's activities in the Persian Gulf region. The Iran-Iraq War, which continued until 1988, alarmed Iraq's Arab neighbors in the Gulf. First and foremost, they feared a victory for revolutionary Iran. Short of that, they worried that the war would bring violence to their own shores or impair their ability to ship oil to world markets. Thus the Gulf Arab states increasingly looked to Washington for protection. Exploiting the opening, the United States bulked up its military forces in the area. The three to five U.S. Navy ships that had patrolled the Gulf since the late 1940s were augmented to a fleet of thirty by 1988. Officially, the Reagan administration remained neutral in the Iran-Iraq War, but unofficially it tilted in favor of Iraq, which it saw as the lesser evil. (The administration's arms-for-hostages dealings with Iran in the mid-1980s were a spectacular, though relatively minor, exception to this rule.) In 1987–1988, responding to Iran's attacks on the maritime oil exports of Arab countries supporting Iraq, the United States provided naval escorts for Kuwaiti oil tankers transiting the Gulf; soon the U.S. Navy was skirmishing directly with Iranian gunboats. These events underscored the Gulf Arab regimes' increasing reliance on the United States for their security—a dependence that grew even more pronounced in the war's unsettled aftermath.[9]

Compounding the Gulf Arab states' sense of vulnerability in the 1980s was a simultaneous contraction in their oil revenues. During the early phase of the Iran-Iraq War, the global oil market was subject to two contradictory influences: an upward pressure on prices resulting from war-related disruptions of exports from the Gulf; and a shrinkage in world demand for Middle Eastern oil in particular, a delayed consequence of consumer nations' responses to previous price increases. Initially, the inflationary pressure prevailed, with OPEC's price surging above forty dollars per barrel in some markets before settling at thirty-four dollars per barrel in October 1981. Over the next few years, however, the contrary trend dominated. After the wrenching OPEC price hikes of late 1973, many of the industrialized nations had taken steps to reduce their dependence on Middle Eastern oil. They mandated fuel efficiency standards, imposed higher gas taxes, invested in public transportation, and built nuclear power plants. They also increased their reliance on non–Middle Eastern sources of petroleum: the U.S. government built a pipeline to carry Alaskan crude to the lower forty-eight states, while the British government invested heavily in developing North Sea reserves. These various measures were pursued haltingly and unevenly—the U.S. commitment to public transportation, for example, was far weaker than that of many other industrialized nations—but their cumulative effect, by about 1983, was a marked decline in global demand for oil in general and an even sharper drop in demand for oil from the Middle East. OPEC had priced itself out of its commanding market share.[10]

The Gulf Arab states' first response to the situation, and that of OPEC generally, was to reduce output. In March 1982, OPEC mandated for its members an overall production limit of 18 million barrels per day (MBD), down from 31 MBD in 1979. (Several OPEC members cheated, however, by exceeding their quotas.) Saudi Arabia, which had lowered its production from 10.4 to 8.5 MBD in October 1981, made a series of further reductions, bottoming out at 2.2 MBD in the summer of 1985. The purpose of the reduced supply had been to maintain OPEC's thirty-four-dollars-per-barrel price, but this proved impossible. In March 1983, the cartel lowered its per-barrel price to twenty-nine dollars; several more reductions followed. In 1986, crude oil prices sank as low as seven dollars per barrel. Saudi oil revenues for that year were $18 billion, a stunning drop from their high point of nearly $111 billion in 1981. The revenues of other Arab oil producers shriveled in like proportion. Collapsing oil revenues severely damaged the economies of oil-poor Arab states, as many of them relied heavily on workers' remittances from oil-rich countries.[11]

Of course, no economic circumstances are permanent. In the coming decades the price of oil would rise again and fall; Arab producers would recover market share and lose it many times over. Never again, however, would the Arab nations as a whole enjoy the combined economic, military, and psychological leverage they had wielded in the middle years of the 1970s—a leverage magnified by the fact that America's own international prospects had then seemed so dismal. By the 1990s, that peculiar juxtaposition of rising Arab fortunes and falling American ones was a hazy memory, supplanted by a stark new reality in which each of those trajectories had been inverted. The Soviet Union had vanished, a significant setback for would-be Arab challengers of U.S. hegemony (though one anticipated by the rapid decline of Moscow's regional influence in the 1980s). The United States, having led an international military coalition (including several Arab states) to expel Iraq from Kuwait in 1991, now dominated the Persian Gulf as never before and commanded unparalleled military power and diplomatic influence throughout the Arab world. Washington remained central to the Arab-Israeli peace process, which, though now formally incorporating Arafat's PLO, surreally enabled Israel's continuing colonization of the West Bank.[12]

There was no shortage of Arab opposition to these circumstances. Yet by the turn of the twenty-first century the locus of Arab resistance had shifted, with ominous implications for America's further involvement in the region. Arab governments, no longer possessing the strategic leverage to extract modest concessions from the United States (such as a more evenhanded policy on Palestine), had ceded the field of resistance to nonstate actors, especially Islamist organizations operating under al-Qa'ida's loose auspices. Such groups not only launched grisly attacks against American and other civilians but also harbored geopolitical ambitions—the elimination of Israel, the overthrow of established Arab regimes, even the restoration of the caliphate—that Washington could not begin to accommodate.[13] The violent extremism of these challengers, coupled with the collective weakness of the Arab states, made stepped-up U.S. intervention in the region seem both necessary and feasible. The decision to invade Iraq in 2003 was a clear, if wildly misdirected, product of such thinking. By the second decade of the twenty-first century, the exorbitant costs of that intervention had convinced most Americans that the direct policing of Arab societies was an unsustainable course. And yet the scaling back of such measures produced chaotic spectacles that stimulated demands for redoubled policing.[14] No end lay in sight.

Few Americans in the mid-1970s, apart from "Miles Ignotus" and his fellow neoconservative fantasists, would have recommended a full-scale U.S. military intervention in a major Arab country on the Persian Gulf. Such a scenario was indeed alien to the zeitgeist of the era. But decisions made, opportunities missed, and patterns established in that decade helped to create conditions in which misadventures of this sort could eventually come to pass.

Regarding the domestic dimensions of the U.S.-Arab encounter in the 1970s, especially as they related to Arab American and Arab-friendly activism and discourse, this book has tried to complicate our understanding. In examining this decade (and later ones, too), it is tempting to stress the degree to which dominant American attitudes about the Middle East stigmatized and marginalized Arab Americans and their views. Actually, the mingling of these external and domestic realms in the seventies produced a sort of double movement: contentious international events that alienated Arab Americans and made their position in American society seem more precarious were often accompanied by, and sometimes inseparable from, developments that mitigated those very processes.

The mitigation usually took one of two forms. In the first pattern, Arab American activists revolted against what they saw as a deplorable status quo and thereby gained strength, cohesion, experience, and visibility. Examples include the public protests against U.S. and Israeli policies that occurred throughout the decade (and reached a crescendo during the 1973 Arab-Israeli War), as well as activists' responses to president Richard Nixon's domestic antiterrorism measures in 1972–1973 and to the Abscam affair in 1980. In the second pattern, U.S. officials—even while pursuing policies that antagonized most Arab American activists—forged alliances with Arab actors or performed rituals of inclusion that had the effect of creating some Arab-friendly space at home. Illustrating this latter phenomenon are Kissinger's public chumminess with Arab leaders during his "shuttle diplomacy" and Washington's eager solicitation of petrodollar investments after 1973. (Of course, petrodollars nurtured pro-Arab constituencies *and* provoked nativist hostility; there is indeed nothing simple about this story.)

One consequence of these trends was that, over the course of the decade, Arab American activists acquired greater sophistication in navigating such mainstream American institutions as Congress, the news media, the entertainment industry, and universities. Another was that in some elite American circles—academia, business, middle- and high-brow journalism, mainstream African American politics, elements of the "think tank" community, certain Christian dominations, and elsewhere—sympathetic outlooks on Arab society, culture, and politics became more prevalent and articulate. To be sure, in other public realms, such as popular entertainment, advertising, mass-circulation journalism, and pro-Israel discourse, anti-Arab portrayals remained hostile or grew even more so. But even in these areas the affirming influence was not entirely absent.

Over the decades since the 1970s, Arab American communities have undergone significant changes in their makeup, experiences, and organizing trajectories. Numbering something over a million in 1980, the Arab American population has grown to around four million by the second decade of the twenty-first century. Although Christians remain in the majority, their share of that population has declined from about four-fifths in the early 1980s to perhaps two-thirds today.[15] In view of the prominent role that Islamism has played in the U.S.-Arab encounter in recent decades, it is not surprising that the American public often conflates the status of Arab Americans with that of American Muslims. And, to the extent that this conflation has impinged on the lives of Arab Americans of all religious backgrounds, perception becomes reality. Public attitudes regarding Islam were far more peripheral to the Arab American experience in the 1970s, gaining prominence only at the end of the decade, in response to revolutionary upheaval in non-Arab Iran.

For all of these changes, however, the concept of the double movement remains a useful one for making sense of Arab American political life since 1980. In subsequent decades, as in the 1970s, America's troubled relations with the Middle East made life difficult for Arab Americans, sometimes exceedingly so, but they resisted in ways that gained them strength and visibility. In the 1980s, the Reagan administration's showy confrontations with Mu'ammar Qaddafi, along with some high-profile acts of Arab terrorism abroad, fueled a domestic backlash against Arabs in America, occasionally taking the form of hate crimes. In October 1985, a bomb planted in the

Los Angeles offices of the American-Arab Anti-Discrimination Committee killed Alex Odeh, the ADC's West Coast regional director. And yet, partly in reaction to that backlash, the 1980s were a golden age of Arab American political organizing. The ADC's membership grew from five thousand in late 1981 to twenty-five thousand in early 1991. (Abdeen Jabara was the group's president from 1986 to 1990.) Arab Americans played key roles in the Reverend Jesse Jackson's insurgent presidential runs of 1984 and 1988, with former ADC codirector James Zogby serving as a deputy campaign manager in 1984 and as the national cochair in 1988.[16]

Also echoing the 1970s, the mitigation of stigma sometimes took the form of official and mainstream acts of recognition and inclusion. In the 1990s, to combat political Islam's more militant standard-bearers, the administration of president Bill Clinton publicly insisted that Islamic and Western societies shared values and interests in common, called for "dialogue" with moderate Islamists throughout the world, and commemorated Muslim holidays along with Christian and Jewish ones. While these gestures were by their nature cosmetic, they fostered a somewhat more welcoming atmosphere for Muslim American and Arab American activists and commentators. Increasingly in the public discourse of the 1990s, the etiquette of diversity was extended to Arab Americans and Muslim Americans. At about the same time that it became obligatory to refer to the "men and women" of the U.S. armed forces, public speakers began appending "and mosques" to their homilies about America's churches and synagogues.[17]

In parts of American academia, the affirmation of Arab and Muslim perspectives was even more pronounced, a trend both symbolized and advanced by the remarkable success of Edward Said's trenchant monograph *Orientalism*. First published in 1978, the book argued that the production of Western knowledge about non-Western and especially Middle Eastern societies was inseparable from, and tended to reproduce, the West's domineering and often imperial relationship with the non-Western "Other." *Orientalism* had its critics, including some who shared Said's sympathy for the victims of Western domination. From the early 1980s on, however, the work exerted extraordinary influence on, and sometimes helped to create, several fields of inquiry in the academic humanities: colonial studies, postcolonial theory, discourse analysis, poststructuralism, and the like. Within Middle East studies (a geographically defined field in which these methodological approaches were increasingly pursued), Said's claims met with initial resistance, which over time gave way to wide and enthusiastic acceptance. At its annual meeting in 1998, the Middle East Studies Association (MESA) held a special plenary session to mark the twentieth anniversary of *Orientalism*'s publication. "The praise heaped on Said on this occasion for his contribution to . . . Middle East studies," writes the historian Zachary Lockman, ". . . indicated the extent to which the field had changed, with a great many scholars who were broadly sympathetic to the intellectual thrust (if not every aspect or detail) of the critique advanced by Said . . . now holding leadership positions within MESA and in the field as a whole." Continuing a trend that first gained impetus in the 1970s, an ever-larger share of the field's practitioners had kinship ties to the Middle East.[18]

Said's intellectual critique had global application, but it radiated from an Arab-friendly core. Even as *Orientalism* transformed academia, Said himself gained increasing prominence in the United States as an advocate for Palestinian rights, generally supportive of Yasser Arafat's leadership in the 1980s, sharply critical of it in the 1990s and early 2000s.[19] (Said died in 2003.) This fact, coupled with *Orientalism*'s focus on Western treatments of Middle Eastern themes, infused Saidian studies as a whole with at least an implicit sympathy—and sometimes an overt one—for Palestinian and Arab efforts to resist U.S. and Israeli policies and the ideologies sustaining them. Scholarship and activism combined to nourish an Arab-friendly sphere.

Of course, the attacks of September 11, 2001, and their aftermath sharply recast the Arab American experience. The societal forces stigmatizing, marginalizing, and even physically endangering Arabs and Muslims in America acquired unprecedented power, reach, and virulence. In the weeks and months after 9/11, U.S. authorities arrested, detained, interrogated, and deported hundreds of individuals, mostly foreign nationals from Arab and Muslim countries. Officially, these measures were directed at noncitizens, but they contributed to a climate of public hysteria in which those with perceived ties to the Arab and Muslim worlds, regardless of citizenship status, endured harassment, defamation, and sometimes outright violence. The domestic reaction to 9/11 thus combined the most menacing features of the Nixon administration's antiterrorism measures of 1972–1973 and of the American public's response to the Iranian hostage crisis of 1979–1981: the official dragnet from the first case and the undifferentiated societal hostility from the second. On both counts, though (and hardly surprisingly, given the nature and scale of the nation's trauma), the extent of the post-9/11 backlash was much greater.[20]

In the years since 2001, the societal hostility has become, in some ways, even more prominent. Fueling it have been the genuine threats that Islamist terrorists continue to pose to the U.S. "homeland," along with less rational fears, promoted by a tirelessly resourceful Islamophobic cottage industry, that domestic Muslims are corrupting the nation's cultural and civic institutions. In the 2010s, anti-Muslim sentiment has found expression in public protests against the establishment of mosques and Muslim community centers in cities throughout the country, in calls for barring all Muslims from entering the United States, and in legislative efforts to combat the imaginary threat that Sharia (Islamic law) might be imposed on American citizens.[21]

Even in the post-9/11 era, however, the forces of mitigation, though hardly a match for the stigmatizing pressures, have been readily evident. The climate of hostility and intolerance following the 2001 attacks produced a fresh surge of Arab American and Muslim American activism, spurring the formation of new organizations and alliances that brought the concerns of Arab and Muslim communities to national attention and thus modestly blunted the backlash. Such efforts have continued to shape the landscape of ethnic and national politics. In long-established discursive realms, such as academia and print journalism, and in newer ones, like the blogosphere, critics with no kinship ties to the Middle East decry U.S. military intervention in the region and the defamation of Arabs and Muslims at home. Government officials and mainstream cultural arbiters continue to insist that people of Arab and Muslim background are integral members of the American community.[22]

To be sure, other mainstream commentators say exactly the opposite, and even the most cordial official embraces of Arabs and Muslims are sometimes inseparable from efforts to monitor those communities or to facilitate U.S. military operations in the Middle East. The FBI conducts "outreach" in Arab American enclaves and eagerly seeks Arabic-speaking recruits. The U.S. military and the CIA sponsor Arab American cultural festivals. "A U.S. Army rock-climbing wall towered over kebob and falafel stands," the bemused editors of an academic Arab American anthology observe of a series of such events from the mid-2000s.[23] The strands of affirmation, cooptation, surveillance, and coercion become, in the end, impossible to disentangle.

At home and abroad, the U.S.-Arab encounter follows a rhythm and a logic peculiar to our own era. Only in the most general ways do the actors in this contemporary drama connect the challenges of today with those of forty years earlier, and many, of course, have no personal memory of that past. Yet the tumultuous events of the 1970s, during which Americans and Arabs first came into extended contact with one another, yielded patterns and pathways that powerfully shaped their relations over subsequent decades and remain visible today. We are just beginning to understand this intricate legacy.

Acknowledgments

My first book covered a period of about four years. In my acknowledgments, I sheepishly reported that my efforts to produce the volume had exceeded that duration by a considerable margin. This time, I set out to chronicle a whole decade. It took me longer than *that* to get the job done. My work would have been even slower, and in some ways impossible, without the help of a great many people and institutions.

I began this book as a faculty member at the University of Chicago and did the bulk of the work while teaching at the University of California, Santa Barbara. In each place, both the department of history and the wider institution were generous with financial support and teaching releases, and both schools provided the stimulating teaching and research environments so necessary for open, searching, and original scholarship. I am especially thankful for the many intellectual and personal friendships I have enjoyed at UC Santa Barbara, my academic home since 2005.

Over the course of my research, I received lengthy fellowships from the Smith Richardson Foundation and the Woodrow Wilson International Center for Scholars, the first allowing me to pursue the project from home in Chicago, the second transporting me to Washington, DC, for a full academic year. It is impossible to overstate the value of that uninterrupted time or, in the case of the Wilson Center fellowship, the opportunity to conduct extensive research in the nation's capital and to partake of the Center's remarkable intellectual ferment. I also received, during my years of research, priceless assistance from the archivists and staff at the Library of Congress, the National Archives and Records Administration, Britain's National Archives, four Presidential Libraries, the Hoover Institution Library and Archives, the Arab American National Museum, the Immigration History Research Center, and numerous other libraries. The digitizing of archival materials has revolutionized historical research, so I must also thank the countless individuals, all unknown to me, who have made it possible to penetrate the inner sanctums of the national security state while sprawled out on a couch in a T-shirt and sweatpants.

I am grateful, too, to the many historical actors who allowed me to interview them, communicated with me by mail or e-mail, shared documents with me, or attached names to faces in old photographs: James G. Abourezk, Nabeel Abraham, M. Cherif Bassiouni, Paul Findley, Elaine C. Hagopian, Lee Hamilton, Abdeen Jabara, Walid Khalidi, Donald McHenry, Fouad Moughrabi, the late Robert B. Oakley, Gregory Orfalea, Thomas Pickering, William B. Quandt, John P. Richardson, the late Richard Shadyac, Jack G. Shaheen, Michael Sterner, Joe Stork, Ghada Talhami, Michael Van Dusen, Fawzi Yaqub, and James Zogby. Susan Welsh kindly donated to me materials that had belonged to her late parents, Elizabeth Scott and Richard Scott.

At the University of Chicago, UC Santa Barbara, and the Wilson Center, several undergraduate and graduate students performed heroic service as research assistants: Melissa Borja, Omar Cheta, Patrick Kennedy, Christopher Marshall, Matthew McDonald, Maria Ponomarenko, Donna Rosenberg, and James Smith. The opportunity to teach, collaborate with, and learn from students at all levels has been an incalculable benefit to my scholarship.

I am delighted that this book is appearing in Cornell University Press's outstanding United States in the World series. I couldn't hope for better scholarly company. Paul Kramer and Mark Bradley, the original series editors, and Alison Kalett, Cornell's former acquisitions editor, recruited me for the series. Mark subsequently assumed special responsibility for my book, offering insightful and encouraging comments and advice. Alison's successor as acquisitions editor, Michael McGandy, oversaw the project for most of its long life, tactfully inquiring from time to time about my progress on the manuscript (sorry, Michael, I worked as fast as I could) and patiently walking me through each stage of evaluation, revision, editing, and production. Several other Cornell people have been particularly helpful in preparing the book for publication: Bethany Wasik, Ange Romeo-Hall, Kerrie Maynes, Dina Dineva, and Susan Barnett. Still others at the press, whose names I don't know, have labored with dedication and professionalism to bring this volume to completion; my sincere thanks to them as well. I am grateful, too, to other publishers. Portions of the manuscript previously appeared in my book chapters, "The Politics of Stalemate: The Nixon Administration and the Arab-Israeli Conflict, 1969–73" (*The Cold War in the Middle East: Regional Conflict and the Superpowers, 1967–73*, ed. Nigel J. Ashton, Routledge, 2007), and "The Weight of Conquest: Henry Kissinger and the Arab-Israeli Conflict" (*Nixon in the World: American Foreign Relations, 1969–1977*, ed. Fredrik Logevall and Andrew Preston, Oxford University Press, 2008).

I would be nowhere without the criticism, encouragement, and advice of fellow scholars. Several anonymous reviewers read the book prospectus or full manuscript for Cornell; they caught numerous errors and offered a host of excellent suggestions for improving the book. Thomas Borstelmann, Douglas Little, Melani McAlister, and Hugh Wilford read the entire manuscript as well and were similarly incisive in their comments. Many other colleagues and friends critiqued portions of the book, discussed the project with me in ways that helped me make it better, shared documents and research tips, or collaborated on related projects that ultimately enriched the book. They include Seth Anziska, Nigel Ashton, Laila Ballout, Paul Chamberlin, Nathan Citino, Elizabeth Cobbs, Bruce Cumings, Craig Daigle, John Lewis Gaddis, Charles Glaser, Petra Goedde, Peter Hahn, Tsuyoshi Hasegawa, Geraint Hughes, Clea Lutz Hupp, Hussein Ibish, Richard Immerman, Matthew Jacobs, Laura Kalman, John Tofik Karam, Rosemary Kelanic, Rashid Khalidi, Betty Koed, Mark Lawrence, Fredrik Logevall, Ussama Makdisi, Victor McFarland, Robert McMahon, Pamela Pennock, Andrew Preston, Jeremi Suri, and David Wight. Meriting particular mention is the warm and generous support of the Red Line Group of Washington, DC, that extraordinary assemblage of scholars and friends I got to know during my fellowship year at the Wilson Center: Marie-Therese Connolly, Mary Ellen Curtin, Matthew Dallek, Deirdre Moloney, Philippa Strum, Wendy Williams, and especially Robyn Muncy.

Over the course of these labors, my parents and siblings offered loving support, as they have done throughout my life. My parents-in-law and sisters-in-law, and their families, blessed me with the same, while kindly hosting me during my many research trips to Washington, DC, the Twin Cities, and the San Francisco Bay Area.

The book is dedicated to my wife, Elizabeth Teare, and to my daughter, Dorothy Teare Yaqub, who arrived just about the time I was starting the research. I could not possibly describe all of the ways that Elizabeth and Dorothy have sustained me and my work. What chiefly stands out is the wonderful home they have made for me, a hive of exuberance, creativity, and passionate engagement that somehow doubles as a haven for serene and appreciative reflection.

Notes

Abbreviations Used in the Notes and Bibliography

AAD	Access to Archival Databases
AAUG	Association of Arab American University Graduates
ACJME	American Committee for Justice in the Middle East
ACLU	American Civil Liberties Union
ANERA	American Near East Refugee Aid
BHL	Bentley Historical Library
CL	Jimmy Carter Presidential Library
DOS	Department of State
DNSA	Digital National Security Archive
EMUL	Eastern Michigan University Library
FL	Gerald R. Ford Presidential Library
FBI documents	declassified FBI documents
FCO	Foreign and Commonwealth Office
FRUS	*Foreign Relations of the United States*
GUL	Georgetown University Library
HAK/ME	Henry A. Kissinger / Middle East
HAK/Telcons	Henry A. Kissinger Telephone Conversations
HILA	Hoover Institution Library and Archives

HL	Hornbake Library
IHRC	Immigration History Research Center
LC	Library of Congress
MSHS	Minnesota State Historical Society
NAAA	National Association of Arab Americans
NARA	National Archives and Records Administration
NL	Richard M. Nixon Presidential Library
NSA Memcons	National Security Adviser, Memoranda of Conversation
NSC/ME	National Security Council /Middle East
NSC/Saunders	NSC Files, Harold H. Saunders Files
PHRC	Palestine Human Rights Campaign
PUL	Princeton University Library
RAC	Remote Access Capture
RG	Record Group
SNF	Subject Numeric Files
TL	Tamiment Library
TNA	The National Archives (Great Britain)
UAL	University of Arkansas Library
UNCL	University of North Carolina Library
UNISPAL	United Nations Information System on the Question of Palestine
USDL	University of South Dakota Library
UUL	University of Utah Library
WHCF	White House Central Files
WSAG	Washington Special Action Group

Introduction

1. Godfrey Jansen, *Why Robert Kennedy Was Killed: The Story of Two Victims* (New York: The Third Press, 1970), 205.

2. A.S. "Doc" Young, "Bells Toll Again as America 'Dies,'" *Los Angeles Times*, June 9, 1968, A1, 12B. Some of the journalistic commentary quoted in this section was first quoted in Jansen, *Why Robert Kennedy Was Killed*. To acquire the full context (and sometimes the full wording) of these quotations, I have, when possible, consulted the original sources.

3. Editorial, *Boston Globe*, June 6, 1968, 10.

4. Jansen, *Why Robert Kennedy Was Killed*, 48–153, 185–96. Kennedy, of course, was hardly the only U.S. politician to trumpet Israel's cause, which was especially popular in the months following the 1967 War. But as a senator from New York, a state with many Jewish voters, he had been unusually forceful in his pro-Israel statements and unusually disparaging of Arab countries. Ibid., 175–96. Also setting Kennedy apart was the progressive, caring persona he cultivated during his presidential campaign. He presented himself as the champion of inner-city blacks, Latino migrant workers, young opponents of the Vietnam War, and other disadvantaged or disaffected elements within U.S. society. Sirhan himself was drawn to this aspect of Kennedy's appeal and thus all the more outraged by his pro-Israel stance. In 1980, Sirhan recalled that Kennedy was "my hero . . . until he betrayed my opinion of him" by advocating more arms for Israel. *Sarasota (FL) Herald Tribune*, September 27, 1980, A2.

5. Editorial, *New York Times*, June 5, 1968, 46; *New York Times*, June 6, 1968, 32; Jerry Landauer, "Does the Press Inspire Assassins?," *Wall Street Journal*, July 18, 1968, 16. Pamela Pennock successfully refutes Jansen's claim that U.S. news coverage systematically ignored the Arab-Israeli dimensions of Sirhan's crime. But it is true that editorials, columns, and op-ed pieces, as opposed to "straight" news stories, rarely addressed those dimensions. Jansen, *Why Robert Kennedy Was Killed*, 212–17; Pennock, *Linkages on the Left: Arab American Activism in the 1960s–1970s* (Chapel Hill: University of North Carolina Press, forthcoming).

6. *Newsweek*, March 24, 1969, 38.

7. *New York Times*, June 9, 1968, 65. For quotations of other Arab editorials in this vein, see Jansen, *Why Robert Kennedy Was Killed*, 220–21.

8. *Washington Post*, April 9, 1969, A3.

9. David A. Korn, *Assassination in Khartoum* (Bloomington, IN: Indiana University Press, 1993), 32–33.

10. Jansen, *Why Robert Kennedy Was Killed*, 217–19. Fueling fears of retaliation were news reports that, days after Sirhan's crime, a Jordanian grocer in Chicago had been killed in apparent reprisal for Kennedy's murder. *Chicago Tribune*, June 11, 1968, A2; *Washington Post*, June 17, 1968, A4. It turned out, however, that the killing of the grocer, a West Bank Palestinian, resulted from a personal dispute unrelated to the Sirhan/Kennedy case. *Chicago Daily Defender*, July 24, 1968, 3, 10; *Chicago Tribune*, June 27, 1969, A4.

11. James G. Abourezk, *Advise and Dissent: Memoirs of South Dakota and the U.S. Senate* (Chicago: Lawrence Hill, 1989), 69; Abourezk, interview with the author, December 19, 2007.

12. Abdeen M. Jabara, foreword to Jansen, *Why Robert Kennedy Was Killed*, 6–12; Dan E. Moldea, *The Killing of Robert F. Kennedy: An Investigation of Motive, Means, and Opportunity* (New York: W.W. Norton, 1995), 130.

13. Letter to the editor, *New York Times*, June 18, 1968, 46; *New York Times*, March 4, 1969, 18; *Chicago Tribune*, June 6, 1968, 5.

14. Robert Fraga, "Sirhan/Kennedy: An Essay on Political Violence," *Middle East Newsletter*, May–June 1969, 4–6.

15. M[uhammad] T. Mehdi, *Kennedy and Sirhan: Why?* (New York: New World Press, 1968), 81.

16. A rare exception was the columnist Max Lerner, who warned that Arab resentments, which he accorded no legitimacy, would spawn future attacks against the West. "If Americans think they will be immune," he wrote, "they have the example of Sirhan B. Sirhan to reflect on." Lerner, "Attacks on Airliners Must Stop, Preferably by International Act," *Los Angeles Times*, February 21, 1969, D9.

17. Eliot Fremont-Smith, "Kennedy: Memorials and Assaults," *New York Times*, November 22, 1968, 45. To be sure, some right-of-center politicians, such as California governor Ronald Reagan and Los Angeles mayor Sam Yorty, along with a few conservative commentators, highlighted Sirhan's Arab origins. Their purpose, however, was not to warn that U.S. policies had antagonized Arabs to the point of provoking retaliation but, rather, to refute the claim that Sirhan's crime reflected a "sick" American society. The assassination, Reagan insisted, represented nothing more than "the violence of war in the Middle East imported by an alien." *Washington Post*, June 7, 1968, A8; *Los Angeles Times*, June 14, 1968, 3; Christopher Emmet, "The Media and the Assassinations," *National Review*, July 30, 1968, 749.

18. Bruce J. Schulman, *The Seventies: The Great Shift in American Culture, Society, and Politics* (New York: Free Press, 2001); Laura Kalman, *Right Star Rising: A New Politics, 1974–1980* (New York: W.W. Norton, 2010); Daniel J. Sargent, *A Superpower Transformed: The Remaking of American*

Foreign Relations in the 1970s (New York: Oxford University Press, 2015); Thomas Borstelmann, *The 1970s: A New Global History from Civil Rights to Economic Inequality* (Princeton, NJ: Princeton University Press, 2013); Judith Stein, *Pivotal Decade: How the United States Traded Factories for Finance in the 1970s* (New Haven, CT: Yale University Press, 2010).

19. John W. Dower, *War Without Mercy: Race and Power in the Pacific War* (New York: Pantheon, 1986); Dower, *Embracing Defeat: Japan in the Wake of World War II* (New York: W. W. Norton, 1999); Naoko Shibusawa, *America's Geisha Ally: Reimagining the Japanese Enemy* (Cambridge, MA: Harvard University Press, 2006); Paul A. Kramer, *The Blood of Government: Race, Empire, the United States, and the Philippines* (Chapel Hill: University of North Carolina Press, 2006); Mark P. Bradley, *Imagining Vietnam and America: The Making of Postcolonial Vietnam, 1919–1950* (Chapel Hill: University of North Carolina Press, 2000); Frank Costigliola, "'Unceasing Pressure for Penetration': Gender, Pathology, and Emotion in George Kennan's Formation of the Cold War," *Journal of American History* 83, no. 4 (March 1997): 1309–39; Petra Goedde, *GIs and Germans: Culture, Gender, and Foreign Relations, 1945–1949* (New Haven, CT: Yale University Press, 2003); David C. Engerman, *Know Your Enemy: The Rise and Fall of America's Soviet Experts* (New York: Oxford University Press, 2009); Mary Ann Heiss, "Real Men Don't Wear Pajamas: Anglo-American Cultural Perceptions of Mohammed Mossadeq and the Iranian Oil Nationalization Dispute," in *Empire and Revolution: The United States and the Third World since 1945*, ed. Peter L. Hahn and Mary Ann Heiss, 178–94 (Columbus: Ohio State University Press, 2001).

20. David A. Korn, *Stalemate: The War of Attrition and Great Power Diplomacy in the Middle East, 1967–1970* (Boulder, CO: Westview Press, 1992); Korn, *Assassination in Khartoum*; Kenneth W. Stein, *Heroic Diplomacy: Sadat, Kissinger, Carter, Begin, and the Quest for Arab-Israeli Peace* (New York: Routledge, 1999); Walter J. Boyne, *The Two O'Clock War: The 1973 Yom Kippur Conflict and the Airlift that Saved Israel* (New York: Thomas Dunne Books, 2002); Craig Daigle, *The Limits of Détente: The United States, the Soviet Union, and the Arab-Israeli Conflict, 1969–1973* (New Haven, CT: Yale University Press, 2012).

21. Douglas Little, *American Orientalism: The United States and the Middle East since 1945* (Chapel Hill: University of North Carolina Press, 2002); William B. Quandt, *Peace Process: American Diplomacy and the Arab-Israeli Conflict since 1967* (1993, repr., Berkeley: University of California Press, 2001); Avi Shlaim, *War and Peace in the Middle East: A Critique of American Policy* (New York: Viking, 1994); Burton I. Kaufman, *The Arab Middle East and the United States: Inter-Arab Rivalry and Superpower Diplomacy* (New York: Twayne Publishers, 1996); H.W. Brands, *Into the Labyrinth: The United States and the Middle East, 1945–1993* (New York: McGraw-Hill, 1994); Peter L. Hahn, *Crisis and Crossfire: The United States and the Middle East since 1945* (Washington, DC: Potomac Books, 2005); Michael B. Oren, *Power, Faith, and Fantasy: America in the Middle East, 1776 to the Present* (New York: W.W. Norton, 2007); Ussama Makdisi, *Faith Misplaced: The Broken Promise of U.S.-Arab Relations, 1820–2001* (New York: PublicAffairs, 2010).

22. Examples of general treatments appear in the previous footnote. Studies of U.S. relations with particular countries or groups include Lloyd Gardner, *The Road to Tahrir Square: Egypt and the United States from the Rise of Nasser to the Fall of Mubarak* (New York: New Press, 2011); Peter L. Hahn, *Missions Accomplished? The United States and Iraq since World War I* (New York: Oxford University Press, 2012); Clea Lutz Hupp, *The United States and Jordan: Middle East Diplomacy during the Cold War* (London: I.B. Tauris, 2014); Kathleen Christison, *Perceptions of Palestine: Their Influence on U.S. Middle East Policy* (1999, repr., Berkeley, CA: University of California Press, 2001); Paul Thomas Chamberlin, *The Global Offensive: The United States, the Palestine Liberation Organization, and the Making of the Post-Cold War Order* (New York: Oxford University Press, 2012.

23. Examples of the latter include Janice J. Terry, *Mistaken Identity: Arab Stereotypes in Popular Writing* (Washington, DC: American-Arab Affairs Council, 1985); Melani McAlister, *Epic Encounters: Culture, Media, and U.S. Interests in the Middle East, 1945–2001* (2001, repr., Berkeley: University of California Press, 2005); Tim Jon Semmerling, *"Evil" Arabs in American Popular Film: Orientalist Fear* (Austin: University of Texas Press, 2006); Alex Lubin, *Geographies of Liberation: The Making of an Afro-Arab Political Imaginary* (Chapel Hill, NC: University of North Carolina Press, 2014); Zachary Lockman, *Contending Visions of the Middle East: The History and Politics of Orientalism* (New York: Cambridge University Press, 2004); Gregory Orfalea, *The Arab Americans: A History* (Northampton, MA: Olive Branch Press, 2005).

24. Stein, *Heroic Diplomacy*, 268; Robert Dallek, *Nixon and Kissinger: Partners in Power* (New York: HarperCollins, 2007), 619; Asaf Siniver, "US Foreign Policy and the Kissinger Stratagem," in *The Yom Kippur War: Politics, Legacy, Diplomacy*, ed. Asaf Siniver (New York: Oxford University Press, 2013), 99. Kissinger himself, not surprisingly, belongs to this school. See Henry A. Kissinger, *Years of Renewal* (New York: Simon & Schuster, 1999), 347.

25. Steven L. Spiegel, *The Other Arab-Israeli Conflict: Making America's Middle East Policy, from Truman to Reagan* (Chicago: University of Chicago Press, 1985), 312–14; Robert Schulzinger, *Henry Kissinger: Doctor of Diplomacy* (New York: Columbia University Press, 1989), 238–40; Chamberlin, "The Cold War in the Middle East," in *The Routledge Handbook of the Cold War*, ed. Craig Daigle and Artemy M. Kalinovsky (London: Routledge, 2014), 172.

26. Elaine C. Hagopian, "Minority Rights in a Nation-State: The Nixon Administration's Campaign against Arab-Americans," *Journal of Palestine Studies* 5, no. 1/2 (Autumn 1975–Winter 1976): 97–114; Louise Cainkar, "The Social Construction of Difference and the Arab American Experience," *Journal of American Ethnic History* 25, no. 2–3 (Winter–Spring 2006): 245–50; Nadine Naber, *Arab America: Gender, Cultural Politics, and Activism* (New York: New York University Press, 2012), 36–39.

27. McAlister, *Epic Encounters*, 2.

28. One exception was the Princeton historian Bernard Lewis, who in a 1976 article did present the U.S.-Arab relationship in such starkly civilizational terms. Lewis, "The Return of Islam," *Commentary*, January 1976, 39–49. Lewis's lament that his own observations on the topic had failed to penetrate American public discourse, while a self-serving rhetorical device, genuinely reflected the relative novelty of his perspective at this time.

29. I also sometimes use the word "militant" to describe an attitude of anger, defiance, and urgency and a propensity for bold action, whether violent or nonviolent. The adjective is more often attached to radicals, but not exclusively so. Again, I mean nothing pejorative by it. Many of those meriting the label doubtless felt they were appropriately militant, given the injustices they faced.

30. Simon C. Smith, *Ending Empire in the Middle East: Britain, the United States, and Post-War Decolonization, 1945–1973* (London: Routledge, 2012), 7–127; Jeffrey R. Macris, *The Politics and Security of the Gulf: Anglo-American Hegemony and the Shaping of a Region* (London: Routledge, 2010), 108–15, 133–39, 155–56; Philip C. Naylor, *A History of North Africa*, rev. ed. (2009, repr., Austin: University of Texas Press, 2015), 179–92.

31. Charles D. Smith, *Palestine and the Arab-Israeli Conflict*, 4th ed. (Boston: Bedford/St. Martin's, 2001), 181–206, 223–50, 261–76, 278–81.

32. Salim Yaqub, *Containing Arab Nationalism: The Eisenhower Doctrine and the Middle East* (Chapel Hill: University of North Carolina Press, 2004), 88–97, 111–12, 119–21, 138–40, 205–36; Little, *American Orientalism*, 127–37, 206–11; Macris, *Politics and Security*, 100–101, 145–51; Madawi Al-Rasheed, *A History of Saudi Arabia*, 2nd ed. (2002, repr., Cambridge: Cambridge University

Press, 2010), 90–92; Robert O. Freedman, *Soviet Policy toward the Middle East since 1970* (New York: Praeger, 1982), 22–24.

33. In the early aftermath of Israel's creation in 1948, the United States formally maintained that Israel should relinquish the territory it had acquired in excess of the lands earmarked for the Jewish state in the United Nations partition resolution of 1947. Similarly, in late 1948 the United States voted in favor of a UN General Assembly resolution calling for the repatriation of Palestinians displaced from their homes in what became Israel, provided they were willing to live in peace with the new state. In 1949, president Harry S. Truman tried to compel Israel's compliance on both matters, but he abandoned the effort after encountering Israeli resistance. Apart from president John F. Kennedy's unsuccessful attempt, in the early 1960s, to resolve the refugee issue by negotiation, Washington made no further effort to implement its official policies on these questions. Spiegel, *Other Arab-Israeli Conflict*, 45–46, 110–17; Christison, *Perceptions of Palestine*, 89–90, 105.

34. Daniel Yergin, *The Prize: The Epic Quest for Oil, Money, and Power* (New York: Simon and Schuster, 1991), 567–68; Freedman, *Soviet Policy*, 35–36.

35. Quandt, *Peace Process*, 23–52; Freedman, *Soviet Policy*, 31–33.

36. An important exception was Tunisia's president, Habib Bourguiba, who first in 1965 and again in 1968 called for a negotiated settlement between the Arab states and Israel. The Shiloah Center for Middle Eastern and African Studies, *Middle East Record, 1968* (Jerusalem: Israel Universities Press, 1973), 185, 237.

37. Malcolm H. Kerr, "Introduction," in *The Elusive Peace in the Middle East*, ed. Malcolm H. Kerr (Albany: State University of New York Press, 1975), 9–11; Yair Evron, "Two Periods in the Arab-Israeli Strategic Relations, 1957–1967; 1967–1973," in *From June to October: The Middle East Between 1967 and 1973*, ed. Itamar Rabinovich and Haim Shaked (New Brunswick, NJ: Transaction Books, 1978), 97.

38. Daigle, *Limits of Détente*, 24.

1. The Politics of Stalemate

1. *Washington Post*, December 10, 1968, A1; *Chicago Tribune*, December 12, 1968, 4.

2. In 1976, however, president Gerald R. Ford appointed William Scranton U.S. ambassador to the United Nations, a position Scranton held until Ford left office early the following year.

3. Combined U.S economic and military aid to Israel amounted to approximately $94 million in fiscal year (FY) 1970, $634 million in FY 1971, $430 million in FY 1972, and $493 in FY 1973. The 1971 figure reflected a spike in military aid related to the escalation of the Egyptian-Israeli War of Attrition in 1970 (see main text below), the year in which Congress determined 1971 aid levels. Clyde R. Mark, *Israel: U.S. Foreign Assistance*, updated April 26, 2006, http://fas.org/sgp/crs/mideast/IB85066.pdf (accessed July 11, 2015), 13.

4. Fouad Ajami, *The Arab Predicament: Arab Political Thought and Practice since 1967* (Cambridge: Cambridge University Press, 1981), 24–75; Fauzi M. Najjar, "The Egyptian Press Under Nasser and al-Sadat," in *Arab Civilization: Challenges and Responses*, ed. George N. Atiyeh and Ibrahim Oweiss (Albany: State University of New York Press, 1988), 336–38; William Rugh, *Arab Mass Media: Newspapers, Radio, and Television in Arab Politics* (Westport, CT: Praeger, 2004), 37, 52.

5. Helena Cobban, *The Palestinian Liberation Organisation: People, Power, and Politics* (Cambridge: Cambridge University Press, 1984), 28–44; Yezid Sayigh, *Armed Struggle and the Search for a State: The Palestinian National Movement, 1949–1993* (Oxford: Clarendon Press, 1997), 95–142, 174–84, 219–20.

6. Sayigh, *Armed Struggle*, 237; Alan Hart, *Arafat: Terrorist or Peacemaker?* (London: Sidgwick & Jackson, 1984), 285–88; Cobban, *Palestinian Liberation Organisation*, 145–47.

7. Roham Alvandi, *Nixon, Kissinger, and the Shah: The United States and Iran in the Cold War* (New York: Oxford University Press, 2014), 29–37; W. Taylor Fain, *American Ascendance and British Retreat in the Persian Gulf Region* (New York: Macmillan, 2008), 175–91.

8. Walter LaFeber, *The American Age: United States Foreign Policy at Home and Abroad*, 2nd ed., *1750 to the Present* (1989, repr., New York: W. W. Norton, 1994), 638, 640; Alvandi, *Nixon, Kissinger, and the Shah*, 37–39, 46–47.

9. Alison Pargeter, *Libya: The Rise and Fall of Qaddafi* (New Haven, CT: Yale University Press, 2012), 35–48; Ronald Bruce St John, *Libya and the United States: Two Centuries of Strife* (Philadelphia: University of Pennsylvania Press, 2002), 78–84; Douglas Little, "To the Shores of Tripoli: America, Qaddafi, and the Libyan Revolution, 1969–89," *International History Review* 35, no. 1 (2013): 72–74.

10. John K. Cooley, *Libyan Sandstorm* (New York: Holt, Rinehart and Winston, 1982), 14–16; Pargeter, *Libya*, 48–53.

11. Among the Arab states seeking to recover territory occupied in 1967, Egypt and Jordan immediately accepted Resolution 242, whereas Syria initially rejected it. In March 1972, Syria accepted the resolution on condition that its implementation resulted in a full Israeli withdrawal from occupied territory and in the restoration of Palestinian rights. Alasdair Drysdale and Raymond A. Hinnebusch, *Syria and the Middle East Peace Process* (New York: Council on Foreign Relations, 1991), 105–6.

12. Charles D. Smith, *Palestine and the Arab-Israeli Conflict*, 4th ed. (Boston: Bedford/St. Martin's, 2001), 303–7; William B. Quandt, *Peace Process: American Diplomacy and the Arab-Israeli Conflict since 1967*, rev. ed. (Berkeley: University of California Press, 2001), 46–47; Little, *American Orientalism: The United States and the Middle East since 1945* (Chapel Hill: University of North Carolina Press, 2002), 282; Lyndon B. Johnson, address to B'nai B'rith meeting, September 10, 1968, *Department of State Bulletin*, October 7, 1968, 348.

13. Smith, *Arab-Israeli Conflict*, 311–12; Muhammad Hasanayn Haykal, *Uktubir 73: Al-silah wa-al-siayasa* [October '73: Arms and politics] (Cairo: Markaz al-Ahram lil-tarjimah wa-al-nashr, 1993), 106. For a full account of the War of Attrition, see David A. Korn, *Stalemate: The War of Attrition and Great Power Diplomacy in the Middle East, 1969–1970* (Boulder, CO: Westview Press, 1992).

14. Little, *American Orientalism*, 285.

15. Kissinger, *White House Years* (Boston: Little, Brown, 1979), 352, 354.

16. Quandt, *Peace Process*, 59.

17. Kissinger, *White House Years,* 564; William Safire, *Before the Fall: An Inside View of the Pre-Watergate White House* (Garden City, NY: Doubleday, 1975), 565–66; Richard M. Nixon to William P. Rogers, May 26, 1971, Record Group 59 (hereafter RG 59), Office of the Secretary, Office Files of William P. Rogers (hereafter Rogers Files), box 25, folder: "WPR—President Nixon," National Archives and Records Administration, College Park, MD (hereafter NARA).

18. Rafael Medoff, *Jewish Americans and Political Participation: A Reference Handbook* (Santa Barbara, CA: ABC-Clio, 2002), 193–96; Safire, *Before the Fall*, 564–75.

19. Nixon to Kissinger, September 22, 1969, in Bruce Oudes, ed., *From the President: Richard Nixon's Secret Files* (New York: Harper & Row, 1989), 49.

20. Quandt, *Peace Process*, 63–64.

21. Benny Morris, *Righteous Victims: A History of the Zionist-Arab Conflict, 1881–1999* (New York: Alfred A. Knopf, 1999), 350–52; Korn, *Stalemate*, 165–76; U.S. Interests Section, Cairo, to Department of State (hereafter DOS), tel #2278, September 20, 1969, National Security Council Files, Country Files, Middle East (hereafter NSC/ME), box 635, folder: "UAR Vol. II, 01 Sep 69–31 Jan 70," Richard M. Nixon Presidential Library, Yorba Linda, CA (hereafter NL).

22. A narrow waterway lying between the southern tip of the Sinai Peninsula and the west coast of Saudi Arabia, the Strait of Tiran is Israel's sole maritime outlet to the Red Sea and Indian Ocean. Cairo's announced blockade of the strait in May 1967 had served as Israel's casus belli in the ensuing June War.

23. Quandt, *Peace Process*, 67–68; Korn, *Stalemate*, 157–61; Steven L. Spiegel, *The Other Arab-Israeli Conflict: Making America's Middle East Policy, from Truman to Reagan* (Chicago: University of Chicago, 1985), 186–87; Rogers to Nixon, December 8, 1969, NSC/ME, box 650, folder: "Middle East Negotiations 12/69," NL.

24. Rogers quoted in Korn, *Stalemate*, 160.

25. Korn, *Stalemate*, 154, 158, 161–63; U.S. Embassy, Tel Aviv, to DOS, tel #4640, December 23, 1969, NSC/ME, box 605, folder: "Israel Vol. III Sept 69–28 Feb 70 (part 2) (2 of 3)," NL. Meir's visitor was senator Mark Hatfield of Oregon.

26. Richard M. Nixon, *The Memoirs of Richard Nixon* (New York: Grosset & Dunlap, 1978), 479.

27. Sisco later recalled that Nixon often telephoned him during this period to receive updates on the negotiations and offer words of support, which Sisco presumably passed on to Rogers. Korn, *Stalemate*, 154.

28. Kissinger, *White House Years*, 372, 376.

29. Yitzhak Rabin, *The Rabin Memoirs* (Boston: Little, Brown, 1979), 162; telephone conversation, Kissinger and Rogers, December 11, 1969, Henry A. Kissinger Telephone Conversations, Chronological File, box 3, folder: "1969 9–16 Dec," NL.

30. Kissinger to Nixon, October 2, 1969, NSC/ME, box 644, folder: "Middle East—General, Vol. II (Oct 69–Jan 70) [2 of 2]," NL; Leonard Garment, *Crazy Rhythm: My Journey from Brooklyn, Jazz, and Wall Street to Nixon's White House* (Cambridge, MA: Da Capo, 2001), 192.

31. Korn, *Stalemate*, 161, 163–64; Robert Stephens, *Nasser: A Political Biography* (New York: Simon and Schuster, 1972), 526–27; *New York Times*, December 7, 1969, 26; U.S. Interests Section, Cairo, to DOS, tel #2750, November 18, 1969, NSC/ME, box 635, folder: "UAR Vol. II, 01 Sep 69–31 Jan 70," NL; DOS to U.S. Interests Section, Cairo, tel #5669, January 14, 1970, NSC/ME, box 635, folder: "UAR Vol. II, 01 Sep 69–31 Jan 70," NL.

32. Mahmoud Riad, *The Struggle for Peace in the Middle East* (London: Quartet Books, 1981), 114; Ashraf Ghorbal, *Mudhakkirat Ashraf Ghurbal: Su'ud wa-inhiyar 'alaqat Misr wa-Amrika* [The memoirs of Ashraf Ghorbal: The rise and fall of Egypt's and America's relations] (Cairo: Markaz al-Ahram lil-tarjimah wa-al-nashr, 2004), 60.

33. Quandt, *Peace Process*, 68; Avi Shlaim, *Lion of Jordan: The Life of King Hussein in War and Peace* (London: Penguin, 2007), 310; Yehuda Lukacs, *Israel, Jordan, and the Peace Process* (1997, repr., Syracuse, NY: Syracuse University Press, 1999), 107.

34. Korn, *Stalemate*, 164.

35. Ibid., 165–88.

36. Egypt's existing surface-to-air missile, the SA-2, which the Soviets had also provided, was far less effective against low-flying aircraft, and generally slower and more cumbersome, than was the SA-3. Haykal, *The Road to Ramadan* (New York: Quadrangle, 1975), 84; Korn, *Stalemate*, 168, 191–92.

37. Haykal, *Road to Ramadan*, 83–87; Haykal, *Uktubir 73*, 111–13; Korn, *Stalemate*, 190–92, 197–98.

38. Korn, *Stalemate*, 192, 225, 252; Morris, *Righteous Victims*, 358.

39. Kissinger, *White House Years*, 568, 570–75; U.S. Interests Section, Cairo, to DOS, tel #340, February 13, 1970, NSC/ME, box 635, folder: "UAR Vol. III 1 Feb–30 April 70," NL; attachment to Theodore L. Eliot to Kissinger, February 23, 1970, NSC/ME, box 605, folder: "Israel Vol. III Sept 69–28 Feb 70 (part 2) (1 of 3)," NL.

40. Korn, *Stalemate,* 201–2; Rabin, *Memoirs*, 171; memorandum of conversation, Nixon and Rabin, March 18, 1970, Digital National Security Archive, George Washington University, Washington, DC (hereafter DNSA), KT00110.

41. Memorandum of conversation, Nixon and Rabin, March 18, 1970, DNSA, KT00110. Rabin's account of this exchange in his memoirs was both more dramatic and more ambiguous. Rabin recalled that Nixon, with what appeared to be "a strange glint in his eye," asked, "'How do you feel about those missiles being manned by the Russians? Have you considered attacking them?' Totally flabbergasted, I blurted out: 'Attack the Russians?'" Rabin wrote that he said nothing further on the matter and was unsure whether Nixon was actually recommending an attack on the SA-3s or merely probing Israel's intentions. Rabin, *Memoirs*, 172–73.

42. Quandt, *Peace Process*, 72–73; Korn, *Stalemate*, 242–43, 245–47.

43. Korn, *Stalemate*, 232–33; Morris, *Righteous Victims*, 359.

44. Haykal, *Road to Ramadan*, 92–93, 95; Haykal, *Uktubir 73*, 118–19.

45. Quandt, *Peace Process*, 74; Rabin, *Memoirs*, 178–79; Korn, *Stalemate*, 255–58, 263.

46. Korn, *Stalemate*, 263–67, 287.

47. Morris, *Righteous Victims*, 362; Korn, *Stalemate*, 208, 269.

48. Yoram Meital, *Egypt's Struggle for Peace: Continuity and Change, 1967–1977* (Gainesville: University Press of Florida, 1997), 73–74; Korn, *Stalemate*, 270; *Wall Street Journal*, July 30, 1970, 1; *Washington Post*, August 1, 1970, A15.

49. Kamal S. Salibi, *A Modern History of Jordan* (London: I.B. Tauris, 1993), 236; Nigel J. Ashton, *King Hussein of Jordan* (New Haven, CT: Yale University Press, 2008), 144–45; *New York Times*, September 8, 1970, 1. On September 30, the PFLP released the remaining hostages in exchange for three PFLP members imprisoned in Switzerland. Victor D. Comras, *Flawed Diplomacy: The United Nations and the War on Terrorism* (Washington, DC: Potomac Books, 2010), 15.

50. Cobban, *Palestinian Liberation Organisation*, 45–46; Hart, *Arafat*, 288–96.

51. Cobban, *Palestinian Liberation Organisation*, 46.

52. Salibi, *Crossroads to Civil War, 1958–1976* (Delmar, NY: Caravan Books, 1976), 39–42; Sayigh, *Armed Struggle*, 189–91; Mark Tessler, *A History of the Israeli-Palestinian Conflict* (Bloomington: Indiana University Press, 1994), 451–54; Farid el Khazen, *The Breakdown of the State in Lebanon, 1967–1976* (Cambridge, MA: Harvard University Press, 2000), 146–48.

53. Rogers to Nixon, October 27, 1969, NSC/ME, box 620, folder: "Lebanon Vol. I Jan 69–31 Jan 1970 (1 of 3)," NL; U.S. Embassy, Beirut, to DOS, tel #3881, May 9, 1969, NSC/ME, box 620, folder: "Lebanon Vol. I Jan 69–31 Jan 1970 (2 of 3)," NL; DOS to U.S. Embassy, Beirut, tels #70266 and 75036, May 6 and 12, 1969, NSC/ME, box 620, folder: "Lebanon Vol. I Jan 69–31 Jan 1970 (3 of 3)," NL.

54. Salibi, *Crossroads*, 42–44; Tessler, *Israeli-Palestinian Conflict*, 455; U.S. Embassy, Beirut, to DOS, tel #9738, November 25, 1969, NSC/ME, box 620, folder: "Lebanon Vol. I Jan 69–31 Jan 1970 (1 of 3)," NL.

55. Alain Gresh, *The PLO: The Struggle Within* (London: Zed Books, 1985), 36; Cobban, *Palestinian Liberation Organisation*, 48–49; Sayigh, *Armed Struggle*, 246–53.

56. Ashton, *Hussein*, 144; Sayigh, *Armed Struggle*, 253–59.

57. Sayigh, *Armed Struggle*, 250–65; Ashton, *Hussein*, 147–48; Craig Daigle, *The Limits of Détente: The United States, the Soviet Union, and the Arab-Israeli Conflict, 1969–1973* (New Haven, CT: Yale University Press, 2012), 147–49; Patrick Seale, *Asad of Syria: The Struggle for the Middle East* (Berkeley: University of California Press, 1988), 158.

58. Ashton, *Hussein*, 148–51; U.S. Embassy, Amman, to DOS, September 21, 1970, U.S. Department of State, *Foreign Relations of the United States* (hereafter *FRUS*, with dates and volume number), *1969–1976*, 24:787; "Middle East: SITREP at 0700 hours," September 21, 1970, Prime Minister's Office Records 15/124, The National Archives, Kew, London, United Kingdom.

59. Talcott Seelye, who led a special State Department task force on the Jordan crisis, later insisted that "Moscow's involvement in fomenting the crisis did not exist to the best of our knowledge. In fact, we had reliable intelligence reports indicating that the Soviets sought to restrain Syria." Quoted in Donald Neff, *Fallen Pillars: U.S. Policy towards Palestine and Israel since 1945* (Washington, DC: Institute for Palestine Studies, 1995), 175.

60. Daigle, *Limits of Détente*, 145–46, 149.

61. Ibid., 146, 149; telephone conversation, Kissinger, Rogers, and Sisco, September 20, 1970, *FRUS, 1969–1976*, 24:788–89; telephone conversations, Nixon and Kissinger, n.d. [September 20, 1970], and September 21, 1970, *FRUS, 1969–1976*, 790–95, 810–11.

62. Ashton, *Hussein*, 150–54; Shlaim, *Lion of Jordan*, 330–32.

63. Daigle, *Limits of Détente*, 152; Shlaim, *Lion of Jordan*, 330; *New York Times,* September 21, 1970, 1, 17; editorial note, *FRUS, 1969–1976*, 24:767, note 2.

64. Daigle, *Limits of Détente*, 152–53; Nadav Safran, *Israel—The Embattled Ally* (1978, repr., Cambridge, MA: Harvard University Press, 1981), 454–55; Robert G. Rabil, *Syria, the United States, and the War on Terror in the Middle East* (Westport, CT: Praeger, 2006), 48.

65. Ashton, *Hussein*, 154–55; Shlaim, *Lion of Jordan*, 333–34.

66. Sayigh, *Armed Struggle*, 266–67; Ashton, *Hussein*, 155; Shlaim, *Lion of Jordan*, 334–35.

67. Said K. Aburish, *Arafat: From Defender to Dictator* (New York: Bloomsbury, 1998), 114; Sayigh, *Armed Struggle*, 268–81.

68. See, for example, Seymour M. Hersh, *The Price of Power: Kissinger in the Nixon White House* (New York: Summit, 1983), 249; Naseer H. Aruri, *Dishonest Broker: The U.S. Role in Israel and Palestine* (Cambridge, MA: South End Press, 2003), 20–21; Little, *American Orientalism*, 106; Quandt, *Peace Process*, 83; Safran, *Israel*, 455–56.

69. Haykal, *Road to Ramadan*, 98–100; Bahjat Abu-Gharbiya, *Min mudhakkirat al-munadil Bahjat Abu-Gharbiya: Min al-nakbah ila al-intifadah, 1949–2000* [From the memoirs of the fighter Bahjat Abu-Gharbiya: From the catastrophe to the uprising, 1949–2000] (Beirut: al-Mu'assasah al-'Arabiya lil-dirasat wa-al-nashr, 2004), 441.

70. Cooley, *Libyan Sandstorm*, 10; Haykal, *Road to Ramadan*, 69–71, 76–77, 185–86.

71. St John, *Libya and the United States*, 91–92; Little, "To the Shores of Tripoli," 74–75. As the United States could now launch submarine- and carrier-based ballistic missiles from the Mediterranean, local airbases such as Wheelus Field were less central to U.S. military strategy. Still, the Pentagon feared that a compelled withdrawal of its forces from Libya would damage U.S. prestige. P. Edward Haley, *Qaddafi and the United States since 1969* (New York, Praeger, 1984), 19; Little, "To the Shores of Tripoli," 76.

72. For evidence of such covert planning, see Little, "To the Shores of Tripoli," 77–80.

73. Ibid., 76–78; Qaddafi quoted in ibid., 79.

74. Ibid., 94–95; Haykal, *Sphinx and Commissar: The Rise and Fall of Soviet Influence in the Arab World* (London: Collins, 1978), 198–202.

75. Quandt, *Peace Process*, 88–89.

76. U.S. Interests Section, Cairo, to DOS, tel #263, February 8, 1971, NSC/ME, box 637, folder: "UAR Vol. VI 01 Jan 71–31 May 71," NL; U.S. Interests Section, Cairo, to DOS, tel #478, March 6, 1971, Henry A. Kissinger Office Files, Country Files, Middle East (hereafter HAK/ME), box 129, folder: "Middle East—NODIS/CEDAR/PLUS 1971 [1 of 2]," NL; Quandt, *Peace Process*, 89.

77. Rogers quoted in Daigle, *Limits of Détente*, 166; "Scenario for Seeking to Break Impasse on Middle East," March 8, 1971, HAK/ME, box 129, folder: "Middle East [Israel, Jordan, Egypt] [Oct 69–May 71] [2 of 2]," NL.

78. Kissinger to Nixon, February 28, 1971, HAK/ME, box 129, folder: "Middle East [Israel, Jordan, Egypt] [Oct 69–May 71] [2 of 2]," NL; Kissinger to Nixon, March 9, 1971, HAK/ME, box 129, folder: "Middle East [Israel, Jordan, Egypt] [Oct 69–May 71] [2 of 2]," NL.

79. Nixon quoted in Daigle, *Limits of Détente*, 167.

80. For a description of those signals, see Salim Yaqub, "The Politics of Stalemate: The Nixon Administration and the Arab-Israeli Conflict, 1979–73," in *The Cold War in the Middle East: Regional Conflict and the Superpowers, 1967–73*, ed. Nigel J. Ashton, (London: Routledge, 2007), 45–46.

81. Daigle, *Limits of Détente*, 168; Haldeman, *The Haldeman Diaries: Inside the Nixon White House* (1994, repr., New York: Berkeley Books, 1995), 332.

82. Rogers visited Turkey, Saudi Arabia, Lebanon, Jordan, Egypt, and Israel.

83. U.S. Embassy, Tel Aviv, tel #2660, May 7, 1971, National Security Council Files, Harold H. Saunders Files, Middle East Negotiations Files, box 1162, folder: "Jarring Talks May 1–9, 1971 (3 of 3), NL; Rogers/Sadat quoted in editorial note, *FRUS, 1969–1976*, 13:709.

84. Haykal, *Uktubir 73*, 134. For much of the 1950s and 1960s, Egyptian-Saudi relations had been mutually antagonistic, but they became somewhat less strained following the shared Arab debacle of 1967. Relations improved further with the ascendancy of Sadat, who was more outwardly pious than Nasser had been and treated Saudi Arabia's King Faisal with greater respect. Steven M. Walt, *The Origins of Alliances* (Ithaca, NY: Cornell University Press, 1987), 111, 120.

85. Memorandum of conversation, Rogers, Meir, et al., May 6, 1971, *Declassified Documents Reference System* (Detroit, MI: Thomson/Gale, 1998), document #CK3100548322.

86. Nixon quoted in Daigle, *Limits of Détente*, 178–79; Haldeman, *Diaries*, 347–48, 354.

87. Nixon to Rogers, May 26, 1971, Rogers Files, box 25, folder: "WPR—President Nixon," NARA.

88. Spiegel, *Other Arab-Israeli Conflict*, 206–7; *New York Times*, August 2, 1971, 7.

89. Daigle, *Limits of Détente*, 183–85; Rogers quoted in ibid., 185; Kissinger quoted in editorial note, *FRUS, 1969–1976*, 13:712.

90. Nixon quoted in editorial note, *FRUS, 1969–1976*, 13:712 (italics in original).

91. Kissinger was key to engineering Nixon's high-profile and domestically popular visits to the People's Republic of China and the Soviet Union in February and May 1972, respectively. Over 1972, Kissinger shaped and implemented Nixon's strategy of first escalating the Vietnam War and then moving toward a settlement. Although Kissinger's Vietnam role received sharp criticism from commentators at the time and historians thereafter, it—along with his actions regarding China and the Soviet Union—secured his status as Nixon's chief foreign policy architect. Robert Dallek, *Nixon and Kissinger: Partners in Power* (New York: HarperCollins, 2007), 285–456.

92. National Security Council meeting, July 16, 1971, DNSA, KT00308, 5.

93. William B. Quandt, *Decade of Decisions: American Policy toward the Arab-Israeli Conflict, 1967–1976* (Berkeley: University of California, 1977), 143; Sisco and Meir quoted in Daigle, *Limits of Détente*, 189–90.

94. Kissinger, *White House Years*, 1285.

95. Memorandum of conversation, Nixon and Andrei Gromyko, September 29, 1971, *FRUS, 1969–1976*, 13:1052–55; memorandum of conversation, Nixon and Kissinger, September 30, 1971, *FRUS, 1969–1976*, 13:1065, 1065; memoranda of conversation (U.S. and Soviet versions), Kissinger and Dobrynin, October 9, 15, 30, November 4, 1971, in *Soviet-American Relations: The Détente Years, 1969–1972* (Washington, DC: U.S. Government Printing Office, 2007), 488–90, 492–93, 496–97, 505, 509–514.

96. Ghorbal, *Mudhakkirat*, 81. Although it is unlikely that Kissinger expressed such sentiments openly in his meetings with Ghorbal, he may well have communicated them obliquely, as they represented his genuine view of the situation. In May 1969, Kissinger told Ambassador Rabin that Moscow's "clients had lost the 1967 war. They would lose the next war. . . . The United States is under no obligation to get Nasser's territory back for him." Memorandum of

conversation, Kissinger, Rabin, et al., May 13, 1969, NSC/ME, box 604, folder: "Israel Vol I. (1 of 2)," NL.

97. Tape recording of conversation, Nixon, Meir, Kissinger, and Rabin, December 2, 1971, available on the website nixontapeaudio.org, http://nixontapeaudio.org/chron2/rmn_e628c.mp3 (accessed August 31, 2015). For a pithier but substantively similar rendition of this exchange, see Rabin, *Memoirs*, 209.

98. Haldeman, *Diaries*, 486–87; Rogers to Nixon, February 2, 1972, HAK/ME, box 134, folder: "Rabin—1972 Vol 3. [1 of 1]," NL; "Summary Memorandum of Conversations," February 2, 1972, HAK/ME, box 134, folder: "Rabin—1972 Vol 3 [1 of 1]," NL; *New York Times*, February 6, 1972, 1.

99. Daigle, *Limits of Détente*, 206–11; memorandum of conversation (U.S. and Soviet versions), Leonid Brezhnev, Kissinger at al., April 24, 1972, *Soviet-American Relations*, 765–66, 769–73.

100. U.S.-Soviet communiqué, May 29, 1972, *Public Papers of the Presidents of the United States: Richard Nixon, 1972* (Washington, DC: Government Printing Office, 1974), 640; Sadat, *In Search of Identity*, 229; Haykal, *Uktubir 73*, 257.

101. Morris, *Righteous Victims*, 390–91; Quandt, *Peace Process*, 95–96; Kissinger, *White House Years*, 1295–56; Kissinger, *Years of Renewal* (New York: Simon & Schuster, 1999), 354.

102. Kissinger, *White House Years*, 1295, 1298–1300; Henry A. Kissinger, *Years of Upheaval* (Boston: Little, Brown, 1982), 205; Ghorbal, *Mudhakkirat*, 70; Kissinger to Nixon, February 22, 1973, HAK/ME, box 131, folder: "Egypt/Ismail Vol II January–February, 1973 [1 of 1]," NL.

103. Alvandi, *Nixon, Kissinger, and the Shah*, 28–29, 46–64.

104. Daniel Yergin, *The Prize: The Epic Quest for Oil, Money, and Power* (New York: Simon & Schuster, 1991), 577–83; *Wall Street Journal*, September 9, 1970, 11.

105. Testimony of Robert I. Brougham, June 7, 1972, *U.S. Interests in and Policy toward the Persian Gulf: Hearings before the Subcommittee on the Near East of the Committee on Foreign Affairs, House of Representatives, 92nd Congress, Second Session* (Washington, DC: U.S. Government Printing Office, 1972), 59.

2. A Stirring at the Margins

1. *New York Times*, June 10, 1967, 35, 67; Edward W. Said, "The Arab Portrayed" (1968), reprinted in *The Arab-Israeli Confrontation of June 1967: An Arab Perspective*, ed. Ibrahim Abu-Lughod (Evanston, IL: Northwestern University Press, 1970), 1.

2. Said, "Arab Portrayed," 1–9; Association of Arab American University Graduates (hereafter AAUG) *Newsletter*, June 1969, 1.

3. Information about David S. Thompson, who died in 2007, is available in his obituary in *Princeton Alumni Weekly*, February 13, 2008, http://paw.princeton.edu/issues/2008/02/13/sections/memorials/6227/index.xml (accessed September 7, 2015).

4. Another online obituary, dated November 7, 2007, notes that Thompson was "born in Assiut, Egypt" and "educated in Egypt until he was 15 years old." http://www.towntopics.com/nov0707/obits.html (accessed September 7, 2015).

5. AAUG *Newsletter*, June 1969, 1.

6. Philip M. Kayal, "Report: Counting the 'Arabs' among Us," *Arab Studies Quarterly* 9, no. 1 (Winter 1987): 102; Gregory Orfalea, *The Arab Americans: A History* (Northampton, MA: Olive Branch Press, 2005), 79–94, 152–53; Samir Khalaf, "The Background and Causes of Lebanese/Syrian Immigration to the United States before World War I," in *Crossing the Waters:*

Arabic-Speaking Immigrants to the United States before 1940, ed. Eric J. Hooglund (Washington, DC: Smithsonian Institution Press, 1987), 18–19, 21; Alixa Naff, "Arabs in America: A Historical Overview," in *Arabs in the New World: Studies on Arab-American Communities,* ed. Sameer Y. Abraham and Nabeel Abraham (Detroit: Wayne State University Press, 1983), 14–17, 23–24.

7. Kayal, "Counting the 'Arabs' among Us," 102; Hatem I. Hussaini, "The Impact of the Arab-Israeli Conflict on Arab Communities in the United States," in *Settler Regimes in Africa and the Arab World: The Illusion of Endurance*, ed. Ibrahim Abu-Lughod and Baha Abu-Laban (Wilmette, IL: Medina University Press, 1974), 202–6; Orfalea, *Arab Americans*, 156–57; Elaine C. Hagopian, "The Institutional Development of the Arab-American Community in Boston: A Sketch," in *The Arab-Americans: Studies in Assimilation*, ed. Elaine C. Hagopian and Ann Paden (Wilmette, IL: Medina University Press, 1969), 71–79. For recent treatments of Arab American political activism in the first half of the twentieth century, see Sarah M.A. Gualtieri, *Between Arab and White: Race and Ethnicity in the Early Syrian American Diaspora* (Berkeley: University of California Press, 2009), 81–112; Hani J. Bawardi, *The Making of Arab Americans: From Syrian Nationalism to U.S. Citizenship* (Austin: University of Texas Press, 2014).

8. Author's tally of country-by-country U.S. Immigration and Naturalization Service data in Appendix 3 of Orfalea, *Arab Americans*, 438–89; Kayal, "Counting the 'Arabs' among Us," 100–103; Naff, "Arabs in America," 24.

9. National Association of Arab Americans (hereafter NAAA), meeting of the board of directors, December 15, 1973, Abdeen Jabara Papers, box 12, folder: "Activities—NAAA Membership Guidelines," Bentley Historical Library, University of Michigan, Ann Arbor, MI (hereafter BHL).

10. Helen Hatab Samhan, "Not Quite White: Race Classification and the Arab-American Experience," in *Arabs in America: Building a New Future*, ed. Michael W. Suleiman (Philadelphia: Temple University Press, 1999), 209–24; Suad Joseph, "Against the Grain of the Nation—The Arab-," in Suleiman, *Arabs in America*, 268.

11. Of course, there were other Americans bearing kinship ties to countries with which U.S. relations were hostile. In none of these other instances, however, was the ethnic group in question so universally linked to despised international actors. Indeed, in some cases—such as that of Cuban Americans—the immigrant groups were generally seen as *allies* of the United States against the governments of their nations of origin.

12. For critical analyses of U.S. press coverage of the 1967 War, see Leslie Farmer, "All We Know Is What We Read in the Papers: A Study of U.S. Press Coverage of the Middle East Crisis," *Middle East Newsletter*, February 1968, 1–5; Michael W. Suleiman, "American Mass Media and the June Conflict," Abu-Lughod, *Arab-Israeli Confrontation*, 138–54.

13. Frank Getlein, "Nasser Can Claim All Credit for War," *Janesville (WI) Daily Gazette*, June 16, 1967, 6; Raymond Moley, "Ass in Lion's Skin," *Newsweek*, June 26, 1967, 80; *Life*, "1.3 Million Causes of Tension," June 23, 1967, 4.

14. *Newsweek*, June 19, 1967, 35; *Time*, June 16, 1967, 17.

15. Jackie Mason, "Jokes about Marriage, the Six-Day War, Modern Warfare, Performed Live on the Ed Sullivan Show/1968," Amazon Digital Services, 2010; Isaac Asimov, *Isaac Asimov's Treasury of Humor* (New York: Houghton Mifflin, 1971), 235; Andrew Furman, *Israel through the Jewish-American Imagination: A Survey of Jewish-American Literature on Israel, 1928–1995* (Albany: State University of New York Press, 1997), 39.

16. *Playboy*, December 1967, 235.

17. AAUG, *The First Decade, 1967–1977* (Washington, DC: AAUG, 1977), n.p. [3–4].

18. Rashid Bashshur to Hagopian, n.d. [c. 1976], AAUG Papers, box 23, folder: "Board Meeting Minutes—1976," Eastern Michigan University Library, Ypsilanti, MI (hereafter EMUL);

Bashshur, "Unfulfilled Expectations: The Genesis and Demise of the AAUG," *Arab Studies Quarterly* 29, no. 3/4 (Summer/Fall 2007): 9.

19. Bashshur to Hagopian, n.d. [c. 1976], AAUG Papers, box 23, folder: "Board Meeting Minutes—1976," EMUL; "Resolution," n.d. [August 1967], AAUG Papers, box 16, folder: "Correspondence Secretary 1968 (Jabara)," EMUL.

20. Bashshur, "Unfulfilled Expectations," 12–13; Jabara, interview with the author, February 13, 2008.

21. Affidavit by Jack A. French, August 27, 1979, American Civil Liberties Union (hereafter ACLU) Records, MC#001, box 1453, folder: "Jabara v. Kelley Privacy Act," Princeton University Library, Princeton, NJ (hereafter PUL).

22. The female members were Ghada Talhami and Soumaya Talhami. See attendance list in AAUG *Newsletter*, Spring 1968, 4. The two women, both of them Palestinian, were graduate students at the time; Soumaya was the sister of Ghada's husband, Ayoub Talhami, a Palestinian civil engineer. Ghada Talhami's communication with the author, June 12, 2013. Ghada Talhami went on to become a professor of politics at Lake Forest College in Illinois and a prolific author on Palestinian, Egyptian, and Syrian history and politics.

23. AAUG Bylaws, n.d. [late 1967 or early 1968], Alfred M. Lilienthal Papers, box 18, folder: "Association of Arab-American University Graduates, Inc.," Hoover Institution Library and Archives, Stanford, CA (hereafter HILA); AAUG *Newsletter*, Spring 1968, 4.

24. Jabara, interview with the author, February 13, 2008; Hagopian, "Reversing Injustice: On Utopian Activism," *Arab Studies Quarterly* 29, no. 3/4 (Summer/Fall 2007): 59; Michael W. Suleiman, "'I Come to Bury Caesar, Not to Praise Him': An Assessment of the AAUG as an Example of an Activist Arab-American Organization," *Arab Studies Quarterly* 29, no. 3/4 (Summer/Fall 2007): 81.

25. Jabara, interview with the author, February 13, 2008; Hagopian, interview with the author, January 8, 2011; Elaine Hagopian, "Ibrahim and Edward," *Arab Studies Quarterly* 26, no. 4 (Fall 2004): 5, 7; Edward Said, "My Guru," *London Review of Books*, December 13, 2001, 19.

26. Hagopian, "Ibrahim and Edward," 6.

27. Jabara to Hassan Sharif, October 4, 1968, AAUG Papers, box 16, folder: "Correspondence Secretary 1968 (Jabara)," EMUL; Jabara, interview with the author, February 13, 2008.

28. AAUG, General Assembly meeting minutes, December 7, 1969, AAUG Papers, box 26, folder: "General Assembly Meeting Minutes—1969," EMUL; Abu-Lughod to Suleiman, December 10, 1969, Suleiman Papers, box 31A, folder: "AAUG," Arab American National Museum, Dearborn, MI; "Report on 3rd Annual AAUG Convention," October 29–November 1, 1970, Fayez A. Sayegh Papers, box 229, folder 2, University of Utah Library, Salt Lake City, UT (hereafter UUL); M. Cherif Bassiouni, interview with the author, July 15, 2008; *Chicago Tribune*, December 11, 1968, D21.

29. Bassiouni, "The AAUG: Reflections on a Lost Opportunity," *Arab Studies Quarterly* 29, no. 3/4 (Summer/Fall 2007): 29–30.

30. AAUG *Newsletter*, Spring 1968, 1; AAUG *Newsletter*, December 1969, 6; AAUG *Newsletter*, March 1970, 6; AAUG *Newsletter*, December 1970, 4; "Resolutions, 5th Annual Convention," November 10–12, 1972, AAUG Papers, box 26, folder: "General Assembly Resolution 1972," EMUL.

31. AAUG *Newsletter*, Spring 1968, 4; Old Executive Committee to members, January 1970, AAUG Papers, box 19, folder: "Correspondence Membership Renewal—1970," EMUL; Bassiouni, "The State of the Association," Third Annual Convention, October 30, 1970, AAUG Papers, box 14, folder: "Correspondence President 1970 (Bassiouni)," EMUL; Abu-Laban, Presidential Address, Sixth Annual Convention, October 19, 1973, AAUG Papers, folder: "Correspondence President—1973 (Abu Laban)", EMUL.

32. Bassiouni, interview with the author, July 15, 2008.

33. The August 1973 AAUG *Newsletter* listed chapters in Detroit, Greater Cincinnati, Illinois, Los Angeles, Louisiana, Minnesota, New England, New York City, Northern California, North Carolina, Ohio, Washington, DC, and Washington State.

34. *New York Times*, November 13, 1972, 8; Abdeen Jabara, "The AAUG: Aspirations and Failures," *Arab Studies Quarterly* 29, no. 3/4 (Summer/Fall 2007): 16. Zachary Lockman acknowledges the AAUG's impact on Middle East studies in this general period, but he erroneously writes that the group was formed in the late 1970s. Lockman, *Contending Visions of the Middle East: The History and Politics of Orientalism* (New York: Cambridge University Press, 2004), 171.

35. Jabara, interview with the author, February 13, 2008; Suleiman, "Assessment of the AAUG," 82; Rashid Bashshur to Jabara, n.d. [Spring 1973], AAUG Papers, box 14, folder: "Committee on the Future of the AAUG," EMUL.

36. Philip M. Kayal and Joseph M. Kayal, *The Syrian-Lebanese in America: A Study in Religion and Assimilation* (New York: Twayne Publishers, 1975), 219–22; "Lebanese-Syrian Assn. of San Diego Sends Open Letter to President-Elect Nixon," *Heritage*, January 18, 1969, 5, 8; "Statement of the Midwest Federation of Syrian-Lebanese Clubs Presented to the National Security Council and the State Department," October 19, 1972, Jabara Papers, box 10, folder: "Activities—Harassment of Arab-Americans—Correspondence, 1972–1973, #2," BHL.

37. *Heritage*, January 4, 1969, 4; *Heritage*, July 1, 1972, 4; *Lebanese American Journal*, January 2, 1969, 1, 4; *Lebanese American Journal*, January 4, 1969, 8, 9; *Lebanese American Journal*, January 16, 1969, 1, 7; *Lebanese American Journal*, December 25, 1969, 1, 7; *Lebanese American Journal*, March 12, 1970, 12; *Lebanese American Journal*, December 21, 1972, 5; *American Syrian-Lebanese Leader*, April 1973, 1, 9; *American Syrian-Lebanese Leader*, May 1973, 3, 8.

38. In April 1969, the Anti-Defamation League of B'nai B'rith (ADL) claimed that the OAS had ten thousand members. This figure must have been a significant exaggeration, as it exceeded the total number of Arab students in the United States at the time, and OAS membership was generally limited to students. In September 1972, the Immigration and Naturalization Service estimated there were nine thousand Arab students in the country, and this number was surely smaller in 1969. *New York Times*, April 21, 1969, 13; Nabeel Abraham, communication with the author, September 10, 2015; A[ndrew] J. Decker to E[dward] S. Miller, September 25, 1972, declassified FBI documents, Intelwire, http://news.intelwire.com/2010/12/fbi-records-reveal-details-of-nixon-era.html (accessed July 19, 2014; no longer posted but downloaded copy in author's possession).

39. *New York Times*, March 11, 1968, 4; *Chicago Daily Defender*, August 20, 1970, 6; Lewis Young, "American Blacks and the Arab-Israeli Conflict," *Journal of Palestine Studies* 2, no. 1 (Autumn 1972): 78; Robert G. Weisbord and Richard Kazarian, Jr., *Israel in the Black American Perspective* (Westport, CT: Greenwood Press, 1985), 36. See also Pamela Pennock, "Third World Alliances: Arab-American Activists in American Universities, 1967–1973," *Mashriq & Mahjar* 4 (2014): 55–78.

40. *Chicago Tribune*, February 6, 1969, 14; *New York Times*, February 4, 1969, 13; *New York Times*, February 10, 1969, 2; *New York Times*, May 23, 1970, 1, 6; *New York Times*, April 10, 1972, 17; *New York Times*, October 8, 1973, 1, 17; *New York Times*, October 15, 1973, 17; AAUG *Newsletter*, December 1973, 10.

41. *New York Times*, October 9, 1970, 30; *Washington Post*, November 7, 1971, 4, *Action*, January 15, 1973, 1; *American-Syrian-Lebanese Leader*, June/July 1974, A. The fire damage forced ACAAR to suspend publication of its newsletter, *Action*, until February 1976. *New York Times*, February 22, 1976, 34.

42. The full run of the *Link*, the first issue of which is dated September 1968, is available in facsimile form on the Americans for Middle East Understanding website, at http://www.ameu.org/The-Link/Archives.aspx?page=1 (accessed August 31, 2015).

43. American Near East Refugee Aid (ANERA), press releases, January 23 and February 13, 1970, Lilienthal Papers, box 70, folder: "Arab American Organizations," HILA; "Statement for Presentation to Under Secretary Richardson," January 26, 1970, Lilienthal Papers, box 70, folder: "Arab American Organizations," HILA.

44. Copies of American Committee for Justice in the Middle East (ACJME) position papers can be found in Lilienthal Papers, box 69, folder: "American Committee for Justice in the Middle East," HILA; in Walter Mondale Papers, 153.K.5.6F, folder: "Foreign Relations 1–2, Middle East, 2 of 3," Minnesota State Historical Society, St. Paul, MN; and in Frank Maria Papers, box 110, folder 3, Immigration History Research Center, University of Minnesota, Minneapolis, MN. See also David L. Hendry to "Editor," *New York Times*, December 3, 1971, 40. For the predominance of women in the ACJME, see Bernice Espy Hicks to Lilienthal, February 8, 1971, Lilienthal Papers, box 70, folder: "Arab American Organizations," HILA.

45. David G. Nes, "Report on Visit to Texas, Arizona, California and Colorado," November 2–16, 1970, Sayegh Papers, box 243, folder 8, UUL; statement presented to undersecretary of state Elliot L. Richardson, October 6, 1969, J. William Fulbright Papers, Second Acquisition, box 40, folder: "Foreign Relations Committee, Middle East, 1961–1964, 1969," University of Arkansas Library, Fayetteville, AR (hereafter UAL).

46. For an excellent account of AFME's founding, activities, and downfall, see Hugh Wilford, *America's Great Game: The CIA's Secret Arabists and the Shaping of the Modern Middle East* (New York: Basic Books, 2013), 113–32, 177–85, 234–44, 292–93. See also Sol Stern, "A Short Account of International Student Politics & the Cold War with Particular Reference to the NSA, CIA, Etc.," *Ramparts*, March 1967, 31; *New York Times*, February 17, 1967, 1, 16; *New York Times*, February 17, 1967, 1, 16. In June 1977, AFME changed its name to AMIDEAST. See *COSERV Across the USA* (newsletter of the National Council for Community Services to International Visitors), April 1978, 3, https://services.lsit.ucsb.edu/imp/view.php?popup_view=1&mailbox=INBOX&index=152793&actionID=view_attach&id=2&mimecache=7f7a7647614ec640bd5d493d4e9e1b40 (accessed October 14, 2014). I am grateful to Professor Wilford for informing me about this source, and for sharing additional information about the AFME-CIA relationship. Hugh Wilford, communication with the author, June 15, 2015.

47. This surmise is based on the fact that, by 1967, CIA support for AFME was already seen in clandestine circles as a relic of a bygone era, preserved mainly by bureaucratic inertia. The appetite for continuing the association with AFME was rapidly diminishing; for funding additional Arabist groups, it was virtually nonexistent. See Wilford, *America's Great Game*, 291–92.

48. For lists of AMEU's board of directors, see archived issues of the *Link* at http://www.ameu.org/The-Link/Archives.aspx?page=1 (accessed August 31, 2015). For ANERA's officers, see archived issues of the *ANERA Newsletter* at http://www.anera.org/resources/newsletters/ (accessed August 31, 2015).

49. In January 1975, the *Washington Post* reported that according to Arnold Forster, general counsel of the ADL, AMEU received $86,300 in seed money from Aramco in 1968. Forster did not disclose the source of his information, but in a separate interview John M. Sutton, AMEU's president, acknowledged that Aramco was a major backer of his organization. In that same article, the *Post* reported that from 1968 to 1970 ANERA received about $250,000 from Aramco and its subsidiary oil companies. *Washington Post*, January 9, 1975, A1, A8.

50. Peter Johnson and Joe Stork, "MERIP: The First Decade," *MERIP Reports*, October–December 1981, 50–52. Most of MERIP's founding members, including Johnson and Stork,

had been active in the Committee of Returned Volunteers, which mobilized veterans of the Peace Corps and other voluntary organizations to oppose the Vietnam War. Ibid., 50; Joe Stork, communication with the author, August 31, 2012.

51. NCC statements quoted in Peter Johnson, "Mainline Churches and United States Middle East Policy," in *American Church Politics and the Middle East*, ed. Basheer K. Nijim (Belmont, MA: Association of Arab American University Graduates, 1982), 80–82; and in K. L[loyd] Billingsley, *From Mainline to Sideline: The Social Witness of the National Council of Churches* (Lanham, MD: University Press of America, 1990), 127–28.

52. Paul D. Garrett and Kathleen A. Purpura, *Frank Maria: A Search for Justice in the Middle East* (Bloomington, IN: AuthorHouse, 2007), 323–27; Johnson, "Mainline Churches," 81.

53. The American Friends Services Committee, *The Search for Peace in the Middle East*, rev. ed. (Greenwich, CT: Fawcett Publications, 1970), 98–101, 114–15.

54. At the bottom of an April 1970 memorandum describing Bolling's entreaties, National Security Council Middle East analyst Harold Saunders wrote, "I have talked with Bolling a dozen times over the past two years about this paper—most recently 6:10–7:20 pm. There is nothing else I can do." L[awrence] Higby to Alexander Haig, April 10, 1970, National Security Council Files, Country Files, Middle East, box 645, "Middle East—General Vol III Feb 20–May 70," Richard M. Nixon Presidential Library, Yorba Linda, CA. The AFSC began its study in 1968; hence Saunders's reference to his "two years" of exposure to the project.

55. H.R. Haldeman, *The Haldeman Diaries: Inside the Nixon White House* (1994, repr., New York: Berkeley Books, 1995), 347.

56. For information on Elmer Berger, see Jack Ross, *Rabbi Outcast: Elmer Berger and American Jewish Anti-Zionism* (Washington, DC: Potomac Books, 2011). For Edmund Hanauer, see Ross, *Rabbi Outcast*, 160; Edmund Hanauer, letter to editor, *Boston Globe*, September 14, 1967, 30; clipping, Edmund Hanauer, "Israel Must Open Its Doors to Palestinians," *Boston Evening Globe*, October 26, 1971, George McGovern Papers, box 98, folder: "Isreal [sic] 1972," PUL. For Allan Solomonow, see Ross, *Rabbi Outcast*, 157. For Noam Chomsky, see Chomsky, *Peace in the Middle East? Reflections on Justice and Nationhood* (New York: Pantheon, 1974). For I.F. Stone, see *Los Angeles Times*, January 14, 1968, K3.

57. U.S. Embassy, Beirut, to Department of State (hereafter DOS), tel #4563, June 9, 1970, Record Group 59 (hereafter RG 59), Subject Numeric Files (hereafter SNF), POL LEB-US, box 2448, National Archives and Records Administration, College Park, MD (hereafter NARA).

58. In the fall of 1970, AUB had 550 faculty members, about a quarter of whom were American. Of the approximately four thousand students, 223 were American. Most of the remaining faculty and students were Arab. *Washington Post*, November 26, 1970, K11.

59. In September 1968, *Newsday* reported that Aramco had awarded AJME a grant of $7,500, to be disbursed over two years. Extract from *Newsday*, September 24, 1968, William E. Mulligan Papers, box 12, folder 23, Georgetown University Library, Washington, DC (hereafter GUL). Fawzi Yaqub, a founding member of AJME (and the author's father), recalls that around this time Aramco awarded the group a larger sum, in the neighborhood of $15,000. Fawzi Yaqub, interview with the author, August 7, 2012.

60. According to the *Christian Science Monitor*, by June 1968 AJME was sending ten thousand copies of its newsletter to recipients in the United States. By June 1970, it was sending fifteen thousand. *Christian Science Monitor*, June 18, 1968, 4; *Christian Science Monitor*, June 5, 1970, 3.

61. *Middle East Newsletter*, December 1969, 11; extract from *Newsday*, September 24, 1968, Mulligan Papers, box 12, folder 23, GUL; *Christian Science Monitor*, June 18, 1968, 4; *Christian Science Monitor*, June 5, 1970, 3; *Newsweek*, October 5, 1970, 68.

62. U.S. Embassy, Beirut, to DOS, tels #3091, April 19, 1970, and #10139, November 25, 1970, SNF, POL 23–8 LEB, box 2447, NARA; *Washington Post*, November 26, 1970, K11; *Chicago Tribune*, November 27, 1970, 2; *Daily Star*, November 27, 1970, 1–2.

63. In January 1970, AUB vice president Robert Crawford joined several other distinguished Americans, including ANERA president John H. Davis and Frank Maria, representative of the Antiochian Orthodox Christian Archdiocese of North America, in presenting a statement to Undersecretary of State Richardson calling on the United States to recognize "the inalienable rights of the Palestinian people" and to refrain from arming Israel further. "Statement for Presentation to Under Secretary Richardson," January 26, 1970, SNF, POL NEAR E, box 2492, NARA. Two months later, when the Nixon administration was considering providing Israel with additional Phantom aircraft (see previous chapter), AUB president Samuel Kirkwood told Joe Sisco that such a move was unnecessary because "Israel had clearly demonstrated its air superiority and it is quite obvious that Israel is far stronger than the Arabs militarily." Memorandum of conversation, Kirkwood, Sisco, et al., March 10, 1970, SNF, POL 27 ARAB-ISR, box 2493, NARA.

64. Kirkwood to Richardson, May 6, 1970, SNF, POL 23–8 LEB, box 2447, NARA.

65. *Newsweek*, October 5, 1970, 68; *Newsweek*, October 19, 1970, 11–12; memorandum of conversation, Kirkwood, John Irwin, and Andrew Killgore, November 16, 1970, SNF, POL 13–10-ARAB, box 2043, NARA; recollection of the author, who lived in Beirut from 1966 to 1981 and first heard the term "Guerrilla U." in 1976.

66. Jill Derby to members, August 7, 1968, Mulligan Papers, box 12, folder 13, GUL; *Middle East Newsletter*, January–February 1969, 15; open letter to Richard Nixon, n.d. [early 1970], RG 59, Lot Files, Lot 74D308, Records Relating to Egypt, 1966–1975, box 6, folder: "American University in Cairo, 1970," NARA.

67. Statement presented to Undersecretary of State Richardson, October 6, 1969, Fulbright Papers, Second Acquisition, box 40, folder: "Foreign Relations Committee, Middle East, 1961–1964, 1969," UAL; *Middle East Newsletter*, August–September 1971, 16.

68. *Free Palestine*, April 1971, 2, 6.

69. Report from Kuwait to CIA headquarters, February 23, 1971, attachment, Robert C. Young to John H.F. Shattuck, May 20, 1975, Jabara Papers, box 3, folder: "FBI—Background Information (1971–82), #1," BHL.

70. Affidavit by Jack A. French, August 27, 1979, ACLU Records, MC#001, box 1453, folder: "Jabara v. Kelley Privacy Act," PUL.

71. *Christian Science Monitor*, February 8, 1973, 6; AAUG *Newsletter*, June 1973, 4; *Los Angeles Times*, January 18, 1974, E1, E8; *Los Angeles Times*, April 14, 1974, 8; *News Circle,* April 1974, 1 5, 10; *News Circle,* May 1974, 1, 6, 8; *Daily Star*, April 15, 1973, 7, 8.

72. *Middle East Newsletter*, July 1970, 6, 7; AAUG *Newsletter*, March 1971, 4.

73. Rowland Evans and Robert Novak, "Israel's Triumph Over 3 Foes," *Washington Post*, February 4, 1972, A25.

74. James G. Abourezk, *Advise and Dissent: Memoirs of South Dakota and the U.S. Senate* (Chicago: Lawrence Hill, 1989), 7–95, 203–5; *New York Times*, June 4, 1972, 47.

75. Abourezk to Marvin Bailin, March 30, 1972, Abourezk Papers, box 649, folder: "Letters to Friends in S. Dakota on the Middle East," University of South Dakota Library, Vermillion, SD; clipping, *Congressional Record*, September 19, 1972, SNF, POL LEB-US, box 2448, NARA.

76. Because of his outspokenness on Vietnam, his association with George McGovern, and his pro-labor record, Abourezk received substantial financial support from liberal Democrats across the country and from national labor unions. Both sectors tended to be strongly pro-Israel. *Chicago Tribune*, October 10, 1972, 14; *Washington Post*, October 29, 1972, A3.

77. Abourezk, *Advise and Dissent*, 99–100; Richard Shadyac, interview with Gregory Orfalea, March 15, 1983, Orfalea Papers, box 3, folder: "Q–S," GUL, 15–16; clipping, Southern Federation of Syrian Lebanese American Clubs, *The Official Bulletin*, January 1972, Lilienthal Papers, box 70, folder: "Arab American Organizations," HILA; Shadyac to "Friend," n.d. [1972], Lilienthal Papers, box 69, folder: "Abourezk, James," HILA; *News Circle*, June 1972, 1, 4; *News Circle*, October 1972, 1, 6; Ira N. Forman, "The Politics of Minority Consciousness: The Historical Voting Behavior of American Jews," in *Jews in American Politics*, ed. L. Sandy Maisel (Lanham, MD: Rowman and Littlefield, 2001), 153.

78. *New York Times*, December 16, 1969, 3; *Washington Post*, September 2, 1970, A1, A7; *Washington Post*, March 24, 1971, A9; *Chicago Tribune*, March 24, 1971, 12.

79. Notes of meetings held on October 15 and 25, November 2 and 16, and December 11, 1971, February 12 and April 14, 1972, AAUG Papers, box 43, folder: "National Association of Arab Americans (NAAA)," EMUL; Shadyac, interview with Orfalea, March 15, 1983, Orfalea Papers, box 3, folder "Q-S," GUL, 16–17.

80. Shadyac, interview with Orfalea, March 15, 1983, Orfalea Papers, box 3, folder "Q-S," GUL, 17, 19.

81. Ibid., 20–22.

82. Prepared remarks, Peter S. Tanous to Sisco, February 27, 1973, and to Saunders, February 28, 1973, Jabara Papers, box 12, folder: "Activities—NAAA Membership Guidelines," BHL; Tanous, Woodrow W. Woody, and Minor George to William P. Rogers, April 16, 1973, Jabara Papers, box 12, folder: "Activities—NAAA Correspondence, 1973–1974," BHL; *Action*, May 7, 1973, 4; *Christian Science Monitor*, May 12, 1973, 6.

83. Minor George résumé, Jabara Papers, box 11, folder: "Activities—Lebanon—Resumes," BHL; NAAA, transcript of first annual convention, June 29–30, 1973, Jabara Papers, box 12, folder: "Activities—NAAA Membership Guidelines," BHL, 3, 6, 7, 19, 27, 44–45.

84. F[uad] K. Taima to Jabara, May 4, 1972, AAUG Papers, box 29, folder: "Correspondence-1972," EMUL; Hagopian to Jabara, May 6, 1972, AAUG Papers, box 29, folder: "Correspondence-1972," EMUL; Jabara to Board of Directors and Committee on the Future of the Association, April 18, 1973, AAUG Papers, box 14, folder: "Committee on the Future of the AAUG," EMUL, Jabara to members of Committee on Future of Association, July 19, 1973, AAUG Papers, box 29, folder: "Correspondence-1972," EMUL

85. Jabara to Board of Directors and Committee on the Future of the Association, April 18, 1973, AAUG Papers, box 14, folder: "Committee on the Future of the AAUG," EMUL; Abu-Lughod to members of the Committee on the Future of the Association, July 25, 1973, AAUG Papers, box 29, folder: "Correspondence-1972," EMUL.

86. Hagopian to Jabara, July 24, 1973, AAUG Papers, box 14, folder: "Committee on the Future of the AAUG," EMUL.

3. From Munich to Boulder

1. Elaine C. Hagopian, "The Institutional Development of the Arab-American Community of Boston: A Sketch," in *The Arab-Americans: Studies in Assimilation*, ed. Elaine C. Hagopian and Ann Paden (Wilmette, IL: Medina University Press, 1969), 71, 76–79, 82–83.

2. Elaine C. Hagopian, "Minority Rights in a Nation State: The Nixon Administration's Campaign against Arab-Americans," *Journal of Palestine Studies* 5, no. 1/2 (Autumn 1975–Winter 1976): 100–102, 104, 106, 112.

3. See, for example, Louise Cainkar, "Thinking Outside the Box: Arabs and Race in the United States," in *Race and Arab Americans before and after 9/11: From Invisible Citizens to Visible Subjects*, ed. Amaney Jamal and Nadine Naber, 46–80 (Syracuse, NY: Syracuse University Press, 2008); Naber, "'Look, Mohammed the Terrorist is Coming!': Cultural Racism, Nation-Based Racism, and the Intersectionality of Oppressions after 9/11," in Jamal and Naber, *Race and Arab Americans*, 276–304.

4. Louise Cainkar, "The Social Construction of Difference and the Arab American Experience," *Journal of American Ethnic History* 25, no. 2–3 (Winter–Spring 2006): 245–50; Nadine Naber, *Arab America: Gender, Cultural Politics, and Activism* (New York: New York University Press, 2012), 36–39; Sarah M.A. Gualtieri, *Between Arab and White: Race and Ethnicity in the Early Syrian American Diaspora* (Berkeley: University of California Press, 2009), 169–79, 61–118. Some scholars couch the transformation in racial terms, arguing that, whereas in earlier decades Arab Americans were seen as white (or nearly so), since the 1970s they have been "racialized" as nonwhite—a status Arab Americans themselves have increasingly embraced. See, for example, Paul Spickard, *Almost All Aliens: Immigration, Race, and Colonialism in American History and Identity* (New York: Routledge, 2007), 425; Naber, "Introduction," in Jamal and Naber, *Race and Arab Americans*, 39; Cainkar, "Thinking Outside the Box," in Jamal and Naber, *Race and Arab Americans*, 46–80. For a challenge to the "racialization" paradigm, see Andrew Shryock, "Moral Analogies of Race: Arab American Identity, Color Politics, and the Limits of Racialized Citizenship," in Jamal and Naber, *Race and Arab Americans*, 81–113.

5. Susan M. Akram, "The Aftermath of September 11, 2001: The Targeting of Arabs and Muslims in America," *Arab Studies Quarterly* 24, no. 2/3 (Spring/Summer 2002): 68–69; Naber, "Introduction," in Jamal and Naber, *Race and Arab Americans*, 34–35.

6. *Los Angeles Times*, November 27, 1978, 6.

7. See, for example, Yousef Munayyer, "FBI Takes Step Back on Civil Rights," *Detroit Free Press*, October 16, 2008, available without pay wall on website of American Arab Anti-Discrimination Committee (ADC), http://www.adc.org/media/press-releases/2008/october-2008/adc-op-ed-on-fbi-guidelines-in-detroit-free-press/ (accessed August 30, 2015); James Zogby, "Arab Americans and Law Enforcement: Rights at Risk," November 10, 2012, http://www.huffingtonpost.com/james-zogby/arab-americans-and-law-en_b_2109335.html (accessed August 30, 2015).

8. Abdeen Jabara, interview with Janice J. Terry, July 20, 1994, Terry Papers, box 1, Bentley Historical Library, University of Michigan, Ann Arbor, MI (hereafter BHL).

9. Said K. Aburish, *Arafat: From Defender to Dictator* (New York: Bloomsbury, 1998), 123–25; Alan Hart, *Arafat: Terrorist or Peacemaker?* (London: Sidgwick & Jackson, 1984), 337–38, 349; Paul Thomas Chamberlin, *The Global Offensive: The United States, the Palestine Liberation Organization, and the Making of the Post-Cold War Order* (New York: Oxford University Press, 2012), 191–92.

10. Mark Ensalaco, *Middle Eastern Terrorism: From Black September to September 11* (Philadelphia: University of Pennsylvania Press, 2008), 28, 33–34; John K. Cooley, *Green March, Black September: The Story of the Palestinian Arabs* (London: Frank Cass, 1973), 124–25; *Los Angeles Times*, December 16, 1972, A27; *New York Times*, May 10, 1972, 1, 2; *Washington Post*, May 19, 1972, A27.

11. Aaron J. Klein, *Striking Back: The 1972 Munich Olympics Massacre and Israel's Deadly Response* (New York: Random House, 2005), 35–70; *Time*, September 18, 1972, 22–29.

12. Klein, *Striking Back*, 56, 71–76.

13. G.M. Drury, "Digital Video Broadcasting by Satellite," in *Satellite Communication Systems*, ed. B.G. Evans, 3rd. ed. (1999, repr., Stevenage, UK: Institution of Engineering and Technology, 2008), 398–99; Melani McAlister, *Epic Encounters: Culture, Media, and U.S. Interests in the Middle East since 1945* (2001, repr., Berkeley: University of California Press, 2005), 178–80.

14. In addition to condemnation from the United States, Canada, and Western European countries, statements of sharp disapproval emanated from the Soviet Union, Czechoslovakia, Hungary, Poland, Yugoslavia, India, and the Philippines. *Los Angeles Times*, September 6, 1972, A11, A13; *Los Angeles Times*, September 7, 1972, A23; *New York Times*, September 7, 1972, 19.

15. *Washington Post*, September 6, 1972, A11; *Washington Post*, September 16, 1972, A12; *New York Times*, September 7, 1972, 19; *New York Times*, September 8, 1972, 12; *New York Times*, September 13, 1972, 3; *Los Angeles Times*, September 11, 1972, B8; Department of State (hereafter DOS) to U.S. Embassy, Tel Aviv, et al., tel #162332, September 6, 1972, National Security Council Files, Harold H. Saunders Files, Middle East Negotiations Files (hereafter Saunders Files), box 1169, folder: "Middle East—Jarring Talks, September 1–30, 1972 (3 of 3)," Richard M. Nixon Presidential Library, Yorba Linda, CA (hereafter NL).

16. Ensalaco, *Middle Eastern Terrorism*, 43; Jeffrey David Simon, *The Terrorist Trap: America's Experience with Terrorism*, 2nd ed. (1994, repr., Bloomington: Indiana University Press, 2001), 106–7; John K. Cooley, *Libyan Sandstorm* (New York: Holt, Rinehart and Winston, 1982), 159–228; P. Edward Haley, *Qaddafi and the United States since 1969* (New York: Praeger, 1984), 35–55; Douglas Little, "To the Shores of Tripoli: America, Qaddafi, and the Libyan Revolution, 1969–89," *International History Review* 35, no. 1 (2013): 80–82.

17. Book-length treatments of this assassination program include Klein, *Striking Back*; George Jonas, *Vengeance: The True Story of an Israeli Counter-Terrorist Team* (New York: Simon & Schuster, 2005); Simon Reeve, *One Day in September: The Full Story of the 1972 Munich Olympics Massacre and the Israeli Revenge Operation "Wrath of God"* (New York: Arcade Publishing, 2006). The program also was the subject of the 2005 film *Munich*, directed by Steven Spielberg and distributed by Universal Studios.

18. *Time*, September 25, 1972, 24; *Time*, October 2, 1972, 31; Chamberlin, *Global Offensive*, 163–64.

19. U.S. UN Delegation to DOS, tel #3446, September 25, 1972, Saunders Files, box 1169, folder: "Middle East—Jarring Talks, September 1–30, 1972 (2 of 3)," NL; DOS to U.S. Embassy, Tel Aviv, et al., tel #188750, October 16, 1972, Saunders Files, box 1169, folder: "Middle East—Jarring Talks, September 1–30, 1972, folder 4," NL.

20. See, for example, *Chicago Tribune*, September 7, 1972, 10; *Los Angeles Times*, September 7, 1972, 2.

21. All of these examples, dated September 6 or 7, 1972, come from a compilation of news commentaries prepared by an unspecified Israeli consulate, titled *No Nation Can Ignore Arab Terrorists: An American Press Commentary* (1972) and housed in the library of the University of California, Santa Barbara.

22. Editorials, *New York Times*, September 8, 1972, 32, September 11, 1972, 36, and September 20, 1972, 46; editorial, *Los Angeles Times*, September 19, 1972, B6; editorial, *Washington Post*, September 12, 1972, A20; William Raspberry, "Arab-Israel Grievances," *Washington Post*, September 13, 1972, A15.

23. *ANERA Newsletter*, September/October 1972, 1.

24. *Boston Globe*, September 24, 1972, 43. The coalition consisted of the AAUG's New England chapter, the American Arabic Association of Boston, the Department of Near Eastern Affairs of the Antiochian Orthodox Christian Archdiocese of North America, Christians Committed to Justice and Reconciliation in Palestine, and SEARCH for Justice and Equality in Palestine.

25. *MERIP Reports*, September/October1972, 13; *Los Angeles Times*, September 24, 1972, H4.

26. Nixon quoted in Timothy Naftali, *Blind Spot: The Secret History of American Counterterrorism Policy* (New York: Basic Books, 2005), 59.

27. *Washington Post*, September 7, 1972, A1, A12; Joseph Sisco to [David] Abshire, NSC Files, White House Special Files, Staff Member and Office Files, Richard C. Tufaro, box 1, folder: "Secret Attachments (#2)," NL.

28. Taped conversation, Nixon, Henry M. Kissinger, et al., September 6, 1972, U.S. Department of State, *Foreign Relations of the United States* (hereafter *FRUS*, with dates and volume number), 1969–1976, vol. E1, doc. 93, https://history.state.gov/historicaldocuments/frus1969-76ve01 (all of the remaining *FRUS* citations are regular volumes; only the citations in endnotes 28, 29, 30 are electronic); Naftali, *Blind Spot*, 58.

29. DOS to U.S. Embassy, London, et al., September 9, 1972, *FRUS, 1969–1976*, vol. E1, doc. 99; Rogers to Nixon, September 18, 1972, *FRUS, 1969–1976*, doc. 102. In the fall of 1972, the United States supported a proposal by UN secretary-general Kurt Waldheim for the creation of an ad hoc General Assembly committee to explore ways of apprehending and punishing the perpetrators of international terrorism. Over the ensuing months, however, a coalition of Arab, Third World, and Soviet bloc nations broadened the mandate of the committee to include investigating "the underlying causes which give rise to such acts of violence," making specific reference to "the inalienable right to national self-determination and independence of all peoples under colonial and racist regimes and other forms of alien domination." These terms of reference diminished the likelihood of vigorous international action against violence of the sort committed in Munich. Victor D. Comras, *Flawed Diplomacy: The United Nations and the War on Terrorism* (Washington, DC: Potomac Books, 2010), 18–24.

30. Memorandum of conversation, Nixon, Rogers, et al., September 6, 1972, *FRUS, 1969–1976*, vol. E1, doc. 94; taped conversation, Nixon, Kissinger, et al., September 6, 1972, *FRUS, 1969–1976*, doc. 95.

31. Nixon to William P. Rogers, September 25, 1972, *Department of State Bulletin*, October 23, 1972, 475–76; Naftali, *Blind Spot*, 59–60.

32. Clipping, *National Observer*, November 18, 1972, Jabara Papers, box 10, folder: "Harassment of Arab-Americans—Press Clippings," BHL.

33. *New York Times*, April 24, 1975, 7.

34. See, for example, U.S. Consulate, Hamburg, to DOS, tel #0853, July 11, 1973, Central Foreign Policy Files, Electronic Telegrams, Access to Archival Databases (hereafter AAD), 1973HAMBUR00853, National Archives and Records Administration, College Park, MA (hereafter NARA); U.S. Embassy, Paris, to DOS, tel #19052, July 11, 1973, AAD, 1973PARIS19052, NARA; U.S. Embassy, Jidda, tel #3020, July 19, 1973, AAD, 1973JIDDA03020, NARA; U.S. Embassy, Kuwait, to DOS, tels #2697, July 29, 1973, AAD, 1973KUWAIT02697, and #0991, March 14, 1974, AAD, 1974KUWAIT00991, NARA; U.S. Consulate, Antwerp, tel #0195, June 19, 1974, AAD, 1974ANTWER00195, NARA; U.S. Embassy, Cairo, tel #4471, June 21, 1974, AAD, 1974CAIRO04471, NARA.

35. *Chicago Tribune*, July 13, 1975, 6; Clarence M. Kelley to Kissinger, April 9, 1974, declassified FBI documents, Intelwire, http://news.intelwire.com/2010/12/fbi-records-reveal-details-of-nixon-era.html (accessed July 19, 2014; no longer posted, but downloaded copy in author's possession) (hereafter FBI documents); "Operation Boulder," n.d. [c. 1974], FBI documents; F.S. Putman to W.R. Wannall, March 6, 1975, FBI documents.

36. A[ndrew] J. Decker to E[dward] S. Miller, September 25, 1972, FBI documents; Decker to Miller, September 20, 1972, FBI documents. For Decker's FBI position in 1972, see *Washington Post*, February 9, 1978, A11.

37. Clipping, *National Observer*, November 18, 1972, Jabara Papers, box 10, folder: "Activities—Harassment of Arab-Americans—Press Clippings," BHL; affidavit by Radi el-Natsha, October 26, 1972, Jabara papers, box 10, folder: "Activities—Harassment of Arab-Americans—

Testimonials and Miscellaneous, 1972–1974," BHL; affidavit by Jamil Azzah, October 1972, Jabara papers, box 10, folder: "Activities—Harassment of Arab-Americans—Testimonials and Miscellaneous, 1972–1974"; statement by Joseph Shikhani, January 10, 1973, Jabara papers, box 10, folder: "Activities—Harassment of Arab-Americans—Testimonials and Miscellaneous, 1972–1974," BHL; M. Cherif Bassiouni to L. Patrick Gray, November 7, 1972, Jabara Papers, box 10, folder: "Activities—Harassment of Arab-Americans, 1972–1979 #1," BHL; "Grazie" (Graziella Figi) to Jabara, December 9, 1972, Jabara papers, box 10, folder: "Activities—Harassment of Arab-Americans, 1972–1979 #1," BHL.

38. Organization of Arab Students, press release, January 8, 1972 [misdated: 1973], Jabara Papers, box 13, folder: "Operation Boulder—Press Clippings, #2," BHL; Edward Djeridjian to Armin Meyer, February 23, 1973, Record Group 59 (hereafter RG 59), Lot Files, Records Relating to Lebanon, box 3, folder: "SY-1 Security—General Lebanon 1973," NARA; Joe Stork and René Theberge, "Any Arab or Others of a Suspicious Nature . . . ," *MERIP Reports*, February 1973, 3.

39. Also lacking are statistics on gender breakdown, though it appears that virtually all of the interview subjects were male. Boulder's visa screening procedures, by contrast, were applied to all Arab applicants of both sexes.

40. *Los Angeles Times*, September 26, 1972, A1, A13; *New York Times*, October 5, 1972, 1, 4; *New York Times*, October 7, 1972, 13.

41. This was true enough in early 1973, but the situation became murkier in the spring and summer of that year. On March 7, unexploded bombs were discovered in two cars parked outside Israeli bank buildings in New York City. One of the cars contained stationery with Black September Organization letterhead. The BSO was not, however, known to print letterhead. On April 16, shots were fired into a Washington, DC, apartment, and the words "Black September" were found spray-painted on the side of the building. The Jordanian ambassador to the United States had previously resided in the apartment and may have been the target. In July, an unknown assailant shot and killed an Israeli diplomat in Washington. The Voice of Palestine in Cairo claimed responsibility, but no forensic evidence linked the crime to any Arab individuals or group. Kameel B. Nasr, *Arab and Israeli Terrorism: The Causes and Effects of Political Violence, 1936–1993* (Jefferson, NC: McFarland & Co., 1996), 64.

42. In October 1970, a bomb went off in the PLO's offices in New York, causing extensive property damage but no fatalities or injuries. An anonymous woman telephoned the United Press International to say the bomb had been planted in retaliation for "Hijack blackmail"—presumably a reference to the Popular Front for the Liberation of Palestine actions of the previous month (see chapter 1). The woman signed off with the words "Never again," a JDL slogan. *New York Times*, October 7, 1970, 1, 9.

43. *Christian Science Monitor*, January 22, 1973, 5; AAUG *Newsletter*, June 1973, 1; AAUG *Newsletter*, August 1973, 7: Hagopian, "Minority Rights," 114.

44. In May 1974, the Department of Justice and the FBI publicly admitted that they had exchanged information about Abdeen Jabara—who had himself come under government scrutiny (see main text below)—with "Jewish, Zionist or Israeli organizations." *Argus Press* (Owosso, MI), May 22, 1974, 16. This revelation, joined to the reasonable supposition that information about other investigative targets had been similarly disseminated, only strengthened the AAUG's conviction that the whole domestic antiterrorism program had been launched at Israel's behest. A more plausible scenario, however, is that U.S. authorities started their investigations for reasons of their own and, having done so, sought help from organizations with a longer track record of monitoring Arabs in America: Israeli spy agencies and American Zionist groups such as the Anti-Defamation League.

45. *New York Times*, October 29, 1972, E4; M. Cherif Bassiouni, "The 'Special Measures' and Some AAUG Public Action," in Bassiouni, *The Civil Rights of Arab-Americans: "The Special Measures,"* (North Dartmouth, MA: Association of Arab-American University Graduates, 1974), 30–32, 34, 47–48; testimonies and affidavits in Jabara Papers, box 10, folder: "Activities—Harassment of Arab-Americans—Testimonials and Miscellaneous, 1972–1974," BHL; Jabara to Mel Wulf, November 27, 1972, Jabara Papers, box 10, folder: "Activities—Harassment of Arab-Americans, 1972–1979, folder #1," BHL.

46. Steve Hollopeter to Jabara, December 8, 1972, Jabara Papers, box 10, folder: "Activities—Harassment of Arab-Americans, 1972–1979, folder #1," BHL; James F. Greene to Jabara, November 9, 1972, quoted in Bassiouni, "Special Measures," 40–41.

47. Jamal Nassar to Jabara, November 8, 1974, Jabara Papers, box 10, folder: "Activities—Harassment of Arab-Americans—Testimonials and Miscellaneous, 1972–1974," BHL; Nurad Farah to Jabara, January 28, 1975, Jabara Papers, box 10, folder: "Activities—Harassment of Arab-Americans—Testimonials and Miscellaneous, 1972–1974," BHL; list and description of FBI visits, n.d. [c. Fall 1974], Jabara Papers, box 13, folder: "Operation Boulder—Correspondence & Miscellaneous," BHL. The INS's abusive treatment of Joseph Shikhani occurred on November 29, 1972, that is, after Greene's November 9 mea culpa (see main text above). But Shikhani did not allege that the INS officers had asked him political questions.

48. Jabara to "Members and Friends," October 24, 1972, quoted in Bassiouni, "Special Measures," 36–37.

49. Bassiouni to Nixon, October 11, 1972, quoted in Bassiouni, "Special Measures," 28; clipping, *Independent-Press-Telegram* (Long Beach, CA), November 8, 1972, Jabara Papers, box 10, folder: "Harassment of Arab-Americans—Press Clippings," BHL; AAUG *Newsletter*, August 1973, 6.

50. *New York Times*, October 29, 1972, E4; clipping, *Militant*, December 15, 1972, Jabara Papers, box 13, folder: "Operation Boulder—Press Clippings, #2," BHL.

51. Jabara, "Operation Arab: The Nixon Administration's Measures in the United States after Munich," in Bassiouni, *Civil Rights*, 8, 13, 14; Jabara to Greene, November 3, 1972, quoted in Bassiouni, "Special Measures," 42.

52. *New York Times*, October 29, 1972, E4. The ad's sponsors included the American Arabic Association of Boston (an offshoot of the Syrian and Lebanese American Federation of the Eastern States), the Antiochian Archdiocese of Toledo, Ohio, and the Washington, DC, chapter of the World Lebanese Cultural Union.

53. Bassiouni, interview with the author, July 15, 2008; David Price, "How the FBI Spied on Edward Said," *CounterPunch*, January 13–15, 2006, http://www.counterpunch.org/2006/01/13/how-the-fbi-spied-on-edward-said/ (accessed August 30, 2015).

54. In 1974, Diab served as president of the Holy Land Fund, a Palestinian charity.

55. Clipping, *National Observer*, November 18, 1972, Jabara Papers, box 10, folder: "Harassment of Arab-Americans—Press Clippings," BHL.

56. Jabara, interview with the author, February 13, 2008; affidavit by Jack A. French, August 27, 1979, American Civil Liberties Union (hereafter ACLU) Records, MC#001, box 1453, folder: "Jabara v. Kelley Privacy Act," Princeton, NJ: Princeton University Library (hereafter PUL). On July 2, 1973, the FBI made another unsuccessful attempt to interview Jabara.

57. Jabara, interview with the author, February 13, 2008; *Washington Post*, February 5, 1975, A2.

58. *Washington Post*, February 5, 1975, A2; *Newsweek*, October 16, 1972, 25; Brief for Plaintiff, U.S. Court of Appeals, Sixth Circuit, No. 80–1391, February 26, 1981, ACLU Records, MC#001, box 1454, folder: "Jabara v. Webster, et al.," PUL, 10; *Detroit Free Press*, October 20, 1972, 7C.

59. Robert B. Oakley to Thomas J. Scotes, October 20, 1972, RG 59, Lot Files, Records Relating to Lebanon, box 1, folder: "DEF-1 General Lebanon 1972," NARA.

60. Price, "How the FBI Spied on Edward Said"; memorandum of conversation, Walid Khalidi, David Korn, et al., November 20, 1972, RG 59, Subject Numeric Files, POL 27 ARAB-ISR, NARA. I am grateful to Paul Chamberlin for sharing this document with me.

61. Bill Anderson, "U.S. Out to Thwart New Terrorism," *Chicago Tribune*, March 16, 1973, 18; *Washington Post*, March 18, 1973, A1, A3.

62. *New York Times*, May 24, 1973, 1, 34.

63. *New York Times*, May 25, 1973, 1, 17; *Newsweek*, June 18, 1973, 32. *Newsweek* was mistaken about the time of the burglary, which occurred in the fall, not the spring, of 1972. *New York Times*, August 18, 1976, 1, 16.

64. AAUG *Newsletter*, June 1973, 1.

65. AAUG *Newsletter*, August 1973, 6–7; AAUG *Newsletter*, October 1973, 7; Jabara, "IRS Proposes to Revoke AAUG Tax Exemption: Another Form of Political Harassment," in Bassiouni, *Civil Rights*, 49–54. The AAUG's tax-exempt status was restored in October 1974. Hassan S. Haddad, presidential address, AAUG annual convention, October 25–27, 1974, AAUG Papers, box 14, folder: "Correspondence President—1974 (Haddad)," Eastern Michigan University Library.

66. Jabara to Mel Wolfe [*sic:* Wulf], December 26, 1972, Jabara Papers, box 3, folder: "Litigation—FBI—Correspondence—1972," BHL; John Shattuck to Jabara, May 2, 1973, Jabara Papers, box 3, folder: "Litigation—FBI—Correspondence—1973," BHL; Jabara to Shattuck, June 7, 1973, Jabara Papers, box 3, "FBI—Correspondence, 1973," BHL.

67. To be sure, by 1970 the FBI had been publicly linked to some notorious abuses of power, including the police killing of the Chicago Black Panther Party leader Fred Hampton in December 1969. But the most significant revelations of FBI misconduct, such as the 1971 exposure of the Bureau's Counter-Intelligence Program (COINTELPRO) and the stories of FBI abuses that broke alongside Watergate, had not yet occurred. Over four decades later, Jabara recalled that news of COINTELPRO did not make much of an impression on him at the time and that it took subsequent revelations, especially those related to Watergate, to alter his view of U.S. officialdom. This is understandable: following the initial, fragmentary exposure of COINTELPRO in the spring of 1971, the program's full dimensions and implications were slow to emerge in national news coverage. Jabara, communication with the author, September 6, 2015; Tim Weiner, *Enemies: A History of the FBI* (New York: Random House, 2012), 293.

68. Jabara, interview with the author, February 13, 2008.

69. AAUG *Newsletter*, June 1974, 1; *Washington Post*, February 5, 1975, A2; *Washington Post*, August 3, 1977, A12; affidavit by Jack A. French, August 27, 1979, ACLU Records, MC#001, box 1453, folder: "Jabara v. Kelley Privacy Act," PUL; "Arab Terrorist Activities: Internal Security—Middle East," February 20, 1975, FBI documents.

70. *New York Times*, July 8, 1979, 15; *New York Times*, November 7, 1982, 28; *Jabara v. Webster*, no. 80–1391, October 21, 1982, http://www.leagle.com/decision?q=1982963691F2d272_1915.xml/JABARA%20v.%20WEBSTER (accessed August 30, 2015); Michael R. Fischbach, "Government Pressure against Arabs in the United States," *Journal of Palestine Studies* 14, no. 3 (Spring 1985): 91–92.

71. See, for example, House Judiciary Committee, *Surveillance: Hearings before the Subcommittee on Courts, Civil Liberties, and the Administration of Justice, February 6, 18, March 4, 18, 21, May 22, June 26, July 25, September 8, 1975* (Washington, DC: U.S. Government Printing Office, 1975), 105–23, 136–37; House Judiciary Committee, *Foreign Intelligence Surveillance Act: Hearings before the Subcommittee on Courts, Civil Liberties, and the Administration of Justice, April 12, May 5, June 2, 1976* (Washington, DC: U.S. Government Printing Office, 1976), 37–51.

72. Charlie Savage, *Power Wars: Inside Obama's Post-9/11 Presidency* (Boston: Little, Brown and Company, 2015), 170–223, 555–626.

4. Rumors of War—and War

1. Donald Neff, *Warriors Against Israel* (Brattleboro, VT: Amana Books, 1988), 124–25, 141–53, 156–70, 173–88.

2. Memorandum of conversation, Edward Heath, Richard M. Nixon, et al., February 2, 1973, Prime Minister's Office Records 15/1764, The National Archives, Kew, London, United Kingdom (hereafter TNA); Richard M. Nixon, *The Memoirs of Richard Nixon* (New York: Grosset & Dunlap, 1978), 786–87.

3. Telephone conversation, Henry A. Kissinger and Joseph Sisco, February 22, 1973, Henry A. Kissinger Telephone Conversations, Chronological File (hereafter HAK/Telcons), box 18, folder: "1973 22–26 Feb," Richard M. Nixon Presidential Library, Yorba Linda, CA (hereafter NL); Kissinger to Nixon, February 23, 1973, U.S. Department of State, *Foreign Relations of the United States* (hereafter *FRUS*, with dates and volume number), *1969–1976*, 25:70, 70, note 3, 71, note 7.

4. Memorandum of conversation, Nixon, Hafiz Ismail, et al., February 23, 1973, *FRUS, 1969–1976*, 25:72–78; memorandum of conversation, Kissinger and Ismail, February 26, 1973, Henry A. Kissinger Office Files, Country Files, Middle East (hereafter HAK/ME), box 130, folder: "Saunders Memoranda—Sensitive Egypt/Hafez Ismail (1 of 2)," NL, 1, 3, 6, 9, 10; Harold Saunders to Kissinger, February 21, HAK/ME, box 130, folder: "Saunders Memoranda—Sensitive Egypt/Hafez Ismail (1 of 2)," NL, 2; Henry A. Kissinger, *Years of Upheaval* (Boston: Little, Brown and Company, 1982), 212–16; Muhammad Hasanayn Haykal, *Uktubir 73: Al-silah wa-al-siayasa* [October '73: Arms and politics] (Cairo: Markaz al-Ahram lil-tarjimah wa-al-nashr, 1993), 272–79.

5. Anwar Sadat, *In Search of Identity: An Autobiography* (New York: Harper & Row, 1978), 238, 288; Haykal, *Uktubir 73*, 280.

6. Craig Daigle, *The Limits of Détente: The United States, the Soviet Union, and the Arab-Israeli Conflict, 1969–1973* (New Haven, CT: Yale University Press, 2012), 259; Kissinger, *Years of Upheaval*, 222; Haykal, *The Road to Ramadan* (New York: Quadrangle, 1975), 203.

7. Kim McQuaid, *The Anxious Years: America in the Vietnam-Watergate Era* (New York: Basic Books, 1989), 191–200; Stanley I. Kutler, *The Wars of Watergate: The Last Crisis of Richard Nixon* (New York: Alfred A. Knopf, 1990), 274–89; Stephen E. Ambrose, *Nixon*, vol. 3, *Ruin and Recovery* (New York: Simon & Schuster, 1991), 66–94.

8. Kissinger, *Years of Upheaval*, 78.

9. "Excerpts from President Sadat's Speech," March 26, 1973, National Security Council Files, Harold H. Saunders Files, Middle East Negotiations Files (hereafter Saunders Files), box 1171, folder: "Middle East—Jarring Talks—March 1–31, 1973 (1 of 2)," NL, 7; *Newsweek*, April 9, 1973, 44–45, 49.

10. Unabridged transcript of Sadat's *Newsweek* interview, March 29, 1973, appended to Richard T. Kennedy to Brent Scowcroft, March 31, 1973, Saunders Files, box 1171, folder: "Middle East—Jarring Talks—March 1–31, 1973 (2 of 2)," NL. Sadat's reference to direct talks with Israel was omitted from the published version of the interview.

11. U.S. Interests Section, Cairo, to Department of State (hereafter DOS), #0998, April 4, 1973, Central Foreign Policy Files, Electronic Telegrams, Access to Archival Databases (hereafter AAD), 1973CAIRO00998, National Archives and Records Administration, College Park, MD (hereafter

NARA); DOS to White House et al., tel #092092, May 15, 1973, AAD, 1973STATE092092, NARA; Kissinger to Nixon, April 26, 1973, Saunders Files, box 1171, folder: "Middle East—Jarring Talks—April 1–30, 1973 (2 of 2)," NL.

12. Although Jordan, too, aspired to reclaim lost territory, it was not a credible partner in an inter-Arab military coalition. The crippling economic and territorial losses Jordan had suffered in 1967 left it unready for war, and King Hussein was a well-known skeptic regarding the military option. Jordan also remained diplomatically isolated in the Arab world on account of its violent expulsion of the Palestine Liberation Organization in 1970–1971. Nigel J. Ashton, *King Hussein of Jordan: A Political Life* (New Haven, CT: Yale University Press, 2008), 170.

13. Sadat, *In Search of Identity*, 241; Moshe Ma'oz, *Asad, the Sphinx of Damascus: A Political Biography* (London: Weidenfeld and Nicolson, 1988), 86–88.

14. Yoram Meital, *Egypt's Struggle for Peace, 1967–1977* (Gainesville: University Press of Florida, 1997), 115; Patrick Seale, *Asad of Syria: The Struggle for the Middle East* (Berkeley: University of California Press, 1988), 196–97.

15. Saad Shazly, *The Crossing of the Suez* (San Francisco: American Mideast Research, 1980), 36–37. Shazly wrote that only under "the most favorable conditions," such as a major Israeli retreat in the Sinai—a remote possibility—would the second phase of the Egyptian military plan go into effect. Ibid., 37.

16. Neff, *Warriors*, 108–9; *Time*, February 12, 1973, 28–29.

17. David Korn, *Assassination in Khartoum* (Bloomington: Indiana University Press, 1993), 6–9, 22–23, 30–33, 104, 129, 202.

18. Korn, *Assassination*, 49–50, 102–3, 110–21, 133–34.

19. Korn, *Assassination*, 148–51, 226; Michael Sterner, interview with the author, July 20, 2010. Several hours before Nixon's press conference, the Jordanian government announced over its official radio station that it would "accept no bargaining with these criminals" in Khartoum. Evidently, though, the Black September operatives regarded Jordan's King Hussein as an American puppet and remained convinced that Nixon could order the king to release the Palestinian prisoners. Thus Nixon's public rejection of Black September's demands appears to have been far more consequential than that of the Jordanian government. Korn, *Assassination*, 138–39, 152.

20. Korn, *Assassination*, 168–80.

21. U.S. Embassy, New Delhi, to DOS, tel #3040, March 16, 1973, AAD, 1973NEWDE03040, NARA. The U.S. government did know the whereabouts of Salah Khalaf, who continued to operate openly in Beirut (see main text below).

22. U.S. Embassy, Rabat, to DOS, tel #01390, March 29, 1973, Record Group 59 (hereafter RG 59), Subject Numeric Files, 1970–73 (hereafter SNF), POL 13–10 Arab, box 2046, NARA; DOS to U.S. Interests Section, Cairo, tel #056953, March 28, 1973, enclosing U.S. Embassy, Sanaa, to DOS, tel #488, March 26, 1973, SNF, 1970–73, POL 23–8, box 1987, NARA. I am grateful to Paul Chamberlin for sharing these documents with me.

23. DOS to U.S. Interests Section, Algiers, et al., tel #042486, March 8, 1973, National Security Council Files, Country Files, Middle East (hereafter NSC/ME), box 666, folder: "Middle East (Fedayeen) Black September Group (9/72–3/73)," NL.

24. U.S. Embassy, Beirut, to DOS, tel #02967, March 14, 1973, #03245, March 21, 1973, NSC/ME, box 621, folder: "Lebanon Vol III Jan 71–Oct 73 (2 of 3)," NL.

25. *Newsweek*, April 23, 1973, 35–36; *Time*, April 23, 1973, 19–20; Farid el Khazen, *The Breakdown of the State in Lebanon, 1967–1976* (Cambridge, MA: Harvard University Press, 2000), 203–4; Mark Ensalaco, *Middle Eastern Terrorism: From Black September to September 11* (Philadelphia: University of Pennsylvania Press, 2008), 53–54.

26. U.S. Embassy, Beirut, to DOS, tel #04172, April 10, 1973, AAD, 1973BEIRUT04172, NARA.

27. DOS to U.S. Interests Section, Cairo, tel #070305, April 14, 1973, quoting U.S. Embassy, Beirut, to DOS, tel #04352, April 10, 1973, AAD, 1973STATE070305, NARA; *Time*, April 23, 1973, 20; el Khazen, *Breakdown*, 205; Kamal S. Salibi, *Crossroads to Civil War: Lebanon, 1958–1976* (Delmar, NY: Caravan Books, 1976), 66–67.

28. U.S. Embassy, Beirut, to DOS, tel #04974, April 30, 1973, AAD, 1973BEIRUT04974, NARA; *Newsweek*, April 23, 1973, 35; *Time*, April 23, 1973, 23; *Time*, May 14, 1973, 40; el Khazen, *Breakdown*, 206–7; Salibi, *Crossroads*, 67–68.

29. *Time*, May 21, 1973, 43; el Khazen, *Breakdown*, 207–8.

30. U.S. Embassy, Beirut, to DOS, tel #05205, May 8, 1973, AAD, 1973BEIRUT05205, NARA; el Khazen, *Breakdown*, 208–11; *Time*, May 28, 1973, 43.

31. U.S. Embassy, Beirut, to DOS, tels #05205, #05251, and #05437, May 8, 9, and 12, 1973, AAD, 1973BEIRUT05205, 1973BEIRUT05251, 1973BEIRUT05437, NARA.

32. Salibi, *Crossroads*, 69–70.

33. Daniel Yergin, *The Prize: The Epic Quest for Oil, Money, and Power* (New York: Simon & Schuster, 1991), 589–91; James E. Akins, "The Oil Crisis: This Time the Wolf Is Here," *Foreign Affairs* 51, no. 3 (April 1973): 464–69; *Time*, April 2, 1973, 23; *New York Times*, April 19, 1973, 53.

34. See, for example, M[orris] A. Adelman, "Is the Oil Shortage Real?: Oil Companies as OPEC Tax Collectors," *Foreign Policy* 9 (Winter 1972–1973): 80–82, 91. Adelman's *Foreign Policy* article, which preceded Akins's *Foreign Affairs* article, criticized earlier expressions of the Akins thesis.

35. *New York Times*, May 16, 1973, 6.

36. Yergin, *Prize*, 594–95.

37. Memorandum of conversation, Kissinger, Zaki Yamani, et al., April 17, 1973, NSC/ME, box 630, folder: "Saudi Arabia Vol IV May 1973–December 31, 1973 (2 of 4)," NL, 1, 2, 5.

38. U.S. Senate Foreign Relations Committee, *Hearings before the Subcommittee on Multinational Corporations, February 20, 21, March 27, 28, 1974*, part 7 (Washington, DC: U.S. Government Printing Office, 1974), Exhibit 7, 504, 506.

39. Ibid., Exhibit 8, 509.

40. DOS to U.S. Embassy, Bogota, et al., tel #096585, May 19, 1973, AAD, 1973STATE096585, NARA; telephone conversation, Kissinger and Kenneth Rush, May 29, 1973, HAK/Telcons, box 20, folder: "1973 16–30 May," NL.

41. Josip Broz Tito to Nixon, January 18, 1973, RG 59, SNF, POL 15–1, U.S.-Nixon, box 2712, NARA; Nixon to Tito, May 1, 1973, RG 59, SNF, POL 15–1, U.S.-Nixon, box 2712, NARA; Giovanni Leone to Nixon, n.d. [c. February 1973], Saunders Files, box 1171, folder: "Middle East—Jarring Talks—February 1–28, 1973 (1 of 4)," NL; Nixon to Leone, March 22, 1973, Saunders Files, box 1171, folder: "Middle East—Jarring Talks—March 1–31, 1973 (2 of 2)," NL; Kissinger to Nixon, April 26, 1973, Saunders Files, box 1171, folder: "Middle East—Jarring Talks—April 1–30, 1973 (2 of 2)," NL; memorandum of conversation, Nixon, Haile Salassie, et al., May 15, 1973, NSC Files, Presidential/HAK Memcons, box 1027, folder: "Memcons April–Nov 1973 HAK + Presidential (5 of 5)," NL; Geraint Hughes, "Britain, the Transatlantic Alliance, and the Arab-Israeli War of 1973," *Journal of Cold War Studies* 10, no. 2 (Spring 2008): 16.

42. Kissinger, *Years of Upheaval*, 297–98; memorandum of conversation, Nixon, Leonid Brezhnev, et al., June 23, 1973, *FRUS, 1969–1976*, 25:220–22.

43. Memorandum of conversation, Nixon, Brezhnev, et al., June 23, 1973, *FRUS, 1969–1976*, 25:222, 224.

44. McQuaid, *Anxious Years*, 207–30.

45. J[ohn] C. Moberly to A[nthony] D. Parsons, June 21, 1973, Foreign and Commonwealth Office 93/231, TNA; memorandum of conversation, Kissinger, Abba Eban, and Simcha Dinitz,

August 17, 1973, Digital National Security Archive, George Washington University, Washington, DC (hereafter DNSA), KT00797, 6, 7.

46. *Washington Post*, July 31, 1973, A11; Mahmoud Riad, *The Struggle for Peace in the Middle East* (London: Quartet Books, 1981), 238.

47. U.S. Embassy, Buenos Aires, to DOS, tel #3762, May 26, 1973, Saunders Files, box 1172, folder: "Middle East—Jarring Talks—May 1–31, 1973 (2 of 3)," NL; *Washington Post*, July 31, 1973, A11.

48. *New York Times*, June 21, 1973, 30 (italics in original); Otto Miller to stockholders, July 26, 1973, reprinted in *News Circle*, September 1973, 3; clipping, *Jewish Telegraphic Agency*, August 6, 1973, Jabara Papers, box 12, folder: "Activities—NAAA Membership Guidelines," Bentley Historical Library, University of Michigan, Ann Arbor, MI (hereafter BHL).

49. *Link*, January/February 1974, 3–5; clippings, *Jewish Telegraphic Agency*, August 6 and 7, 1973, Jabara Papers, box 12, folder: "Activities—NAAA Membership Guidelines," BHL; memorandum of conversation, Kissinger, Eban, and Dinitz, August 17, 1973, DNSA, KT00797, 6.

50. Peter S. Tanous to Miller, August 9, 1973, Jabara Papers, box 12, folder: "Activities—NAAA Correspondence, 1973–1974," BHL; *New Lebanese American Journal*, July 12, 1973, 4. See also *News Circle*, September 1973, 3.

51. AAUG *Newsletter*, October 1973, 6.

52. *New Lebanese American Journal*, August 16, 1973, 4; *ANERA Newsletter*, July–October 1973, 1.

53. James G. Abourezk, *Advise and Dissent: Memoirs of South Dakota and the U.S. Senate* (Chicago: Lawrence Hill Books, 1989), 179, 192–93.

54. Abourezk, *Advise and Dissent*, 179.

55. Yergin, *Prize*, 597; Haykal, *Road to Ramadan*, 268; *Newsweek*, September 10, 1973, 35.

56. Sadat and Asad worried that, once the war was under way, Israel would cross Jordanian territory to mount a counterattack on Syrian forces in the Golan. Without divulging their own intentions (and instead suggesting that Israel itself might break the cease-fire), they got Hussein to agree to deploy forces in northern Jordan to block an Israeli incursion. The Insight Team of the London *Sunday Times*, *The Yom Kippur War* (Garden City, NY: Doubleday, 1974), 86–88; Ashton, *Hussein*, 171.

57. Haykal, *Uktubir 73*, 308–10; Insight Team, *Yom Kippur War*, 88; Seale, *Asad*, 194.

58. Ashton, *Hussein*, 172; Kissinger, *Years of Upheaval*, 459–63.

59. Ashton, *Hussein*, 172–73; David Elazar quoted in Abraham Rabinovich, *The Yom Kippur War: The Epic Encounter that Transformed the Middle East* (New York: Schocken Books, 2004), 49–53.

60. Walter Isaacson, *Kissinger: A Biography* (New York: Simon & Schuster, 1992), 505. From 1969 to 1971, the FBI, with Kissinger's encouragement, tapped the phones of several journalists and government officials suspected of disseminating classified information. Ibid., 212–27.

61. President's news conference, September 5, 1973, *PPP*, 1973, 735; memorandum of conversation, Kissinger, Dinitz, et al., September 10, 1973, *FRUS, 1969–1976*, 25:265; memorandum of conversation, Kissinger, Laureano López Rodó, et al., October 4, 1973, NSC Files, Presidential/HAK Memcons, box 1027, folder: "Memcons—April–Nov 1973 HAK & Presidential (2 of 5)," NL.

62. Neff, *Warriors*, 141–53, 156–70, 173–88; Benny Morris, *Righteous Victims: A History of Zionist-Arab Conflict, 1881–1999* (New York: Alfred A. Knopf, 1999), 400–407, 411–19; Seale, *Asad*, 202–7.

63. *Christian Science Monitor*, October 12, 8; Ahmad 'Abd al-Karim, *Yawmiyat diblumasi 'Arabi: Ghadat Harb Hizayran 1967 wa tada'iyat Harb Tishrin 1973* [Chronicles of an Arab diplomat: The day after the June 1967 War and the fallout from the October 1973 War] (Beirut: Bisan lil-nashr wa-al-tawzi' wa-al-i'lam, 2006), 313; *Daily Star* (Beirut), October 10, 1973, 4; *Daily Star* (Beirut), October 12, 1973, 4; *al-Nahar* (Beirut), October 12, 1973, 8.

64. Neff, *Warriors*, 190–97; Morris, *Righteous Victims*, 415–20; Kissinger, *Years of Upheaval*, 488–95.

65. Kissinger, *Years of Upheaval*, 202; telephone conversation, Kissinger and Alexander Haig, October 7, 1973, *FRUS, 1969–1976*, 25:343; telephone conversation, Nixon and Kissinger, October 8, 1973, *FRUS, 1969–1976*, 25:389.

66. Richard Valeriani, *Travels With Henry* (Boston: Houghton Mifflin, 1979), 32; see also *Newsweek*, November 5, 1973, 42.

67. Kissinger, *Years of Upheaval*, 495–503, 507–15, 525; Morris, *Righteous Victims*, 433–34.

68. Morris, *Righteous Victims*, 407–10, 419–31; Haykal, *Road to Ramadan*, 214–30; Seale, *Asad*, 207–14; Victor Israelyan, *Inside the Kremlin during the Yom Kippur War* (University Park: Pennsylvania State University Press, 1995), 71–72.

69. Yergin, *Prize*, 600–601, 604–5; *Washington Post*, October 10, 1973, A7; U.S. Embassy, Kuwait, to DOS, tel #03765, October 15, 1973, AAD, 1973KUWAIT03765, NARA; William Rugh, *Arab Perceptions of American Foreign Policy during the October War* (Washington, DC: Middle East Institute, 1976), 16–24.

70. Memorandum of conversation, Nixon, Kissinger, Omar Saqqaf, et al., October 17, 1973, *FRUS, 1969–1976*, 25:565–71; *New York Times*, October 18, 1973, 1, 18.

71. Washington Special Action Group (WSAG) meeting, October 17, 1973, *FRUS, 1969–1976*, 25:577–78, 583–84.

72. Yergin, *Prize*, 608–9, 613; *Washington Post*, October 22, 1973, A9; *Newsweek*, October 29, 1973, 85.

73. Yergin, *Prize*, 605–6, 615.

74. Hasia R. Diner, *The Jews of the United States* (Berkeley: University of California Press, 2004), 323; *Newsweek*, October 22, 1973, 99; *Time*, October 29, 1973, 55–56; "The Israeli Lobby: Instant Votes When Needed," *Congressional Quarterly*, October 27, 1973, 2858.

75. "Projections from the conservative available figures," the AAUG *Newsletter* stated, "show that the protests during the eight-week period after Oct. 6 may have involved as many as 120 campuses and the top 70 metropolitan areas bringing about 150,000 persons to some 300 protest rallies." The newsletter did not explain the methodology underlying these extrapolations. AAUG *Newsletter*, December 1973, 1.

76. AAUG *Newsletter*, December 1973, 1; *News Circle*, November 1973, 5; *Chicago Tribune*, October 9, 1973, 2; Mike Kelly, "3,000 Arabs Protest U.S.-Israeli Terror," *Militant*, October 26, 1973, page number not shown, Dan Georgakas Papers, box 2, folder: "Detroit Arabian Community; Protests Against Israeli Aid, 1973," Walter P. Reuther Library, Wayne State University Archives, Detroit, MI.

77. On October 7, Kissinger spoke by phone with New York Mayor John Lindsay, who reported on the pro-Israeli and pro-Arab demonstrations occurring that day near UN headquarters (see main text below). Lindsay said the situation was under control but joked that he would bill the State Department for police overtime. Telephone conversation, Kissinger and Lindsay, October 7, 1973, Kissinger, *Crisis: The Anatomy of Two Major Foreign Policy Crises* (New York: Simon & Schuster, 2003), 107. This is the only recorded instance in which pro-Arab activism intruded on Kissinger's October War deliberations. Even on this occasion, Kissinger's attention was on pro-Israeli demonstrators: his call to Lindsay was occasioned by a report that some of them were physically menacing Egypt's diplomatic mission in New York. WSAG meeting, October 7, 1973, *FRUS, 1969–1976*, 25:354.

78. *New York Times*, October 8, 1973, 1, 17; *Chicago Tribune*, October 9, 1973, 2.

79. AAUG *Newsletter*, December 1973, 10–11; *News Circle*, November 1973, 1; *Los Angeles Times*, October 15, 1973, 3; Ishmael Ahmed, "Organizing an Arab Workers Caucus," *MERIP Reports* 34 (January 1975): 19.

80. Kelly, "3,000 Arabs Protest."

81. AAUG *Newsletter*, December 1973, 10–11; *Washington Post*, October 20, 1973, A29; *Los Angeles Times*, October 22, 1973, 3B; *New York Times*, October 15, 1973, 17.

82. *New York Times*, October 8, 1973, 17; *New York Times*, October 15, 1973, 17; AAUG *Newsletter*, December 1973, 10.

83. *Daily Star* (Beirut), October 17, 1973, 5; *Daily Star* (Beirut), October 18, 1973, 5; *Middle East Newsletter*, Summer/Fall 1973, 15.

84. *Los Angeles Times*, October 15, 1973, 3; *News Circle*, November 1973, 12.

85. AAUG *Newsletter*, December 1973, 3; *Time*, October 29, 1973, 55; Kelly, "3,000 Arabs Protest"; *Detroit News*, October 10, 1973, 8A.

86. *Newsweek*, October 29, 1973, 55–56; *Chicago Tribune*, October 9, 1973, 2; *Washington Post*, October 20, 1973, A29.

87. Haykal, *Road to Ramadan*, 230–40; Kissinger, *Years of Upheaval*, 538–44.

88. Kissinger, *Years of Upheaval*, 550–52; Scowcroft to Kissinger, October 20, 1973, *FRUS, 1969–1976*, 25:628; Kissinger to Scowcroft, October 21, 1973, *FRUS, 1969–1976*, 25:632.

89. Kissinger, *Years of Upheaval*, 552; Ambrose, *Nixon*, 3:247–53, 260.

90. Kissinger, *Years of Upheaval*, 552–55, 1246–47.

91. Rabinovich, *Yom Kippur War*, 454–56, 464–65.

92. Kissinger acknowledged in his memoirs that, during his short stop in Israel, "I had indicated that I would understand if there was a few hours' 'slippage' in the cease-fire deadline while I was flying home" so that Israel could improve its position on the ground. Kissinger, *Years of Upheaval*, 569.

93. Walter J. Boyne, *The Two O'Clock War: The 1973 Yom Kippur Conflict and the Airlift that Saved Israel* (New York: St. Martin's Press, 2002), 238–44.

94. Brezhnev to Nixon, n.d. [received October 24, 1973], *FRUS, 1969–1976*, 25:735; Boyne, *Two O'Clock War*, 250–53.

95. Telephone conversation, Nixon and Kissinger, October 24, 1973, DNSA KA11402, 2; Kissinger, *Years of Upheaval*, 581, 585.

96. The evident basis for this statement was the fact that the U.S. government had no reliable information about major military actions taking place *at that moment*. As his memoirs make clear, however, Kissinger had no doubt that Israel had massively violated the cease-fire over the previous two days, and it was now common knowledge that Israeli forces were surrounding the Egyptian Third Army and preventing food, water, and medicine from reaching the troops. Kissinger, *Years of Upheaval*, 568–75.

97. Nixon to Brezhnev, October 25, 1973, *FRUS, 1969–1976*, 25:747–49; Kissinger, *Years of Upheaval*, 586–91.

98. Boyne, *Two O'Clock War*, 256–59; Neff, *Warriors Against Israel*, 287–89.

99. Kissinger, *Years of Upheaval*, 601–11; Morris, *Righteous Victims*, 431.

100. Mark Riyashi, "Nasr min Allah" [A victory from God], *al-Nahar* (Beirut), October 12, 1973, 3.

5. Scuttle Diplomacy

1. *New York Times*, May 14, 1974, 1–2.

2. *New York Times*, May 12, 1974, 1, 40; *New York Times*, May 14, 1974, 1–2; *New York Times*, May 15, 1974, 10. For the erroneous "Jew boys" quotation, see Leonard Garment, *Crazy Rhythm:*

From Brooklyn and Jazz to Nixon's White House (Cambridge, MA: De Capo Press, 2001), 200–201; Roger Mudd, *The Place to Be: Washington, CBS, and the Glory Days of Television News* (New York: PublicAffairs, 2008), 315–16.

3. Memorandum of conversation, Henry A. Kissinger, 'Abd al-Halim Khaddam, et al., May 14, 1974, Digital National Security Archive, George Washington University, Washington, DC (hereafter DNSA), KT01163.

4. The Kilometer 101 talks (see previous chapter) were the sole exception to this rule. They dealt only with military logistics and ended in early 1974.

5. The nine member states were Belgium, Britain, Denmark, France, Holland, Ireland, Italy, Luxembourg, and West Germany.

6. Daniel Möckli, *European Foreign Policy during the Cold War: Heath, Brandt, Pompidou and the Short Dream of Political Unity* (London: I.B. Tauris, 2009), 204; *Washington Post*, November 7, 1973, A26; *Christian Science Monitor*, November 9, 1973, 4; *Los Angeles Times*, November 10, 1973, A4; George W. Ball, "The Chill Realities of Mideast Peace," *Newsweek*, November 5, 1973, 59.

7. Henry A. Kissinger, *Years of Upheaval* (Boston: Little, Brown and Company, 1982), 615.

8. Memorandum of conversation, Gerald R. Ford, Kissinger, and Brent Scowcroft, August 12, 1974, U.S. Department of State, *Foreign Relations of the United States* (hereafter *FRUS*, with dates and volume number), *1969–1976*, 26:403; memorandum of conversation, Kissinger, Yigal Allon, et al., August 1, 1974, *FRUS, 1969–1976*, 26:403, 396.

9. Memorandum of conversation, Ford, Kissinger, et al., September 6, 1974, National Security Adviser, Memoranda of Conversation, 1973–1977 (hereafter NSA Memcons), box 5, Gerald R. Ford Library, Ann Arbor, MI (hereafter FL); Henry A. Kissinger, *Years of Renewal* (New York: Simon & Schuster, 1999), 428. Although Kissinger and his immediate family escaped Nazi Germany in 1938, thirteen members of his extended family later perished in the death camps.

10. Memorandum of conversation, Kissinger, Eban, et al., November 21, 1973, DNSA, KT00918, 2; memorandum of conversation, Kissinger, Golda Meir, Simcha Dinitz, and Peter W. Rodman, December 16, 1973, DNSA, KT00958, 1, 4; memorandum of conversation, Kissinger, Meir, et al., February 27, 1974, DNSA, KT01042, 20.

11. Kissinger, *Years of Upheaval*, 768.

12. Memorandum of conversation, Kissinger, Alec Douglas-Home, et al., December 12, 1973, FCO 82/309 (included in DNSA, KT00948), 11; Kissinger, *Years of Upheaval*, 554, 1247.

13. Kissinger, *Years of Upheaval*, 755.

14. Ibid., 766–70, 782–87, 789–91; William B. Quandt, *Peace Process: American Diplomacy and the Arab-Israeli Conflict since 1967* (Berkeley: University of California Press, 2001), 138–40; Muhammad Hasanayn Haykal, *Uktubir 73: Al-silah wa-al-siayasa* [October '73: Arms and politics] (Cairo: Markaz al-Ahram lil-tarjimah wa-al-nashr, 1993), 727–28; Patrick Seale, *Asad of Syria: The Struggle for the Middle East* (Berkeley: University of California Press, 1988), 226–34.

15. Quandt, *Peace Process*, 140–41; Kissinger, *Years of Upheaval*, 795–98; *New York Times*, December 22, 1973, 9.

16. Daniel Yergin, *The Prize: The Epic Quest for Oil, Money, and Power* (New York: Simon & Schuster, 1991), 613–14, 625; *Christian Science Monitor*, November 9, 1973, 4; *Time*, November 12, 1973, 64.

17. Yergin, *Prize*, 616–17; *Newsweek*, November 12, 1973, 91–92; *Newsweek*, November 19, 1973, 110–11; *Newsweek*, December 31, 1973, 27–28; *Newsweek*, February 18, 1974, 22; *Los Angeles Times*, December 7, 1973, 2; *New York Times*, January 4, 1974, 14; *New York Times*, January 5, 1974, 1, 40; *Chicago Tribune*, February 2, 1974, S1; *Washington Post*, December 25, 1973, C1–C2; *Washington Post*, February 21, 1974, A11.

18. *Gallup Opinion Index*, report no. 104 (February 1974): 4.

19. William F. Buckley, Jr., "And What Has Europe Done for America Lately?" *Los Angeles Times*, November 15, 1973, B7; *New York Times*, November 19, 1973, 4.

20. *Wall Street Journal*, November 6, 1973, 22; editorial, *Chicago Tribune*, November 21, 1973, 10; William Raspberry, "Blackmail—or Diplomacy?" *Washington Post*, November 23, 1973, A31; *Newsweek*, November 26, 1973, 41–42.

21. *Los Angeles Times*, November 20, 1973, A7; *Washington Post*, November 28, 1973, A21; Secretary's Staff Meeting, November 26, 1973, DNSA KT00924, 9; memorandum of conversation, Kissinger, King Faisal, et al., November 8, 1973, DNSA KT00894, 10; *Newsweek*, December 3, 1973, 51–52; Haykal, *Uktubir 73*, 689.

22. Jack Forsyth, "Arab Oil and the 'Zionist Connection,'" *Link*, January/February 1974, 6; *Chicago Tribune*, December 7, 1973, A6; *Los Angeles Times*, December 7, 1973, A7. For evidence of Elmer Berger's authorship of the "More in Sorrow" advertisement, see Berger to Bernice [Espy] Hicks, November 10, 1973, American Jewish Alternatives to Zionism Papers, reel #6, Hoover Institution Library and Archives, Stanford, CA; Berger to Frank Maria, February 4, 1974, Maria Papers, box 90, folder 1, Immigration History Research Center, University of Minnesota, Minneapolis, MN (hereafter IHRC).

23. AAUG *Newsletter*, December 1973, 1; Fayez Sayegh to Ezzedine [Shamsedin], January 31, 1974, Sayegh Papers, box 188, folder 6, University of Utah Library (hereafter UUL), (italics in original); *Chicago Tribune*, November 26, 1973, A3.

24. See, for example, clipping, *Congressional Record*, November 9, 1973, James G. Abourezk Papers, box 59, folder: "107 Detente and the Middle East 11/9/73," University of South Dakota Library, Vermillion, SD (hereafter USDL); clipping, *Sioux Falls Argus-Leader*, October 25, 1973, AAUG Twin Cities Chapter Papers, box 1, folder: "Archives," IHRC, page number not shown; *Chicago Tribune*, November 26, 1973, A3.

25. Clipping, *International Bulletin*, January 28–February 10, 1974, 1, Abourezk Papers, box 651, folder: "Mid East, General Information," USDL. Abourezk visited Lebanon, Syria, Iraq, Kuwait, the United Arab Emirates, Saudi Arabia, Egypt, Jordan, and Israel. James G. Abourezk, *Advise and Dissent: Memoirs of South Dakota and the U.S. Senate* (Chicago: Lawrence Hill Books, 1989), 180.

26. Abourezk, interview with the author, December 19, 2007.

27. Clipping, *St. Paul Pioneer Press*, January 16, 1974, 1–2, Abourezk Papers, box 689, folder: "Egerstrom, Lee, articles—Middle East Trip, 12/26/73 to 1/15/74," USDL. After the conclusion of the Syrian-Israeli disengagement agreement in late May (see main text below), 382 Syrian POWs and 56 Israeli ones were returned home. *Los Angeles Times*, June 6, 1974, 2.

28. Kissinger, *Years of Upheaval*, 809–11, 818, 821–38, 844–45; memorandum of conversation, Kissinger, Meir, et al., January 15, 1974, DNSA, KT00996, 1 (brackets in source text).

29. Memorandum of conversation, Kissinger, Douglas-Home, et al., January 20, 1974, DNSA, KT01006, 14; telephone conversation, Kissinger and Alfred L. Atherton, November 17, 1973, DNSA, KA11612; Richard Valeriani, *Travels With Henry* (Boston: Houghton Mifflin, 1979), 263–64.

30. Valeriani, *Travels With Henry*, 72; caption in photographs section, Valeriani, *Travels With Henry*, n.p.; Kissinger, *Years of Upheaval*, 818; memorandum of conversation, Kissinger, King Hussein, et al., November 8, 1973, DNSA KT00893, 6; *Washington Post*, May 31, 1974, A20; Public Broadcasting System, television documentary, "The 50 Years War: Israel and the Arabs," 1999.

31. Memorandum of conversation, Kissinger, Meir, et al., May 2, 1974, Record Group 59, Records of Henry Kissinger, 1973–77, box 7, folder: "Nodis Memcons, Mar 1974, folder 3" (misfiled), National Archives and Record Administration, College Park, MD (hereafter NARA), 7.

32. Valeriani, *Travels With Henry*, 191–92; memorandum of conversation, Kissinger, Khaddam, et al., May 20, 1974, DNSA, KT01179, 3.

33. *Los Angeles Times*, January 10, 1974, 1, 6, 7; *Chicago Tribune*, April 2, 1974, 1, 15; *Chicago Tribune*, April 3, 1974, 1, 23; editorial, *Wall Street Journal*, May 8, 1974, 20; *Newsweek*, February 18, 1974, 41.

34. Memorandum of conversation, Kissinger, Meir, et al., February 27, 1974, DNSA, KT01042, 9, 15, 30.

35. Ibid., 26.

36. Ibid., 20; memorandum of conversation, Kissinger, Meir, et al., February 27, 1974, DNSA, KT01041, 6.

37. Kissinger, *Years of Upheaval*, 972–73; Quandt, *Peace Process*, 145; memorandum of conversation, Kissinger, Hafiz al-Asad, et al., March 1, 1974, DNSA, KT01047, 11–13, 19–21, 26.

38. Kissinger, *Years of Upheaval*, 892–95; Quandt, *Peace Process*, 143–44, 147; Seale, *Asad*, 240–41; Yergin, *Prize*, 630–32.

39. Kissinger, *Years of Upheaval*, 936, 1042–47; Valeriani, *Travels With Henry*, 217.

40. Memorandum of conversation, Kissinger, Meir, and Rodman, May 6, 1974, *FRUS, 1969–1976*, 26:227; memorandum of conversation, Kissinger, Khaddam, et al., May 16, 1974, DNSA, KT01169, 5; memorandum of conversation, Kissinger, Faisal, et al., May 9, 1974, DNSA, KT01154, 3.

41. Roham Alvandi, *Nixon, Kissinger, and the Shah: The United States and Iran in the Cold War* (New York: Oxford University Press, 2014), 65–91; Abraham Rabinovich, *The Yom Kippur War: The Epic Encounter that Transformed the Middle East* (New York: Schocken Books, 2004), 307–18; memorandum of conversation, Kissinger, Dinitz, and Rodman, March 21, 1974, DNSA, KT01078, 6.

42. The disengagement agreement committed Israel to withdraw from the Syrian territory seized in the October War and from Quneitra; established a UN buffer zone that generally coincided with the October 6 line but bulged westward to place Quneitra on the Syrian side; imposed force limitations on either side of the disengagement line; provided for a POW exchange; and ended a war of attrition that the two countries had waged over the previous several weeks. Quandt, *Peace Process*, 152.

43. *Newsweek*, June 10, 1974, cover; Kissinger, *Years of Upheaval*, 1125–28; Steven L. Spiegel, *The Other Arab-Israeli Conflict: Making America's Middle East Policy, from Truman to Reagan* (Chicago: University of Chicago Press, 1985), 280–83; Stephen E. Ambrose, *Nixon*, vol. 3, *Ruin and Recovery* (New York: Simon & Schuster, 1991), 394–405, 409–17.

44. Memorandum of conversation, Kissinger, Sabah Qabbani, et al., August 8, 1974, National Security Council Files, Presidential/HAK Memcons, box 1029, folder: "Memcons 1 June 1974–8 Aug 1974 HAK & Presidential (1 of 3)," Richard M. Nixon Presidential Library, Yorba Linda, CA.

45. Alan Hart, *Arafat: Terrorist or Peacemaker?* (London: Sidgwick & Jackson, 1984), 383; *Time*, November 12, 1973, 59; *Washington Post*, January 14, 1974, A1, A16–17.

46. Hart, *Arafat*, 378–79; *Washington Post*, February 18, 1974, A7; *New York Times*, April 13, 1974, 3; *New York Times*, April 20, 1974, 13; *Time*, April 22, 1974, 36; *Time*, May 27, 1974, 24–26, 28, 31–32.

47. Alain Gresh, *The PLO: The Struggle Within: Towards an Independent Palestinian State* (London: Zed Books, 1985), 168.

48. Paul Thomas Chamberlin, *The Global Offensive: The United States, the Palestine Liberation Organization, and the Making of the Post-Cold War Order* (New York: Oxford University Press, 2012), 239–44; Quandt, *Peace Process*, 157–58.

49. Quandt, *Peace Process*, 159. No Western European governments voted in favor of the UN resolution to grant the PLO observer status, but Austria, France, Greece, and Sweden abstained

on the measure; Britain, Denmark, Iceland, Ireland, Italy, Luxembourg, the Netherlands, Norway, and West Germany joined the United States in opposing it. In October 1974, a more limited General Assembly resolution, to invite the PLO to participate in the plenary debate on Palestine, won the support of France, Greece, Ireland, Italy, Norway, and Sweden. The remaining Western European countries either opposed the resolution (as did the United States) or abstained. United Nations Information System on the Question of Palestine (UNISPAL), Resolution 3210, October 14, 1974, http://unispal.un.org/UNISPAL.NSF/0/2A1CF8A3EA4D1F0385256230005AFFEE, and Resolution 3237, November 22, 1974, http://unispal.un.org/UNISPAL.NSF/0/512BAA69B5A32794852560DE0054B9B2 (both pages accessed September 7, 2015).

50. *Wall Street Journal*, November 14, 1974, 14; *New York Times*, November 14, 1974, 22–23; *New York Times*, November 15, 1974, 18.

51. Shafiq al-Hout, *My Life in the PLO: The Inside Story of the Palestinian Struggle* (New York: Pluto Press, 2011), 123; AAUG *Newsletter*, December 1974–March 1975, cover page; Elaine C. Hagopian, "Reversing Injustice: On Utopian Activism," *Arab Studies Quarterly* 29, no. 3/4 (Summer/Fall 2007): 63.

52. Quandt, *Peace Process*, 159–62.

53. Seale, *Asad*, 257.

54. Kissinger, *Years of Renewal*, 402, 409; Quandt, *Peace Process*, 162; Kissinger to Ford, March 18, 1975, *FRUS, 1969–1976*, 26:543–44.

55. Kissinger, *Years of Renewal*, 405–21; memoranda of conversation, Kissinger, Rabin, et al., March 22, 1975, *FRUS, 1969–1976*, 26:557, 561.

56. Quandt, *Peace Process*, 163–65; memoranda of conversation, Ford, Kissinger, et al., March 26, 27, and 28, 1975, NSA Memcons, box 10, FL.

57. For examples of criticisms of Israel that Ford administration officials leaked to the press, see, Rowland Evans and Robert Novak, ". . . And President Ford's Reassessment," *Washington Post*, April 3, 1975, A15.

58. Spiegel, *Other Arab-Israeli Conflict*, 296–97; memorandum of conversation, Ford, Harold Wilson, et al., May 30, 1975, NSA Memcons, box 12, FL.

59. Spiegel, *Other Arab-Israeli Conflict*, 297. See chapter 7 for separate treatment of the Lebanese civil war.

60. Alvandi, *Nixon, Kissinger, and the Shah*, 114–20; Kissinger, *Years of Renewal*, 592–96.

61. Quandt, *Peace Process*, 165. For both public and confidential evidence of growing mainstream support for a comprehensive approach at this time, see Stephen S. Rosenfeld, "Israel's Geneva Option," *Washington Post*, March 21, 1975, A26; Zbigniew Brzezinski, "Unmanifest Destiny: Where Do We Go from Here?" *New York Magazine*, March 3, 1975, 53, 55; Zbigniew Brzezinski et al., "Peace in an International Framework," *Foreign Policy*, July 1975, 3–17; Brzezinski to Kissinger, April 4, 1975, Brzezinski Collection, box 8, Jimmy Carter Presidential Library, Atlanta, GA; memorandum of conversation, Kissinger and Middle East experts, May 1, 1975, DNSA, KT01609; Dean Rusk to George W. Ball, May 28, 1975, Ball Papers, box 83, folder 8, Princeton University Library (hereafter PUL).

62. Kissinger to Ford, April 21, 1975, Presidential Country Files, Middle East and South Asia, box 1, folder: "Middle East—General (8)," FL, 16; memoranda of conversation, Ford and Kissinger, April 28 and May 8, 1975, NSA Memcons, box 11, FL.

63. Kissinger, *Years of Renewal*, 428.

64. Whether or not Kissinger really planned to resign, he discussed this intention privately at the time, as well in his memoirs years later. In early April, a *New York Times* article noted, "One American Jew reported that Mr. Kissinger had told him he would resign rather than preside over a 'sell-out' of Israel." *New York Times*, April 7, 1975, 12.

65. Kissinger, *Years of Renewal*, 428–56; Quandt, *Peace Process*, 165–69.

66. Quandt, *Peace Process*, 169–70.

67. U.S. Embassy, Kuwait, tel #3684, September 8, 1975, Central Foreign Policy Files, Electronic Telegrams, Access to Archival Databases (hereafter AAD), 1975KUWAIT03684, NARA; U.S. Embassy, Paris, tel #28449, October 31, 1975, AAD, 1975PARIS028449, NARA; U.S. Embassy, Amman, to Department of State (hereafter DOS), tels #5883 and #8427, September 4 and November 13, 1975, AAD, 1975AMMAN05883 and 1975AMMAN08427, NARA; U.S. Embassy, Jidda, to DOS, tels #6669 and #7347, September 29 and November 3, 1975, AAD, 1975JIDDA06669 and 1975JIDDA07347, NARA; memorandum of conversation, Kissinger, King Hussein, et al., September 3, 1975, Kissinger Reports on USSR, China, and Middle East Discussions, box 5, folder: "August 21–September 1, 1975—Sinai Disengagement Agreement—Vol III (9)," FL, 8.

68. *Al-Nahar* (Beirut), September 4, 1975, 1; *New York Times*, September 6, 1975, 6; *New York Times*, September 7, 1975, 12; *New York Times*, September 21, 1975, 1, 5; *al-Siyasa* (Kuwait), September 7, 1975, 13; U.S. Delegation, New York, tel #4920, October 10, 1975, AAD, 1975USUNN04920, NARA; U.S. Embassy, Tripoli, tels #0937 and #0997, August 21 and September 2, 1975, AAD, 1975TRIPOL00937 and 1975TRIPOL00997, NARA.

69. *Washington Post*, September 18, 1975, A2; *Los Angeles Times*, September 18, 1975, B1–B16; "Prepared Statement on Behalf of the National Association of Arab Americans," *Early Warning System in Sinai: Hearings before the Committee on Foreign Relations, United States Senate, 94th Congress, First Session, October 6 and 7, 1975* (Washington, DC: U.S. Government Printing Office, 1976), 169–72; AAUG *Newsletter*, December 1975, 4.

70. John M. Sutton to Sayegh, November 1, 1974, Sayegh Papers, box 184, folder 2, UUL; Berger to Sayegh, February 10, 1975, Sayegh Papers, box 188, folder 1, UUL.

71. *Time*, June 23, 1975, 17, 20; *New York Times*, June 30, 1975, 1, 10; *Chicago Tribune*, July 27, 1975, A2; *Sarasota (FL) Herald-Tribune*, September 11, 1975 (syndicating a *Congressional Quarterly* story), 7-A; clipping, "Arab-Americans: Getting a Grip on Destiny," *Pittsburgh Press*, October 12, 1975 (page numbers not visible), Maria Papers, box 115, folder 7, IHRC.

72. *New York Times*, June 30, 1975, 10; NAAA statement, June 26, 1975, Gerald R. Ford Presidential Digital Library, http://www.fordlibrarymuseum.gov/library/document/0314/1553144.pdf (accessed September 7, 2015).

73. Gerald Ford had become vice president through presidential appointment and congressional confirmation; he then advanced to the presidency upon Nixon's resignation. Thus in 1976 Ford sought election for the first time, not reelection.

74. DOS to U.S. Embassy, Damascus, tel #281275, November 27, 1975, Presidential Country Files, Middle East and South Asia, box 31, folder: "Syria—State Department Telegrams from SECSTATE—NODIS (5)," FL; Kissinger, *Years of Renewal*, 1056; Seale, *Asad*, 276.

75. Kathleen Christison, *Perceptions of Palestine: Their Influence on U.S. Middle East Policy* (1999, repr., Berkeley: University of California Press, 2001), 147–49; Harold Saunders, prepared statement, *The Palestinian Issue in Middle East Peace Efforts: Hearings before the Special Subcommittee on Investigations of the Committee on International Relations, House of Representatives, 94th Congress, First Session, September 30, October 1, 8, and November 12, 1975* (Washington, DC: U.S. Government Printing Office, 1976, 178–80; R[ichard] J.S. Muir to D[avid] A.S. Blatherwick, December 9, 1975, Foreign and Commonwealth Office (hereafter FCO) 93/777, The National Archives, Kew, London, United Kingdom (hereafter TNA); memorandum of conversation James Callaghan, Kissinger, et al., December 13, 1975, FCO 93/777, TNA.

76. Christison, *Perceptions of Palestine*, 148–49.

77. John J. McCloy to Ball, February 17, 1976, Ball Papers, box 68, folder 13, PUL. McCloy was referring to a March 31, 1975, meeting at the State Department attended by himself, Kissinger, Ball, former secretary of state Dean Rusk, former secretary of defense Robert McNamara, and other prominent former government officials. The State Department's memorandum of this conversation fails to cover the first ninety minutes, and the recorded portions do not capture Kissinger's views on a comprehensive settlement. But they do indicate that most of the attendees, Kissinger included, were highly critical of Israel's substantive positions and negotiating tactics. Memorandum of conversation, Kissinger, Rusk, et al., March 31, 1975, *FRUS, 1969–1976*, 26:606–9.

78. *Toward Peace in the Middle East: Report of a Study Group* (Washington, DC: The Brookings Institution, 1975); memorandum of conversation, Kissinger, Nadav Safran, et al., May 1, 1975, DNSA, KT01609. The dissenter was Rita Hauser, an international lawyer and diplomat who co-authored the Brookings Institution report.

79. *Toward Peace in the Middle East*, 1, 19.

80. The polarization of public discourse on this issue at the time will be evident in the proceeding section. In subsequent scholarship, the following works express sympathy for the UN General Assembly's equation of Zionism with racism: Sami Hadawi, *Bitter Harvest: A Modern History of Palestine* (New York: Olive Branch Press, 1989), 184; Uri Davis, "Naming the Colonizer in Geographical Palestine: Conceptual and Political Double Binds and Their Possible Solution," in *Across the Wall: Narratives of Israeli-Palestinian History*, ed. Ilan Pappé and Jamil Hilal (London: I.B. Tauris, 2010), 401. The following works strongly criticize the General Assembly's action: Avi Beker, *The United Nations and Israel: From Recognition to Reprehension* (Lexington, MA: Lexington Books, 1988), 56–63, 85–88; Gil Troy, *Moynihan's Moment: America's Fight against Zionism as Racism* (New York: Oxford University Press, 2013).

81. In 1949, the United Nations accepted Israel's application for membership on the understanding that Israel would relinquish the territory it had acquired in excess of the 1947 UN partition plan and repatriate the Palestinian refugees. Israel did neither. Hadawi, *Bitter Harvest*, 130–31.

82. Daniel Patrick Moynihan, *A Dangerous Place* (Boston: Little, Brown and Company, 1978), 171–72.

83. Memorandum of conversation, [Michael] Weir, R[obert] Blake, et al., July 21, 1975, FCO 93/777, TNA; U.S. Embassy, Damascus, to DOS, tel #2827, July 25, 1975, AAD, 1975 DAMASC02827, NARA. In an insightful but at times tendentious study, Gil Troy pays only fleeting attention to the role of the Sinai negotiations in galvanizing the diplomatic attacks on Israel in the summer and fall of 1975. He instead attributes those attacks mainly to a long-term Soviet drive to marginalize Israel. Troy, *Moynihan's Moment*, 74–76, 110, 112–13. Although the Soviet dimension merits close attention, it alone cannot tell us much about why the anti-Zionist campaign gathered such powerful momentum in the second half of 1975.

84. *New York Times*, July 15, 1975, 1, 5; *New York Times*, August 31, 1975, 1, 8; Ruth Raeli, *The Steps that Led to United Nations General Assembly Resolution 3379: Elimination of All Forms of Racial Discrimination, November 10, 1975* (n.p.: World Zionist Organization, 1984), 34–42.

85. Raeli, *Steps*, 5–7; U.S. Delegation, New York, #05005, October 1, 1975, AAD, 1975USUNN05005, NARA.

86. The 1965 International Convention on the Elimination of All Forms of Racial Discrimination defines racial discrimination "as any distinction, exclusion, restriction, or preference based on race, color, descent, or national or ethnic origin." Passed as General Assembly Resolution 2106 (XX), December 21, 1965.

87. Fayez Sayegh, *Zionism: "A Form of Racism and Racial Discrimination": Four Statements Made at the U.N. General Assembly* (New York: Office of the Permanent Observer of the Palestine Liberation Organization to the United Nations, 1976), 14.

88. Sayegh noted, for example, that most of Israel's land was jointly controlled by the Israeli government and the Jewish National Fund, each of which operated under a charter banning the sale of its land to non-Jews. Sayegh, *Zionism*, 20.

89. Statement by Ambassador Moynihan, November 10, 1975, *Department of State Bulletin*, December 1, 1975, 791–93.

90. Sayegh, *Zionism*, 38.

91. Moynihan, *Dangerous Place*, 179–80, 181–85, 196–99, 211; statement by Ambassador Moynihan, November 10, 1975, *Department of State Bulletin*, December 1, 1975, 791.

92. As far as can be determined, senator James Abourezk did not take a public position on the UN resolution at the time. The Senate resolution condemning the UN vote was a "unanimous consent" agreement, to which no senator objected but for which no roll call vote was recorded. Betty Koed (Historian of the Senate), communication with the author, July 14, 2015. Asked about the matter nearly four decades later, Abourezk had no specific recollection of the Senate vote but concluded that he must have been absent for it. Had he been present, he said, he would have objected. Abourezk, communication with the author, September 8, 2015.

93. *New York Times*, November 12, 1975, 1, 16; *New York Times*, December 28, 1975, 3; *New York Times*, January 13, 1976, 14; *Washington Post*, November 12, 1975, A1, A10; Anti-Defamation League of the B'nai B'rith, "Big 50 Press Survey: Anti-Zionism and the Nations," November 1975, Moynihan Papers, box 325, folder: Correspondence, General Ba," LC.

94. Arab Information Center display advertisement, *New York Times*, November 23, 1975, E7; letters to the editor, *New York Times*, November 23, 1975, 16; AAUG *Newsletter*, December 1975, 4; reprint, Edmund Hanauer, "Support for U.N. Vote Condemning Zionism," *San Francisco Examiner*, January 19, 1976, Rowland Evans Papers, box 26, folder 7, LC; clipping, Hanauer, "Opinion: Zionism-As-Racism," *National Catholic Reporter*, March 5, 1976, Evans Papers, box 26, folder 7, LC.

95. See, for example, *News Circle*, December 1975, 4, 15; *Voice*, December 1975, 7; *Link*, Winter 1975–1976, 1–15. Although the NAAA appears to have taken no position on the "Zionism is racism" resolution, it did respond to the earlier effort to expel Israel from the United Nation. In August 1975, the NAAA passed a resolution calling on "all nations of the U.N. to exert their individual and collective influence on Israel to force it to comply with the Charter of the U.N, and the duly authorized resolutions passed by the U.N.," thus implicitly opposing the expulsion effort. "As you will see," former NAAA president Richard Shadyac explained to Moynihan in a letter, to which a copy of the NAAA resolution was attached, "[the resolution] does not request that Israel be expelled or suspended from the United Nations." Shadyac to Moynihan, August 22, 1975, attaching NAAA resolution, August 5, 1975, Moynihan papers, box 331, "folder: "Correspondence, General Se-Sh," LC.

96. *New York Times*, November 21, 1975, 3; *New York Times*, November 22, 1975, 1, 5; *New York Times*, November 25, 1975, 6; *Newsweek*, November 24, 1975, 54; *Newsweek*, December 1, 1975, 48; telephone conversation, Kissinger and Rusk, November 22, 1975, DNSA, KA14396.

97. Telephone conversations, Kissinger and William Buffum, November 10 and 11, 1975, DNSA, KA14329 and KA14332.

98. Troy, *Moynihan's Moment*, 191–208, 219–22.

99. For more on the emergence of neoconservatism, see Justin Vaïsse, *Neoconservatism: The Biography of a Movement*, trans. Arthur Goldhammer (Cambridge, MA: The Belknap Press, 2010); John Ehrman, *The Rise of Neoconservatism: Intellectuals and Foreign Affairs, 1945–1994* (New Haven, CT: Yale University Press, 1995).

100. Moynihan, however, disliked the "neoconservative" label. Troy, *Moynihan's Moment*, 10.

101. Anthony Lewis, "The American Dream," *New York Times*, October 13, 1975, 25; Orde Coombs, "The Retreat of the Liberal Sages," *New York Times*, May 17, 1976, 29; Irving Kristol, "What Is a 'Neo-Conservative'?" *Newsweek*, January 19, 1976, 17; *Boston Globe*, May 23, 1976, A1–A2.

102. UNISPAL, S/PV.1879, "The Middle East Problem Including the Palestinian Question," January 26, 1976, http://unispal.un.org/UNISPAL.NSF/0/D0242E9E210D937585256C6E0054DF8A (accessed October 9, 2014); UK Mission, memorandum on UN Security Council meetings on Palestine, February 9, 1976, FCO 93/959, TNA.

103. *Chicago Tribune*, January 18, 1976, 24.

6. Future Shock

1. Herbert Stein and Benjamin Stein, *On the Brink* (New York: Simon and Schuster, 1977).

2. John Woodcock, "Disaster Thrillers: A Literary Mode of Technology Assessment," *Science, Technology, & Human Values* 4, no. 26 (Winter 1979): 37–45; Stephen Keane, *Disaster Movies: The Cinema of Catastrophe* (London: Wallflower, 2001), 19–50.

3. M. Keith Booker and Anne-Marie Thomas, *The Science Fiction Handbook* (Oxford: Wiley-Blackwell, 2009), 70–71.

4. *New York Times*, August 24, 1975, 236; *New York Times*, December 28, 1975, 164. "Newgate Callendar" was a pseudonym used by Harold C. Schonberg, whose main assignment was as music critic for the *New York Times*.

5. See, for example, Robert J. Allison, *The Crescent Obscured: The United States and the Muslim World, 1776–1815* (1995, repr., Chicago: University of Chicago Press, 2000), 107–26.

6. Reeva S. Simon, *The Middle East in Crime Fiction: Mysteries, Spy Novels, and Thrillers from 1916 to the 1980s* (New York: Lillian Barber Press, 1989), 141–92. Simon's criteria for inclusion are considerably broader than mine, incorporating titles published in the United States, Canada, and Britain, story lines that appear to be both apolitical and political, and plots set in all parts of the Middle East. I have used Simon's bibliographic information and plot synopses to isolate U.S.-published titles containing clearly political plots confined to the Arab world.

7. Richard L. Graves, *Cobalt 60* (New York: Stein and Day, 1975); Colin Forbes, *Year of the Golden Ape* (New York: E.P. Dutton, 1974); Thomas Harris, *Black Sunday* (New York: Dell, 1975).

8. Marvin H. Albert, *The Gargoyle Conspiracy* (Garden City, NY: Doubleday, 1975); Alfred Coppel, *Thirty-Four East* (New York: Harcourt Brace Jovanovich, 1974).

9. Barry Schiff and Hal Fishman, *The Vatican Target* (New York: St. Martin's Press, 1978); Sandor Frankel and Webster Mews, *The Aleph Solution* (New York, Stein and Day, 1978). "Webster Mews" was a pseudonym for Jethro K. Lieberman; see http://www.jethrolieberman.com/works.htm (accessed September 7, 2015).

10. Edward A. Pollitz, Jr., *The Forty-First Thief* (New York: Delacorte Press, 1975).

11. Harris, *Black Sunday*, 28; Forbes, *Year of the Golden Ape*, 60–61.

12. Leonard Harris, *The Masada Plan* (New York: Crown Publishers, 1976).

13. Janice J. Terry, *Mistaken Identity: Arab Stereotypes in Popular Writing* (Washington, DC: American-Arab Affairs Council, 1985); Jack G. Shaheen, *Reel Bad Arabs: How Hollywood Vilifies a People* (New York: Olive Branch Press, 2001); Tim Jon Semmerling, *"Evil" Arabs in American Popular Film: Orientalist Fear* (Austin: University of Texas Press, 2006).

14. Forbes, *Year of the Golden Ape*, 314–15; Frankel and Mews, *Aleph Solution*, 107; Graves, *Cobalt 60*, 127.

15. Melani McAlister, *Epic Encounters: Culture, Media, and U.S. Interests in the Middle East, 1945–2001* (2001, repr., Berkeley: University of California Press, 2005), 187–92; Semmerling, *"Evil" Arabs,* 93–101, 109–23; Harris, *Black Sunday*, 171; Frankel and Mews, *Aleph Solution*, 142.

16. Kabakov's concentration camp tattoo is revealed in the hospital scene of the movie version of *Black Sunday*; Tal's is described on page 86 of *Aleph Solution*.

17. Harris, *Black Sunday*, 253; Frankel and Mews, *Aleph Solution*, 188.

18. Harris, *Masada Plan*, 56; Coppel, *Thirty-Four East*, 140, 153; Pollitz, *Forty-First Thief*, 93.

19. As recently as the early 1960s, Jews were barred from many social clubs, and some elite universities placed quotas on the numbers of Jews they admitted. In 1948, the U.S. Supreme Court ruled that restrictive covenants in real estate transactions were unenforceable. Nevertheless, in the late 1950s the Anti-Defamation League produced evidence that such clauses continued to prevent Jews from buying some properties. *Jewish Telegraphic Agency*, January 15, 1962, http://www.jta.org/1962/01/15/archive/anti-defamation-league-reports-discrimination-in-781-clubs-in-u-s (accessed December 19, 2013); Marcia Graham Synnott, *Student Diversity at the Big Three: Changes at Harvard, Yale, and Princeton since the 1920s* (New Brunswick, NJ: Transaction Publishers, 2013), 65–112; Wendy Plotkin, "Restrictive Covenants," in *Anti-Semitism: A Historical Encyclopedia of Prejudice and Persecution*, ed. Richard S. Levy, vol. 1 (Santa Barbara, CA: ABC-CLIO, 2005), 598.

20. Of the authors whose work is discussed in this section, Hal Fishman, Sandor Frankel, Jethro Lieberman ("Webster Mews"), Herbert Stein, and Benjamin Stein publicly identified as Jewish.

21. I am grateful to Robyn Muncy and Melani McAlister for helping me sort through the issues discussed in this paragraph.

22. Mark Ensalaco, *Middle Eastern Terrorism: From Black September to September 11* (Philadelphia: University of Pennsylvania Press, 2008), 96–102; McAlister, *Epic Encounters*, 181–83. The slain Israeli commando was Jonathan Netanyahu, brother of future Israeli prime minister Benjamin Netanyahu.

23. Nick Thimmesch, "Brilliant Israeli Rescue," *Lodi (CA) News-Sentinel*, July 12, 1976, 10; Paul Harvey, "The Israeli Example of Self-Development," *Florence (AL) Times–Tri-Cities Daily*, July 22, 1976, 4; Walter Mondale quoted in McAlister, *Epic Encounters*, 186.

24. Paul Seabury, "It's Time to Consider Force against Arab Oil Nations," *Los Angeles Times*, December 8, 1974, F3; Edward N. Luttwak, "Obsolescent Elites," *Times Literary Supplement*, December 27, 1974, reprinted in Luttwak, *Strategy and Politics: Collected Essays* (New Brunswick, NJ: Transaction Books, 1980), 305–12; Robert W. Tucker, "Oil: The Issue of American Intervention," *Commentary* 59, no. 1 (January 1975): 21–31; Miles Ignotus, "Seizing Arab Oil," *Harper's*, March 1975, 45–62. Luttwak's authorship of the *Harper's* piece was suspected immediately, though he denied it at the time. *Christian Science Monitor*, March 12, 1975, 3. In 2004, Luttwak finally acknowledged writing the article. *Wall Street Journal*, February 4, 2004, A1. For Paul Seabury's role in the neoconservative movement in the 1970s, see Justin Vaïsse, *Neoconservatism: The Biography of a Movement*, trans. Arthur Goldhammer (Cambridge, MA: The Belknap Press, 2010), 101–2, 128, 145. For Luttwak's role, see Vaïsse, *Neoconservatism*, 110; Ben J. Wattenberg, *Fighting Words: A Tale of How Liberals Created Neo-Conservatism* (New York: St. Martin's Press, 2008), 154; John Ehrman, *The Rise of Neoconservatism: Intellectuals and Foreign Affairs, 1945–1994* (New Haven, CT: Yale University Press, 1995), 107, 114, 132. For Robert Tucker's role, see Ehrman, *Rise of Neoconservatism*, 50–54, 56–57, 111.

25. Jack Anderson, "U.S. Officials Mutter against Israel," *Washington Post*, December 17, 1974, B15; Kissinger interview, *Business Week*, January 13, 1975, 69; memorandum of conversation, Gerald Ford, Kissinger, and Brent Scowcroft, January 6, 1975, National Security Adviser, Memoranda of Conversation, 1973–1977 (hereafter NSA Memcons), box 8, Gerald R. Ford Presidential Library, Ann Arbor, MI (hereafter FL).

26. *Wall Street Journal*, February 4, 2004, A1; *Washington Post*, March 20, 1975, A24; Robert Dreyfuss, "The Thirty-Year Itch," *Mother Jones* (March/April 2003), http://motherjones.com/politics/2003/03/thirty-year-itch (accessed September 5, 2015).

27. U.S. Embassy, Jidda, to Department of State (hereafter DOS), #00067, January 5, 1975, Central Foreign Policy Files, Electronic Telegrams, Access to Archival Databases, 1975JIDDA00067, National Archives and Records Administration, College Park, MD; DOS to U.S. Embassy, Jidda, tel #001955, January 5, 1975, Presidential Country Files, Middle East and South Asia, box 28, folder: "Saudi Arabia—State Department Telegrams, from SECTATE—EXDIS," FL; U.S. Embassy Jidda, to DOS, tels #00251 and #00402, January 13 and 20, 1975, Presidential Country Files, Middle East and South Asia, box 29, folder: "Saudi Arabia—State Department Telegrams To SECSTATE (NODIS) (3)," FL; *Washington Post*, March 20, 1975, A24.

28. For the former position, see editorial, *Chicago Tribune*, January 5, 1975, A4; Stephen S. Rosenfeld, "Oil and Military Force," *Washington Post*, January 10, 1975 A22; Tom Wicker, "Stating the Obvious," *New York Times*, January 12, 1975, E17; Barry Blechman, "Force and Diplomacy," *Washington Post*, February 7, 1975, A22. For the latter, see I.F. Stone, "War for Oil," *New York Review of Books*, February 6, 1975, 7–10; and John Sparkman, "Sparkman on Foreign Policy," *Wall Street Journal*, February 13, 1975, 16.

29. *Washington Post*, January 23, 1975, B8.

30. Dreyfuss, "Tinker, Banker, Neocon, Spy: Ahmed Chalabi's Long and Winding Road from (and to?) Baghdad," *American Prospect*, November 18, 2002, http://prospect.org/cs/articles?article=tinker_banker_neocon_spy (accessed September 7, 2015); Dreyfuss, "Thirty-Year Itch"; Dreyfuss, *Devil's Game: How the United States Helped Unleash Fundamentalist Islam* (New York: Henry Holt, 2005), 247–48; *Wall Street Journal*, February 4, 2004, A1.

31. Paul E. Erdman, *The Crash of '79* (New York: Simon and Schuster, 1976); Peter Tanous and Paul Rubinstein, *The Petrodollar Takeover* (New York: G.P. Putnam's Sons, 1975).

32. *Wall Street Journal*, March 21, 1979, 21; Erdman obituary, *New York Times*, April 25, 2007, A25.

33. Erdman, *Crash of '79*, 80, 87, 117, 210, 222, 250.

34. *Washington Post*, August 3, 1975, 160, *Washington Report on Middle East Affairs*, May 17, 1982, 8.

35. Tanous and Rubinstein, *Petrodollar Takeover*, 31, 108–9, 142.

36. See, for example, *New York Times*, July 27, 1975, BR3; *Waycross (GA) Journal-Herald*, September 11, 1975, 11.

37. *Washington Post*, October 10, 1976, A12; Spiro Agnew, "The Truth about My Novel," *Ladies' Home Journal*, May 1974, 99, 159; Agnew, *Go Quietly . . . Or Else* (New York: William Morrow, 1980).

38. Agnew, "Truth about My Novel," 99; *Washington Post*, February 20, 1974, B8.

39. See, for example, William F. Buckley, Jr., "In the Face of U.S. Isolationism, the Answer Is to Make Israel the 51st State," *Los Angeles Times*, July 31, 1972, C7.

40. Spiro Agnew, *The Canfield Decision* (Chicago: Playboy Press, 1976), 175, 245.

41. Ibid., 32, 84.

42. *New York Times*, October 26, 1975, 16–17, 99–101, 106–7; *Washington Post*, October 10, 1976, 1, A12.

43. *Newsweek*, May 24, 1976, 27, ellipses in original; clipping, *More*, July/August 1976, Spiro T. Agnew Papers, unprocessed materials, accession number 1994–067 (hereafter Agnew Papers), box 75, "STA Novel Zionism," Hornbake Library, University of Maryland, College Park, MD (hereafter HL), 17.

44. These activities entailed not just the publication of *The Canfield Decision* but also the distribution of a political newsletter, *Memoranda*, which Agnew was preparing to publish under the auspices of Education for Democracy, a conservative nonprofit foundation he had acquired in the fall of 1975. (It had been formed by students at Indiana University in 1971 and had lain dormant for several years.) The first issue of *Memoranda* appeared in the summer of 1976 and was sent out, Agnew claimed, to fifty thousand recipients. Focusing mainly on foreign affairs, the newsletter combined hard-line anticommunism with sharp criticism of Israeli policies and of U.S. support for Israel. Clipping, Agnew interview, *Emirate News* (United Arab Emirates), July 21, 1976, 5, Agnew Papers, box 77, folder: "Israel," HL.

45. Agnew to Crown Prince Fahd, March 11, 1976, Agnew Papers, box 81, folder: "Saudi Arabia—Khalid bin Abdul Aziz, Also King Faisal," HL; Agnew to Ali Alireza, March 11, 1976, Agnew Papers, box 81, folder: "Saudi Arabia—Khalid bin Abdul Aziz, Also King Faisal," HL.

46. Agnew to Fahd, April 5, 1976, Agnew Papers, box 81, folder: "Saudi Arabia—Khalid bin Abdul Aziz, Also King Faisal," HL.

47. *Pittsburgh Press*, April 8, 1978, 1.

48. John Kenneth Galbraith, "The Canfield Decision," *New York Times*, June 6, 1976, 218; *Newsweek*, May 24, 1976, 104; Richard Condon, "Hail to the Chiefs," *Harper's*, August 1976, 82; David Shaw, "Agnew's Final Solution to the Media Problem," *Los Angeles Times*, May 16, 1976, K1, K8, K10, K11; *Tri-City Herald* (Pasco, Kennewick, and Richland, WA), May 16, 1976, 19; *Tuscaloosa (AL) News*, May 21, 1976, 12; *Eugene (OR) Register-Guard*, May 30, 1976, 14B.

49. *New York Times*, May 12, 1976, 39.

50. *Newsweek*, May 24, 1976, 27; clipping, *Washington Star*, May 23, 1976, Frank Maria Papers, box 47, folder 7, Immigration History Research Center, University of Minnesota, Minneapolis, MN.

51. Clipping, *Washington Star*, May 29, 1976, A6, Agnew Papers, box 75, "STA Novel Zionism," HL; clipping, *More*, July/August 1976, 12, 17, Agnew Papers, box 75, "STA Novel Zionism," HL; *Washington Post*, June 26, 1976, A5; William Safire, "Spiro Agnew and the Jews," *New York Times*, May 24, 1976, 28; Victor Gold, "Agnew Has Simply Sold Out," *New York Times*, May 28, 1976, 20; *Citizen* (Ottawa, Ontario), July 29, 1976, 63.

52. M.T. Mehdi to Agnew, June 25, 1976, Agnew Papers, box 95, folder: "Foundation Newsclips—Misc," HL.

53. *New York Times*, July 31, 1976, 12; Cynthia Rosenwald to Agnew, n.d. [c. August 1976], Agnew Papers, box 75, "STA Novel Zionism," HL; Jerold Hoffberger to Agnew, August 19, 1976, Agnew Papers, box 75, "STA Novel Zionism," HL. See other letters to and from Agnew in this file.

54. *The Canfield Decision* spent four weeks on the *New York Times* best-seller list in the summer of 1976. *New York Times*, July 4, 1976, BR5; *New York Times*, July 11, 1976, 187; *New York Times*, July 25, 1976, 171; *New York Times*, August 1, 1976, 177. In October 1976, the *Washington Post* reported that about 80,000 hard-cover copies of the book had been sold. *Washington Post*, October 10, 1976, A12. Two years later, however, a royalty statement from Playboy Press indicated that the book had sold 34,964 hard-cover copies both domestically and overseas, yielding Agnew $46,920.38 in royalties. Royalty statement, December 31, 1978, Agnew Papers, box 89, folder: "Canfield Decision," HL. It is unclear whether the *Washington Post* was mistaken or was counting in some different way.

55. *New York Times*, July 31, 1976, 12; *Newsweek*, May 24, 1976, 27.

56. Although Fulbright and Ball were good friends who worked along parallel lines on Middle East issues, they seem not to have collaborated directly on such matters.

57. Memorandum of conversation, Kissinger and unidentified interviewer (apparently Theodore White), January 3, 1975, George W. Ball Papers (hereafter Ball Papers), box 17, folder 1,

Princeton University Library (hereafter PUL); James A. Bill, *George Ball: Behind the Scenes in U.S. Foreign Policy* (New Haven, CT: Yale University Press, 1997), 191. Ball's criticism of U.S. partiality toward Israel was one factor in Carter's decision to pass Ball over for secretary of state. Bill, *George Ball*, 192.

58. Fulbright's scenario, which first appeared in the *Washington Star* on July 13, 1975, is reprinted in Edward R.F. Sheehan, *The Arabs, Israelis, and Kissinger* (New York: Reader's Digest Press, 1976), 261–65.

59. Ibid., 261, 264–65.

60. Memorandum of conversation, Ford, Fulbright, and Scowcroft, July 2, 1975, NSA Memcons, box 13, FL.

61. George W. Ball, "How to Save Israel in Spite of Herself," *Foreign Affairs* 55, no. 3 (April 1977): 465–66.

62. Randall Bennett Woods, *Fulbright: A Biography* (New York: Cambridge University Press, 1995), 673; *Washington Post*, January 27, 1976, A2; *Washington Post*, July 18, 1976, 151; *U.S. News and World Report*, March 27, 1978, 26; *New York Times*, April 30, 1978, E4; clipping, *Washington Star*, April 18, 1978, James G. Abourezk Papers, box 649, folder: "Search Info—MERC, Arab Lobby," University of South Dakota Library, Vermillion, SD, A-5.

63. Ball to Jackson, January 3, 1975, Ball Papers, box 59, folder 7, PUL; Ball to Marilyn Berger, September 9, 1975, Ball Papers, box 22, folder 6, PUL; Holmes Alexander, "Lobbies Not Petitioners but Strong-Armed Salesmen," *Rome (GA) News-Tribune*, May 16, 1978, 4.

64. For Fulbright's warnings along these lines, see *New York Times*, November 3, 1974, 68; Fulbright, "Mideast 'Slide toward War,'" *Los Angeles Times*, July 13, 1975, D3. For Ball's, see Ball, "The Looming War in the Middle East and How to Avert It," *Atlantic Monthly*, January 1975, 6–8, 10–11; Ball, "Step by Step to Where?" *Newsweek*, September 15, 1975, 13.

65. For examples of Fulbright's and Ball's infrequent appeals to morality, see Fulbright, opening statement, round table, "Prospects for Peace in the Middle East," American Enterprise Institute, September 26, 1977, Fulbright Papers, Post-Senatorial Papers, box 46, folder 13, University of Arkansas Library, Fayetteville, AR; Ball, "The Disenchantment with Kissinger," *Saturday Review*, June 12, 1976, 21.

66. As discussed in chapters 9 and 10, Saudi Arabia's ability to affect world oil prices simply by altering the volume of its output afforded the kingdom some leverage in international affairs in the mid- and late 1970s. But this, of course, was a far cry from the sort of pressure exerted by an outright embargo.

67. Interview with Fulbright, *Chicago Tribune*, February 18, 1980, 1; Ball, "The Mideast Challenge," *New York Times*, April 1, 1979, E19; interview with Ball, *U.S. News and World Report*, September 3, 1979, 17–18.

7. Fallen Cedar

1. *Los Angeles Times*, July 28, 1976, 4; *Washington Post*, July 28, 1976, A18. Instead of returning to Lebanon, Talcott Seelye stayed in Washington as deputy assistant secretary of state for African affairs, a position he held until 1977. From 1978 to 1981, he served as U.S. ambassador to Syria.

2. *New York Times*, July 28, 1976, 1, 3; Senate Judiciary Committee, Subcommittee to Investigate Problems Connected with Refugees and Escapees, *Humanitarian Problems in Lebanon, Part II, July 29, 1976* (Washington, DC: U.S. Government Printing Office, 1976), 124.

3. Tabitha Petran, *The Struggle Over Lebanon* (New York: Monthly Review Press, 1987), 207–9; *New York Times*, July 25, 1976, 1, 5; memorandum of conversation, Gerald Ford, Henry Kissinger, and Brent Scowcroft, July 19, 1976, National Security Adviser, Memoranda of Conversation, 1973–1977 (hereafter NSA Memcons), box 20, Gerald R. Ford Presidential Library, Ann Arbor, MI (hereafter FL).

4. General treatments of the Lebanese civil war include Kamal S. Salibi, *Crossroads to Civil War, 1958–1976* (Delmar, NY: Caravan Books, 1976); Charles Winslow, *Lebanon: War and Politics in a Fragmented Society* (London: Routledge, 1996); Farid el Khazen, *The Breakdown of the State in Lebanon, 1967–1976* (Cambridge, MA: Harvard University Press, 2000); David Hirst, *Beware of Small States: Lebanon, Battleground of the Middle East* (New York: Nation Books, 2010).

5. The relative decline in Lebanon's Christian population resulted from lower fertility rates and higher levels of emigration among Christians. W.B. Fisher, "Lebanon: Physical and Social Geography," in *The Middle East and North Africa, 2004*, ed. Lucy Dean (London: Europa Publications, 2003), 744.

6. Salibi, *Crossroads to Civil War*, 97–122; Winslow, *Lebanon*, 180–87.

7. William Bazzy, "The Lebanese Problem," March 22, 1976, Frank Maria Papers, box 91, folder 2, Immigration History Research Center, University of Minnesota, Minneapolis, MN (hereafter IHRC); Fred J. Khouri, "The Arab-Israeli Conflict," in *Lebanon in Crisis: Participants and Issues*, ed. P. Edward Haley and Lewis W. Snyder (Syracuse, NY: Syracuse University Press, 1979), 165. See also el Khazen, *Breakdown of the State*, 319.

8. Khouri, "Arab-Israeli Conflict," 165–66; U.S. Embassy, Beirut, to Department of State (hereafter DOS), tel #12637, October 10, 1975, Central Foreign Policy Files, Electronic Telegrams, Access to Archival Databases (hereafter AAD), 1975SBEIRUT12637, National Archives and Records Administration, College Park, MD (hereafter NARA).

9. Petran, *Struggle Over Lebanon*, 169–70; Naomi Joy Weinberger, *Syrian Intervention in Lebanon: The 1975–76 Civil War* (New York: Oxford University Press, 1986), 263, 270–71; Hirst, *Beware of Small States*, 108.

10. Minutes of Washington Special Actions Group meeting, October 10, 1975, U.S. Department of State, *Foreign Relations of the United States* (hereafter *FRUS*, with dates and volume number), *1969–1976*, 26:933.

11. For evidence of Israel's support for the Lebanese Right and of U.S. attitudes regarding that support, see James Stocker, *Spheres of Intervention: The United States and the Struggle for Lebanon, 1967–1976* (Ithaca, NY: Cornell University Press, forthcoming).

12. Salibi, *Crossroads to Civil War*, 122–32; Winslow, *Lebanon*, 187–88; el Khazen, *Breakdown of the State*, 313–15; *New York Times*, October 23, 1975, 5; *Washington Post*, October 30, 1975, A1, A6.

13. Memorandum of conversation, Ford and Kissinger, October 16, 1975, NSA Memcons, box 16, FL.

14. DOS to U.S. Embassy, Paris, tel #239610, October 8, 1975, AAD, 1975STATE239610, NARA; DOS to U.S. Embassy, Tel Aviv, tel #243279, October 11, 1975, AAD, 1975STATE243279, NARA; U.S. Embassy, Tel Aviv, to DOS, tel #6562, October 16, 1975, AAD, 1975TELAV06562, NARA; Stocker, *Spheres of Intervention*; minutes of secretary of state's staff meeting, October 28, 1975, *FRUS, 1969–1976*, 26:945.

15. U.S. Embassy, Beirut, to DOS, tels #13296, October 25, 1975, AAD, 1975BEIRUT13296, and #13409, October 29, 1975, AAD, BEIRUT13409, NARA; DOS to U.S. Embassy, Beirut, tel #260612, November 4 1975, AAD, 1975STATE260612, NARA; Charles Oliver to AJME members, September 23, 1976, and January 12, 1977, William E. Mulligan Papers, box 12, folder 13, Georgetown University Library, Washington, DC; recollection of the author, who attended ACS, and whose father taught at AUB, for the duration of the 1975–1976 Lebanese civil war.

16. Petran, *Struggle Over Lebanon*, 182–89; Salibi, *Crossroads to Civil War*, 146–58; James M. Markham, "Always Fragile: Lebanon, an Artificial Nation May Not Endure," *New York Times*, January 18, 1976, 143.

17. Helen M. Haje, press release, November 17, 1975, James G. Abourezk Papers, box 690, folder: "Arab Meeting—Nov. 15, 1975, Washington, DC," University of South Dakota Library, Vermillion, SD (hereafter USDL); statement by Senator Abourezk, November 15, 1975, James G. Abourezk Papers, box 690, folder: "Arab Meeting—Nov. 15, 1975, Washington, DC," USDL.

18. Statement by Senator Abourezk, November 15, 1975, James G. Abourezk Papers, box 690, folder: "Arab Meeting—Nov. 15, 1975, Washington, DC," USDL. By contrast, the NAAA, consisting mostly of Lebanese Americans, issued a resolution in January 1976 expressing concern for "the welfare of the Lebanese people." *Voice*, February 1976, 3.

19. Elaine C. Hagopian to members, January 27, 1976, Association of Arab American University Graduates (AAUG) Papers, box 15, folder: "President—Elaine Hagopian, 1976," Eastern Michigan University Library, Ypsilanti, MI (hereafter EMUL). *Youngstown (OH) Vindicator*, October 24, 1975, 8. Later in the decade, Father Ashkar would lend overt political support to the Lebanese Right. *Youngstown (OH) Vindicator*, December 2, 1978, 14; program, Joint Lebanese Appeal, Akron, OH, February 25, 1979, Charles Malik Papers, box 103, folder: "American Lebanese League, 1976–1982, nd," Library of Congress, Washington, DC (hereafter LC).

20. Association of Arab American University Graduates, *Lebanon: Two Perspectives* (Detroit: AAUG, 1975), n.p. [1, 4–5].

21. Ibid., n.p. [7].

22. Ibid., n.p. [6–7].

23. *News Circle*, November 1975, 4, 14; *New Lebanese American Journal*, October 2, 1975, 1–2. In 1976, Joanne McKenna, chair of the NAAA Speakers Bureau Committee, did draw up, for delivery in public forums, a detailed and sophisticated presentation on the causes of the Lebanese civil war. Her analysis was similar to the one offered at the start of this chapter (hence the author's description of the talk as "sophisticated"). But the speech was not circulated in print, offered no political prescriptions, and did not constitute an official NAAA position statement. McKenna, "The War in Lebanon," delivered at the Arabian Nights Club of Cleveland, September 17, 1976, Maria Papers, box 47, folder 10, IHRC.

24. A case in point was the somewhat facile claim, advanced by many AAUGers and other progressives, that Lebanon's domestic crisis was primarily a struggle between "haves" and "have-nots." Although one could certainly argue that most Lebanese (and perhaps most Palestinians) would have fared better by struggling on the basis of class interest, few of them actually did so.

25. Another possible explanation for the NAAA's relative silence is that the organization was internally divided over Lebanon. But any such divisions must remain a matter of speculation, as no definitive evidence of them has emerged.

26. ALL, proceedings, May 25, 1976, Malik Papers, box 103, folder: "American Lebanese League, 1976–82, n.d.," LC; ALL, articles of organization, May 25, 1976, box 103, folder: "American Lebanese League, 1976–82, nd," LC; *Washington Post*, October 20, 1978, A13.

27. See, for example, Elias T. Saadi, "Memorandum on Lebanese Refugees," in Senate Judiciary Committee, *Humanitarian Problems in Lebanon, Part II*, 153–54; ALL to Elias Sarkis, November 2, 1976, Malik Papers, box 103, folder: "American Lebanese League, 1976–82, nd," LC.

28. Elias El-Hayek, "Strife in Lebanon: An Attempt at Delineating Its Causes," April 15, 1976, Staff Offices, Special Assistant for Ethnic Affairs, Stephen Aiello Files (hereafter Aiello Files), box 45, folder: "Lebanese(-Americans) 5/78," Jimmy Carter Presidential Library, Atlanta, GA (hereafter CL). For other contemporary analyses mentioning these same factors, see Salibi, *Crossroads to Civil War*; Ray Vicker, "Lebanon's Slipping Establishment," *Wall Street Journal*,

November 26, 1975, 18; James M. Markham, "Always Fragile: Lebanon, an Artificial Nation May Not Endure," *New York Times*, January 18, 1976, 143.

29. El-Hayek, "Strife in Lebanon."

30. Memorandum of conversation, Ford, Middle Eastern religious leaders, et al., April 15, 1976, NSA Memcons, 1973–1977, box 19, FL.

31. Petran, *Struggle Over Lebanon*, 190–94: Winslow, *Lebanon*, 203–5.

32. Patrick Seale, *Asad of Syria: The Struggle for the Middle East* (Berkeley: University of California Press, 1988), 280–81; Itamar Rabinovich, *The War for Lebanon, 1970–1985* (Ithaca, NY: Cornell University Press, 1985), 47–48.

33. Seale, *Asad*, 277, 281–83; Petran, *Struggle Over Lebanon*, 189–90; el Khazen, *Breakdown of the State*, 327–32; Rabinovich, *War for Lebanon*, 48–52; Weinberger, *Syrian Intervention*, 184–92.

34. Weinberger, *Syrian Intervention*, 263; Petran, *Struggle Over Lebanon*, 192, 195–96.

35. Seale, *Asad*, 278–80; Alan Hart, *Arafat: Terrorist or Peacemaker?* (London: Sidgwick & Jackson, 1984), 422–27; Hanna Batatu, *Syria's Peasantry, the Descendants of Its Lesser Notables, and Their Politics* (Princeton, NJ: Princeton University Press, 1999), 298–99; Bassel Salloukh, "Syria and Lebanon: A Brotherhood Transformed," *MERIP Middle East Report* 236 (Fall 2005): 15–16.

36. David Wight, "Kissinger's Levantine Dilemma: The Ford Administration and the Syrian Occupation of Lebanon," *Diplomatic History* 37, no. 1 (January 2013): 155. Kissinger seems to have been less convinced than Asad that a Leftist/PLO victory in Lebanon would provoke Israeli intervention. In a March 24 meeting with other U.S. officials, Kissinger said that the Israelis "wouldn't mind if the PLO took over [in Lebanon] because their position would be easier to maintain in American public opinion if they faced the PLO across their border." Memorandum of conversation, Kissinger, Brent Scowcroft, et al., March 24, 1976, *FRUS, 1969–1976*, 26:969. This may, however, have been an offhand observation rather than a considered opinion.

37. Wight, "Kissinger's Levantine Dilemma," 155, 164–65.

38. Ibid., 159–61.

39. Ibid., 163; Stocker, *Spheres of Intervention*.

40. See, for example, Robert G. Rabil, *Embattled Neighbors: Syria, Israel, and Lebanon* (Boulder, CO: Lynne Reinner, 2003), 51–52; Michael Kerr, "'A Positive Aspect to the Tragedy of Lebanon': The Convergence of U.S., Syrian, and Israeli Interests at the Outset of Lebanon's Civil War," *Israel Affairs* 5, no. 14 (October 2009): 360.

41. Wight, "Kissinger's Levantine Dilemma," 157–58; Stocker, *Spheres of Intervention*; memorandum of conversation, Kissinger, Simcha Dinitz, et al., March 24, 1976, Digital National Security Archive, George Washington University, Washington, DC (hereafter DNSA), KT01920.

42. Wight, "Kissinger's Levantine Dilemma," 164, 168; Stocker, *Spheres of Intervention*; U.S. Embassy, Tel Aviv, to DOS, tel #2403, April 5, 1976, AAD, 1976TELAV02403, NARA; DOS to Damascus, tel #088187, April 13, 1976, AAD, 1976STATE088187, NARA.

43. Memorandum of conversation, Kissinger, Scowcroft, et al., March 23, 1976, *FRUS, 1969–1976*, 26:953; memorandum of conversation, Ford, Kissinger, et al., March 24, 1976, *FRUS, 1969–1976*, 26:959, 959; cabinet meeting, April 14, 1976, NSA Memcons, 1973–77, box 19, FL.

44. Weinberger, *Syrian Intervention*, 209–15; Winslow, *Lebanon*, 208–9; Wight, "Kissinger's Levantine Dilemma," 169–71; Yitzhak Rabin quoted in *New York Times*, June 3, 1976, 6.

45. Mark Tessler, *A History of the Israeli-Palestinian Conflict* (Bloomington: Indiana University Press, 1994), 495; Weinberger, *Syrian Intervention*, 218–22; Petran, *Struggle Over Lebanon*, 205–10.

46. Memorandum of conversation, Ford, Kissinger, and Scowcroft, July 16, 1976, NSA Memcons, box 20, FL; telephone conversation, Kissinger and Leonard Garment, October 1, 1976, DNSA, KA15272.

47. *Washington Post*, June 17, 1976, A1, A6. Estimates of the number of Americans still in Lebanon ranged from 1,400 to 1,800. About 1,000 of them were of Lebanese descent. *New York Times*, June 21, 1976, 1, 13; *New York Times*, July 20, 1976, 3; *Washington Post*, June 18, 1976, A1.

48. *Los Angeles Times*, June 21, B1, B7, B8: *New York Times*, June 21, 1976, 13.

49. Wight, "Kissinger's Levantine Dilemma," 173; U.S. Embassy, Amman, to DOS, tel #3751, July 17, 1976, AAD, 1976AMMAN03751, NARA; DOS to Damascus, tel #180072, July 21, 1976, AAD, 1976STATE180072, NARA; *New York Times*, July 20, 1976, 3.

50. Talcott Seelye, President Ford's special representative in Lebanon following Ambassador Meloy's assassination, placed this motive at the top of a list of possible explanations for the PLO's behavior. He did not mention Kissinger's theory about Soviet-PLO collusion. U.S. Embassy, Beirut, to DOS, tel #6506, July 22, 1976, AAD, 1976BEIRUT06506, NARA.

51. *Los Angeles Times*, July 28, 1976, 4; *Washington Post*, July 28, 1976, A18; *Press-Republican* (Plattsburgh, NY), July 28, 1976, 1. On July 22, Ford sent urgent personal messages to Anwar Sadat and Crown Prince Fahd of Saudi Arabia, asking each of them to press the PLO to cooperate with evacuation efforts. Sadat wrote back to say he had "urgently" appealed for such cooperation from "Arafat and his colleagues." Fahd notified Kissinger that he had contacted Arafat and Kamal Jumblatt, both of whom "promised to do their best to solve [the] problem" but insisted "they cannot assume responsibility alone. They suggest you apply pressure to Syrians and Christians" to ensure security for any overland evacuation. DOS to U.S. Embassy, Cairo, tel #181222, July 22, 1976, AAD, 1976STATE181222, NARA; DOS to U.S. Embassy, Jidda, tel #181225, July 22, 1976, AAD, 1976STATE181225, NARA; U.S. Embassy, Cairo, to DOS, tel #9945, July 22, 1976, AAD, 1976CAIRO09945, NARA; U.S. Embassy, Jidda, to DOS, tel #5087, July 22, 1976, AAD 1976JIDDA05087, NARA.

52. Weinberger, *Syrian Intervention*, 311–13; Kissinger, *Years of Renewal*, 1049–50.

53. *Chicago Tribune*, July 14, 1976, 2; *Nashua (NH) Telegraph*, July 22, 1976, 6; *Victoria (TX) Advocate*, August 19, 1976, 5C.

54. No comprehensive accounting of private funds raised for Lebanon has surfaced. During the fiscal year running from July 1, 1975, to June 30, 1976, American Near East Refugee Aid (ANERA) donated $20,229 to Lebanon's Ministry of Public Health and $5,000 to the Lebanese Red Cross. These figures do not exhaust ANERA's contributions to Lebanon's war victims, however, as the organization disbursed about $600,000 in additional assistance for Palestinians in Lebanon and the Israeli occupied territories; it is unclear how much of this money was spent in Lebanon. In July 1976, the Palestine Arab Fund (PAF), a California-based organization with close ties to al-Fatah, sent about $50,000 worth of medical supplies to war victims in Lebanon. In September 1976, the United Holy Land Fund, a Chicago-based Palestinian charity, reported that its West Coast chapters had shipped over $200,000 in supplies for Palestinian medical relief efforts in Lebanon. (It is possible that this included the PAF shipment.) In June 1977, the AAUG reported raising $10,181 for its Lebanon Emergency Relief Fund. In November 1977, the ALL claimed that its members had raised $3.5 million in medical supplies during the civil war. *ANERA Newsletter*, July–September 1976, 1, 3; *News Circle*, August 1976, 1; "AAUG—Lebanon Emergency Relief Fund, Summary of Account as of 6/13/77," AAUG Papers, box 7, folder: "Lebanon Emergency Relief Fund II," EMUL; *News and Courier* (Charleston, SC), November 13, 1977, 2C. Even if we credit all these reports (which amount to somewhere around $4 million) and multiply them severalfold to account for reports lost to history, we are still left with a figure dwarfed by American Jewish fund-raising on behalf of Israel, which during and shortly after the 1973 Arab-Israeli War amounted to $675 million. Hasia R. Diner, *The Jews of the United States* (Berkeley: University of California Press, 2004), 323.

55. *Victoria (TX) Advocate*, August 19, 1976, 5C; *New Lebanese American Journal*, September 11, 1975, 2; *New Lebanese American Journal*, December 18, 1975, 2, 11; *Voice*, September/October 1976, 1.

56. Spofford Canfield to Nelson Rockefeller, February 4, 1976, White House Central Files (hereafter WHCF), Name File, box 6, folder: "Abourezk, James," FL; *Voice*, February 1976, 2; *Voice*, May/June 1976, 2; *Voice*, September/October 1976, 4. In October 1976, the State Department estimated that Lebanon's reconstruction would require $300 million to $500 million. In January 1977, Lebanese experts put the cost at $3 billion. *New York Times*, October 27, 1976, 3; *Washington Post*, January 13, 1977, A21.

57. Abourezk to Ford, July 26, 1976, White House Congressional Mail File, box 10, folder: "Abourezk, James," FL; Ford to Abourezk, August 15, 1976, WHCF, Name File, box 6, folder: "Abourezk, James," FL; *Voice*, September/October 1976, 1.

58. Press release, July 28, 1976, Abourezk Papers, box 109, folder: "Lebanon: Humanitarian Aid, Etc.," USDL; *Voice*, September/October 1976, 1, 6; *New York Times*, July 30, 1976, 2; *Humanitarian Problems in Lebanon, Part II*, 90–92, 94–96, 131.

59. Telegram, Elaine C. Hagopian to Arab foreign ministers, June 8, 1976, AAUG Papers, box 30, folder: "Meeting Minutes & Correspondence, May–December 1976," EMUL; AAUG *Newsletter*, December 1976, 13; Elaine C. Hagopian, "Reversing Injustice: On Utopian Activism," *Arab Studies Quarterly* 29, no. 3/4 (Summer/Fall 2007): 66.

60. *Chicago Tribune*, June 8, 1976, 3; *Los Angeles Times*, June 9, 1976, B1, B6; *Voice*, May/June 1976, 12.

61. El-Hayek, "Raison D'Etre," n.d., Aiello Files, box 45, folder: "Lebanese 5/79," CL. I am grateful to Laila Ballout for sharing a copy of this document with me. The contents of the pamphlet and a reference to its existence in another ALL document indicate that it was composed after Jimmy Carter's inauguration on January 20, 1977, and no later than early June of that year. ALL, "News Briefs," n.d. [May or June 1977], William Baroody Papers, box 85, folder: "American Lebanese League 1977," LC.

62. El-Hayek, "Raison D'Etre."

63. Petran, *Struggle Over Lebanon*, 203–5; Rabinovich, *War for Lebanon*, 55–56.

64. Petran, *Struggle Over Lebanon*, 215–16; Rabinovich, *War for Lebanon*, 55; Winslow, *Lebanon*, 209.

65. Memorandum of conversation, Ford, Kissinger, and Scowcroft, November 4, 1976, NSA Memcons, box 21, FL.

66. Petran, *Struggle Over Lebanon*, 219–22, 236–63; Hirst, *Beware of Small States*, 121.

67. Petran, *Struggle Over Lebanon*, 218–19, 232–38; Winslow, *Lebanon*, 218–19.

68. Petran, *Struggle Over Lebanon*, 240–41, 244–48; John Chalcraft, *The Invisible Cage: Syrian Migrant Workers in Lebanon* (Stanford, CA: Stanford University Press, 2009), 113; Benny Morris, *Righteous Victims: A History of the Zionist-Arab Conflict, 1881–1999* (New York: Knopf, 1999), 505.

69. AAUG *Newsletter*, March 1978, 1; AAUG *Newsletter*, June 1978, 10–13; NAAA, *Political Focus*, August 1978, 1; *Palestine Human Rights Campaign Bulletin*, May 1978, Paul N. McCloskey Papers, box 276, Hoover Institution Library and Archives, Stanford, CA; Elaine C. Hagopian and Samih Farsoun, eds., *South Lebanon: Special Report No. 2* (Detroit: Association of Arab American University Graduates, 1978); clipping, *Congressional Record*, March 21, 1978, Abourezk Papers, box 641, folder: "Middle East Con Rec. The Israeli Invasion of Lebanon, 3/21/78," USDL.

70. ALL, "News Briefs," n.d. [1977], Baroody Papers, box 85, folder: "American Lebanese League 1977," LC; *News and Courier* (Charleston, SC), November 13, 1977, 1C.

71. *New Lebanese American Journal*, February 27, 1978, 1, 4.

72. Display advertisement, *Washington Post*, July 6, 1978, A15; *Washington Post*, October 20, 1978, A13; hearing, Senate Foreign Relations Committee, Subcommittee on Near Eastern and South Asian Affairs, *The Situation of the Christian Community in Lebanon, August 16, 1978* (Washington, DC: Government Printing Office, 1978), 17; ALL fund-raising programs, Cleveland, October 20, 1978, Los Angeles, November 29, 1978, Youngstown, OH, December 1, 1978, Malik Papers, box 103, folder: "American Lebanese League, 1976–82, nd," LC; clipping, *DuPage Magazine*, December 1978, Malik Papers, box 103, folder: "American Lebanese League, 1976–82, nd," LC; *ALL Dimensions*, December 1978, Malik Papers, box 103, folder: "American Lebanese League, 1976–82, nd," LC.

73. ALL fund-raising programs, Akron, OH, February 25, 1979, Jamaica Plain, MA, April 21, 1979, Malik Papers, box 103, folder: "American Lebanese League, 1976–82, nd," LC. Neither of the Ohio senators appears to have attended an event in Akron at which both had been scheduled to appear. *ALL Dimensions*, March/April, 1979, box 103, folder: "American Lebanese League, 1976–82, nd," LC.

74. Petran, *Struggle Over Lebanon*, 236, 246; C.L. Gates, "The Lebanese Lobby in the U.S.," *MERIP Reports*, December 1978, 17–18; *Los Angeles Times*, October 6, 1978, 1, 11; *Washington Post*, August 3, 1978, A1, A14; *Washington Post*, September 29, 1978, A2.

75. *Washington Post*, October 20, 1978, A13; clipping, *Events*, December 15, 1978, Malik Papers, box 103, folder: "American Lebanese League, 1976–82, nd," LC; *Jewish Telegraphic Agency*, September 13, 1978, http://www.jta.org/1978/09/13/archive/israels-aid-to-lebanon-defended (accessed December 30, 2015).

76. In March 1979, the State Department instructed Talcott Seelye, now serving as the U.S. ambassador in Damascus, to assure Syrian foreign minister 'Abd al-Halim Khaddam that "Syria's role is essential in maintaining peace in Lebanon and in preventing a return to full-scale civil war." Talking points for Seelye-Khaddam conversation, n.d. [c. early March 1979], appended to "US Initiative on the Lebanon," March 12, 1979, Foreign and Commonwealth Office 93/2003, The National Archives, Kew, London, United Kingdom.

8. Camp David Retreat

1. *Lakeland (FL) Ledger*, December 6, 1978, 9B.

2. In his 1982 presidential memoirs, Carter wrote, "The Judeo-Christian ethic and study of the Bible were bonds between Jews and Christians which had always been part of my life. I also believed very deeply that the Jews who had survived the Holocaust deserved their own nation, and that they had a right to live in peace among their neighbors. I considered this homeland for the Jews to be compatible with the teachings of the Bible, hence ordained by God." One can readily accept that Carter's compassion for Holocaust survivors had a Christian basis. But the former president did not explain how the creation of a Jewish state in Palestine, against the wishes of Palestine's non-Jewish majority, reflected the "Judeo-Christian ethic" or was "compatible with the teachings of the Bible." Jimmy Carter, *Keeping Faith: Memoirs of a President* (Fayetteville: University of Arkansas Press, 1982), 274.

3. Carter, *Keeping Faith*, 274–47; Zbigniew Brzezinski, *Power and Principle: Memoirs of the National Security Adviser, 1977–1981* (New York: Farrar, Straus and Giroux, 1983), 5, 83–86; Kathleen Christison, *Perceptions of Palestine: Their Influence on U.S. Middle East Policy* (1999; repr., Berkeley: University of California Press, 2001), 163–65.

4. Cyrus Vance, *Hard Choices: Critical Years in America's Foreign Policy* (New York: Simon & Schuster, 1983), 164–65; Brzezinski, *Power and Principle*, 88; Christison, *Perceptions of Palestine*,

165–66; William B. Quandt, *Camp David: Peacemaking and Politics* (Washington, DC: The Brookings Institution, 1986), 34–35.

5. Quandt, *Camp David*, 34, 36–38; Vance, *Hard Choices*, 163, 164.

6. Quandt, *Camp David*, 36, 39–40, 47–48; Vance, *Hard Choices*, 164, 166, 172–73; Brzezinski, *Power and Principle*, 85–87.

7. Quandt, *Camp David*, 48–49; Vance, *Hard Choices*, 170.

8. Quandt, *Camp David*, 44–47, 50–53, 55–58, 67; Brzezinski, *Power and Principle*, 89–91; telephone conversation, Carter and James Callaghan, May 21, 1977, Prime Minister's Office Records 16/1370, The National Archives, Kew, London, United Kingdom (hereafter TNA); Carter, *Keeping Faith*, 280.

9. Christison, *Perceptions of Palestine*, 170.

10. Brzezinski to Carter, May 20, 1977, Brzezinski Collection, Subject File, box 41, folder: "Weekly Reports (to the President), 1–15 (2/77–6/77)," Jimmy Carter Presidential Library, Atlanta, GA (hereafter CL).

11. In October 1977, for example, Labor leader Shimon Peres criticized the Begin government for agreeing that a non-PLO Palestinian delegation could take part in the Geneva Conference (see main text below), claiming this was tantamount to accepting participation by the PLO itself. *Washington Post*, October 14, 1977, A14.

12. Christison, *Perceptions of Palestine*, 170–71.

13. Moshe Dayan, *Breakthrough: A Personal Account of the Egypt-Israel Peace Negotiations* (New York: Alfred A. Knopf, 1981), 20–21; Vance, *Hard Choices*, 180–84; Quandt, *Camp David*, 77–82.

14. James G. Abourezk, *Advise and Dissent: Memoirs of South Dakota and the U.S. Senate* (Chicago: Lawrence Hill Books, 1989), 177–78; press release, July 20, 1977, Abourezk Papers, box 649, folder: "Press Clippings on Israel," University of South Dakota Library, Vermillion, SD (hereafter USDL); *Los Angeles Times*, July 21, 1977, A18.

15. *New York Times*, March 21, 1977, 1, 3; Quandt, *Camp David*, 48; Middle East staff to Brzezinski, March 29, 1977, Remote Archives Capture (hereafter RAC), NLC-10-1-7-29-1, CL.

16. Quandt, *Camp David*, 85–87.

17. Patrick Tyler, *A World of Trouble: The White House and the Middle East—From the Cold War to the War on Terror* (New York: Farrar, Straus and Giroux, 2009), 187.

18. Quandt, *Camp David*, 57, 67; White House memorandum, July 21, 1977, RAC, NLC-25-74-9-4-0, CL; U.S. Embassy, Damascus, to Department of State (hereafter DOS), tel #4618, July 21, 1977, attachment to White House memorandum NLC-25-74-9-4-0. These documents refer to Mahmoud Abbas by his nom de guerre Abu Mazin.

19. Brzezinski, National Security Council Weekly Report #22, July 22, 1977, Brzezinski Collection, Subject File, box 41, folder: "Weekly Reports (to the President), 16–30 (6/77–9/77)," CL; Quandt, *Camp David*, 86–87.

20. Quandt, *Camp David*, 89, 91; Vance, *Hard Choices*, 188–89.

21. Evening notes, August 16, 1977, RAC, NLC-1-3-4-20-1, CL; DOS to U.S. Embassy, Beirut, August 17, 1977 U.S. Department of State, *Foreign Relations of the United States* (hereafter *FRUS*, with dates and volume number), *1977–1980*, 8:477.

22. U.S. Embassy, Beirut, to DOS, tel #4068, August 19, 1977, RAC, NLC-16-107-6-40-6, CL.

23. U.S. Embassy, Beirut, to DOS, August 23, 1977, *FRUS, 1977–1980*, 8:488–89.

24. *New York Times*, August 27, 1977, 3; Helena Cobban, *The Palestinian Liberation Organisation: People, Power, and Politics* (Cambridge: Cambridge University Press, 1984), 89; Quandt, *Camp David*, 101; U.S. Embassy, Beirut, to DOS, August 19, 1977, *FRUS, 1977–1980*, 8:483; CIA information cable, August 20, 1977, *FRUS, 1977–1980*, 8:486–87, 486–87.

25. Memorandum of conversations, Landrum Bolling and Yasser Arafat, September 9–12, 1977, *FRUS, 1977–1980*, 8:501–2.

26. Ibid., 503–4.

27. Ibid., 505, 511.

28. Cobban, *Palestinian Liberation Organisation*, 89–90; Quandt, *Camp David*, 102.

29. Transcript of recorded conversation, Paul Findley and Yasser Arafat, November 25, 1978, Findley Papers, box 11, folder: "Arafat's Pledge to PF," Hoover Institution Library and Archives, Stanford, CA (hereafter HILA).

30. Quandt, *Camp David*, 102; Vance, *Hard Choices*, 191.

31. Quandt, *Camp David*, 118–19, 120–22; Vance to the White House, August 5, 1977, *FRUS, 1977–1980*, 8:405. Meeting with Ismail Fahmy on September 21, Carter said that the Arab countries participating in the refugee negotiations would be Egypt, Syria, Jordan, Lebanon, Kuwait, Iraq, and perhaps other states. Ismail Fahmy, *Negotiating for Peace in the Middle East* (London: Croon Helm, 1983), 200.

32. Brzezinski, *Power and Principle*, 105; diary entry, August 31, 1977, Henry Brandon Papers, box 10, folder 2, Library of Congress, Washington, DC.

33. In October 1977, construction began on a new Jewish settlement on the outskirts of Jerusalem. The Israeli government had not authorized the settlement but made no effort to prevent its construction. Begin denied it was a new settlement because it was close to an existing one. In January 1978, the Israeli government began building four new settlements in the Sinai. Begin insisted that Moshe Dayan's promised moratorium on settlements was meant to last till the end of calendar year 1977, not for a full year starting in September 1977—an interpretation that contradicted the U.S. record of the Carter-Dayan conversation and the recollection of all of the American participants in the meeting. Quandt, *Camp David*, 161.

34. Memorandum of conversation, Carter, Dayan, et al., September 19, 1977, Brzezinski Collection, Geographic File, box 13, folder: "Middle East—Negotiations: (9/75–9/77)," CL, 1, 10, 14, 15; Brzezinski, *Power and Principle*, 107.

35. Quandt, *Camp David*, 119–20, 122–23. The Soviets initially proposed the phrase "legitimate national rights of the Palestinian people" but removed the word "national" after the Americans objected to it.

36. Steven L. Spiegel, *The Other Arab-Israeli Conflict: Making America's Middle East Policy, from Truman to Reagan* (Chicago: University of Chicago Press, 1985), 338; Congress of Presidents of Major American Jewish Organizations, *Middle East Memo*, October 3, 1977, Allard K. Lowenstein Papers, box 47, folder: "1124 Israel," University of North Carolina Library, Chapel Hill, NC (hereafter UNCL).

37. *Los Angeles Times*, October 6, 1977, A1; *Chicago Tribune*, October 8, 1977, B6; Spiegel, *Other Arab-Israeli Conflict*, 338–89; Quandt, *Camp David*, 126–31; Brzezinski, *Power and Principle*, 108–10; "Working Paper on Suggestions for the Resumption of the Geneva Peace Conference," October 5, 1977, Brzezinski Collection, Geographic File, box 13, folder: "Middle East—Negotiations: (10/77–12/77)," CL.

38. Yoram Meital, *Egypt's Struggle for Peace: Continuity and Change, 1967–1977* (Gainesville: University of Florida Press, 1997), 155–56; Quandt, *Camp David*, 88–89, 96, 109, 118.

39. Dayan, *Breakthrough*, 38–54; Quandt, *Camp David*, 108–10; Meital, *Egypt's Struggle*, 160–63. The Carter administration did not learn about the Dayan-Tuhami meeting until a few days later, when Dayan arrived in Washington and told Vance about it. Vance gave little thought to the meeting, assuming it was simply an effort to clear the path to Geneva. Quandt, *Camp David*, 111.

40. *New York Times*, October 11, 1977, 7, *New York Times*, October 23, 1977, 10; Sadat, *In Search of Identity*, 305–6; Fahmy, *Negotiating for Peace,* 243–46, 253–56; Quandt, *Camp David*, 138–42.

41. Fahmy, *Negotiating for Peace,* 256–61, 265–67; Alan Hart, *Arafat: Terrorist or Peacemaker?* (London: Sidgwick & Jackson, 1984), 434–35.

42. A few hours before Sadat's November 9 speech, U.S. ambassador to Egypt Hermann Eilts learned that Sadat might refer to a possible trip to Jerusalem. Quandt, *Camp David*, 146, note 13.

43. Quandt, *Camp David*, 146–47; Fahmy, *Negotiating for Peace,* 273–78; Ashraf Ghorbal, *Mudhakkirat Ashraf Ghurbal: Su'ud wa-inhiyar 'alaqat Misr wa-Amrika* [The memoirs of Ashraf Ghorbal: The rise and fall of Egypt's and America's relations] (Cairo: Markaz al-Ahram lil-tarjimah wa-al-nashr, 2004), 137–38; Taha al-Farnawani, *al-Sira' al-'Arabi al-Isra'ili fi-damir diblumasi Misri* [The Arab-Israeli conflict in the conscience of an Egyptian diplomat] (Cairo: Dar al-mustaqbal al-'Arabi, 1994), 110–13.

44. *New York Times*, November 10, 1977, A3; *New York Times*, November 16, 1977, A1; Sadat, *In Search of Identity*, 306–9, 311–12.

45. The analysis offered here is based less on anything Sadat said or did in November 1977 than on the positions he took the following December and January (see main text below).

46. Anwar Sadat, *Those I Have Known* (New York: Continuum, 1984), 105.

47. See the text of Sadat's Knesset address, reprinted in Quandt, *Camp David*, 345–55.

48. *New York Times*, December 2, 1977, A10; *New York Times*, 5, 1977, 3; *New York Times*, December 6, 1977, 11.

49. Quandt, *Camp David*, 149–54; Brzezinski, *Power and Principle*, 112–20, 235; Vance, *Hard Choices*, 194–95. Shedding additional light on the Carter administration's thinking are the reports of British diplomats, who consulted closely with their U.S. counterparts. See, for example, UK Embassy, Washington, to Foreign and Commonwealth Office (hereafter FCO), tels #5109 and #5111, November 30, 1977, and #5219, December 7, 1977, FCO 93/1229, TNA.

50. Middle East staff to Brzezinski, February 22, 1977, RAC, NLC 10-1-4-1-4, CL; *Voice* 4, no. 4, n.d. [c. August 1977]: 2; Joseph Baroody to Hubert Humphrey, October 17, 1977, Humphrey Papers, Correspondence Files, Legislative and Administrative, 1971–1978, box 150.J.11.4 (F), folder: "4. Middle East," Minnesota State Historical Society, St. Paul, MN (hereafter MSHS).

51. Telegram, Michael Suleiman to Carter, October 3, 1977, Association of Arab American University Graduates (AAUG) Papers, box 16, folder: "President—Michael Suleiman, 1977," Eastern Michigan University Library, Ypsilanti, MI (hereafter EMUL); Suleiman, presidential address, AAUG, Tenth Annual Convention, October 21, 1977, AAUG Papers, box 16, folder: "President—Michael Suleiman, 1977," EMUL.

52. *Washington Post*, October 24, 1977, A1.

53. Quandt, *Camp David*, 124–25; Fahmy, *Negotiating for Peace,* 252; *New York Times*, November 14, 1977, 7. Because both Said and Abu-Lughod were members of the Palestine National Council, they seemed especially likely candidates for the role Sadat was outlining.

54. *New York Times*, November 16, 1977, A14.

55. *Washington Post*, November 16, 1977, A18. Christopher Hitchens, *Hitch-22: A Memoir* (New York: Twelve, 2010), 386–87. Hitchens situated this event a bit later in the diplomatic chronology than it actually occurred. He wrote that it took place at the time of "the Jimmy Carter-Anwar Sadat-Menachem Begin 'Camp David' deal." Hitchens, *Hitch-22*, 386.

56. *Los Angeles Times*, November 14, 1977, B9.

57. John P. Richardson, "Report on Meeting with Secretary of State Vance," November 18, 1977, AAUG Papers, box 31, folder: "Meeting with President Carter," EMUL; Elaine C. Hagopian, "Ibrahim and Edward," *Arab Studies Quarterly* 26, no. 4 (Fall 2004): 8–9.

58. Richardson, "Report on Meeting with Vance," November 18, 1977, AAUG Papers, box 31, folder: "Meeting with President Carter," EMUL; Mary Haddad Macron to Fayez Sayegh, November 30, 1977, Sayegh Papers, box 359, folder 13, University of Utah Library, Salt Lake

City, UT (hereafter UUL); Hagopian to Sayegh, November 27, 1977, Sayegh Papers, box 380, folder 2, UUL.

59. "Draft Summary of Meeting with President Jimmy Carter," December 15, 1977, AAUG Papers, box 31, folder: "Meeting with President Carter," EMUL. In January 2011, Hagopian informed the author that she had drafted this document.

60. Ibid.

61. Ibid. The ALL had also voiced strong support for Carter's attempt to achieve a comprehensive settlement. In an October 3 public statement, the league praised the October 1 U.S.-Soviet joint communiqué as an effort to advance "the basic human rights of all parties" to the Middle East conflict. "A.L.L. believes that FIRM steps taken now to resolve the Palestinian problem will also help secure Lebanon's territorial integrity, thus stabilizing the entire Middle East and protecting America's vital interests there." Statement quoted in Elias T. Saadi and Paul A. Corey to Humphrey, October 7, 1977, Humphrey Papers, Correspondence Files, Legislative and Administrative, 1971–1978, box 150.J.11.4 (F), folder: "4. Middle East," MSHS.

62. President's news conference, December 15, 1977, *Public Papers of the Presidents of the United States: Jimmy Carter, 1977*, vol. 2 (Washington, DC: Government Printing Office, 1978), 2120; *New York Times,* December 30, 1977, A4.

63. Quandt, *Camp David*, 155–60, 163–65; Mohamed Ibrahim Kamel, *The Camp David Accords: A Testimony* (London: KPI, 1986), 23–27, 53–71. No U.S. officials attended the Ismailia talks in late December; Secretary Vance participated in the Jerusalem talks in mid-January.

64. This paragraph and the next summarize more detailed accounts available in Quandt, *Camp David*, 168–201; and Brzezinski, *Power and Principle*, 239–50.

65. On the diplomatic front, the Carter administration feared that agreeing to sell planes to just one or two of those three nations would alienate the remaining nation or nations. The domestic concern stemmed from the fact none of the sales could proceed without legislative approval. The administration realized that Congress, if permitted to consider each sale individually, would approve the Israeli sale and reject the Egyptian and Saudi ones. The only way to ensure passage of the Arab sales was to tie both of them to the Israeli sale in a "package deal."

66. Cobban, *Palestinian Liberation Organisation*, 94–97; Tabitha Petran, *The Struggle Over Lebanon* (New York: Monthly Review Press: 1987), 240–43; *Washington Post*, April 30, 1978, B3.

67. Nick Thimmesch, "McCloskey Seeks Israeli Bomb Restraint or an Aid Ban," *Chicago Tribune*, April 14 1978, C2; Paul N. McCloskey to "Colleague," April 10, 1978, McCloskey Papers, box 276, untitled folder, HILA; *Washington Post*, March 20, 1978, A15.

68. "Statement of Senator James Abourezk on Lebanon," March 20, 1978, clipping, *Palestine Human Rights Bulletin*, May 1978, McCloskey Papers, box 276, untitled folder, HILA, 4–5; *Washington Post*, May 8, 1978, A6. For more on the NAAA's response to the 1978 Israeli invasion, see chapter 7.

69. *Washington Post*, April 6, 1978, A1, A18; McCloskey to Carter, March 22 and April 10, 1978, McCloskey Papers, box 276, untitled folder, HILA; McCloskey to Simcha Dinitz, April 10, 1978, McCloskey Papers, box 276, untitled folder, HILA; McCloskey to Brzezinski, April 17, 1978, McCloskey Papers, box 276, untitled folder, HILA; McCloskey to Vance, April 10, 1978, Lowenstein Papers, box 47, folder: "1124 Israel," UNCL; McCloskey to Stansfield Turner, April 10, 1978, Lowenstein Papers, box 47, folder: "1124 Israel," UNCL.

70. *Washington Post*, April 6, 1978, A1; Abourezk to McCloskey, April 17, 1978, McCloskey Papers, box 276, untitled folder, HILA; Douglas J. Bennet to McCloskey, n.d. [received May 5, 1978], McCloskey Papers, box 276, untitled folder; *Chicago Tribune*, May 13, 1978, A5.

71. Editorial, *Los Angeles Times*, April 11, 1978, C6; Vance, *Hard Choices*, 209.

72. Carter, *Keeping Faith*, 315; Brzezinski to Carter, July 18, 1978, Brzezinski Collection, Geographic File, box 13, folder: "Middle East—Negotiations: (1/78–7/28/78)," CL.

73. Brzezinski, *Power and Principle*, 250–52; Quandt, *Camp David*, 201–2, 207; Carter, *Keeping Faith*, 315–16.

74. Quandt, *Camp David*, 204.

75. Brzezinski to Carter, n.d. [c. early September 1978], Brzezinski Collection, Geographic File, box 13, folder: "Middle East—Negotiations: (7/29/78–9/6/78)," CL; Vance to Carter, n.d. [c. early 1978], Brzezinski Collection, Geographic File, box 13, folder: "Middle East—Negotiations: (7/29/78–9/6/78)," CL; Quandt, *Camp David*, 212–14.

76. The Israelis ensured this result by carefully monitoring the Camp David agreement's references to Resolution 242, whose preamble asserts "the inadmissibility of the acquisition of territory by war," the legal principle underpinning Israel's obligation to withdraw from the occupied territories. Whereas the Americans and the Egyptians took the standard view that Resolution 242 was relevant to determining the final status of the West Bank and Gaza, the Israelis insisted that it applied only to the bilateral Israeli-Jordanian negotiations expected to unfold concurrently with the multilateral negotiations over the Palestinian areas. "Since in Begin's view King Hussein had no valid claim to the West Bank, and certainly none to Gaza," Quandt later wrote, "the issue of withdrawal should not arise." Unable to dissuade the Israelis on this point, the American team fudged the issue. It drafted a paragraph that described first the multilateral Palestinian negotiations and then the bilateral Israeli-Jordanian ones. "The negotiations," the paragraph continued, "shall be based on all the provisions and principles of UN Security Council Resolution 242." The Israelis could claim that this sentence referred only to the Israeli-Jordanian negotiations; everyone else could claim that it covered both sets of negotiations. Quandt, *Camp David*, 243–45; "A Framework for Peace in the Middle East Agreed at Camp David," reprinted in ibid., 379.

77. Carter wrote in his memoirs, "I explained to [Sadat] the extremely serious consequences of his unilaterally breaking off the negotiations: that his action would harm the relationship between Egypt and the United States, he would be violating his personal promise to me, and the onus for failure would be on him. . . . I told him it would damage one of my most precious possessions—his friendship and our mutual trust." Carter, *Keeping Faith*, 392. A few days after the encounter, Carter reported to Brzezinski that he had also said that Sadat's departure "would probably mean the end of my Presidency because this whole effort will be discredited." Brzezinski, *Power and Principle*, 272.

78. Quandt, *Camp David*, 241, 245.

79. For a detailed presentation of Mohamed Kamel's perspective and that of other Egyptian officials who opposed the Camp David agreement, see Kamel, *Camp David Accords*, 294–382.

80. "Framework for the Conclusion of a Peace Treaty Between Egypt and Israel," reproduced in Quandt, *Camp David*, 381–82.

81. The accords' sole mention of Jerusalem was a reference to Sadat's visit to that city in November 1977. Simultaneously with the signing of the accords, Sadat, Begin, and Carter submitted side letters outlining their governments' respective positions on Jerusalem. Sadat's letter stated that East Jerusalem "is an integral part of the West Bank" and "should be under Arab sovereignty." Begin's letter claimed that "Jerusalem is one city indivisible, the Capital of the State of Israel." Carter's letter referred to previous U.S. statements taking the view that East Jerusalem was Israeli-occupied territory but, on account of its special religious character, held a status different from that of the West Bank. The only mention of Palestinian refugees in the Camp David Accords was in a sentence stating that Israel, Egypt, and "other interested parties" would, in final status negotiations over the West Bank and Gaza, work "to establish agreed procedures for a prompt, just and permanent implementation of the resolution of the refugee problem."

"A Framework for Peace in the Middle East Agreed at Camp David," reprinted in Quandt, *Camp David*, 376, 380; letters from Sadat, Begin, and Carter, September 17, 1978, reprinted in ibid., 385–86.

82. "Framework for Peace in the Middle East Agreed at Camp David," reprinted in ibid., 376–81.

83. Ibid., 247–51, 263–64, 277; Jimmy Carter, *White House Diary* (New York: Farrar, Straus and Giroux, 2010), 256.

84. Quandt, *Camp David*, 277; *Los Angeles Times*, September 22, 1978, B8; *Newsweek*, October 2, 1978, 24–27; Carter, *Keeping Faith*, 405.

85. "NAAA Statement on Camp David Outcome," September 18, 1978, Alfred M. Lilienthal Papers, box 86, folder: "National Association of Arab Americans," HILA; NAAA, *Political Focus*, April 1, 1979, 1; NAAA, *Political Focus*, April 15, 1979, 1; "AAUG statement on the Camp David Summit," September 19, 1978, AAUG Papers, box 16, folder: "President—Fouad Moughrabi 1978," EMUL; Michael S. Sahady to Carter, October 2, 1978, Staff Offices, Special Assistant for Ethnic Affairs, Stephen Aiello Files, box 45, folder: "Lebanese Correspondence, 12/78–7/79," CL. I am grateful to Laila Ballout for providing me a copy of this document.

86. *Chicago Tribune*, September 19, 1978, 5; *Los Angeles Times*, September 19, 1978, A1; *Washington Post*, November 6, 1978, A21; Quandt, *Camp David*, 264–65, 279–80; Nigel J. Ashton, *King Hussein of Jordan: A Political Life* (New Haven, CT: Yale University Press, 2008), 202–6.

87. Quandt, *Camp David*, 277–79, 285–90; Vance, *Hard Choices*, 238, 241–42; Carter, *White House Diary*, 258; Brzezinski, National Security Council Weekly Report #81, December 2, 1978, Brzezinski Collection, Subject File, box 42, folder: "Weekly Report to the President, 71–81 (9/78–12/78)," CL; Brzezinski, *Power and Principle*, 277–78.

88. Quandt, *Camp David*, 290–92; Brzezinski quoted in ibid., 295; Vance, *Hard Choices*, 243.

89. Quandt, *Camp David*, 296. Quandt's contemporaneous account of the meeting contains a terser rendition of Carter's remarks on this issue. Memorandum of conversation, Carter, Vance, et al., February 19, 1979, *FRUS, 1977–1980*, 9:606, 607.

90. Quandt, *Camp David*, 286, 296, 300–301; Vance, *Hard Choices*, 246.

91. Quandt, *Camp David*, 313–14. The text of the memorandum of agreement is reprinted in Dayan, *Breakthrough*, 356–57.

92. *Los Angeles Times*, March 27, 1979, A23; *al-Siyasa* (Kuwait), March 28, 1979, 18. Some Arab observers suspected that Sadat deliberately omitted those passages after hearing anti-Cairo slogans chanted by Palestinian demonstrators congregating across the street from the White House. *Al-Siyasa* (Kuwait), March 28, 1979, 18.

93. *Al-Siyasa* (Kuwait), March 26, 1979, 8; *Al-Siyasa* (Kuwait), March 27, 1979, 5, 16; *Al-Siyasa* (Kuwait), March 28, 1979, 17, 18; *Los Angeles Times*, March 27, 1979, B1, B19; Stein, *Heroic Diplomacy*, 259; memorandum of conversation, Brzezinski, Sadat, et al., March 18, 1979, *FRUS, 1977–1980*, 9:761–63.

94. Mark Tessler, *A History of the Israeli-Palestinian Conflict* (Bloomington: Indiana University Press, 1994), 517–18; Ann Mosely Lesch, *Political Perceptions of the Palestinians on the West Bank and the Gaza Strip* (Washington, DC: The Middle East Institute, 1980), 11–25, 92–95; *Newsweek*, April 2, 1979, 25; *Washington Post*, June 4, 1979, A1, A18. The Israeli guidelines stated that any autonomy provisions extended to the West Bank and Gaza would apply to the inhabitants but not to the land, over which Israel would retain control and on which it would continue to build Jewish settlements. *New York Times*, May 18, 1979, A1, A7.

95. Carter, *White House Diary*, 323, 341; Tessler, *Israeli-Palestinian Conflict*, 518–20. By the end of 1980, there were 12,500 Israeli settlers on the West Bank (excluding East Jerusalem), up from 4,000 in mid-1977. Tessler, *Israeli-Palestinian Conflict*, 520.

96. Quandt, *Camp David*, 302, 313–14.

97. *New York Times*, March 13, 1979, A10; *Chicago Tribune*, March 14, 1979, 8; *Los Angeles Times*, March 27, 1979, B16. For Vance's and Brzezinski's use of the same language, see *Washington Post*, March 19, 1979, A20; *New York Times*, March 20, 1979, A7.

98. Jimmy Carter, *The Blood of Abraham: Insights into the Middle East* (Boston: Houghton Mifflin, 1985), 45.

99. See, for example, *Chicago Tribune*, October 29, 1978, B2; *Williamson (WV) Daily News*, November 4, 1978, 1; *Newsweek*, April 2, 1979, 24.

100. Memorandum of conversation, Carter, Dick Clark, and Robert Hunter, June 22, 1979, National Security Affairs, Subject File, box 37, folder: "Memcons: President, 6/79," CL.

101. For a detailed analysis of public opinion data on the Arab-Israeli conflict in these years, see Richard H. Curtiss, *A Changing Image: American Perceptions of the Arab-Israeli Dispute* (Washington, DC: American Educational Trust, 1982), 189–208.

102. *Washington Post*, February 7, 1978, A9; *New York Times*, April 14, 1978, A1, A10; Curtiss, *Changing Image*, 195, 197; Ghorbal, *Mudhakkirat*, 113.

103. Curtiss, *Changing Image*, 193, 195–200, 210.

104. *Newsweek*, December 5, 1977, 110; *New York Times*, April 30, 1978, E4; memorandum of conversation, Brzezinski, Hussein, et al., March 18, 1979, *FRUS, 1977–1980*, 9:753; A.J.D. Stirling to FCO, February 20, 1979, FCO 93/2212, TNA.

105. See, for example, *Los Angeles Times*, January 3, 1978, B21; *Los Angeles Times*, January 8, 1978, A13; *Los Angeles Times*, February 1, 1978, B1, B14; Anwar Sadat, National Press Club address, excerpts, *New York Times*, February 7, 1978, 4; Sadat, "Egypt's Efforts to Promote Peace, and Israel's Responses," *New York Times*, March 21, 1978, 35.

106. Sara C. Gentry to "Friends," April 1978, Frank Maria Papers, box 63, folder 8, Immigration History Research Center, University of Minnesota, Minneapolis, MN; James Zogby, "Fall Program," n.d. [c. summer 1978], bound compilation of Palestine Human Rights Campaign documents, in possession of James Zogby, Washington, DC; John J. O'Connor, "A Changed Focus on Palestine," *New York Times*, January 14, 1979, D31.

107. George Ball, "The F15 Sale," *Washington Post*, May 15, 1978, A22; *Time*, May 8, 1978, 30–31; *Time*, May 22, 1978, 17–18; *Newsweek*, May 22, 1978, 18–19; *Hearings before the Committee on Foreign Relations, United States Senate, 95th Congress, Second Session, on Proposed U.S. Sales of Fighter Aircraft to Saudi Arabia, Egypt, and Israel, May 3, 4, 5, and 8, 1978* (Washington, DC: U.S. Government Printing Office, 1978).

108. AAUG *Newsletter*, June 1978, 1, 2–3. For news stories mentioning the NAAA's involvement in the arms sales debate, see *Chicago Tribune*, March 19, 1978, 26; *Chicago Tribune*, April 30, 1978, A1; *New York Times*, April 30, 1978, E4; *New York Times*, May 12, 1978, A11; *Washington Post*, May 7, 1978, A14; clipping, *Washington Star*, April 18, 1978, Abourezk Papers, box 649, folder: "Search Info—MERC, Arab Lobby," USDL, A-5.

109. Thimmesch, "The Arabs in Washington," *Saturday Evening Post*, May/June 1979, 135; *Washington Post*, May 12, 1978, A5. As Richardson, with wry amusement, recalled decades later, "We probably got more visibility than we deserved." Richardson, interview with the author, December 13, 2012.

110. *Washington Post*, May 7, 1978, A14; Abourezk to Richardson, June 14, 1978, Abourezk Papers, box 649, folder: "Search Info—MERC, Arab Lobby," USDL.

9. Abdul Enterprises

1. Note for the record, n.d. [apparently October 7, 1977], James G. Abourezk Papers, box 647, folder, "The Fake Shaykh—10/77," University of South Dakota Library, Vermillion,

SD (hereafter USDL); clipping, *National Enquirer*, October 25, 1977, Abourezk Papers, box 647, folder, "The Fake Shaykh—10/77," USDL.

2. Clipping, *National Enquirer*, October 25, 1977, Abourezk Papers, box 647, folder, "The Fake Shaykh—10/77," USDL; clipping, *Pierre (SD) Times*, March 4, 1977 (mislabeled: 1978), Abourezk Papers, box 647, folder, "The Fake Shaykh—10/77," USDL.

3. Daniel Yergin, *The Prize: The Epic Quest for Oil, Money, and Power* (New York: Simon & Schuster, 1991), 633–46; James A. Bill, *The Eagle and the Lion: The Tragedy of American-Iranian Relations* (New Haven, CT: Yale University Press, 1988), 216–17; Andrew Scott Cooper, *The Oil Kings: How the U.S., Iran, and Saudi Arabia Changed the Balance of Power in the Middle East* (New York: Simon & Schuster, 2011), 159–62, 178–79, 200–203, 220, 223–26, 229, 250–55, 276–78, 311, 336.

4. Treasury Department report quoted in David M. Wight, "The Petrodollar Era and Relations between the United States and the Middle East and North Africa, 1969–1980" (PhD diss., University of California, Irvine, 2014), 100; Gad G. Gilbar, *The Middle East Oil Decade and Beyond: Essays in Political Economy* (London: Frank Cass, 1997), 40–42; *Los Angeles Times*, August 18, 1977, E19; *New York Times*, June 15, 1978, D4.

5. *Chicago Tribune*, November 18, 1974, A2; *Washington Post*, December 10, 1974, D10; *New York Times*, February 24, 1975, 9; *New York Times*, March 4, 1975, 43, 49; *Hearings before the Subcommittee on Multinational Corporations of the Committee on Foreign Relations, United States Senate, 94th Congress, First Session, July 16, September 11, 18, October 9, 29, 1975, Part 15* (Washington, DC: U.S. Government Printing Office, 1976), 25, 27, 65–66.

6. *Chicago Tribune*, January 1, 1975, 1, 19; *Los Angeles Times*, January 9, 1975, F11; *New York Times*, March 23, 1975, section 4, 3; *Wall Street Journal*, October 28, 1975, 22; *Hearings on Multinational Corporations*, 25–26, 37–38, 131–32.

7. *Washington Post*, December 1, 1974, A1, A6; *Washington Post*, December 10, 1974, D10; Wight, "Petrodollar Era," 168–70; Diane B. Kunz, *Butter and Guns: America's Cold War Economic Diplomacy* (New York: The Free Press, 1997), 256–57.

8. Wight, "Petrodollar Era," 170–71; Kunz, *Butter and Guns*, 257–58.

9. Wight, "Petrodollar Era," 171–73; Kunz, *Butter and Guns*, 258–59.

10. Wight, "Petrodollar Era," 173–74; U.S. Embassy, Abu Dhabi, to Department of State (hereafter DOS), tel #3045, November 14, 1976, Central Foreign Policy Files, Electronic Telegrams, Access to Archival Databases (hereafter AAD) 1976ABUDH03045, National Archives and Records Administration, College Park, MD (hereafter NARA); U.S. Embassy, Jidda, to DOS, tel #7560, November 18, 1976, AAD, 1976JIDDA07560, NARA.

11. AAD, 1976JIDDA07560, NARA. Assistant secretary of state for Near Eastern affairs Alfred Atherton later wrote to Abourezk that Horan "acted properly in suggesting that he accompany you for your audience with King Khalid" but "obviously pressed matters further than he should have." Atherton to Abourezk, December 3, 1976, Abourezk Papers, box 653, folder: "ME Trip Fall 1976," USDL.

12. Cooper, *Oil Kings*, 359–63; Morris Adelman, *The Genie Out of the Bottle: World Oil since 1970* (Cambridge, MA: The MIT Press, 1996), 159; U.S. Embassy, Abu Dhabi, tel #3045, November 14, 1976, 1976ABUDH03045, NARA.

13. *New York Times*, November 24, 1974, F5; *Wall Street Journal*, June 9, 1975, 5.

14. Harold Robbins, *The Pirate* (New York: Pocket Books, 1974), 103. For Adnan Khashoggi's role as the inspiration for Robbins's protagonist, see *New York Times*, July 6, 1975, Section 3, 1.

15. *Network*, Metro-Goldwyn-Mayer, 1976.

16. I am indebted to Jack G. Shaheen, who, by documenting commercial television shows at the time of their initial broadcast (see main text below), called my attention to all of the programs discussed in this paragraph and the next. Over three decades later, I was able to view

all of the programs online, where they had been previously posted or were available on a pay-per-view basis.

17. "Marathon Angels," *Charlie's Angels*, aired March 7, 1979, Sony Pictures, available at Amazon.com pay-per-view; "The Surrogate," *Trapper John, MD*, aired December 23, 1979, 20th Century Fox, posted online at http://www.youtube.com/watch?v=lQiQN0EQN8M (accessed December 26, 2013).

18. "The Sheik," *CHiPs*, aired November 18, 1978, MGM Television, available at Amazon.com pay-per-view.

19. To confirm the accuracy of his notes, Shaheen frequently requested, and sometimes received, program transcripts from the networks themselves. He recalls that he acquired a videocassette recorder around 1978, though the continuation of transcript requests into 1979 and 1980 suggests that he either obtained the VCR later than he remembers or did not use it as his exclusive means of recording TV content in this period. Shaheen to Barbara Zuckerman, November 13, 1978, Shaheen Papers, box 17, folder: "NBC Letters," Tamiment Library, New York University, New York, NY (hereafter TL); Shaheen to Traviesas, May 25, 1979, Shaheen Papers, box 17, folder: "NBC Letters," TL; Shaheen to Bettye King Hoffman, December 10, 1979, Shaheen Papers, box 17, folder: "NBC Letters," TL; Hoffman to Shaheen, January 4, 1980, Shaheen Papers, box 17, folder: "NBC Letters," TL; Shaheen, telephone conversation with the author, January 3, 2014.

20. Shaheen to Donn O'Brien, January 15, 1980, Shaheen Papers, box 17, folder: "CBS Letters," TL. See also Shaheen to Zuckerman, November 13, 1978, Shaheen Papers, box 17, folder: "NBC Letters," TL; Shaheen to Jack Elinson and Norman Paul, December 14, 1978, Shaheen Papers, box 3, folder: "L.A. Interviews, TV ARAB, Correspondence, 1980s," TL.

21. O'Brien to John P. Richardson, December 19, 1978, Shaheen Papers, box 17, folder: "CBS Letters," TL; Marjorie Holyoak to Cheryl Abdullah, August 21, 1980, Shaheen Papers, box 16, folder: "TV Move, 'The Pirate,'" TL; Van Gordon Sauter to Joanne Myler, November 14, 1977, Shaheen Papers, box 3, folder: "L.A. Interviews, TV ARAB, Correspondence, 1980s," TL.

22. It is difficult to gauge the impact of Shaheen's criticism, and that of others like him, on television content in the late 1970s. Midlevel network executives held cordial meetings with Shaheen and other Arab-friendly critics and repeatedly assured them that their message was getting through. Occasionally, an executive would report that an objectionable episode would not be rebroadcast, but it is not clear that the criticism was a decisive factor in such decisions. Shaheen, *The TV Arab* (Bowling Green, OH: Bowling Green State University Press, 1984), 6, 64, 70; O'Brien to Richardson, December 27, 1978, Shaheen Papers, box 17, folder: "CBS Letters," TL; O'Brien to Shaheen, September 21, 1979, Shaheen Papers, box 17, folder: "CBS Letters," TL; Richardson, memo for the record, n.d. [on or shortly after May 30, 1979], Shaheen Papers, box 17, folder: "NBC Letters," TL; Ralph Daniels to Shaheen, June 8, 1979, Shaheen Papers, box 17, folder: "CBS Letters," TL.

23. O'Brien to Shaheen, December 26, 1979, Shaheen Papers, box 17, folder: "CBS Letters," TL; Shaheen to O'Brien, January 8, 1980, Shaheen Papers, box 17, folder: "CBS Letters," TL.

24. Shaheen, "The Arabs: TV's Most Popular Villain," *Christian Century*, December 13, 1978, 1213–18; Shaheen, "Do Television Programs Stereotype Arabs?," *Wall Street Journal*, October 12, 1979, 23; Shaheen, "Why This Image of a Bloodsucking Blackmailer?," *Voice*, September 10, 1979; ; Shaheen, "The Arab Stereotype on Television," *Link*, April–May 1980, 1–13; clipping, Shaheen, "The Television Arab: Hollywood's Nigger," *Middle East International*, April 13, 1979, 10, Shaheen Papers, box 7, folder: "Articles: Published," TL; clipping, Shaheen, "TV's Dehumanizing Perception of Arabs," *Media Reporter*, Summer 1980, 38–39, Shaheen Papers, box 7, folder: "1970s–1980s," TL.

25. *Los Angeles Times*, April 2, 1978, WS1; *Los Angeles Times*, April 17, 1978, F1, F6; *Los Angeles Times*, April 27, 1978, WS1, WS6; *Los Angeles Times*, July 17, 1978, B3.

26. *Evening News* (Newburgh, NY), January 23, 1975, 1; *Southeast Missourian* (Cape Girardeau, MO), March 7, 1975, 6; Art Buchwald, "Forget the Alamo," *Lewiston (ME) Evening Journal*, January 28, 1975, 4.

27. *New York Times*, March 28, 1975, 1, 24; *Wall Street Journal*, May 14, 1976, 1; *Los Angeles Times*, November 26, 1978, 16; clipping, *Moment*, September 1978, 16, Sayegh Papers, box 48, folder 8, University of Utah Library, Salt Lake City.

28. *Washington Post*, October 10, 1980, B4; *Newsweek*, February 19, 1979, 81.

29. *Washington Post*, November 5, 1977, C1; Nicholas Lemann, "War-Torn Georgetown," *New Republic*, June 2, 1979, 16–19.

30. Paul Findley, *They Dare to Speak Out: People and Institutions Confront Israel's Lobby* (Westport, CT: Lawrence Hill, 1985), 196–201; *New York Times*, February 24, 1981, A13. Libya had made the gift in $150,000 increments, and as of early 1981 the final increment was yet to be disbursed. Thus Georgetown returned $600,000 rather than the full $750,000. *New York Times*, February 24, 1981, A13.

31. *Time*, November 13, 1978, 75; *Newsweek*, February 19, 1979, 81; *Los Angeles Times*, June 7, 1979, A3.

32. Findley, *They Dare to Speak Out*, 189–90; *Fortune*, June 1977, 114–16.

33. Findley, *They Dare to Speak Out*, 191–92; *Chicago Tribune*, August 16, 1978, 1.

34. Findley, *They Dare to Speak Out*, 192–95.

35. *New York Times*, June 10, 1979, 17; *New York Times*, March 4, 1980, A1, D19; *New York Times*, June 6, 1982, 29.

36. Deborah Shapley, "Middle East Studies: Funding Wilts as Arab-U.S. Friendship Flowers," *Science*, July 5, 1974, 42–44; *Los Angeles Times*, April 15, 1979, A4.

37. Matthew F. Jacobs, *Imagining the Middle East: The Building of an American Foreign Policy, 1918–1967* (Chapel Hill: University of North Carolina Press, 2011); Zachary Lockman, *Contending Visions of the Middle East: The History and Politics of Orientalism* (New York: Cambridge University Press, 2004), 121–214. For a polemical treatment that nonetheless provides some useful information about the field's changing ethnic character, see Martin Kramer, *Ivory Towers on Sand: The Failure of Middle East Studies in America* (Washington, DC: Washington Institute for Near East Policy, 2001), 38–39. For more on the later prominence of Edward Said's *Orientalism*, see the epilogue.

38. Connally was notorious for having urged Nixon to destroy the Watergate tapes before they could be turned over to Congress or federal prosecutors, but he was otherwise generally untainted by that scandal. James Reston, Jr., *The Lone Star: The Life of John Connally* (New York: Harper & Row, 1989), 454–55.

39. Reston, Jr., *Lone Star*, 557–58; *New York Times*, December 21, 1977, A1, D11; *New York Times*, December 28, 1977, D1, D9.

40. Andrew Busch, *Reagan's Victory: The Presidential Election of 1980 and the Rise of the Right* (Lawrence: University Press of Kansas, 2005), 45.

41. Reston, Jr., *Lone Star*, 561–68; Samuel Hoskinson, interview with Paul Findley, June 22, 1983, Findley Papers, box 4, folder: "Connally," Hoover Institution Library and Archives, Stanford, CA (hereafter HILA).

42. For a full text of the speech, see the advertisement that the Connally campaign took out in the *Los Angeles Times*, October 12, 1979, C4.

43. Connally referred, for example, to Israel's "policy of creeping annexation of the West Bank." Ibid.

44. "John Connally, Weakling," *New Republic*, October 27, 5; editorial, *New York Times*, October 21, 1979, E20; Maxwell Greenberg and Howard Baker quoted in *Jewish Telegraphic Agency*, October 15, 1979, http://www.jta.org/1979/10/15/archive/connally-under-fire (accessed January 15, 2014).

45. See, for example, George F. Will, "Dear John," *Washington Post*, November 8, 1979, A19; John Chamberlin, "Connally Mideast Plan Unrealistic," *Daily News* (Bowling Green, KY), November 13, 1979, 6.

46. *Washington Post*, October 19, 1979, A3; *Washington Post*, November 6, 1979, A7; *Chicago Tribune*, October 28, 1979, A12; *New York Times*, November 7, 1979, A17.

47. Editorial, *New York Times*, October 21, 1979, E20; Richard Reeves, "Has Connally Been Too Clever?" *Sarasota (FL) Journal*, November 8, 1979, 6-A; George Will, "Characteristic Connally," *Washington Post*, October 18, 1979, A19.

48. Clipping, William Loeb, "Oily John—The Arab Candidate," *Manchester Union Leader*, date obscured [c. late 1979], Findley Papers, box 4, folder: "Connally," HILA; letters, *New York Times*, October 18, 1979, A22.

49. The reference to future revelations was omitted from the version of Anderson's column published in the *Washington Post* (December 12, 1979, C19), but it appeared in numerous other newspapers that syndicated the column. See, for example, *Daily Reporter* (Spencer, IA), December 12, 1979, 4; *Kingman (AZ) Daily Miner*, December 12, 1979, A-4; *Sarasota (FL) Herald-Tribune*, December 12, 1979, 7-A; *Sumter (SC) Daily Item*, December 12, 1979, 17A; *Gadsden (AL) Times*, December 12, 1979, 4; *Deseret News* (Salt Lake City, UT), December 12, 1979, 4A; *Hour* (Norwalk, CT), December 12, 1979, 5; *Bryan (OH) Times*, December 15, 1979, 4.

50. Jack Anderson, "Connally Showed Pro-Arab Bias Early," *Washington Post*, March 12, 1980, E9; *Los Angeles Times*, February 12, 1980, 13.

51. Reston, Jr., *Lone Star*, 579–80, 585–86.

52. Reston, Jr., *Lone Star*, 570, 585; James Reston, "Iowa Burns Myths and Illusions," *Lawrence (KS) Journal-World*, January 24, 1980, 4.

53. The information in this and the next three paragraphs comes primarily from Robert W. Greene, *The Sting Man: Inside Abscam* (New York: E.P. Dutton, 1981).

54. See the recollections of John Good, supervisor of the FBI's Abscam investigation, in *Grapevine*, January/February 2015, http://fbistudies.com/wp-content/uploads/2015/03/FBI-Grapevine-Abscam.pdf (accessed September 20, 2015). *Grapevine* is a journal published by the Society of Former Special Agents of the FBI.

55. *Newsweek*, February 18, 1980, 30–33; *Time*, February 18, 1980, 10, 13–14.

56. For the former view, see editorial, *St. Petersburg (FL) Times*, February 7, 1980, 18A; Lemann, "Putting the House (and Senate) in Order," *Washington Post*, February 10, 1980, D1. For the latter, see editorial, *Washington Post*, February 5, 1980, A16; William Raspberry, "The Catch in the Catch," *Washington Post*, February 6, 1980, A19; Arthur R. Miller, "May One Branch 'Entrap' Another?" *Sarasota (FL) Herald Tribune*, February 24, 1980, 2G.

57. See, for example, Joseph Kraft, "Media Don't Come Off Scot-Free in Abscam," *Los Angeles Times*, February 15, 1980, D7; Meg Greenfield, "Abscammery: Nagging Doubts," *Washington Post*, February 20, 1980, A19.

58. "Letters to the Editor: Abscam," *Washington Post*, February 10, 1980, D6; "Letters: ABSCAM Affair," *St. Petersburg (FL) Times*, February 14, 1980, 23A; *True FBI Files: Abscam*, n.d. (compilation of FBI documents released under the Freedom of Information Act), http://books.google.com/books?id=ZG8M6cljh5YC&printsec=frontcover&dq=abscam+fbi&hl=en&sa=X&ei=G3_sUtHGNsXroASV6YEQ&ved=0CDkQ6AEwAg#v=onepage&q=abscam%20fbi&f=false (accessed June 13, 2015).

59. *News Circle*, February/March 1980, 18; *Christian Science Monitor*, February 21, 1980; *Los Angeles Times*, June 15, 1980, F1; *Spartanburg (SC) Herald Journal*, February 13, 1980, A5.

60. *Washington Post*, February 5, 1980, A4; *News Circle*, February/March 1980, 9; AAUG *Newsletter*, September 1979/March 1980, 7; Mujid Kazimi to AAUG members, February 12, 1980, AAUG Twin Cities Chapter Papers, box 1, Immigration History Research Center, University of Minnesota, Minneapolis, MN; *New York Times*, February 4, 1980, A15.

61. *Washington Post*, February 7, 1980, D1; AAUG *Newsletter*, September 1979/March 1980, 7.

62. Abdeen Jabara to Abourezk, March 2, 1980, Shaheen Papers, box 17, folder: "Various Letters from People & Corp.," TL; James Zogby, interview with the author, July 19, 2010; Abourezk, interview with the author, December 19, 2007.

63. *ADC Report* #1, October 1980, Jabara Papers, box 9, folder, "ADC (American-Arab Anti-Discrimination Committee), 1980–1981," Bentley Historical Library, University of Michigan, Ann Arbor, MI (hereafter BHL); Zogby to ADC members, December 1980, William E. Mulligan Papers, box 12, folder 10, Georgetown University Library, Washington, DC; *Sarasota (FL) Herald-Tribune*, November 8, 1981, 2C; Shaheen, *Abscam: Arabiaphobia in America* (n.d., repr., Washington, DC: American-Arab Anti-Discrimination Committee, 1980); Shaheen, *The Influence of the Arab Stereotype on American Children* (n.d., repr., Washington, DC: American-Arab Anti-Discrimination Committee, 1980 or 1981).

64. *ADC Report* #1, October 1980, Jabara Papers, box 9, folder, "ADC (American-Arab Anti-Discrimination Committee), 1980–1981," BHL; extract from unspecified *ADC Report*, date unknown [c. 1981], Shaheen Papers, box 9, folder: "Anti-Discrimination League," TL; *ADC Report* #7, June 1981, Shaheen Papers, box 9, folder: "Anti-Discrimination League," TL.

65. *ADC Report* #5 and #6, March/April 1981, Shaheen Papers, box 9, folder: "Anti-Discrimination League," TL; Roger Simon, "Arab Fair Game? He Won't Play," *Chicago Sun-Times*, March 5, 1981, reprinted in *ADC Report* #5 and #6; *LA Times*, March 5, 1981, F14.

10. The Center Cannot Hold

1. Walter Fauntroy to Jimmy Carter, November 8, 1979, Association of Arab American University Graduates Papers, box 31, folder: "Correspondence, 1979 (January–December)," Eastern Michigan University Library (hereafter EMUL); *Chicago Tribune*, September 21, 1979, A8; *Washington Post*, September 23, 1979, B1, B3.

2. *Washington Post*, November 18, 1979, A1, A10; *Chicago Tribune*, November 23, 1979, 1, 18.

3. Daniel Yergin, *The Prize: The Epic Quest for Oil, Money, and Power* (New York: Simon & Schuster, 1991), 684–92.

4. Victor R.S. McFarland, "Living in Never-Never Land: The United States, Saudi Arabia, and Oil in the 1970s" (PhD diss., Yale University, 2014), 311–13; R[ichard] J.S. Muir to David Tatham, February 9, 1979, Foreign and Commonwealth Office (hereafter FCO) 93/1819, The National Archives, Kew, London, United Kingdom (hereafter TNA); David Owen to James Callaghan, February 22, 1979, FCO 93/1819, TNA; James Akins to Zbigniew Brzezinski, February 14, 1979, White House Central Files (hereafter WHCF), Subject File, Countries, box CO-52, folder: "CO 134 1/20/77–1/20/81 Confidential," Jimmy Carter Presidential Library, Atlanta, GA (hereafter CL); Andrew I. Killgore to George W. Ball, May 1, 1979, Ball Papers, box 61, folder 16, Princeton University Library, Princeton, NJ (hereafter PUL).

5. McFarland, "Never-Never Land," 313–16; Muir to Tatham, March 9, 1979, FCO 93/1819, TNA; "Saudi Arabia: An Assessment as of January 1, 1980," Remote Access Capture (hereafter RAC), NLC-15-46-8-18-8, CL; *New York Times*, February 27, 1979, A2.

6. Ann Mosely Lesch, *Political Perceptions of the Palestinians on the West Bank and the Gaza Strip* (Washington, DC: The Middle East Institute, 1980), 11–25, 92–95.

7. Paul Findley, *They Dare to Speak Out: People and Institutions Confront Israel's Lobby* (Westport, CT: Lawrence Hill, 1985), 1–12; Findley, interview with the author, July 17, 2008.

8. Findley, *They Dare to Speak Out*, 12–13; transcript of recorded conversation, Findley and Yasser Arafat, November 25, 1978, Findley Papers, box 11, folder: "Arafat's Pledge to PF," Hoover Institution Library and Archives, Stanford, CA; statement by Yasser Arafat, November 25, 1978, Findley Papers, box 11, folder: "Arafat's Pledge to PF," Hoover Institution Library and Archives.

9. Findley, *They Dare to Speak Out*, 13; *Chicago Tribune*, December 2, 1978, S2; Findley, interview with the author, July 17, 2008.

10. According to the spokesman, Arafat told Findley "that it is our right to establish an independent Palestinian state on any part of Palestine that is liberated or evacuated." *Los Angeles Times*, November 28, 1978, B21. This was essentially the same formulation that the PLO had used since 1974. It was silent on the acceptance of Israel but did not exclude it, either.

11. *New York Times*, December 20, 1978, A6; Yezid Sayigh, *Armed Struggle and the Search for State: The Palestinian National Movement, 1949–1993* (Oxford: Clarendon Press, 1997), 441; Douglas Bennet to Helen Meyner, January 24, 1979, WHCF, Subject File, Countries, box CO-48, folder: "CO 120 1/20/77–1/20/81 General," CL.

12. Findley to Carter, April 18, 1979, WHCF, Subject File, Countries, box CO-48, folder: "CO 120 1/20/77–1/20/81 Executive," CL; Bennet to Findley, May 24, 1979, WHCF, Subject File, Countries, box CO-48, folder: "CO 120 1/20/77–1/20/81 Executive," CL.

13. Steven L. Spiegel, *The Other Arab-Israeli Conflict: Making America's Middle East Policy, from Truman to Reagan* (Chicago: University of Chicago, 1985), 373–74.

14. G[raham] S. Burton to "John" [Moberly], May 15, 1979, FCO 93/2176, TNA.

15. Summary, senior-level meeting, July 25, 1979, U.S. Department of State, *Foreign Relations of the United States* (hereafter *FRUS*, with dates and volume number), *1977–1980*, 9:886–87; UK Embassy, Washington, tels #1863, July 10, 1979, and #2120, July 30, 1979, FCO 93/2176, TNA; Zbigniew Brzezinski, *Power and Principle: Memoirs of the National Security Adviser, 1977–1981* (New York: Farrar, Straus and Giroux, 1983), 439.

16. For Findley's role as an intermediary, see *Washington Post*, August 17, 1979, A14; for Walid Khalidi's, see memorandum of conversation, John Gunther Dean and Harold Saunders, July 27, 1979, RAC, NLC-131-12-3-13-5, CL. Regarding Landrum Bolling, on July 26 U.S. ambassador to Lebanon John Gunther Dean reported on his meeting that day with Bolling, who had seen Arafat days earlier. Bolling spoke of "Arafat's interest in a new UNSC resolution which would reaffirm the fundamental principles of UNSC Resolution 242." Dean noted that Bolling was returning to Washington to meet with U.S. officials, including Saunders. There is no specific indication that Bolling conveyed to Arafat the U.S. government's request for delay, but Bolling clearly was in a position to do so, and it seems likely that he participated in this effort. U.S. Embassy, Beirut, to Department of State (hereafter DOS), tel #4168, July 26, 1999 [misdated: 1979], RAC, NLC-131-2-10-4-9, CL.

17. UK Mission, New York, to FCO, tel #806, July 30, 1979, FCO 93/2176, TNA; memorandum of conversation, Dean and Walid Khalidi, July 31, 1979, RAC, NLC-131-1-2-19-3, CL; Bartlett C. Jones, *Flawed Triumphs: Andy Young at the United Nations* (Lanham, MD: University Press of America, 1996), 130.

18. See, for example, editorial, *Washington Post*, July 11, 1979, A22; George W. Ball, "Mideast Oil: Countdown to Trouble," *Washington Post*, August 14, 1979, A19; Morton Kondracke, "What the Saudis Want for Their Oil," *Chicago Tribune*, August 4, 1979, 9.

19. UK Embassy, Washington, tel #2255, August 9, 1979, FCO 93/2176, TNA; "Evening Report—Middle East," August 10, 1979, RAC, NLC-25-124-6-13-7, CL.

20. *Chicago Tribune*, August 6, 1979, 2; *Chicago Tribune*, August 8, 1979, 16.

21. U.S. Embassy, Cairo, to DOS, August 19, 1979, *FRUS, 1977–1980*, 9:905–8; UK Embassy, Cairo, tel #656, August 20, 1979, FCO 93/2176, TNA; UK Embassy, Washington, tel #2355, August 20, 1979, FCO 93/2176, TNA.

22. UK Embassy, Washington, tels #2370, August 21, 1979, and #2379, August 22, 1979, FCO 93/2176, TNA; Jones, *Flawed Triumphs*, 140.

23. Jones, *Flawed Triumphs*, 109–26, 131–32.

24. Andrew J. DeRoche, *Andrew Young: Civil Rights Ambassador* (Wilmington, DE: Scholarly Resources, 2003), 111–13; Jones, *Flawed Triumphs*, 132–34, 139–40; Jimmy Carter, *White House Diary* (New York: Farrar, Straus and Giroux, 2010), 351, 352; *Washington Post*, August 20, 1979, A1, A16.

25. On August 16, a panel of black leaders including Vernon Jordan, president of the National Urban League; Benjamin Hooks, executive director of the National Association for the Advancement of Colored People; and Coretta Scott King, widow of Martin Luther King, Jr., issued a statement expressing regret that Carter had accepted Young's resignation. The statement cited news reports that another American diplomat, U.S. ambassador to Austria Milton A. Wolf, had himself recently met with a PLO official without suffering any repercussions. *Los Angeles Times*, August 17, 1979, B1, B11. Wolf had indeed met in Vienna with Issam Sartawi, a top aide to Arafat, as part of the general U.S. effort to encourage PLO moderation. In early July, while in Vienna for talks with Austrian chancellor Bruno Kreisky, Arafat had not objected to Kreisky's declaration that the PLO's goal "is not the destruction of the state of Israel." Wolf subsequently met with Sartawi, apparently to confirm that Arafat truly accepted Kreisky's characterization. When the State Department learned of the meeting, which was unauthorized, it merely reminded Wolf of the ban on contact with the PLO. Wolf, however, had not misled the department, as Young would do a month later. *Los Angeles Times*, August 16, 1979, 1, 9; *Los Angeles Times*, August 18, 1979, 1, 10.

26. Salim Yaqub, "Our Declaration of Independence: African Americans, Arab Americans, and the Arab-Israeli Conflict, 1967–1979," *Mashriq & Mahjar* 3, no. 1 (2015): 18–20.

27. AAUG *Newsletter*, July 1979, 8.

28. *Washington Post*, August 22, 1979, A5; *Chicago Tribune*, August 21, 1979, 2; *Los Angeles Times*, September 11, 1979, B11; TransAfrica, "Message to the President on the Resignation of Ambassador Andrew Young and on United States Relations with the Middle East and with Africa," n.d. [c. September 1979], in *Afro-Americans Stand Up for Middle East Peace*, ed. James Zogby and Jack O'Dell (Washington, DC: Palestine Human Rights Campaign, 1980), 38.

29. *Chicago Tribune*, August 26, 1979, 16; Fauntroy, statement at the Black Leadership Meeting, August 22, 1979, Abdeen Jabara Papers, box 9, folder: "Activities—Black/Arab Coalition, 1979–1983," Bentley Historical Library, University of Michigan, Ann Arbor, MI (hereafter BHL); AAUG *Newsletter*, September/October 1980, 9.

30. Clipping, *Jerusalem Post*, September 27, 1979, page number not shown, FCO 93/2198, TNA; M[ichael] P.V. Hannam to M[ichael] K. Jenner, September 27, 1979, FCO 93/2198, TNA; *Washington Post*, September 30, 1979, A16; *Los Angeles Times*, September 30, 1979, A5. Arafat said the PLO would establish a state in "any part of Palestine from which Israel will withdraw." It would then try, by diplomatic means, to expand the territory of that state. *Los Angeles Times*, September 30, 1979, A5.

31. *Chicago Tribune*, September 12, 2; *Chicago Tribune*, September 30, 1979, 4; *Los Angeles Times*, October 14, 1979, 2, 3.

32. *Chicago Tribune*, September 24, 1979, D8; *Washington Post*, September 26, 1979, C1, C7; *New York Times*, October 17, 1979, D22; *New York Times*, October 30, 1979, A15; Nabeel Abraham

to *New York Times*, October 18, 1979, AAUG Papers, box 16, folder: "President—Samih Farsoun 1979," EMUL; AAUG *Newsletter*, December 1979/March 1980, 1–2.

33. Yaqub, "Our Declaration," 23.

34. John C. Moberly to John A. Robinson, September 28, 1979, FCO 93/2198, TNA.

35. *New York Times*, September 2, 1979, 10; William "Buddy" Carter, *Billy Carter: A Journey through the Shadows* (Atlanta: Longstreet, 1999), 186.

36. Douglas Little, "To the Shores of Tripoli: America, Qaddafi, and the Libyan Revolution, 1969–89," *International History Review* 35, no. 1 (2013): 80–82; Graham R. Lawes to Roger Tomkys, May 26, 1977, FCO 93/1013, TNA; R[aymond] L. Balfour to Jenner, March 21, 1978, FCO 93/1378, TNA; testimony of David D. Newsom, *Hearings before the Subcommittee to Investigate the Activities of Individuals Representing the Interests of Foreign Governments of the Committee on the Judiciary of the United States, 96th Congress, Second Session, Volume II, August 4, 6, 19, 20, 21, 22, September 4, 5, 8, 10, 16, 17, October 2, 1980* (Washington, DC: U.S. Government Printing Office, 1981), 10.

37. The Hague Convention of 1970 obligated signatory states to outlaw and punish acts of international hijacking of civilian aircraft.

38. P. Edward Haley, *Qaddafi and the United States since 1969* (New York: Praeger, 1984), 69–70; U.S. Embassy, Tripoli, to DOS, tel #00806, June 20, 1977, Access to Archival Databases, TRIPOL00806; clipping, *Christian Science Monitor*, October 25, 1978, FCO 93/1376, TNA; Muir to Jenner, November 8, 1978, FCO 93/1376, TNA; Bennet to Jacob Javits, February 13, 1979, Abraham Ribicoff Papers, box 653, folder: "Libyan/US Relations, 1979," Library of Congress, Washington, DC (hereafter LC); Newsom testimony, *Hearings on Activities of Individuals*, 11.

39. For accounts of the "Arab-American Dialogue," see Georgie Anne Geyer, "A Rare Dialogue in Libya," *Washington Post*, October 25, 1978, A15; Press Committee, First Arab-American Dialogue, *The Arab-American People's Dialogue*, October 12, 1978, Fulbright Papers, Post-Senatorial Papers, box 48, folder 9, University of Arkansas Library, Fayetteville, AR; [Harry F. Kern,] *Foreign Reports*, October 18, 1978, Fulbright Papers, Post-Senatorial Papers, box 48, folder 9; Federation of American Scientists, *F.A.S. Public Interest Report*, December 1978, Fulbright Papers, Post-Senatorial Papers, box 13, folder 2; NAAA, *Political Focus*, November 1, 1978, 1.

40. U.S. Senate Judiciary Committee, *Inquiry into the Matter of Billy Carter and Libya, Report* (Washington: U.S. Government Printing Office, 1980), 9–10. For Buddy Carter's sensitive and unflinching account of his father's personal travails in these years, see Carter, *Billy Carter*, 121–93.

41. *Inquiry into the Matter of Billy Carter*, 2–3, 6–7, 8–9, 11, 63, note 3; Haley, *Qaddafi*, 151–52, 178–79.

42. *Inquiry into the Matter of Billy Carter*, 3–6, 7–9, 11, 15–16; Haley, *Qaddafi*, 178–80, 186, 188.

43. Newsom testimony, *Hearings on Activities of Individuals*, 11.

44. *Los Angeles Times*, June 30, 1979, A5; UK Embassy, Washington, tel #1617, June 20, 1979, FCO 93/1869, TNA; P[atrick] M. Nixon to D[avid] A. Wright, n.d. [received August 7, 1979], FCO 93/1869, TNA; Qaddafi to Carter, August 27, 1979, FCO 93/1869, TNA; Nixon to Wright, August 29, 1979, FCO 93/1869, TNA; J. A[drian] Fortescue to John M. Crosby, October 12, 1979, FCO 93/1869, TNA; Haley, *Qaddafi*, 150–51.

45. *New York Times*, September 3, 1979, A2; *Chicago Tribune*, September 3, 1979, 2; Newsom testimony, *Hearings on Activities of Individuals*, 12.

46. David Farber, *Taken Hostage: The Iran Hostage Crisis and America's First Encounter with Radical Islam* (Princeton, NJ: Princeton University Press, 2005), 112–14, 127–42.

47. *Inquiry into the Matter of Billy Carter*, 21–26, 26, note 18.

48. John K. Cooley, *Libyan Sandstorm* (New York: Holt, Rinehart and Winston, 1982), 261–62. For an exploration of Musa al-Sadr's life, disappearance, and significance, see Fouad

Ajami, *The Vanished Imam: Musa al Sadr and the Shia of Lebanon* (Ithaca, NY: Cornell University Press, 1986). Kai Bird cites unnamed "Palestinian sources" as asserting that Qaddafi had al-Sadr executed, without indicating how those sources were in a position to know. Bird, *The Good Spy: The Life and Death of Robert Ames* (New York: Crown Publishers, 2014), 206.

49. Haley, *Qaddafi*, 188; *Inquiry into the Matter of Billy Carter*, 25–27.

50. *New York Times*, December 3, 1979, A1, A14; UK Embassy, Tripoli, tels #303, #313, and #315, December 3 and 7, 1979, FCO 93/1869, TNA; transcript of interview with Qaddafi, December 10, 1979, FCO 93/1869, TNA; Newsom testimony, *Hearings on Activities of Individuals*, 13; *Los Angeles Times*, December 6, 1979, B16; *Inquiry into the Matter of Billy Carter*, 29, note 31.

51. *New York Times*, November 8, 1979, A10; *Chicago Tribune*, November 8, 1979, 2. Since leaving office in the late 1960s, Ramsey Clark had moved steadily leftward. During 1979, he had come out in opposition first to the shah's regime and then to Israeli military operations in Lebanon. See *Washington Post*, January 19, 1979, A16; *Washington Post*, January 23, 1979, A10; *Washington Post*, January 28, 1979, A16; press release, "Ramsey Clark and Others Call for End to Israeli Raids on Lebanon," August 27, 1979, Ball Papers, box 64, folder 9, PUL; NAAA, *Political Focus*, October 1, 1979, 3–4. Presumably, the Carter administration hoped that Clark's anti-shah record would placate the new Iranian government. Whether or not his recent positions on Israel were a factor in the administration's selection of Clark for the Iran mission, those stances presumably helped him, in some way, gain access to the PLO.

52. *New York Times*, November 8, 1979, A10; Khalidi, interview with the author, June 28, 2012.

53. *Chicago Tribune*, November 9, 1979, 4; *Chicago Tribune*, November 10, 1979, 1, 5; *Chicago Tribune*, November 16, 1979, 2; *Los Angeles Times*, November 9, 1979, 1, 6; *Los Angeles Times*, November 11, 1979, A8; *Washington Post*, November 15, 1979, A1; memorandum of conversation, Dean and Khalidi, November 9, 1979, RAC, NLC-131-12-5-23-2, CL; UK Mission, New York, to FCO, tel #1542, November 14, 1979, FCO 93/2062, TNA.

54. *Washington Post*, November 18, 1979, A1, A10; Cyrus Vance to Arafat, November 25, 1979, RAC, NLC-131-1-3-8-4, CL. Vance's message was sent in written form to Ambassador Dean, who delivered it orally to Khalidi, who in turn conveyed it to Arafat.

55. UK Embassy, Washington, to FCO, tel #3903, November 26, 1979, FCO 93/2062, TNA.

56. U.S. Embassy, Beirut, tel #6543, November 25, 1979, RAC, NLC-131-1-3-7-5, CL; Dean, memorandum, n.d. [November 26 or 27, 1979], RAC, NLC-131-1-3-8-4, CL; memorandum of conversation, Dean and Khalidi, November 27, 1979, RAC, NLC-131-1-3-9-3, CL; Vance to Arafat, November 30, 1979, RAC, NLC-131-1-3-12-9, ibid. CL; Khalidi, interview with the author, June 28, 2012.

57. *Washington Post*, November 10, 1979, A18; memorandum of conversation, Dean and Basil Aql, November 19, 1979, RAC, NLC-131-1-3-3-9, CL.

58. Memorandum of conversation, Dean and Khalidi, December 6, 1979, RAC, NLC-131-1-3-16-5, CL; *Washington Post*, December 6, 1979, A26. Perhaps Khalidi was able, after all, to influence Arafat directly. The following day, the PLO chairman informed Vance (via Khalidi and then Dean) that he, Arafat, was sending a message to Khomeini "explaining the ultra sensitive Lebanese spectrum in view of the talk about Iranian volunteers coming to the south of Lebanon." Arafat to Vance, December 7, 1979, RAC, NLC-131-1-3-17-4, CL. The Iranian "volunteers" came anyway. By late January, somewhere between fifty and one hundred of them had entered Lebanon via Syria. The Popular Front for the Liberation of Palestine and other Palestinian splinter groups welcomed the new arrivals, whereas al Fatah leaders were discomfited by their presence. The local Shia population, reported the British embassy, "has offered them normal hospitality (food and shelter), but has reacted coldly to [their] revolutionary zeal and sloganeering." UK Embassy, Beirut, tel #ZJGR0124, January 29, 1980, FCO 93/2423, TNA. See also UK Embassy, Tel Aviv, tel #UHGR0028, January 21, 1980, FCO 93/2423, TNA.

59. *New York Times*, August 15, 1980, A10; *Washington Post*, March 18, 1981, A14. For George Otis's self-presentation and worldview, see Otis, *Voice of Hope* (Van Nuys, CA: High Adventure Ministries, 1983). I am grateful to Laila Ballout for calling my attention to Otis's radio project.

60. All of these events are recounted in Yaroslav Trofimov, *The Siege of Mecca: The Forgotten Uprising in Islam's Holiest Shrine and the Birth of al Qaeda* (New York: Doubleday, 2007).

61. Trofimov, *Siege of Mecca*, 229–32, 242–45; Steve Coll, *Ghost Wars: The Secret History of the CIA, Afghanistan, and bin Laden, from the Soviet Invasion to September 10, 2001* (New York: Penguin Press, 2004), 79–88.

62. *Los Angeles Times*, January 10, 1980, B7; *New York Times*, February 14, 1980, A1; John K. Cooley, *Unholy Wars: Afghanistan, America, and International Terrorism* (1999, repr., London: Pluto Press 2000), 34–38.

63. The Begin government's accelerated construction of Jewish settlements in the West Bank, for example, gave a modest boost to Arab American lobbying efforts on Capitol Hill. In June 1980, partly in response to pressure from the NAAA and the PHRC, senator Adlai Stevenson III of Illinois offered an amendment to reduce U.S. aid to Israel by $150 million, approximately the amount Israel spent each year on settlements. The amendment was defeated by an 85–7 vote, but the fact that it was considered at all suggested some erosion in senatorial support for Israel. Gregory Orfalea, *The Arab Americans: A History* (Northampton, MA: Olive Branch Press, 2005), 231–33; PHRC memorandum, March 13, 1980, PHRC book, in the possession of James Zogby, Washington, DC; *Chicago Tribune*, June 18, 1980, 2.

64. *Chicago Tribune*, November 8, 1979, 2; *Chicago Tribune*, November 13, 1979, 2; *Los Angeles Times*, November 11, 1979, A3, A26; *Los Angeles Times*, September 12, 1980, G1; *Los Angeles Times*, February 12, 1981, 11; *Los Angeles Times*, February 14, 1981, B3; *New York Times*, November 18, 1979, 14; *Washington Post*, December 12, 1979, 28; *Washington Post*, June 27, 1980, A13; *Washington Post*, November 20, 1980, VA1; *Eugene (OR) Register-Guard*, December 9, 1979, 5A.

65. NAAA, *Political Focus*, November 15, 1979, Staff Offices, Ethnic Affairs, Stephen Aiello Files (hereafter Aiello Files), box 38, folder: "Arab(-American) Newsletters 10/79–7/80," CL, 4; NAAA, *Political Focus*, December 15, 1979, 1, 4; *News Circle*, April 1980, 9; AAUG *Newsletter*, December 1979/March 1980, 9; *Voice*, Winter 1979, Maria Papers, box 48, folder 5, Immigration History Research Center, University of Minnesota, Minneapolis, MN (hereafter IHRC), 1.

66. *New York Times*, July 17, 1980, A14; *Washington Post*, July 19, 1980, A1, A5. In fact, the chairman of Carter's reelection committee, none other than Robert Strauss, who had stepped down as special Middle East envoy in late 1979, insisted he had never authorized "the creation of an Arab/American Committee or any other ethnic committee," preferring to enlist supporters of different backgrounds through a single "umbrella ethnic committee." Evidently, Shadyac had been appointed by a lower-level campaign staffer without Strauss's knowledge. Campaign officials were further chagrined when Shadyac was quoted in the press saying that Arab Americans, unlike their Jewish counterparts, were not prone to dual loyalty. *New York Times*, July 25, 1980, A10; Strauss to Shadyac, July 17, 1980, Special Adviser to the President—Moses, box 19, folder: "Shadyac, Richard, 7/22/80," CL; memorandum for the President, July 22, 1980, Special Adviser to the President—Moses, box 19, folder: "Shadyac, Richard, 7/22/80," CL; note to campaign staff, n.d. [July 1980], Aiello Files, box 35, folder: "Shadyac (Richard; Arab-Americans) 4/78–7/80," CL.

67. James Sams to Carter, July 25, 1980, Aiello Files, box 12, folder: "Arabs 2/80–12–80," CL.

68. *New York Times*, July 15, 1980, A1, A14; *Los Angeles Times*, July 23, 1980, A7, A10; *Inquiry into the Matter of Billy Carter*, 60–69. The controversy was even more painful to Billy's wife and children, who had been ill prepared for his initial celebrity, let alone for his subsequent disgrace. Carter, *Billy Carter*, 177–93.

69. *New York Times*, May 16, 1980, A5; *New York Times*, August 22, 1980, A2; Haley, *Qaddafi*, 121.

70. Haley, *Qaddafi*, 122–25, 127–30; U.S. State Department, press guidance, n.d. [May 1980], FCO 93/2338, TNA.

71. Haley, *Qaddafi*, 127; U.S. State Department, note to Libyan People's Bureau, May 2, 1980, FCO 93/2338, TNA; *New York Times*, May 9, 1980, A11. Although all four Libyan officials had attended American universities, only one of them was registered in the spring term of 1980, in his case at the University of Miami. *New York Times*, May 9, 1980, A11.

72. Haley, *Qaddafi*, 127; *New York Times*, May 8, 1980, A1, A19; *New York Times*, May 9, 1980, A11.

73. NAAA, *Voice*, April 1976, 1–3; *Voice*, January 1977, 2–3.

74. N[abeel] Abraham to M[ajid] Kazimi and A[bdeen] Jabara, May 20, 1980, Jabara Papers, box 13, folder: "Palestine Human Rights Campaign, Correspondence, 1979–1980," BHL; AAUG *Newsletter*, July–August 1980, 4. The September–October *Newsletter* carried an opinion piece by Abdeen Jabara denouncing the suppression of dissent in Egypt. Jabara referred in the piece to "recent news reports of assassinations in Europe and the Middle East of prominent Arab political figures, activists, exiles and refugees" and noted that representatives of some Arab regimes had "readily acknowledged" such violent measures, saying they were "being implemented to 'safeguard the revolution.'" Jabara did not mention Libya by name. AAUG *Newsletter*, September–October, 1980, 5.

75. Abraham, communications with the author, September 10 and 11, 20115. For an Arab American Republican's resistance to anti-Tripoli discourse, see Frank Maria, "Libyan Friendship Important to the United States," July 24, 1980, Maria Papers, box 120, folder 1, IHRC. Evidently, this document is a draft of an open letter to senator Birch Bayh of Indiana, chair of the Senate committee investigating "Billygate," copies of which Maria sent to the White House and the news media. Paul D. Garrett and Kathleen A. Purpura, *Frank Maria: A Search for Justice in the Middle East* (Bloomington, IN: AuthorHouse, 2007), 567.

76. Haley, *Qaddafi*, 130–33; *New York Times*, May 21, 1981, 1. In fact, Edwin Wilson is the subject of several monographs. See Joseph P. Goulden and Alexander W. Raffio, *The Death Merchant: The Rise and Fall of Edwin P. Wilson* (New York: Simon & Schuster, 1984); Peter Maas, *Manhunt: The Incredible Pursuit of a CIA Agent Turned Terrorist* (New York: Random House, 1986); Joseph J. Trento, *Prelude to Terror: Edwin P. Wilson and the Legacy of America's Private Intelligence Network* (New York: Carrol & Graf, 2005).

77. Extract of DOS cable to unknown recipient(s), tel #277512, date not shown [October 1980], FCO 93/2338, TNA; Haley, *Qaddafi*, 202–18, *New York Times*, October 24, 1980, A8; Congressional Research Service, "CRS Issue Brief for Congress: Libya," updated April 10, 2002, http://fpc.state.gov/documents/organization/9577.pdf (accessed December 2, 2014), 6.

78. Accounts of the Iran-Iraq War include Shahram Chubin and Charles Tripp, *Iran and Iraq at War* (London: I.B. Tauris, 1988); Edgar O'Ballance, *The Gulf War* (London: Brassey's Defense Publishers, 1988); and Stephen C. Pelletiere, *The Iran-Iraq War: Chaos in a Vacuum* (New York: Praeger, 1992). For up-to-date essays on particular aspects of the war, see Nigel J. Ashton and Bryan Gibson, eds., *The Iran-Iraq War: New International Perspectives* (London: Routledge, 2013).

79. Jeffrey R. Macris, *Politics and Security of the Gulf: Anglo-American Hegemony and the Shaping of a Region* (London: Routledge, 2010), 208–10; Douglas Little, *American Orientalism: The United States and the Middle East since 1945* (Chapel Hill: University of North Carolina Press, 2002), 151–52.

80. From the start of the Iran-Iraq War, journalists and scholars have speculated that the Carter administration, eager to place additional pressure on Iran, gave a "green light" to Iraq's attack on that country. In a careful study, Chris Emery surveys these accounts and persuasively argues that the administration, while aware of prior border tensions between the two countries,

did not bless the Iraqi attack in advance. Chris Emery, "Reappraising the Carter Administration's Response to the Iran-Iraq War," in Ashton and Gibson, *Iran-Iraq War*, 149–77.

81. O'Ballance, *Gulf War*, 51–53; Emery, "Carter Administration's Response," 169; *Los Angeles Times*, October 29, 1980, 1, 12; U.S. Embassy, Amman, to DOS, tels #7516 and #7517, September 24, 1980, RAC NLC-6-42-4-23-0, CL; Edmund Muskie to Carter, October 15, 1980, National Security Affairs, Subject File, box 23, folder: "Evening Reports (State): 10/80," CL.

82. Emery, "Carter Administration's Response," 165–69; Brzezinski, *Power and Principle*, 504; *Washington Post*, September 23, 1980, A1, A10; *New York Times*, September 29, 1980, 12.

83. Brzezinski, *Power and Principle*, 452–54; Brzezinski to Carter, October 3, 1980, Brzezinski Collection, Subject File, box 42, folder: "Weekly Reports (to the President), 151–61 (8/80–12/80)," CL; *New York Times*, October 25, 1980, 6.

84. "Discussion Paper: Policy Ramifications of Iran-Iraq Conflict," attachment to Peter Tarnoff to Brzezinski, October 14, 1980, RAC, NLC-132-82-2-8-4, CL.

85. Yergin, *Prize*, 711–12; *Los Angeles Times*, October 19, 1980, 1, 5; *Washington Post*, October 20, 1980, A1, A12; *New York Times*, October 27, 1980, D6.

86. "Saudi Arabia: An Assessment as of October 1980," October 27, 1980, RAC, NLC-15-47-1-8-5, CL.

87. Gary Sick, *All Fall Down: America's Fateful Encounter with Iran* (London: I.B. Tauris, 1985), 310–18.

88. *Washington Post*, September 6, 1980, A6; *Chicago Tribune*, September 8, 1980, D2; Ronald Reagan, address to B'nai B'rith Forum, September 3, 1980, White House Staff and Office Files, Geoffrey Kemp Files, RAC box 3, folder: "Israel—Settlements, 1981," Ronald Reagan Presidential Library, Simi Valley, CA.

89. Betty Glad, *An Outsider in the White House: Jimmy Carter, His Advisors, and the Making of American Foreign Policy* (Ithaca, NY: Cornell University Press, 2009), 273–78.

90. AAUG *Newsletter*, September–October, 1980, 13, 16. The figures included Joseph Churba, a former Air Force intelligence official who in the early 1960s had associated with Meir Kahane, later the founder of the Jewish Defense League. They also included the neoconservative intellectuals Robert W. Tucker and Robert Luttwak, both of whom had advocated U.S. intervention in Saudi Arabia in the mid-1970s (see Chapter Six). The preparers of the AAUG *Newsletter* were evidently unaware of Luttwak's anonymous authorship of the *Harper's* piece, but they did note that Luttwak "has written, in Israel, advocating Israeli military action against Arab oil fields." Ibid., 16.

91. Fortescue to John E. Holmes, December 2, 1980, FCO 93/2601, TNA; memorandum of conversation, Douglas Hurd and Thomas Farmer, October 14, 1980, FCO 93/2601, TNA.

92. Abdallah Najjar to NAAA president and executive director, November 11, 1980, Maria Papers, box 46, folder 4, IHRC; Moberly to J[ohn] Graham, December 17, 1980, FCO 93/2601, TNA; *Washington Post*, November 30, 1980, A2.

Epilogue

1. John P. Miglietta, *American Alliance Policy in the Middle East, 1945–1992: Iran, Israel, and Saudi Arabia* (Lanham, MD: Lexington Books, 2002), 144; *Los Angeles Times*, September 22, 1982, 11; *Wall Street Journal*, October 1, 1982, 34.

2. *Wall Street Journal*, October 1, 1982, 34.

3. Born in Egypt in 1944, Youssef Ibrahim moved to the United States in 1969 and later became a U.S. citizen. In 1984 *Washington Report on Middle East Affairs*, a journal published

by retired U.S. Foreign Service officers, called him "the only first-generation Arab immigrant who has a major job on a top American newspaper." Ibrahim won a George Polk award for his reporting on energy affairs during 1983. *Washington Report on Middle East Affairs*, April 2, 1984, http://www.wrmea.org/1984-april-2/personality-youssef-m.-ibrahim.html (accessed December 31, 2014).

4. Seth P. Tillman, *The United States in the Middle East: Interests and Obstacles* (Bloomington: Indiana University Press, 1982), 276–77. To be sure, at either end of the spectrum of views forming this international consensus, some parties used veiled language. In the Paris Declaration of March 1979, the European Economic Community called for a comprehensive settlement that "must translate into fact the right of the Palestinian people to a homeland." The statement stopped short, however, of explicitly calling for a Palestinian state. Similarly, in September 1982, the PLO and all of the Arab states except Libya issued a peace plan affirming the right of all states in the Middle East, including a newly established Palestinian one, to live in peace and security. The recognition of Israel was implied rather than spelled out. Bichara Khader, "Europe and the Arab-Israeli Conflict 1973–1983: An Arab Perspective," in *European Foreign Policy-Making and the Arab-Israeli Conflict*, ed. D. Allen and A. Pijpers (The Hague: Martinus Nijhoff Publishers, 1984), 171; Kathleen Christison, *Perceptions of Palestine: Their Influence on U.S. Middle East Policy* (1999, repr., Berkeley: University of California Press, 2002), 212–13.

5. One such exception was an outline of a territorial settlement that president Bill Clinton presented to Israeli and Palestinian negotiators in December 2000, proposing Israel's withdrawal from 94 to 96 percent of the West Bank and its annexation of the remainder. But Clinton unveiled these "parameters" just a month before leaving office, and his successor, George W. Bush, did not pursue them. Terje Rød-Larsen, Nur Laiq, and Fabrice Aidan, eds., *The Search for Peace in the Arab-Israeli Conflict: A Compendium of Documents and Analysis* (Oxford: Oxford University Press, 2014), 461–62.

6. An arguable exception to this rule was president John F. Kennedy's dispatching in 1963 of an Air Force squadron to patrol the skies of Saudi Arabia during the latter's proxy war with Egypt over Yemen. The American squadron did not, however, engage in actual hostilities. A clearer exception was a 1981 skirmish between U.S. and Libyan warplanes over the Gulf of Sidra (or Sirte) during which two Libyan planes were shot down. The United States deployed the armed forces in its unsuccessful effort to rescue the American hostages in Iran in 1980, but Iran, of course, is not an Arab country. Douglas Little, *American Orientalism: The United States and the Middle East since 1945* (Chapel Hill: University of North Carolina Press, 2002), 238–39, 244; John K. Cooley, *Libyan Sandstorm* (New York: Holt, Rinehart and Winston, 1982), 266–69.

7. Patrick Tyler, *A World of Trouble: The White House and the Middle East—from the Cold War to the War on Terror* (New York: Farrar, Straus and Giroux, 2009), 267–90, 290–302, 304–11; Galia Golan, *Soviet Policies in the Middle East: From World War II to Gorbachev* (Cambridge: Cambridge University Press, 1990), 126–37.

8. P. Edward Haley, *Qaddafi and the United States since 1969* (New York: Praeger, 1984), 247–49; Douglas Little, "To the Shores of Tripoli: America, Qaddafi, and the Libyan Revolution, 1969–89," *International History Review* 35, no. 1 (2013): 83–93.

9. Jeffrey R. Macris, *The Politics and Security of the Gulf: Anglo-American Hegemony and the Shaping of a Region* (London: Routledge, 2010), 213–17, 221; Steven Hurst, *The United States and Iraq since 1979: Hegemony, Oil, and War* (Edinburgh: Edinburgh University Press, 2009), 40–47, 52–66. Following Iraq's invasion of Kuwait in 1990, Saudi Arabia allowed the United States to station hundreds of thousands of U.S. troops on its soil, while Kuwait, of course, relied primarily on U.S. military forces to rid itself of Iraqi occupation. After Iraq was ousted from Kuwait in 1991, only about five thousand U.S. troops remained in Saudi Arabia, but the United States maintained an extensive military infrastructure in the kingdom and in several other Gulf

Arab states, most of which welcomed the continued U.S. presence. Macris, *Politics and Security*, 224–28, 232.

10. Daniel Yergin, *The Prize: The Epic Quest for Oil, Money, and Power* (New York: Simon & Schuster, 1991), 711–14, 717–18.

11. Yergin, *Prize*, 718–21, 745–51; Abbas Alnasrawi, *Arab Nationalism, Oil, and the Political Economy of Dependency* (New York: Greenwood Press, 1991), 141–45, 200; Daryl Champion, *The Paradoxical Kingdom: Saudi Arabia and the Momentum of Reform* (New York: Columbia University Press, 2003), 80; Bahgat Korany, "The Middle East since the Cold War: Initiating the Fifth Wave of Democratization?," in *International Relations of the Middle East*, ed. Louise Fawcett, 3rd ed. (2005, repr., Oxford: Oxford University Press, 2013), 83; Kiren Aziz Chaudhry, *The Price of Wealth: Economies and Institutions in the Middle East* (Ithaca, NY: Cornell University Press, 1997), 2, 4, 269–93.

12. Berch Berberoglu, *Turmoil in the Middle East: Imperialism, War, and Political Instability* (Albany: State University of New York Press, 1999), 11, 121; Christison, *Perceptions of Palestine*, 274–311.

13. Treatments of al-Qa'ida's rise in the 1990s include Peter L. Bergen, *Holy War, Inc.: Inside the Secret World of Osama bin Laden* (New York: Simon & Schuster, 2002); Steve Coll, *Ghost Wars: The Secret History of the CIA, Afghanistan, and bin Laden, from the Soviet Invasion to September 10, 2001* (New York: Penguin Press, 2004); and Lawrence Wright, *The Looming Tower: Al-Qaeda and the Road to 9/11* (New York: Knopf, 2006).

14. For treatments of the Iraq War's prelude, execution, and aftermath, see Terry Anderson, *Bush's Wars* (New York: Oxford University Press, 2011); Michael Isikoff and David Corn, *Hubris: The Inside Story of Spin, Scandal, and the Selling of the Iraq War* (New York: Crown, 2006); Thomas E. Ricks, *Fiasco: The American Military Adventure in Iraq* (London: Penguin, 2006); and John S. Duffield and Peter J. Dombrowski, eds., *Balance Sheet: The Iraq War and U.S. National Security* (Stanford, CA: Stanford University Press, 2010).

15. Philip M. Kayal, "Report: Counting the 'Arabs' among Us," *Arab Studies Quarterly* 9, no. 1 (Winter 1987): 100–103; Anan Ameri, "Arab American Immigration," in *Daily Life of Arab Americans in the 21st Century*, ed. Ameri and Holly Arida (Santa Barbara, CA: Greenwood, 2012), 2; *Jewish Week*, June 10, 1983, 7; Fariborz Ghadar, *Becoming American: Why Immigration Is Good for Our Nation's Future* (Lanham, MD: Rowman and Littlefield, 2014), 31.

16. Nabeel Abraham, "Anti-Arab Racism and Violence in the United States," in *The Development of Arab-American Identity*, ed. Ernest McCarus (Ann Arbor: University of Michigan Press, 1994), 161–77; Gregory Orfalea, *The Arab Americans: A History* (Northampton, MA: Olive Branch Press, 2005), 257–63, 265; *Sarasota (FL) Herald-Tribune*, November 8, 1981, 2C; July 20, 1986, 19; editorial, *New York Times*, January 29, 1991, A20; Suad Joseph, "Against the Grain of the Nation—The Arab-," in *Arabs in America: Building a New Future*, ed. Michael W. Suleiman (Philadelphia: Temple University Press, 1999), 266–67.

17. Fawaz A. Gerges, *America and Political Islam: Clash of Cultures or Clash of Interests?* (Cambridge: Cambridge University Press, 1999), 86–114.

18. Edward W. Said, *Orientalism* (New York: Pantheon Books, 1978); Zachary Lockman, *Contending Visions of the Middle East: The History and Politics of Orientalism* (New York: Cambridge University Press, 2004), 182–216. In 1992, the Middle East Studies Association's president estimated that half of MESA's membership was of Middle Eastern background. Martin Kramer, *Ivory Towers on Sand: The Failure of Middle East Studies in America* (Washington, DC: Washington Institute for Near East Policy, 2001), 39.

19. Said argued that, in joining the U.S.-brokered Israeli-Palestinian peace process in the early 1990s, Arafat effectively surrendered long-standing Palestinian national claims. Said's observations on the Palestine issue from the late 1970s to the early 2000s are found in his

books *The Question of Palestine* (New York: Times Books, 1979); *After the Last Sky: Palestinian Lives* (New York: Pantheon Books, 1986); *The Politics of Dispossession: The Struggle for Palestinian Self-Determination, 1969–1994* (New York: Pantheon Books, 1994); *Peace and Its Discontents: Essays on Palestine in the Middle East Peace Process* (New York: Vintage Books, 1996); *The End of the Peace Process: Oslo and After* (New York: Pantheon Books, 2000); *From Oslo to Iraq and the Road Map* (New York: Pantheon Books, 2004).

20. Louise Cainkar, "Thinking Outside the Box: Arabs and Race in the United States," in *Race and Arab Americans before and after 9/11: From Invisible Citizens to Visible Subjects*, ed. Amaney Jamal and Nadine Naber (Syracuse, NY: Syracuse University Press, 2008), 53–57; Helen Hatab Samhan, "Public and Political Life," in Ameri and Arida, *Daily Life of Arab Americans*, 182–88.

21. *New York Times*, December 6, 2015, A1; *New York Times*, December 8, 2015, A1; Yaser Ali, "Shariah and Citizenship: How Islamophobia Is Creating a Second-Class Citizenry in America," *California Law Review* 100, no. 4 (August 1, 2012): 1054–56, 1061–66.

22. Samhan, "Public and Political Life," 171–72, 188–89.

23. Nabeel Abraham, Sally Howell, and Andrew Shryock, "The Terror Decade in Arab Detroit: An Introduction," in *Arab Detroit 9/11: Life in the Terror Decade*, ed. Nabeel Abraham, Sally Howell, and Andrew Shryock (Detroit: Wayne State University Press, 2011), 5–10.

Bibliography

Official Archives

Great Britain

The National Archives (TNA), Kew.

Foreign and Commonwealth Office Files.
Prime Minister's Office Records.

The United States

Jimmy Carter Presidential Library (CL), Atlanta, GA.

Zbigniew Brzezinski Collection.
National Security Affairs.
Remote Access Capture (RAC).
White House Central Files (WHCF).

Gerald R. Ford Presidential Library (FL), Ann Arbor, MI.

National Security Adviser, Memoranda of Conversation (NSA Memcons).

National Security Council, Memoranda of Conversation.
Presidential Country Files.
White House Central Files (WHCF).
White House Congressional Mail File.

Richard M. Nixon Presidential Library, Yorba Linda, CA (NL).

Henry A. Kissinger Office Files.
Henry A. Kissinger Telephone Conversations (HAK/Telcons).
National Security Council Files (NSC).
White House Special Files.

Ronald W. Reagan Presidential Library, Simi Valley, CA.

White House Staff and Office Files.

National Archives and Records Administration (NARA), College Park, MD.

General Records of the Department of State, Record Group (RG) 59.

Personal and Organizational Collections

Abourezk, James G., Papers. University of South Dakota Library (USDL), Vermillion, SD.
Agnew, Spiro T., Papers. Hornbake Library (HL), University of Maryland, College Park, MD.
American Alternatives to Zionism Papers. Hoover Institution Library and Archives (HILA), Stanford, CA.
Association of Arab American University Graduates Papers. Eastern Michigan University Library (EMUL), Ypsilanti, MI.
Association of Arab American University Graduates Twin Cities Chapter Papers. Immigration History Research Center (IHRC), University of Minnesota, Minneapolis, MN.
Ball, George W., Papers. Princeton University Library (PUL), Princeton, NJ.
Baroody, William, Papers. Library of Congress (LC), Washington, DC.
Brandon, Henry, Papers. Library of Congress (LC), Washington, DC.
Evans, Rowland, Papers. Library of Congress (LC), Washington, DC.
Findley, Paul, Papers. Hoover Institution Library and Archives (HILA), Stanford, CA.
Fulbright, J. William, Papers. University of Arkansas Library (UAL), Fayetteville, AR.
Georgakas, Dan, Papers. Walter P. Reuther Library, Wayne State University Archives, Detroit, MI.
Humphrey, Hubert H., Papers. Minnesota State Historical Society (MSHS), St. Paul, MN.
Jabara, Abdeen, Papers. Bentley Historical Library (BHI), University of Michigan, Ann Arbor, MI.
Lilienthal, Alfred M., Papers. Hoover Institution Library and Archives (HILA), Stanford, CA.

Lowenstein, Allard K., Papers. University of North Carolina Library (UNCL), Chapel Hill, NC.

McCloskey, Paul N., Papers. Hoover Institution Library and Archives (HILA), Stanford, CA.

McGovern, George, Papers. Princeton University Library (PUL), Princeton, NJ.

Malik, Charles, Papers. Library of Congress (LC), Washington, DC.

Maria, Frank, Papers. Immigration History Research Center (IHRC), University of Minnesota, Minneapolis, MN.

Mondale, Walter F., Papers. Minnesota State Historical Society (MSHS), St. Paul, MN.

Moynihan, Daniel Patrick, Papers. Library of Congress (LC), Washington, DC.

Mulligan, William E., Papers. Georgetown University Library (GUL), Washington, DC.

Orfalea, Gregory, Papers. Georgetown University Library (GUL), Washington, DC.

Ribicoff, Abraham, Papers. Library of Congress (LC), Washington, DC.

Sayegh, Fayez A., Papers. University of Utah Library (UUL), Salt Lake City, UT.

Shaheen, Jack G., Papers. Tamiment Library (TL), New York University, New York, NY.

Suleiman, Michael, Papers. Arab American National Museum, Dearborn, MI.

Terry, Janice J., Papers. Bentley Historical Library (BHL), University of Michigan, Ann Arbor, MI.

Published Documents

Early Warning System in Sinai: Hearings before the Committee on Foreign Relations, United States Senate, 94th Congress, First Session, October 6 and 7, 1975. Washington, DC: U.S. Government Printing Office, 1976.

Hearings before the Committee on Foreign Relations, United States Senate, 95th Congress, Second Session, on Proposed U.S. Sales of Fighter Aircraft to Saudi Arabia, Egypt, and Israel, May 3, 4, 5, and 8, 1978. Washington, DC: U.S. Government Printing Office, 1978.

Hearings before the Subcommittee on Multinational Corporations of the Committee on Foreign Relations, United States Senate, 94th Congress, First Session, July 16, September 11, 18, October 9, 29, 1975, Part 15. Washington, DC: U.S. Government Printing Office, 1976.

Hearings before the Subcommittee to Investigate the Activities of Individuals Representing the Interests of Foreign Governments of the Committee on the Judiciary of the United States, 96th Congress, Second Session, Volume II, August 4, 6, 19, 20, 21, 22, September 4, 5, 8, 10, 16, 17, October 2, 1980. Washington, DC: U.S. Government Printing Office, 1981.

House Judiciary Committee. *Foreign Intelligence Surveillance Act: Hearings before the Subcommittee on Courts, Civil Liberties, and the Administration of Justice, April 12, May 5, June 2, 1976.* Washington, DC: U.S. Government Printing Office, 1976.

House Judiciary Committee. *Surveillance: Hearings before the Subcommittee on Courts, Civil Liberties, and the Administration of Justice, February 6, 18, March 4, 18, 21, May 22, June 26, July 25, September 8, 1975.* Washington, DC: U.S. Government Printing Office, 1975.

Kissinger, Henry A. *Crisis: The Anatomy of Two Major Foreign Policy Crises*. New York: Simon & Schuster, 2003.

Oudes, Bruce, ed. *From the President: Richard Nixon's Secret Files*. New York: Harper & Row, 1989.

The Palestinian Issue in Middle East Peace Efforts: Hearings before the Special Subcommittee on Investigations of the Committee on International Relations, House of Representatives, 94th Congress, First Session, September 30, October 1, 8, and November 12, 1975. Washington, DC: U.S. Government Printing Office, 1976.

Public Papers of the Presidents of the United States: Jimmy Carter, 1977. Vol. 2. Washington, DC: Government Printing Office, 1978.

Public Papers of the Presidents of the United States: Richard Nixon, 1972. Washington, DC: Government Printing Office, 1974.

Senate Foreign Relations Committee, Subcommittee on Near Eastern and South Asian Affairs. *The Situation of the Christian Community in Lebanon, August 16, 1978*. Washington, DC: Government Printing Office, 1978.

Senate Judiciary Committee, Subcommittee to Investigate Problems Connected with Refugees and Escapees. *Humanitarian Problems in Lebanon, Part II, July 29, 1976*. Washington, DC: U.S. Government Printing Office, 1976.

Soviet-American Relations: The Détente Years, 1969–1972. Washington, DC: U.S. Government Printing Office, 2007.

U.S. Department of State. *Foreign Relations of the United States, 1969–1976*. Vols. 13, 24, 25, 26, E1.

U.S. Department of State. *Foreign Relations of the United States, 1977–1980*. Vols. 8, 9.

U.S. Interests in and Policy toward the Persian Gulf: Hearings before the Subcommittee on the Near East of the Committee on Foreign Affairs, House of Representatives, 92nd Congress, Second Session. Washington, DC: U.S. Government Printing Office, 1972.

U.S. Senate Foreign Relations Committee. *Hearings before the Subcommittee on Multinational Corporations, February 20, 21, March 27, 28, 1974*. Part 7. Washington, DC: U.S. Government Printing Office, 1974.

U.S. Senate Judiciary Committee. *Inquiry into the Matter of Billy Carter and Libya, Report*. Washington: U.S. Government Printing Office, 1980.

Online Documents

Declassified Documents Reference System, Gale Digital Collections. Accessed January 15, 2016. http://gdc.gale.com/products/declassified-documents-reference-system/.

Digital National Security Archive (DNSA), George Washington University, Washington, DC. Accessed January 15, 2016. http://nsarchive.chadwyck.com/marketing/index.jsp.

Gerald Ford Presidential Digital Library. Accessed September 7, 2015. http://www.fordlibrarymuseum.gov/library/docs.asp.

Luke A. Nichter, ed. Nixontapes.org. Accessed August 31, 2015.
United Nations Information System on the Question of Palestine (UNISPAL). Accessed September 7, 2015. http://unispal.un.org/unispal.nsf/udc.htm.
U.S. Department of State, Access to Archives Database, National Archives and Records Administration. Accessed January 15, 2016. http://aad.archives.gov/aad/.

Interviews

Abourezk, James G., December 19, 2007.
Bassiouni, M. Cherif, July 15, 2008.
Findley, Paul, July 17, 2008.
Hagopian, Elaine C., January 8, 2011.
Jabara, Abdeen, February 13, 2008.
Khalidi, Walid, June 28, 2012.
Richardson, John P., December 13, 2012
Shaheen, Jack G., January 3, 2014.
Sterner, Michael, July 20, 2010
Yaqub, Fawzi, August 7, 2012.
Zogby, James, July 19, 2010.

Newspapers and Periodicals

AAUG *Newsletter*
Action
ADC Report
Al-Ahram (Cairo)
ALL Dimensions
American Prospect
American Syrian-Lebanese Leader
ANERA Newsletter
Argus Press (Owosso, MI)
Atlantic Monthly
Boston Globe
Bryan (OH) Times
Business Week
Chicago Daily Defender
Chicago Tribune
Christian Century
Christian Science Monitor
Citizen (Ottawa, Ontario)
Cleveland Plain Dealer

Columbia (SC) Record
Commentary
Congressional Quarterly
COSERV Across the USA
CounterPunch
Daily News (Bowling Green, KY)
Daily Reporter (Spencer, IA)
Daily Star (Beirut, Leb.)
Department of State Bulletin
Deseret News (Salt Lake City, UT)
Detroit Free Press
Detroit News
DuPage Magazine
Eugene (OR) Register-Guard
Evening Independent (St. Petersburg, FL)
Evening News (Newburgh, NY)
Florence (AL) Times–Tri-Cities Daily
Foreign Affairs
Foreign Policy
Free Palestine
Gadsden (AL) Times
Gallup Opinion Index
Grapevine
Harper's
Heritage
Hour (Norwalk, CT)
Janesville (WI) Daily Gazette
Jewish Telegraphic Agency
Kingman (AZ) Daily Miner
Ladies' Home Journal
Lakeland (FL) Ledger
Lawrence (KS) Journal-World
Lebanese American Journal
Lewiston (ME) Evening Journal
Life
Link
Lodi (CA) News-Sentinel
London Review of Books
Los Angeles Times
MERIP Reports
Middle East Newsletter
Mother Jones
Al-Nahar (Beirut)
Nashua (NH) Telegraph

National Review
New Lebanese American Journal
New Republic
News and Courier (Charleston, SC)
News Circle
Newsweek
New York Review of Books
New York Times
New York Magazine
Palestine Human Rights Campaign Bulletin
Pittsburgh Press
Playboy
Political Focus
Press-Republican (Plattsburgh, NY)
Princeton Alumni Weekly
Rome (GA) News-Tribune
Sarasota (FL) Herald Tribune
Sarasota (FL) Journal
Saturday Evening Post
Saturday Review
Al-Siyasa (Kuwait)
Southeast Missourian (Cape Girardeau, MO)
Spartanburg (SC) Herald Journal
St. Petersburg (FL) Times
Sumter (SC) Daily Item
Time
Tri-City Herald (Pasco, Kennewick, and Richland, WA)
Tuscaloosa (AL) News
U.S. News and World Report
Victoria (TX) Advocate
Voice
Wall Street Journal
Washington Post
Washington Report on Middle East Affairs
Waycross (GA) Journal-Herald
Williamson (WV) Daily News
Youngstown (OH) Vindicator

Books, Articles, and Dissertations

ʻAbd al-Karim, Ahmad. *Yawmiyat diblumasi ʻArabi: Ghadat Harb Hizayran 1967 wa tadaʻiyat Harb Tishrin 1973* [Chronicles of an Arab diplomat: The day after the June 1967 War and the fallout from October 1973 War]. Beirut: Bisan lil-nashr wa-al-tawziʻ wa-al-iʻlam, 2006.

Abourezk, James G. *Advise and Dissent: Memoirs of South Dakota and the U.S. Senate.* Chicago: Lawrence Hill Books, 1989.

Abraham, Nabeel, Sally Howell, and Andrew Shryock, eds. *Arab Detroit 9/11: Life in the Terror Decade.* Detroit: Wayne State University Press, 2011.

Abraham, Sameer Y., and Nabeel Abraham, eds. *Arabs in the New World: Studies on Arab-American Communities.* Detroit: Wayne State University Press, 1983.

Abu-Gharbiya, Bahjat. *Min mudhakkirat al-munadil Bahjat Abu-Gharbiya: Min al-nakbah ila al-intifadah, 1949–2000* [From the memoirs of the fighter Bahjat Abu-Gharbiya: From the catastrophe to the uprising, 1949–2000]. Beirut: al-Mu'assasah al-'Arabiya lil-dirasat wa-al-nashr, 2004.

Abu-Lughod, Ibrahim, ed. *The Arab-Israeli Confrontation of June 1967: An Arab Perspective.* Evanston, IL: Northwestern University Press, 1970.

Abu-Lughod, Ibrahim, and Baha Abu-Laban, eds. *Settler Regimes in Africa and the Arab World: The Illusion of Endurance.* Wilmette, IL: Medina University Press, 1974.

Aburish, Said K. *Arafat: From Defender to Dictator.* New York: Bloomsbury, 1998.

Adelman, Morris. *The Genie Out of the Bottle: World Oil since 1970.* Cambridge, MA: The MIT Press, 1996.

Agnew, Spiro. *The Canfield Decision.* Chicago: Playboy Press, 1976.

——. *Go Quietly . . . Or Else.* New York: William Morrow, 1980.

Ajami, Fouad. *The Arab Predicament: Arab Political Thought and Practice since 1967.* Cambridge: Cambridge University Press, 1981.

——. *The Vanished Imam: Musa al Sadr and the Shia of Lebanon.* Ithaca, NY: Cornell University Press, 1986.

Akram, Susan M. "The Aftermath of September 11, 2001: The Targeting of Arabs and Muslims in America." *Arab Studies Quarterly* 24, no. 2/3 (Spring/Summer 2002): 61–118.

Albert, Marvin H. *The Gargoyle Conspiracy.* Garden City, NY: Doubleday, 1975.

Ali, Yaser. "Shariah and Citizenship: How Islamophobia Is Creating a Second-Class Citizenry in America." *California Law Review* 100, no. 4 (August 1, 2012): 1027–68.

Allen, D., and A. Pijpers, eds. *European Foreign Policy-Making and the Arab-Israeli Conflict.* The Hague: Martinus Nijhoff Publishers, 1984.

Allison, Robert J. *The Crescent Obscured: The United States and the Muslim World, 1776–1815.* 1995. Reprint, Chicago: University of Chicago Press, 2000.

Alnasrawi, Abbas. *Arab Nationalism, Oil, and the Political Economy of Dependency.* New York: Greenwood Press, 1991.

Alvandi, Roham. *Nixon, Kissinger, and the Shah: The United States and Iran in the Cold War.* New York: Oxford University Press, 2014.

Ambrose, Stephen E. *Nixon.* Vol. 3, *Ruin and Recovery.* New York: Simon & Schuster, 1991.

Ameri, Anan, and Holly Arida, eds. *Daily Life of Arab Americans in the 21st Century.* Santa Barbara, CA: Greenwood, 2012.

American Friends Services Committee. *The Search for Peace in the Middle East.* Rev. ed. Greenwich, CT: Fawcett Publications, 1970.

Anderson, Terry. *Bush's Wars.* New York: Oxford University Press, 2011.

Aruri, Naseer H. *Dishonest Broker: The U.S. Role in Israel and Palestine.* Cambridge, MA: South End Press, 2003.

Ashton, Nigel J., ed. *The Cold War in the Middle East: Regional Conflict and the Superpowers, 1967–73.* London: Routledge, 2007.

——. *King Hussein of Jordan: A Political Life.* New Haven, CT: Yale University Press, 2008.

Ashton, Nigel J., and Bryon Gibson, eds. *The Iran-Iraq War: New International Perspectives.* London: Routledge, 2013.

Asimov, Iassac. *Isaac Asimov's Treasury of Humor.* New York: Houghton Mifflin, 1971.

Association of Arab American University Graduates. *The First Decade, 1967–1977.* Washington, DC: AAUG, 1977.

——. *Lebanon: Two Perspectives.* Detroit: AAUG, 1975.

Atiyeh, George N., and Ibrahim Oweiss, eds. *Arab Civilization: Challenges and Responses.* Albany: State University of New York Press, 1988.

Bashshur, Rashid. "Unfulfilled Expectations: The Genesis and Demise of the AAUG." *Arab Studies Quarterly* 29, no. 3/4 (Summer/Fall 2007): 7–13.

Bassiouni, M. Cherif, ed. "The AAUG: Reflections on a Lost Opportunity." *Arab Studies Quarterly* 29, no. 3/4 (Summer/Fall 2007): 21–32.

——. *The Civil Rights of Arab-Americans: "The Special Measures."* North Dartmouth, MA: Association of Arab American University Graduates, 1974.

Batatu, Hanna. *Syria's Peasantry, the Descendants of Its Lesser Notables, and Their Politics.* Princeton, NJ: Princeton University Press, 1999.

Bawardi, Hani J. *The Making of Arab Americans: From Syrian Nationalism to U.S. Citizenship.* Austin: University of Texas Press, 2014.

Beker, Avi. *The United Nations and Israel: From Recognition to Reprehension.* Lexington, MA: Lexington Books, 1988.

Berberoglu, Berch. *Turmoil in the Middle East: Imperialism, War, and Political Instability.* Albany: State University of New York Press, 1999.

Bergen, Peter L. *Holy War, Inc.: Inside the Secret World of Osama bin Laden.* New York: Simon & Schuster, 2002.

Bill, James A. *The Eagle and the Lion: The Tragedy of American-Iranian Relations.* New Haven, CT: Yale University Press, 1988.

——. *George Ball: Behind the Scenes in U.S. Foreign Policy.* New Haven, CT: Yale University Press, 1997.

Billingsley, K. L[loyd]. *From Mainline to Sideline: The Social Witness of the National Council of Churches.* Lanham, MD: University Press of America, 1990.

Bird, Kai. *The Good Spy: The Life and Death of Robert Ames.* New York: Crown Publishers, 2014.

Booker, M. Keith, and Anne-Marie Thomas. *The Science Fiction Handbook.* Oxford: Wiley-Blackwell, 2009.

Borstelmann, Thomas. *The 1970s: A New Global History from Civil Rights to Economic Inequality.* Princeton, NJ: Princeton University Press, 2013.

Boyne, Walter J. *The Two O'Clock War: The 1973 Yom Kippur Conflict and the Airlift That Saved Israel.* New York: Thomas Dunne Books, 2002.

Bradley, Mark P. *Imagining Vietnam and America: The Making of Postcolonial Vietnam, 1919–1950.* Chapel Hill: University of North Carolina Press, 2000.

Brands, H.W. *Into the Labyrinth: The United States and the Middle East, 1945–1993.* New York: McGraw-Hill, 1994.

Brookings Middle East Study Group. *Toward Peace in the Middle East: Report of a Study Group*. Washington, DC: The Brookings Institution, 1975.

Brzezinski, Zbigniew. *Power and Principle: Memoirs of the National Security Adviser, 1977–1981*. New York: Farrar, Straus and Giroux, 1983.

Busch, Andrew. *Reagan's Victory: The Presidential Election of 1980 and the Rise of the Right*. Lawrence: University Press of Kansas, 2005.

Cainkar, Louise. "The Social Construction of Difference and the Arab American Experience." *Journal of American Ethnic History* 25, no. 2–3 (Winter–Spring 2006): 243–78.

Carter, Jimmy. *The Blood of Abraham: Insights into the Middle East*. Boston: Houghton Mifflin, 1985.

——. *Keeping Faith: Memoirs of a President*. Fayetteville, AR: University of Arkansas Press, 1982.

——. *White House Diary*. New York: Farrar, Straus and Giroux, 2010.

Carter, William "Buddy." *Billy Carter: A Journey Through the Shadows*. Atlanta: Longstreet, 1999.

Chalcraft, John. *The Invisible Cage: Syrian Migrant Workers in Lebanon*. Stanford, CA: Stanford University Press, 2009.

Chamberlin, Paul Thomas. *The Global Offensive: The United States, the Palestine Liberation Organization, and the Making of the Post-Cold War Order*. New York: Oxford University Press, 2012.

Champion, Daryl. *The Paradoxical Kingdom: Saudi Arabia and the Momentum of Reform*. New York: Columbia University Press, 2003.

Chaudhry, Kiren Aziz. *The Price of Wealth: Economies and Institutions in the Middle East*. Ithaca, NY: Cornell University Press, 1997.

Chomsky, Noam. *Peace in the Middle East? Reflections on Justice and Nationhood*. New York: Pantheon, 1974.

Christison, Kathleen. *Perceptions of Palestine: Their Influence on U.S. Middle East Policy*. 1999. Reprint, Berkeley: University of California Press, 2001.

Chubin, Shahram, and Charles Tripp. *Iran and Iraq at War*. London: I.B. Tauris, 1988.

Cobban, Helena. *The Palestinian Liberation Organisation: People, Power, and Politics*. Cambridge: Cambridge University Press, 1984.

Coll, Steve. *Ghost Wars: The Secret History of the CIA, Afghanistan, and bin Laden, from the Soviet Invasion to September 10, 2001*. New York: Penguin Press, 2004.

Comras, Victor D. *Flawed Diplomacy: The United Nations and the War on Terrorism*. Washington, DC: Potomac Books, 2010.

Congressional Research Service. "CRS Issue Brief for Congress: Libya." Updated April 10, 2002. Accessed December 2, 2014. http://fpc.state.gov/documents/organization/9577.pdf.

Cooley, John K. *Green March, Black September: The Story of the Palestinian Arabs*. London: Frank Cass, 1973.

——. *Libyan Sandstorm*. New York: Holt, Rinehart and Winston, 1982.

——. *Unholy Wars: Afghanistan, America, and International Terrorism*. 1999. Reprint, London: Pluto Press, 2000.

Cooper, Andrew Scott. *The Oil Kings: How the U.S., Iran, and Saudi Arabia Changed the Balance of Power in the Middle East.* New York: Simon & Schuster, 2011.

Coppel, Alfred. *Thirty-Four East.* New York: Harcourt Brace Jovanovich, 1974.

Costigliola, Frank. "'Unceasing Pressure for Penetration': Gender, Pathology, and Emotion in George Kennan's Formation of the Cold War." *Journal of American History* 83, no. 4 (March 1997): 1309–39.

Curtiss, Richard H. *A Changing Image: American Perceptions of the Arab-Israeli Dispute.* Washington, DC: American Educational Trust, 1982.

Daigle, Craig. *Limits of Détente: The United States, the Soviet Union, and the Arab-Israeli Conflict, 1969–1973.* New Haven, CT: Yale University Press, 2012.

Daigle, Craig, and Artemy M. Kalinovsky, eds. *The Routledge Handbook of the Cold War.* London: Routledge, 2014.

Dallek, Robert. *Nixon and Kissinger: Partners in Power.* New York: HarperCollins, 2007.

Dayan, Moshe. *Breakthrough: A Personal Account of the Egypt-Israel Peace Negotiations.* New York: Alfred A. Knopf, 1981.

Dean, Lucy, ed. *The Middle East and North Africa, 2004.* London: Europa Publications, 2003.

DeRoche, Andrew J. *Andrew Young: Civil Rights Ambassador.* Wilmington, DE: Scholarly Resources, 2003.

Diner, Hasia R. *The Jews of the United States.* Berkeley: University of California Press, 2004.

Dower, John W. *Embracing Defeat: Japan in the Wake of World War II.* New York: W. W. Norton, 1999.

——. *War without Mercy: Race and Power in the Pacific War.* New York: Pantheon, 1986.

Dreyfuss, Robert. *Devil's Game: How the United States Helped Unleash Fundamentalist Islam.* New York: Henry Holt, 2005.

Drysdale, Alasdair, and Raymond A. Hinnebusch. *Syria and the Middle East Peace Process.* New York: Council on Foreign Relations, 1991.

Duffield, John S., and Peter J. Dombrowski, eds. *Balance Sheet: The Iraq War and U.S. National Security.* Stanford, CA: Stanford University Press, 2010.

Ehrman, John. *The Rise of Neoconservatism: Intellectuals and Foreign Affairs, 1945–1994.* New Haven, CT: Yale University Press, 1995.

El Khazen, Farid. *The Breakdown of the State in Lebanon, 1967–1976.* Cambridge, MA: Harvard University Press, 2000.

Engerman, David C. *Know Your Enemy: The Rise and Fall of America's Soviet Experts.* New York: Oxford University Press, 2009.

Ensalaco, Mark. *Middle Eastern Terrorism: From Black September to September 11.* Philadelphia: University of Pennsylvania Press, 2008.

Erdman, Paul E. *The Crash of '79.* New York: Simon and Schuster, 1976.

Evans, B. G., ed. *Satellite Communication Systems.* 3rd ed. 1999. Reprint, Stevenage, UK: Institution of Engineering and Technology, 2008.

Fahmy, Ismail. *Negotiating for Peace in the Middle East.* London: Croon Helm, 1983.

Fain, W. Taylor. *American Ascendance and British Retreat in the Persian Gulf Region.* New York: Macmillan, 2008.

Farber, David. *Taken Hostage: The Iran Hostage Crisis and America's First Encounter with Radical Islam*. Princeton, NJ: Princeton University Press, 2005.

Al-Farnawani, Taha. *Al-Sira ' al- 'Arabi al-Isra'ili fi-damir diblumasi Misri* [The Arab-Israeli conflict in the conscience of an Egyptian diplomat]. Cairo: Dar al-mustaqbal al-'Arabi, 1994.

Fawcett, Louise, ed. *International Relations of the Middle East*. 3rd ed. 2005. Reprint, Oxford: Oxford University Press, 2013.

Findley, Paul. *They Dare to Speak Out: People and Institutions Confront Israel's Lobby*. Westport, CT: Lawrence Hill, 1985.

Forbes, Colin. *Year of the Golden Ape*. New York: E.P. Dutton, 1974.

Frankel, Sandor, and Webster Mews. *The Aleph Solution*. New York, Stein and Day, 1978.

Freedman, Robert O. *Soviet Policy toward the Middle East since 1970*. New York: Praeger, 1982.

Furman, Andrew. *Israel through the Jewish-American Imagination: A Survey of Jewish-American Literature on Israel, 1928–1995*. Albany: State University of New York Press, 1997.

Gardner, Lloyd. *The Road to Tahrir Square: Egypt and the United States from the Rise of Nasser to the Fall of Mubarak*. New York: New Press, 2011.

Garment, Leonard. *Crazy Rhythm: My Journey from Brooklyn, Jazz, and Wall Street to Nixon's White House*. Cambridge, MA: Da Capo Press, 2001.

Garrett, Paul D., and Kathleen A. Purpura. *Frank Maria: A Search for Justice in the Middle East*. Bloomington, IN: AuthorHouse, 2007.

Gerges, Fawaz A. *America and Political Islam: Clash of Cultures or Clash of Interests?* Cambridge: Cambridge University Press, 1999.

Ghadar, Fariborz. *Becoming American: Why Immigration Is Good for Our Nation's Future*. Lanham, MD: Rowman and Littlefield, 2014.

Ghorbal, Ashraf. *Mudhakkirat Ashraf Ghurbal: Su'ud wa-inhiyar 'alaqat Misr wa-Amrika* [The memoirs of Ashraf Ghorbal: The rise and fall of Egypt's and America's relations]. Cairo: Markaz al-Ahram lil-tarjimah wa-al-nashr, 2004.

Gilbar, Gad G. *The Middle East Oil Decade and Beyond: Essays in Political Economy*. London: Frank Cass, 1997.

Glad, Betty. *An Outsider in the White House: Jimmy Carter, His Advisors, and the Making of American Foreign Policy*. Ithaca, NY: Cornell University Press, 2009.

Goedde, Petra. *GIs and Germans: Culture, Gender, and Foreign Relations, 1945–1949*. New Haven, CT: Yale University Press, 2003.

Golan, Galia. *Soviet Policies in the Middle East: From World War II to Gorbachev*. Cambridge: Cambridge University Press, 1990.

Golden, Peter. *Quiet Diplomat: A Biography of Max M. Fisher*. New York: Cornwall, 1992.

Goulden, Joseph P., and Alexander W. Raffio. *The Death Merchant: The Rise and Fall of Edwin P. Wilson*. New York: Simon & Schuster, 1984.

Graves, Richard L. *Cobalt 60*. New York: Stein and Day, 1975.

Greene, Robert W. *The Sting Man: Inside Abscam*. New York: E.P. Dutton, 1981.

Gresh, Alain. *The PLO: The Struggle Within: Towards an Independent Palestinian State*. London: Zed Books, 1985.

Gualtieri, Sarah M.A. *Between Arab and White: Race and Ethnicity in the Early Syrian American Diaspora*. Berkeley: University of California Press, 2009.

Hadawi, Sami. *Bitter Harvest: A Modern History of Palestine*. New York: Olive Branch Press, 1989.

Hagopian, Elaine C. "Ibrahim and Edward." *Arab Studies Quarterly* 26, no. 4 (Fall 2004): 3–22.

——. "Minority Rights in a Nation-State: The Nixon Administration's Campaign against Arab-Americans." *Journal of Palestine Studies* 5, no. 1/2 (Autumn 1975–Winter 1976): 97–114.

——. "Reversing Injustice: On Utopian Activism." *Arab Studies Quarterly* 29, no. 3/4 (Summer/Fall 2007): 57–73.

Hagopian, Elaine C., and Ann Paden, eds. *The Arab-Americans: Studies in Assimilation*. Wilmette, IL: Medina University Press, 1969.

Hagopian, Elaine C., and Samih Farsoun, eds. *South Lebanon: Special Report No. 2*. Detroit: Association of Arab American University Graduates, 1978.

Hahn, Peter L. *Crisis and Crossfire: The United States and the Middle East since 1945*. Washington, DC: Potomac Books, 2005.

——. *Missions Accomplished? The United States and Iraq since World War I*. New York: Oxford University Press, 2012.

Hahn, Peter L., and Mary Ann Heiss, eds. *Empire and Revolution: The United States and the Third World since 1945*. Columbus: Ohio State University Press, 2001.

Haldeman, H.R. *The Haldeman Diaries: Inside the Nixon White House*. 1994. Reprint, New York: Berkeley Books, 1995.

Haley, P. Edward. *Qaddafi and the United States since 1969*. New York: Praeger, 1984.

Haley, P. Edward, and Lewis W. Snyder. *Lebanon in Crisis: Participants and Issues*. Syracuse, NY: Syracuse University Press, 1979.

Harris, Leonard. *The Masada Plan*. New York: Crown Publishers, 1976.

Harris, Thomas. *Black Sunday*. New York: Dell, 1975.

Hart, Alan. *Arafat: Terrorist or Peacemaker?* London: Sidgwick & Jackson, 1984.

Haykal, Muhammad Hasanayn. *The Road to Ramadan*. New York: Quadrangle, 1975.

——. *Sphinx and Commissar: The Rise and Fall of Soviet Influence in the Arab World*. London: Collins, 1978.

——. *Uktubir 73: Al-silah wa-al-siayasa* [October '73: Arms and politics]. Cairo: Markaz al-Ahram lil-tarjimah wa-al-nashr, 1993.

Hersh, Seymour M. *Price of Power: Kissinger in the Nixon White House*. New York: Summit, 1983.

Hirst, David. *Beware of Small States: Lebanon, Battleground of the Middle East*. New York: Nation Books, 2010.

Hitchens, Christopher. *Hitch-22: A Memoir*. New York: Twelve, 2010.

Hooglund, Eric J. *Crossing the Waters: Arabic-Speaking Immigrants to the United States before 1940*. Washington, DC: Smithsonian Institution Press, 1987.

Al-Hout, Shafiq. *My Life in the PLO: The Inside Story of the Palestinian Struggle*. New York: Pluto Press, 2011.

Hughes, Geraint. "Britain, the Transatlantic Alliance, and the Arab-Israeli War of 1973." *Journal of Cold War Studies* 10, no. 2 (Spring 2008): 3–40.

Hupp, Clea Lutz. *The United States and Jordan: Middle East Diplomacy during the Cold War*. London: I.B. Tauris, 2014.

Hurst, Steven. *The United States and Iraq since 1979: Hegemony, Oil and War.* Edinburgh: Edinburgh University Press, 2009.

Insight Team of the London *Sunday Times. The Yom Kippur War.* Garden City, NY: Doubleday, 1974.

Isaacson, Walter. *Kissinger: A Biography.* New York: Simon & Schuster, 1992.

Isikoff, Michael, and David Corn. *Hubris: The Inside Story of Spin, Scandal, and the Selling of the Iraq War.* New York: Crown, 2006.

Israelyan, Victor. *Inside the Kremlin During the Yom Kippur War.* University Park, PA: Pennsylvania State University Press, 1995.

Jabara, Abdeen. "The AAUG: Aspirations and Failures." *Arab Studies Quarterly* 29, no. 3/4 (Summer/Fall 2007): 15–19.

Jacobs, Matthew F. *Imagining the Middle East: The Building of an American Foreign Policy, 1918–1967.* Chapel Hill, NC: University of North Carolina Press, 2011.

Jamal, Amaney, and Nadine Naber, eds. *Race and Arab Americans before and after 9/11: From Invisible Citizens to Visible Subjects.* Syracuse, NY: Syracuse University Press, 2008.

Jansen, Godfrey. *Why Robert Kennedy Was Killed: The Story of Two Victims.* New York: The Third Press, 1970.

Jonas, George. *Vengeance: The True Story of an Israeli Counter-Terrorist Team.* New York: Simon & Schuster, 2005.

Jones, Bartlett C. *Flawed Triumphs: Andy Young at the United Nations.* Lanham, MD: University Press of America, 1996.

Kalman, Laura. *Right Star Rising: A New Politics, 1974–1980.* New York: W.W. Norton, 2010.

Kamel, Mohamed Ibrahim. *The Camp David Accords: A Testimony.* London: KPI, 1986.

Kaufman, Burton I. *The Arab Middle East and the United States: Inter-Arab Rivalry and Superpower Diplomacy.* New York: Twayne Publishers, 1996.

Kayal, Philip M. "Report: Counting the 'Arabs' among Us." *Arab Studies Quarterly* 9, no. 1 (Winter 1987): 98–104.

Kayal, Philip M., and Joseph M. Kayal, *The Syrian-Lebanese in America: A Study in Religion and Assimilation.* New York: Twayne Publishers, 1975.

Keane, Stephen. *Disaster Movies: The Cinema of Catastrophe.* London: Wallflower, 2001.

Kerr, Malcolm, ed. *The Elusive Peace in the Middle East.* Albany, NY: State University of New York Press, 1975.

Kerr, Michael. "'A Positive Aspect to the Tragedy of Lebanon': The Convergence of U.S., Syrian, and Israeli Interests at the Outset of Lebanon's Civil War." *Israel Affairs* 5, no. 14 (October 2009): 355–71.

Kissinger, Henry A. *White House Years.* Boston: Little, Brown, 1979.

——. *Years of Renewal.* New York: Simon & Schuster, 1999.

——. *Years of Upheaval.* Boston: Little, Brown, 1982.

Klein, Aaron J. *Striking Back: The 1972 Munich Olympics Massacre and Israel's Deadly Response.* New York: Random House, 2005.

Korn, David A. *Assassination in Khartoum.* Bloomington: Indiana University Press, 1993.

——. *Stalemate: The War of Attrition and Great Power Diplomacy in the Middle East, 1969–1970.* Boulder, CO: Westview Press, 1992.

Kramer, Martin. *Ivory Towers on Sand: The Failure of Middle East Studies in America.* Washington, DC: Washington Institute for Near East Policy, 2001.

Kramer, Paul A. *The Blood of Government: Race, Empire, the United States, and the Philippines.* Chapel Hill: University of North Carolina Press, 2006.

Kunz, Diane B. *Butter and Guns: America's Cold War Economic Diplomacy.* New York: The Free Press, 1997.

Kutler, Stanley I. *The Wars of Watergate: The Last Crisis of Richard Nixon.* New York: Alfred A. Knopf, 1990.

LaFeber, Walter. *The American Age: United States Foreign Policy at Home and Abroad.* 2nd ed., *1750 to the Present.* 1989. Reprint, New York: W. W. Norton, 1994.

Lesch, Ann Mosely. *Political Perceptions of the Palestinians on the West Bank and the Gaza Strip.* Washington, DC: The Middle East Institute, 1980.

Levy, Richard S., ed. *Anti-Semitism: A Historical Encyclopedia of Prejudice and Persecution.* Vol. 1. Santa Barbara, CA: ABC-CLIO, 2005.

Little, Douglas. *American Orientalism: The United States and the Middle East since 1945.* Chapel Hill: University of North Carolina Press, 2002.

——. "To the Shores of Tripoli: America, Qaddafi, and the Libyan Revolution, 1969–89." *International History Review* 35, no. 1 (2013): 70–99.

Lockman, Zachary. *Contending Visions of the Middle East: The History and Politics of Orientalism.* New York: Cambridge University Press, 2004.

Lubin, Alex. *Geographies of Liberation: The Making of an Afro-Arab Political Imaginary.* Chapel Hill, NC: University of North Carolina Press, 2014.

Lukacs, Yehuda. *Israel, Jordan, and the Peace Process.* 1997. Reprint, Syracuse, NY: Syracuse University Press, 1999.

Luttwak, Edward N. *Strategy and Politics: Collected Essays.* New Brunswick, NJ: Transaction Books, 1980.

Maas, Peter. *Manhunt: The Incredible Pursuit of a CIA Agent Turned Terrorist.* New York: Random House, 1986.

Macris, Jeffrey R. *The Politics and Security of the Gulf: Anglo-American Hegemony and the Shaping of a Region.* London: Routledge, 2010.

Maisel, L. Sandy, ed. *Jews in American Politics.* Lanham, MD: Rowman and Littlefield, 2001.

Makdisi, Ussama. *Faith Misplaced: The Broken Promise of U.S.-Arab Relations, 1820–2001* New York: PublicAffairs, 2010.

Ma'oz, Moshe. *Asad, the Sphinx of Damascus: A Political Biography.* London: Weidenfeld and Nicolson, 1988.

Mark, Clyde R. *Israel: U.S. Foreign Assistance*, updated April 26, 2006. Accessed July 11, 2015. http://fas.org/sgp/crs/mideast/IB85066.pdf.

McAlister, Melani. *Epic Encounters: Culture, Media, and U.S. Interests in the Middle East, 1945–2001.* 2001. Reprint, Berkeley: University of California Press, 2005.

McCarus, Ernest, ed. *The Development of Arab-American Identity.* Ann Arbor: University of Michigan Press, 1994.

McFarland, Victor R.S. "Living in Never-Never Land: The United States, Saudi Arabia, and Oil in the 1970s." PhD diss., Yale University, 2014.

McQuaid, Kim. *The Anxious Years: America in the Vietnam-Watergate Era.* New York: Basic Books, 1989.

Medoff, Rafael. *Jewish Americans and Political Participation: A Reference Handbook*. Santa Barbara, CA: ABC Clio, 2002.

Mehdi, M[uhammad] T. *Kennedy and Sirhan: Why?* New York: New World Press, 1968.

Meital, Yoram. *Egypt's Struggle for Peace: Continuity and Change, 1967–1977*. Gainesville: University of Florida Press, 1997.

Miglietta, John P. *American Alliance Policy in the Middle East, 1945–1992: Iran, Israel, and Saudi Arabia*. Lanham, MD: Lexington Books, 2002.

Möckli, Daniel. *European Foreign Policy during the Cold War: Heath, Brandt, Pompidou, and the Short Dream of Political Unity*. London: I.B. Tauris, 2009.

Moldea, Dan E. *The Killing of Robert F. Kennedy: An Investigation of Motive, Means, and Opportunity*. New York: W.W. Norton, 1995.

Morris, Benny. *Righteous Victims: A History of Zionist-Arab Conflict, 1881–1999*. New York: Alfred A. Knopf, 1999.

Moynihan, Daniel Patrick. *A Dangerous Place*. Boston: Little, Brown and Company, 1978.

Mudd, Roger. *The Place to Be: Washington, CBS, and the Glory Days of Television News*. New York: PublicAffairs, 2008.

Naber, Nadine. *Arab America: Gender, Cultural Politics, and Activism*. New York: New York University Press, 2012.

Naftali, Timothy. *Blind Spot: The Secret History of American Counterterrorism Policy*. New York: Basic Books, 2005.

Nasr, Kameel B. *Arab and Israeli Terrorism: The Causes and Effects of Political Violence, 1936–1993*. Jefferson, NC: McFarland & Co., 1996.

Naylor, Philip C. *A History of North Africa*. Rev. ed. 2009. Reprint, Austin: University of Texas Press, 2015.

Neff, Donald. *Fallen Pillars: U.S. Policy towards Palestine and Israel since 1945*. Washington, DC: Institute for Palestine Studies, 1995.

——. *Warriors Against Israel*. Brattleboro, VT: Amana Books, 1988.

Nijim, Basheer K., ed. *American Church Politics and the Middle East*. Belmont, MA: Association of Arab American University Graduates, 1982.

Nixon, Richard M. *The Memoirs of Richard Nixon*. New York: Grosset & Dunlap, 1978.

O'Ballance, Edgar. *The Gulf War*. London: Brassey's Defense Publishers, 1988.

Oren, Michael B. *Power, Faith, and Fantasy: America in the Middle East, 1776 to the Present*. New York: W.W. Norton, 2007.

Orfalea, Gregory. *The Arab Americans: A History*. Northampton, MA: Olive Branch Press, 2005.

Otis, George. *Voice of Hope*. Van Nuys, CA: High Adventure Ministries, 1983.

Oudes, Bruce, ed. *From the President: Richard Nixon's Secret Files*. New York: Harper & Row, 1989.

Pappé, Ilan, and Jamil Hilal, eds. *Across the Wall: Narratives of Israeli-Palestinian History*. London: I.B. Tauris, 2010.

Pargeter, Alison. *Libya: The Rise and Fall of Qaddafi*. New Haven, CT: Yale University Press, 2012.

Parker, Richard B. *The Politics of Miscalculation in the Middle East*. Bloomington: Indiana University Press, 1993.

Pelletiere, Stephen C. *The Iran-Iraq War: Chaos in a Vacuum*. New York: Praeger, 1992.

Pennock, Pamela. *Linkages on the Left: Arab American Activism in the 1960s–1970s*. Chapel Hill: University of North Carolina Press, forthcoming.

Peterson, M.J. *The UN General Assembly*. London: Routledge, 2006.

Petran, Tabitha. *The Struggle Over Lebanon*. New York: Monthly Review Press, 1987.

Pollitz, Edward A., Jr. *The Forty-First Thief*. New York: Delacorte Press, 1975.

Quandt, William B. *Camp David: Peacemaking and Politics*. Washington, DC: The Brookings Institution, 1986.

——. *Decade of Decisions: American Policy toward the Arab-Israeli Conflict, 1967–1976*. Berkeley: University of California, 1977.

——. *Peace Process: American Diplomacy and the Arab-Israeli Conflict since 1967*. Rev. ed. Berkeley: University of California Press, 2001.

Rabil, Robert G. *Embattled Neighbors: Syria, Israel, and Lebanon*. Boulder, CO: Lynne Reinner, 2003.

Rabin, Yitzhak. *The Rabin Memoirs*. Boston: Little, Brown, 1979.

Rabinovich, Abraham. *The Yom Kippur War: The Epic Encounter That Transformed the Middle East*. New York: Schocken Books, 2004.

Rabinovich, Itamar. *The War for Lebanon, 1970–1985*. Ithaca, NY: Cornell University Press, 1985.

Rabinovich, Itamar, and Haim Shaked, eds. *From June to October: The Middle East Between 1967 and 1973*. New Brunswick, NJ: Transaction Books, 1978.

Raeli, Ruth. *The Steps That Led to United Nations General Assembly Resolution 3379: Elimination of All Forms of Racial Discrimination, November 10, 1975*. N.p.: World Zionist Organization, 1984.

Al-Rasheed, Madawi. *A History of Saudi Arabia*. 2nd ed. 2002. Reprint, Cambridge: Cambridge University Press, 2010.

Reeve, Simon. *One Day in September: The Full Story of the 1972 Munich Olympics Massacre and the Israeli Revenge Operation "Wrath of God."* New York: Arcade Publishing, 2006.

Reston, James, Jr. *Lone Star: The Life of John Connally*. New York: Harper & Row, 1989.

Riad, Mahmoud. *The Struggle for Peace in the Middle East*. London: Quartet Books, 1981.

Ricks, Thomas E. *Fiasco: The American Military Adventure in Iraq*. London: Penguin, 2006.

Robbins, Harold. *The Pirate*. New York: Pocket Books, 1974.

Rød-Larsen, Terje, Nur Laiq, and Fabrice Aidan, eds. *The Search for Peace in the Arab-Israeli Conflict: A Compendium of Documents and Analysis*. Oxford: Oxford University Press, 2014.

Ross, Jack. *Rabbi Outcast: Elmer Berger and American Jewish Anti-Zionism*. Washington, DC: Potomac Books, 2011.

Rugh, William. *Arab Mass Media: Newspapers, Radio, and Television in Arab Politics*. Westport, CT: 2004.

——. *Arab Perceptions of American Foreign Policy during the October War*. Washington, DC: Middle East Institute, 1976.

Sadat, Anwar. *In Search of Identity: An Autobiography*. New York: Harper & Row, 1978.

——. *Those I Have Known*. New York: Continuum, 1984.

Safire, William. *Before the Fall: An Inside View of the Pre-Watergate White House*. Garden City, NY: Doubleday, 1975.

Safran, Nadav. *Israel—The Embattled Ally*. 1978. Reprint, Cambridge, MA: Harvard University Press, 1981.

Said, Edward W. *After the Last Sky: Palestinian Lives*. New York: Pantheon Books, 1986.

——. *The End of the Peace Process: Oslo and After*. New York: Pantheon Books, 2000.

——. *From Oslo to Iraq and the Road Map*. New York: Pantheon Books, 2004.

——. *Orientalism*. New York: Pantheon Books, 1978.

——. *Peace and Its Discontents: Essays on Palestine in the Middle East Peace Process*. New York: Vintage Books, 1996.

——. *The Politics of Dispossession: The Struggle for Palestinian Self-Determination, 1969–1994*. New York: Pantheon Books, 1994.

——. *The Question of Palestine*. New York: Times Books, 1979.

Salibi, Kamal S. *Crossroads to Civil War, 1958–1976*. Delmar, NY: Caravan Books, 1976.

——. *The Modern History of Jordan*: London: I.B. Tauris, 1993.

Salloukh, Bassel. "Syria and Lebanon: A Brotherhood Transformed." *MERIP Middle East Report* 236 (Fall 2005): 14–21.

Sargent, Daniel J. *A Superpower Transformed: The Remaking of American Foreign Relations in the 1970s*. New York: Oxford University Press, 2015.

Savage, Charlie. *Power Wars: Inside Obama's Post-9/11 Presidency*. Boston: Little, Brown and Company, 2015.

Sayegh, Fayez. *Zionism: "A Form of Racism and Racial Discrimination": Four Statements Made at the U.N. General Assembly*. New York: Office of the Permanent Observer of the Palestine Liberation Organization to the United Nations, 1976.

Sayigh, Yezid. *Armed Struggle and the Search for State: The Palestinian National Movement, 1949–1993*. Oxford: Clarendon Press, 1997.

Schiff, Barry, and Hal Fishman. *The Vatican Target*. New York: St. Martin's Press, 1978.

Schulman, Bruce J. *The Seventies: The Great Shift in American Culture, Society, and Politics*. New York: Free Press, 2001.

Schulzinger, Robert. *Henry Kissinger: Doctor of Diplomacy*. New York: Columbia University Press, 1989.

Seale, Patrick. *Asad of Syria: The Struggle for the Middle East*. Berkeley: University of California Press, 1988.

Semmerling, Tim Jon. *"Evil" Arabs in American Popular Film: Orientalist Fear*. Austin: University of Texas Press, 2006.

Shaheen, Jack G. *Abscam: Arabiaphobia in America*. N.d. Reprint, Washington, DC: American-Arab Anti-Discrimination Committee, 1980.

——. *The Influence of the Arab Stereotype on American Children*. N.d. Reprint, Washington, DC: American-Arab Anti-Discrimination Committee, 1980 or 1981.

——. *Reel Bad Arabs: How Hollywood Vilifies a People*. New York: Olive Branch Press, 2001.

——. *The TV Arab*. Bowling Green, OH: Bowling Green State University Press, 1984.

Shazly, Saad. *The Crossing of the Suez*. San Francisco: American Mideast Research, 1980.

Sheehan, Edward R.F. *The Arabs, Israelis, and Kissinger*. New York: Reader's Digest Press, 1976.

Shibusawa, Naoko. *America's Geisha Ally: Reimagining the Japanese Enemy*. Cambridge, MA: Harvard University Press, 2006.

The Shiloah Center for Middle Eastern and African Studies. *Middle East Record, 1968*. Jerusalem: Israel Universities Press, 1973.

Shlaim, Avi. *Lion of Jordan: The Life of King Hussein in War and Peace*. New York: Alfred A. Knopf, 2008.

——. *War and Peace in the Middle East: A Critique of American Policy*. New York: Viking, 1994.

Sick, Gary. *All Fall Down: America's Fateful Encounter with Iran*. London: I.B. Tauris, 1985.

Simon, Reeva S. *The Middle East in Crime Fiction: Mysteries, Spy Novels, and Thrillers from 1916 to the 1980s*. New York: Lillian Barber Press, 1989.

Siniver, Asaf, ed. *The Yom Kippur War: Politics, Legacy, Diplomacy*. New York: Oxford University Press, 2013.

Smith, Charles D. *Palestine and the Arab-Israeli Conflict*. 4th ed. New York: St. Martin's Press, 2001.

Smith, Simon C. *Ending Empire in the Middle East: Britain, the United States, and Post-War Decolonization, 1945–1973*. London: Routledge, 2012.

Spickard, Paul. *Almost All Aliens: Immigration, Race, and Colonialism in American History and Identity*. New York: Routledge, 2007.

Spiegel, Steven L. *The Other Arab-Israeli Conflict: Making America's Middle East Policy, from Truman to Reagan*. Chicago: University of Chicago, 1985.

Stein, Herbert, and Benjamin Stein. *On the Brink*. New York: Simon and Schuster, 1977.

Stein, Judith. *Pivotal Decade: How the United States Traded Factories for Finance in the 1970s*. New Haven, CT: Yale University Press, 2010.

Stein, Kenneth W. *Heroic Diplomacy: Sadat, Kissinger, Carter, Begin, and the Quest for Arab-Israeli Peace*. New York: Routledge, 1999.

Stephens, Robert. *Nasser: A Political Biography*. New York: Simon and Schuster, 1972.

St John, Ronald Bruce. *Libya and the United States: Two Centuries of Strife*. Philadelphia: University of Pennsylvania Press, 2002.

Stocker, James. *Spheres of Intervention: The United States and the Struggle for Lebanon, 1967–1976*. Ithaca, NY: Cornell University Press, forthcoming.

Suleiman, Michael W., ed. *Arabs in America: Building a New Future*. Philadelphia: Temple University Press, 1999.

——. "'I Come to Bury Caesar, Not to Praise Him': An Assessment of the AAUG as an Example of an Activist Arab American Organization." *Arab Studies Quarterly* 29, no. 3/4 (Summer/Fall 2007): 75–95.

Suri, Jeremi. *Henry Kissinger and the American Century*. Cambridge, MA: Harvard University Press, 2007.

Synnott, Marcia Graham. *Student Diversity at the Big Three: Changes at Harvard, Yale, and Princeton since the 1920s*. New Brunswick, NJ: Transaction Publishers, 2013.

Tanous, Peter, and Paul Rubinstein. *The Petrodollar Takeover*. New York: G.P. Putnam's Sons, 1975.

Terry, Janice J. *Mistaken Identity: Arab Stereotypes in Popular Writing*. Washington, DC: American-Arab Affairs Council, 1985.

Tessler, Mark. *A History of the Israeli-Palestinian Conflict*. Bloomington: Indiana University Press, 1994.

Tillman, Seth P. *The United States in the Middle East: Interests and Obstacles*. Bloomington: Indiana University Press, 1982.

Trento, Joseph J. *Prelude to Terror: Edwin P. Wilson and the Legacy of America's Private Intelligence Network*. New York: Carrol & Graf, 2005.

Trofimov, Yaroslav. *The Siege of Mecca: The Forgotten Uprising in Islam's Holiest Shrine and the Birth of al Qaeda*. New York: Doubleday, 2007.

Troy, Gil. *Moynihan's Moment: America's Fight Against Zionism as Racism*. New York: Oxford University Press, 2013.

Tyler, Patrick. *A World of Trouble: The White House and the Middle East—from the Cold War to the War on Terror.* New York: Farrar, Straus and Giroux, 2009.

Vaïsse, Justin. *Neoconservatism: The Biography of a Movement*. Translated by Arthur Goldhammer. Cambridge, MA: The Belknap Press, 2010.

Valeriani, Richard. *Travels with Henry*. Boston: Houghton Mifflin, 1979.

Vance, Cyrus. *Hard Choices: Critical Years in America's Foreign Policy*. New York: Simon & Schuster, 1983.

Walt, Stephen M. *The Origins of Alliances*. Ithaca, NY: Cornell University Press, 1987.

Wattenberg, Ben J. *Fighting Words: A Tale of How Liberals Created Neo-Conservatism*. New York: St. Martin's Press, 2008.

Weinberger, Naomi Joy. *Syrian Intervention in Lebanon: The 1975–76 Civil War*. New York: Oxford University Press, 1986.

Weisbord, Robert G., and Richard Kazarian, Jr. *Israel in the Black American Perspective*. Westport, CT: Greenwood Press, 1985.

Wight, David. "Kissinger's Levantine Dilemma: The Ford Administration and the Syrian Occupation of Lebanon." *Diplomatic History* 37, no.1 (January 2013): 144–77.

——. "The Petrodollar Era and Relations between the United States and the Middle East and North Africa, 1969–1980." PhD diss., University of California, Irvine, 2014.

Wilford, Hugh. *America's Great Game: The CIA's Secret Arabists and the Shaping of the Modern Middle East*. New York: Basic Books, 2013.

Winslow, Charles. *Lebanon: War and Politics in a Fragmented Society*. London: Routledge, 1996.

Woods, Randall Bennett. *Fulbright: A Biography*. New York: Cambridge University Press, 1995.

Wright, Lawrence. *The Looming Tower: Al-Qaeda and the Road to 9/11*. New York: Alfred A. Knopf, 2006.

——. *Thirteen Days in September: Carter, Begin, and Sadat at Camp David*. New York: Alfred A. Knopf, 2014.

Yaqub, Salim. *Containing Arab Nationalism: The Eisenhower Doctrine and the Middle East*. Chapel Hill: University of North Carolina Press, 2004.

——. "Our Declaration of Independence: African Americans, Arab Americans, and the Arab-Israeli Conflict, 1967–1979." *Mashriq & Mahjar* 3 no. 1 (2015): 12–29.

Yergin, Daniel. *The Prize: The Epic Quest for Oil, Money, and Power*. New York: Simon & Schuster, 1991.

Zogby, James, and Jack O'Dell, eds. *Afro-Americans Stand Up for Middle East Peace*. Washington, DC: Palestine Human Rights Campaign, 1980.

Index

Page numbers followed by letter *f* refer to figures.